D0849897

THE INTERSECTION OF RACE, CLASS, AND GENDER IN MULTICULTURAL COUNSELING

The Intersection of Race, Class, and Gender in Multicultural Counseling

WITHDRAWN

Donald B. Pope-Davis ▪ Hardin L. K. Coleman ▪ Editors

Sage Publications, Inc.
International Educational and Professional Publisher
Thousand Oaks ▪ London ▪ New Delhi

36l.06
7.6l9l
2 00 l

For information:

Sage Publications, Inc.
2455 Teller Road
Thousand Oaks, California 91320
E-mail: order@sagepub.com

Sage Publications Ltd.
6 Bonhill Street
London EC2A 4PU
United Kingdom

Sage Publications India Pvt. Ltd.
M-32 Market
Greater Kailash I
New Delhi 110 048 India

Printed in the United States of America

Library of Congress Cataloging-in-Publication Data

Main entry under title:

The intersection of race, class, and gender in multicultural counseling / edited by
Donald Pope-Davis and Hardin L.K. Coleman.
   p. cm.
Includes bibliographical references and index.
ISBN 0-7619-1158-8 (hc)
1. Minority women—Counseling of. 2. Cross-cultural counseling.
I. Pope-Davis, Donald. II. Coleman, Hardin L. K.
HQ1150 .I58 2000
361'.06'089—dc21
                                        00-010050

01   02   03   10   9   8   7   6   5   4   3   2   1

Acquiring Editor:	Nancy Hale
Production Editor:	Diana E. Axelsen
Editorial Assistant:	Victoria Cheng
Typesetter/Designer:	Marion Warren
Indexer:	Mary Mortensen
Cover Designer:	Michelle Lee

CONTENTS

PART II: Integrating Class, Gender, and Race Into Counseling Theory and Counseling Training

PART III: Theory to Practice

PART IV: Conclusion

INTEGRATING MULTICULTURAL COUNSELING THEORY

An Introduction

Hardin L. K. Coleman
Donald B. Pope-Davis

Anyone who believes in the theory of ethnic identity that has evolved from Cross's (1971) seminal work has to be very excited about this book. As this theory has evolved (Atkinson, Morten, & Sue, 1993; Cross, 1991; Helm, 1993; Phinney, 1989), ethnic identity is thought to be developed as the individual passes through a series of stages. In many ways, our understanding of multicultural counseling has evolved in a similar pattern. The pre-encounter stage began with the creation of the counseling profession, with its focus on a universalist model that emphasized an intrapsychic model of development shared by the whole of humankind. This model dominated both training programs and clinical practice well into the 1970s, when we came to understand the degree to which traditional counseling practices were failing to meet the needs of ethnic minorities and others who did not fit the mainstream psychology on which these practices were based. At this time, the creation of community mental health centers was bringing more lower-income and ethnic minority clients into contact with counselors. These encounters were not always pretty. This encounter phase of development led to the creation of a field of study that focused on the needs of ethnic minorities in counseling. Unlike the impression given by Fowers and Richardson in their 1996 article on multiculturalism in the *American Psychologist,* this focus in counseling did not meet with overwhelming acceptance. In fact, it was often met with hostility and rejection.

These experiences led to a major shift in the manner in which issues related to cultural factors were addressed by the counseling profession, both in the clinical and scientific communities, that paralleled the immersion-emersion stages of ethnic identity. Increasingly, those who were interested in these issues withdrew into communities of kind who shared common assumptions about the role of culture in counseling and the lack of appreciation for context that dominated traditional psychology. During this period, an infrastructure was created to support this exploration, including but not limited to Divisions 35, 44, and 46 in the American Psychological Association (APA) and a proliferation of ethnic- and gender-specific treatment programs across the country. Although initially stimulated by rejection from mainstream groups, this process quickly allowed those who were concerned with cultural factors in counseling to develop a positive sense of commitment to an important issue facing psychology and the nation. This led to the internalization of the role that culture plays in our lives.

This book represents an attempt to apply that identity to the fullest extent. Currently, when the term *multicultural* is used, too many people assume we are talking about issues related to ethnicity and are, therefore, ignoring the concerns of women, gays, lesbians, bisexuals, and those who are differently abled. This assumption is legitimately rooted in the immersion-emersion stages of development when the focus was on developing positive group identity and individuals would discuss their exploration of multiculturalism in terms of their particular group membership. We believe we are at the point of developing an integrated view of multiculturalism that will allow us, as individuals and professionals, to incorporate all aspects of our selves and not just the one(s) that are most physically obvious (e.g., gender or race). To achieve that goal, we need to articulate models of how cultural factors affect development, how they interact with the counseling process, and how we can systematically examine these processes. The authors who have contributed to this book offer a variety of perspectives that will support the process of articulating these models.

In this introductory chapter, we will briefly outline an ecological model of behavior, give an example of how it integrates the many factors of culture within the counseling process, and suggest a case-based model of inquiry that can serve to improve our understanding of these issues. We will then describe the manner in which we have organized the chapters in this book to show how an ecological model of multicultural counseling has evolved and is being used in the field.

Ecological Model of Behavior

The field of addictions counseling, with the development of a biopsychosocial (BPS) model for assessment and treatment (Donovan & Marlatt, 1988), has provided an excellent model for thinking about the etiology of behavior in a nonlinear manner. The BPS emphasizes the reality that behavior is an outcome of the interactions between biology, psychology, and sociology. The major drawback of the BPS is that it still emphasizes the intrapsychic process of development. One of the great contributions of multicultural theory is that it places equal emphasis on contextual variables to explain behavior as it does the intrapsychic variables.

Elsewhere, Coleman (1995) describes just such an ecological model that gives equal credence to contextual and intrapsychic variables. An ecological model assumes that behavior is organized and not caused. It also assumes that individuals are active agents in making sense of their environment. It is this interaction between the individual as a meaning-making agent and his or her social environment that simultaneously accounts for the stability of behavior across generations and its change. The fact that behavior is organized by multiple factors is exactly why the field of multiculturalism needs to integrate all cultural factors into its theoretical frameworks. Neither ethnicity, gender, nor class stands alone in creating our behavior patterns. What we need to focus on is not how each of these factors independently contributes to a behavior pattern but also how they do so in an interactive manner. Here is an example.

Slavin, Ranier, McCreary, and Gowda (1991) present a model for how minority status affects the stress process. In this model, they build on the formulation of Lazarus and Folkman (1984) that an individual's reaction to a stressor is determined by his or her appraisal of that stressor. Slavin et al. identify the manner in which minority status can influence the nature of the stressor, the appraisal of the event, the available coping strategies, and the evaluation of the resolution of the stress reaction. An integrated multicultural model of stress would also include the role of class and gender in the process. For example, gender often has an impact on what is viewed as a stressful event. In a workshop for mental health workers recently run by the first author, the female participants were quite articulate about the fact that the cleanliness of their homes was a stressor for them regardless of who was responsible for the cleaning. Certainly, all the data suggest that women are still perceived as the primary caregivers for children and are expected to fill that role. Cultural group membership has a significant influence on the type of behaviors that are acceptable to use to cope with a stressor. It is class, however, that will determine the resources that an individual brings to bear to support his or her coping efforts.

In work with a African American mother who has a bipolar disorder and four children, one of us found that she was providing a caring and nurturing home for her children, even though one child suffered from depression, and the others were falling behind in their acquisition of reading skills. Her lower-income status was the biggest hurdle to managing the stressors in her life. It prevented her from accessing sufficient mental health support for herself, respite care for the family, and academic services for the children. The experience of racial discrimination, coupled with the gendered expectation of her role with her children and compounded by her lack of resources, served as significant triggers for her disorder. Treatment must address these cultural factors as well as intrapsychic issues if it is to be effective. Unfortunately, it is not the burdens in her life that get her referred for treatment. That occurs when she reverts to traditional patterns of child rearing when her children are out of line with American middle-class parenting values—in this case, spanking. It is then that she interfaces with the mental health system when referred by the Department of Health and Human Services. How to effectively work within the complex interactions of her culture, her gender, and her class is the challenge for mental health professionals.

IMPLICATIONS FOR COUNSELOR EDUCATION

Preparing counselors to meet this challenge is the responsibility of counselor educators. Recently, several authors have outlined an ambitious agenda for the competencies that counselor education programs need to teach their students (Arredondo et al., 1996; Sue, Ivey, & Pedersen, 1996). The core competencies that they suggest students acquire are awareness of one's own cultural identity, understanding and knowledge of clients' worldviews, and learning culturally appropriate techniques. Many counseling programs have made great strides in accomplishing the first two goals. It is at the practicum level where students really learn these techniques, and we need to start focusing our training concerns on the on-site supervisors who have not yet been trained in a multicultural perspective. One of the great responsibilities of counselor education programs is to serve as a training resource for professionals in the field to help increase their level of multicultural competence so that they are in a better position to serve their clients as well as their students.

IMPLICATIONS FOR MULTICULTURAL COUNSELING RESEARCH

One way to improve the multicultural competence of our supervisors is to work with them as scientists to improve our knowledge base of what techniques work best with which clients. Over the past decade, research in issues related to cultural factors has proliferated. Within the counseling field, however, we have done a better job of describing the problem than solving it. At this point, we concur with Sue et al. (1996) that we need to turn to qualitative methods to improve our understanding of multicultural counseling. Specifically, we advocate the use of case studies to examine what type of culturally relevant interventions works with which clients. We suggest that scientists work with practicum students and their supervisors to develop exemplars of best practices. This will encourage our students to be self-reflective about their work, encourage the supervisor to engage with the cultural factors in counseling, and allow us, as educators and scientists, to develop reality-based standards of best practice. We encourage the editors of the journals that have traditionally been receptive to multicultural counseling research (*The Counseling Psychologist, Journal of Counseling Psychology, Journal of Multicultural Counseling and Development, Journal of Counseling and Development*) to regularly set aside issues for the publication of these case-based explorations.

CONCLUSION

This is an exciting moment. As our understanding of cultural factors grows, we are better able to address the challenges and take advantage of the opportunities involved in working in a culturally diverse society. To really develop an integrated practice of multicultural counseling, we advocate paying equal attention to the scientist and practitioner as we develop standards of best practice.

As you read the chapters in this book, we hope you share our excitement. We have organized the book so that it builds from a sense of the experience of how one develops in a pluralistic society to how one can creatively work with individuals from a multicultural perspective to assist them in achieving their full potential in a society that is at once rife with discrimination, oppression, and the promise of equal treatment and opportunity for all. In the first part, the chapters will focus on issues that relate to identity development in a pluralistic society, with a focus on the interplay between the structural variables of race, class, and gender and the various ways in which individuals make meaning of those variables in their own lives. The second part presents theories on how to integrate issues of class, gender, and race into counseling theory and the training of counselors. The third part presents a variety of ways in which these theories can be put into practice. The final chapter of the book represents what we believe is an excellent integrated model for counseling in a pluralistic society. The model proposed by D'Andrea and Daniels pulls together the issues of race, class, and gender as they relate to practice and shows us how we can deal with these in a respectful and caring manner.

We hope you find these chapters as informative and stimulating as we have. We thank the authors for their hard and good work that is represented in this book. We also want to thank our wives, Gail and Sara, for their support in this process and for providing us on a daily basis the great rewards that come when you live in a world that actively integrates the positive that comes from individuals from all races, classes, and each gender.

References

Arredondo, P., Toporek, R., Brown, S. P., Jones, J., Locke, D. C., Sanchez, J., & Stadler, H. (1996). Operationalization of the multicultural counseling competencies. *Journal of Multicultural Counseling and Development, 24,* 42-78.

Atkinson, D., Morten, G., & Sue, D. (1993). *Counseling American minorities* (4th ed.). Dubuque, IA: Brown & Benchmark.

Coleman, H. L. K. (1995). Strategies for coping with cultural diversity. *The Counseling Psychologist, 23,* 722-740.

Cross, W. E., Jr. (1971). The Negro-to-Black conversion experience: Toward a psychology of Black liberation. *Black World, 20*(9), 13-31.

Cross, W. E., Jr. (1991). *Shades of Black: Diversity in African American identity.* Philadelphia: Temple University Press.

Donovan, D. M., & Marlatt, G. A. (Eds.). (1988). *Assessment of addictive behaviors.* New York: Guilford.

Fowers, B. J., & Richardson, F. C. (1996). Why is multiculturalism good? *American Psychologist, 51,* 609-621.

Helm, J. E. (1993). *Black and White racial identity: Theory, research, and practice.* Westport, CT: Praeger.

Lazarus, R. S., & Folkman, S. (1984). *Stress, appraisal, and coping.* New York: Springer.

Phinney, J. (1989). Stages of ethnic identity development in minority group adolescents. *Journal of Early Adolescence, 9,* 34-49.

Slavin, L. A., Ranier, K. L., McCreary, M. L., & Gowda, K. K. (1991). *Journal of Counseling and Development, 70,* 156-164.

Sue, D. W., Ivey, A. E., & Pedersen, P. B. (1996). *A theory of multicultural counseling and therapy.* Pacific Grove, CA: Brooks/Cole.

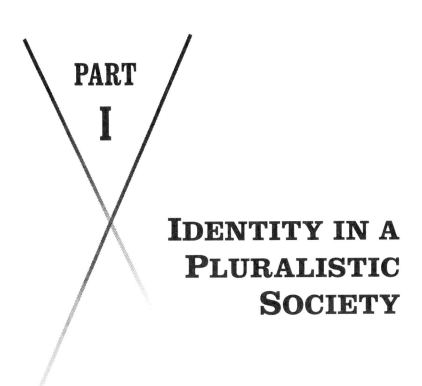

PART

I

IDENTITY IN A
PLURALISTIC
SOCIETY

THE CULTURAL CONSTRUCTION OF LATINAS

Practice Implications of Multiple Realities and Identities

Alberta M. Gloria
University of Wisconsin–Madison

*Soy un amasamiento, I am an act of kneading, of uniting and joining that
not only has produced both a creature of darkness and a creature of light,
but also a creature that questions the definitions of light and dark and
gives them new meanings.*
—Anzaldúa (1987, p. 81)

The reality of a Latina is *un choque,* a cultural collision constructed from numerous experiences and identities that form her new and unique existence. That
is, she integrates multiple roles and realities that shape her social experiences
and structures (Anzaldúa, 1987), particularly those realities ascribed to her by

AUTHOR'S NOTE: Because of the many identities that construct my reality as a Chicana/
Latina, I extend my sincerest thanks and appreciation to Jeffrey S. Hird and Hyun-nie Ahn for
their personal support in my writing of this chapter. This chapter is dedicated to my father, Albert
Gloria. I received the Ninth Annual Women of Color Psychologies Award (1999) from Division
35 (Psychology of Women) of the American Psychological Association for this chapter.

the values, traditions, assumptions, and biases of the larger society (Hurtado, 1989). As such, a bidirectional process occurs whereby a Latina is influenced by societal perceptions while she creates her reality from dynamic cultural factors, including race/ethnicity, gender, socioeconomic status, language, sexual orientation, physical and mental capabilities, spirituality, immigration status, levels of acculturation and traditionality, ethnic identity, educational and professional status, age, and roles within her families and communities. Although these dimensions have subjective meaning and salience for each Latina, they provide multiple contexts for understanding Latina identities in relation to self, family, community, and society.

Although considerable debate exists regarding the most appropriate term or label by which to identify Latinas (Hayes-Bautista & Chapa, 1987; Melville, 1988; Portes & Truelove, 1987; Treviño, 1987), the term *Latina* will be used in this chapter because it reflects both race/ethnicity and gender. *Latinas* will refer to Mexican-, Cuban-, Puerto Rican-, and South and Central American-descended women currently residing in the United States. Despite the current argument regarding the "correct" or most appropriate terminology for Latinos (see Oboler, 1995), Padilla (1995) asserted that social and cultural "politics" are secondary to the psychological implications of the self-referents used. Although the debate concerning the use and nuances of terminologies is beyond the scope of this chapter, use of the term *Latina* is not intended to negate or minimize the varied realities experienced by these women.

Holding a lower socioeconomic status relative to White women, White men, and racial/ethnic minority men, Latinas endure a triple oppression (Flores-Ortiz, 1995; Vasquez, 1984, 1994). That is, a Latina is a racial/ethnic minority, a woman, and often a member of the lowest socioeconomic class (Ortiz, 1994; Rivers, 1995; Vasquez, 1984). Furthermore, Latinas are often "physically segregated from the rest of society . . . suffer[ing] a disproportionate share of social and economic instability" (Giachello, 1996, p. 122). For instance, Comas-Díaz (1988) stated that a Puerto Rican-descended woman "must simultaneously stand against a society outside her community that discriminates against her as a Puerto Rican and a society within her community that demands her submissiveness as a woman" (p. 22). Similarly, Mexican-descended women endure "triple oppression by virtue of their sex, lower socioeconomic status and the internal male dominance (machismo) inherent in the Mexican-American culture" (Vasquez, 1984, p. 20).

Despite general descriptors that characterize Latinas, numerous differences exist between and within Latino groups and subgroups. Given that Latinos originate from more than 20 different countries (Giachello, 1996), no single or "typical" Latino population (García & Marotta, 1997; Queralt, 1984) or "typical" Latina exists (Ortiz, 1994). The assumption of a "typical" Latina is further dispelled given that Latinas vary by age, ethnic identity, geographical location, generational status, level of acculturation, and socioeconomic status (Comas-Díaz, 1994; Giachello, 1996; Vasquez, 1984, 1994).

Given the between- and within-group heterogeneity of Latinas, this chapter will focus primarily on the integration and salience of multiple Latina identities and realities. The first section provides a contextual basis for the chapter, reviewing selected demographic and historical issues for women descended from Mexico, Puerto Rico, Cuba, and Central and South America. The next section describes the salience of race/ethnicity and gender for Latinas. In the third section, additional identities for Latinas (i.e., educational and professional status, immigration status, and sexual orientation) will briefly be discussed. The fourth section outlines current concerns regarding theory development for women of color, Latinas in particular. A review of three Latina-focused counseling approaches is presented in the fifth section. That is, integrative theory (Comas-Díaz, 1994), *un grupo de apoyo para mujeres* (a Latina support group) (Arredondo, 1991), and *la conciencia de la mestiza* (a new consciousness) (Anzaldúa, 1987) are addressed. Finally, attitudes and beliefs, types of knowledge, and skills are proposed for conceptualizing and providing culturally sensitive and competent counseling services to Latinas.

OVERVIEW OF WOMEN DESCENDED FROM MEXICO, PUERTO RICO, CUBA, AND CENTRAL AND SOUTH AMERICA

Latinos represent 9.6% of the total U.S. population (Giachello, 1996), an underestimation given the number of undocumented individuals residing in the United States. Furthermore, Latinos comprise many distinct subgroups from North, Central, and South America (Chapa & Valencia, 1993; García & Marotta, 1997), each having different economic and political reasons for migration (Rogler, 1994). Currently, individuals of Mexican descent constitute the largest group of Latinos (60%), followed by Puerto Rican-descended (12%) and Cuban-descended (5%) individuals (Chapa & Valencia, 1993). Although South and Central American-descended individuals comprise 22% of the U.S. Latino population, their between-group differences (e.g., ethnicity, national origin) have often been overlooked in the literature (Bean & Tienda, 1987; Marín & Marín, 1991). Furthermore, South and Central American- descended Latinos are commonly referred to as "Other" Latinos by researchers (Chapa &

Valencia, 1993; Ginorio, Gutiérrez, Cauce, & Acosta, 1995; Marín & Marín, 1991).

Given the numerous subgroups of Latinos, only individuals of Mexican, Puerto Rican, and Cuban ancestry will be reviewed specifically. Latinos of Central and South American ancestry will be reviewed as a group. The following section is intended to provide not in-depth information about Latinas but a brief overview from which counselors can contextualize and conceptualize the multiple realities (e.g., social, political, economic, and historical dimensions) of their Latina clients.

Mexican-Descended Women

Latinos of Mexican heritage generally reside in the Southwest (Marín & Marín, 1991) and Midwest (Chapa & Valencia, 1993). With the subjugation of the indigenous Indian populations by the Spaniards in the 16th century, Mexicans became mestizos (i.e., comprising many different races) (Anzaldúa, 1987; Bean & Tienda, 1987). By the end of the Mexican-American War in 1848, many Mexican-descended individuals who had migrated to the present southwestern United States (which was then Mexico) had their land annexed by the U.S. government with the Treaty of Guadalupe Hidalgo (Marín & Marín, 1991). As a result of geographical proximity to Mexico, continued migration, and extensive economic history with the United States, Mexican-descended individuals have the greatest degree of generational heterogeneity compared to other Latino groups (Bean & Tienda, 1987). Ironically, Mexican-descended individuals continue to experience social and political discrimination in the United States yet are strangers in their native homeland (Anzaldúa, 1987).

Mexican-descended women are the youngest Latina group (median age = 24.6 years) and have the largest mean family size of 4.0 people. Furthermore, these women have the lowest median female income of $10,098 per year, with less than half (46.2%) of those 25 years or older having completed 4 years of high school or more. Less than one fifth (19.4%) of Mexican-descended women are heads of their household, with 46% of these families living in poverty (U.S. Bureau of the Census, 1994).

Puerto Rican-Descended Women

Although Latinos of Puerto Rican heritage have lived in the United States for more than a century, a mass immigration of Puerto Ricans occurred after

World War II in response to economic opportunities in the United States (Bean & Tienda, 1987; Payton, 1985). Many Puerto Rican-descended Latinos returned to their homeland during the 1960s and 1970s, thereby creating a slow "revolving-door migration" through the 1980s (Marín & Marín, 1991; Moore & Pinderhughes, 1995). Despite Puerto Rico's status as a U.S. commonwealth, U.S. economic and social policies have been minimally committed to enhancing the Puerto Rican economy. As such, Puerto Rican-descended individuals have been integrated into U.S. society as "second class citizenry" (Bean & Tienda, 1987). Currently, many Puerto Rican-descended Latinos live in the Northeast (Chapa & Valencia, 1993), specifically in New York and New Jersey (Marín & Marín, 1991). Despite strong cultural ties to both Puerto Rico and the United States, second-generation Puerto Rican-descended Latinos born in New York self-identify as *Nuyoricans,* a term reflecting their experience as living between two countries and their marginalization in Puerto Rico and the United States (Bean & Tienda, 1987).

Puerto Rican-descended women are slightly older than Mexican-descended women (median age = 26.9 years) and have a smaller mean family size of 3.3 people. Furthermore, they have the highest median female income of $14,200 as compared to other Latina groups, with 59.8% of those 25 years or older having completed 4 or more years of high school. Approximately two fifths (40.5%) of Puerto Rican-descended women (the most of any Latina group) are heads of their household, with nearly two thirds (60.3%) of these families living in poverty (U.S. Bureau of the Census, 1994).

Cuban-Descended Women

Cuban-descended Latinos generally live in the Southeast (Chapa & Valencia, 1993), concentrated in Florida (Marín & Marín, 1991) and, to a lesser degree, in California (Los Angeles), New Jersey, New York, Illinois (Chicago), and Texas (Bernal, 1982; Queralt, 1984). Cuban-descended individuals have Spanish and African ancestry, as the indigenous population was virtually eradicated (Bernal, 1982). Although Cuban-descended communities existed in the United States as early as the 1870s (Marín & Marín, 1991), many individuals were political refugees and arrived during one of three migration waves: (a) following the Cuban Revolution in 1959, (b) after the Bay of Pigs invasion in 1961 (Payton, 1985), and (c) during the immigration of *Marielitos* (individuals who left Cuba from the Mariel port) in the 1980s (Oboler, 1995). The first two waves of political refugees were provided training and placement services (Marín &

Marín, 1991; Moore & Pinderhughes, 1995); however, those in the third wave were placed in detainment camps and not offered similar economic opportunities. The perception that Cuban immigrants are economically successful as a result of U.S. government intervention has promoted a social distancing between individuals of Cuban descent and other Latinos (Queralt, 1984).

Cuban-descended women are the oldest of all Latina groups (median age = 43.6 years) and also have the smallest mean family size of 3.1 people. Although 62.1% of those 25 years or older have completed 4 years of high school or more, the median female income is $14,117. Less than one fifth (19.4%) of Cuban-descended women are heads of their household (U.S. Bureau of the Census, 1994).

Central or South American-Descended Women

Although use of the term *Other Latinos* for Central or South American-descended women is a function of convenience for governing agencies and academic researchers (much like the use of the terms *Latino* and *Hispanic* [Portes & Truelove, 1987]), this group is the most diverse and heterogeneous by national origin and sociodemographic characteristics (Bean & Tienda, 1987; Marín & Marín, 1991). Many of these individuals left their homelands seeking increased educational and employment opportunities and refuge from political change (Marín & Marín, 1991).

Central and South American Latino-descended individuals are the second largest Latino group in the United States (Chapa & Valencia, 1993), but they are largely not identified or discussed in the literature because of their sociodemographic and national heterogeneity (Bean & Tienda, 1987; Ginorio et al., 1995). Central American-descended individuals (e.g., Costa Rica, Nicaragua, Panama) and South American-descended individuals (e.g., Colombia, Venezuela) reside predominately in New York and San Francisco (Paniagua, 1994). Also identified as "Other" Latinos, many Salvadorians, Guatamalans, Nicaraguans, and Dominicans came to the United States as refugees from political oppression (Marín & Marín, 1991; Moore & Pinderhughes, 1995). Given that the United States has not acknowledged their refugee status, Central and South American Latinos remain among the poorest in the nation, living as undocumented workers with minimal job security and low wage earnings (Moore & Pinderhughes, 1995).

Central and South American-descended women have a median age of 28.6 years and a mean family size of 3.6 people. Despite their status as the most educated of all Latina groups, with 62.9% of individuals 25 years or older having completed 4 years of high school or more, the median female income is only $10,249. One of every four (24.7%) Central or South American-descended women is the head of her household, and half (51.3%) of these families live in poverty (U.S. Bureau of the Census, 1994). These demographics should be viewed cautiously given their representation of numerous countries and ethnicities.

In summary, the vast differences in sociocontextual and sociohistorical experiences underscore the heterogeneity in realities between and within Latina groups. Given these differences, counselors must integrate sociopolitical and sociohistorical influences into their conceptualization and treatment of Latina clients. In addition, racial/ethnic and gender influences are salient mediators of Latina realities that warrant extensive consideration by mental health professionals. Therefore, the following section will examine the salience of race/ethnicity, gender, and the interaction of race/ethnicity and gender in Latina identities.

CONSTRUCT SALIENCE: RACE/ETHNICITY VERSUS GENDER

> Ethnic women may find themselves in a double bind; that is, a choice to address women's issues is seen by ethnic men as contradictory to their work on ethnic problems. On the other hand, a choice to address ethnic issues may be seen by White women as negation of female status. (Santos de Barona & Reid, 1992, p. 97)

The interrelationships of race/ethnicity and gender are not easily addressed because each construct is dynamic as a function of individual and societal change (Griscom, 1979). That is, the salience or importance ascribed to each construct may change across personal, social, political, and environmental contexts. The danger in emphasizing sexism, both in theory and practice, is in overlooking or de-emphasizing racism and in effect perpetuating the focus on gender as a "White elitist movement" (Griscom, 1979, p. 11). At the same time, an overemphasis on race/ethnicity neglects Latinas' gender. Thus, a multifaceted framework that examines the interaction effects of gender and race/ethnicity within context is necessary when counseling women of color (Reid & Comas-Díaz, 1990). In the following section, identity issues will be discussed relative to Latinas as women and as racial/ethnic minorities.

Identity as a Woman or a Woman of Color?

The race/ethnicity and gender literatures typify the experiences of women of color, failing to consider between-group differences by race/ethnicity and culture. Although there are indeed similarities among different racial/ethnic minority women, clustering women of color into a single group minimizes and negates distinct and important differences. The belief that gender is the common bond for all women renders women of color invisible (Brown, 1990; Espín, 1993, 1994). That is, the portrayal of "raceless" or "nonethnic" women denies the social, environmental, and cultural realities and identities of women of color. Furthermore, Reid and Kelly (1994) indicated that the study of the "universal woman" focuses only on While middle-class women. As such, inherent to any discussion of women is the need to integrate racial/ethnic issues. Although addressing commonalities of gender deconstructs images and symbols of women, understanding the role of race/ethnicity *and* gender promotes an understanding of the contexts and experiences of all women (Mullings, 1994).

For instance, there is an unfounded belief that all women experience the same socialization and oppression (Reid, 1994). "The egocentricity of this belief has allowed us to accept a psychology of women that treats the middle-class experience as totally representative, if not the totality, of women's worlds" (Reid, 1993, p. 135). By focusing on the universality of women's struggles, the impact of racial/ethnic minority group membership is overlooked and therefore minimized (Tarver-Behring, 1994). Given the within-group heterogeneity among Latinas, assuming similarities among Latina subgroups negates significant historical, economical, social, and cultural differences.

Womanhood is constructed differently for racial/ethnic minority women than for White women (Hurtado, 1989), differently for subgroups of racial/ethnic minority women (Davenport & Yurich, 1991), and differently within groups of racial/ethnic women as well (Ortiz, 1994). Hurtado (1989) indicated that White women have a wider range of choices (e.g., identify or not identify with White culture) and rewards (e.g., power, status, or both) for identifying with the White culture. That is, inherent in the nature of race privilege is the ability not to recognize race/ethnicity and to have the option of choosing racial/ethnic salience (Waters, 1990). For women of color, however, no options exist; Latinas are not perceived or viewed as White, regardless of attempts by others or Latinas to identify or conform to White culture.

In understanding the choice of attending to race/ethnicity or gender, Eberhardt and Fiske (1994) contended that racial/ethnic minority groups are more segregated from each other than are women and men. That is, an individual living in the United Statesis more likely to have minimal contact with racial/ethnic minorities than to have contact with members of the opposite sex. Furthermore, the degree of segregation will directly influence the formulation and content of racial/ethnic minority and gender stereotypes (Fiske & Stevens, 1993). Given that stereotypes contain both descriptive (i.e., information about what a "typical" group member is like) and prescriptive (i.e., information about what a group member "should" be like) elements (Eberhardt & Fiske, 1994), racial/ethnic minority stereotypes tend to be primarily descriptive, whereas gender stereotypes are both descriptive and prescriptive. That is, racial/ethnic stereotypes include descriptive characterizations (e.g., lazy, dirty, uneducated), whereas female gender stereotypes are descriptive (e.g., passive, weak, hysterical) and prescriptive (e.g., "should" be accommodating to others, "should" be "feminine"). In extending this argument, stereotypes derived from both race/ethnicity and gender, as they occur for Latinas and other women of color, would be even more difficult to dispel.

Examining the salience of race/ethnicity and gender, Abrahams (1996) conducted 50 in-depth interviews with 11 Latina and 39 Anglo women regarding their empowerment from community participation. The primary motive for Latinas' participation was race/ethnicity, which helped them shape their career choices, strengthen their ties to the Latino community, and unite in their collective identity as Latinas. For the Anglo women, race/ethnicity was not a conscious impetus for community commitment. Rather, gender was identified as the most salient factor contributing to their empowerment. That Latinas and White women ascribed different subjective meanings to race/ethnicity, and gender indicates that race/ethnicity and gender must be considered across sociocultural and sociopolitical contexts.

Identity as a Racial/Ethnic Minority or a Woman of Color?

Both race/ethnicity and gender are identified within the term *Latina.* That is, the word *Latino* is nongendered, referring to both males and females, whereas the word *Latina* is gender specific, identifying females only. Recently, scholars have added the endings "o/a" or "a/o" to the term *Latino* (i.e., Latino/a,

Latina/o), enabling readers to clearly identify the gender of the group being discussed. Controversy exists, however, regarding the use of the o/a or a/o suffix (Dernersesian, 1993), as the use of o/a identifies race/ethnicity first, whereas a/o identifies gender first.

Considered a political and ideological conflict, particularly by male Latinos, the "splitting of [Latino] subjectivity" has been criticized as oppositional to Latino interests because gender is identified before race/ethnicity (Dernersesian, 1993). Although the split in subjectivity between race/ethnicity and gender has occurred at a grammatical level (i.e., spelling), the sociopolitical shift in Latina identity stems from deep-rooted sociocultural and sociopolitical issues. That is, Dernersesian argued that Latinas have been omitted from group characterizations or systems that privileged male identities and subjectivities, as evidenced by Latinas being subsumed under the term *Latino*. Latinas have subsequently challenged the male-oriented characterization of Latinas by subverting gender and racial/ethnic identities and proclaiming their self-defined and subjective realities. As a result, the a/o or o/a suffix culturally and politically underscores the presence of Latinas by providing a context of gender for the term *Latino* (Dernersesian, 1993). Given the differences in salience that may be ascribed to race/ethnicity and gender, assessing a Latina's self-identification (e.g., Latina, Latino, Chicano) and the meaning she gives to her self-definition is critical. That is, this information can help counselors to contextualize (a) a Latina's self-defined reality; (b) the influences of race/ethnicity, gender, and the race/ethnicity by gender interaction on her worldview and the world's view of her; and (c) the degree to which she is influenced by societal oppressions. Understanding the complexities of race/ethnicity, gender, and their interaction will also allow counselors to further clarify the self, cultural, and community expectations and assumptions of Latinas in their multiple roles. Although identity development for women of color most often occurs within a context of family and community (Santos de Barona & Reid, 1992), role and identity conflicts often occur between the expectations of family and community and those of the dominant White culture (Reid, 1994). Some of these conflicts will be highlighted in the next section.

Although this section has focused specifically on the integration of race/ethnicity and gender into Latina identity, numerous other identities form the experiences, realities, and roles of Latinas. Because it is beyond the scope of this chapter to fully address all of the many Latina identities that exist, three factors in particular will be discussed. That is, the mediating and moderating influences of education, immigration, and sexual orientation will be highlighted.

T RAVERSING LATINA IDENTITIES: EDUCATION, IMMIGRATION, AND SEXUAL ORIENTATION

Identifying and Defining Identities

In struggling for self-definition and meaning within a racist and sexist society, Latinas' boundaries between self, family, and community often overlap (Abrahams, 1996). As such, the need to identify, understand, and bridge identities is key to promoting Latina well-being. The guiding assumption of this section, therefore, is that the integration and balance of multiple identifications across and within multiple contexts can occur by finding membership and meaning in cultural subgroups.

Educational and Professional Status. Succeeding in high school and higher education is particularly difficult for Latinas because they often need to overcome financial need, racism, alienation, isolation, and environments that often are only minimally tolerant of diversity (Gloria, 1997; Ponterotto, 1990; Secada et al., 1998; Vasquez, 1982). The relationship of educational level to socioeconomic or class status is well documented and thus has direct implications for Latina social identities. For instance, professional women of color not only face difficulties of balancing family, community, and work relationships (Arredondo, 1991), but they must also (a) link their professional aspirations with community needs, (b) serve as the conscience (e.g., racial/ethnic and gender) of their organization or institution, (c) prove their professional competency, and (d) find outlets to express anger regarding the aforementioned stressors (Comas-Díaz & Greene, 1994). Despite the energy required to juggle academic and home cultures (Fiske, 1988) and maintain a sense of cultural congruence (Gloria & Robinson-Kurpius, 1996), Latinas who are students or professionals must somehow balance family and career goals with cultural values and roles (Arredondo, 1991; Vasquez, 1982).

Immigration Status. Many Latinas struggle to define new identities and roles as a result of immigrating to a new country (Vargas-Willis & Cervantes, 1987). That is, many Latina immigrants experience racism for the first time as a "minority" group member when they enter the United States (Arredondo, 1991). Furthermore, Latina immigrants face many premigration stressors, including (a) leaving family members (including children) behind with hopes of reuniting with them after establishing financial stability, (b) entering the United States without proper documents, and (c) needing to learn English to traverse different communities. Furthermore, Latina immigrants often experience migration stressors of displacement, alienation, and loss of personal control, status, and community (Sciarra & Ponterotto, 1991; Vargas-Willis & Cervantes, 1987). Postmigration stressors include acculturation, unemployment, marital and family relationships, physical and psychological traumas (e.g., physical torture or political persecution), and societal oppression and discrimination (Cienfuegos & Monelli, 1983; Espín, 1987; Ginorio et al., 1995; Vargas-Willis & Cervantes, 1987). As a result of these experiences, assuming an identity as an "immigrant" or "minority" and adapting within a new country can be a lifelong process (Ginorio et al., 1995).

Sexual Orientation. Latina lesbians and bisexuals need to traverse the lesbian/bisexual community, Latino and Latina communities, and predominately heterocentric White communities (Morales, 1990, 1992). In extending the triple-oppression concept discussed earlier (Rivers, 1995; Vasquez, 1984), Latina lesbians and bisexuals may experience a "quadruple oppression" as a member of a racial/ethnic minority group, a woman, a socioeconomically disadvantaged individual, and a "sexual minority" (Yep, 1995, p. 207). Latina lesbians/bisexuals must assume and balance multiple identities (de Monteflores, 1986) because of multidimensional oppressions. Because gender roles within Latina/o families and culture are well established and many heterocentric values and behaviors are expected (Greene, 1994), homophobia within Latina/o cultures is often more intense than within White cultures (Morales, 1992). Consequently, identifying as a lesbian or bisexual may be viewed within Latino communities as a "treasonous" act against both family and culture (Greene, 1994). For instance, Mexican-descended lesbians are often perceived as a threat to the established male order of dominance within communities (Trujillo, 1991).

Balancing Identities

A bi- or multicultural identification by definition implies an alliance to two or more cultures either by choice or by force (Ayala-Vazquez, 1979). Thus, Latinas must have a clear understanding of their value systems and contexts to create and maintain balance of their multiple realities (Comas-Díaz, 1994). The efforts required to balance identities often press Latinas to draw on their emotional or psychic reserves (Anzaldúa, 1987, 1990). Addictive behaviors, depression, psychosomatizations, and stress or anxiety are common concerns of Latinas who must traverse multiple realities (Comas-Díaz & Greene, 1994). Consequently, counselors need to help Latinas access formal and informal support systems to facilitate their clients' emotional, social, and environmental well-being.

For instance, counselors would most likely consider different support systems, attend to different oppressions, and help to balance different identities for a client who identifies as a lesbian Latino woman versus a Latina lesbian. Based on self-identification, a lesbian Latino woman places the salience of her multiple identities first on her sexual identity, followed by race/ethnicity with gender subsumed. In contrast, a Latina lesbian places her primary focus on her integrated race/ethnicity and gender identity, followed by sexual identity. Understanding the self-ascribed and societal-imposed meanings for Latinas across contexts can help counselors to understand the multiple realities and identities of Latinas. Consequently, therapeutic approaches that address context, identities, and multiple realities are needed when working with Latinas. In the following section, three context-specific counseling approaches that address multiple identities and contexts for Latinas will be reviewed.

CURRENT THERAPEUTIC APPROACHES FOR COUNSELING LATINAS

The Assumed Invisibility of Latinas in Feminist Theory

Given that many theories fail to address cultural, environmental, political, and social issues, counselors have employed feminist theory to create counseling frameworks for Latinas and women of color. Although the application of feminist theory to Latinas has merit, many scholars have questioned the utility and validity of feminist theory for women of color (Brown, 1990; Espín, 1993, 1994, 1995; Kanuha, 1990; Mays & Comas-Díaz, 1988). For instance,

> Feminist therapy and feminist therapy theory have been developed by and with white women. Currently, feminist theory is neither diverse nor complex in the reality it reflects. It has been deficient from the start in its inclusiveness of the lives and realities of women of color, poor working class women, non-North American women, women over sixty-five, or women with disabilities. (Brown, 1990, p. 3)

Mays and Comas-Díaz (1988) argued that the basic tenets of feminist theory omit Latinas and other women of color from theoretical consideration. For
instance, the premise that the oppression of women is the most fundamental or
salient oppression for all women perpetuates the myth of a universal woman,
negating racial/ethnic and cultural differences (Espín, 1995; Mays &
Comas-Díaz, 1988). Feminist theory also posits that as a group, women have
more in common (i.e., gender) than do women of color and men of color (i.e.,
race/ethnicity) (Mays & Comas-Díaz, 1988). Cogently argued by Espín (1995),
women of color are "simply unknown to most white feminists and considered
irrelevant by people in their own ethnic group" (p. 127).

Because the realities of women of color are often invalidated (Espín,
1995), many women-of-color researchers and practitioners refuse to identify
with feminist theory given its cultural biases and denial of other racial/ethnic
and cultural identities (Kanuha, 1990). Mays and Comas-Díaz (1988) indicated
that the "primacy of gender division tended to ignore the strong realities of ethnicity, race, culture, and class bonds in the lives of ethnic minority group members" (p. 229). Instead, attending to empowerment issues within sociocultural
contexts is imperative to ensure that feminist theory contributes to theoretical
and conceptual understandings (e.g., mental health, identity) of women of color
(Espín, 1994).

Counseling approaches that reflect and integrate multiple Latina contexts
and realities are needed to provide culturally competent and relevant services.
Although several clinical applications to counseling Latinas have been developed (Davenport & Yurich, 1991; Ponterotto, 1989; Ramírez, 1987), three approaches or philosophies developed by and for Latinas will be emphasized
here. These approaches include the integrative approach (Comas-Díaz, 1994),
un grupo de apoyo para mujeres (Arredondo, 1991), and *la conciencia de la
mestiza* (Anzaldúa, 1987, 1990).

Integrative Approach

The work of the prominent scholar Lillian Comas-Díaz includes numerous
books and journal articles that specifically address therapeutic issues and counseling approaches with Latinas (Puerto Rican-descended women in particular)
and women of color. The integrative approach to self-concept development for
women of color encompasses gender, race/ethnicity, and the interaction of
race/ethnicity and gender (Comas-Díaz, 1994). Within the integrative approach, the counselor prompts Latinas to (a) reclaim or recover their sense of

self through positive self-esteem and attribution; (b) achieve dignity through self-efficacy, mastery, and determination; and (c) transform their self and situation by developing a critical consciousness. This *conscientização* involves the "awareness and restoration of dignity and self-perception by recognizing the ability to transform one-self and one's world" (Comas-Díaz, 1994, pp. 290-291). In promoting self-understanding, Comas-Díaz argued that counselors need to help Latinas define and understand their (a) womanhood, (b) identity conflicts (e.g., sexual, class, ethnic, and gender), and (c) spirituality (e.g., sense of oneness and harmony with the universe). Furthermore, both the client and the counselor need to address their gender and ethnoracial realities to connect internal experiences with the Latina's contextual realities.

Un Grupo de Apoyo Para Mujeres (A Support Group for Women)

Another prominent scholar is Patricia Arredondo, whose work has been instrumental in defining multicultural competencies and standards for counseling (Sue, Arredondo, & McDavis, 1992). Arredondo (1991) described a psychoeducational support group for Latina immigrants or "women in transition who must face multiple changes [and multiple realities] simultaneously" (p. 150). The group addressed eight culturally relevant topic areas, each attempting to empower women in their new roles and functions in their new communities and country. Group foci were (a) personal introductions, (b) information about health services, (c) information about community services and resources, (d) change and adjustment concerns, (e) expectations regarding their children's education, (f) parenting issues, (g) stress and anxiety management, and (h) personal well-being and support. This psychoeducational group approach is also applicable with other Latina subgroups, including Latina lesbians and/or professionals. Although topical foci may need to be redefined, the premise of the group is generalizable as counselors integrate different social contexts (e.g., family, work, environment) with different relational contexts (e.g., partner, mother, daughter).

La Conciencia de la Mestiza (The Conscience of the Mestiza)

Although not necessarily an approach to counseling, an important contextual framework for providing psychological services to Latinas was conceptualized by Gloria Anzaldúa (1987, 1990), a widely respected Latina novelist and poet. Identified as a "new consciousness" or *la conciencia de la mestiza,* each individual is conceptualized as the totality of different identities that create a new and unique consciousness, rather than as separate identities. Mestizo/a means a summative mixture of cultures and identities (Anzaldúa, 1987) or a dynamic and synergistic intermingling of cultural, physical, psychological, and spiritual dimensions (Ramírez, 1982). More specifically, a *mestizaje* consciousness simultaneously perceives multiple realities, moves from convergent to divergent thinking (Anzaldúa, 1987), and listens to many voices simultaneously (Anzaldúa, 1990). Hurtado (1989) succinctly described the *mestizaje* consciousness as a dynamic entity that "simultaneously rejects and embraces—so not as to exclude—what it rejects" (p. 855).

In helping Latina clients traverse "borders" of cultures or identities (e.g., White world vs. Latina/o world, woman vs. Latina, traditional vs. contemporary Latina/o cultural values), counselors can address the emotional stress resulting from balancing identities. Given that women of color often cannot fully participate in their traditional cultures (vis-à-vis sexism) or in White culture (vis-à-vis racism), they often experience a sense of alienation and isolation (Anzaldúa, 1987). Thus, counselors can help Latina clients generate a support system to successfully navigate cultures and ascribe meaning to their roles (Arredondo, 1991), thereby achieving congruence between real and perceived selves (Comas-Díaz, 1994).

PROPOSED CULTURAL COUNSELING COMPETENCIES FOR WORKING WITH LATINAS

In helping Latina clients to balance identities within different contexts, the integrative, *un grupo de apoyo para mujeres,* and *la conciencia de la mestiza* approaches provide counselors with frameworks from which to provide culturally relevant services. However, applications of the approaches are not "recipes" or formulas intended to circumvent the development of multicultural competencies (Olmedo & Parron, 1981). Rather, continuous development of culturally relevant knowledge and skills and deconstruction of negative attitudes and beliefs about Latinas allow counselors to provide competent and appropriate psychological services to Latinas.

Extending the work of Sue et al. (1992), the following multicultural competencies are proposed. Although not intended to be exhaustive, these guidelines provide a conceptual foundation for counselors working with Latinas.

Attitudes and Beliefs

1. Counselors are aware of their personal attitudes, assumptions, and stereotypes about Latinas. Counselors consciously avoid the assumption that all women (and all Latinas) construct and experience contexts similarly (Brown, 1990).
2. Counselors are aware of the multiple identities that construct Latina realities, whereby race/ethnicity is not assumed to be the primary identity for Latinas, and gender is not assumed to be the primary issue for women of color (Moraga & Anzaldúa, 1981).
3. Counselors espouse a "difference equals diversity" attitude when Latina values, beliefs, and behaviors are different from their own.
4. Counselors are willing to continuously examine their own values and increase their knowledge regarding Latinas' economic, historical, social, and cultural contexts.
5. Counselors consider environmental, social, historical, and political variables that affect Latinas and avoid pathologizing or blaming Latina/o culture for presenting issues or concerns. That is, counselors should not assume that a Latina client understands her stressors and resulting symptoms, as many Latinas do not conceptualize their concerns as a function of specific etiological factors (Vargas-Willis & Cervantes, 1987).

Types of Knowledge

1. Counselors are familiar with the social, historical, environmental, and political factors that affect different Latina groups (i.e., Mexican-, Puerto Rican-, Cuban-, South and Central American-descended individuals) (see Bean & Tienda, 1987; Oboler, 1995) and subgroups (e.g., lesbians, immigrants, and professionals) (see Comas-Díaz & Greene, 1994). Counselors also understand that no "typical" Latina exists.
2. Counselors understand the issues inherent in gender role socialization and the splitting of subjectivities (a/o and o/a) for Latinas (see Dernersesian, 1993).
3. Counselors are familiar with Latina/o cultural values (e.g., *familismo, respecto, simpata, personalismo, marianismo, hembrismo*). Similarly, counselors are familiar with how these values influence

the counseling process (see Comas-Díaz & Greene, 1994; Marín & Marín, 1991; Morales, 1992; Paniagua, 1994).

4. Counselors have a working understanding of mestizo consciousness (see Anzaldúa, 1987, 1990; Ramírez, 1983).
5. Counselors are aware of the ramifications of excluding Latinas in theory and service delivery (see Hurtado, 1989; Reid & Kelly, 1994).

Skills

1. Counselors can assess the salience and ascribed meaning given to the different identities faced by Latinas and are able to integrate these subjectivities into the counseling process. That is, counselors can assess the psychological implications of self-referents used by Latina clients (Padilla, 1995).
2. Counselors can help Latinas integrate and attend to the stress of their multiple roles and identities. For instance, counselors can assess the roles and meanings ascribed to Latinas by family, community, and work or career and help clients to find balance and bridge their roles.
3. Counselors can establish and maintain a Latino community resource network. For instance, counselors can access a bilingual facilitator if a Latina prefers conducting therapy in Spanish.
4. Counselors are flexible in assuming different therapeutic roles for Latinas (e.g., adviser, change agent, facilitator, consultant) (see Atkinson, Thompson, & Grant, 1993).
5. Counselors actively facilitate change in the lives of Latinas through institutional and structural change in society (Espín, 1993).

SUMMARY

The multiple realities experienced by Latinas create numerous conceptual complexities for counselors (Griscom, 1979). That is, counselors must continuously develop their cultural competencies with Latinas by (a) expanding their consciousness and counseling abilities and (b) examining their assumptions and stereotypes. Three context-specific counseling approaches have been described for counselors to help Latinas traverse and bridge their different realities (Anzaldúa, 1987; Flores-Ortiz, 1993, 1995; Lugones, 1990). In summary, counselors must move beyond their tendency to assess others through myopic lenses of either race/ethnicity or gender and examine the interactive influences and socialization processes of various identities and constructs (Comas-Díaz, 1994; Davenport & Yurich, 1991).

References

Abrahams, N. (1996). Negotiating power, identity, family, and community: Women's community participation. *Gender and Society, 10,* 768-796.

Anzaldúa, G. (1987). *Borderlands/La frontera: The new mestiza.* San Francisco: Aunt Lute.

Anzaldúa, G. (1990). La conciencia de la mestiza: Towards a new consciousness. In G. Anzaldúa (Ed.), *Making face, making soul/Haciendo caras: Creative and critical perspectives by feminists of color* (pp. 377-389). San Francisco: Aunt Lute.

Arredondo, P. (1991). Counseling Latinas. In C. C. Lee & B. L. Richardson (Eds.), *Multicultural issues in counseling: New approaches to diversity* (pp. 143-156). Alexandria, VA: American Association for Counseling and Development.

Atkinson, D. R., Thompson, C. E., & Grant, S. K. (1993). A three-dimensional model for counseling racial/ethnic minorities. *The Counseling Psychologist, 21,* 257-277.

Ayala-Vazquez, N. (1979). The guidance and counseling of Hispanic females. *Journal of Non-White Concerns, 7,* 114-121.

Bean, F. D., & Tienda, M. (1987). *The Hispanic population of the United States.* New York: Russell Sage.

Bernal, G. (1982). Cuban families. In M. McGoldrick, J. K. Pearce, & J. Giordano (Eds.), *Ethnicity and family therapy* (pp. 187-207). New York: Guilford.

Brown, L. S. (1990). The meaning of a multicultural perspective for theory-building in feminist theory. In L. S. Brown & M. P. P. Root (Eds.), *Diversity and complexity in feminist therapy* (pp. 1-17). New York: Haworth.

Chapa, J., & Valencia, R. R. (1993). Latino population growth, demographic characteristics, and educational stagnation: An examination of recent trends. *Hispanic Journal of Behavioral Sciences, 15,* 165-187.

Cienfuegos, A., & Monelli, C. (1983). The testimony of political repression as a therapeutic instrument. *American Journal of Orthopsychiatry, 54,* 43-51.

Comas-Díaz, L. (1988). Mainland Puerto Rican woman: A sociocultural approach. *Journal of Community Psychology, 16,* 21-31.

Comas-Díaz, L. (1994). An integrative approach. In L. Comas-Díaz & B. Greene (Eds.), *Women of color: Integrating ethnic and gender identities in psychotherapy* (pp. 287-318). New York: Guilford.

Comas-Díaz, L., & Greene, B. (1994). Women of color with professional status. In L. Comas-Díaz & B. Greene (Eds.), *Women of color: Integrating ethnic and gender identities in psychotherapy* (pp. 347-388). New York: Guilford.

Davenport, D. S., & Yurich, J. M. (1991). Multicultural gender issues. *Journal of Counseling and Development, 70,* 64-71.

de Montefiores, C. (1986). Notes on the management of difference. In T. S. Stein & C. J. Cohen (Eds.), *Contemporary perspective on psychotherapy with lesbians and gay men* (pp. 73-101). New York: Plenum.

Dernersesian, A. C. (1993). And, yes . . . the earth did part: On the splitting of Chicana/o subjectivity. In A. de la Torre & B. M. Pesquera (Eds.), *Building with our hands: New directions in Chicana studies* (pp. 34-56). Los Angeles: University of California Press.

Eberhardt, J. L., & Fiske, S. T. (1994). Affirmative action in theory and practice: Issues of power, ambiguity, and gender versus race. *Basic and Applied Social Psychology, 15,* 201-220.

Espín, O. M. (1987). Psychological impact of migration on Latinas: Implications for psychotherapeutic practice. *Psychology of Women Quarterly, 11,* 489-503.

Espín, O. M. (1993). Feminist therapy: Not for or by White women only. *The Counseling Psychologist, 21,* 103-108.

Espín, O. M. (1994). Feminist theories. In L. Comas-Díaz & B. Greene (Eds.), *Women of color: Integrating ethnic and gender identities in psychotherapy* (pp. 265-286). New York: Guilford.

Espín, O. M. (1995). On knowing you are the unknown: Women of color constructing psychology. In J. Adeleman & G. Enguídanos (Eds.), *Racism in the lives of women: Testimony, theory, and guides to antiracist practice* (pp. 127-136). Binghamton, NY: Harrington Park.

Fiske, E. B. (1988). The undergraduate Hispanic experience: A case of juggling two cultures. *Change, 20,* 29-33.

Fiske, S. T., & Stevens, L. E. (1993). What's so special about sex? Gender stereotyping and discrimination. In S. Oskamp & M. Cessions (Eds.), *Gender issues in contemporary society: The Claremont symposium on applied psychology* (pp. 173-196). Newbury Park, CA: Sage.

Flores-Ortiz, Y. G. (1993). La mujer y la violencia: A culturally based model for the understanding and treatment of domestic violence in Chicana/Latina communities. In N. Alarcón, R. Castro, E. Pérez, B. Pesquera, A. S. Riddell, T. D. Rebolledo, C. Sierra, & P. Zavella (Eds.), *Chicana critical issues: Mujeres activas en letras y cambio social* (pp. 169-182). Berkeley, CA: Third Woman Press.

Flores-Ortiz, Y. G. (1995). Psychotherapy with Chicanas at midlife: Cultural/clinical considerations. In J. Adeleman & G. Enguídanos (Eds.), *Racism in the lives of women: Testimony, theory, and guides to antiracist practice* (pp. 251-259). Binghamton, NY: Harrington Park.

García, J. G., & Marotta, S. (1997). Characterization of the Latino population. In J. G. García & M. C. Zea (Eds.), *Psychological interventions and research with Latino populations* (pp. 1-14). Boston: Allyn & Bacon.

Giachello, A. L. (1996). Latino women. In M. Bayne-Smith (Ed.), *Race, gender, and health* (pp. 121-171). Thousand Oaks, CA: Sage.

Ginorio, A. B., Gutiérrez, L., Cauce, A. M., & Acosta, M. (1995). Psychological issues for Latinas. In H. Landrine (Ed.), *Bringing cultural diversity to feminist psychology: Theory, research, and practice* (pp. 241-263). Washington, DC: American Psychological Association.

Gloria, A. M. (1997). Chicana academic persistence: Creating a university-based community. *Education and Urban Society, 30,* 107-121.

Gloria, A. M., & Robinson-Kurpius, S. E. (1996). The validation of the Cultural Congruity Scale and the University Cultural Environment Scale with Chicano students. *Hispanic Journal of Behavioral Sciences, 18,* 533-549.

Greene, B. (1994). Lesbian women of color: Triple jeopardy. In L. Comas-Díaz & B. Greene (Eds.), *Women of color: Integrating ethnic and gender identities in psychotherapy* (pp. 389-427). New York: Guilford.

Griscom, J. L. (1979). Sex, race, and class: Three dimensions of women's experience. *The Counseling Psychologist, 8,* 10-11.

Hayes-Bautista, D. E., & Chapa, J. (1987). Latino terminology: Conceptual bases for standardized terminology. *American Journal of Public Health, 77,* 61-68.

Hurtado, A. (1989). Relating to privilege: Seduction and rejection in the subordination of White women and women of color. *Signs: Journal of Women in Culture and Society, 14,* 833-855.

Kanuha, V. (1990). The need for an integrated analysis of oppression in feminist therapy ethics. In H. Lerman & N. Porter (Eds.), *Ethics in feminist therapy* (pp. 24-35). New York: Springer.

Lugones, M. (1990). Playfulness, "world"-traveling, and loving perception. In G. Anzaldúa (Ed.), *Making face, making soul/Haciendo caras: Creative and critical perspectives by feminists of color* (pp. 390-402). San Francisco: Aunt Lute.

Marín, G., & Marín, B. V. (1991). *Research with Hispanic populations.* Newbury Park, CA: Sage.

Mays, V. M., & Comas-Díaz, L. (1988). Feminist therapy with ethnic minority populations: A closer look at Blacks and Hispanics. In M. A. Dutton-Douglas & L. E. Walker (Eds.), *Feminist psychotherapies: Integration of therapeutic and feminist systems* (pp. 228-251). Norwood, NJ: Ablex.

Melville, M. B. (1988). Hispanics: Race, class, or ethnicity? *Journal of Ethnic Studies, 16,* 67-83.

Moore, J., & Pinderhughes, R. (1995). The Latino population: The importance of economic re-structuring. In M. L. Anderson & P. H. Collins (Eds.), *Race, class, and gender* (pp. 227-260). Belmont, CA: Wadsworth.

Moraga, C., & Anzaldúa, G. (1981). *This bridge called my back: Writing by radical women of color.* Watertown, MA: Persephone.

Morales, E. S. (1990). HIV infection and Hispanic gay and bisexual men. *Hispanic Journal of Behavioral Sciences, 12,* 212-222.

Morales, E. S. (1992). Latino gays and Latina lesbians. In S. Dworkin & F. Gutiérrez (Eds.), *Counseling gay men and lesbians: Journey to the end of the rainbow* (pp. 125-139). Alexandria, VA: American Association for Counseling and Development.

Mullings, L. (1994). Images, ideology, and women of color. In M. B. Zinn & B. T. Dill (Eds.), *Women of color in U.S. society* (pp. 265-289). Philadelphia: Temple University Press.

Oboler, S. (1995). *Ethnic labels, Latino lives: Identity and the politics of (re)presentation in the United States.* Minneapolis: University of Minnesota Press.

Olmedo, E. L., & Parron, D. L. (1981). Mental health of minority women: Some special issues. *Professional Psychology, 12,* 103-111.

Ortiz, V. (1994). Women of color: A demographic overview. In M. B. Zinn & B. T. Dill (Eds.), *Women of color in U.S. society* (pp. 13-40). Philadelphia: Temple University Press.

Padilla, A. M. (1995). Introduction to Hispanic psychology. In A. M. Padilla (Ed.), *Hispanic psychology: Critical issues in theory and research* (pp. xi-xxi). Thousand Oaks, CA: Sage.

Paniagua, F. A. (1994). *Assessing and treating culturally diverse clients: A practical guide.* Thousand Oaks, CA: Sage.

Payton, C. R. (1985). Addressing the special needs of minority women. *New Directions for Student Services, 29,* 75-90.

Ponterotto, J. G. (1987). Counseling Mexican Americans: A multimodal approach. *Journal of Counseling and Development, 65,* 308-312.

Ponterotto, J. G. (1990). Racial/ethnic minority and women students in higher education: A status report. *New Directions for Student Services, 52,* 45-59.

Portes, A., & Truelove, C. (1987). Making sense of diversity: Recent research on Hispanic minorities in the United States. *Annual Review of Sociology, 13,* 359-385.

Queralt, M. (1984). Understanding Cuban immigrants: A cultural perspective. *Social Work, 29,* 115-121.

Ramírez, M. (1982). *Psychology of the Americas.* Elmsford, NY: Pergamon.

Reid, P. T. (1993). Poor women in psychological research: Shut up and shut out. *Psychology of Women Quarterly, 17,* 133-150.

Reid, P. T. (1994). The real problem in the study of culture. *American Psychologist, 49,* 524-525.

Reid, P. T., & Comas-Díaz, L. (1990). Gender and ethnicity: Perspective on dual status. *Sex Roles, 22,* 397-408.

Reid, P. T., & Kelly, E. (1994). Research on women of color: From ignorance to awareness. *Psychology of Women Quarterly, 18,* 477-486.

Rivers, R. Y. (1995). Clinical issues and interventions with ethnic minority women. In J. F. Aponte, R. Y. Rivers, & J. Wohl (Eds.), *Psychological interventions and cultural diversity* (pp. 181-198). Boston: Allyn & Bacon.

Rogler, L. H. (1994). International migrations. *American Psychologist, 49,* 701-708.

Santos de Barona, M., & Reid, P. T. (1992). Ethnic issues in teaching the psychology of women. *Teaching of Psychology, 19,* 96-99.

Sciarra, D. T., & Ponterotto, J. G. (1991). Counseling the Hispanic bilingual family: Challenges to the therapeutic process. *Psychotherapy, 28,* 473-479.

Secada, W. G., Chavez-Chavez, R., Garcia, E., Munoz, C., Oakes, J., Santiago-Santiago, I., & Slavin, R. (1998, February). *No more excuses: The final report of the Hispanic Dropout Project.* Washington, DC: Office of Bilingual Education and Minority Languages Affairs, U.S. Department of Education.

Sue, D. W., Arredondo, P., & McDavis, R. J. (1992). Multicultural counseling competencies and standards: A call to the profession. *Journal of Counseling and Development, 70,* 477-486.

Tarver-Behring, S. (1994). White women's identity and diversity: Awareness from the inside out. *Feminism and Psychology, 4,* 206-208.

Treviño, F. (1987). Standardized terminology for Hispanic populations. *American Journal of Public Health, 77,* 69-72.

Trujillo, C. (Ed.). (1991). *Chicana lesbians: The girls our mothers warned us about.* Berkeley, CA: Third Woman Press.

U.S. Bureau of the Census. (1994). *The Hispanic population in the United States: March 1993* (Series CPR, No. 455). Washington, DC: Government Printing Office.

Vargas-Willis, G., & Cervantes, R. C. (1987). Consideration of psychological stress in the treatment of the Latina immigrant. *Hispanic Journal of Behavioral Sciences, 9,* 315-329.

Vasquez, M. J. T. (1982). Confronting barriers to the participation of Mexican American women in higher education. *Hispanic Journal of Behavioral Sciences, 4,* 147-165.

Vasquez, M. J. T. (1984). Power and status of the Chicana: A social-psychological perspective. In J. L. Martinez, Jr., & R. H. Mendoza (Eds.), *Chicano psychology* (2nd ed., pp. 269-287). New York: Academic Press.

Vasquez, M. J. T. (1994). Latinas. In L. Comas-Díaz & B. Greene (Eds.), *Women of color: Integrating ethnic and gender identities in psychotherapy* (pp. 114-138). New York: Guilford.

Waters, M. C. (1990). *Ethnic options: Choosing identities in America.* Berkeley: University of California Press.

Yep, G. A. (1995). Communicating the HIV/AIDS risk to Hispanic populations. In A. M. Padilla (Ed.), *Hispanic psychology: Critical issues in theory and research* (pp. 196- 212). Thousand Oaks, CA: Sage.

CHAPTER

2

Self-in-Relation Theory and African American Female Development

Va Lecia L. Adams
Teresa D. LaFromboise
Stanford University

I wear a mask. My mask keeps people from knowing how I really feel. If they know the real me, they can hurt me. People at school think I'm an angry Black girl, but I'm not. I'm just afraid—afraid of being hurt. My mask hides my sadness, my disappointment, and my loneliness. I guess I do want people to see me, to see the real me without the mask. But I don't know who to trust. I am a stranger at school and at home. Even my mom doesn't understand me anymore. Things weren't always this way. I wish Mom and I were close again. I want her to understand me and know what I am really feeling.

—17-year-old Mother-Daughter Relational
Group Therapy participant

This chapter describes the development, implementation, and pilot evaluation of a group therapy intervention with African American female adolescents and their mothers. The Mother-Daughter Relational Group Therapy intervention takes a relationship-focused approach to enhance the quality of mother-daughter relationships and foster the capacity of daughters to cope with issues that concern them. In addition to background information about relational and Afrocentric theories, the applicability of relational theory to intervention with

African-descended women and prevention with African American female ado-lescents is reviewed. Results of the process and the outcome evaluation of the pilot intervention are outlined in detail for direction in further refinement of re-lational group therapy efforts with this population. Finally, implications of this work for counseling intervention development and future research are dis-cussed.

The Self and Self-in-Relation Theory

Like most other adolescents, African American females are confronted with personal challenges related to difficulties involved in establishing a stable sense of self (Leadbeater & Way, 1996). Erikson's (1963) model of human de-velopment suggests that a critical task of adolescence is to overcome a crisis of identity by pursuing and ultimately acquiring autonomy and independence. Al-though the tenets of Erikson's theory explain aspects of adolescent develop-ment from a Western cultural perspective, many groups throughout the world question its relevance to other cultures (Markus & Kitayama, 1998).

Highlighting the limitations of Erikson's (1963) model of human develop-ment, feminist theorists suggest that women in European American contexts, for one reason or another, develop a sense of self that emphasizes the mainte-nance of connection to others rather than autonomy from others. As opposed to a sense of self being formed and stabilized through individuation, it is proposed that for females, the gendered sense of self in European American contexts is set within a framework of care, connection, and relationships. According to Gilligan (1982) and Miller (1991), the self, as described by the West and in tra-ditional psychology, does not accurately depict women's experiences. In fact, Miller (1976) argued that rather than developing a self that is separate or inde-pendent from others, women grow and develop a sense of self in "relation" to others.

An alternative theory of development that describes important aspects of women's psychological development and interventions aimed at enhancing the well-being of women and girls has been developed by Stone Center research-ers. According to this theory, psychological advancement involves a process of differentiation and expansion in relationships rather than separation-individua-tion (Genero, Miller, Surrey, & Baldwin, 1992; Miller, 1988). The construct "self-in-relation" is tied to the idea of the "self" found in theories of childhood and psychological development. It involves the recognition that for women, the primary experience of self is relational (Surrey, 1991). In other words, a woman's sense of self is developed and shaped in the context of relationships.

Relationships have been reported to foster psychological well-being in females (Gilligan, 1982; Gilligan, Rogers, & Tolman, 1991; Jordan, Kaplan, Miller, Stiver, & Surrey, 1991; Miller, 1988). Surrey (1991) defined *relationship* as "an experience of emotional and cognitive intersubjectivity: the ongoing, intrinsic inner awareness and responsiveness to the continuous existence of the other or others and the expectation of mutuality in this regard" (p. 61). This definition implies that the act of being in a relationship involves a sense of knowing oneself and others through a process of mutual relational interaction and sharing.

Within this paradigm, movement toward mutuality is key to relational development. Genero et al. (1992) defined *mutuality* as the bidirectional exchange of feelings, thoughts, and activity between individuals in relationships. Jordan (1991) noted that "growth-enhancing relationships are characterized by mutual respect, honesty, understanding, and recognition; they engender the capacity for caring, sense of courage, and the ability to act" (p. 1).

Mutually empathic and mutually empowering relationships help to protect young girls from constructing restricted and distorted images of themselves and from developing a sense of unworthiness and powerlessness in relationships (Miller, 1988). In light of this, it is expected that movement toward mutuality in a relational context would lead to psychological growth (Genero et al., 1992).

The Self and Afrocentric Theory

Afrocentric scholars also question the relevance of the Eriksonian developmental model. They offer an alternative perspective, which is particularly useful in exploring the experiences of African-descended people. Afrocentric theory highlights the differences between the Western worldview—its focus on individualism and autonomy—and the African ethos, which emphasizes cooperation and interdependence. White and Parham (1990) outlined several African principles that make up the African American self:

> The African world view begins with a holistic conception of the human condition. There is no mind-body or affective-cognitive dualism, the human organism is conceived as a totality made up of a series of interlocking systems.

This total person is simultaneously a feeling, experiencing, sensualizing, sensing, and knowing human being living in a dynamic, vitalistic world where everything is interrelated and endowed with the supreme force of life. There is a sense of alikeness, intensity, and animation in the music, dance, song, language, and lifestyles of Africans. (p. 15)

Unlike Western ideology, which views the individual as a separate entity, African philosophies consider the tribe to be the basic human unit (White & Parham, 1990). In the African system, the collective is valued over the autonomous individual as a means of survival. Thus, the Cartesian premise, "I think, therefore I am," which is foundational to the Western view of the self, is in direct contrast to the African view, "We are, therefore I am."

Research suggests that African American girls' experiences, much like those of European American girls, are lacking in models of human development. Pastor, McCormick, and Fine (1996) argued that barriers associated with racism, sexism, and classism make it difficult, if not impossible, for ethnic girls to pursue tasks such as autonomy and independence that Erikson (1963) featured in his model.

African American girls also may resist Western notions of individualism that view the self as separate from others (Robinson & Ward, 1991). In their study on personal and ethnic identity values and self-esteem among Black and Latino adolescent girls, Rotheram-Borus, Dopkins, Sabate, and Lightfoot (1996) found similar evidence to support this contention. In integrating their personal identity, ethnic girls in their study were found to prefer to lose themselves in a group identity or passively await the natural emergence of their true selves than to go through a process of individuation.

These authors are not suggesting that females are the only group whose experiences are missing in Western theories of development. Indeed, traditional psychology also has failed to accurately depict the experiences of men in general (Bergman, 1991), particularly African American men (Wade, 1994). In fact, African American males tend to be left out of models of development altogether, or they are presented in contrast to white males and depicted as violent, threatening, and hostile. Yet, research suggests that African American males who are reared in nurturing (African-centered) environments are just as likely as African American females to prefer and practice relational ways of being, that is, connection and wholeness in the context of relationships.

However, societal mandates and structures that emphasize individuation and rugged individualism encourage young boys to distance themselves from their mothers and to engage in gender role activities. These and other forces make it particularly difficult for African American males to develop into relational beings. Clearly, research that explores African American male development and the applicability of the self-in-relation model to African American males is needed. Yet, due to our interest in the development of ethnic minority women, the focus of this work is on the experiences of African American female adolescents.

African American Female Selves
and Self-in-Relation Theory

The African American female self is multifaceted. In addition to being shaped by the nature and quality of the relationships that she is in, the self is affected by gender politics, her race, and her socioeconomic status (hooks, 1993). She is constantly confronted with having to cope with the interlocking "isms" to which her race, gender, and social location make her susceptible (Greene, 1994). This is due to the multiple contexts in which she is located. The relational model's emphasis on the role of oppression and male-female power imbalances make it particularly conducive to structuring an intervention for African American adolescents and women, who are often confronted with multiple levels of oppression and discrimination.

In reviewing the literature, a connection seems to emerge between what the self-in-relation theory proposes as the key to healthy development in women and themes that have emerged from Afrocentric theory. These themes are the value placed on relationships with parents, friends, and extended family; the importance of trust and honesty; the need to be heard and understood; and the desire for connection (Cauce et al., 1996; Robinson & Ward, 1991). The self-in-relation theory also seems to capture a central aspect of African American women's development—namely, their attempt to establish a sense of self that integrates ethnic pride and commitment to family and community (Turner, 1997).

According to the relational model, the mother-daughter relationship is critical to a female child's development of a sense of self (Surrey, 1991). Similarly, the mother-daughter relationship is depicted as a source of strength to African American female adolescents (e.g., Cauce et al., 1996). The relationship a daughter has with her mother has the potential to shape her self-esteem, her ability to be empathetic, her tendency toward nurturing, her view of women, and her "connection" with others (Jordan et al., 1991). In describing the role many African American mothers play in their daughters' lives, Ward (1996) noted,

> In the safety of the homespace of care, nurturance, refuge, and truth, black mothers have learned to skillfully weave lessons of critical consciousness into moments of intimacy between a parent and child and to cultivate resistance against beliefs, attitudes, and practices that can erode a black child's self-confidence and impair her positive identity development. (pp. 85-86)

As would be expected, these researchers also found that African American daughters viewed their mothers as a central source of support.

According to Collins (1991) and hooks (1993), African American girls must be taught how to survive in the interlocking oppressive structures of race, class, and gender while learning how to transcend those stifling structures. In a qualitative study that assessed closeness, conflict, and control within African American mother-daughter relationships, Cauce et al. (1996) observed that African American mothers frequently modeled for their daughters successful approaches to coping with racism and sexism.

Although African American girls are encouraged to be strong and self-sufficient, they are also expected to remain connected (closely tied) to their immediate and extended families. Unlike their male counterparts, most have not had to face societal and familial pressure to individuate, allowing them to stay nested in caring and nurturing parent-child relationships. Thus, the self-in-relation model with its emphasis on the mother-daughter bond, the importance of connection, and the centrality of relationships is especially attractive to African Americans. We believe that the relational model is particularly useful for understanding and designing interventions for African American female adolescents.

Development of the Relational Intervention

The potential utility of a relational approach to therapy based on the self-in-relation model has been addressed by a number of scholars (e.g., Fedele & Harrington, 1990; Vasquez & Ling Han, 1995). A relational approach involves the promotion of four salient healing factors. These include the validation of one's experience, empowerment to act in relationships, development of self-empathy, and mutuality. Validation involves a sense of knowing that one's experiences are understood by another person. A relational view of empowerment involves one's capacity both to be moved by and to move others (Surrey, 1991). Self-empathy includes the ability to have compassion for and to fully accept oneself (Fedele & Harrrington, 1990). Mutuality is the ability to tune into the inner experience of another at cognitive and affective levels (Jordan, 1991).

The effectiveness of group therapy is well documented (Yalom, 1985). Research suggests that group interventions can be effective therapeutic tools for ethnic minority clients in general (LaFromboise & Graff Low, 1998; Vasquez & Ling Han, 1995) and for African American females in particular (Boyd-Franklin, 1991; Gibbs, 1998). Fedele and Harrington (1990) suggested that group therapy is an ideal environment to enhance women's mutual relational connection.

The Stone Center model provides a useful framework for the development of group therapy interventions (Vasquez & Ling Han, 1995). The interactive and relationship-focused nature of the theory promotes connection and healing in the context of relationships. When healing and growth are encouraged in the context of a group, participants experience a sense of vitality and connection from joining with other females on issues particularly salient to women (Jordan et al., 1991). The relational model promotes a sense of mutual support and connection—which involves being understood and understanding others (Turner, 1997). With particular attention paid to the promotion of the healing factors of validation, empowerment, empathy, and mutuality, females experience a sense of vitality and strength that flows from mutually supportive interactions that occur in the group. The Mother-Daughter Relational Group Therapy intervention was also informed by current literature on African American female adolescents and interviews with African American female adolescents and mothers.

The Mother-Daughter Relational Group Therapy intervention was developed by the first author based on the work cited above and her experience delivering services to African American adolescents. In 1997, a pilot investigation was conducted to evaluate whether a relational intervention with African American female adolescents and their mothers was likely to strengthen the relationship girls have with their mothers (increase mutuality) and enhance their ability to cope with issues that concern them. Specifically, the purpose of this pilot study was to explore the applicability of the self-in-relation model to African American female development and the relevance of the construct of mutuality with this population.

To this end, a therapy group ($n = 4$) and a wait-list control group ($n = 4$) were recruited from California schools, churches, and community centers. Participants were asked to take part in the intervention to help researchers explore approaches to improving African American mother-daughter relationships and to help mental health practitioners improve services offered to African American female adolescents. The African American female adolescents (ages 15-17) and the mothers and grandmothers who were the primary caregivers of the female adolescents (hereafter referred to as mothers) were from low- and middle-income families.

Components of Mother-Daughter
Relational Group Therapy

An explanation of the themes of the Mother-Daughter Relational Group Therapy intended to enhance the mother-daughter relationship is provided below. Whole-group and mother-daughter exercises employed during the intervention to facilitate understanding and application are also described. Homework was assigned at the end of each session, and each mother-daughter pair was asked to maintain an ongoing journal in which they were to note personal reflections related to concepts discussed in the group. Both cognitive behavioral and interpersonal approaches to therapy were emphasized during the eight group therapy sessions. What follows is a brief description of each session of the mother-daughter group therapy intervention.

Introduction to Relational Group Therapy. In this session, participants introduced themselves, discussed why they had decided to participate in the group, and shared what they hoped to gain from the process. After consent forms were signed, issues of confidentiality and the format of group therapy interventions were discussed. During the last half of the session, mother-daughter pairs participated in an "ice-breaker" that required each group member to compose a poem from several words that she had pulled out of a fishbowl and to share the poem with the group. The fishbowl included words such as *dark, cloud, space, freedom, black, care, cave,* and *sky* from poems, articles, and short stories.

During this initial session, one young woman constructed a poem that described movement through a dark, cavelike space that opened up into a bright, warm sky full of light. Another daughter created verses that described emotional pain resulting from racism and prejudice. After all the writings were shared, group members discussed their impression of what had been read and the personal meaning they derived from the poems.

At first, the participants were doubtful of their ability to produce poetry from the fishbowl words—saying to themselves, "I can't do this" or "my poem is going to be silly." After receiving feedback from the group and hearing the participants share the feelings that the words evoked, the person sharing the poem seemed to experience a sense of relief and positive feelings. Such feelings of vitality came from knowing that they were able to create something, in less than a minute, that could produce positive energy and feelings in another human being—a vivid example of the relational component of connection.

This session introduced the participants to the powerful exchange that can occur between women and girls in therapy. From a relational perspective, the exercise provided participants with an opportunity to influence others and in turn to be influenced by others—a notion at the heart of the self-in-relation model. The session also created a space for the mothers and daughters to give voice to their experiences in a creative manner and allowed the discussion to move to a deeper level of sharing without requiring the participants to disclose personal information.

Relational Validation. Session 2 focused on personal validation. The session exercise provided both mothers and daughters an opportunity to discuss aspects of one another's personal qualities that they most appreciated. Thus, the girls and their mothers learned how to engage in the mutual exchange of explicit discourse, displaying appreciation and support within their relationships.

One pair remarked during this session that they had never actually verbalized their feelings to each other in front of other people. With the support of the other participants in the group, the daughter told her mother how much she enjoyed spending time with her. She also showed that she appreciated the support and care her mother provided her, particularly during difficult times. Fighting back tears, her mother expressed her gratitude for what was said and explained that she appreciated how strong and courageous her daughter had become. Her mother also stated that she was proud of the wonderful attitude her daughter displayed, particularly the cooperative way she had been behaving recently. The other pairs engaged in a similar exchange, which created an atmosphere of warmth, care, and mutual acceptance. This session prompted participants to reflect on several positive aspects of their relationship and acknowledge each other's strengths.

Relational Mutuality. In this session, an explanation of mutuality and its role in relationships was presented. The potential shift from unilateral authority in parent-adolescent relationships during adolescence to one of mutuality and cooperation was encouraged (Galambos & Ehrenberg, 1997). For example, the mother-daughter pairs were encouraged to communicate honestly and practice accepting each other unconditionally, and they were presented information on the possible barriers to connection in relationships such as mistrust and unresolved hurts. The group also explored various approaches to decreasing relational conflict (e.g., listening empathically and showing respect for the other person's opinion) and ways to reconnect after a disagreement.

During the mutuality exercise, one of the girls in the group expressed her appreciation for her mother's caring and nonjudgmental nature. She also described her love and commitment to her mother and thanked her for being a wonderful role model and friend. She discussed an occasion when she had turned to her mother for support and advice and described how her mother's response had helped her get through a difficult period in her life. She mentioned another occasion on which she had helped her mother make it through a stressful period, and she expressed what it meant to her to be able to assist her mother in that manner. She told the group that she loves partnering with her mother because it allows her to contribute to the well-being of the family. This young woman further reflected on the way her mother's honesty about her own life experiences had enhanced her ability to be honest and forthright in their relationship.

Another mother admitted that she was worried about her upcoming retirement and how that transition could possibly affect her family financially. She was particularly concerned about whether she would be able to afford to send her daughters to college. In response, one of her daughters said that she understood her mother's concerns and that she was certain that things would work out as long as the family continued to work together.

This session allowed the daughters to experience what it feels like to be heard and understood by their mothers. It also enabled them to relate to their mothers more than they had been able to in the past and experience their mothers as more human—with everyday problems and issues to handle. It also gave the mothers permission to share their concerns with their daughters, which helped to shatter the "supermom" image. This session attempted to promote authentic sharing and connection in the context of relationships. It nurtured a sense of oneness and mutual support in the mother-daughter pairs, and it laid the foundation for future sharing.

Relational Empowerment. In Session 4, the mother-daughter dyads learned how to create opportunities for mutual growth in their relationships. The members of the mother-daughter pairs were encouraged to give each other permission to develop uniqueness while still remaining connected to one another. An emphasis was placed on the importance of displaying and communicating unconditional acceptance and love. The session exercise involved the pairs learning how to create a space in the relationship for nonjudgmental sharing that celebrates "diversity"—differing opinions, views, and perspectives. During the exercise, daughters shared some of their long- and short-term goals and discussed specific ways they wanted their mothers to support them in reaching their goals.

One mother admitted to concerns that she might be stifling her two daughters' growth by overly controlling them. When her behavior was challenged by the group, she explained that she was operating out of a sense of fear that she would make the same mistakes with her younger daughters that she had made with her older daughters—that they would end up pregnant and lose their opportunity to attend college. She admitted that she had been unfair to them because their behavior up to that point had been commendable. She apologized for her lack of trust and asked them to forgive her. She was then encouraged by the other participants to ask her daughters to teach her how to support and help them grow within the context of the relationship.

After hearing her mother admit to her shortcomings, one of the daughters expressed her frustration, saying, "I feel like I can never do enough . . . like I can never please you. I've never been in trouble, I don't go out, and yet you still don't trust me. . . . It just isn't fair." The two daughters asked their mother to show her trust in them by giving them a little more freedom (e.g., telephone time, permission to go out with girlfriends from school). Their mother promised to do so, and they agreed to report back on their progress. The other mothers in the group said that they could relate to this mother's concerns and that they had also been confronted with similar challenges. They encouraged her to continue providing her daughters support while allowing them to have more autonomy.[1]

Later in this session, one of the mothers encouraged the girls in the group to prepare themselves for the stumbling blocks (e.g., cultural mistrust, discrimination) that could arise in their lives as African American females. Confronted with various forms of discrimination, African American women and girls often experience hopelessness and disempowerment. The aim of this session was to empower girls in the context of the mother-daughter relationship so that they might learn how to become agents in their own lives.

Relational Masks and the Hidden Self. In this session, participants explored reasons why women often silence themselves in relationships. The group listed some of the feelings women and girls are likely to mask such as anger, fear, and sadness, as well as the more socially acceptable emotions of happiness and joy. The participants discussed the importance of honesty and trust in their mother-daughter relationships and the sense of emptiness they experience when they are unable to be authentic with each other. During the session exercise, the members of the mother-daughter pairs discussed the masks they often wear with one another and suggested ways to help each other be more honest and authentic in the relationship, such as expressing interest in how each of them is "really" feeling or being available to talk when the other person is ready.

During this session, one of the girls explained that she uses her mask to hide her fear that students at school dislike her. She said, "I use the mask to keep from causing conflict." She discussed her sense of discomfort in telling people how she really feels because she believes that they may not like her if she does. In the group, the participants discussed some of the safe places in their lives where masks can be put down and real voices can emerge. Some of the girls identified the relationship they have with their mothers as one of the few safe relationships they have in which they can "be real about their feelings."

The girls and the women discussed some of the societal mandates around which emotions are or are not acceptable for women. The girls suggested that they often mask feelings of anger, fear, and sadness because society and sometimes their families say that those feelings are inappropriate. Some of the girls indicated that their masks project false smiles and screen silenced pain. One girl explained, "Sometimes my mask reflects joy when I'm really feeling sad and alone." Another girl remarked, "The cold and intimidating stare conceals my desire to be close to and to be heard by my friends and family."

hooks (1993) suggests that one's ability to mask or hide feelings is viewed by many as a positive characteristic and a sign of strength in the Black community. The women and girls in the group often de-emphasized their pain and past difficulties in keeping with the injunction to "be strong at all costs" that permeates African American life. This attempt to mask any sign of vulnerability has been a crucial aspect of coping among African American females (hooks,

1993). Yet relational ways of being emphasize the importance of women having an outlet and safe place where they can take off their masks and engage in authentic sharing.

This session encouraged participants to collectively unmask their true selves—their voices, feelings, and beliefs—which according to hooks (1993) is an important act of resistance to sex and race oppression. With the intervention's focus on authenticity and honesty, the African American female adolescents and their mothers were given the opportunity to put down their masks and begin to speak the truth about their feelings and their relationships.

Relational Scars: Healing Past Hurts. Session 6 focused on the relational scars that are often created in mother-daughter relationships. The role of forgiveness in bringing about relational healing was emphasized. Each group member was encouraged to recall times when she had been hurt by her mother or daughter and then describe how the incident made her feel. The mother or daughter who was listening was then encouraged to try to take the other person's perspective and experience the hurt the other had shared. After one member of the dyad had expressed her past hurt, the other was given the opportunity to respond and ask for forgiveness.

One young girl reminded her mother of a time when she had accused her of lying. She stated that it had really hurt her to learn that her mother did not trust her. She said that the situation made her feel separated from her mother, and she explained that she wanted to have her mother's trust back. She promised that she would always try to be honest with her mother. The mother, in turn, apologized for not listening to her and for not giving her an opportunity to explain the situation thoroughly. She then promised to try to be more understanding and trusting in the future.

One mother asked her daughter why she would not allow her to help her any longer—why she had shut her out of her life. The mother, with tears running down her face, pleaded for an explanation. The young girl told her mother that she did not need her help and that she found her mother to be too critical. The young girl had distanced herself from her mother because she tended to put her down and compare her to others, which hurt her greatly. The two of them worked through some of this in the group. With the support of the other group members, they began to soften and acknowledge the role each of them played in the deterioration of the relationship.

In this session, the mothers and daughters were asked to explore their relational scars. In light of the fact that the literature suggests that African American girls and women often have a difficult time revealing their weakness, this session gave the participants permission to show their feelings and vulnerabilities in the group. The brutality inflicted on African American women through systems of oppression has left psychological wounds (hooks, 1993), which affect everyday interpersonal relationships.

Relational Communication. In this session, the pairs were encouraged to discuss some barriers to effective communication that they had experienced in their relationships. They were further asked to specify the skills that they had learned in the group that enhanced their ability to relate to each other. The participants were encouraged, during their discussions with each other, to focus on hearing "from the perspective of the other"—not only to focus on their own voice and desire to be heard but also to demonstrate a willingness to hear and, more important, understand what the other person is communicating.

During this session, a mother-daughter pair reported that they were at an impasse in their ability to communicate relationally. The young girl said that she felt her mother "never listened," and her mother explained that she felt like she was not given credit for the extent to which she had improved since joining the group. During the session, the pair practiced communication skills designed to promote a sense of safety, authenticity, and connection in the relationship. The other mother-daughter pairs participated in a similar exchange. The mothers and daughters ended the session by sharing their goals for improving communication skills in the future.

The purpose of this session was to expose the pairs to two-way communication that de-emphasized the self and instead highlighted the relationship—the bidirectional exchange of emotions, thoughts, and feelings between two individuals within the relationship.

Relational Self-Empathy. In the final session, the group was introduced to the notion of self-empathy, that is, the ability to forgive oneself and take responsibility for one's own mistakes. Each participant was encouraged to share a past mistake, failure, or experience so that she could grow to understand herself better. Challenges faced by members of the group while learning to provide support and the importance of understanding difficulties experienced by others were underscored. In bringing closure to the group, each participant was asked to share how she felt the mother-daughter relationship had improved over the course of the intervention. Each then stated her relational goals for the future.

One mother, speaking through her tear-filled voice, told her daughter and the group that she had to forgive herself for having low expectations of her daughter. She explained that she never believed that she was capable of going on to college and pursuing an intellectually challenging career. She asked forgiveness for not supporting and encouraging her daughter more, particularly in her academic pursuits. She turned to her daughter and said, "I was absolutely wrong about you and your potential . . . after watching you grow up all of these years, I can see that you are one of the most stable, mature, and intelligent young women I have ever known." The young girl, with tears in her eyes, expressed her forgiveness and admitted that she had also wondered if she could do all of the things other females in the family were doing. She then thanked her mother for addressing the issue.

Another mother said she needed to forgive herself for being too protective of her daughter and limiting her sense of autonomy. She admitted to hovering at times and acknowledged that she might be smothering her daughter. She explained that she was afraid that her daughter might become resentful someday. The daughter expressed appreciation for her mother's sensitivity and assured her that she did not resent her.

Many of the girls said that they were going to miss the group and that they planned to continue to practice some of the skills they had learned there. In addition to the skill-building exercises, the intervention focused on a number of qualities and characteristics within the affective domains of personality development—identity in terms of gender, race, and culture. The messages shared in this group addressed issues related to self-identity and self-worth and hence self-esteem. Messages also touched on group identity and belonging as well as the importance of self-discipline and personal motivation in reaching long- and short-term goals.

EVALUATION OF THE RELATIONAL INTERVENTION PILOT TEST

Anecdotal Support

To ascertain the participants' reactions to the intervention and the extent to which they found the relational group therapy relevant to their experiences, we solicited responses from each session with a feedback form addressing the following questions: How was the session? How much did you participate? Were the activities relevant to your life? What did you like most and what did you like the least about this session? What was the most important thing you learned from this session?

Process results for each session indicate that the intervention was deemed to be very interesting and relevant to their experiences as African American females. The female adolescent participants reported that they valued the group and appreciated having the opportunity to express their feelings. Likewise, mothers reported that the group helped them to better understand the relationship they have with their daughters and learn ways to improve the quality of that bond. Mothers stated that they particularly enjoyed learning the relational concepts and having an opportunity to hear how other mother-daughter pairs handled conflict.

Regarding the introduction to the relational group therapy session, daughters reported that they enjoyed expressing themselves through the writing of poetry, appreciated being understood, and learned that everyone is unique and everyone's opinion is important. The mothers enjoyed the session's emphasis on creativity. They liked the open nature of the discussion and the opportunity to share their feelings and hear the feelings and ideas of other group members. In noting what she learned, one mother wrote, "We can all have different opinions and approaches to the same set of circumstances. We can all be creative if given the opportunity to be or do so."

In the relational validation session, all of the daughters reported that they liked the mutual appreciation exercise, which allowed them to hear how their mothers feel about them, and they also liked the opportunity to share their feelings about their mothers. Most mothers reported that they now realize the need to share how they feel about their daughters more often.

Most of the daughters reported that they enjoyed the name tag switch game in the relational mutuality session. During this exercise, each mother-daughter pair switched name tags so that each daughter became her mother and each mother became her daughter. The daughters reported that they enjoyed playing the role of their mothers and describing their mothers as if they were actually them. Many of the daughters noted that the most important thing they learned was how their mothers perceived them. The mothers found the name tag switch game to be enjoyable as well. They reported that they liked hearing how much the other mother-daughter pairs in the group know about each other.

The daughters responded favorably to the discussion and the activities in the relational empowerment session. Some of the girls particularly liked having the opportunity to tell their mothers what they needed from them with regard to support. Others explained that they liked discussing their goals and ways they plan to attain them. In terms of what they learned, one daughter wrote, "I learned that I have a lot to look forward to." Another daughter noted, "You can do anything you want, all you have to do is put your mind to it." Overall, the mothers enjoyed sharing their "secret" desires and concerns without feeling ashamed. In reporting the most important thing that she learned, one mother wrote, "Relational empowerment is a good thing that encourages growth, trust, confidence, and constructive decision making."

In the relational masks and the hidden self session, most of the daughters reported that the most important thing they learned was that it is important to learn how to express their feelings with people they can trust. One girl wrote, "Since we all wear masks at times, it is important not to judge people based on the look they are projecting." Many reported that what they most liked about the session was the discussion about the masks they themselves wear to hide their feelings. The mothers enjoyed the examples provided by their daughters regarding the masks that women as a group tend to wear. One of the mothers explained that she became sensitized to the way that people wear masks to protect themselves.

All of the daughters enjoyed expressing their feelings and past hurts honestly in the session titled "Relational Scars: Healing Past Hurts." Although some of the daughters particularly enjoyed sharing how they felt, others appreciated having the opportunity to apologize to their mothers for things they had done in the past. Most of the girls learned the value of expressing their "true" feelings. For example, one of the daughters wrote that the most important thing that she learned was that she could be real and honest with her friends, her family, and with other African American women. The mothers responded enthusiastically to this session and reported that they loved the discussion that evolved from the session activities. One mother explained that she liked having the opportunity to express how she had been hurt by her daughter and to also ask her daughter for forgiveness for things she had done to her. In terms of what she learned, that same mother noted that she now has a better understanding of how difficult expressing past hurts can be but that the expression of those hurts is freeing and healing.

The activities and discussion in the relational communication session also received favorable feedback. Some of the girls reported that the session helped them learn ways to express their opinions more authentically. For example, one of the daughters said that what she liked most about the session was that participants "spoke from the heart." Although some girls focused on their need to improve listening skills to enhance the relationship they have with their mothers, one girl focused on the difficulty she has revealing her emotions to other people. She explained that she learned that she needs to put down her mask to improve communication with others. In keeping with responses given by the daughters, the mothers indicated that they learned that their daughters often hide how they really feel from them.

Regarding the relational self-empathy session, all of the girls reported that they enjoyed learning more about themselves. Although one participant explained that she particularly liked having the opportunity to express herself on a deeper level, another noted that she learned that it is okay to express her feelings and that she does not have to always focus on pleasing everyone. Most of the girls explained that the discussion and activities in this session taught them how to begin to forgive and accept themselves.

Likewise, the mothers indicated an appreciation for the level of sharing that occurred in the session. One mother reported that what she liked most about the session was that the group members were given the opportunity to be honest and to "free themselves" through the process of self-forgiveness. Most of the mothers indicated that they enjoyed having the opportunity to confront certain issues in their lives and forgive themselves for slights or wrongdoings associated with those issues.

Outcome Support

The Mutual Psychological Development Questionnaire (Genero et al., 1992) and the Daily Hassles Questionnaire (Rowlison & Felner, 1988) were administered to all participants pre- and posttreatment. The wait-list control group participants were administered the instruments within the same time frame as the therapy group participants.

The Mutual Psychological Development Questionnaire (MPDQ) (Genero et al., 1992) is a 22-item self-report inventory derived from six conceptual mutuality elements: empathy, engagement, authenticity, zest, diversity, and empowerment (see Genero et al., 1992). Initially, this measure was designed to assess perceived mutuality in close adult relationships. The questionnaire asks respondents to rate a relationship from both their own perspective and the perspective of the other person in the relationship. Respondents then rate items in response to the following two sentences: "When we talk about things that matter to [the other person], I am likely to . . ." and "When we talk about things that matter to me, [the other person] is likely to . . ." on a 6-point Likert scale (*never, rarely, occasionally, more often than not, most of the time,* and *all of the time*). With scores ranging from 1 to 6 on each item, an average score of 4 or less indicates low mutuality. The scale is reported by Genero and colleagues (1992) to have high internal consistency (alpha reliability coefficient = .87 to .93). The MPDQ was adapted to measure perceived mutuality in the mother-daughter relationship for this intervention.

The mean posttest mutuality score was 3.48 for the control group and 4.85 for the intervention group, a decrease of .12 relative to the pretest for the control group and an increase in the score for the intervention group of .44. The difference between the control and intervention groups' pre- to posttest scores on the MPDQ was statistically significant ($p < .05$), based on the results of the Mann-Whitney U test.

The Daily Life Hassles Questionnaire (DLHQ) (Rowlison & Felner, 1988) was used to assess the extent to which adolescents are able to cope with daily hassles. The 81-item self-report inventory was adapted by Barbara Guthrie for the Female Adolescent Substance Experience Study (see Guthrie, 1997). The items represent typical day-to-day concerns of children and adolescents (e.g., not being a part of the popular group, not having enough money). Participants were asked to report whether the event being rated occurred in the last week or in the last month and to rate the extent to which the event was a hassle for them using a Likert rating scale from 1 (*not a hassle*) to 4 (*a very big hassle*). A total hassle score is derived by summing the item ratings. The initial DLHQ had excellent internal consistency (reliability coefficient alpha = .95) (Rowlison & Felner, 1988).

The control group posttest mean daily hassles score was 2.60; the intervention group posttest mean daily hassles score was 1.50. Although the control group's daily hassles score increased by .43, the intervention group's score decreased by .52. However, a comparison of the pre- to posttest changes on the DLHQ using the Mann-Whitney U test failed to detect a statistically significant effect.

These findings suggest that a relational group therapy intervention may be effective with African American female adolescents and that the self-in-relation model may be helpful in understanding African American female development. The difference between the mean posttest scores on mutuality indicates that the intervention was effective in increasing perceived mutuality between the young women and their mothers. Not only was there greater change made by the intervention group, but each control group member's score on mutuality also decreased, and all of the subjects' scores in the intervention group increased from pretest to posttest. A look at the daily hassles scores suggests that the intervention also helped participants cope more effectively with their problems. Although differences in changes from pre- to posttesting for treatment and control groups were observed, statistical significance was not achieved on scores for daily hassles.

Discussion

The observed increase in mutuality is assumed to be due to the intense focus on increasing mutuality in the mother-daughter relationship that occurred in each session. The expected decrease in daily hassles was hypothesized to be mediated by an increase in mutuality in the participants' relationships with their mothers. In other words, the strengthened connection between the participants and their mothers was expected to decrease the extent to which the daughters perceived their problems to be a hassle. The fact that this study produced an equivocal effect on daily hassles may suggest that mutuality does not have a significant moderating effect on stress. However, this speculation would be somewhat contrary to previous research on the beneficial effects of mutuality in relationships (Genero et al., 1992; Jordan, 1991; Powell, Denton, & Mattsson, 1995). It may be more likely that the brief nature of the intervention was more conducive to enhancing mutuality scores but that the brevity, coupled with the small number of participants, was not sufficient to produce a statistically significant change in hassle scores.

The complex nature of African American adolescent coping styles may require that interventions that attempt to help African American youth cope with stress more effectively also nurture the adolescents' ability to take a stance against their stressors or daily life challenges (Myers, 1989). This exploratory investigation was unable to confirm the extent to which increased mutuality in mother-daughter relationships improves coping with hassles or other stressors. However, these preliminary results support the worth of further research on the relationship between mutuality and coping and the inclusion of specific coping skills in future intervention protocols.

Much like our findings, Kaplan, Klein, and Gleason's (1991) research on mother-daughter relationships at Wellesley College revealed the applicability of the self-in-relation theory to the development of female adolescents and the relationships they have with their mothers. Kaplan et al. found that girls in their study were more interested in strengthening their relationships with their mothers than in individuating. Much like the young girls who participated in this intervention, the young women in the Wellesley study described their relationships with their mothers as among the most important in their lives but noted that they also occasionally had difficulties expressing themselves to the extent that they felt that they had been heard and understood by their mothers.

This intervention emphasizes ways in which youth and their parents can interact to bolster their mutual development, and it is a potentially useful example of a collaborative structure for culturally relevant service delivery. This work recognizes the influence the parent-child relationship can have on positive youth development. It addresses the problem of distancing between mothers and daughters during this developmental period, and it also helps prepare the female adolescent for positive adult roles (as a parent, friend, mentor, future community advocate). Unlike other clinical interventions for ethnic minority youth that are often problem focused, this intervention focuses on the wonderful potential that lies within female adolescents. Conceptually, this work fits with new calls for youth development as

> an ongoing process in which all young people are engaged and invested, and through which young people seek ways to meet their basic physical and social needs and to build the competencies and connections they perceive as necessary for survival and success. (Hyman, 1999, p. 13)

By focusing on relational development, empowerment strategies, and the value of authenticity, this intervention enhanced the potential for positive relational outcomes for participants. By inviting the mothers to participate in the intervention, cultural norms for standards of behavior were easily included so that the intervention was deemed culturally appropriate and a context-sensitive service. This process also formally recognized the mothers' social capital as role models and community advocates. Thus, this intervention could be thought of as a community-based support in that relationships, expectations, and messages from adults and peers were exchanged. Overall, this intervention sought to strengthen youth skills and foster positive youth attitudes and provide increased opportunities for quality youth experiences.

Several implications for psychologists, school counselors, school or community administrators, and staff emerge from this intervention development and evaluation project. First, it is important that interactions with African American girls in the schools and community-based organizations be supportive—relational—and nonconfrontational. Every attempt should be made to include the voices of African American adolescents in all aspects of their educational and social planning (e.g., PTA meetings, clubs, churches). Such

inclusiveness will empower young African American girls and possibly improve their self-concept.

Second, the results of this study emphasize the importance of being authentic, empathetic, and trustworthy in working with African American female
adolescents. Educators and counseling professionals working with this population should plan to spend a fair amount of time building trust and rapport on ini-
tiation of the relationship.

Future research on mutuality in the mother-daughter relationships of African American females is warranted. Research suggests that African American
females are socialized to be strong, self-reliant, and independent (hooks, 1993).
Work is being done to explore how African American women define mutuality in light of the socialization messages they receive with regard to being
self-reliant and strong (Adams, 1999). Continued research that uses the voices
of African American females would expand our understanding of the notion of
mutuality and potentially expose the extent to which the meaning of mutuality
differs across cultures.

Note

1. Real growth and movement toward mutual empowerment were evident in the
mother-daughter relationships described in this session. The mother put a phone line in the girls'
rooms, and they behaved responsibly in their use of the phone. The daughters did not let their
grades drop—a concern expressed by the mother. The mother also allowed them to have a little
more time with their girlfriends. In response to that growth in the relationship, the two girls experienced a sense of empowerment, which came from feeling trusted and valued by their mother. They
eventually applied to college and received scholarships to a 4-year university. Their relationship
with their mother is much more open, and they report an increased ability to be honest and authentic with one another.

References

Adams, V. (1999). *The relationship between perceived mother-daughter mutuality and coping in
    African American female adolescents.* Unpublished doctoral dissertation, Stanford Univer-
    sity, Stanford, CA.
Bergman, S. J. (1991). *Men's psychological development: A relational perspective* (Work in prog-
    ress, No. 48). Wellesley, MA: Stone Center, Wellesley College.
Boyd-Franklin, N. (1991). Recurrent themes in the treatment of African American women in
    group psychotherapy. *Women and Therapy, 11,* 25-40.
Cauce, A. M., Hiraga, Y., Graves, D., Gonzales, K., Ryan-Finn, K., & Grove, K. (1996). African
    American mothers and their adolescent daughters: Closeness, conflict, and control. In B. J.

Leadbeater & N. Way (Eds.), *Urban girls: Resisting stereotypes, creating identities* (pp. 100-116). New York: New York University Press.

Collins, P. H. (1991). *Black feminist thought: Knowledge, consciousness, and the politics of empowerment.* New York: Routledge & Kegan Paul.

Erikson, E. (1963). *Childhood and society* (2nd ed.). New York: Norton.

Fedele, N. M., & Harrington, E. A. (1990). *Women's groups: How connections heal* (Work in progress, No. 47). Wellesley, MA: Stone Center, Wellesley College.

Galambos, N. L., & Ehrenberg, M. F. (1997). The family as health risk and opportunity: A focus on divorce and working families. In J. Schulenberg, J. L. Maggs, & K. Hurrelmann (Eds.), *Health risks and developmental transitions during adolescence* (pp. 139-160). Cambridge, UK: Cambridge University Press.

Genero, N. P., Miller, J. B., Surrey, J., & Baldwin, L. M. (1992). Measuring perceived mutuality in close relationships: Validation of the Mutual Psychological Development Questionnaire. *Journal of Family Psychology, 6,* 36-48.

Gibbs, J. T. (1998). African American adolescents. In J. T. Gibbs & L. N. Huang (Eds.), *Children of color: Psychological interventions with minority youth* (pp. 171-214). San Francisco: Jossey-Bass.

Gilligan, C. (1982). *In a different voice: Psychological theory of women's development.* Cambridge, MA: Harvard University Press.

Gilligan, C., Rogers, A. G., & Tolman, D. L. (Eds.). (1991). *Women, girls and psychotherapy: Reframing resistance.* Binghamton, NY: Harrington Park.

Greene, B. (1994). African American women. In L. Comas-Díaz & B. Greene (Eds.), *Women of color: Integrating ethnic and gender identities in psychotherapy* (pp. 10-29). New York: Guilford.

Guthrie, B. J. (1997). *African American adolescent female health promotion: An ethnic and gender specific substance prevention framework.* Unpublished manuscript.

hooks, b. (1993). *Sisters of the yam: Black women and self-recovery.* Boston: South End.

Hyman, J. B. (1999). *Spheres of influence.* Baltimore: Annie E. Casey Foundation.

Jordan, J. V. (1991). *The movement of mutuality and power* (Work in progress, No. 53). Wellesley, MA: Stone Center, Wellesley College.

Jordan, J. V., Kaplan, A. G., Miller, J. B., Stiver, I. P., & Surrey, J. L. (Eds.). (1991). *Women's growth in connection: Writings from the Stone Center.* New York: Guilford.

Kaplan, A. G., Klein, R., & Gleason, N. (1991). Women's self development in late adolescence. In J. V. Jordan, A. G. Kaplan, J. B. Miller, I. P. Stiver, & J. L. Surrey (Eds.), *Women's growth in connection: Writings from the Stone Center* (pp. 122-142). New York: Guilford.

LaFromboise, T. D., & Graff Low, K. (1998). American Indian children and adolescents. In J. T. Gibbs & L. N. Huang (Eds.), *Children of color: Psychological interventions with minority youth* (pp. 112-138). San Francisco: Jossey-Bass.

Leadbeater, B. J., & Way, N. (Eds.). (1996). *Urban girls: Resisting stereotypes, creating identities.* New York: New York University Press.

Markus, H. R., & Kitayama, S. (1998). The cultural psychology of personality. *Journal of Cross-Cultural Psychology, 29*(1), 63-87.

Miller, J. B. (1976). *Toward a new psychology of women.* Boston: Beacon.

Miller, J. B. (1988). *Connections, disconnections and violations* (Work in progress, No. 33). Wellesley, MA: Stone Center, Wellesley College.

Miller, J. B. (1991). The development of a women's sense of self. In J. V. Jordan, A. G. Kaplan, J. B. Miller, I. P. Stiver, & J. L. Surrey (Eds.), *Women's growth in connection: Writings from the Stone Center* (pp. 11-27). New York: Guilford.

48   IDENTITY IN A PLURALISTIC SOCIETY

Myers, H. F. (1989). Urban stress and the mental health of Afro-American youth: An
    epidemiologic and conceptual update. In R. L. Jones (Ed.), *Black adolescents* (pp. 123-154).
    Berkeley, CA: Cobb & Henry.
Pastor, J., McCormick, J., & Fine, M. (1996). Makin' homes: An urban girl thing. In B. J. Lead-
    beater & N. Way (Eds.), *Urban girls: Resisting stereotypes, creating identities* (pp. 15-43).
    New York: New York University Press.
Powell, J. W., Denton, R. D., & Mattsson, A. (1995). Adolescent depression: Effects of mutuality
    in the mother-daughter dyad and locus of control. *American Orthopsychiatric Association, 65,*
    263-273.
Robinson, T., & Ward, J. V. (1991). "A belief in self far greater than anyone's disbelief": Culti-
    vating resistance among African American female adolescents. In C. Gilligan, A. G. Rogers,
    & D. L. Tolman (Eds.), *Women, girls and psychotherapy: Reframing resistance* (pp. 87-103).
    Binghamton, NY: Harrington Park.
Rotheram-Borus, M. J., Dopkins, S., Sabate, N., & Lightfoot, M. (1996). Personal and ethnic iden-
    tity, values, and self-esteem among Black and Latino Adolescent girls. In B. J. Leadbeater &
    N. Way (Eds.), *Urban girls: Resisting stereotypes, creating identities* (pp. 35-52). New York:
    New York University Press.
Rowlison, R. T., & Felner, R. D. (1988). Major life events, hassles, and adaptation in adolescence:
    Confounding in the conceptualization and measurement of life stress and adjustment revisited.
    Journal of Personality and Social Psychology, 55, 432-444.
Surrey, J. L. (1991). The "self-in-relation": A theory of women's development. In J. V. Jordan,
    A. G. Kaplan, J. B. Miller, I. P. Stiver, & J. L. Surrey (Eds.), *Women's growth in connection:
    Writings from the Stone Center* (pp. 51-67). New York: Guilford.
Turner, C. W. (1997). Clinical applications of the Stone Center theoretical approach to minority
    women. In J. V. Jordan (Ed.), *Women's growth in diversity: More writings from the Stone Cen-
    ter* (pp. 74-90). New York: Guilford.
Vasquez, M. J. T., & Ling Han, A. (1995). Group interventions and treatment with ethnic minori-
    ties. In J. F. Aponte, R. Y. Rovers, & J. Wohl (Eds.), *Psychological interventions and cultural
    diversity* (pp. 109-127). Needham Heights, MA: Allyn & Bacon.
Wade, J. C. (1994). African American fathers and sons: Social, historical, and psychological con-
    siderations. *Families in Society, 75,* 561-570.
Ward, J. V. (1996). Raising resisters: The role of truth telling in the psychological development of
    African American girls. In B. J. Leadbeater & N. Way (Eds.), *Urban girls: Resisting stereo-
    types, creating identities* (pp. 85-99). New York: New York University Press.
White, J. L., & Parham, T. A. (1990). *The psychology of Blacks: An African American perspective.*
    Englewood Cliffs, NJ: Prentice Hall.
Yalom, I. D. (1985). *The theory and practice of group psychotherapy* (3rd ed.). New York: Basic
    Books.

THE INTERACTION OF RACE AND GENDER IN AFRICAN AMERICAN WOMEN'S EXPERIENCES OF SELF AND OTHER AT A PREDOMINANTLY WHITE WOMEN'S COLLEGE

Lisa R. Jackson
Boston College

I find I am constantly being encouraged to pluck out some one aspect of myself and present this as the meaningful whole, eclipsing or denying the other parts of self. But this is a restrictive and fragmenting way to live. My fullest concentration of energy is available to me only when I integrate all the parts of who I am, openly, allowing power from particular sources of my living to flow back and forth freely through all my different selves, without the restrictions of externally imposed definition.
—Lorde (1984, pp. 120-121)

In this chapter, I discuss the intersection of race and gender in the self-definition of African American women in predominantly white environments. To do this, I draw on the findings of a recent study (Jackson, 1996, 1998) where I interviewed African American women at a predominantly white women's college (PWC) about their definition of self as informed by both their race and their gender. I explore the phenomenon of a "both/and" experience for these women and the ramifications for their psychological and emotional well-being.

The experiences of African American women have been largely ignored by psychology research (Thomas & Miles, 1995). When they are included in studies, African American women are either compared to white women, implying that the study of African American women alone is inappropriate (some have called this approach "methodologically deficient") (Landrine, Klonoff, & Brown-Collins, 1995), or they are considered relative to African American men, indicating that as a group, African American women do not warrant independent research attention.

In drawing attention to African American women, this chapter heeds the advice of Smith and Stewart (1983) and Reid and Comas-Díaz (1990) and takes an interactive approach to examining both race and gender within the self-concept of African American women. First, I explain the work of Oyserman and Markus (1993), whose theory of a sociocultural self I use as a framework for the research study I share in this chapter. This is followed by a discussion of the sociocultural and historical contexts of African American women's lives, emphasizing the work of Patricia Hill Collins (1991). I then review existing literature on the college experiences of African American women generally. Last and most important, I share the words of five African American women at a small predominantly white women's college. Their definition of self in terms of race and gender, as well as their experiences and perspectives about race and gender on their college campus, provides insight into the psychological and emotional needs of women of color in predominantly white environments. In addition, the information they share challenges the assumption of a shared women's experience at a school where, as one woman described it, "the archetype and prototype for a woman is a white woman, a straight white woman at that."

THE SOCIOCULTURAL SELF

The sociocultural model of the self developed by Oyserman and Markus (1993) serves as the theoretical framework for the analysis and interpretation of the interview data collected in the study presented in this chapter. They argue that the self cannot be studied void of its sociocultural context. They posit that the self comprises many self-conceptions. These self-conceptions are the ways in which a person perceives of who he or she is within larger sociocultural contexts. Some self-conceptions are more permanent and are the result of repeated experiences (e.g., constantly experiencing the self in terms of a particular racial group membership); others are more temporary and function only in a given moment. The more permanent self-conceptions are called *self-schemas:* "cognitive generalizations about the self, derived from past experiences, that organize and guide the processing of self-related information contained in the individual's social experience" (Markus, 1977, p. 64).

In explaining their theory, Oyserman and Markus (1993) state the complexity of determining the role of a particular sociocultural context within a person's self-definition:

> These embedded contexts are nested, with the influence of each being mediated by the constraints placed on it by all the others. The main point is that these effects cannot be easily disentangled. One is not a woman and a Catholic and an Hispanic and creative and sympathetic, but a sympathetic, creative, Catholic woman (or perhaps instead a Catholic, Hispanic, creative, sympathetic woman). The independent contribution of each sociocultural context to one's self or identity cannot be evaluated. Each attribute or identifying feature both provides meaning to, and recruits meaning from, all the others. The resulting self is some melding, collaging, or weaving together of one's various sociocultural influences (which metaphor is most appropriate here is important but at this point it is an empirical question). (p. 195)

In the case of African American women, it is often assumed that race takes priority over gender in self-definition. However, depending on the salience of race and gender in a given situation and the sociocultural and historical contexts, both race and gender appear to be simultaneously central to the self.

Although the sociocultural framework of the self provides a way of conceptualizing self as a multifaceted and dynamic construct, given the multiple contexts that can inform the identity of any given person or group of people, Oyserman and Markus (1993) leave to researchers the task of identifying the relevant sociocultural contexts of their research participants. Few studies have used this framework to explore the self and its construction (see Oyserman, Gant, & Ager, 1995), explicitly considering the sociocultural contexts of the lives of study participants. The following section explores the sociocultural and historical contexts relevant to the lives of African American women.

THE SOCIOCULTURAL AND HISTORICAL CONTEXT OF AFRICAN AMERICAN WOMEN'S LIVES

Much of the scholarly research on African American women focuses on their dual status as women and ethnic minorities in U.S. society. This status is commonly referred to as *double jeopardy* or *double bind* (Greene, 1994; Lykes, 1983; Reid, 1984). As Beverly Greene (1994) points out, African American women have to deal with maintaining their West African-based culture in a society where non-European cultures are denigrated and devalued, as well as with being a woman in a patriarchal, sexist society. In addition, African American women are often pushed and pulled by two separate communities. The African American community typically identifies racism as the most pervasive oppressive force in society. Therefore, an African American woman's efforts should be focused within the African American community so that the community as a whole can make progress as a "race" (Reid, 1984). White women form the other community that admonishes African American women for not participating in "feminist" efforts to fight sexism. By not joining in this cause, white women argue that sexism will flourish in the African American community (Reid, 1984). However, forging such an allegiance with white women can make African American women feel that they have to identify African American men as sexist oppressors. To do so can result in African American women being perceived as "siding with the enemy" by the African American community.

To handle this double jeopardy, African American women develop a variety of adaptive strategies (Collins, 1991; Greene, 1994; Lykes, 1983). Depending on the type of environment they are in and the people present, some African American women will ignore the stressors put on them as a result of their race or gender status. Others will tackle such stressors head-on in an effort to contradict negative stereotypes. Collins (1991) suggests that the controlling stereotypical images that serve to objectify and negatively define the existence of African American women in this society force individual women to resist the stressors that stem from double jeopardy. Such resistance can be vocal or silent but always represents doing something that counters the expectations of others (e.g., being academically successful when the stereotype of African Americans is that they are not intelligent).

Greene (1994) points to racial socialization as a determinant of adaptive strategy choice among African American women. Focusing on the stress related to racism, Greene says that African American women must be able to clearly identify and label racism, have access to role models for appropriate response choices to racism, and receive emotional support in their efforts to understand racism. Responses to the stressors stemming from double jeopardy will in part be determined by the individual experiences of women in each of these three areas. Regardless of the adaptive strategies, the psychological reality of African American women requires creative coping skills, deft negotiating skills, and strength to maintain overall self-integrity.

> A major element of psychological reality for African American women involves integrating the influences of the majority culture without internalizing the accompanying devaluing messages that are the result of its racism and sexism. This leaves African American women with the challenge of developing coping mechanisms in response to racism and sexism, negotiating the discriminatory barriers that result from institutional racism and sexism, and addressing the full range of life's normal and catastrophic stressors. (Greene, 1994, p. 16)

Although the double-jeopardy approach offers one perspective for understanding African American women's lives, it is limited for at least two reasons. First, it perpetuates the problem of treating race and gender as separate factors. Although it considers both, it focuses on race as the primary factor in an African American woman's life and gender as the secondary factor. Little effort is made to understand the interaction of race and gender. The second problem with this approach is that it focuses on African American women as victims in an oppressive society. Although it is true that African American women have to tackle racism and sexism in this society, focusing on them as victims negates that which is powerful and positive about their dual status. In addition, although researchers may identify African American women as victims, the women do not define themselves as such. Work by Lawrence-Lightfoot (1994); Lykes (1983); Angelou (1993); Hull, Scott, and Smith (1982); and many others shows how African American women are often change agents, active intellectually, politically, and spiritually. Instead of behaving as victims, African American women work very hard at defining who they are and creating paths for success in their lives (Collins, 1991; James & Farmer, 1993).

In a departure from the double-jeopardy approach, Patricia Hill Collins (1991) offers Black feminist thought as a way to interpret the experiences of African American women.

> I suggest that Black feminist thought consists of specialized knowledge cre-
> ated by African American women which clarifies a standpoint of and for
> Black women. In other words, Black feminist thought encompasses theoret-
> ical interpretations of Black women's reality by those who live it. (p. 22)

Collins (1991) argues that Black women experience overlapping social and political oppressions based on a variety of sociocultural factors (e.g., race, gender,
class, sexual orientation). To focus on any one of these factors alone would minimize the role of the others, creating a false representation of African American
women's experiences.

Collins points to "a system of interlocking race, class, and gender oppression" (p. 222) as that which largely determines the experiences of African
American women in this country. African American women experience a
both/and existence such that who they are is at all times defined by both race and
gender.

RESEARCH ON AFRICAN AMERICAN WOMEN COLLEGE STUDENTS

In seeking to understand how college success is influenced by campus context
and students' backgrounds, Allen (1992) examined the academic performance
of African Americans who attended predominantly white colleges and universities (PWCUs) and those who attended historically Black colleges and universities (HBCUs). He found that student perceptions of support and responses to
various challenges have a greater impact on academic experiences than does
prior academic achievement.

> The way a student perceives and responds to events in the college setting
> will differentiate his or her college experience and shape his or her college
> outcomes. What he or she does when confronted with difficult subject mat-
> ter, how he or she handles the uncertainty of new situations, and how adept
> he or she is in help-seeking behavior will ultimately determine whether a
> student's college experience is positive or negative. (p. 39)

Academic achievement was highest for participants with high educational
aspirations, who believed that their school choice was correct, and who had
positive relations with faculty at either HBCUs or PWCUs. African Americans

at PWCUs had lower current grades, higher high school grades, and fewer positive relationships with faculty than those African Americans attending HBCUs. With regard to gender, at both PWCUs and HBCUs, African American women reported higher confidence and high school grades than males but lower occupational aspirations. These lower aspirations were not in line with the women's strong academic performance. In terms of predictor variables for occupational aspirations, gender of the student and racial composition of the school had the highest predictive value.

Although Allen's (1992) study provides a view of college experiences for African American students, he fails to consider some factors. Although he does consider the racial composition of each school and the gender of his participants, he does not consider the gender composition of each school. All of the schools in his study are coeducational (they are also all state supported, not private). As a result, he is unable to speak to the experience of an all-women's school context for African American women. Allen does make the comment that some of his findings suggest an interaction effect for race and gender in terms of student outcomes. However, he states that such interaction is not the focus of the study, and he therefore does not explore the interaction.

A second example of research on African American college students is Jacqueline Fleming's (1984) prominent study that spanned 3 years and compared the experiences of African American and white students at 11 predominantly white colleges and universities (PWCUs) and 7 historically Black colleges and universities (HBCUs). At both types of schools, Fleming found that although men have the most difficulty with interpersonal relations, African American women are plagued by doubts about their academic competence:

> They [black women] invariably set lower goals than men. They perform more poorly in math. They experience more anxiety during competition and express more dissatisfaction with their performance than men. But black women's competence anxieties are out of proportion with some of the objective facts of their competitive abilities. While it is true that they perform worse than men in math, they do perform well in verbal tasks and show the most improvement in their verbal skills from freshman to senior year. (p. 144)

Fleming (1984) found that African American women who attend PWCUs are more socially assertive and independent than those women who attend HBCUs. Although they do not show the academic gains of women at HBCUs, they do show gains in their ability to work under pressure, be assertive, act as role models, use coping skills, and focus on career goals. On the downside, African American women who attend PWCUs are often ostracized for their assertiveness and experience more failed relationships and isolation. Fleming concludes that an environment with fewer African American males results in increased unhappiness at the same time it provides greater career development opportunities.

As with Allen's (1992) work, Fleming's (1984) study addresses a wide range of issues affecting the lives of African Americans in college. Unlike many researchers, she does consider carefully the position of African American women. She does this both at coeducational schools and at an all-women's HBCU. The site she omits, however, is the women's PWC.

Carroll (1982) addresses the unique situation of African American women on predominantly white coeducational campuses. She reminds us that these women experience both racial and gender discrimination on campus. In addition, there are rarely African American women professors or administrators to serve as role models. The result is that women create strong peer groups and derive models of success from each other. Citing the work of Willie and Levy (1972), Carroll posits that African American women do better socially and academically on campuses where there are large numbers of other African Americans. This provides women an opportunity to develop a community or extended family, providing academic and social support.

The literature on the experiences of African American women (or women of color) at predominantly white women's colleges is virtually nonexistent. Of the studies that focus on single-sex education, those that look at women's colleges ignore the presence of African American women and other women of color (Crosby et al., 1994; Miller-Bernal, 1993; Riordan, 1992; Whitt, 1994). One explanation given for this absent attention is given by Smith, Wolf, and Morrison (1995), whose sample included 160 women who attended all-women's colleges and 764 women who attended coeducational institutions. In this total sample, the authors argue that the number of women of color was so small in the total sample that it was "impossible to include race/ethnicity as a meaningful variable in this study" (p. 250).

Statistics on enrollment for women's colleges are not regularly reported distinctly in national education databases. A report put out by the National Center for Education Statistics in 1979 indicated that within the 125 colleges that were identified as women's colleges, 8,382 of the 109,549 students enrolled were African American. More recent data tell us that 7% of the 14,646 women who received bachelor's degrees in 1985 were African American (Touchton & Davis, 1991).

Although they are small in number, the dilemma of measuring the experiences of these women points to the limitations of quantitative research methods in studying the experiences of underrepresented groups on certain college campuses. This should not mean that because their numbers are small, the experiences of African American women and other women of color are not worth understanding. All colleges and universities, whether coeducational or single-sex institutions, should strive to meet the psychological, educational, and emotional needs of all their students. To do this effectively, they must recognize and understand the sociocultural contexts of the lives of their students.

To achieve this understanding, educators and service providers must listen to the voices of African American women as they integrate their multiple cultural and personal identities into a coherent sense of self. The developmental competencies and challenges that college-age women face provide an excellent lens through which to view the process of integrating these identities. To help us hear that process more directly, I will share the themes that emerged from interviews with women at a predominantly white women's college.

The interviews come from a larger study involving four colleges and universities and 135 African American women (see Jackson, 1996, for a full presentation of the study). Five women from Berton (a pseudonym), a private, predominantly white women's college, participated in one-on-one interviews as part of the study. Interviews ran from 1 to 2 hours and covered topics including what it means to be a woman and an African American, how they made the decision to attend the school in which they are currently enrolled, experiences of racism and sexism, and interactions with faculty, staff, and students on their campus.

Berton College was founded in 1852 as a seminary institution and became a college in 1885. The school's academic purpose, as stated in its bulletin, is "broad-based education in the liberal arts." One of the more interesting things about how the school that is presented to the public is the emphasis on what type of people Berton students will be once they graduate from the school:

> We hope that when our students leave Berton, they will go on to lead valuable and fulfilling lives. We want them to appreciate and understand the complexity and diversity of human communities and the world in which we

live. We want them to be people who make a difference to those communities and to the world—because they have learned how to observe, think,
question, imagine, and speak out when they see a need on principles they
know to be their own.

Berton's student population is small—only 800 undergraduate students.
When graduate students are added (both male and female), the number slightly
exceeds 1,000. The ethnic breakdown of the undergraduate student body is as
follows: 15.7% are Asian American, 8.4% are African American, 4.3% are Hispanic, 61.5% are white, and 6.5% are designated as international students. In
terms of faculty, 52% of the 150 full-time professors are women.[1]

In terms of resources available concerning race or gender studies, Berton
offers a women's studies and ethnic studies major. Although there is a major in
Hispanic studies, there is not an African American studies major or African
studies major. There is the Black Women's Collective, a women-of-color student organization, and an organization for lesbian women of color called Queer
Melanin.

When I first made contact with the associate dean of students at Berton,
who introduced me to the Black Women's Collective, she indicated that there
was a certain amount of discontent among Berton African American students.
In fact, the meeting I attended to recruit study participants was considered an
"emergency meeting" by students. All African Americans on campus, including staff and faculty, were invited to discuss how African Americans were relating to one another on campus. Issues such as "being Black enough," ostracizing
staff who received promotions, and student responsibility to African Americans in the local community outside the walls of Berton were addressed.

In addition to this activity, two stories made the campus paper in the month
I began recruitment. The first story concerned a lawsuit filed by an African
American woman faculty member charging that Berton engaged in "racial harassment" and discrimination against her. The suit claims, among other things,
that she was evicted from promised faculty housing and denied tenure. The second story was about a paper called "Interrogations" that was disseminated to
students, faculty, and staff. This paper contained essays that focused on white
bourgeoisie privilege. In addition to factual information about "Interrogations,"
the campus paper also solicited student responses to the essays. All of the above
activities suggest that at the time of recruitment and data collection, race was a
salient issue on the Berton campus.

THE INTERSECTION OF RACE AND GENDER: BLACK WOMEN AT BERTON COLLEGE

As is revealed in the interviews, the definition of self for Berton African American women is inextricably connected to the environment they are in. The core themes described below must be considered in light of this, for as Collins (1991) points out and as my larger study shows (Jackson, 1996), these themes manifest themselves differently depending on the racial and gender composition of the school.

Emotional Safety

Each of the five women at some point during the interviews talked about how unsafe Berton was for their mental and emotional health or about how "crazy" people were on the campus. Fern (all names are pseudonyms), in response to whether she felt safe on the campus, said the following:

> I mean it depends on how you define *safe*. I mean emotionally this is not a safe place for women of color. You have to seek out other people to support you. You couldn't just thrive here on your own; it would be emotionally devastating.

Terry talked about how she had mostly "associates" on campus and had a difficult time trusting people. She did not go out of her way to make friends because in general she felt that women at Berton were crazy:

> **Jackson:** Do you think you will eventually make friends here with people?
> **Terry:** It's not a priority because like I said, the people here are crazy.

Eileen, who is a dance major, spoke about how the stress of racism on the campus would sometimes manifest itself in her body physically. During her sophomore year, she traveled in India, largely because of the difficult time she was having at Berton.

> **Eileen:** But leaving all had to do with this school.

Jackson: What were some of the reasons that you wanted to leave?

Eileen: One is during that entire sophomore year [I felt] totally unsupported and isolated, because of speaking out and people not talking to you.

Jackson: OK.

Eileen: Of being labeled as the person who's always angry and always, um, so therefore people don't communicate and don't talk to you. So therefore, you're dealing with things alone.

Jackson: Right.

Eileen: You know, subtle things, next to you, where you go to the bathroom and you see a sign or something.

Jackson: Hmm.

Eileen: Um, yeah. That's stuff drove me crazy.

Here's what Phyllis and Stephanie had to say about emotional safety:

Phyllis: I don't know if this is a college thing or whatever but everybody's really high-strung. We're always having nervous breakdowns and stuff about something. Every time I see another Black woman, it's like we are both losing our minds.

Stephanie: And so I have to go outside to look for things. That's something I realize, like keeping my friends like on an even keel because Berton is not a safe environment for women of color.

Berton does have a counseling center on campus. However, only one woman mentioned using its services. There is an African American woman who is the adviser for women of color. She is not a counselor by training, and because she is also the associate dean of students, she spends much of her time keeping up with students' academic activities and progress.

In addition to feeling that Berton is not an "emotionally safe" place, all five women shared that at one time or another, they experienced depression, some for as long as a year. This depression was often the result of feeling isolated and alienated. As mentioned above by Eileen, some of the alienation came as a result of feeling that being angry or expressing emotion was not accepted by others on campus. Stephanie, in talking about her interactions with professors, had this to say: "Then there are faculty that [think], 'Damn women of color—angry women of color.'"

Proving Self to Others

In light of all the debates surrounding affirmative action, each of the women readily gave an example of proving to others that they deserved to be at Berton. This was emotionally draining and angering. For Terry, her grades were a large part of her self-definition: "It's like, that as an African American woman, those grades are me. Those grades are me." Later, when talking about what it means to her to be an African American, she said, "I was really upset at myself last semester when my grades were bad because I didn't want people to think, oh well, she's here 'cause she's Black. No wonder she couldn't do it, you know?" Stephanie responds to such negative stereotypes about Blacks and affirmative action in this way:

> I notice a lot of people are like, "Well, people say I got here on affirmative action." I'm like, "Well who's doing your homework?" You got here. Who's doing your homework? If it's affirmative action, cool. Who's doing your work?

This issue can also get complicated when students feel they receive grades they did not deserve. For Stephanie and Phyllis, it was that professors gave them high grades for work they felt deserved lower grades. The reason they gave was that professors were probably worried that they would be labeled as racist if they gave African American students low grades.

One of the consequences of constantly having to prove yourself to others is the development of self-doubt. Phyllis hopes that over time she will gain more confidence in her abilities and skills: "I got skills and I got talents, but I'm just too afraid to use them, 'cause I'm just scared I'm going to fail." In identifying major issues in her life currently, Fern remembers the difficulties she had with self-esteem the previous year:

> Yeah, self-esteem issues, I mean, it's kind of weird 'cause I've always been built up, but then I found myself having self-doubt and it is environmental. And so, I've worked on that, and as I've gotten closer to my friends, it's been easier to just feel confident.

Intragroup Relations

Although women had little difficulty talking about their conflict with white women on campus, there were also examples of tension within groups of African American women or women of color. As racism produced tension between Blacks and whites, homophobia produced tension between Blacks:

> **Stephanie:**   On this campus, you know, a lot of women of color are homophobic, you know. A lot of white women are very racist. A lot of white lesbians are very racist, and so it's like, if you are queer and of color, you find people to stick with . . . yeah . . . so we have Queer Melanin.

Not being "Black enough" was also a problem. Terry was equally wary of women of color and white women due to this: "Women of color generally, but it's in my experience with the Black women, you know. It seems as if people are constantly questioning how 'ethnic' you are, you know?" Eileen expressed the same concern:

> **Jackson:**   What does being African American mean?
> **Eileen:**   Well, let's see, it still means—first of all, what it means to me is I recognize I can be who I am and claim that as African American, that's one thing I recognize.
> **Jackson:**   OK.
> **Eileen:**   Um, and yeah. I think that's probably the key thing. Is that because I've been told that I'm not Black enough.

Sometimes, women of color just do not see eye to eye.

> **Fern:**   It's just been really hard because people are working on a really large project, and like I and some other like two or three other women of color like had an issue with one of their statements. We thought it was xenophobic and exclusionary to people outside of this country and that just caused a rift. There was already somewhat of a rift between us, for some weird reason, but I didn't feel it as much, and I thought, just because we're women of color in this environment which is somewhat hostile towards us, that we could just pull it together and be there for one another. But we had this big meeting,

just all of us women of color who came, and a lot of things happened in that meeting that were hurtful.

The Consequences of Choosing a White Women's College

All five of the women came to Berton for essentially the same reasons. The campus is aesthetically pleasing, class size is small, it is close to home, and it is a women's college. Once at Berton, women found that some of their expectations were met; others were not. Stephanie discovered that classes were not always small and that just because Berton was all women, it did not mean that who she was as a woman was valued. As for the attractive campus, "It is very, very beautiful. Unfortunately that hides a multitude of sins. But it is really pretty."

Phyllis, who had been homeless on and off during her childhood, felt that Berton offered her things that other women probably took for granted:

But there's so much here I never had access to. Like food all the time. I like being able to eat and eat a lot. And just computers whenever I want. And I got my own room. For the first time in my life. My own bed. I can decorate my own. My own phone.

As for things she did not like about Berton, Phyllis felt there was a lot of pressure to conform in terms of sexuality. She felt there were two choices, either to be homophobic and hated for that or to be lesbian or pretend you are lesbian to fit in. She also did not like that there were so few Black women for her to have as friends. Those who were there worked so hard most of the time that they did not have time to cultivate friendships.

Terry came to Berton because it was close to home. She also got hooked by Berton's "empowerment message." She felt that the women at Berton had confidence and were very outspoken. These are traits she hoped to develop in herself. She liked that it was small and felt that helped her be academically successful. The size also provided her with a sense of community. The primary thing she did not like about Berton was the following:

Everything is so politicized—I'm not saying that's a bad thing, or to ignore issues, but too many people on this campus, I mean they come from little hick towns and they don't know what's going on. And it's just really frustrating. And then, everything is an issue so you try to go to the administration with these issues and to some extent there's not enough communication between the administration and the president; she doesn't care. And that, that makes it a lot harder. It makes you feel like, well why am I even bothering to fight for these things? I should just get my education.

Eileen got hooked on Berton through their promotional materials. Before coming, however, she knew about the racial tension on campus. She decided to come anyway because for her, the pros outweighed the cons. The primary pro was that she got to develop her own major. As for fulfilling her expectations, she found that in general, the atmosphere on Berton's campus was one of stagnation:

> In terms of thinking processes, what can or can't be done even though they give you this idea of freedom of choices you can make. When you try you do that, they tell you you can't do that, and they tell you just like that—"No. You can't do that." And you sit there and you have to fight for it, you know.

Fern came to Berton for the same reasons as the other women. However, she feels that as a result of being at Berton, she is changing as a person in a way that scares her.

> And I've changed a lot from high school, just because of the environment and I don't feel completely good about how I'm changing as a human being, 'cause I'm beginning to close myself off to like white people, just because I can't deal with a lot of the racism that goes on here, so I choose to be around people who I identify with—women of color, and . . . so it's hard because in high school I was a total people's advocate—everybody's rights. And now, I don't know, the picture's changing and so that's kind of scary and it's not really well accepted in a way either.

What will be remembered by these women once they leave Berton? The struggle, first and foremost. The loneliness and the depression. How hard it was to be a Black student on Berton's campus. But just as other college students, these African American women will remember their friendships and their fun times. They will also carry with them a sense of pride that they survived a difficult time and earned a degree that, it is hoped, will take them where they want to go. Phyllis shared an interesting point of view about what she would remember and why:

Jackson: When you are long gone from this place. . . .
Phyllis: I will speak very favorably.
Jackson: How will you—yeah, will you?
Phyllis: Oh definitely. It bothers me that people speak bad about it. It's like, I have to graduate from here. This is where I'm going to get my B.A. from. I would like for it to have a good reputation in the future, like it does now.

Even though Phyllis has experienced severe depression during her time at Berton and has had a difficult time with financial aid and relationships with other students and faculty, she still wants to feel good about Berton. She wants to hold on to that which is positive—Berton's reputation.

Some of the women talked about remembering their own personal growth. Fern said she will remember "the struggle. Just to remember, to stay true to myself. All the growing too." Terry, who was only a freshman at the time of this study, felt she had already grown since her time at Berton:

Probably just me growing as a person because I've grown so much since I've been here. Just learning how to deal with other people, learning how to deal with issues. Learning when to just shut off and shut the world out and do the task at hand. So far, if I were to leave right now, that would be what I would take.

Stephanie summarizes all that she will take with her when she leaves—the good and the bad. She wants people to know her experience and to appreciate her success:

Stephanie: Partners that I'm going to be tight with for life. We've been through a lot, you know, a lot. The education here at Berton is a really good education. You just have to plow through a lot of bullshit to get it.
Jackson: Right!
Stephanie: But, you know, that degree that says Stephanie, Berton College, graduate June 1997. You know, it's worth it, but it's a lot of

hard work here, you know. A lot of energy, a lot of hard work, blood, sweat, and tears. So I have to tell people that.

The women in this study decided to attend a predominantly white women's college with the expectation that they would find a community among other women, that they would receive a good education in an aesthetically appealing environment, and that the school would provide them with opportunities beyond its walls once they finished. Although these expectations were met, there were other consequences of attending such a school that the women had not anticipated. Relationships with other Black women were sometimes complicated by sexual orientation and standards of "Blackness" that were exclusive (i.e., not being "Black enough"). Relationships with white women on campus were complicated by racism. The African American women in the study found they had to work hard to survive experiences of hostility, isolation, and depression on campus and that they often only had each other to turn to for support.

DISCUSSION: DEFINING SELF IN TERMS OF DIFFERENCE—BEING "BOTH/AND"

Although all of the women decided to come to Berton because it was a women's college, being African American for all of them and being lesbian for four of them made self-definition possible mostly in terms of difference. It was very important to the women, when asked about what it meant to be a woman or if they considered themselves feminist, that I understand their responses in terms of their race as well as their gender. In talking about how she would describe herself to someone who did not know her, Fern's multiple positions all took center stage: "Well, they should definitely know that I'm African American and that I'm a woman and that I'm lesbian and that I'm a runner and that I'm very devoted to things that I believe in."

Terry's response to defining feminism reflects the responses of other women as well. She cannot simply be a feminist—it is much more complicated than that:

I don't know that I am—I'm pro-woman, but I don't know if I'm a feminist. Um, I would have to be a Black feminist, because I think in communities there's definitely a difference from Black feminists than there is from white women because they can afford to say, "We hate our men" and go on about their business, basically. I can't do that.

Both Terry and Stephanie point to how the issues for African American and white women are different, although they share their gender.

Terry: It's hard for me to be down with that because the people that are preaching feminist this, feminist that are white women and we're, we're fighting two different battles here. And I mean, their failure to recognize that—their conscious failure to recognize that—is a total turnoff to me.

Stephanie: And then people hear that Berton—oh all women, we can all just be women here. You know. But the archetype and prototype for a woman is a white woman, a white straight woman at that. So if you happen to be African American or Latina or Chinese and you happen to be bi- or questioning or queer—oh my gosh! Just forget it! And then there's the white lesbians who go, "I'm a lesbian, therefore I know your pain." And, "Your pain is so empowering to me." And you're like, "Oh God." It's weird here bordering on surreal.

In many ways, these responses speak to the experience of double jeopardy (Greene, 1994). Although located within a community of women, the women in this study had to deal with the consequences of also being African American within a predominantly white context. These women explain that the dual status of African American women produces experiences that are positioned outside the experiences of white women. In addition, they must continuously prove themselves to others in the Berton community to fight negative stereotypes about their academic ability as African American women. To handle the resulting stress of this experience, the women at Berton developed adaptive strategies that included creating a community of support (Carroll, 1982), participating in political activities, and speaking out in classes and with peers about racism and sexism.

Although these women experienced double jeopardy, they worked very hard at not viewing themselves as victims with no recourse. Instead, as evidenced by the quotes earlier, they framed their existence at Berton as a "both/and" (Collins, 1991) experience. By doing this, they engage in work on the self that recognizes the multiple sociocultural contexts in which they are located (Oyserman & Markus, 1993). They move toward an integrated self, pushing at the boundaries imposed on them by the institution they attend and by the larger society.

Colleges and universities work with students at a very critical time of their identity development. As with most college students at this time in their lives, the road to an integrated sense of self is not smooth. Such development is further complicated for African American women who seek to create an identity that represents multiple sociocultural contexts at the same time they are located within a predominantly white environment. Unfortunately, Berton has provided few opportunities for these women to experience and thus develop an integrated self, aspired to by Audre Lorde (1984) in the opening quote of this chapter.

Although it is important that service providers (either at a higher education institution or in another setting) understand the ways in which a person defines who he or she is and therefore understands the world, it is equally important that the context in which that definition is made is understood. For the African American women at Berton, although the school they attend is an all-women's college, this does not negate their racial status. This status affects the experiences they have in that environment, as well as the way they decide to interpret and handle such experiences.

To provide a psychologically healthy and "emotionally safe" environment for African American women and to support the development of an integrated self-definition that grows out of an experience of self as "different" or as "object," service providers must create services with an understanding of the multiple interacting sociocultural contexts that define the lives of these women. Such services should be administered by service providers who share the sociocultural and historical experience of being African American women or who have been adequately trained to work with African American women (of varying sexual orientations). Such providers will likely be aware of the needs and challenges that exist for African American women in predominantly white environments such as the need for an African American community that can provide emotional support in an "emotionally unsafe" environment and the pressure to be academically competent in the face of negative stereotypes. As Greene (1994) points out, it is important for African American women to have role models available who can offer them guidance and emotional support in identifying and responding to racism.

In addition, institutions must verbally and actively support the efforts of African American students to create safe emotional spaces. Without such spaces, African American students are not likely to make themselves vulnerable to the potential psychological threat they often experience in interethnic interactions and relationships. All such efforts can increase the opportunities for African American women in predominantly white environments to develop an integrated sociocultural self.

Note

1. These data were obtained from Berton's World Wide Web page and their college bulletin in 1996. Ethnicity of faculty was not available in either of these documents or in any of the other published materials to which I was given access.

References

Allen, W. R. (1992). The color of success: African American college student outcomes at predominantly white and historically Black public colleges and universities. *Harvard Educational Review, 62*(1), 26-44.

Angelou, M. (1993). *Wouldn't take nothing for my journey now.* New York: Random House.

Carroll, C. M. (1982). Three's a crowd: The dilemma of the Black woman in higher education. In G. T. Hull, P. B. Scott, & B. Smith (Eds.), *All the women are white, all the Blacks are men, but some of us are brave: Black women's studies* (pp. 115-128). New York: The Feminist Press.

Collins, P. H. (1991). *Black feminist thought: Knowledge, consciousness, and the politics of empowerment.* New York: Routledge Kegan Paul.

Crosby, F., Allen, B., Culbertson, T., Wally, C., Morith, J., Hall, R., & Nunes, B. (1994). Taking selectivity into account, how much does gender composition matter? A re-analysis of M. E. Tidball's research. *NWSA Journal, 6*(1), 107-118.

Fleming, J. (1984). *Blacks in college.* San Francisco: Jossey-Bass.

Greene, B. (1994). African American women. In L. Comas-Díaz & B. Greene (Eds.), *Women of color: Integrating ethnic and gender identities in psychotherapy* (pp. 10-29). New York: Guilford.

Hull, G. T., Scott, P. B., & Smith, B. (Eds.). (1982). *All the women are white, all the Blacks are men, but some of us are brave: Black women's studies.* New York: The Feminist Press.

Jackson, L. R. (1996). *Race and gender schema in the self-concept of African American college women.* Unpublished doctoral dissertation, Stanford University, Stanford, CA.

Jackson, L. R. (1998). Expanding the definition of diversity: The influence of both race and gender in the lives of African American college women. *Review of Higher Education, 21*(4), 359-375.

James, J., & Farmer, R. (Eds.). (1993). *Spirit, space and survival: African American women in (white) academe.* New York: Routledge Kegan Paul.

Landrine, H., Klonoff, E. A., & Brown-Collins, A. (1995). Cultural diversity and methodology in feminist psychology: Critique, proposal, empirical example. In H. Landrine (Ed.), *Bringing cultural diversity to feminist psychology: Theory, research, and practice* (pp. 55-75). Washington, DC: American Psychological Association.

Lawrence-Lightfoot, S. (1994). *I've known rivers: Loves of loss and liberation.* New York: Addison-Wesley.

Lorde, A. (1984). *Sister outsider.* Freedom, CA: Crossing.

Lykes, M. B. (1983). Discrimination and coping in the lives of Black women. *Journal of Social Issues, 39*(3), 79-100.

Markus, H. (1977). Self-schemata and processing information about the self. *Journal of Personality and Social Psychology, 35,* 63-78.

Miller-Bernal, L. (1993). Single-sex versus coeducational environments: A comparison of women students' experiences at four colleges. *American Journal of Education, 102,* 23-54.

Oyserman, D., Gant, L., & Ager, J. (1995). A socially contextualized model of African American identity: Possible selves and school persistence. *Journal of Personality and Social Psychology, 69*(6), 1216-1232.

Oyserman, D., & Markus, H. R. (1993). The sociocultural self. In J. Suls (Ed.), *Psychological perspectives on the self: The self in social perspective* (Vol. 4, pp. 1216-1232). Hillsdale, NJ: Lawrence Erlbaum.

Reid, P. T. (1984). Feminism versus minority group identity: Not for Black women only. *Sex Roles, 10*(3/4), 247-255.

Reid, P. T., & Comas-Díaz, L. (1990). Gender and ethnicity: Perspectives on dual status. *Sex Roles, 22*(7/8), 397-408.

Riordan, C. (1992). Single- and mixed-gender colleges for women: Educational, attitudinal, and occupational outcomes. *Review of Higher Education, 15*(3), 327-346.

Smith, A., & Stewart, A. (1983). Approaches to studying racism and sexism in Black women's lives. *Journal of Social Issues, 39*(3), 1-15.

Smith, D., Wolf, L., & Morrison, D. (1995). Paths to success: Factors related to the impact of women's colleges. *Journal of Higher Education, 66*(3), 245-266.

Thomas, V. G., & Miles, S. E. (1995). Psychology of Black women: Past, present, and future. In H. Landrine (Ed.), *Bringing cultural diversity to feminist psychology: Theory, research, and practice* (pp. 303-330). Washington DC: American Psychological Association.

Touchton, J. G., & Davis, L. (1991). *Fact book on women in higher education.* New York: Macmillan.

Whitt, E. J. (1994). "I can be anything!" Student leadership in three women's colleges. *Journal of College Student Development, 35,* 198-207.

Willie, C., & Levy, J. (1972). Black is lonely. *Psychology Today, 5*(10), 50-80.

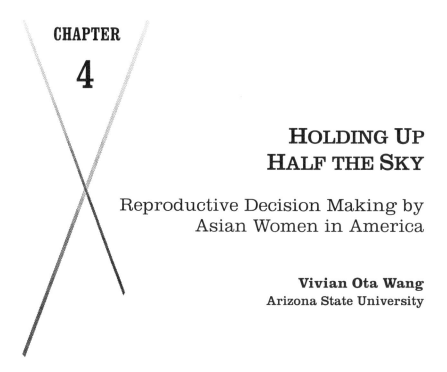

CHAPTER

4

HOLDING UP
HALF THE SKY

Reproductive Decision Making by
Asian Women in America

Vivian Ota Wang
Arizona State University

As the fastest growing racial-ethnic population in the United States, Asian and
Pacific Islanders' historical, cultural, and language heterogeneity serves as a
distinctive and important group characteristic. In the United States, Asian and
Pacific Islanders represent a multifaceted group of people with ancestral and
cultural ties to Asia and the Pacific Islands (Leong, 1986; Sue & Sue, 1990;
Takaki, 1989). These ties include all countries east of Pakistan as well as the nations of South Asia, Southeast Asia, East Asia, Melanesia, and Polynesia
(Barringer, 1993). As a group, they numbered 8.8 million in 1994, up from 7.3
million in 1990 and accounting for approximately 3% of the U.S. total population. The population of this group has been projected to increase to more than
12 million people by the year 2001. It should be noted that in the 1990 U.S. Census, 76% of Asians and Pacific Islanders were from one of five ethnicities: Chinese, Filipino, Japanese, Asian Indian, and Korean. Other ethnic groups (Vietnamese, Cambodian, Laotian, Thai, and Hmong) accounted for an additional
19%, with Pacific Islanders (Hawaiian, Samoan, Guamanian, Tongan, Fijian,

Paluan, Northern Mariana Islander, Tahitian) comprising the remaining 5% (National Heart, Lung, and Blood Institute, 1998).

Nevertheless, a critical evaluation of the underlying values for Asian women regarding reproductive decision making is essential in order to understand who these racialized and gendered women are, because for them, reproductive decision making and womanhood often have been intimately linked. Ultimately involving choices beyond contraception options, concerns about fertility, effects of contraception on future fertility, reproductive technologies, adoption, pregnancy terminations, child care, how many and what gender of children people desire, and when to bear children become especially relevant because each choice affects lifelong decisions. For example, one of the first reproductive decisions made has been whether to have children. Although women in general have been socialized to expect to bear children and to become mothers, women who choose not to become mothers and those who experience fertility problems often have been viewed as deviating from socially sanctioned norms (Phoenix, Woollett, & Lloyd, 1991; Veevers, 1980).

Reproductive decisions often have been explained using economic models of costs and benefits of bearing children. Such models have assumed that attitudes operate in rational ways to influence decisions about family size or the use of contraceptive method. For instance, people who want fewer children or want to delay starting their family have been assumed to use contraceptives or use them more effectively than those who want larger families or do not want to delay having children (Porter, 1990). Unfortunately, women making reproductive decisions within their own racial-cultural context of attitudes and ideas *and* a broader White U.S. racial-cultural milieu often find themselves needing to reconcile different and even conflicting messages about what is appropriate and for whom. Thus, explanations of reproductive decision making need to reach beyond discussions of economic costs and benefits to examine the context of interpersonal relationships and racial-cultural expectations and prescriptions around childbearing, child rearing, and womanhood. It is important that both theoretically and practically, the diversity and variability in Asian women's attitudes, identities, and experiences be recognized and validated. Sources of within-group variability need to be identified and understood if reproductive decision making is to be made relevant to the lives of all Asian women. In this regard, racial and womanist identity models may be useful when examining this within-group variability.

Women from Asian groups are by no means homogeneous. Instead of reducing these women to a list of culture-specific differences and similarities describing *what* they are, in this chapter, I will attempt to understand *who* they are as racial and gendered people by describing the filial piety that joins many of their experiences in issues related to reproductive decision making.

FIVE, FOUR, THREE: CONFUCIANISM AND THE SOCIAL CODES OF ROLES AND EXPECTATIONS OF ASIAN WOMEN

The social roles in many Asian cultures have been traced to the prescriptions of the Chinese scholar Confucius (551-479 B.C.). By furnishing an ethical rationale, Confucius developed a framework for exercising power through social codes of conduct that have endured to the present day. Confucius's thinking on morality and, by extension, true and pure knowledge assumed a fundamental and indisputable distinction between right and wrong. He contended that power and subordination to authority were to be inculcated in family systems through a series of behavioral codes that prescribed socially appropriate expectations and relationships (Hu, 1960, pp. 157-170). *Wu lun,* or the "five relationships," is the Confucian social code that has defined and advocated "proper" behavior between ruler and subject, father and son, elder and younger brother, husband and wife, and friend and friend (Latourette, 1957). Based on these five relationships, Confucius derived "four virtues" (*si de*) and "three obediences" (*san cong*) for the expectations and behavior of women.

He prescribed the *si de,* or "four virtues," as (a) "women's virtue" (*fu de*), which dictated how women should behave in agreement with "feudal ethics"; (b) "women's speech" (*fu yan*), which required women to talk less and speak properly at the correct place and right time; (c) "women's appearance" (*fu rong*), which instructed women to be graceful and pleasant; and (d) "women's tasks" (*fu gong*), which demanded women perform domestic chores dutifully and willingly. His "three obediences" referred to the requirements of women at different developmental stages of their lives. A woman was first to obey her father before marriage; second, obey her husband after marriage; and third, obey her son when widowed (Hu, 1988). These Confucian behavioral codes not only have created the expectation that women will "walk behind men" but also have reinforced clearly defined gender roles in strict patriarchal family structures. In this sense, Confucian filial piety has provided culturally defined patriarchal power and authority, leaving the status of women institutionally underclassed.

In view of the fact that filial piety may be generalized to authority relationships beyond the family, it has become a potent determinant of not only intergenerational but also superior-subordinate relationships. For example, filial piety has justified absolute authority of adults over children, veneration for the aged, and, by extension, the authority of those senior in generation and gender (men) over those junior in rank. Ho (1996) has argued that although some of its component ideas (e.g., obedience) are shared by other cultures, filial piety has surpassed all other social and ethical codes in its historical continuity, the proportion of humanity under its governance (more than 40% of the world population), and the all-encompassing nature of its precepts.

For centuries, filial piety has served as a guiding principle governing patterns of socialization. Using specific codes of conduct throughout the length of a person's life span, continuity was maintained by authoritarian moralism through the following five social codes: (a) obeying and honoring one's parents, (b) providing for the material and mental well-being of one's aged parents, (c) performing the ceremonial duties of ancestral worship, (d) avoiding harm to one's body and conducting oneself to bring honor and not disgrace to the family name, and (e) ensuring the continuity of the family line by bearing sons (Ho, 1987, 1996). Thus, not so surprisingly, when examining themes related to continuities and discontinuities, authoritarian moralism and collectivism have been traced to the Confucian ethic of filial piety. Ho (1989a) has suggested that

> authoritarian moralism (vs. democratic-psychological orientation) and collectivism (vs. individualism) capture succinctly the distinctive character of Chinese socialization patterns. The former entails impulse control (vs. Expression); the latter entails interdependence (vs. Autonomy) and conformism (vs. unique individuation). Authoritarian moralism and collectivism underlie both the traditional and the contemporary ideologies governing socialization, and thus, preserve its continuity. (p. 144)

Authoritarian moralism has embodied two salient features of Confucian-based cultures: (a) a hierarchical ranking of authority in the family and in educational and sociopolitical institutions and (b) a pervasive application of moral precepts as a primary standard against which people are judged. Consequently, the absolute authority placed on parents has been both a cause and consequence of this authoritarianism. In this regard, moralism, with its overriding emphasis on the development of a moral character through education, has predisposed parents to be moralistic rather than psychologically oriented. Thus, parents have been expected to treat their children of all ages in terms of whether their conduct meets some external moral criteria (e.g., childbearing) rather than in terms of sensitivity to their internal needs, feelings, and aspirations. Children have been expected to be transformed into adults who exercise impulse control, behave properly, and fulfill, above all, their filial obligations (Ho, 1987).

Wu (1996) has advocated that despite geographical separation and ideological differences, a socialization of shared basic values and practices among many Asian cultural groups exists (e.g., the expectation of children to obey and respect their elders). Wu and Xue (1995) have shown that despite sharing some general values on child rearing from their European counterparts, Chinese parents' approaches to socialization have remained quite different. They showed no significant differences regarding acculturation of child-rearing attitudes among Chinese Americans regardless of years away from their country of origin. In addition, among their study's participants, parents reported valuing success for one's family and adhering to parental strictness and discipline, thus supporting parents' rights and positions of authority. They have concluded that the socialization and development of a "Chinese" identity among descendants of Chinese emigrants and overseas Chinese have been retained through some of the basic elements of Confucian filial piety. Thus, they have suggested that their work strengthens a common belief of other scholars (Bond, 1988; Hsu, 1981; Wu & Tseng, 1985) that Confucian traditions have enjoyed an enduring historical and cultural continuity (Wu & Xue, 1995).

GENDER IDENTITY: ROLES AND EXPECTATIONS OF ASIAN WOMEN

According to the traditional patriarchal structure of filial piety, inequity between sons and daughters begins at birth. As described in one of the early works of Chinese poetry, *The Book of Poetry* (as quoted by Croll, 1978, p. 23),

When a son is born
Let him sleep on the bed,
Clothe him with fine clothes,
And give him jade to play with.
How lordly his cry is!
May he grow up to wear crimson
And be the lord of the clan and the tribe.

When a daughter is born,
Let her sleep on the ground,

Wrap her in common wrappings,
And give her broken tiles for playthings.
May she have no faults, no merits of her own
May she well attend to food and wine,
And bring no discredit to her parents.

This favoritism of sons over daughters has been a manifestation of filial piety where expectations exist for the son to sustain and add to the legacy of his family's name, perform ceremonial tasks, and support his parents in their old age. In turn, the son has the right to inherit the father's property and prestige. Conversely, a daughter has been expected to eventually leave her family home and join her husband and his family after marriage. As a wife, her responsibility is bearing sons. Being a member of her husband's household also may preclude her from participating in ceremonial rituals for her own parents or having a claim to their family traditions and inheritances.

In education, gendered differential role strain also has existed in Confucian-influenced cultures. Historically, in China, since the sixth century, only men, rich or poor, were allowed to take the imperial examinations based on Confucian teachings (Hsu, 1955). In 1905, when the imperial examinations were abolished (before the decline of the Manchu dynasty and the establishment of the People's Republic), traditional respect for a man's scholarship continued to be evinced, with a college degree replacing the imperial one. For women, education was seen as endangering the "feminine" virtues set forth by Confucius; a woman's status in life was to be a devoted helper and bearer of many male grandchildren for her future mother-in-law.

Only within the past century, with the influence of Western religious missionaries, has there been educational emancipation of women in China, with a number of Christian schools and colleges having been established. It was not until 1910 that these schools began to provide women with the same educational opportunities as men (Bond, 1996). Although their educational ambitions have been enlarged, these women have not been immune from the centuries of Confucian legacies that have shaped the cultural worldviews of women's expected roles and behaviors.

For example, in the late 1960s, Fong and Peskin (1969) described how in the first legal waves of mass Asian immigration since 1924, people migrating from one cultural environment to another continued to maintain culturally ingrained emotional meanings of essential social roles. With two cultures as different as Asian and White American, they hypothesized that new meanings for social roles would conflict with previously held roles, creating difficulties for individual coping, adjustment, and personal identity development. Moreover, they suggested that such incongruities were more pronounced for one gender than the other and thus posed more unique issues around racial and gender identity for Asian women. In their study, Fong and Peskin hypothesized that Asian women college students would have greater conflict with and rebellion against role expectations than their Asian male counterparts in the United States. Using the Femininity Scale of the California Personality Inventory (CPI), Fong and Peskin showed that both men and women observed more Confucian values of modesty, patience, and reserve. They also showed that unlike their male counterparts, Asian women were caught in an inescapable dilemma of satisfying their anti-Confucian educational ambitions in the American educational system while being faced with the antifeminist values of Confucian-based parental expectations. Thus, filial piety followed Asian women to the United States.

GENDER IDENTITY: ASIAN WOMEN'S LIFE CYCLES

In many respects, expectations throughout family life cycles have taken different courses for Asian woman and men. For a man, these expectations have developed into an undisputed form in his family position and role as the "guarantor" of the family's continued existence by linking the succession of generations of ancestors and descendants. For a woman, the meaning of the succession of generations in the family into which she was born has been irrelevant. Until she herself becomes a mother-in-law, an event that can only occur when her son marries a woman (based on Confucian social codes), his wife holds the lowest rank in her in-law's household, with neither a room nor a place to call her own. Thus, for many Asian women, their gender identity has developed through their multiple roles of a daughter-in-law, a mother bearing the heir needed by her husband's family, and a mother-in-law (Sich, 1988). Within this context of the significance traditionally accorded children in Confucian-based cultures, many Asian woman have experienced familial and social pressures to bear children, particularly healthy sons. This can be seen today in family planning and women's health programs in which many Asian women continue to invest in modern and traditional measures designed to promote the birth of a son.

With the pressure of successfully birthing a son and the importance of succession for Asian women, Morgan, Rindfuss, and Parnell (1984) studied Asian couples in conjugal relationships. In their sample of Japanese men and women, most participants were found to place less importance on the romantic love aspects of their relationships and emphasized the significance of having children to preserve the linkage between past and future generations. To some degree, this also may have explained the reasons why childlessness may be a less attractive option for many of these couples.

Kumagai (1995) expanded on Morgan et al.'s (1984) study, showing conjugal relationships between Japanese couples as institutionally driven rather than for love and companionship. Kumagai found that due to the psychological and physical absences of fathers in households, many mothers compensated for their limited marital relationships by intensifying their relationships with their children, especially their sons, thus providing another example of a vertical generational patriarchal system. In some cases, some mother-child relationships have been so intense that mothers have regarded their children as their own personal property. In this sense, Doi (1962) has described this attachment as *amae,* wherein a person asks and receives another person's benevolence and indulgent support. In return, the recipient is obligated to be dutiful and to repay the family. Thus, reciprocity and interdependency have been perpetuated.

Yi (1988) has discussed the reciprocal obligations of children and their parents to one another as being dictated by Confucian analects. In this case, reciprocity has created a cultural mechanism of interdependence between children and their parents, thus ensuring parental care both economically and emotionally as they age. In this respect, filial piety has broader implications in those societies where the elderly depend on their children for support. As in the case of the People's Republic of China, if infant and child mortality rates continue to increase, a substantial proportion of women who have had one child (who may or may not be male) may find themselves alone without support in their old age. At least for now, filiation has endured, with a great majority of the elderly living with one of their married children, typically the older son.

Asian Woman Identity: Reproductive Decision Making

For many Asian women, the cultural meaning of womanhood and gender identity has been intimately linked and must be examined within the cultural lens of

Confucian social codes of conduct. Many Western psychologists, consistent with their individualistic worldview, have generally studied reproductive decision making as a matter of individual choice, thus focusing on individual decision-making processes (Adler, 1979). On the other hand, other socially oriented scholars have been more interested in how social and environmental factors influence fertility decisions, fertility outcomes, and definitions of womanhood. In this regard, a couple's reproductive decision making has not been new in fertility research. Since the increasing usage of birth control measures worldwide and the improving effectiveness of fertility regulations, fertility discussions and reported preferences have become increasingly consistent with actual fertility outcomes.

Despite concerns about the increasing numbers of children born to Asian women, especially in developing countries, there have been only limited attempts to explore reproductive decision making by women, especially from indigenous and immigrant Asian ethnic communities. For example, although most Asian women have been socially expected to bear children and become mothers, those who choose not to become mothers or experience fertility problems have been considered deviant, abnormal, and stigmatized (Phoenix et al., 1991; Veevers, 1980; Wang & Marsh, 1992).

Women from different Asian ethnic communities have made reproductive decisions within the context of attitudes and ideas in their own culture and the wider culture in which they live. Thus, reproductive decisions have gone beyond choices about contraceptive methods and have reached into the concept of womanhood. For many of these women, their decisions have required them to reconcile different and conflicting ideas and questions about wanting or not wanting versus expecting to have children, family size, the method of contraception, spacing of children, gender of the children, infertility, the use of assisted reproductive technologies, miscarriages, and pregnancy terminations.

Although ideas and attitudes may have changed more rapidly in some Asian communities than others, the Confucian influence of filial piety and gender preference for sons has continued to transcend reproductive decision making for many Asian women and their families. For example, Woollett, Dosanjh-Matwala, and Hadlow (1991) showed that Asian women who used contraception to limit family size reportedly preferred families of two or three children with a mix of gender. In many respects, their findings were similar to those for non-Asian women in their study. However, the gender of the children was reported as having a greater salience for Asian women who reported less positive feelings about having a preponderance of girls in their family.

In another study, Nemeth and Bowling (1985) examined the preferential lactation practices of mothers of infants in Korea and reported that a significant percentage of increased early fertility may be deliberate and related to the desire for sons. In their study, decreases in birth intervals were found among women whose first two children were girls. Consistent with male preferences, women who had sons were found more likely to differentially breast-feed their sons over daughters. Nemeth and Bowling suggested that women without sons were not breast-feeding in order to shorten the lactation periods and accelerate the potential of conceiving another child, preferably a son. When asked, these mothers most often reported their desire for sons as future security and support later in life.

Although Asian women's socioeconomic level and occupational status have improved over time, the patriarchal tradition of Confucianism has continued to be deeply rooted in present social structures (Johnson, Nathan, & Rawski, 1985; Kaufman, 1983; Li, 1993; Poston & Gu, 1987; Wang, 1988). For example, one salient feature for some Asian women has been their lower status in the family and kinship system, regardless of their or their family's occupation or educational level. Influenced by the Confucian three bonds of obedience of obeying fathers when young, husbands when married, and adult sons when widowed, these women live in a cultural-family environment that has not allowed for their individual racialized and gendered identities to develop. Thus, in many families, women have been marginal members lacking the power in decision making on the matters of the family and reproductive decisions. For example, a husband may have consulted with his parents about how many children he and his wife should have rather than first discussing this with his wife.

Espenshade and Ye (1994) have argued that the structural component of minority group status and lower fertility rates in the United States has been dependent on the additional efforts made by minority group members to overcome discrimination and achieve equality. Using a sample of 4,508 Chinese American women, they found that the extra effort Asian women made in combating structural discrimination had been negatively related to their fertility. Showing that institutionalized discrimination against Chinese American women was widespread, these women have been frequently unable to convert educational attainment into occupational status at the same rate as White women. Consequently, they have been found to try harder or make more sacrifices in their pursuit of social and economic equality. However, those who have been successful have paid a personal price in terms of lower fertility and a reduction of time and energy available for childbearing and rearing.

PSYCHOLOGICAL APPROACHES TO RACIAL AND GENDER IDENTITY DEVELOPMENT

Because race and gender have been more than visible group demographic variables, racial and womanist identity scholars have proposed understanding race and gender on a more individual psychological basis of personality development. On the basis of internal levels of identification with one's race and gender through ego differentiation, within-group differences have been proposed in racial and gender identity development models as a means to understand the psychological perspectives people hold about themselves and others as racial-cultural-gendered beings. For example, according to Black racial identity theory (and, more broadly, people of color identity theory), Black people's racial identity develops from (a) overvaluing and idealizing White cultural norms (preencounter), (b) feeling confusion as they try to understand their previously held beliefs of White superiority and Black inferiority (encounter), (c) affirming "Blackness" and denigrating "Whiteness" by becoming involved in an idealized African cultural heritage and withdrawing from society (immersion-emersion), and (d) integrating a positive Black identity while maintaining a balanced perspective of "Whiteness" (internalization). In White racial identity theory, White people's racial identity develops from (a) being unaware of their own racial group membership and ignoring the race of others, and, when differences are acknowledged, culture is seen in those unlike themselves (contact); (b) feeling guilty over their own internal standards and societal norms about race and overidentifying with Blacks (disintegration); (c) rejecting Blacks and overidealizing Whiteness (reintegration); (d) intellectualizing racial issues (pseudo-independence); and (e) internalizing a positive White identity by both an emotional and intellectual appreciation for and respect of racial differences and similarities (autonomy) (Helms, 1995).

The development of a womanist identity model has been an extrapolation of the racial and racial-cultural identity developmental literature (Atkinson, Morten, & Sue, 1979; Cross, 1971; Downing & Roush, 1985; Helms, 1984) and has proposed that "women's abandonment of external definitions and adaptation of internal standards of womanhood occur through a stage-wise developmental process" (Ossana, Helms, & Leonard, 1992, p. 403). In Helms's (1984)

womanist identity model, the first womanist level (preencounter) has been typi-
fied by acceptance of traditional gender roles and denial of socialization
and gendered cultural bias. The second womanist level (encounter) has involved questioning and confusion about gender roles for oneself and in society.
Immersion-emersion, the third womanist level, has been characterized by
rejection of traditional gender roles through idealizing women and rejecting
men. In the final level, the woman has developed an internally defined
womanist identity without undue dependence on either traditional or feminist
viewpoints.

Helms's (1984) womanist identity model has fundamentally differed from
more traditional feminist identity development models (e.g., Downing &
Roush's [1985] feminist model of identity) on several important points. On one
hand, the feminist identity models have placed greater emphasis on changing
women's perceptions of the role of women compared to that of men, and they
have assumed that a healthy identity includes a political feminist orientation.
On the other hand, Helms has suggested that her womanist identity model sub-
sumes the feminist identity model by proposing a womanist's identity development as being personal and ideologically flexible; it may or may not incorporate political feminism and social activism. Thus, a greater emphasis has been
placed on how a woman "comes to value herself as a woman regardless of her
chosen role" (Ossana et al., 1992, p. 403).

In a study conducted by Ossana et al. (1992), internalization womanist attitudes (e.g., internally denied and integrated female identity without undue reliance on either traditional roles or feminist viewpoint) were positively related to
self-esteem as compared to encounter womanist attitudes (e.g., questioning and
confusion about gender roles). Immersion-emersion womanist attitudes (e.g.,
externally based feminist stance, hostility toward men, idealization of women)
were negatively related to levels of self-esteem. (It should also be noted that
Pyant & Yanico [1991] and Carter & Parks [1996] have shown that for Black
women, their level of racial identity and not gender role attitudes has not been
predictive of mental health.)

Although gaps currently exist in the literature on Asian womanist identity
development, Chow (1987) was able to show, using Bem's (1974) theoretical
formulation of androgyny, that Asian women who were masculine and androgynous achieved higher levels of occupational attainment, a greater degree of
work satisfaction, and higher levels of self-esteem than those with feminine and
undifferentiated sex role identity. Similarly, Ossana et al. (1992) found that androgynous Asian American women had higher levels of self-esteem and greater
work satisfaction than those with other types of sex role identity.

Also interested in the intersection of racial and gender identity, Woollett, Marshall, Nicolson, and Dosanjh (1994) have shown the fluidity of gender and ethnic identity development of women of Asian origin and the ways in which their racial-gender identity has been informed by specific contexts or circumstances in their lives. For example, as cited by Woollett et al., Asian women in their study were dichotomized as being "Asian" and "Western."

> In some ways, I'm more traditional [Asian] and some things I'm more broad-minded [Western]. . . . (*More traditional?*) In family, wise might be. Respect for patients, respect for elders, and things like that. I believe in our religion. I try and practice it but not really 100 per cent. I had an arranged marriage. (*Westernized?*) I'm not shy and I don't mind talking with boys and communicating with anyone. I wouldn't mind going out. So it depends on the circumstances. . . .
>
> I think by Indian standards I'm westernized but I think I'm an in-between. I can adjust well to both cultures. I can speak the language pretty well so I can communicate with the elderly. Because I like Indian "dos" I can mix there as well. The things with the western culture is that I like discos and all that. When I say I'm more westernized according to the Indian culture it's the way I think, in that I don't believe in staying where you are. I think you should [go] forward in life in everything you do. (p. 129)

Their study demonstrated some of the varied and complex ways gender has influenced Asian women's constructions of their racial-ethnic womanist identity and highlighted a number of ways in which gender had differing significance for women in informing their racial-gendered identity.

FUTURE AREAS OF MULTICULTURAL RESEARCH AND COUNSELING

For centuries, filial piety has played a major role in governing some Asian cultural expectations and behaviors throughout a person's life span. What has been remiss is how little interest exists in studying filial piety from a psychological perspective. Although scholars have developed counseling models using acculturation and racial and ethnic identity for working with Asians or individuals with multiple identities (Carter, 1995; Herring, 1995; Kitano, 1989; Poston, 1990; Reynolds & Pope, 1991; Root, 1985, 1990; Winn & Priest, 1993), what has continued to be unclear is how filial piety influences Asian women's identity development, especially around issues of reproduction, disenfranchisement, and empowerment. In this regard, a more systematic examination of inter- and intragroup variation of the psychological dimensions of filial piety is needed to better inform clinicians and researchers alike of *who* Asian women are.

To date, only a very few researchers have examined filial piety through instrument development (Yeh & Yang, 1989), educational level, gender (Ho, Hong, & Chiu, 1993), socioeconomic status, and filial behavior (Ho, 1994; Ho, 1989a, 1989b). Although scholars have recognized the social influences of filial piety as a basic ethic governing intergenerational and, by extension, interpersonal relationships in some Asian societies, how expectations of filial piety have influenced Asian women's gender identity in the United States has not been well described or examined in the literature and is worthy of investigation.

In cases of reproductive decision making and infertility of Asian women, large gaps currently exist in the medical and psychologically oriented research and clinical literatures. Given the growing clinical and medical advances in the field of assisted reproductive technologies, it will become more important to determine if these voids in the literature and service provision have been due to social-political barriers (e.g., unavailability of egg and sperm donors), personal reasons, or cultural factors (e.g., Confucianism).

In addition, it is imperative for scholars and clinicians to recognize within-group variability and the complexity of beliefs, attitudes, and experiences of Asian women and *not* create one-dimensional profiles of how to work with Asian women. Asian American women's ideas, experiences, and the meanings that events may have for them cannot be assumed merely based on knowing their race and gender. Informed by life changes related to relationships and reproductive decisions about choosing to have children, racial and womanist identity developments are fluid and change over time. Because these changes are not due merely to increasing familiarity with the White American culture or how long women have been living in the United States, racial and womanist identity developmental models raise difficulties for acculturation and other paradigms that employ simplistic forms of racial and gender categorizations, assessments, and treatment plans.

Ultimately, mental health and other medical professionals will have to venture beyond simplistic notions and stereotypes of Asian women and their families (e.g., Asian women have familial support, are collectivistic) toward more sensitive and appropriate assessments and interventions based on the multitude of racial and womanist identity status combinations. By becoming curious about *who* an Asian woman is rather than *what* one imagines her to be, clinicians and scholars alike can begin contextualizing and integrating aspects of race and gender from the vantage point of what an Asian woman's version is of what it means to be herself as an Asian woman making reproductive decisions. For example, what if, by examining the ways in which Asian women experience reproductive decision making, issues and processes may in fact be similar (or not) to other women from other racial-cultural groups? Then, questions about the ways in which attitudes and experiences vary within and between communities should be asked and explored. Extending studies to include other racial-cultural women and men will clearly bring into focus the need to (a) examine the social-cultural-political context in which reproductive decision making occurs and (b) consider the provision of appropriate services for all women. This is even more important because all too frequently, Asian women have been considered problematic, holding beliefs and practices that are incongruent with current medical and psychological models. Instead of finding ways in which their beliefs, attitudes, and behaviors can be modified to make them better consumers, greater knowledge and awareness of the varied racialized and gendered experiences of Asian women should ensure more culturally responsive services, thus ensuring overall better health for everyone.

Thus, investigating and understanding what it means to be an Asian woman in the United States and the psychological benefits and consequences from a contemporary and developmental perspective are imperative if clinicians and scholars are to be more sensitively attuned to the phenotypic and psychological variability of race and gender for Asian women. If the Chinese saying that "women hold up half the sky" is true, research can help describe who these women are, what they are holding up, and the rewards and consequences for the choices they have made or have been made for them.

References

Adler, N. A. (1979). Decision models in population research. *Journal of population 2*(3), 187-202.
Atkinson, D. R., Morten, G., & Sue, D. W. (1979). A minority identity development model. In D. R. Atkinson, G. Morten, & D. W. Sue (Eds.), *Counseling American minorities: A cross-cultural perspective* (pp. 35-47). Dubuque, IA: William C. Brown.
Barringer, H. (1993). *Asians and Pacific Islanders in the United States*. New York: Russell Sage.
Bem, S. L. (1974). The measurement of psychological androgyny. *Journal of Consulting and Clinical Psychology, 42*, 155-162.
Bond, M. H. (1988). Finding universal dimensions of individual variation in multicultural studies of values: The Rokeach and Chinese value surveys. *Journal of Personality and Social Psychology, 55*, 1009-1015.

Bond, M. H. (1996). *The handbook of Chinese psychology.* Hong Kong: Oxford University Press.

Carter, R. T. (1995). *The influence of race and racial identity in psychotherapy: Toward a racially inclusive model.* New York: John Wiley.

Carter, R. T., & Parks, E. E. (1996). Womanist identity and mental health. *Journal of Counseling & Development, 74,* 484-489.

Chow, E. N. -L. (1987). The influence of sex-role identity and occupational attainment on the psychological well being of Asian American women. *Psychology of Woman Quarterly, 11,* 69-82.

Croll, E. (1978). *Feminism and socialism in China.* London: Routledge.

Cross, W. E. (1971). Negro-to-Black conversion experience: Toward a new psychology of Black liberation. *Black World, 20*(9), 13-27.

Doi, L. T. (1962). Amae—A key concept for understanding Japanese personality structure. *Psychologia, 5,* 1-7.

Downing, N. E., & Roush, K. L. (1985). From passive acceptance to active commitment: A model of feminist identity development for women. *The Counseling Psychologist, 12,* 153-165.

Espenshade, T. J., & Ye, W. (1994). Differential fertility within an ethnic minority: The effect of "trying harder" among Chinese-American women. *Social Problems, 41*(1), 97-113.

Fong, S. L. M., & Peskin, H. (1969). Sex-role strain and personality adjustment of China-born students in America: A pilot study. *Journal of Abnormal Psychology, 74*(5), 563-567.

Helms, J. E. (1984). Toward a theoretical explanation of the effects of race on counseling: A Black and White model. *The Counseling Psychologist, 12,* 153-165.

Helms, J. E. (1995). An update of Helm's White and people of color racial identity models. In J. G. Ponterotto, J. M. Casas, L. A. Suzuki, & C. M. Alexander (Eds.), *Handbook of multicultural counseling* (pp. 181-198). Thousand Oaks, CA: Sage.

Herring, R. G. (1995). Developing biracial ethnic identity: A review of the increasing dilemma. *Journal of Multicultural Counseling and Development, 23,* 29-38.

Ho, D. Y. F. (1987). *Family therapies with minorities.* Newbury Park, CA: Sage.

Ho, D. Y. F. (1989a). Socialization in contemporary mainland China. *Asian Thought and Society, 14,* 136-149.

Ho, D. Y. F. (1989b). Continuity and variation in Chinese patters of socialization. *Journal of Marriage and the Family, 51,* 149-163.

Ho, D. Y. F. (1994). Filial piety, authoritarian moralism, and cognitive conservatism in Chinese societies. *Genetic, Social, and General Psychology Monographs, 120,* 347-365.

Ho, D. Y. F. (1996). Filial piety and its psychological consequences. In M. H. Bond (Ed.), *The handbook of Chinese psychology* (pp. 143-154). Hong Kong: Oxford University Press.

Ho, D. Y. F., Hong, Y. Y., & Chiu, C. Y. (1993, May). *Filial piety and family-matrimonial traditionalism in Chinese societies.* Paper presented at the International Conference on Moral Values and Moral Reasoning in Chinese Societies, Academia Sinica Conference Center, Taipei.

Hsu, F. L. K. (1955). *Americans and Chinese.* London: Cresset.

Hsu, F. L. K. (1981). *Americans and Chinese: Passage to differences* (3rd ed.). Honolulu: University of Hawaii Press.

Hu, S. M. (1960). *China.* New Haven, CT: HRAG Press.

Hu, S. M. (1988). The Chinese family: Continuity and change. In B. Birns & D. F. Hay (Eds.), *The different faces of motherhood* (pp. 119-135). New York: Plenum.

Johnson, D., Nathan, A. J., & Rawski, E. S. (1985). *Popular culture in late Imperial China.* Berkeley: University of California Press.

Kaufman, J. (1983). *A billion and counting: Family planning campaigns and policies in the People's Republic of China.* San Francisco: San Francisco Press.

Kitano, H. H. L. (1989). A model for counseling Asian Americans. In P. B. Pedersen, J. G. Draguns, W. L. Lonner, & J. E. Trimble (Eds.), *Counseling across cultures* (3rd ed., pp. 139-152). Honolulu: University of Hawaii Press.

Kumagai, F. (1995). Families in Japan: Beliefs and realities. *Journal of Comparative Family Studies, 26*(1), 135-163.

Latourette, K. S. (1957). *A short history of the Far East.* New York: Macmillan.

Leong, F. T. L. (1986). Counseling and psychotherapy with Asian-Americans: Review of the literature. *Journal of Counseling Psychology, 33*(2), 196-206.

Li, L. (1993). Chinese women's participation in fertility discussions. *International Journal of Sociology of the Family, 23,* 33-42.

Morgan, S. P., Rindfuss, R. R., & Parnell, A. (1984). Modern fertility patterns: Contrasts between the United States and Japan. *Population and Development Review, 10*(1), 19-40.

National Heart, Lung, and Blood Institute. (1998). *Caring families for heart health: Promoting healthy hearts for Asian American and Pacific Islanders: A background report.* Washington, DC: National Institutes of Health, Office of Prevention, Education, and Control, National Heart, Lung, and Blood Institute.

Nemeth, R. J., & Bowling, J. M. (1985). Son preference and its effects on Korean lactation practices. *Journal of Biosocial Science, 17,* 451-459.

Ossana, S. M., Helms, J. E., & Leonard, M. M. (1992). Do "womanist" identity attitudes influence college women's self-esteem, and perceptions of environmental bias? *Journal of Counseling & Development, 70,* 402-408.

Phoenix, A., Woollett, A., & Lloyd, E. (Eds.). (1991). *Motherhood: Meanings, practices, and ideologies.* London: Sage.

Porter, M. (1990, September). *Free to choose? A study of contraceptive risk taking.* Paper presented at the 10th Anniversary Conference, Society for Reproductive and Infant Psychology, University of Cambridge, Cambridge, UK.

Poston, D. L., & Gu, B. (1987). Socioeconomic development, family planning, and fertility in China. *Demography, 24*(4), 531-551.

Poston, C. W. S. (1990). The biracial identity development model: A needed addition. *Journal of Counseling and Development, 69,* 153-155.

Pyant, C. T., & Yanico, B. J. (1991). Relationship of racial identity and gender-role attitudes to Black women's psychological being. *Journal of Counseling Psychology, 38,* 315-322.

Reynolds, A. L., & Pope R. L. (1991). The complexities of diversity: Exploring multiple oppressions. *Journal of Counseling & Development, 70,* 174-180.

Root, M. P. P. (1985). Guidelines for facilitating therapy with Asian American clients. *Psychotherapy, 22,* 349-356.

Root, M. P. P. (1990). Resolving "other" status: Identity development of biracial individuals. In L. S. Brown & M. P. Root (Eds.), *Diversity and complexity in feminist therapy* (pp. 185-206). Binghamton, NY: Harrington Park.

Sich, D. (1988). Childbearing in Korea. *Social Sciences in Medicine, 27*(5), 497-504.

Sue, D. W., & Sue, D. (1990). *Counseling the culturally different: Theory and practice* (2nd ed.). New York: John Wiley.

Takaki, R. (1989). *Strangers from a different shore: A history of Asian Americans.* New York: Penguin.

Veevers, J. E. (1980). *Childless by choice.* Toronto: Butterworths.

Wang, F. (1988). The role of individual's socioeconomic characteristics and the government family planning program in China's fertility decline. *Population Research and Policy Review, 7,* 255-276.

Wang, V., & Marsh, F. H. (1992). Ethical principles and cultural integrity in health care delivery: Asian ethnocultural perspectives in genetic services. *Journal of Genetic Counseling, 1*(1), 81-92.

Winn, N. N., & Priest, R. (1993). Counseling biracial children: A forgotten component of multicultural counseling. *Family Therapy, 20*(1), 28-36.

Woollett, A., Dosanjh-Matwala, N., & Hadlow, J. (1991). Reproductive decision making: Asian women's ideas about family size, and the gender and spacing of children. *Journal of Reproductive and Infant Psychology, 9,* 237-252.

Woollett, A., Marshall, H., Nicolson, P., & Dosanjh, N. (1994). Asian women's ethnic identity: The impact of gender and context in the accounts of women bringing up children in East London. *Feminism & Psychology, 4,* 119-132.

Wu, D. Y. H. (1996). Chinese childhood socialization. In M. H. Bond (Ed.), *The handbook of Chinese psychology* (pp. 143-154). Hong Kong: Oxford University Press.

Wu, D. Y. H., & Tseng, W. S. (1985). Introduction: The characteristics of Chinese culture. In W. S. Tseng & D. Y. H. Wu (Eds.), *Chinese culture and mental health* (pp. 3-13). New York: Academic Press.

Wu, D. Y. H., & Xue, S. A. (Eds.). (1995). *Socialization of Chinese children.* Shanghai: Shanghai Educational Literature Press. (in Chinese)

Yeh, K. H., & Yang, K. S. (1989). Cognitive structure and development of filial piety: Concepts and measurement. *Bulletin of the Institute of Ethnology, 56,* 131-169. (in Chinese)

Yi, Z. (1988). Changing demographic characteristics and the family status of Chinese women. *Population Studies, 42,* 183-203.

CHAPTER

5

POSTTRAUMATIC STRESS DISORDER and the MINORITY EXPERIENCE

Farah A. Ibrahim
Howard University

Hifumi Ohnishi
Michigan State University

This chapter expands on an emerging hypothesis that when racial and cultural minorities enter counseling for psychological difficulties, they may be misdiagnosed if the traditional approach to diagnosis is taken (i.e., the difficulties are endogenous to the individual). We propose that both exogenous and endogenous factors must be considered, along with an examination of the number of stressors the individual faces in daily life. We also contend that the diagnostician must consider posttraumatic stress disorder as a viable primary hypothesis or as a secondary diagnosis, given the racial, gender, and class dynamics of the United States. The critical variable that underlies these issues and their impact on an individual is trauma and stress because of race, gender, or social class. Because these three variables are out of a person's control, when issues put an individual in a traumatic or stressful situation, considerable damage can result. Although several hypotheses posit the positive outcomes of such stressors, the emphasis in this chapter is on considering negative outcomes of traumatic stress, assessment for their identification, and appropriate treatment strategies.

Sources of Trauma: Personal and Environmental

This section will briefly review the sources of stress that may lead to a series of traumas or a traumatic event that may become a precursor to posttraumatic stress disorder. These include personal variables (identity development as an ethnic minority, acculturation stress, identity resolution, personality, gender issues, and class factors) and environmental variables such as racism and discrimination.

Personal Variables

Identity Development of Nondominant Groups. Psychological literature presents many hypotheses regarding minority identity development (Helms, 1995; Ibrahim, Ohnishi, & Sandhu, 1997; Sue, 1981; Sue & Sue, 1991). The corollaries of the identity development paradigms address many dimensions in which the minority person's identity develops differently from that of individuals who represent the mainstream. It is contended that a key element is missing in conceptions of minority identity development. This pertains to the lack of attention given to the impact of living in a society that does not tolerate differences (race, class, gender, sexual orientation, people with disabilities, etc.). These systemic inequities are particularly painful for people who live in a system that espouses the principles of liberty, equality, and fraternity for all its citizens. Yet, in practice, these principles are not operationalized in everyday life in U.S. societies. They function as ideals that the United States aspires to uphold.

To understand how members of nondominant groups develop their identity and come to terms with their place in a social system, we will use Berry's (1980) conceptualization of acculturation and adaptation for immigrants. We believe that his conception may help explain the variability in adaptation to a culture that has a powerful dominant group and several nondominant groups at various stages of acculturation and adaptation (from indigenous people to people who came or were brought here several hundred years ago to recent immigrants). This conceptualization also will help to clarify stress experienced in response to acculturation, racism, sexism, class issues, and marginalization or exclusion.

Berry (1980) presents a model of acculturation that classifies different strategies to cope with or adjust to a new culture. He presents four modes of acculturation: integration, assimilation, segregation, and marginalization. *Integration* involves retention of one's ethnic identity while incorporating components of the dominant culture. *Assimilation* results in relinquishing one's cultural identity and assuming the beliefs, values, assumptions, and attitudes of the majority group. *Separation* occurs when an individual chooses to withdraw from the dominant system. This is different from segregation (forced separation of ethnic groups). *Marginalization* occurs when a person cannot identify with his or her own cultural group or the majority culture. In both the integration and the separation modes of acculturation, the person decides to retain the primary cultural identity. However, these acculturation modes do not give the same outcome in terms of adjustment. In Berry's model, integration is the healthiest resolution in a pluralistic society (Berry, Poortinga, Segall, & Dasen, 1992).

Research suggests that these modes are differently related to health and psychosocial adjustment and personality variables such as cognitive styles, coping strategies, and reactions to stressful life events. Acculturation in this model is viewed as consisting of a number of phases or different forms of contact between the ethnic group and the majority group (Aponte, Rivers, & Wohl, 1995; Berry & Kim, 1988; Berry, Kim, Minde, & Mok, 1987). We accept the bidirectional process of acculturation, in which the ethnic person is assimilated into the majority culture but also retains his or her ethnic culture and identity. The majority culture in this model is also affected and changes over time due to contact (Aponte et al., 1995). Sodowsky, Lai, and Plake (1991) recommend that both the assimilated and the retained components must be assessed to obtain an accurate assessment of an individual's level of acculturation.

Acculturation—a complex, multifaceted, and multidimensional process—is situation driven (a person may adopt different acculturation options depending on the situation) (Cuellar, Harris, & Jasso, 1980; Olmedo, 1979; Sodowsky et al., 1991). The acculturation options and status available to a person are influenced by most moderator variables; these include but are not limited to socioeconomic status, gender, and residence (including years of residence in the United States, ethnic density in the neighborhood, and familial and social networks) (Aponte et al., 1995; Garcia & Lega, 1979; Ibrahim, 1992a, 1992b, 1994; Ibrahim et al., 1997). Kitano (1989) cautions that acculturation and ethnic identity are not synonymous processes but are separate conceptual elements. Helms (1990a, 1990b) clarifies that acculturation focuses on the person's values, beliefs, and behaviors, and ethnic identity is the process and outcome of integrating a person's racial/ethnic aspects into his or her overall self-concept and identity.

Berry (1980) notes that the mode of acculturation is important to consider in determining stress. In his model, marginalized individuals have the highest level of stress. People who choose separation as an acculturation option also have high stress. Individuals who choose assimilation as an acculturation option are in the intermediate range for stress. Those who pursue integration are minimally stressed. In Berry's model, stress level increases when a person or group is excluded, despite the acculturation option chosen. Other factors that affect acculturation stress are status, age, gender, number of partners, social support, ethnic association, and acceptance or prestige of one's group; the less accepted have additional barriers and stressors, such as discrimination and exclusion.

Key psychological variables that can ease acculturation and reduce the stress associated with it include expectations, knowledge of culture and language, level of education, values, self-esteem, identity status confusion, rigidity, flexibility, and cognitive style. Taft (1977) notes that not all individuals deal with acculturation pressures similarly. Similar to Berry's (1980) conceptualization regarding acculturation and stress, Taft's research shows that people who cope well do well on five variables: social-emotional adjustment, ethnic and national identity, cultural competence, social absorption, and role acculturation.

Personality Variables. Krystle (1978) maintains that there is profound personality change because of trauma in the management of emotional expression and interpersonal communication. According to him, there is (a) loss of capacity to use community supports, (b) chronic recurrent depression with feelings of despair, (c) psychosomatic symptoms, (d) emotional anesthesia or blocked ability to react effectively, and (e) an inability to recognize and make use of emotional reactions. The result is a robotlike existence, without fantasy and empathy for others, often accompanied by chronic physical illness, alcoholism, or drug dependence.

The fear and rage that racial and ethnic, religious, language, and lifestyle minorities and women experience result in higher rates of self-medication through alcohol and drug dependence or through prescribed medications for severe depression and anxiety disorders. Blaming the victims in this scenario does not do justice to the situation or addresses the problem (i.e., a system that creates problems for those within it, if they are identified in any way as "different"). Being different creates fear in this society. Starting with early adolescence, the primary demands that young people face require similarity. Ethnocultural minorities in such a system pay a high psychological and emotional price for marginal membership due to their "differentness."

Women of Color. Women of color have dual identities. Both these identities are ascribed a lower or secondary status, identified as *double jeopardy* (Lerner, 1986). Sandoval (1990) maintains that as a result, they are at the bottom of the ladder in terms of subordination and have the least power. Researchers hold that psychological explanations of male domination and subordination of women and children across ethnic groups, social classes, and cultures are associated with abuse of power, the objectification of women, and the association of individualism with interpersonal violence (Brownmiller, 1975; Hall, Hirschman, Graham, & Zaragoza, 1993; Herman, 1990; Holtzworth-Munroe, Beatty, & Anglin, 1995; Koss et al., 1994; Triandis, Bontempo, Villareal, Assai, & Lucca, 1988). Therefore, Root (1996) maintains that women of color in the United States experience cumulative effects of abuse of power through disenfranchisement, dislocation, and objectification.

Women of color live in a racist, sexist, and exclusionary society and are at higher risk for becoming victims of poverty, violence, institutional racism, and sexism. These trauma factors create despair, anger, and frustration in their daily lives. These circumstances include contextual threats through the interplay of the domination by gender, race, and ethnicity that threaten their safety, limit their mobility, and denigrate their self-worth (Root, 1996). Root (1996) suggests that these experiences comprise a foundation for insidious trauma among women of color that results in a decreased sense of optimism, risk of displaced anger, and sometimes a self-centered isolation for the survival of the spirit.

ENVIRONMENTAL FACTORS THAT CONTRIBUTE TO POSTTRAUMATIC STRESS DISORDER

Race, Class, and Gender Discriminations

Discrimination is practiced against racial-cultural groups, very poor and lower middle-class individuals of all ethnic groups, people with disabilities from all ethnic groups, and women. These groups are at particular risk of being subjected to discrimination in everyday life. Several stressors are linked to discrimination and exclusion because of race, class, and gender, and these stressors are directly related to trauma and its aftermath. Race-related traumas are the most obvious, given the politics of race in the United States. The stressors listed above are further aggravated when they are tied to class, disability, and gender issues (Ogbu, 1979).

Social-Historical Factors as Stressors. The effects of the negative social-historical conditions of ethnic and racial minorities on the mainstream population are guilt and shame. Evidence that these feelings exist is especially obvious during "affirmative action" or "diversity" workshops, where majority group members feel they cannot identify with individuals who are racist, sexist, ageist, or homophobic. These reactions are most dangerous for this group since they symbolize group guilt or shame regarding the maltreatment of the culturally different to benefit the economy and the well-being of the people in control of the economy—as with African Americans and slavery, Asian Americans and the labor need of the 19th century, the later concentration camp experience of Japanese Americans, and the Native American and Latino American (Mexico and Puerto Rico) experiences of loss of land, culture, languages, family system, and so on to provide land and its benefits to the colonists.

In reality, whether people came to this subcontinent voluntarily or involuntarily or were already here, whenever people have been culturally, racially, or ethnically different from the mainstream or the majority group that has power (control of government, the judiciary, law enforcement, schools, and other community institutions), they have been mistreated (Takaki, 1993). People who represent the mainstream or are the majority group in power are comfortable in creating power hierarchies under them that replicate their power structure and hegemony. African Americans are finally being recognized as a minority group that has been denied access to opportunity. Recently, Latino Americans have started to gain similar recognition. Native Americans and Asian Americans are still invisible as minorities and are not afforded access to affirmative action programs in several parts of the United States. With Asian Americans, colleges and universities in California are trying to restrict their access to education by imposing a quota on how many Asian Americans the school can absorb. If we study the history of Native Americans and Asian Americans, they have not been treated any better. Yet on a scale of powerlessness and misery, they are evaluated as better off. These tactics re-create the colonial stance of divide and rule and keep the misery and trauma index high for minorities who remain culturally different and excluded from the American Dream (Ibrahim et al., 1997). This situation also forces ethnic minorities to fight among themselves for a very small slice of the American pie that has been apportioned for "minorities."

Race-Related Stressors. Loo (1994) states that race-related stressors include verbal and physical assaults, racial stigmatization, disassociation from self, and marginalization. Verbal and physical assaults reduce minority group members to a stereotype and treat them as nonhuman. Reduction to a stereotype makes it easier to see the person as a nonperson, and physical assaults are easier on nonhumans than humans. Consider the case of an Asian American high school student in the Midwest. She is told by her mainstream peers that "slant eyes go back to China" and "Chinks or yellow monkeys go back to the zoo." This student has also experienced being spit on because of her ethnicity. Another case is of an African American graduate student in New England who is told by his instructor to sit in the back of the classroom. When he responds with shock, he is told it is a joke, and he needs to learn to take a joke. These are self-reports by minority group members. Experiences such as these create stress, and the accumulated stress over the life span can lead to posttraumatic stress disorder (PTSD), given that acculturation to mainstream society requires minority group members to internalize this stress. Risk factors for PTSD will be higher when a person's circumstances also include poverty, less valued gender (female), a disability, or an alternative lifestyle. As these variables are added to the minority ethnocultural index, the powerlessness factors increase and cause intense frustration and rage.

Racial stigmatization is a result of prejudice. Prejudice can be acted out verbally and nonverbally (Henley, 1977; Word, Zanna, & Cooper, 1974). Root (1993) considers racial stigmatization an insidious form of trauma that is a low level but constant threat to the self. Such experiences lead to Loo's (1994) hypothesis that American minorities experience cognitive-affective discordance between their schema of themselves as Americans and the identity given to them by others. Such an identity has experienced a broad representation of hatred and rejection. To highlight cognitive-affective discordance, we should consider the case of a Cuban American soldier stationed in Cuba during the Cuban American war. The soldier identifies himself as an American soldier. However, the identity ascribed to the soldier by his peers (as a Cuban) and as similar to us results in cognitive-affective discordance and severe psychological distress.

Dissociation from self occurs when an individual attempts to reduce conflict by ignoring or avoiding discrepant information about the self. This occurs when incoming information does not match with the perception of one's self-identity (Loo, 1994). For example, consider a Mexican American border police officer who daily confronts conflict in arresting Mexicans who are illegally crossing the border. Furthermore, the racial slurs and epithets used about the illegal Mexican aliens and the mistreatment of the illegal aliens may pose additional stress for the police officer. He may have a difficult time dissociating from the illegal immigrants. The cognitive dissonance inherent in this situation will cause the Mexican American border police officer to have severe psychological distress. The only mode of coping in such a conflict situation would be to dissociate from the emotional pain.

Marginalization occurs when people experience feelings of alienation. Stonequist (1935) notes that marginalization occurs when people have lost cultural and psychological contact with both their traditional culture and the larger society. Furthermore, he asserts that when acculturation is imposed, it is tantamount to ethnocide. When stabilized in the nondominant group, it is marginality. According to Stonequist's (1935) conceptualization, the marginal personality develops when a person subscribes to more than one ethnic group heritage. Therefore, the individual becomes a "marginal" member of all groups. Poston (1990) states that if marginality exists, it is not an individual personality problem. It implies that there is prejudice within society, and it is an internalization of the biases inherent in the available cultural systems.

Trauma and the Culturally Different. McGoldrick, Pearce, and Giordano (1996) maintain that the trauma experienced by an immigrant group on arrival in the United States stays within the unconscious of that group for many generations, even after a group has achieved presumed "parity" in economic terms. Portes and Rumbaut (1990) show that traumatic events experienced by any group migrating to the United States affects the psyche of that group for a considerable time. The stress of migration with the additional trauma of marginality and exclusion has a negative impact on adjustment and acculturation.

Marsella, Friedman, Gerrity, and Schurfield (1996) state that the traumas experienced by people because of societal and environmental oppression can result in PTSD. They also highlight that in the past decade, there has been heightened awareness regarding the impact of trauma, especially repeated trauma and its effect on the adjustment of various ethnocultural groups. Marsella et al. also contend that specific responses differ across ethnocultural groups. These responses are also mediated by class and gender. In addition, the intensity of the trauma is directly related to the opportunities available to the individual. If people are economically stable or have unlimited funds, they can construct their world to avoid traumatic experiences and emotional abuse.

The impact of stigmatization, exclusion, marginality, and verbal and physical assaults can be reduced by economic affluence. Not everyone will respond
to trauma and emotional abuse with a psychological breakdown or PTSD. A
psychological breakdown can be directly linked to lack of resilience due to poverty and other moderator variables that may increase stress, such as an alternative lifestyle, a less valued gender, a physical or psychological disability, and so
on. Wilson (1989) notes in his person-environment model of traumatic stress
that the subjective experience and reaction to trauma are influenced by dimensions of traumatic experience (level of threat and loss), the experience of
trauma (alone or with a group), the structure of trauma (single or multiple
stressors), and the posttraumatic milieu (support or the trauma membrane; rituals; cultural, social, or individual attitudes toward the traumatized; opportunity
to reintegrate). The environmental stressors are not appropriately addressed by
the mental health literature when being a minority is not recognized as a risk
factor, or the usual mode of labeling is conducted that creates the perception
that somehow the individual who needs mental health services has a weakness
or a propensity to the disorder. This thinking blames the victim and revictimizes
the individual by labeling the person with the problem (or a psychological
weakness), instead of considering the damage that marginality, exclusion, and
oppression can inflict on people.

Class Factors as Stressors. Aponte et al. (1995) note that social class is a moderator variable in the treatment of ethnic and racial minorities. This variable is
difficult to categorize because sometimes income or educational level is used to
define socioeconomic level. This variable must be coupled with environmental
factors such as place of residence (urban, suburban, or rural) and the impact of
that on social support available to the client. Trauma resolution is directly related to the social support available to the client, in terms of the trauma membrane and how it protects and supports the client in times of major distress.

Research across a variety of community and clinical samples shows a
strong relationship between socioeconomic status and rates of psychopathology, use of mental health services, and effectiveness of these services
(Comas-Díaz & Griffith, 1988; Gaw, 1993; Wierzbicki & Pecarik, 1993). In all
the available reviews of the literature, persons from low socioeconomic status
(SES) evidently have a higher rate of psychopathology and have a lower rate of
using mental health services. The research has not clearly identified whether
the higher rates are due to ethnic background or social class issues. Aponte et al.
(1995) argue that coming from a lower social class can make one vulnerable to a

larger number of stressors. They also note that low social class ethnic people experience more victimization (stressful life experiences) with higher vulnerability due to lower resources, and they have more additive burdens and are subject to chronic burdens (long-term personal and situational stressors) (Dohrenwend & Dohrenwend, 1981; Lorion & Felner, 1986). Aponte et al. caution that despite these data, it is quite possible for low SES ethnic people to function effectively in society and be "resilient" (p. 30). Social and familial support accounts for the resiliency. The two broad sources of structural support identified in the literature are social embeddedness and perceived or functional support (Barrera, 1986).

Diagnosis of PTSD

What specific acculturation process and what specific set of environmental and personality variables would predispose a minority person to PTSD? Why PTSD and not another diagnostic category to classify the psychological difficulties faced by racial and ethnic minorities, gays and lesbians, women, people with disabilities, language and religious minorities, and the elderly? We contend that the symptoms experienced by these groups have been misclassified as anxiety disorders, adjustment disorders, affective disorders, and so on. This has occurred due to the misperception that we have a level playing field and all are exposed to similar stressors, without considering how the stress of being a minority (coupled with the stress of racism, sexism, classism, handicapism, homophobia, etc.), the various acculturative processes, and environmental and personality factors may increase risk as a result of repeated trauma that forces people to endure systems that practice racism, sexism, homophobia, and so on.

To consider PTSD as a viable diagnosis for racial and cultural minorities, we need to evaluate the categories of PTSD in the *Diagnostic and Statistical Manual of Mental Disorders*, fourth edition (*DSM-IV*) (American Psychiatric Association, 1994) and consider how they may apply. In addition, we need to consider what specific environmental and personal factors, when coupled with minority status, may put a person at risk for PTSD.

DSM-IV Diagnostic Criteria:
Posttraumatic Stress Disorder

This disorder is characterized by the following:

A. The person has been exposed to a traumatic event in which both of the following were present:

1. The person experienced, witnessed, or was confronted with an event or events that involved actual or threatened death or serious injury or a threat to the physical integrity of self or others.
2. The person's response involved intense fear, helplessness, or horror. *Note:* In children, this may be expressed instead by disorganized or agitated behavior.

B. The traumatic event is persistently reexperienced in at least one (or more) of the following ways:

1. Recurrent and intrusive distressing recollections of the event, including images, thoughts, or perceptions. *Note:* In young children, repetitive play may occur in which themes or aspects of the trauma are expressed.
2. Recurrent distressing dreams of the event. *Note:* In children, there may be frightening dreams without recognizable content.
3. Acting or feeling as if the traumatic event were recurring (includes a sense of reliving the experience, illusions, hallucinations, and dissociative flashback episodes, including those that occur on awakening or when intoxicated). *Note:* In young children, trauma-specific reenactment may occur.
4. Intense psychological distress at exposure to internal or external cues that symbolize or resemble an aspect of the traumatic event.

C. Persistent avoidance of stimuli associated with the trauma and numbing of general responsiveness (not present before the trauma) as indicated by three (or more) of the following:

1. Efforts to avoid thoughts, feelings, or conversations associated with the trauma
2. Efforts to avoid activities, places, or people that arouse recollections of the trauma
3. Inability to recall an important aspect of the trauma
4. Markedly diminished interest or participation in significant activities
5. Feelings of detachment or estrangement from others

6. Restricted range of affect (e.g., unable to have loving feelings)
7. Sense of foreshortened future (e.g., does not expect to have a career, marriage, children, or a normal life span)

D. Persistent symptoms of increased arousal (not present before the trauma), as indicated by two (or more) of the following:

1. Difficulty falling or staying asleep
2. Irritability or outbursts of anger
3. Difficulty concentrating
4. Hypervigilance
5. Exaggerated startle response

E. Duration of the disturbance (symptoms in Criteria B, C, and D) is more than 1 month.

F. The disturbance causes clinically significant distress or impairment in social, occupational, or other important areas of functioning (American Psychiatric Association, 1994, pp. 209-211).

Traumatic Stress

Wilson (1989) proposes a person-environment approach to traumatic stress reactions. Several researchers support a need for interactional models that specify how several variables work together to create social-psychological-biological processes (Aronoff & Wilson, 1985; Kenrick & Funder, 1988). In the stress and coping research, an interactional approach has been suggested for many years (Wilson, 1989).

Historically, traumatic neurosis has been understood in terms of physiological causation as a primary determinant (i.e., concussions, spinal cord injury, etc.) and as a stimulus to altering psychological functioning (Trimble, 1981, 1985). Wilson (1989) notes that Freud had originally proposed an intrapsychic mechanism, in which the ego was overwhelmed by excessive stimulation from stressful life events. Once the ego was traumatized, other stimuli similar to the original stressor could instigate the original trauma. This theory, according to Wilson, was an early formulation of posttraumatic stress disorder.

Freud (1916/1966) later abandoned the external stressor theory and moved to the Oedipal theory of neurosis. He no longer accepted that an external event or set of events led to neurotic symptoms. He did, however, accept that constitutional factors would determine how the ego responds to trauma.

Since World War II, several researchers have proposed models of stress, coping, and adaptation that allow for the onset of psychopathology as an interactive effect of the severity and duration of extreme stress and the personality attributes of the individual (Hocking, 1970). Horowitz (1986) proposes a model that is similar to Loo's (1993, 1994) model of cognitive-affective discordance that leads to PTSD. Horowitz suggests that psychopathology results from incongruence between self-schemata and unassimilated information (affect and imagery) from the trauma. Marmar and Horowitz (1988) add that the stress syndrome involves a cycle of oscillations between episodes of intrusive imagery and avoidance of the trauma-laden imagery and affect. Lifton (1976, 1979, 1988), in his seminal work, suggests that trauma affects psychoformative processes (changes in self-structure, including but not limited to a sense of stasis, separation, disintegration, a loss of continuity, decentering, numbing, and a changed view of the world). Posttraumatic adaptation is determined by several classes of variables that include (a) the nature and dimensions of trauma, (b) personality attributes, (c) the recovery environment, and (d) the coping resources of the individual (Dohrenwend & Shrout, 1984; Green, Wilson, & Lindy, 1985; Lazarus & Folkman, 1984; Raphael, 1987; Wilson, 1989). Researchers also maintain that these variables interact in influencing both pathological and nonpathological forms of adaptation to stressful life events (Everstine & Everstine, 1993; Wilson, 1989).

Wilson (1989) notes that the critical variable is the *subjective* experience of the person in a traumatic event or series of traumatic events. In addition, individual variables such as personality traits, cognitive style, gender, and intelligence affect the way in which stressful events are appraised, perceived, and processed. It is important in an interactional model of trauma to consider how excessive stress alters personality functioning in pathological (PTSD, dysthymia, major depression, dissociative reactions, adjustment reactions, anxiety disorders, substance abuse or self-medication, and personality alteration) and nonpathological ways (positive personality alteration and character change, intensification of specific stages of ego development, psychosocial acceleration in ego development, changes in prepotency in the motive [need] hierarchy, and alteration in belief, attitudes, and values), as well as its influence over the life span. In addition, the cultural environment of the person must be considered because the meaning assigned to events can never be culture free (Wilson, 1989).

Most racial, ethnic, religious, languages, lifestyle, and age (e.g., children and the elderly) minorities have experienced overt and covert threats to their well-being. Psychological literature is replete with instances in which a minority person reports fear living in a certain neighborhood or driving through a certain part of town because his or her life would be threatened. The cross burnings and the lynchings are still fresh in the minds of African Americans, Mexican Americans, and Native Americans as things that happen to real people on this subcontinent. People who have historically lived their lives under threat and have been separated and segregated from the mainstream carry these historical events in their subconscious as group trauma. This trauma persists and influences their behavior. Stress-related disorders are highest among minorities and women in the U.S. workplace (Hatfield, 1990; Keita & Jones, 1990).

Although it is accepted that war veterans and refugees suffer from PTSD (Eisenbruch, 1991; Espino, 1991; Lin, 1986; Litz, 1992; McGuire, 1990; Miller, Goreczny, & Perconte, 1992; Schlenger, Kulka, Fairbank, & Hough, 1992), it is not considered an acceptable hypothesis that racial, ethnic, religious, language, and lifestyle minorities could be suffering from an environmentally induced and maintained disorder. Potts (1994) has already made a case for a classification within the PTSD literature that addresses civilian trauma. When people who belong to any of these "protected" groups fall prey to a stress-related disorder, they are generally blamed for their lack of resilience or generalized weakness or propensity to the disorder. Sue and Sue (1991) recommend that in counseling minorities, we must emphasize the reduction of their need to take responsibility for events and situations beyond their control. They contend that many psychological conflicts occur in an individual who does not have control over his or her destiny yet believes that he or she is in control. Similarly, Helms (1990a, 1990b) notes that the process of healthy minority identity development seeks to establish the reality of the situation as it influences an individual's primary group in an ongoing system.

Knowledge about social cultural oppression creates justified rage for oppressed groups. This is a necessary response before evolving into a healthy identity by recognizing injustice and what is right with one's group. When these identity phases are appropriately negotiated, the risk of falling prey to PTSD is greatly reduced. When minority youth are not educated about the promotion of healthy minority identity development or they are not taught to accept the rage and anger connected with the injustices in the system, they will remain stuck. Therefore, denial or lack of acceptance of the history of the nation or cultural groups within it does not promote healthy identity development for any member (dominant or nondominant group members) of this society. We believe that denial creates a system similar to an addictive society that parallels the beliefs and behaviors of an addicted person (Schaef, 1987). Suppression or lack of confrontation of the history and current conditions in this society becomes the root cause of dysfunction for people who benefit from racism, sexism, and classism and for those who suffer because of these problems in a society.

Psychological Trauma as a Result of the Minority Experience

Racism is the key variable in the psychological trauma that minority group members face. Racism is the denigration or subordination of minority groups, because of racial or cultural characteristics, that creates a sense of inferiority in such groups. A racist perspective has allowed many members of the majority group to believe that the disproportionate amount of power and wealth that they have is justified. Furthermore, this perspective has been justified and has led to efforts by the dominant group to impose a pervasive sense of powerlessness that the latter will not try to disrupt the status quo.

Kardiner and Ovesey (1966) note that the African American personality is severely affected by racism. Every pathological trait in African Americans is attributable to difficult living conditions. They note that African Americans have been required to adapt to the same culture and same goals as Euro-Americans, without the opportunities to achieve these goals. This creates a significant amount of stress and anxiety. The impact of such conditions has created an African American personality that at best can be called a caricature of the White personality, instead of a mature African American personality (Parsons, 1990). We contend that similar stress operates for ethnic minority groups and for women from all cultural groups. The standard for appropriate conduct, looks, behavior, achievement, and so on is exemplified by White Anglo-Saxon values (Takaki, 1993). Because this value system is a derivation of patriarchal values and belief system, women within this system from all ethnic groups automatically become second-class citizens. In addition, when we consider the high value placed on achievement and the opportunities for achievement that are available to ethnic minority males and all women, the frustration index rises and stress level increases.

Pinderhughes (1986) postulates that prejudice is "hardwired" in the average human psyche, and social relationships are built on "differential bonding" and affiliative-affectionate drives toward in-group members. Furthermore, differentiative-aggressive drives are maintained toward out-group members. According to her, the 400-year history of African Americans has been characterized by the attribution of negative traits to them by the dominant culture and population. This is a deliberate and systematic process. Pinderhughes suggests that as a result of this history, most Americans retain significant prejudice toward racial and ethnic minorities. Pinderhughes (1982) also notes that African Americans, to cope with this oppression, have developed a survival system that she labels the "victim system." This system advocates cooperation within the group to combat powerlessness; strict obedience to authority in the context of oppression, strength, toughness of character, and present time orientation (because the past is painful and the future is unknown); and a belief in luck and magic and spirituality. This system also creates the conditions for identification with the aggressor.

Bessel van der Kolk (1987) holds that psychological damage can and does result from terrifying life experiences. Generally, responses to trauma have been described as a phasic reliving and denial, with alternating intrusive and numbing responses. The intrusive responses are hyperreactivity, explosive aggressive outbursts, startle responses, intrusive recollections as nightmares and flashbacks, and reenactments of the situations reminiscent of the trauma. The denial by society of any trauma associated with the minority experience can possibly create a fixation for individuals who do suffer from the anxiety of living with an active Ku Klux Klan, cross burnings, and symbols that represent lynching.

Racism and Intergenerational Posttraumatic Disorder

Experiencing violence, abuse, exclusion, and lack of access to opportunity due to ethnocultural and gender variables can lead to PTSD and extend beyond the first generation to several following generations. Loo (1993) notes that race-related discrimination is a form of traumatic stress that is due to intentional, external human design. Essed (1990) suggests that repeated exposure to racial discrimination affects the victim. Duran, Guillory, and Tingley (1992) state that a blatant example of a personal threat is the forced acculturation experienced by minorities in the United States. These conditions, experienced over several generations, can lower resilience (as noted in the PTSD descriptor in the *DSM-IV*) on psychological and biological variables. The resulting condition is intergenerational PTSD.

Evidence for this hypothesis comes from reports that the rate of alcoholism and drug abuse is higher among minority populations. Currently, the Native American community faces a crisis in dealing with excessive rates of alcoholism and fetal alcohol syndrome (Streissguth, LaDue, & Randels, 1988; Weisner, Weibel-Orlando, & Long, 1994). Alcohol and substance abuse is a destructive coping mechanism for individuals with PTSD because of racism, discrimination, and acculturative stress (Berlin, 1987; Yates, 1987).

Loo (1994) proposed a conceptual framework for race-related PTSD. According to this framework, (a) cumulative racism is traumatic; (b) such trauma violates basic cognitive assumptions about the world, causing a shift within the cognitive schema that starts to separate the traumatized person from others in the social system; (c) a new behavioral repertoire (social behaviorism) is required that contradicts an earlier behavioral repertoire; and (d) stress results from the negation of bicultural identity, denial of one aspect (i.e., American), and denigration of the other aspect (e.g., Asian/African/Native/Latino) by a requirement to behave in the same manner as the majority group (considered the incorporation of American norms).

Resolutions to Race, Gender, and Class Traumas

There are several resolutions to trauma because of race, gender, and class issues. Some of these have positive outcomes, and some have negative outcomes. These include cumulative racism as trauma, cognitive schema theory, social behaviorism, and bicultural identity theory.

Cumulative Racism as Trauma. A brief summary of Loo's (1994) conceptual framework follows: Race-related trauma, a form of traumatic stress, is due to intentional, external human design (PTSD-IHD) (Loo, 1993). Symptoms such as chronic depression and insomnia experienced by Japanese Americans who were interned in U.S. concentration camps during World War II are an example of race-related trauma that has had chronic effects. Studies on African American women in White-dominated organizations show similar results of cumulative stress due to racism, resulting in chronic problems (Parsons, 1985; Root, 1992). Essed (1990) notes that delineated marginalization (denied access to positions of power, nonrecognition, underestimation, nonacceptance, and obstruction of mobility) and containment (adverse reactions of the dominant group, especially power or authority figures in organizations, to assertive behavior of the dominated group's pursuit of equality, justice, and power) are elements of everyday racism. Similar lack of access and frustration is experienced by women and lower social class individuals.

Cognitive Schema Theory. Cognitive schema theory has been proposed by several researchers (Horowitz, 1976, 1979; Mancuso, 1977; McCann, Sakheim, & Abrahamson, 1988). Cognitive schema theory maintains that individuals derive beliefs and expectations about themselves and others, either positive or negative, in response to life experiences and are shaped by gender and sociocultural background. If this cognitive system is continually discrepant with an individual's daily experience, a conflict arises in the cognitive schema that needs resolution (Mancuso, 1977). Trauma is an event that generally shatters the victim's basic assumptions (Figley, 1985; Foa, Steketee, & Olasoz-Rothbaum, 1989; Janoff-Bulman, 1985).

Trauma also can be understood as involving cognitive discordance due to violations of basic beliefs (Horowitz, 1979; Loo, 1993). Parsons (1990) presents an example of cognitive discordance in African American self-identity development as characterized by internalization of socially projected images of the African self as unworthy, incompetent, and stupid. Being descendents of American slaves and the servility, personal dejection, and low self-esteem associated with these experiences still lurk deep within the unconscious mind of African Americans. These are also reinforced by experiences of everyday racism and can become a powerful source of problems and induce a psychological state that interferes with interactions and communication.

Social Behaviorism. Staats (1968a, 1968b, 1975) defines social behaviorism as behavioral repertoires that fall within emotional-motivational, language-cognitive, and sensory-motor domains, and these determine how a person will experience a certain situation. For example, during World War II, Japanese Americans were called "Japs" and "slant eyes" and subjected to slogans, such as "kill Japs" and "hate Japs," and they were removed from society and placed in concentration camps in several parts of the world, including the United States, Canada, and several South American countries.

Staats (1975) notes that the emotional-motivational element of prejudiced labeling can be interpreted as a personal threat, experienced as anxiety, and accompanied by physiological arousal, which can lead to feelings of self-hate. In essence, social behaviorism asserts that learning a new behavioral repertoire is difficult if it contradicts a previously learned repertoire. Therefore, all racist acts would be interpreted as similar or close to the World War II experience for Japanese Americans.

Bicultural Identity. Achieving a bicultural identity is an adaptive response to being raised in an ethnic environment different from the ethnicity of the majority group. It is the process that helps minority group members to learn two distinct behavioral repertoires for two specific environments (Cross, 1987; Valentine, 1971). Berry (1980), in a multidimensional model of acculturation, proposes that minority persons may differ in regard to whether they consider it desirable to maintain relationships with European Americans and with their ethnic and cultural identity. According to Loo (1994), people with an integrationist mode of acculturation value their ethnic and cultural identity while striving for acceptance by the dominant majority group.

Loo (1994) proposes that greater stress is experienced when the bicultural mode of acculturation and desire for integration (among the bicultural elements of identity) are deterred by stigmatizing experiences that deny people the dignity of their ethnic identity. For example, bicultural Arab Americans may concurrently fear being called "terrorists" by other Americans, even as they believe themselves to be Americans. This may cause Arab Americans to fear being stigmatized as disloyal to their country and can lead to feeling threats to their lives (Loo, 1994). LaFromboise, Coleman, and Gerton (1993) note that individuals who can develop a bicultural identity are better equipped to deal with the difficulties of living in a multicultural context than those who do not.

Coping With Persistent Stress

To cope with the persistent stress of race/ethnicity-related exclusion and abuse, people who are not exposed to healthy, resilient environments that provide a supportive membrane and enhance positive identity development will develop identities that either deny their identity or develop complicated and psychologically, physically, and emotionally damaging coping behaviors. These coping behaviors become part of a family's identity and are later treated as a singular psychological problem or, at the most, are given a dual diagnosis that is eventually treated. Uba (1994) notes that individual differences in ethnic identity occur in the degree to which individuals have experienced racism and the ways in which they have responded to racism. Furthermore, experiences with racism lead to a denial of one's ethnic identity or overidentification with one's ethnocultural group. When individuals sense a threat because of membership in a minority group, they may decide not to own any sense of ethnic consciousness.

The rise in the belief in Anglo-Saxon superiority in the 19th century openly justified genocidal policies toward Native Americans and people of color (Horsman, 1981). Minority group members in the United States experienced forced acculturation, racism, exclusion from opportunities, and other discriminations. The trauma experienced by Native Americans and other minority groups in the nation lives on in their unconscious mind (McGoldrick et al., 1996). Choney, Berryhill-Paapke, and Robbins (1995) show in a study of acculturation of Native Americans that the results of severe intergenerational trauma without any interventions have led to the highest rates of alcohol consumption in the United States. Berlin (1987) and Yates (1987) both report that in an attempt to alleviate the sense of hopelessness and loss of identity, Native Americans have developed a coping strategy of high alcohol consumption to numb the senses. Currently, fetal alcohol syndrome and fetal alcohol effect are a significant threat to the survival of Native Americans (Streissguth et al., 1988). Other outcomes of the untreated intergenerational PTSD are suicides, homicides, accidental deaths and injuries, thefts, social discord, unemployment, and epidemic divorce rates among Native American communities (Price, 1975).

Similar destructive coping mechanisms such as substance abuse habits are common among other minority groups, including African Americans, Asian Americans, Caribbean Americans, and Latino Americans. Hough, Canino, Abueg, and Gusman (1996) report that Mexican Americans can expect to have higher stress levels than the average population due to their experience of migration, immigration, prejudice, discrimination, fewer social resources, and language barriers. These stress factors increase various forms of traumatic violence among Mexican Americans (e.g., a higher proportion of children are maltreated and women are battered in this population).

These malfunctioning behaviors and psychological patterns as adaptive responses result in high rates of unemployment, high levels of interpersonal dysfunction, physical and psychological comorbidity, child abuse, poverty, and divorce (Brinson & Treanor, 1988; Keane & Wolfe, 1990; Potts, 1994; Resnick, Foy, Donahue, & Miller, 1989). These destructive patterns are passed on to the children in these groups, and they also become subject to PTSD. Fitzpatrick and Boldizer (1993) report that in a survey of 221 inner-city African Americans, 21.7% indicated that they were suffering from PTSD. Researchers report that children of parents with PTSD have several adjustment problems, including academic difficulties, mood and anxiety problems, and behavior disturbances (including primary PTSD symptoms such as nightmares and ruminations).

Cases: Minorities Experiencing
Posttraumatic Stress Disorder

Case 1: Misdiagnosed as Paranoid Disorder

An Asian immigrant professional woman is suffering from extreme anxiety and depression. She believes that her boss and her company are out to get her. The organization she works for became extremely concerned because of her paranoid and bizarre behavior. They sought a consultation from a local psychologist who is an expert on cultural issues in psychotherapy.

The psychologist helps the organization recognize that in reaction to her distress, they have created the exact circumstances that are creating stress and difficulties for this employee. She reassures them that they need to be more supportive and act less suspicious of the troubled employee. The organization and the woman's boss are educated about the anxiety a culturally different employee may feel. Furthermore, they are educated about the history of the United States and the cultural attitudes toward people who do not represent the mainstream; her behavior reflects reality, not a paranoid condition. It was also learned during an interview with the unhappy worker that she was extremely disillusioned by the reality of race relations in the United States. She truly believed that this was a land of opportunity. Now she knows that it is a land of opportunity but only for European Americans and their progeny.

Case 2: Misdiagnosed as Explosive Personality Disorder

An African American male, in his mid-20s, is diagnosed with explosive personality disorder. The individual has a history of explosive anger episodes since early childhood. He grew up in a housing project in an inner-city environment. He was surrounded by desperate people, drug users and abusers, and murderers and victims. Considering the client's environment and his experiences since early childhood, it is difficult to conclude whether he is suffering from explosive personality disorder or from PTSD.

The client reports recurrent dreams—nightmares about the events and the environment in which he was raised. He continues to feel completely frustrated by his helplessness to change his world and move on with his life emotionally. The trauma of his childhood environment has taken over his life. He denigrates himself for not moving on. Consequently, he blames himself for circumstances that are beyond his control. The counseling intervention here seems to have exacerbated the original problem by making the client feel that he is failing. Because the intervention does not consider or include the impact of environmental variables or does not provide any outlet for giving the client experiences that may help or empower him to influence the social system, he remains powerless. A major consequence of not properly diagnosing the problem is that the intervention may alleviate some symptoms but may leave the client unable to achieve his full potential or come to terms with the conditions that have created the problem.

CONSIDERATIONS FOR A DIAGNOSIS OF PTSD AS A RESULT OF THE MINORITY EXPERIENCE

In essence, we propose that several factors can contribute to healthy or maladaptive adjustment. The risk factors are race, gender, cultural orientation, ethnic identity, acculturation to mainstream culture, social class, educational level, disability status, and lifestyle. Moderator variables that can facilitate or obstruct adjustment include accumulated stress because of racism, sexism, class variables, coping strategies, cognitive and affective style of a person, personality variables, intellectual ability level, previous trauma, accumulated trauma, and family of origin resilience factors. Outcomes can be positive or negative. Positive outcomes include increased ethnic or racial pride, a bicultural identity, and identity resolution to the integration phase (Berry, 1980; LaFromboise et al., 1993). Negative outcomes can include psychological problems, including PTSD. These will be mediated by the above moderator variables and will determine how the individual will resolve the trauma of exclusion and marginality.

Assessment for PTSD

We recommend a multisystem assessment before a diagnosis or a treatment strategy. Because no empirical research exists to support the hypothesis we propose, we are using a complex interpretation of several theoretical statements and empirical studies to accept the viability of the hypothesis that cumulative stress over time, as a result of one's race, gender, and social class, may lead to psychological difficulties, which would be appropriately identified as posttraumatic stress disorder. Identification as an affective disorder, adjustment disorder, or anxiety disorder may provide a partial resolution to the client in treatment.

The assessment becomes key in this process. The first step in the assessment process must include a cultural and gender identity assessment. We recommend using the Cultural Identity Checklist (Ibrahim, 1993, in press) as a springboard to identify issues that are relevant to the client in terms of cultural/ethnic identity; gender; social class; religious orientation; life stage concerns; clarification of the impact of living in urban, suburban, or rural environments; family of origin issues; and place in the family system. Using this checklist, the clinician can identify issues that may have been traumatic or stressful over the life span. The Cultural Identity Checklist will specifically clarify cultural, gender, and class dimensions. The assessment can also help in identifying the client's strengths (personality variables, cognitive style, intellectual ability, and coping style) and the limits (negative life experiences because of racism, sexism, class issues, growing up in a threatening family or community environment, etc.). The strengths can be used in the therapeutic process as a foundation for positive coping. The limits can assist in identifying counseling goals and appropriate coping strategies.

The second step in clarifying the client's cultural, ethnic, and gender identity involves clarifying the client's worldview. This will entail using a scale such as the Scale to Assess World View (Ibrahim & Kahn, 1984, 1987). The client's worldview, once assessed, will help in setting goals that will be meaningful for the client and in ensuring that the goals are consistent with the client's worldview and ethnic-cultural socialization. This assessment will also assist in understanding the client's subjective experience of pain, stress, and trauma. The client's values, rather than the therapist's assumptions, must determine the meaning of the experiences that have brought the client to counseling. This recommendation is in line with experts on trauma resolution (Everstine & Everstine, 1993; Wilson, 1989).

In addition, we recommend an understanding of the client's acculturation level and an assessment of the client's developmental stage to clarify the type of intervention that would be most effective given the acculturation stage and developmental level specific to cognitive development (Berry, 1980; Padilla, 1980). For women, we recommend an additional assessment to clarify their identity status. These assessments will assist in making the intervention client specific and relevant.

In terms of trauma assessment, Everstine and Everstine (1993) recommend using the Everstine Trauma Response Index (ETRI), an instrument that has been specifically designed to determine psychological trauma. It describes the trauma response qualitatively and quantitatively. It provides definitive descriptions of symptoms of trauma or trauma-related behavior. This facilitates the client's providing a structure to the amorphous, chaotic thoughts that trauma creates. ETRI has similar conceptual assumptions as earlier instruments, surveys, and tests that were conceived to measure stress such as the Social Readjustment Scale and the Life Experiences Survey.

Implications for Treatment

Before embarking on any therapeutic strategy, it is important to cast a therapeutic intervention within the following structure (Ibrahim, 1998): (a) recognize the sociopolitical history of the group and the diversity within the group. What are the implications of both these variables for the specific client you are planning to work with? (b) How is trauma conceptualized in the client's cultural context? (c) What are the culturally accepted coping mechanisms (religion, spirituality, kinship, or social support groups)? (d) What are the gender-specific issues relevant to the client? (e) What specific recommendations would you make for therapy?

Two specific treatments that could be very effective in this context are Parsons's (1990) posttraumatic psychocultural therapy and Ivey's (1995) psychotherapy as liberation therapy. We also recommend cognitive-behavioral approaches that combine several modalities to assist in the process of helping the client to come to terms with the trauma and gain control of his or her life. In addition, it is critical that schools employ preventive measures that incorporate multicultural identity models in psychosocial developmental programs such as developmental guidance interventions to increase resilience, cultural, ethnic, and gender pride (Ibrahim, 1992a, 1992b, 1994). A third approach that is gaining momentum in the field to treat psychological trauma is called *eye movement desensitization and reprocessing* (EMDR) (Shapiro, 1989). This is a new and controversial approach that has shown quick results for people suffering from long-term results of psychological trauma.

Parsons (1990) proposes a posttraumatic psychocultural therapy that aims to achieve integration of the self-identity system at each successive life stage. The therapy attempts a systematic exploration of intrapsychic/dynamic and extra/ecologic factors to alleviate psychological and social symptoms resulting from stigmatization and social impediments due to race or cultural identity. Posttraumatic psychocultural therapy emphasizes the following: (a) focusing on the client's real or fantasized experience of racial discrimination and exclusion, (b) strengthening the client's capacity to actively engage in effecting social change through meaningful engagement and prosocial behavior, (c) egalitarian sharing of power in the treatment relationship (we recommend that guidelines for clients from specific cultural groups are followed; some cultural groups may find an egalitarian relationship difficult), and (d) assisting clients to gain insight into their problems and increase their ability to make meaningful connections with historical events and present symptomology, complaints, and behavior patterns.

Ivey (1995) proposes a psychotherapy as liberation therapy that focuses on expanding the client's consciousness by emphasizing seeing oneself and others in relation to the cultural and social context. This approach is based on Paulo Friere's (1979) theory espoused in *Pedagogy of the Oppressed.* The theory

(a) helps the client to understand the self in relation and move from a naive understanding of the oppression to naming and resistance, (b) helps the client to expand his or her understanding for naming the issue and the mode of resistance needed to move to the next phase of development, (c) helps the client expand his or her understanding of reflection and redefinition and start a dialogue that takes a multiperspective approach, and (d) helps the client to integrate the multiple perspectives into their ongoing consciousness and apply it to the events in their lives and to their families, community, cultural group, and society to bring about personal, social, and cultural change.

EMDR (Shapiro, 1989) is a controversial treatment that claims to resolve longstanding traumatic memories within a few sessions. During this treatment, the client is asked to hold in mind an image of the trauma, a negative self-cognition, negative emotions, and related physical sensations about the trauma. While doing so, the client is instructed to move his or her eyes quickly and laterally back and forth for about 15 to 20 seconds following the therapist's fingers. Other forms of left-to-right alternating stimulation (auditory or tactile) are also used sometimes (Wilson, Becker, & Tinker, 1995). The client is asked to then report the images, cognitions, emotions, and physical sensations that emerge. This recursive procedure continues until desensitization of troubling material is complete and positive self-cognitions have replaced the previous negative self-cognitions.

Shapiro (1989), in her initial report on the procedure, reported that EMDR significantly reduced anxiety associated with a traumatic memory and increased the perceived validity of positive cognitions within a single session. Later, case reports supported the efficacy of EMDR (Kleinknecht & Morgan, 1992; Levin, 1993; Lipke & Botkin, 1992; Spector & Huthwaite, 1993; Wolpe & Abrams, 1991). Wilson et al. (1995) reported the results of a well-controlled study that showed positive outcomes using EMDR. In addition, they noted that as traumatic memory was desensitized, general functioning of the participants improved. They do caution that although EMDR showed promise in the treatment of traumatic memories, the reasons for its effectiveness were not clear.

Blake, Abueg, Woodward, and Keane (1993) reviewed the effectiveness of various treatments for PTSD. Research in this domain is limited; they concluded that exposure therapies showed better outcomes than psychodynamic approaches. EMDR has a number of elements that are not typical of exposure therapies, although imaginal exposure is involved. Wilson et al. (1995) showed that in a much shorter time than exposure therapies, EMDR brought the participants to within normal range on the outcome measures.

Cultural Aspects in Treatment

PTSD is a dysfunction that implicates biological, psychological, and social aspects that are all influenced by ethnocultural factors such as cultural conceptions of health and disease, perceptions and definitions of trauma, conception of the person, and standards concerning normality and abnormality
(Marsella et al., 1996). It is necessary to develop sensitivity to possible cultural
influences in the treatment process. The following highlights cultural considerations that may enhance treatment for minority clients with PTSD.

African Americans. Allen (1996) notes that race permeates any subject related
to American society. According to him, "The presence of African Americans in
this country, as a group feared, yet depended on, has predisposed this country to
enormous internal conflict obscured by race" (p. 233). Allen further comments
that the conflict is intensified because the treatment of African Americans has
been a violation of fundamental principles of human rights.

West (1993) describes PTSD among African Americans as nihilism. He
notes,

> Nihilism is to be understood here as philosophic doctrine. . . . It is, far more,
> the lived experience of coping with a life of horrifying meaninglessness,
> hopelessness, and (most important) lovelessness. The frightening result is
> numbing detachment from others and a self destructive disposition toward
> the world. (p. 23)

In working with African American clients, it is recommended that the
trauma and therapy be placed in the context of life experiences that include
class variables, including employment and unemployment, gender issues as
they apply to relationships, educational level, social and medical problems,
health care delivery systems, racial discrimination in the schools, and financial
difficulties (Allen, 1996).

It is recommended that clinical settings for African American clients are
racially integrated (Penk & Allen, 1991). This recommendation is made in view
of the African American client's hyperawareness of problematic clinical settings. This client group is cognizant of racial and ethnic diversity among the
staff. These observations may not be mentioned spontaneously, although they
create a more natural environment for the client.

It is critically important to be aware of the diversity among African Americans. There are currently several distinct groups in the United States (McGoldrick et al., 1996). These groups include the African Americans who were brought 400 years ago: Jamaicans, immigrant groups from Africa (specifically Nigeria and Ethiopia), South Americans, Caribbean groups, and Haitians. Some of the recent immigrants may be trauma survivors from wars in their homelands. It is important to be sensitive to previous traumatic events because significant trauma also may be occurring in adjustment to the United States.

Asian Americans. In working with Asian Americans, Abueg and Chun (1996) recommend understanding the heterogeneous cultural context of Asian American groups and the meaning of trauma within it. Coping mechanisms vary across Asian American cultural groups, along with affect and spiritual dimensions. It is critical to understand the client's cultural, social, political, historical, religious, and acculturation level, as well as the client's personal understanding of the interaction of these variables.

It is significant to note that most Asian Americans do not identify with Asian culture exclusively, although their primary traumatization comes from acquaintances and peers who are not Asian but want them to act exclusively as stereotypes of Asians. There are also significant variations in gender, class, educational level, and identification with culture of origins. Gender hierarchy in Asian American culture imposes a major stressor on the women, who are socialized in a patriarchal model. Asian Americans perceive a power hierarchy in the United States that is race and gender based. They perceive White males as number one, White women as number two, Asian men as number three, and Asian women as number four on the race-gender-class hierarchy (Ibrahim, 1992a, 1992b). In this context, regardless of primary cultural orientation (Chinese, Japanese, Korean, etc.), Asian American women experience considerably more stress and trauma due to racism, exclusion, lack of opportunity, their fourth-class status, and their belief in fatalism and stoicism. There is a much higher incidence of justifiable rage being turned on themselves.

Portes and Rumbaut (1990) reported higher rates of suicide for Asian immigrants. It is also important to note that Asian American women have the highest suicide rate among all ethnic and cultural groups in the United States (Ibrahim, 1994). Stoicism, the common cultural trait among all Asian American groups, must be reexamined in the context of trauma interventions. Electing to suffer quietly and coping with PTSD and recurrent depression without seeking help may result in serious consequences, such as suicide.

It would be beneficial to help define the nature of PTSD and differentiate it from the definition of mental illness as understood by the client. The element of shame and loss of face must be addressed if therapy is going to proceed. Otherwise, premature termination may occur. We believe that a large part of the therapeutic process must be allocated to educating the client about trauma and its impact over the life span. The cultural meaning of psychological distress in the United States and Asian American cultural systems must be clarified, and common ground must be found with the client.

In working with Asian American clients, process variables must be addressed. Communication styles will differ from White, African, and Latino therapists. For example, Asian American clients, especially first generation, use nonverbal and indirect communication styles more than any other ethnic group. Therefore, the therapists must understand and use various communication styles sensitively and effectively.

Western therapy must incorporate religious principles from various religions dominant in Asia, such as Buddhism, Taoism, Shintoism, Hinduism, Zoroastrianism, and Islam. The inclusion of spiritual factors as healing agents would provide a holistic intervention. Furthermore, Canda and Phaobtong (1992) believe that the religious aspects are very important as coping mechanisms for certain Asian ethnic groups that are recent immigrants. Two therapeutic approaches proposed by Loo (1993) and Gusman et al. (1996) incorporate spiritual elements for Asian American clients with PTSD and show positive outcomes.

Spanish-Speaking Americans. This population is very diverse, with various sociopolitical histories in the United States ranging from the time of the Alamo to the recent wave of migration that includes a large number of refugees. Although there are several cultural commonalities, there are also large differences in terms of the trauma experienced from the perspective of an invaded people, or a protectorate, or trauma as a result of being a recent immigrant with language difficulties. It becomes critically important to evaluate the client's cultural identity, acculturation level, identification with a faith, ability to speak English, educational level, social class, and gender variables before an assessment of psychological dysfunction or the intervention is undertaken (Ibrahim, 1991, 1993). Culture-specific responses to acute stress must be understood and not labeled as psychopathology. These include dissociation, somatic complaints, and the culturally endogenous symptoms such as *ataques de nervious* (Hough et al., 1996).

Cervantes and Castro (1985) note, along with others, that the degree of trauma or stress reported from an event can be attenuated or intensified by culture-specific patterns of appraisal of the event. Hough et al. (1996) stress that the culture of Spanish-speaking people may "normalize" stress. According to Paz (1961), the Mexican American man can be characterized as closed, defensive, and tending to express resignation, stoicism, and indifference to suffering. These traits normalize stress and lead to the belief that it is less traumatic. Hough et al. also suggest that among some Mexican American men, a need to be in control may make traumatic events that induce helplessness extremely difficult to cope with. According to them, a clinical generalization suggests that there may be two specific pathological adaptations to this helplessness, "one that is passive introspective and severely depressed, versus a highly reactive, angry, and potentially explosive response" (p. 326). They recommend that because clinical work and research rest on constructivist assumptions, it is critical that a therapist focus on the cognitive style of the Spanish-speaking client and his or her perceptions of the potentials of traumatic events and their outcome in terms of mental health status.

Native Americans. Native Americans have experienced severe and cumulative trauma (Manion et al., 1996; Robin, Chester, & Goldman, 1996). Therefore, accurate assessment of each Native American client is necessary to enable an effective treatment regimen that addresses substance abuse and mental health problems. Lira, Becker, and Catillo (1988) recommend that several factors must be considered in working with Native American clients. These include the following: (a) The nature and extent of prolonged and repeated trauma must be documented to have an understanding of the history of trauma among Native Americans; (b) the impact of a single, acute traumatic incident within the context of cumulative multigenerational trauma must be examined; and (c) the concept of community trauma must be developed because Native American reservation residents are often collectively affected by traumatic events because of the close and interwoven relationships that typify these communities.

Given the commonality of intergenerational PTSD among Native American populations, it is critical to focus on educating the community, especially the youth, about PTSD, along with alcoholism and substance abuse to prevent the youth from becoming victims of the system.

Manion et al. (1996) recommend that culture-specific healing strategies must be used to heal victims of intergenerational PTSD. According to them, these ceremonies extend the biomedical perspective and have a positive healing and social effect beyond the individual that is the focus of the intervention. They note that the healing ceremony derives its power from the "meaning-making aspects and the coherence engendering qualities of the healing ritual" (p. 275). Wilson (1989) recommends using prevention strategies via Native American ceremonies to heal the young and to prevent adaptation to trauma through alcoholism and substance abuse.

Conclusion

This chapter makes a case that the minority experience of everyday life in the United States can lead to posttraumatic stress disorder. It reviews the stressors that minority populations face on a daily basis in the school, the streets, the community, and the workplace. Furthermore, the role of race, gender, and class in adaptation to everyday life and its impact on adjustment are presented. Considerations for treatment interventions are also presented. It is argued that a human-caused trauma is perpetuated by a society that values one race over others, and this evaluation exacerbates the difficulties that people face as a result of other constraining variables such as gender and class.

References

Abueg, F. R., & Chun, K. M. (1996). Traumatization stress among Asians and Asian Americans. In A. J. Marsella, M. J. Friedman, E. T. Gerrity, & R. M. Scurfield (Eds.), *Ethnocultural aspects of posttraumatic stress disorder* (pp. 285-299). Washington, DC: American Psychological Association.

Allen, I. M. (1996). PTSD among African Americans. In A. J. Marsella, M. J. Friedman, E. T. Gerrity, & R. M. Scurfield (Eds.), *Ethnocultural aspects of posttraumatic stress disorder* (pp. 209-238). Washington, DC: American Psychological Association.

American Psychiatric Association. (1994). *Diagnostic and statistical manual of mental disorders* (4th ed.). Washington, DC: Author.

Aponte, J. E., Rivers, R. Y., & Wohl, J. (1995). *Psychological interventions and cultural diversity.* Boston: Allyn & Bacon.

Aronoff, J., & Wilson, J. P. (1985). *Personality in the social process.* Hillsdale, NJ: Lawrence Erlbaum.

Barrera, M. (1986). Distinction between social support concepts, measures and models. *American Journal of Community Psychology, 14,* 413-445.

Berlin, I. N. (1987). Effects of changing Native American cultures on child development. *Journal of Community Psychology, 13,* 299-306.

Berry, J. W. (1980). Acculturation as varieties of adaptation. In A. M. Padilla (Ed.), *Acculturation: Theory, models and some new findings* (pp. 9-25). Boulder, CO: Westview.

Berry, J. W., & Kim, U. (1988). Acculturation and mental health. In P. R. Dasen, J. W. Berry, & N. Sartorius (Eds.), *Health and cross-cultural psychology: Toward applications* (pp. 207-236). Newbury Park, CA: Sage.

Berry, J. W., Kim, U., Minde, T., & Mok, D. (1987). Comparative studies of acculturative stress. *International Migration Review, 21,* 491-511.

Berry, J. W., Poortinga, Y. H., Segall, M. H., & Dasen, P. R. (1992). *Cross-cultural psychology: Research and applications.* Cambridge, UK: Cambridge University Press.

Blake, D. D., Abueg, F. R., Woodward, S. H., & Keane, T. M. (1993). Treatment efficacy of posttraumatic stress disorder. In T. R. Giles (Ed.), *Handbook of effective psychotherapy* (pp. 195-236). New York: Plenum.

Brinson, T., & Treanor, V. (1988). Alcoholism and post-traumatic disorder among Vietnam veterans. *Alcoholism Treatment Quarterly, 5,* 65-82.

Brownmiller, S. (1975). *Against our will: Men, women, and rape.* New York: Bantam.

Canda, E. R., & Phaobtong, T. (1992). Buddhism as a support system for Southeast Asian refugees. *Social Work, 37,* 61-67.

Cervantes, R. C., & Castro, F. G. (1985). Stress, coping and Mexican American mental health: A systematic review. *Hispanic Journal of Behavioral Science, 7,* 1-73.

Choney, S. K., Berryhill-Paapke, E., & Robbins, R. R. (1995). The acculturation of American Indians. In J. G. Ponterotto, J. M. Casas, L. A. Suzuki, & C. M. Alexander (Eds.), *Handbook of multicultural counseling* (pp. 73-92). Thousand Oaks, CA: Sage.

Comas-Díaz, L., & Griffith, E. E. H. (1988). *Clinical guidelines in cross-cultural health.* New York: John Wiley.

Cross, W. E., Jr. (1987). A two-factor theory of Black identity: Implications for the study of identity development in minority children. In J. S. Phinney & M. J. Rotheram (Eds.), *Children's ethnic socialization: Pluralism and development* (pp. 117-133). Newbury Park, CA: Sage.

Cuellar, I., Harris, L. C., & Jasso, R. (1980). An acculturation scale for Mexican American normal and clinical populations. *Hispanic Journal of Behavioral Sciences, 2,* 199-217.

Dohrenwend, B. P., & Shrout, P. E. (1984). "Hassles" in the conceptualization and measurement of life stress variables. *American Psychologist, 40,* 780-786.

Dohrenwend, B. S., & Dohrenwend, B. P. (1981). Hypothesis about stress processes linking social class to various types of psychopathology. *American Journal of Community Psychology, 9,* 146-159.

Duran, E., Guillory, B., & Tingley, P. (1992, October). *Domestic violence in Native American communities: The effects of intergenerational post traumatic stress.* Paper presented at the Veteran's Administration Conference on Post Traumatic Stress Disorder, Oklahoma City, OK.

Eisenbruch, M. (1991). From post traumatic stress disorder to cultural bereavement: Diagnosis of Southeast Asian refugees. *Social Sciences Medicine, 33,* 673-680.

Espino, C. M. (1991). Trauma and adaptation: The case of Central American children. In F. L. Ahearn & J. L. Athey (Eds.), *Refugee children: Theory, research, and services* (pp. 106-124). Baltimore, MD: John Hopkins University Press.

Essed, P. (1990). Black women's perceptions of racism in the Netherlands. *International Journal of Group Tension, 10,* 123-143.

Everstine, D. S., & Everstine, L. (1993). *The trauma response.* New York: Norton.

Figley, C. R. (1985). Introduction. In C. R. Figley (Ed.), *Trauma and its wake: The study and treatment of post-traumatic stress disorder* (pp. xvii-xvi). New York: Brunner/Mazel.

Fitzpatrick, K. M., & Boldizer, J. P. (1993). The prevalence and consequences of exposure to violence among African American youth. *Journal of Child and Adolescent Psychiatry, 32,* 424-430.

Foa, E. B., Steketee, G., & Olasoz-Rothbaum, B. (1989). Behavioral/cognitive conceptualizations of post-traumatic stress disorder. *Behavioral Therapy, 20,* 155-176.

Freud, S. (1966). *Introductory lectures on psychoanalysis.* New York: Liveright. (Original work published 1916)

Friere, P. (1979). *Pedagogy of the oppressed.* New York: Herder & Herder.

Garcia, M., & Lega, L. T. (1979). Development of a Cuban ethnic identity questionnaire. *Hispanic Journal of Behavioral Sciences, 1,* 247-261.

Gaw, A. C. (1993). *Culture, ethnicity and mental illness.* Washington, DC: American Psychiatric Association.

Green, B., Wilson, J. P., & Lindy, J. (1985). Conceptualizing post-traumatic stress disorder: A psychosocial framework. In C. R. Figley (Ed.), *Trauma and its wake: The study and treatment post-traumatic stress disorder* (pp. 66-93). New York: Bruner/Mazel.

Gusman, F. E., Stewart, J., Young, B. H., Rinely, S. J., Abueg, F. R., & Blake, D. D. (1996). A multicutlural developmental approach for treating trauma. In A. J. Marsella, M. J. Firedman, E. T. Gerrity, & R. M. Scurfield (Eds.), *Ethnocultural aspects of posttraumatic stress disorder* (pp. 439-458). Washington, DC: American Psychological Association.

Hall, G. C., Hirschman, R., Graham, J. R., & Zaragoza, M. S. (1993). *Sexual aggression: Issues in etiology, assessment, and treatment.* New York: Taylor & Francis.

Hatfield, M. O. (1990). Stress and the American worker. *The American Psychologist, 45,* 1162-1164.

Helms, J. E. (1990a). *Black and White racial identity theory, research, and practice.* Westport, CT: Greenwood.

Helms, J. E. (1990b). Three perspectives on counseling and psychotherapy with visible racial/ethnic minority clients. In F. C. Serafica, A. I. Schwebel, R. K. Russell, P. D. Isaac, & L. B. Myers (Eds.), *Mental health of ethnic minorities* (pp. 171-201). New York: Praeger.

Helms, J. E. (1995). An update of Helms's White and people of color racial identity models. In J. G. Ponterotto, J. M. Cass, L. A. Suzuki, & C. M. Alexander (Eds.), *Handbook of multicultural counseling* (pp. 181-198). Thousand Oaks, CA: Sage.

Henley, N. M. (1977). *Body politics: Power, sex, and nonverbal communication.* Englewood Cliffs, NJ: Prentice Hall.

Herman, J. L. (1990). Sex offenders: A feminist perspective. In W. L. Marshall, D. R. Laws, & H. E. Barbaree (Eds.), *Handbook of sexual assault: Issues, theories, and treatment of the offender* (pp. 177-193). New York: Plenum.

Hocking, F. (1970). Psychiatric aspects of extreme environmental stress. *Diseases of the Nervous System, 8,* 542-545.

Holtzworth-Munroe, A., Beatty, S. B., & Anglin, K. (1995). The assessment and treatment of marital violence: An introduction for the marital therapist. In N. S. Jacobson & A. S. Gurman (Eds.), *Clinical handbook of couple therapy* (pp. 317-339). New York: Guilford.

Horowitz, M. (1976). *Trauma and recovery.* New York: Basic Books.

Horowitz, M. (1979). Psychological response to serious life events. In V. Hamilton & D. M. Warburton (Eds.), *Human stress and cognition* (pp. 235-263). New York: John Wiley.

Horowitz, M. J. (1986). *Stress response syndromes* (2nd ed.). Northvale, NJ: Jason Aronson.

Horsman, R. (1981). *Race and manifest destiny.* Cambridge, MA: Harvard University Press.

Hough, R. L., Canino, G. J., Abueg, F. R., & Gusman, F. D. (1996). PTSD and related stress disorders among Hispanics. In A. J. Marsella, M. J. Firedman, E. T. Gerrity, & R. M. Scurfield

(Eds.), *Ethnocultural aspects of posttraumatic stress disorder* (pp. 209-238). Washington, DC: American Psychological Association.

Ibrahim, F. A. (1991). The contribution of cultural worldview to generic counseling and development. *Journal of Counseling and Development, 70,* 13-19.

Ibrahim, F. A. (1992a). Asian American women: Identity issues. *Women Studies Quarterly.*

Ibrahim, F. A. (1992b, April). *Identity development from a culture and gender perspective.* Symposium chaired at the annual meeting of the American Counseling Association, Baltimore, MD.

Ibrahim, F. A. (1993). Existential world view theory: Transcultural counseling. In J. McFadden (Ed.), *Transcultural counseling* (pp. 28-58). Alexandria, VA: American Counseling Association.

Ibrahim, F. A. (1994). Asian American women and suicidal behavior in Asian Americans. In S. Canetto & D. Lester (Eds.), *Women and suicidal behavior* (pp. 110-143). New York: Springer.

Ibrahim, F. A. (1998, April). *Assessment and treatment strategies for post traumatic stress disorder (PTSD): The minority experience.* Paper presented at the annual meeting of the American Counseling Association, Indianapolis, IN.

Ibrahim, F. A. (in press). Transcultural counseling: Existential world view theory and cultural identity. In J. McFadden (Ed.), *Transcultural counseling: Bilateral and international perspectives* (2nd ed.). Alexandria, VA: American Counseling Association.

Ibrahim, F. A., & Kahn, H. (1984). *Scale to assess world view.* Unpublished copy-written scale, University of Connecticut, Storrs.

Ibrahim, F. A., & Kahn, H. (1987). Assessment of world view. *Psychological Reports, 60,* 163-176.

Ibrahim, F. A., Ohnishi, H., & Sandhu, D. (1997). Asian American identity development: South Asian Americans. *Journal of Multicultural Counseling and Development, 25,* 34-50.

Ivey, A. E. (1995). Psychotherapy as liberation: Toward specific skills and strategies in multicultural counseling. In J. E. Ponterotto, J. M. Casas, L. A. Suzuki, & C. M. Alexander (Eds.), *Handbook of multicultural counseling* (pp. 53-72). Thousand Oaks, CA: Sage.

Janoff-Bulman, R. (1985). The aftermath of victimization: Rebuilding shattered assumptions. In C. R. Figley (Ed.), *Trauma and its wake* (pp. 36-61). New York: Brunner/Mazel.

Kardiner, A., & Ovesey, L. (1966). *The mark of oppression.* New York: Meridian.

Keane, T. M., & Wolfe, J. (1990). Comorbidity in post-traumatic stress disorder: An analysis of community and clinical studies. *Journal of Applied Social Psychology, 20,* 1776-1788.

Keita, G. P., & Jones, J. M. (1990). Reducing adverse reaction to stress in the work place. *American Psychologist, 45,* 1137-1141.

Kenrick, D. T., & Funder, D. (1988). Profiting from controversy: Lessons from the person-situation debate. *American Psychologist, 43,* 15-23.

Kitano, H. H. L. (1989). A model for counseling Asian Americans. In P. B. Pedersen, J. G. Draguns, W. J. Lonner, & J. E. Trimble (Eds.), *Counseling across cultures* (3rd ed., pp. 139-151). Honolulu: University of Hawaii Press.

Kleinknecht, R. A., & Morgan, M. P. (1992). Treatment of post-traumatic stress disorder with eye movement desensitization. *Journal of Behavior Therapy and Experimental Psychiatry, 23,* 43-50.

Koss, M. P., Goodman, L., Browne, A., Fitzgerald, L. F., Keit, G. P., & Russo, N. F. (1994). *No safe haven: Violence against women at home, at work, and in the community.* Washington, DC: American Psychological Association.

Krystle, H. (1978). Trauma and affects. *Psychoanalytical Study of Children, 33,* 81-116.

LaFromboise, T., Coleman, H. L. K., & Gerton, J. (1993). Psychological impact of biculturalism: Evidence and theory. *Psychological Bulletin, 114,* 395-412.

Lazarus, R. S., & Folkman, S. (1984). *Stress, appraisal and coping.* New York: Springer.

Lerner, G. (1986). *The creation of patriarchy.* New York: Oxford University Press.

Levin, C. (1993, July-August). The enigma of EMDR. *Family Therapy Networker,* pp. 75-83.

Lifton, R. J. (1976). *The life of the self.* New York: Simon & Schuster.

Lifton, R. J. (1979). *The broken connection.* New York: Simon & Schuster.

Lifton, R. J. (1988). Understanding the traumatized self: Imagery, symbolization, and transformation. In J. P. Wilson, Z. Harel, & B. Kahana (Eds.), *Human adaptation to extreme stress: From the Holocaust to Vietnam* (pp. 85-106). New York: Plenum.

Lin, K. -M. (1986). Psychopathology and social disruption in refugees. In C. L. Williams & J. L. Westermeyer (Eds.), *Refugee mental health in resettlement countries* (pp. 61-73). Washington, DC: Hemisphere.

Lipke, H., & Botkin, A. (1992). Brief case studies of eye movement desensitization and reprocessing with chronic post-traumatic stress disorder. *Psychotherapy, 29,* 591-595.

Lira, E., Becker, D., & Catillo, M. I. (1988, June). *Psychotherapy with victims of political repression in Chile: A therapeutic and political challenge.* Paper presented at meeting of the Latin American Institute of Mental Health and Human Rights, Santiago, Chile.

Litz, B. T. (1992). Emotional numbing in combat related post-traumatic stress disorder: A critical review and reformulation. *Clinical Psychology Review, 12,* 417-432.

Loo, C. M. (1993). An integrative-sequential model of treatment for PTSD: A case study of the Japanese American interment and redress. *Clinical Psychology Review, 13,* 89-117.

Loo, C. M. (1994). Race-related PTSD: The Asian American Vietnam veteran. *Journal of Traumatic Stress, 7,* 637-656.

Lorion, R. P., & Felner, R. D. (1986). Research on mental health interventions with the disadvantaged. In S. L. Garfield & A. E. Bergin (Eds.), *Handbook of psychotherapy and behavior change* (3rd ed., pp. 739-775). New York: John Wiley.

Mancuso, J. C. (1977). *Current motivational models in the elaboration of personal construct theory.* Lincoln: University of Nebraska Press.

Manion, S., Beals, J., O'Nell, T., Piasecki, J., Bechtold, D., Keane, E., & Jones, M. (1996). Wounded spirits, ailing hearts: PTSD and related disorders among Americans Indians. In A. J. Marsella, M. J. Friedman, E. T. Gerrity, & R. M. Schurfield (Eds.), *Ethnocultural aspects of posttraumatic stress disorder* (pp. 255-283). Washington, DC: American Psychological Association.

Marmar, C. R., & Horowitz M. J. (1988). Diagnosis and phase-oriented treatment of post-traumatic stress disorder. In J. P. Wilson, Z. Harel, & B. Kahana (Eds.), *Human adaptation to extreme stress: From the Holocaust to Vietnam* (pp. 48-65). New York: Plenum.

Marsella, A. J., Friedman, M. J., Gerrity, E. T., & Schurfield, R. M. (Eds.). (1996). *Ethnocultural aspects of posttraumatic stress disorder.* Washington, DC: American Psychological Association.

McCann, I. L., Sakheim, D. K., & Abrahamson, D. J. (1988). Trauma and victimization: A model of psychological adaptation. *Counseling Psychology, 16,* 531-594.

McGoldrick, M., Pearce, J. K., & Giordano, J. (1996). *Ethnicity and family therapy.* New York: Guilford.

McGuire, B. (1990). Post traumatic stress disorder: A review. *Irish Journal of Psychology, 11,* 1-23.

Miller, D. J., Goreczny, A. J., & Perconte, S. T. (1992). Comparison of symptom distress between World War II ex-POWs and Vietnam combat veterans with post-traumatic stress disorder. *Journal of Anxiety Disorders, 6,* 41-46.

Ogbu, J. U. (1979). Social stratification and socialization of competence. *Anthropology and Education Quarterly, 10,* 3-20.

Olmedo, E. (1979). Acculturation: A psychometric perspective. *American Psychologist, 34,* 1061-1070.

Padilla, A. M. (1980). *Acculturation: Theory, models, and some new findings.* Boulder, CO: Westview.

Parsons, E. R. (1985). The intercultural setting: Encountering Black Vietnam veterans. In S. Sonneberg, A. Blank, & J. Talbott (Eds.), *The trauma of war: Stress and recovery in Vietnam veterans* (pp. 361-387). Washington, DC: American Psychiatric Press.

Parsons, E. R. (1990). Post-traumatic psychocultural therapy (PTpsyCT): Integration of trauma and shattering social labels of the self. *Journal of Contemporary Psychotherapy, 20,* 237-258.

Paz, O. (1961). *The labyrinth of solitude, life and thought in Mexico.* New York: Grove.

Penk, W. E., & Allen, I. M. (1991). Clinical assessment of post-traumatic stress disorder (PTSD) among American minorities who served in Vietnam. *Journal of Traumatic Stress, 4,* 41- 66.

Pinderhughes, C. A. (1982). Paired differential bonding in biological, psychological, and social system. *American Journal of Social Psychiatry, 2,* 5-14.

Pinderhughes, C. A. (1986). The American racial dilemma: A social psychiatric formulation. *American Journal of Social Psychiatry, 6,* 107-113.

Portes, A., & Rumbaut, R. G. (1990). *Immigrant America: A portrait.* Berkeley: University of California Press.

Poston, S. S. C. (1990). The biracial identity development model: A needed addition. *Journal of Counseling and Development, 69,* 152-155.

Potts, M. K. (1994). Long-term effects of trauma: Post-traumatic stress among civilian internees of the Japanese during World War II. *Journal of Clinical Psychology, 50,* 681-698.

Price, J. A. (1975). An applied analysis of North American Indian drinking patterns. *Human Organization, 34,* 17-26.

Raphael, B. (1987). *When disaster strikes.* New York: Humanities Press.

Resnick, H. S., Foy, D. W., Donahue, C. P., & Miller, E. N. (1989). Antisocial behavior in post-traumatic stress disorder in Vietnam veterans. *Journal of Clinical Psychology, 45,* 860-866.

Robin, R. W., Chester, B., & Goldman, D. (1996). Cumulative trauma among Native Americans. In A. J. Marsella, M. J. Friedman, E. T. Gerrity, & R. M. Scurfield (Eds.), *Ethnocultural aspects of posttraumatic stress disorder* (pp. 239-253). Washington, DC: American Psychological Association.

Root, M. P. P. (1992). Reconstructing the impact of trauma on personality. In L. S. Brown & M. Ballou (Eds.), *Personality and psychopathology* (pp. 229-625). New York: Guilford.

Root, M. P. P. (1993). Reconstructing the impact of trauma on personality. In M. Ballou & L. Brown (Eds.), *Theories of personality and psychopathology: Feminist reappraisal* (pp. 25-48). New York: Guilford.

Root, M. P. P. (1996). Women of color and traumatic stress in "domestic captivity": Gender and race as disempowering status. In A. J. Marsella, M. J. Firedman, E. T. Gerrity, & R. M. Scurfield (Eds.), *Ethnocultural aspects of posttraumatic stress disorder* (pp. 363-387). Washington, DC: American Psychological Association.

Sandoval, C. (1990). Feminism and racism: A report on the 1981 National Women's Studies Association Conference. In G. Anzaldua (Ed.), *Making face, making soul (Haciendo caras): Creative and critical perspectives by women of color* (pp. 55-71). San Francisco: Aunt Lute.

Schaef, A. W. (1987). *When society becomes an addict.* New York: Norton.

Schlenger, W. E., Kulka, R. A., Fairbank, J. A., & Hough, R. L. (1992). The prevalence of post-traumatic stress disorder in the Vietnam generation: A multimodal, multisource, assessment of psychiatric disorder. *Journal of Traumatic Stress, 5,* 333-363.

Shapiro, F. (1989). Eye movement desensitization: A new treatment for post-traumatic stress disorder. *Journal of Behavior Therapy and Experimental Psychiatry, 20,* 211-217.

Sodowsky, G. R., Lai, E. W., & Plake, B. S. (1991). Moderating effects of socio-cultural variables on acculturation attitudes of Hispanics and Asian Americans. *Journal of Counseling and Development, 70,* 76-86.

Spector, J., & Huthwaite, M. (1993). Eye-movement desensitization to overcome post-traumatic stress disorder. *British Journal of Psychiatry, 163,* 106-108.

Staats, A. W. (1968a). *Learning language, and cognition.* New York: Holt, Rinehart & Winston.

Staats, A. W. (1968b). Social behaviorism and human motivation: Principles of the attitude-reinforce discriminative system. In A. G. Greenwald, T. C. Brock, & T. M. Ostrom (Eds.), *Psychological foundations of attitudes* (pp. 33-66). New York: Academic Press.

Staats, A. W. (1975). *Social behaviorism.* Homewood, IL: Dorsey.

Stonequist, E. B. (1935). The problem of the marginal man. *American Journal of Sociology, 14,* 1-12.

Streissguth, A. P., LaDue, R. A., & Randels, S. P. (1988). *A manual on adolescents and adults with fetal alcohol syndrome with special reference to American Indians.* Seattle: University of Washington, Department of Psychiatry and Behavioral Sciences.

Sue, D. W. (1981). *Counseling the culturally different: Theory and practice.* New York: John Wiley.

Sue, D. W., & Sue, D. (1991). *Counseling the culturally different* (2nd ed.). New York: John Wiley.

Taft, R. (1977). Coping with unfamiliar cultures. In N. Warren (Ed.), *Studies in cross-cultural psychology* (pp. 121-151). London: Academic Press.

Takaki, R. (1993). *A different mirror.* Boston: Little, Brown.

Triandis, H. C., Bontempo, R., Villareal, M. J., Assai, M., & Lucca, N. (1988). Individualism and collectivism: Cross-cultural perspectives on self-in-group relationships. *Journal of Personality and Social Psychology, 54,* 323-338.

Trimble, M. R. (1981). *Post-traumatic neurosis.* Chicester, UK: Wiley.

Trimble, M. R. (1985). Post-traumatic stress disorder: History of a concept. In C. R. Figley (Ed.), *Trauma and its wake: The study and treatment of post-traumatic stress disorder* (pp. 5-14). New York: Bruner/Mazel.

Uba, L. (1994). *Asian Americans.* New York: Guilford.

Valentine, C. A. (1971). Deficit, difference, and bicultural models of Afro-American behavior. *Harvard Educational Review, 41,* 137-157.

van der Kolk, B. A. (1987). *Psychological trauma.* Washington, DC: American Psychiatric Association.

Weisner, T. S., Weibel-Orlando, J. C., & Long, J. (1994). "Serious drinking," "White man's drinking," and "tee totaling": Drinking level and styles in an urban American Indian population. *Journal of Studies on Alcohol, 45,* 237-250.

West, C. (1993). *Race matters.* Boston: Beacon Press.

Wierzbicki, M., & Pecarik, G. (1993). A meta-analysis of psychotherapy dropout. *Professional Psychology: Research and Practice, 24,* 190-195.

Wilson, J. P. (1989). *Trauma, transformation and healing: An integrative approach to theory, research, and post-traumatic therapy.* New York: Bruner/Mazel.

Wilson, S. A., Becker, L. A., & Tinker, R. H. (1995). Eye movement desensitization and reprocessing (EMDR) treatment for psychologically traumatized individuals. *Journal of Consulting and Clinical Psychology, 63,* 928-937.

Wolpe, J., & Abrams, J. (1991). Post-traumatic stress disorder overcome by eye movement desensitization: A case report. *Journal of Behavior and Experimental Psychiatry, 22,* 39-43.

Word, C. O., Zanna, M. P., & Cooper, J. (1974). The nonverbal mediation of self-fulfilling prophecies in interracial interaction. *Journal of Experiential Social Psychology, 10,* 109-120.

Yates, A. (1987). Current status and future directions of research on the American Indian child. *American Journal of Psychiatry, 144,* 1135-1142.

CHAPTER

6

EXPANDING OUR
UNDERSTANDING OF
MULTICULTURALISM

Developing a Social Class
Worldview Model

William M. Liu
University of Iowa

Multiculturalism seeks to understand people within their context (Leach & Carlton, 1997) (e.g., race, culture, gender, and class). But among the many contextual factors that are related to a person's lived experiences, social class seems to be one of the least understood constructs in psychology (Frable, 1997). Although the extant literature agrees that social class is a pervasive and important dimension of a person's life that must be understood and examined, often social class is treated as a singular variable and used to infer a person's social class "thinking."

We do know that social class or socioeconomic status (SES) is linked to almost every area of a person's life. For example, SES is related to occupational attainment (Geoghehan, 1997; Hacker, 1997; Hollingshead, 1975), job satisfaction (National Institutes of Mental Health [NIMH], 1995), disordered eating (Thompson, 1994), educational achievement (So, 1987; Wright, 1978), intelligence (Brody, 1997; Ceci & Williams, 1997), acculturation (Sodowsky, Lai, & Plake, 1991), interracial relationships (Jo, 1992), tobacco and alcohol use (Adler et al., 1994), and physical activity (Adler et al., 1994). SES is also related to major risk factors involved in mental illness (e.g., stress, lack of social relationships, etc.), such that mental illness seems to be more prevalent among those in the lower classes (NIMH, 1995). Thus, treatment of mental illness should be sensitive to SES.

In counseling, SES has been associated with the effectiveness of therapy (Carter, 1991; Ivey, Ivey, & Simek-Morgan, 1993; Katz, 1985; Sue, Ivey, & Pedersen, 1996), career counseling (Luzzo, 1992), the supervision relationship (Brown & Landrum-Brown, 1995), service delivery (Brabeck, Walsh, Kenny, & Comilang, 1997; Carlson & Rosser-Hogan, 1993; Nicks, 1985), hospitalization and treatment (Bulhan, 1985), and diagnosis (Adler et al., 1994; Eaton & Muntaner, 1999). SES is also a factor in counseling values in that middle-class values such as time-limited therapy, verbal ability, appointment keeping, and psychological mindedness (Sue & Sue, 1990) may all be related to how well the therapeutic relationship evolves as well as to the counseling outcome. The pervasiveness of middle-class values may extend from the areas counselors are typically employed. Arguably, a privileged population skews counseling's science and practice (Sue, 1999), and because many counseling psychologists seem to be employed in departments of psychology, counseling, and educational psychology at colleges and universities (33.9%); in independent practice (21.5%); or in university counseling centers (17.8%) (Watkins, Lopez, Campbell, & Himmell study, as cited in Gelso & Fretz, 1992, p. 14), counseling psychology practice may be biased. The remaining 26.8% of counseling psychologists are employed at community mental health care centers, general and mental hospitals, outpatient clinics, and medical schools (Watkins et al. study, as cited in Gelso & Fretz, 1992). Because SES is such a pervasive factor in counseling, it would be beneficial to explore the complexities of SES and how it affects counseling relationships, treatment, and outcome.

In research, SES has been problematically defined and explored, and hence SES has been difficult to understand (Frable, 1997). The extant literature often uses SES as a descriptor for research participants (e.g., the participants were all middle class) or as a variable to control for deviation among other constructs (Frable, 1997). Typically, the problem of SES in research emerges from (a) the subjective identification method (e.g., "what class do you think you belong to?"), which seems to invite uncontrolled variation in how people interpret class distinctions, or (b) the linking of descriptor variables (e.g., income) to a static class status (e.g., middle class). Consequently, the problem is that researchers may not explore the variability within each of the socioeconomic groups. Instruments that have attempted to assess social status and SES are problematic because they may be too general, use occupation as the main indicator for social status, or measure prestige (Miller, 1964). All these current methods of measuring social class complicate our understanding because within-group variation is usually not explored.

The problem with SES in research reflects the multiple ways that SES is defined. Proposed definitions of SES often include prestige, power, income, wealth and property, in-group and out-group behavior, lifestyle, and leisure and consumption behavior (Argyle, 1994). The variables considered range from objective indicators of class such as income and educational level to perceptual variables such as power, prestige, and lifestyle. With such a multiplicity of intrapsychic and external variables, a clear understanding of how people construct their social class and perceive their social class world is difficult to discern. In addition, many of the samples used do not reflect the general U.S. population (e.g., convenient sampling of college students or individuals with college degrees), which poses a limitation on research applicability (Fitzgerald & Betz, 1994). Consequently, these counseling and research concerns may not only influence the applicability of counseling theories, but if psychology does not respond to these issues, the field may become obsolete as a resource for many people (Hall, 1997).

Because SES is a variable in counseling and research and has been problematically operationalized in the past, researchers need to explore and refine SES to better understand it. Thus, to take on the task of articulating a clearer understanding of SES, I will discuss some historical considerations of SES and provide a brief overview of how SES has been conceptualized and studied in the sociological literature. Second, I will discuss the literature on the role SES has in psychological research. In addition, I will attempt to bridge sociological and psychological research to expose areas that are not covered. From the literature reviews, one will start to understand the number of different variables that have been linked to SES and how these elements may be useful in redefining SES. Third, a critique of previous models of SES will help elucidate the strengths and limitations of, and what has been learned from, the preceding research. Fourth, I will attempt to rethink SES as an intrapsychic cognitive process called the *social class worldview model (SCWM)* and provide a case example for illustration. Finally, I will provide counseling implications and considerations for future research.

The Current Understanding of SES and Class

This chapter focuses on rearticulating the understanding of SES and exploring SES as a phenomenological experience (i.e., SES subjectivity). Many issues surrounding SES are contentious and debatable, but others are not. For example, there are clear correlations between one's economic and monetary resources with good mental health (Triandis, 1989), educational opportunities, and life expectancy (Adler et al., 1994). The goal of this chapter is to stretch definitions of SES and investigate the way people make sense and think of their world according to SES. Because it appears that "social class" operates from indices such as income, occupation, and education, many previous attempts to understand a person's social class have been predicated on these areas. These narrower definitions of SES usually employ class-demographic variables (e.g., level of income, level of education, and type of occupation), which are assumed to be objective measures to assess one's SES. The class-demographic variables appear to be interval or ratio measurement-level variables but are likely to be ordinal level. That is, at the ordinal level of measurement, there is an agreed-on difference in the levels, but the difference between the levels is unclear and open to subjectivity.

Earlier definitions using class-demographic variables also typically situate people into a particular "class" and assume homogeneity in how they define and interpret the meaningfulness of income, education, and occupation within their class. The assumption is that people have agreed to a common definition and understanding of these class-demographic variables (i.e., everyone agrees to the importance of education) and have a common understanding of what it takes to belong to a particular "class" (i.e., one should make $45,000 and have a "white-collar" job to belong in the middle class). The challenge is to examine the assumption of homogeneity within "classes" and to explore how SES is made meaningful in people's lives.

Underlying most SES theories are the historical contexts in which they are created. For instance, Karl Marx's theory of class in the late 19th century is highly influenced by the Industrial Revolution and by the societal and cultural changes occurring at the time (Gilbert & Kahl, 1993). According to Marx, societies are "shaped by their economic organization" (Gilbert & Kahl, 1993, p. 4), and individuals within these stratified classes reflect their relationship to modes of production and capital. Thus, the capitalists or bourgeoisie own the means of production, and the workers or proletariat have to "sell their labor" to earn a living wage (Gilbert & Kahl, 1993).

During the same era, another sociologist, Max Weber, also critiqued class, ideology, and economic processes (Gilbert & Kahl, 1993). Weber distinguishes between class and status, defining class as "groupings of people according to their economic position. Class situation or membership is defined by the economic opportunities and life chances an individual has in the labor, commodity, and credit markets" (Gilbert & Kahl, 1993, p. 8). Weber defines status as a shared lifestyle and opportunity between people in a certain social class. These lifestyles and opportunities stratify people within the same class; for example, although a professor and a plumber may make the same income (class), they have different lifestyles and occupy different statuses. Lifestyles are then linked to the life chances and the kinds of social class mobility that one has. In effect, then, although income may help to situate a person within a particular class, other variables (e.g., lifestyle and opportunity) play a role in prestige, mobility, and life chances.

One of the problems with Marx's and Weber's theories stems from the historical contexts of their original writings. Pervasive in the industrial era was the castelike stratification of peoples. However, today, social classes in the United States are perceived to be more permeable. In addition, Marx and Weber failed to fully account for the impact of race and gender on social class, and in the United States, these theories are limited in application. These initial theories also posit static class and status positions from which people exist and operate. One thing that is clear from Weber's definition is that class and status operate interdependently on each other, even though they may mean different things. In essence, it seems that Weber is describing "classes" within a "class," even while using different words to describe this stratification. This confusion in terminology is reflected in the extant literature wherein the terms *class* and *status* are used interchangeably.

Confusing terminology aside, Marx and Weber do provide valuable insights into the architecture of social stratification. For both theorists, these classes or statuses are hypothetically framed by nonpermeable boundaries between classes, and stratification operates from larger social pressures. It is believed that people act according to the norms of each class and status, such that the maintenance of their class position is important. People also believe that their class position is important through the development of class consciousness, which, Marx and Weber argue, arises from class positions, revolution, and resistance to class oppression. But still, this theory is problematic because it assumes people are relatively homogeneous in class consciousness within that class or status.

Another concern left virtually unexplored by Marx and Weber are the number of different factors involved in the way people form their impression about class and status (which will be discussed later). Although social scientists have taken on the challenge of exploring SES and have attempted to develop a clearer definition, most of the extant literature refers to SES, class, or both. This confusing use of SES, class, and status as interchangeable descriptors of a complex phenomenon only led to greater confusion and a "less clear" understanding of SES. To be consistent and clear throughout this chapter, socioeconomic status and class (SESC) will refer to the current use and understanding throughout the literature review. SESC pertains to the various ways a person's class-demographic characteristics influence his or her experiences, worldview, and position in a social hierarchy. The use of SESC does not necessarily involve other variables that may affect one's SCWM, such as saliency of social class, the awareness or attitudes of one's SESC, lifestyle, or relationship with cohorts. Instead, SESC reflects the current understanding and use in research. *Social class issues* will refer to knowledge of economic inequality, discrimination, and stratification and how these issues are incorporated into a person's worldview. *Lower class* alludes to those who may be employed in menial labor (unskilled or semiskilled) or not working at all (impoverished) (Argyle, 1994). *Working class* typically refers to people employed in "blue-collar" occupations, whereas *middle* and *upper class* often imply people in "white-collar" or professional work (nonmanual labor) (Argyle, 1994).

Multiple Determinants of SESC

Elements of SESC

Most of the current literature focuses on how stratification occurs or how individuals respond to social class issues as a function of their SESC. Much of the understanding developed for psychological research has been distilled from sociological literature, but the problem for psychology is that sociologists often focus on the macroeffects rather than intrapsychic or microeffects of SESC. Nevertheless, psychology can build an understanding of SESC from the sociological literature. In order to elucidate the conditions that create stratification and link macro- and intrapsychic effects in the United States, Gilbert and Kahl (1993) propose nine different variables. The first three variables are economic variables: occupation, income, and wealth. The next three variables center on (a) a person's status and personal prestige (e.g., prestige may come from having the respect of neighbors; deference from others), (b) association (e.g., interacting with those in the same social class), and (c) socialization, or the "process through which an individual learns the skills, attitudes, and customs needed to participate in the life of the community" (p. 13). The third set of two variables is related to the politics of stratification and focuses on power and class consciousness. Power is defined as "the potential of individuals or groups to carry out their will even over the opposition of others" (p. 13), and class consciousness is the "degree to which people at a given level in the stratification system are aware of themselves as a distinctive group with shared political and economic interests" (p. 13). The ninth variable focuses on the concept of succession and mobility. This concept examines the manner in which children inherit their parents' class position (succession) and the opportunity to ascend the class system (mobility) (p. 14).

Perhaps the best example of familial transmission of SESC may be seen through a perusal of *The New York Times* marriage announcements section. The short biographies for each couple contain pertinent social class information, such as parents' occupation and education and the brides' and grooms' occupations and educational levels. The information provided (a) establishes the economic and educational status of the families, their personal prestige, the people in their cohort, and the culture they inhabit and (b) perhaps predicts how the couple will carry on or succeed their SESC position.

Family, Peer, and Cohort Groups

From the other variables that Gilbert and Kahl (1993) delineated, it appears that cohorts, association, and socialization patterns are important in shaping how people understand their SESC and the SESC of others. Another function of these cohort and peer groups seems to be the establishment of norms for behaviors and attitudes (Kelly & Evans, 1995). These cohort referent groups assist the person in believing that he or she is normal or prototypical of that group. To that end, the person begins to see himself or herself as average within that group because the person is able to locate others who are "above" and "below" him or her, which allows the person to infer relative "middleness" within the SESC group (Kelly & Evans, 1995). Therefore, when people speak of middleness or middle classhood, they may be implying that they are in the "middle" of their cohort group and not necessarily "middle class" with regard to the class-demographic indices. Furthermore, if people use their immediate cohorts to define *middle classhood,* then it follows that multiple interpretations of middle classhood would appear to be independent of income level. For instance, one could imagine that developing a political consensus among the middle class would be difficult if New York Governor George Pataki believes that the middle class are those households making $175,000 a year (Roberts, 1997), whereas President Clinton's cohort group consists of those with assets ranging from $600,000 to $35 million (Babcock & Saffir, 1997). With the average American household making $35,492 per year (Vobejda & Chandler, 1997), conflicting worldviews seem inevitable.

If there are multiple interpretations of what constitutes middle class, what could possibly weave together all these potentially disparate views? One possible answer may be the ideology that the middle class subscribes to reflect the "American Dream" of class mobility and equality of life opportunities achieved through personal effort and thrift. This ideology is important because when "everyone has a fair chance of gaining admission to social groups with various status positions . . . status differences between groups are felt to be legitimate" (Ellemers, Knippenberg, & Wilke, 1990, p. 245). Without such ideology, the reality of class stratification in the United States would probably create class conflict (Takaki, 1993) and fracture any attempt to develop consensus. Thus, the American Dream ideology seems to help people make sense of their SESC environment and is probably most potent when the cohort group members reinforce each other about the ideology.

Cultural, Human, and Social Capital

Another role of the peer group is to shape how a person conceptualizes and interprets his or her SESC environment through personal and social networks and socialization. Determining his or her SESC environment allows the individual to define the "culture" and "values" of the group (Erikson, 1996; Walker, 1995). That is, it is assumed that every "culture" has a value system, and people are indoctrinated into these cultural value systems. These cultural value systems not only evaluate the worth of material belongings (e.g., brand of car) but also place worth on personal characteristics (e.g., skin color, educational level). Because cultural value systems may be unique to specific cohort and peer groups, one's sense of worth may be limited to that particular culture at a specific time. Thus, people develop a kind of "cultural capital" that has currency within a particular cultural value system, and the cultural capital then helps to establish the mobility one has within that SESC group.

Another way to look at cultural capital is by examining how cultural capital differs between people and groups. For example, language is a form of capital and has been used to demarcate urban from rural peoples (Argyle, 1994; Giles & Copeland, 1991; Tyler, 1989). Those from "lower classes" are perceived to use language that has less concrete information, fewer illustrations, and is more egocentric (Schatzman & Strauss, 1955) than the language of more affluent "classes." Thus, if someone were to move from a lower-class group to a higher one, the individual would have to cultivate the language styles of the higher-class group to "fit in" or "pass" as a member of that class group. Other forms of cultural capital that differentiate between people and groups may be one's family, neighborhood, or style of dress. People learn to negotiate these differences to either hide or accentuate class distinctions.

Cultural capital is confusing because it includes objective (e.g., language) and subjective (e.g., peer group) resources of a person. One way to better understand cultural capital may be to discriminate between the elements within cultural capital. Thus, other forms of capital that individuals may possess are social capital and human capital (Lin, 1999). Human capital can be described as qualities that individuals develop, refine, and invest in that allow them access to greater resources and an opportunity toward social mobility (Lin, 1999). Examples of human capital are education, occupational experience, and interpersonal skills. Social capital, though, consists of interpersonal contacts and ties that also allow a person access to greater resources and upward social mobility (Lin, 1999). Examples of social capital are connections that people may have as a result of their family's economic status, the parents' occupations, and social networks. Lin (1999) argues that although human capital is important, most good jobs obtained by people are a result of networking rather than the merits of an individual's human capital. Consequently, those who have low social capital also need to invest monies into developing human capital. Those with high social capital are likely to have high human capital because they may have better access to educational and occupational resources and better training, and they associate in circles of peers who enhance their social capital (Lin, 1999). Lin suggests that human capital has the greatest impact on an individual when social capital is low, and human capital has the least influence on a person's life when social capital is high. That is, the returns on human capital decrease as social capital increases (Lin, 1999).

Illustrating the importance of human and social capital, Weiss (2000) reported a developing problem over the Scholastic Aptitude Test (SAT). He found that many time extensions on the SAT are now given to middle-class White men who have been recently diagnosed with a learning disability. With extra time, the likelihood that a better score increased (i.e., human capital). Weiss (2000) discovered that this diagnosis and time extension were far more likely among White middle-class men than among the racial minority students in public schools (Weiss, 2000). Social capital was most apparent in this group as Weiss (2000) described how parents who shopped for psychologists who gave diagnoses of a learning disorder were referred to other parents wanting the same diagnoses.

Materialism

One's social class may be related to the meaningfulness of money in his or her life (Furnham & Argyle, 1998). But ownership of money is not the only significant way to mark a person's social class. Rather, symbols of one's monetary worth are often as important as money. Thus, the drive to own symbols of money and class is defined as materialism (Furnham & Argyle, 1998). A statement such as, "Brand names are very important" (Faludi, 1999, p. 110) reflects an individual's attention toward markers of social prestige, one's SESC social group, and mobility. Yet often, the drive to own these symbols and status to fill an emotional void leaves the pursuer frustrated and depressed (Furnham & Argyle, 1998). Dittmar (1992) reports a study that found people who rated high on a measure of materialism often were "less happy, and they were more often disappointed or anxious after buying things" (p. 164). One could infer that the expectancy of emotional fulfillment could stir feelings of anxiety learned from previous failures.

Materialism is not a unique concept for only Western countries. Ger and Belk (1996) found that among a sample of 1,729 college students from France, Britain, Germany, the United States, Sweden, Turkey, New Zealand, Israel, Romania, Ukraine, Thailand, and India, those who were the most "materialistic" were not necessarily from Westernized nations. What is materialism, though? Richins and Rudmin (1994) state that when people put material possessions and the acquisition of material objects as the most important part of feeling satisfied with their lives and feeling well and judging their own and others' success by their possessions, then they may be described as materialistic.

Those who may be described as materialistic can be dissatisfied with their lives because they establish a standard of living for themselves that is based on referent groups that are far removed from their current situation (Sirgy, 1998). Some researchers have found that individuals from disrupted families are often more materialistic and prone to compulsive consumption than those from intact families (Rindfleisch, Burroughs, & Denton, 1997). Consequently, those prone to materialism may already feel dissatisfied with their lives, and the pursuit of material objects allows avoidance of their sadness.

Classism

Classism is defined here as prejudice and discrimination based on social class resulting from individuals from different perceived social classes. Classism is not only a downward phenomenon in that perceived higher-class individuals are prejudiced toward lower classes, but classism can also occur from lower to upper classes. Classism may be such a significant oppressing force that people struggling to adapt to perceived classism in their environment experience anxiety and stress.

One example of how people negotiate these markers of class distinction comes from a study by Granfield (1991). In this study of law students from lower- and working-class backgrounds within a prestigious private law school, Granfield found multiple strategies employed by students that allowed them to "pass" as middle-class and upper-class students (i.e., the peer or cohort group they existed within and aspired to be). He speculated that that the transition from one context to another (i.e., lower to upper class) accentuated the students' feelings of inadequacy to cope in this new environment (Frable, 1997). That is, this movement made it apparent for some of these lower- and working-class students that they needed to learn the cultural norms and expectations of their new cohort and peer group. The students may have felt inadequate because they did not know how to make sense of their new environment and peer group or how to make sense of new SESC information. These students reported feeling a dissonance between their SESC and their current environment, as well as a sense of "class stigma" that created SESC identity conflicts (Granfield, 1991). Students feeling this conflict often learned to negotiate these SESC hurdles by hiding their SESC of origin, as well as by finding various ways to blend into their new surroundings. For some of these students, blending in (i.e., passing) often meant buying new clothes or taking on middle- and upper-class mannerisms (Granfield, 1991). For other students, their working- and lower-class backgrounds became a source of empowerment, such that they would purposely wear unprofessional clothing or act in ways that conflicted with the "upper-class" cultural norm (Granfield, 1991). Consequently, although students believed in and valued a good education, they were also aware of their cultural capital deficiencies. They were motivated to find appropriate coping mechanisms to feel a part of the school's culture and assist their matriculation. For these students from a "lower" economic background, SESC issues became salient when they entered a prestigious school and interacted with a new cohort group. These students employed various strategies to cope with their sense of "stigma." The coping strategy ranged in behavior and attitude from aligning with the cultural expectations to maintaining the distance in the SESC between themselves and their law school cohorts.

Moving from class to class also can have certain effects on women. For instance, when women moved from lower classes to higher classes, there was a tendency for more disordered eating to occur (Thompson, 1994). Thompson (1994) speculates that ideals of beauty change from class to class, such that thinness was valued as a part of middle-class culture, and their status was dependent on upholding this aesthetic. Another example of class stigma, as a result of moving from a higher class to a lower class, is from a study by Grella (1990). She looked at the impact that divorce has on women's SESC standing and found that divorced women appear to experience a real economic and subjective decline in their SESC status and often encounter a kind of "class" stigma resulting from their drop in status (Grella, 1990). Grella notes that the women experiencing the economic decline and class stigma reported feelings of depression and anxiety.

Social class stigma or classism also has a relationship to intellectual performance. Croizet and Claire (1998) found among 128 undergraduates from poor backgrounds that when they were presented with a test of "intellectual ability," these students tended to perform more poorly than when they were presented with the same exam that was described as a nondiagnostic assessment of intellectual ability. The authors speculate that students from poor backgrounds are aware of the stigma they carry, and this susceptibility to a stereotype impaired their performance. Thus, the stigma of being from lower classes, an internalized oppression, can be activated in a seemingly innocuous environment.

The Protestant Work Ethic Attitude

An important component in how an individual determines his or her SESC attitude is the subscription to the Protestant work ethic (PWE). The PWE has been shown to be an underlying construct in much of the extant literature on SESC (Furnham, 1984). The PWE can be defined as a construct with the following components: asceticism (thrift), hard work and self-discipline, postponement of gratification, control over one's life, frugality, and conservative political sentiments (Furnham, 1984; Mirels & Darland, 1990).

Some argue that as a person gets higher in the social hierarchy, he or she is more likely to endorse the PWE and a sense that status differences are legitimate (Argyle, 1994; Heaton, 1987). This may be especially true if one also believes that there are no barriers to gaining admission to any status group and that mobility within the structure is relatively unencumbered (Ellemers et al., 1990). In one study of 119 college students and the PWE, results showed that those who endorse the PWE were also likely to score high on scales of achievement, endurance, willpower, self-discipline, and order (Mirels & Darland, 1990). Conversely, those who scored high on the PWE scored low in impulsiveness and autonomy (Mirels & Darland, 1990).

The PWE also has been associated with the type of attributions made toward someone who is poor or impoverished. Middle-class individuals tended to make attributions that focused on personality dispositions (e.g., the problem of the poor is due to their lack of effort and ability), whereas lower- or working-class individuals tended to make attributions that addressed the situation (e.g., the problem with being poor is due to prejudice and low wages) (Argyle, 1994; Furnham, 1984; Segalman, 1968).

For those who embrace the PWE attitude, certain "cultural" messages about SESC and social class issues were probably transmitted when growing up. If this person has chosen to adopt these PWE cultural messages, then the likelihood of having a lifestyle that reflects the values of the PWE is high. Similarly, these individuals are also inclined to associate with others who are compatible and reaffirm their attitudes and worldview. Hence, such attitudes may be a function of socialization and of how one interacts with a cohort group.

Sesc and psychology

SESC, Counseling, Research, and Mental Health Issues

In psychological research, Jones and Thorne (1987) propose that SESC is an important dimension to study because there is tremendous in-group variability that occurs along educational or economic lines. Thus, if SESC is not attended to or explicated, then it becomes difficult to determine what underlies particular psychological phenomena (Jones & Thorne, 1987; Kagitcibasi, 1989). Even with this recommendation, Graham (1992) found that SESC was not always reported in psychological studies. She concluded that SESC should always be reported; especially "in comparative racial studies, the reporting of SES information should be mandatory" (Graham, 1992, p. 638). Problematically, though, even when SESC information is reported, Helms (1992) argues that income (an index of a person's SESC) may have different meaning in Black and White groups. If these differences are indeed real, then it would be prudent to redefine between-group differences.

Extant research on SESC and mental health has shown that SESC is related to several counseling issues (Adler et al., 1994). Attrition from therapy (Garfield, 1994; Mays, 1985; Sue & Sue, 1990) and depression (Ying, 1988), for example, may be related to SESC. Those clients who live in poverty may expect more pragmatic advice than focus on insight (Garfield, 1994; Sue & Sue, 1990) and may have difficulty keeping appointments (Atkinson, Morten, & Sue, 1993; Garfield, 1994; Sue & Sue, 1990). Furthermore, those clients from lower economic backgrounds also have been diagnosed more frequently with character disorders or psychoses than upper-income individuals (Beutler, Machado, & Neufeldt, 1994; Haase, cited in Bulhan, 1985), and lower SES individuals have suffered less resolution of their counseling issues (Hillerbrand, 1988). Counselors should then be aware of the SESC biases they may possess and how these biases affect the therapy relationship and process (Robinson, 1993).

Because SESC contributes to the therapeutic relationship, it is important to understand the impact. In a study of counseling dyads that examined the effects of race and SESC, 12 White and African American participants were asked to judge a hypothetical client and counselor dyad on various dimensions such as attraction, skill of the counselor, cognitive similarity between client and counselor, helpfulness of the counselor, and counselor's valuing of the client. The hypothetical dyads were either same race or mixed race, and the client and counselor could be from the lower, middle, or upper class. The results showed that when the study participants believed the client and counselor were of the same race and SESC, the various dimensions (e.g., helpfulness and skill of the counselor) were rated high; when the client and counselor were dissimilar in race and SESC, the participants judged lower on the dimensions (Sladen, 1982). The study may show that people, using themselves as a gauge, perceive race and SESC to be important components in the way people relate to each other, and incongruence in either or both dimensions (i.e., people from different cohort groups) can lead to potential conflict or a poor therapeutic relationship.

Another concern about SESC for counseling psychologists is the area of career counseling. SESC seems to be a significant "lens" through which people understand the world of work (Sharf, 1992; Tracey, 1997). However, the current understanding of career issues from research may be limited due to the sample used in most career research (i.e., college students). Fitzgerald and Betz (1994) note that 25% of the workforce have college degrees, yet 80% of the career research is based on college students and other professionals. These authors point out that it "is fair to say that we know almost nothing about the career choice process in the majority of the population: those who do not attend college, are not White, and are of lower socioeconomic status" (p. 106). Consequently, counseling psychology finds itself unprepared to serve the non-college-educated population. Other limitations of career theories may be that individuals who are struggling for economic survival are less likely to view self-actualization and self-realization as a goal (Fitzgerald & Betz, 1994) and may find career counseling not applicable to their daily lives. Thus, because there may be such differences in the values placed on the goals or rationale of career counseling, contemporary career theories need to be transformed to reflect and respond to a greater range of clients.

The Relationship Between One's Group of Origin and SESC

SESC may influence a person's early experiences and expectations of the environment. Children, as young as those in kindergarten, have shown an awareness to social class distinctions (King, 1997). The notion that children are aware of social class and potentially behave in classist ways is important. The literature until now has explored the meaning of social class among adults where indices such as income, education, and occupation level are associated with subjective SESC. However, if children are aware of social class distinctions, and because they operate relatively absent of income, education, and occupational distinctions, then a subjective social class schema can exist without a strict adherence to adult indices of social class. The class research on children highlights the importance of socialization messages about social class and how people may use that information to construct a framework to understand their social class world. Just as important, though, is people's perception of social class, which acts as a foundation from which people act on their environment and thus create social class.

Because parent-child relationships affect the ways children perceive their SESC environment, children often perpetuate the social class worldview of their parents (Tulkin, 1973; Tulkin & Kagan, 1972). For example, Kohn (cited in Bronfenbrenner, 1986) found that working-class men who had to comply with authority in the workplace stressed obedience as a value, whereas middle-class men who were given some autonomy in the workplace expected their children to be self-directed and independent. Those parents in occupations characteristic of the working class (e.g., highly supervised, not autonomous) may have a sense of hopelessness and alienation that "undermines beliefs about the possibility of control in other aspects of life" (NIMH, 1995, p. 106). As a result, these "working-class" parents may be less "emotionally supportive . . . [and less] able to provide them [children] with responsible, stimulating environments" (NIMH, 1995, p. 106). Children in these different environments may then inculcate the values and beliefs of their parents about work, the world, and their own self-efficacy and future opportunities.

As the children grow, early economic and environmental deficiencies affect how they perform in school and further affect their sense of SESC. In a study of 398 mid-grade adolescents (45% were male and 51% of the sample were White) from a poor rural area, economic disadvantage was inversely related to academic and socioemotional development. Youth in homes with parents who held low-skill and low-income jobs performed more poorly than youth from homes with parents who were semiprofessional and semiskilled (Felner et al., 1995). The youth with parents of a low occupational status reported greater maternal rejection and feelings of alienation in school and experienced major stressful events when compared to those youth with parents of a higher occupational status (Felner et al., 1995). With all of these external stressors, children from environments of economic disadvantage may be more aggressive than those who are not economically disadvantaged (Guerra, Huesmann, Tolan, Van Acker, & Eron, 1995). Finally, these youth may experience greater life stress events (e.g., parent's loss of work) and accept aggression as a legitimate coping mechanism (Guerra et al., 1995). As a result, the way they view the world (i.e., hostile and unpredictable) may then affect how they view their own economic and educational future (i.e., limited).

Such disruption of positive child development has educational implications well beyond grade school. Often, children who do not achieve in early education are placed into groups that tend to reflect economic and educational stratification. Educational tracking, for example, is one major program that reproduces stratification by selecting those who will go to college and those who will not (Colclough & Beck, 1986). Youth from economically disadvantaged backgrounds may find that they are sorted into educational "tracks" that place them in non-college-bound directions more than those from advantaged backgrounds (Colclough & Beck, 1986). Early tracking is important because future aspirations are often solidified by the eighth grade (Hanan, 1996). For instance, in one study of 25,000 teenagers over 6 years (1988-1994), income was found to be more important than race, ethnicity, sex, or scores on achievement tests in "determining the expectations and future education of the group" (Hanan, 1996, p. A11). The study was conducted by the National Opinion Research Center at the University of Chicago and used self-administered questionnaires, computer-assisted interviews, and telephone and live interviews to collect data. Of the teenagers who were followed, 48% of the low-income students went to community colleges, and 37% went to 4-year colleges. Compare this finding to the fact that 74% of the most affluent group went to 4-year colleges and only 23% of this affluent group went to 2-year colleges. One may infer that a societal stratification is re-created through education, which in turn may limit life chances as well.

Summary of the Sociological and
Psychological Literature on SESC

From the literature reviews, it appears that multiple variables may be involved in SESC (e.g., Gilbert & Kahl, 1993). Of these various elements that go into a person's SESC, the cohort and peer group seem to play an important role in establishing SESC norms and expectations. When a person alternates between peer and cohort groups (Granfield, 1991; Grella, 1990), there may be a sense of SESC stigma that arises from the shifting between groups. Often, people have to learn the norms and expectations of their new group to alleviate their sense of anxiety and stigma.

The psychological literature reveals that SESC needs to be carefully defined if differences within a group and between groups are to be understood. SESC was shown to affect the process and outcome of therapy (i.e., social and vocational) as well as how the therapeutic relationship develops. The literature also demonstrates a link between SESC and early developmental issues. Specifically, SESC was linked to the values and the way values are imparted to children, how children relate to each other, and the kinds of life opportunities they receive. Yet with all of this information, some clarification is still in order. In addition, how does this information assist us in developing a new understanding of SESC?

Assessing PREVIOUS THEORIES OF SOCIAL ECONOMIC STATUS AND CLASS

What becomes apparent in most of the extant literature is the confusing and confounded ways SESC has been used (Argyle, 1994; Frable, 1997). Although there have been some gains made in understanding the architecture of SESC in society and advancements made in understanding the role SESC plays in psychology, limitations arise because of these definitional problems. Most of the studies and theories still rely on specific class-demographic variables (i.e., income, education, and occupation) to determine a person's class or status. What is unclear is the relative contribution of each variable in positioning a person within a certain class or status. Another problem is that class-demographic variables are used to imply that certain indices are prevalent in some groups but not in others. These class-demographic variables are used as a leap to identify specific "classes" (e.g., middle class) and infer a particular "class thinking." Although many other variables are outlined as contributors to a person's SESC, it is difficult to discern how previous researchers have used these variables in their studies. It seems that most researchers have assumed that once people are placed in a class or are allowed to choose what class they believe they belong to, then people will consistently behave and think from that class. Similarly, people within that class should also behave like others who are placed into or who self-identify with that class. Because of the wide variation that may arise in how people see their SESC world, it may not be surprising that in some studies, SESC becomes a less than useful explanatory variable.

Another concern that contributes to the problematic use of SESC in studies may be the various ways that class and status are used. It may appear at times that the manner in which researchers operationalize SESC varies to the point that these divergent conceptualizations of SESC do not even refer to the same construct (Weber, 1995). These different definitions may reflect the researcher's personal experience, sociohistorical or sociopolitical context, and even region of the country. To proceed with an assessment of previous theories of SESC, one must first have a better understanding of status and class from the extant literature. However, what becomes apparent, even in attempting to clarify the difference between status and class, is the difficulty of discriminating between the two.

Clarifying the Definitions of Status and Class

First, *status* refers seemingly to a perceived position within an economic hierarchy but does not necessarily refer to a cohort group or community. Usually, this subjective position is determined from an individual's assessment of various elements that include class-demographic indices but also other components that have been socially determined to be markers of a particular status. Like signposts on a road, these socially determined markers (e.g., lifestyle, consumption or consumer pattern, neighborhood) usually help a person establish what status he or she has. For instance, Coleman and Rainwater's (1978) survey results of 900 participants found that income, education, and occupation were the best predictors of a family's status. The status that a person believes he or she has may not necessarily refer to a specific socioeconomic group and may also be context dependent. For instance, people may vary in how they interpret the meaningfulness of income or education level depending on the socially constructed "markers" to which people look and the context in which they live (e.g., $50,000 may mean different things to people in Manhattan and in Iowa City). And because $50,000 may mean different things in these two cities because of cost-of-living expenses, lifestyle and life opportunities are different. Thus, status may not be a static phenomenon or easily determined by looking at certain indices (e.g., graduate students often live below the economic poverty line but are considered part of society's intellectual elite).

Second, class seems to refer to a group who share similar characteristics derived from a combination of shared class-demographic characteristics (e.g., home, income, education) (Gilbert & Kahl, 1993) and life chances or opportunities (Hout, Brooks, & Manza, 1996; Thompson, 1995; Weber, 1995). People see themselves as part of a class with commonality to others in that class through the development of class consciousness. Focusing on class differences has been favored because class-demographic variables often are related to an assumed stratification of class groups. Hollingshead used these objective indices as the basis for his Two-Factor Index of Social Position (Hollingshead, 1975; Hollingshead & Redlich, 1958). In the two-factor model, occupation, education, sex, and marital status served as the major determinants of one's class standing. Hollingshead assumed that classes were static, and people within them were homogeneous (i.e., people within a given "class" agree that they belong to a similar group and share same circumstances) (Gilbert & Kahl, 1993; Jackman & Jackman, 1973). The problem with focusing only on classes and class consciousness is the assumption that "class" is basically determined to be the same everywhere one goes, and therefore people within a class share the same class consciousness. That is, someone from a middle class in Boston would see himself or herself in the same situation as a middle-class person in Duluth. Yet one could easily argue that the variables used (e.g., level of income and education) take on different meanings based on the context (i.e., rural vs. urban) or situation (i.e., what peer or cohort group one is around). Without exploring the within-group differences, one could make the error of assuming homogeneity within these classes and expecting people to have a common understanding of their SESC.

Areas Overlooked by Extant SESC Theories

Besides not taking the context of a person into consideration, another area of confusion seems to lie in the shift between the psychological (individual) and the sociological (societal) level of analysis. That is, conclusions drawn from large groups of people (e.g., between classes or statuses) are then suggested to be representative of an individual's worldview. This shifting makes comparisons between studies difficult because people seem to focus on variables they deem salient to their population of interest. Furthermore, rather than looking explicitly at the intrapsychic process of SES, class, and status, there is an attempt to distill subjectivity from focusing on external descriptors. Basically, it would be similar to assume that all African Americans think alike because they share similar phenotypic features. Although phenotype is a salient feature in how people think about themselves as racial beings, it is not the only variable (i.e., racial minority status confers various factors that affect one's "racial identity"); the assumption that these phenotypic features determine or constrain a person's worldview would be erroneous.

Many of the assumptions posited in current SESC theories may be problematic for a variety of reasons that include the following: using homogeneous samples such as college students (Furnham, 1984), constructing class as a strict hierarchy (Boston, 1991; Eder, 1993), not considering the role of race in forming class configurations (Boston, 1991), not developing a multidimensional conceptualization of SESC (Argyle, 1994), not looking at the "shared values" within an SESC (Eder, 1993), and not considering the importance of the individual's peer relationships (Jackman & Jackman, 1973). Boston (1991) suggests that to do SESC research effectively, one needs to (a) define or identify the boundaries of the basic classes, (b) identify correlations between classes and forms of class consciousness, and (c) analyze the interaction between racial subordination and class composition and determine the current effects of economic and social development of class configurations. Although these criticisms inform future research, these recommendations still retain the notion of definitive SESC groups as well as the homogeneity within SESC. Sociological literature provides some foundation to understand how people act and respond to their socioeconomic environment, but psychology needs to move beyond the use of SESC groupings as a means to determine a person's worldview or internal experience of SESC to an individualistic or phenomenological understanding of SESC.

The psychological literature seems to show that there are significant relationships between one's SESC and effectiveness and success in counseling, positive development, educational opportunities, and life chances. Most of the psychological research is premised on sociological interpretations of SESC (i.e., discreet statuses and a hierarchical class system) that link class-demographic characteristics with a person's subjective experience of SESC (e.g., Hollingshead Index of Social Position). What seems to be missing is an understanding of the cognitive process of how that worldview functions, how it may have been developed, and its connections with a person's behavior.

The best theory of SESC that helps establish a foundation for developing a SESC cognitive-processing model seems to come from Gilbert and Kahl (1993). In their theory, nine variables are outlined as principle determinants of a person's SESC (i.e., occupation, income, wealth, personal prestige, association, socialization, power, class consciousness, and succession and mobility). Gilbert and Kahl do a good job of outlining the various parts that comprise one's

SESC, but some appear difficult to operationalize as intrapsychic variables. Thus, other ways to measure such phenomena may be to evaluate the relative influence of others on the individual, measure how the individual relates to important "others" in his or her environment, and investigate the strategies people employ to cope with stratification pressure. Another aspect that psychology may distill from Gilbert and Kahl's theory is the importance of early socialization and succession in framing an individual's SESC schemata. However, with all the insights provided by their theory, there are still some shortcomings. For example, the authors did not specify the weight each component may play in determining a person's SESC outlook. They also overlooked the way that the variables interact with each other and how this interaction contributes to the development of a person's SESC. Because there are nine different variables and an environmental (sociohistorical) context to consider, it is difficult to imagine that each variable plays an equally salient role in a person's SESC formation. Hence, it is important to understand how these different variables interact with each other and what role they play in a person's SESC formation.

Throughout the literature review, it is apparent that the peer and cohort groups play important roles in early socialization, SESC succession, and maintenance of one's SESC. The peer and cohort group plays such central roles because people always see themselves as part of a social group, and these groups have significance (i.e., affective) for the individual (Abrams & Hogg, 1990). However, not everyone has the same commitment and identification with their peer and cohort group. Thus, another area of variation may come from the different ways people identify and use their peer and cohort group as a point of reference in developing their SESC. For instance, when people feel threatened because they are a part of a certain group, they may either distance themselves from the group or immerse themselves in the group as a means to retain their positive sense of self (Abrams & Hogg, 1990; Brewer, 1979; Brown, 1984; Doosje, Ellemers, & Spears, 1995; Ellemers et al., 1990; Jetten, Spears, & Manstead, 1996; Spears, Doosje, & Ellemers, 1997). This sense of distancing or immersion also may occur with other groups that are significant in the person's life (e.g., family). Consequently, information about the effect of group's on a person's attitudes and behaviors should serve an integral part in any new definition of SESC.

Because there is such confusion about what comprises a particular "class" or how people determine their "status," a fundamental question driving this redefinition of SESC is, "Is there a need to place people in a particular 'class' (e.g., middle class) to understand their SESC thinking?" My conclusion is quite possibly no. As stated earlier, it seems that past researchers fluctuated between focusing on class-demographic variables and strict "classes" in which people can be assigned, and from there, researchers inferred a class worldview. The problem is that most researchers focused on only a few variables and did not examine the number of different elements that contribute to a person's SESC. What may be useful is to ask people to identify their SESC (e.g., lower class, middle class) to understand how they see themselves and how they orient themselves toward others. Finally, what was also left unclear was how the different elements of one's SESC interacted with each other and how within-group variability could be examined. Hence, based on assessments of previous theories, there is a need for a new model.

Developing the SCWM Model

In developing a new way to conceptualize social class, one theory that we can borrow from is social constructionism. In social constructionism, the premise is that reality is created internally by the person's perception of his or her world. The way the individual acts on those perceptions functions to create the reality they internally perceive. For instance, the extant literature argues that race and gender are social constructions (Pope-Davis & Liu, 1998) because although physical differences do exist, differences are reified according to the perceiver's worldview of how difference is to be understood.

If we extend social constructionism to the area of social class, then it is possible to argue that there is no "one" objective social class in our world but multiple social classes because each individual constructs social class around him or her. This is not to say, for example, that poverty or income inequality does not exist. What social constructionism argues is that poverty or income inequality exists because people with certain resources see their social class world in a certain way that compels them to behave in such a way as to create or maintain income inequality. Thus, the premise of the proposed new model to understand social class proposes that social class does not actually exist but is created by perceivers.

The problem is that at the present time, no theories in the existing literature address how one develops an SESC worldview or subjectivity. Thus, the cognitive process that people employ to create a SESC worldview is left unexamined in previous theories and studies. In addition to and perhaps as a result of the dearth of subjective SESC information, there does not seem to be any literature that concentrates on how a subjective SESC may be an important component in counseling. The literature does, however, suggest important areas to consider in developing an understanding of the SESC cognitive processes.

Social class is retained and redefined to name the intrapsychic phenomena being studied because (a) individuals perceive differences in groups and individuals according to class-demographic characteristics; (b) individuals are interested in either maintenance or mobility between these perceived groups; (c) inequality exists in how the system distributes resources and therefore life chances and opportunities, and people acknowledge this fact; and (d) these phenomena are socially constructed and influenced by the person's context.

In describing the SCWM, the term *worldviews* is used because it reflects the underlying concept and idea of this model. To clarify, a worldview may be defined as a "pattern of beliefs, behavior, and perceptions that is shared by a population based on similar socialization and life experiences . . . [and] is a predisposition, not a trait; it changes substantially depending on the ecological context" (Watts, 1994, pp. 52-53). "World views are not only composed of our attitudes, values, opinions, and concepts, but also they may affect how we think, make decisions, behave, and define events" (Sue & Sue, 1990, p. 137). Sue and Sue (1999) elaborate further by saying that worldviews can be seen as a framework that makes sense of how the world works.

Kluckhohn and Strodtbeck (1961) are often referred to when speaking of worldviews. Rather than elaborate on their theories, it may be helpful to give an overview of the four dimensions that ground their worldview model. Kluckhohn and Strodtbeck assume that there are salient "core dimensions" (Sue & Sue, 1990, p. 138) that are salient for all people. Briefly, the first dimension is time (i.e., what is the temporary focus of human life?). Answers may be the past, present, or future. The second dimension is human activity (i.e., what is the modality of human activity?). Answers may be *being, being and in-becoming,* and *doing.* The third dimension is social relations (i.e., how are human relationships defined?). *Lineal, collateral,* and *individualistic* may be possible answers. Finally, the fourth dimension is people-nature relationships (i.e., what is the relationship of people to nature?). Answers can range from *subjugation of nature, harmony with nature,* or *mastery of nature* (Sue & Sue, 1990, p. 139). Worldviews then represent the social class based on socialized experiences of a particular person within a milieu that constructs patterns of values, beliefs, attitudes, behaviors, and perceptions. Moreover, worldviews allow one to best understand issues such as social and class mobility and changes in values over time.

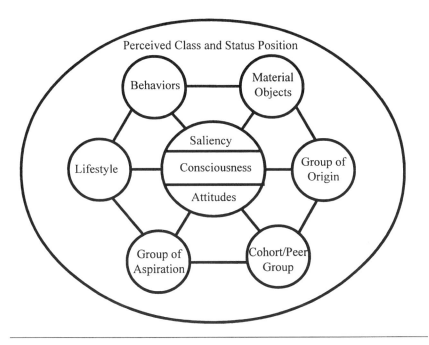

Figure 6.1. Perceived Class and Status Position

The Cognitive Process of the SCWM

Based on the need to understand the cognitive process that underlies a person's SESC, I propose a new model of social class called the social class worldview model (SCWM). The SCWM builds on the previous theories but elaborates on the relationship between hypothetical social class constructs and how people perceive social class and behave from a certain SCWM. The SCWM is a cognitive-processing model. It is predicated on the following components: (a) the domain of social class saliency, consciousness, and attitudes; (b) the domain of social class referent groups that comprise the group of origin, the peer and cohort group, and the group of aspiration; (c) the social class lifestyle; (d) the relationship to material objects; (e) the SCWM behavior; and (f) perceived class and status position (see Figure 6.1).

The SCWM shows the various domains and the theoretical relationship between them. Most apparent is that perceived class and status position exists as the background. The rationale is that the perceived class and status position is likely the most available indicator of a person's social class world and is perhaps the most easily accessible. As one ventures into the worldview, the surrounding elements of behaviors, lifestyle, material objects, and referent groups are the next area that may be delved into. Finally, I suggest that the most difficult domain to articulate exists within the center and provides the "hub" for the other domains.

The SCWM is a cognitive-processing model from which an individual is able to develop a coherent and consistent picture of both the outside and intrapsychic worlds. Coherence is important because the individual must make sense of what occurs around him or her and still maintain a positive sense of self. The person's SCWM helps make sense of the individual's behaviors, subjective identification with a "class" (e.g., middle class), and the actions of others. Each domain serves to indicate the importance that domain has on the overall SCWM of the individual. For instance, more focus on materialism may indicate the relative importance material goods have in maintaining the overall homeostasis of that person's SCWM.

The focus of the SCWM is on how people make meaning in and sense of their particular occupation, education level, or income rather than how these indices situate them within an objective economic hierarchy. Also, the principle behind the SCWM is the maintenance of homeostasis. That is, the function of the SCWM is premised on encoding information based on existing schemas, retaining consistency in cognitions and behaviors, and explaining what occurs in the environment in a fashion that resonates with the individual's SCWM schemas. Because the SCWM is a cognitive network, any change in one aspect of the model implies a cascading effect on the rest of the system.

Cognitive homeostasis is an important concept in the SCWM. Conflicts may arise when the SCWM of the individual is incompatible with class-demographic indices such as income, human capital indices such as social networks, and human capital indices such as educational level. For instance, a focus on materialism that exceeds a person's ability to purchase all that is needed to maintain an internal sense of SCWM homeostasis may result in feelings of stress and anxiety. Consequently, the person finds himself or herself needing to change his or her SCWM to accommodate the objective reality of the situation. Thus, the feeling that one needs to change his or her SCWM and the actual adaptation are two potential sources of stress and anxiety that the individual attempts to ease or avoid.

Domain Definitions of the SCWM

Below are definitions for the various domains in the SCWM. The domain definitions overlap with one another. However, to clearly identify what each domain represents, I make the definitions in each section seem independent of the others. Some brief examples are given to illustrate how each component theoretically functions.

The Domain of Social Class Saliency, Consciousness, and Attitudes

Saliency represents how meaningful and significant social class is to the person. The saliency of social class and its issues varies from person to person. Saliency implies that there is some awareness or consciousness of a social economic and class system in operation and that not everyone shares the same opportunities.

One way in which social class becomes apparent and salient may be when the person's SCWM cannot fully explain what is occurring in the environment or in an experience. An experience that disrupts the capacity of the SCWM to explain a particular experience may cause social class to be meaningful for the person at that moment. If the person possesses the cognitive maturity to process complex information, the SCWM system may mature and evolve to help the individual explain, understand, and cope with this new situation. For example, social class may become salient when one feels underdressed or when one is speaking with others who appear to be highly educated. Social class becomes meaningful because there is a dissonance between the way a person conceptualizes the self in regards to social class (e.g., "I am middle class") and the apparent inability to fit into a situation the person believes he or she should be in (e.g., "others will not see me as middle class if I cannot mirror their customs or match their standards").

Consciousness implies the degree to which an individual has an awareness that he or she belongs to a social class system and that social class plays a role in his or her life. Durant and Sparrow (1997) describe class consciousness as the meaning social class has as it is related to an awareness of the factors that influence one's social class position. Factors contributing to one's awareness are things such as the correct behavior, lifestyle, and those things contributing to status inequality (Durant & Sparrow, 1997). There are those who may not be completely aware of social class issues and do not see social class in operation. These people may have a difficult time explaining and articulating issues such as social mobility or poverty, even though they know it exists. Conversely, others may be very conscious of social class and may have a SCWM that interprets the environment in terms of consistent discrimination. These people who are highly conscious of social class may see either frequent oppression against a minority group or unfair barriers placed in front of "hardworking" individuals.

Some people may not be conscious of a social class system and may have difficulty explaining their own feelings of marginalization and seek alternative ways to explain their experiences. For example, a White first-year student from a lower-class or working-class environment who comes to a college counseling center with feelings of isolation may be experiencing a kind of social class environmental transition. This White student, who is the first in his or her social group to attend college, may feel unprepared to deal with the academic pressures, as well as with the added burden of negotiating social class expectations unfamiliar to him or her. The client may be struggling with social class identification issues (i.e., new referent group). The client may be afraid to ask questions that reveal his or her "ignorance" of middle-class college cultural rules. Also, an individual who feels alienated may not be able to understand his or her sense of isolation or marginalization. It may be possible that a person in this situation may identify with a marginalized racial group (e.g., African Americans) as a means to explain the sense of isolation. That is, the person identifies his or her sense of class marginalization with racial marginalization and may take on the values, customs, and attitudes of that racial group as a means of coping. Thus, exploring what the client is experiencing in terms of social class expectations may help to illuminate underlying issues related to the presenting problem. In this case, social class issues are salient to this student, but he or she may not be aware of how social class operates (i.e., he or she is a part of a social class system).

Attitudes are the feelings, beliefs, attributions, and values related to social class. Most social class attitudes are shaped by early developmental messages, socialization, and experiences from significant caretakers and peer and cohort groups. Although these early attitudes may be introjected, continued developmental and life experiences serve to moderate these attitudes and eventually form a personalized attitude array. The attitudes of an individual also imply that there is a certain value and belief system in relation to class-demographic indices (e.g., education, income, occupation, place of residence), as well as to how he or she relates to reference groups (i.e., competitive or cooperative) and how a lifestyle is chosen. The value and belief system also governs the level of prestige these class-demographic indices may have (e.g., a degree from Harvard may have more currency than a degree from a state university). Of course, the value a particular class-demographic index has is related to how others in a cohort group value that characteristic (e.g., a certain occupation). Thus, attitudes typically reflect the norm of a chosen cohort group but are constantly mediated by the person's future goals and aspirations.

One way people develop social class attitudes is through introjecting the attitudes of significant others (e.g., parents). Adult experiences have not challenged these early introjects, and thus the individuals continue to espouse the same attitudes as their parents. For instance, individuals from lower-, working-, or middle-class groups may subscribe wholly to the idea of freedom in "class" mobility (i.e., if one works hard enough, one can rise to the top) because their parents either believed in it or wanted their children to believe in it. Therefore, when these individuals perceive of an "unfair" advantage that another person has (e.g., affirmative action), they may feel anger or disgust. That is, they do not believe others are supposed to receive such privileges because it challenges either their own history of struggle or sense of entitlement. Their feelings of hostility toward people in the "unfairly advantaged" group reflect the introjected attitudes. Because these individuals who feel anger or disgust are likely to immerse themselves in a cohort group that is similar to them, their anger is validated and normalized. They may be perplexed by others who do not share their attitude toward the "advantaged group" because it seems to them that everyone around them shares the same feelings and beliefs.

In contrast, some may reject the attitudes of significant others and seek to define their own worldview (e.g., political beliefs). This redefinition of values and beliefs may result from an attempt to individuate from parents and significant others. Thus, any value, belief, or feeling that is linked with parents or significant others is rejected. One possible outcome is that these persons develop a value and belief system that stands in direct opposition to parents, peers, and significant others. To develop a worldview that is congruent with their experiences, these individuals also shift their reference groups (e.g., cohort group) to include only those people who symbolize opposition to the original attitude and group. Choice in lifestyle and one's relationship to material commodities also adjusts to accommodate the change in attitudes. In this case, individuals may come from a very economically privileged background but suddenly immerse themselves in lower- or working-class groups. These people will likely say that the lower- or working-class value and belief systems offer them a sense of meaning that they were unable to find in their privileged system of beliefs and values. Their attitudes, however, are still linked to the group of origination because the new attitude must remain in opposition to the "original" group.

The Domain of Social Class Referent Groups

Referent groups of orientation refer to the people (past, present, and future) in an individual's life who help guide the development of an SCWM as well as steer behavior (e.g., Ellemers et al., 1990). It makes sense, then, that the degree to which a person identifies with a particular group (i.e., feels alike or sameness with it) influences whether that group shapes a person's SCWM and behavior. For instance, Granfield's (1991) research on lower-class law students shows how identification with a particular referent group determines the principle strategy employed in dealing with the social class dissonance (e.g., identification with or distancing from the cohort group) that resulted from moving from one group to another. Referent groups are also important because they may ascribe an individual with an SESC (i.e., people may act toward a person as if he or she belonged to a certain "class"). This ascription of SESC influences the person's SCWM and behavior because the person must respond to the social class attributions and expectations. That is, through the socialization of one's referent group of origin, one begins to interpret and understand his or her position within a society, as well as the opportunities for mobility.

Three reference groups of orientation are associated with a person's SCWM. The first is the group of origination. This group is likely to consist of the home environment in which the individual was raised and functions as the main source of early social class socialization. Most significant in this group are the early caretakers, relatives, and peers.

The second reference group is the cohort group, representing those who are like the individual in worldview and behavior. It is conceivable that the cohort group is also similar to the individual in class-demographic characteristics (e.g., income); however, this does not have to be the case. The cohort group is likely to consist of people with whom the individual spends the most time and with whom he or she feels "average" and "normal." Significantly, the social class cohort group also provides the individual a sense of normality in SCWM because most of them share the same SCWM.

The third group of reference is the group of social class aspiration. This is the group that may have a pronounced influence on the person's SCWM because it represents the group to which the individual would like to belong and thus helps shape the individual's goals. The aspired group may represent one that is of higher prestige or greater on some class-demographic index, and it is esteemed because it provides a valuable goal for which to strive. Importantly, the aspired group represents the perceived "natural" outcome of current SCWM and behaviors. For instance, those in the lower or middle class who work hard and believe that the American economic class system is ascendable may hope one day to be a part of an upper-class group. Values, beliefs, and behaviors are geared toward being accepted into this group of aspiration.

All three groups influence a person in different ways, and not all may function equally. For example, a person growing up in a wealthy and privileged environment may feel that the group of aspiration is not of great concern because maintenance, not mobility, is the key concern. For those who are in poverty and do not believe that they have the resources to escape poverty, the cohort group may be the most significant because it helps the individual survive. The group of aspiration plays a limited role because immediate concerns may take precedence over future needs.

The Relationship to Material Objects

The focus on material objects is an important part of the SCWM because it assumes that social class is relatively invisible. That is, unlike race or gender, social class, absent the material objects we wear and surround ourselves with, is virtually impossible to detect. Thus, I would argue that social class, in regard to how an individual chooses and uses material objects to reflect his or her SCWM, is a type of performance. In effect, the individual's use of material objects "performs" or manifests the individual's SCWM for others.

Relationship with material commodities represents the use of objects deemed to be important in maintaining coherence and stability in the SCWM. The importance of material possessions also reflects the salience of this dimension when evaluating others. In a survey of 168 students ages 14 to 26, those who tended to be more materialistic also were likely to favor a person who owned expensive possessions than a person who lacked these possessions

(Dittmar & Pepper, 1994). That is, if material possessions are important in the maintenance of one's life, then it will also be a meaningful determinant in evaluating others (Dittmar & Pepper, 1994).

These material commodities tend to be objects that are associated with or symbolic of a lifestyle and SCWM and are supposed to be consistent with how others in the reference groups (e.g., origin, cohort, aspired) value those commodities (Dittmar, 1994; Richins & Rudmin, 1994). Material possessions have been found to be important reflections of the self as well as crucial indicators of status and life satisfaction (Dittmar, 1994; Richins & Rudmin, 1994). The meaning and import of such objects vary according to the perceiver (Richins & Rudmin, 1994). There are also normative expectations for material commodities that arise from one's SCWM and one's cohort groups. For example, a new computer for a graduate student is probably highly prized. The commodity (computer) is an object that is valued among the cohort group (other graduate students), is seen as a necessity among the group of origin (family), and helps the graduate student move closer to the aspired group (e.g., those who have graduated and other professionals). Hence, one is expected to have a computer. On the other hand, although a trip to Cancun is highly prized, it may not be a reasonable expectation among certain referent groups, or completely consonant with a graduate student's SCWM. Thus, material objects, along with referent group expectations, help regulate one's SCWM.

The Social Class Lifestyle

Lifestyle alludes to the manner in which one would like to live his or her life according to the SCWM. However, lifestyle is also a feature of socialization within a particular social class (Hendry, Kloep, & Olsson, 1998). The lifestyle is related to the behavioral manifestation of the SCWM and is linked to the groups of reference and the individual's relationship with material commodities. The lifestyle represents the way people organize their SCWM and economic resources to carry out a preferred pattern of action and behaviors. As a result, the lifestyle that is congruent with one's SCWM generates a sense of accomplishment and fulfillment. This affirmation is fed back into the SCWM system to maintain homeostasis. This is not to say that everyone is happy with his or her lifestyle. Rather, a sense of accomplishment and fulfillment is a result of conducting oneself consonant with one's SCWM. Again, the reference groups help to provide a sense of reasonable expectations for one's lifestyle and help to rein in behaviors (e.g., lavish spending) unless the person has chosen to change reference groups. If that is the case, then the SCWM has probably changed as well, and new norms and expectations are generated.

The Behavior of Social Class

The SCWM behavior is the action part of the SCWM model and should reflect the person's SCWM cognitions. The behaviors are meant to be the overt manifestation of a person's SCWM and are perceived to be the appropriate behaviors necessary to reflect one's perceived social class. In essence, it is another "performative" element of a person's SCWM. Behaviors important for an individual to maintain a middle-class worldview may revolve around speaking correct English, having good table manners, or knowing how to "walk" correctly. These behaviors are important because they can become telltale signs that the individual does not belong to a particular class group in which he or she is trying to "pass."

Perceived Class and Status Position

The perceived class and status position refers to the answer most people would give when asked, "What is your social class or SES?" The answer provides the researcher or clinician the basic foundation from which to develop further inquiries into the individual's SCWM. The answer also provides a glimpse into the perceived pressures the individual has placed on himself or herself to reflect that perceived position. Thus, when a person answers that he or she is middle class but is a first-year student in college coming from a lower-working-class background, one may begin to explore how he or she derived that conclusion. In addition, assessment in other areas of the person's SCWM affords the clinician an opportunity to understand the specific areas that may be causing stress or anxiety (e.g., attempting to live a certain lifestyle, having problems buying material objects, or feeling uncomfortable around an aspirational group).

What About Income, Education, and Occupation?

Because much of the literature emphasizes income, education, and occupation as important class-demographic indicators of social class, ignoring their significance within this model would be impossible. However, how are demographic indices integrated into a phenomenological model of social class? Indices such as income, education, and occupation function as objective parameters within which a person's SCWM has to operate. These indices that represent the human, cultural, and social capital of a person define the boundaries that individuals cannot go beyond regardless of their SCWM. For instance, if a person focuses on obtaining material objects as the sole symbol of his or her social class, money and resources that allow one to purchase material objects are a specific limitation and act to moderate the individual's relationship to material objects. Similarly, if people seek to be a part of the intellectual elite of a society but do not have the requisite educational experiences (human capital) and social networks (social capital), then regardless of how much they orient themselves toward that group, they will be limited from actually obtaining status and position within that aspirational group.

In Grella's (1990) example of women experiencing anxiety and stress due to a divorce and a shift downward in social class, one may argue that some of the stress may come from the intersection of their SCWM as middle class and their income level. Thus, the trappings of a middle-class lifestyle may include being fashionable, dining out, and taking vacations that help to maintain a woman's middle-class SCWM. However, when faced with a limited income and reduced resources, the maintenance of such a lifestyle becomes difficult. Consequently, although the women attempt to maintain a middle-class SCWM, practically everything around them does not allow them to sustain that orientation. Stress and anxiety may result as the women attempt to reorient themselves and seek homeostasis.

Case Example

To give a better illustration of how the SCWM can be used in a counseling context to gather information and conceptualize a client's issues, I provide a case example of a counseling client.

The client was a 21-year-old White male heterosexual college student who was still 2 years away from graduating and was experiencing difficulty choosing a major. When asked his social class, he described himself as working middle class because he did not identify with the middle-class students on campus, but rather saw himself needing to work to achieve and maintain his middle classhood. He seemed to be more interested in working full-time as a technical apprentice than in graduating. He prized his ability to earn money and pay for "everything," even though he spent most of his money on his hobby of building custom trucks. The client stated that his goals for college were different from his father's (e.g., his father wanted him to have a white-collar job, and the client did not think that was important). The client also hoped to retire early in life. He remarked about his feeling of isolation on campus. He was not dating anyone at the time of counseling and expressed frustration at not being able to find someone suitable for him.

Using the SCWM in counseling revealed pertinent information about the client's situation, issues, and worldview that may not have been apparent when using conventional SESC assessments (e.g., "tell me what class you belong to"). For instance, to recap what has been said earlier, current SESC assessment may only focus on the "class" of the client without really exploring all the other possible elements that contribute to a client's SCWM. Moreover, in assessing someone's SESC, the close-ended questions may revolve around how much money one makes, level of education, and type of job as a means to situate the person within a particular "class." The SCWM, however, allows the counselor a number of different places from which to begin an assessment rather than only focusing on the client's class. Thus, open-ended questions may focus on what money or education means to the individual to better understand how the client views his or her world.

The model, then, with its various components, affords the counselor various access routes to the person's SCWM. For the client, information gathering may seem more seamless and coherent. For the counselor, most client information can be reinterpreted to gain an understanding about the client's SCWM. Because the counselor is getting information about multiple aspects of a client's life that are related to his or her SCWM, and this information about the client is not necessarily specific to a client's class, these insights and information about the client can be connected to presenting issues and thus provide a better understanding of the client. The information about the client's SCWM can also be reflected back to him or her to help the client understand how his or her SCWM influences other aspects of the client's life.

Using this case, rather than saying to the client that he or she has a worldview that reflects middle-class values, the counselor can help the client understand how early socialization experiences (e.g., a working-class father who eventually became middle class and imparted strong middle-class values) helped to shape certain attitudes about himself or herself and the world. In addition, the counselor can link peer and cohort pressures and expectations with how the client views himself or herself and how the client is coping or not coping with these expectations. It may be that the client's inability to cope with class expectations may leave the client feeling marginalized from the cohort or peer group. Also, what may not be addressed in counseling, when using only class information about the client, is how the client views his or her future and which groups help to establish goals for the client.

For the client, it was clear that early retirees were the group of aspiration. This client could explore the "lifestyle" that he would like to have and how the lifestyle fit into his current SCWM. Because this client's group of aspiration was early retirees, and he valued his leisure time to work on his expensive trucks, there appeared to be a discrepancy between his future goal and current behavior. This may have arisen because he chose to identify highly with both groups simultaneously rather than placing his aspirations within a long-term plan of action. Thus, it was not surprising to hear that the client felt somewhat distant from both his peer group at school and the cohort group that worked on trucks. For him, the peer group that worked on trucks was working class with no real aspiration to retire early. Similarly, the peer group at school was described as having "professional" aspirations (e.g., white-collar work) with no real interest in his trucks. Because he split his identification between the two groups, he felt marginalized from both as well.

His hobby of working on trucks seemed to be an interesting area to explore. At one point, counseling focused on the meaning or significance that these trucks had as "material objects" to him. That is, the counselor explored the extent to which he had his sense of self tied to these trucks and what these trucks or objects gave him in return. Building and showing his trucks as part of a car club gave him a sense of belonging and competency with a peer group. In addition, the trucks were "flashy," so he was able to receive attention from driving and showing his trucks. His interest in trucks also reflected his interest in manual labor and working-class hobbies, but he was still interested in getting his college diploma (a middle-class value). He did not appear completely invested in a college education or professional vocations but seemed to be more interested in the idea of getting a college degree (i.e., diploma) so he could somehow "get rich." Thus, he said that he could not date women in college because they tended to want "professionally" oriented men rather than working-class men. For this client, social class was salient, but because he was not necessarily conscious of social class issues or able to identify with one reference group, he felt alienated from multiple groups. As a result, because he did not understand how to make sense of his marginalization, he tended to avoid addressing social class entirely. The current milieu also suggests that the economy is doing well. This belief in a strong economy may help the client feel comfortable with spending large amounts of money on his hobby rather than saving it.

To summarize the conceptualization of the client within the SCWM, it was apparent that the client, even though he was in a middle-class educational environment, did not necessarily share the same values of the educational environment. That is, one would hope that people would pursue a college education for the personal growth associated with higher education (a middle-class value). Instead, the client valued the currency afforded in society to a college diploma more than the learning or personal growth. Part of his feeling of isolation could have arisen from not subscribing to middle-class or working-class values. Also, although he would like to retire early in his life (i.e., lifestyle and group of aspiration), it appears that his behaviors are not consonant with these goals (e.g., spends all of his money on trucks). The SCWM did allow the counselor a better understanding of the client's behaviors and motivations and helped the counselor make sense of some contradictions in the client's behaviors. Vocational and personal counseling did occur but with a better understanding of how the client valued an education, jobs, and money and how his cohort groups influenced his decisions.

Counseling, Practice, and Research Implications

As society changes and social class issues become more salient (Arax, Curtius, & Nelson, 2000; Rifkin, 2000), psychologists need to have a better understanding of how social class is related to people's lives and experiences (Palmer, 1996; Soriano, Soriano, & Jimenez, 1994). It is not enough to just say counselors should briefly consider the social class of the individual as a potential factor influencing the therapeutic relationship, but rather the counselor could use the way the client conceptualizes his or her social class worldview to understand the client better. Consequently, the counselor is provided more ways to work with the client and allowed more information about what is contributing to the client's current crisis.

This consideration may be more important on college and university campuses where socialization into middle classhood (Alford, 2000) is as important as an education (Butler, 1991; Moses, 1990) and where entrance is perceived as acceptance into "elite" society (Gose, 2000; Weiss, 2000). College students may come to counselors with anxieties that may stem from their fear of failure. That is, the client may present with poor grades, depression, or poor class attendance, which may be related to how the client conceptualizes the college environment within his or her SCWM. For instance, if the client focuses on material goods and a lifestyle that nurtures the development of social capital, the academic demands may not be given attention. Thus, the client begins to fail courses and still desperately wants to stay in college but for what may seem the wrong reasons.

Another way to understand social class among this group of students is to start discussing these issues during orientation. Presently, many minority orientation programs introduce students to the possibility of racism during their collegiate experience. Similarly, women students are exposed to various campus resources and offices for assistance around gender discrimination. Yet, one area that is overlooked is the potential class crises that may arise for students. That is, as Granfield (1991) noted among law students entering into an elite academic environment, many students approached the situation without much parental and peer guidance. Stress could accumulate as a consequence of trying to "pass" as middle class. Thus, it may be beneficial in environments such as this to normalize students' anxieties and acknowledge the difficulty of trying to navigate a new "classed" environment unfamiliar to them. Social class workshops and programs such as dining etiquette may be promoted as career enhancement events. Thus, one may subtly acknowledge the importance of social class and the possibility of social class crises and conflicts but not make students feel that they stand out and are not like their peers.

Counselors who focus specifically on the academic crisis without a full understanding of what may be contributing to the current event may find the client not returning. The client may feel misunderstood because the counselor focuses on symptoms rather than on potential causes of stress. The implication for the counselor is that the client should begin to develop an awareness of what compels particular behaviors, attitudes, and beliefs. This is not to moralize which beliefs and attitudes are right or wrong but instead is a way for the client to gain insight into his or her own intrapsychic world and to develop new behavioral patterns and strategies.

Currently, I am unaware of any research on the subjective experience of social class. As a means to empirically investigate this theoretical model, I have developed a preliminary scale that comprises the domains described earlier. However, future research should examine the ways people create an understanding of their social class world and how they see social class in others and themselves. A shift away from using only class-demographic variables would allow the researcher to understand the within-group variability necessary to fully illuminate the intersection of race, gender, and class.

Future research should also consider gathering information from non-college-age participants. Although convenience of the sample facilitates research at times, social class research can benefit from participants who are not from a specific age range and socialized into middle-class life. An investigation that uses non-college-age participants can also inform clinical practice because, as Fitzgerald and Betz (1994) have already argued, our understanding of people is limited to a certain population.

Finally, research into social class and examining within-group variation can help psychology better understand the population it serves. Hall (1997) mentioned the need to internally transform itself to reflect the population served or risk obsolescence. A social class understanding is one means by which psychology and counseling can stay relevant and current with the communities that it serves.

The SCWM is a step toward fully examining the various ways people differ and are similar. Adding a fuller understanding of social class to the growing literature in areas of sexuality, race, and gender research can only enhance our clinical and research practice. Consequently, psychology and counseling can better meet the needs of a changing community.

References

Abrams, D., & Hogg, M. A. (1990). An introduction to the social identity approach. In D. Abrams & M. A. Hogg (Eds.), *Social identity theory: Constructive and critical advances* (pp. 1-9). New York: Springer-Verlag.

Adler, N. E., Boyce, T., Chesney, M. A., Cohen, S., Folkman, S., Kahn, R. L., & Syme, S. L. (1994). Socioeconomic status and health: The challenge of the gradient. *American Psychologist, 49,* 15-24.

Alford, S. M. (2000). A qualitative study of the college social adjustment of Black students from lower socioeconomic communities. *Journal of Multicultural Counseling and Development, 28,* 2-15.

Arax, M., Curtius, M., & Nelson, S. S. (2000, January 9). California income gap grows amid prosperity. *Los Angeles Times,* pp. A1, A16, A17.

Argyle, M. (1994). *The psychology of class.* New York: Routledge.

Atkinson, D. R., Morten, G., & Sue, D. W. (1993). (Eds.). *Counseling American minorities: A cross-cultural perspective* (4th ed.). Dubuque, IA: William C. Brown.

Babcock, C. R., & Saffir, B. J. (1997, July 24). In wealth, Clinton team doesn't look like America. *The Washington Post,* p. A19.

Beutler, L. E., Machado, P. P., & Neufeldt, S. A. (1994). Therapist variables. In A. E. Bergin, & S. L. Garfield (Eds.), *Handbook of psychotherapy change* (4th ed., pp. 229-269). New York: John Wiley.

Boston, T. (1991). Race, class and political economy: Reflections on an unfinished agenda. In A. Zegeye, L. Harris, & J. Maxted (Eds.), *Exploitation and exclusion: Race and class in contemporary U.S. society* (pp. 142-157). New York: Hans Zell.

Brabeck, M., Walsh, M. E., Kenny, M., & Comilang, K. (1997). Interprofessional collaboration for children and families: Opportunities for counseling psychology in the 21st century. *The Counseling Psychologist, 25,* 615-636.

Brewer, M. B. (1979). In-group bias in the minimal intergroup situation: A cognitive-motivational analysis. *Psychological Bulletin, 86,* 301-324.

Brody, N. (1997). Intelligence, schooling, and society. *American Psychologist, 52,* 1046-1050.

Bronfenbrenner, U. (1986). Ecology of the family as a context for human development: Research perspectives. *Developmental Psychology, 22,* 723-742.

Brown, M. T., & Landrum-Brown, J. (1995). Counselor supervision: Cross-cultural perspectives. In J. G. Ponterotto, J. M. Casas, L. A. Suzuki, & C. M. Alexander (Eds.), *Handbook of multicultural counseling* (pp. 263-286). Thousand Oaks, CA: Sage.

Brown, R. J. (1984). The effects of intergroup similarity and cooperative versus competitive orientation on intergroup discrimination. *British Journal of Social Psychology, 23*(1), 21-33.

Bulhan, H. A. (1985). Black Americans and psychopathology: An overview of research and theory. *Psychotherapy, 22,* 370-378.

Butler, J. E. (1991). Retention and recruitment of minority faculty: Defeating the Sisyphean syndrome. *Metropolitan Universities, 1*(4), 65-73.

Carlson, E. B., & Rosser-Hogan, R. (1993). Mental health status of Cambodian refugees ten years after leaving their homes. *American Journal of Orthopsychiatry, 63,* 223-231.

Carter, R. T. (1991). Cultural values: A review of empirical research and implications for counseling. *Journal of Counseling and Development, 70,* 164-173.

Ceci, S. J., & Williams, W. M. (1997). Schooling, intelligence, and income. *American Psychologist, 52,* 1051-1058.

Colclough, G., & Beck, E. M. (1986). The American educational structure and the reproduction of social class. *Sociological Inquiry, 56,* 456-476.

Coleman, R. P., & Rainwater, L. (1978). *Social standing in America: New dimensions of class.* New York: Basic Books.

Croizet, J. C., & Claire, T. (1998). Extending the concept of stereotype and threat to social class: The intellectual underperformance of students from low socioeconomic backgrounds. *Personality and Social Psychology Bulletin, 24,* 588-594.

Dittmar, H. (1992). *The social psychology of material possessions.* Hemel Hempstead, UK: Harvester Wheatsheaf.

Dittmar, H. (1994). Material possessions as stereotypes: Material images of different socio-economic groups. *Journal of Economic Psychology, 15,* 561-585.

Dittmar, H., & Pepper, L. (1994). To have is to be: Materialism and person perception in working-class and middle-class British adolescents. *Journal of Economic Psychology, 15*(2), 233-251.

Doosje, B., Ellemers, N., & Spears, R. (1995). Perceived intragroup variability as a function of group status and identification. *Journal of Experimental Social Psychology, 31,* 410-436.

Durant, T. J., & Sparrow, K. H. (1997). Race and class consciousness among lower-and middle-class Blacks. *Journal of Black Studies, 27*(3), 334-351.

Eaton, W. W., & Muntaner, C. (1999). Socioeconomic stratification and mental disorder. In A. V. Horwitz & T. L. Scheid (Eds.), *A handbook for the study of mental health* (pp. 259-283). New York: Cambridge University Press.

Eder, K. (1993). *The new politics of class: Social movements and cultural dynamics in advanced societies.* Newbury Park, CA: Sage.

Ellemers, K., Knippenberg, A., & Wilke, H. (1990). The influence of permeability of group boundaries and stability of group status on strategies of individual mobility and social change. *British Journal of Social Psychology, 29,* 233-246.

Erikson, B. H. (1996). Culture, class, and connections. *American Journal of Sociology, 102,* 217-251.

Faludi, S. (1999). *Stiffed: The betrayal of American men.* New York: William Morrow.

Felner, R. D., Brand, S., DuBois, D. L., Adan, A. M., Mulhall, P. F., & Evans, E. G. (1995). Socio-economic disadvantage, proximal environmental experiences, and socioemotional and academic adjustment in early adolescence: Investigation of a mediated effects model. *Child Development, 66,* 774-792.

Fitzgerald, L. F., & Betz, N. E. (1994). Career development in a cultural context: The role of gender, race, class, and sexual orientation. In M. L. Savikas & R. W. Lent (Eds.), *Convergence in career development theories* (pp. 103-117). Palo Alto, CA: CPP Books.

Frable, D. E. S. (1997). Gender, racial, ethnic, sexual, and class identities. *Annual Review Psychology, 48,* 139-162.

Furnham, A. (1984). The protestant work ethic: A review of the psychological literature. *European Journal of Social Psychology, 14,* 87-104.

Furnham, A., & Argyle, M. (1998). *The psychology of money.* New York: Routledge.

Garfield, S. L. (1994). Research on client variables in psychotherapy. In A. E. Bergin & S. L. Garfield (Eds.), *Handbook of psychotherapy change* (4th ed., pp. 190-228). New York: John Wiley.

Gelso, C. J., & Fretz, B. R. (1992). *Counseling psychology.* New York: Harcourt Brace.

Geoghehan, T. (1997, June 3). Overeducated and underpaid. *The New York Times,* p. A25.

Ger, G., & Belk, R. W. (1996). Cross-cultural differences in materialism. *Journal of Economic Psychology, 17*(1), 55-77.

Gilbert, D., & Kahl, J. (1993). *The American class structure: A new synthesis* (4th ed.). Belmont, CA: Wadsworth.

Giles, H., & Copeland, N. (1991). *Language contexts and consequences.* Milton Keynes: Open University Press.

Gose, B. (2000, January 14). Measuring the value of an Ivy degree. *Chronicle for Higher Education,* pp. A52-A53.

Graham, S. (1992). "Most of the subjects were White and middle class": Trends in published research on African Americans in selected APA journals. *American Psychologist, 47,* 629-639.

Granfield, R. (1991). Making it by faking it: Working-class students in an elite academic environment. *Journal of Contemporary Ethnography, 20,* 331-351.

Grella, C. E. (1990). Irreconcilable differences: Women defining class after divorce and downward mobility. *Gender and Society, 4*(1), 41-55.

Guerra, N. G., Huesmann, L. R., Tolan, P. H., Van Acker, R., & Eron, L. D. (1995). Stressful events and individual beliefs as correlates of economic disadvantage and aggression among urban children. *Journal of Clinical and Consulting Psychology, 63,* 518-528.

Hacker, A. (1997). *Money: Who has how much and why.* New York: Scribner.

Hall, C. C. I. (1997). Cultural malpractice: The growing obsolescence of psychology with the changing U.S. population. *American Psychologist, 52,* 642-651.

Hanan, W. H. (1996, June 17). Income found to predict education level better than race. *The New York Times,* p. A11.

Heaton, T. B. (1987). Objective status and class consciousness. *Social Science Quarterly, 68,* 611-620.

Helms, J. E. (1992). Why is there no study of cultural equivalence in standardized cognitive ability testing? *American Psychologist, 47,* 1083-1101.

Hendry, L. B., Kloep, M., & Olsson, S. (1998). Youth, lifestyle and society: A class issue. *Childhood: A Global Journal of Child Research, 5*(2), 133-150.

Hillerbrand, E. (1988). The relationship between socioeconomic status and counseling variables at a university counseling center. *Journal of College Student Development, 29,* 250-254.

Hollingshead, A. B. (1975). *Four factor index of social status.* Unpublished manuscript, Yale University.

Hollingshead, A. B., & Redlich, F. C. (1958). *Social class and mental illness: A community study.* New York: John Wiley.

Hout, M., Brooks, C., & Manza, J. (1996). The persistence of classes in post-industrial societies. In D. J. Lee & B. S. Turner (Eds.), *Conflicts about class: Debating inequality in late industrialism* (pp. 49-59). New York: Longman.

Ivey, A. E., Ivey, M. B., & Simek-Morgan, L. (1993). *Counseling and psychotherapy: A multicultural perspective* (3rd ed.). Needham Heights, MA: Allyn & Bacon.

Jackman, M. R., & Jackman, R. W. (1973). An interpretation of the relation between objective and subjective social class status. *American Sociological Review, 38,* 569-582.

Jetten, J., Spears, R., & Manstead, A. S. R. (1996). Intergroup norms and intergroup discrimination: Distinctive self-categorization on social identity effects. *Journal of Personality and Social Psychology, 71,* 1222-1233.

Jo, M. H. (1992). Korean merchants in the Black community: Prejudice among the victims of prejudice. *Ethnic and Racial Studies, 15,* 395-411.

Jones, E. E., & Thorne, A. (1987). Rediscovery of the subject: Intercultural approaches to clinical assessment. *Journal of Clinical and Consulting Psychology, 55,* 488-495.

Kagitcibasi, C. (1989). Family and socialization in cross-cultural perspective: A model of change. In J. J. Berman (Ed.), *Nebraska symposium on Motivation: Vol. 37. Cross cultural perspectives* (pp. 135-200). Lincoln: University of Nebraska Press.

Katz, J. H. (1985). The sociopolitical nature of counseling. *The Counseling Psychologist, 13,* 615-624.

Kelly, J., & Evans, M. D. R. (1995). Class and class conflict in six Western nations. *American Sociological Review, 60,* 157-178.

King, E. W. (1997). Social class in the lives of young children: Cross cultural perspectives. *Education and Society, 15*(1), 3-12.

Kluckhohn, F. R., & Strodtbeck, F. L. (1961). *Variations in value orientations.* Evanston, IL: Row and Peterson.

Leach, M. M., & Carlton, M. A. (1997). Toward defining a multicultural training philosophy. In D. B. Pope-Davis & H. L. K. Coleman (Eds.), *Multicultural counseling competencies: Assessment, education and training, and supervision* (pp. 184-208). Thousand Oaks, CA: Sage.

Lin, N. (1999). Social networks and status attainment. *Annual Review of Sociology, 25,* 467-487.

Luzzo, D. A. (1992). Ethnic group and social class differences in college students' career development. *Career Development Quarterly, 41*(2), 161-173.

Mays, V. M. (1985). The Black American and psychotherapy: The dilemma. *Psychotherapy, 22,* 379-388.

Miller, D. C. (1964). *Handbook of research design and social measurement.* New York: David McKay.

Mirels, H. L., & Darland, D. M. (1990). The Protestant work ethic and self-characterization. *Personality and Individual Difference, 11,* 895-898.

Moses, Y. T. (1990). The challenge of diversity: Anthropological perspectives on university culture. *Education and Urban Society, 22*(4), 402-412.

National Institutes of Mental Health (NIMH). (1995). *Basic behavioral science research for mental health: A national investment* (NIH No. 95-3682). Washington, DC: Author.

Nicks, T. L. (1985). Inequalities in the delivery and financing of mental health services for ethnic minority Americans. *Psychotherapy, 22,* 469-476.

Palmer, P. (1996). Pain and possibilities: What therapists need to know about working-class women's issues. *Feminism and Psychology, 6*(3), 457-462.

Pope-Davis, D. B., & Liu, W. M. (1998). The social construction of race: Implications for counseling psychology. *Counseling Psychology Quarterly, 11,* 151-161.

Richins, M. L., & Rudmin, F. W. (1994). Materialism and economic psychology. *Journal of Economic Psychology, 15,* 217-231.

Rifkin, J. (2000, January 13). Behind the merger hype: Hypercapitalism. *Los Angeles Times,* p. B9.

Rindfleisch, A., Burroughs, J. E., & Denton, F. (1997). Family structure, materialism, and compulsive consumption. *Journal of Consumer Research, 23*(4), 312-325.

Roberts, S. (1997, May 8). Another kind of middle-class squeeze. *The New York Times,* Section 4, pp. 1, 6.

Robinson, T. (1993). The intersection of gender, class, race, and culture: On seeing clients whole. *Journal of Multicultural Counseling and Development, 21,* 50-58.

Schatzman, L., & Strauss, A. (1955). Class and modes of communication. *American Journal of Sociology, 60,* 329-338.

Segalman, R. (1968). The Protestant ethic and social welfare. *Journal of Social Issues, 24,* 125-141.

Sharf, R. S. (1992). *Applying career development theory to counseling.* Pacific Grove, CA: Brooks/Cole.

Sirgy, M. J. (1998). Materialism and quality of life. *Social Indicators Research, 43*(3), 227-260.

Sladen, B. J. (1982). Effects of race and socioeconomic status on the perception of process variables in counseling. *Journal of Counseling Psychology, 29,* 560-566.

So, A. Y. (1987). High-achieving disadvantaged students: A study of low SES Hispanic language minority youth. *Urban Education, 22*(1), 19-35.

Sodowsky, G. R., Lai, E. W. M., & Plake, B. S. (1991). Moderating effects of sociocultural variables on acculturation attitudes of Hispanic and Asian Americans. *Journal of Counseling and Development, 70,* 194-204.

Soriano, M., Soriano, F. I., & Jimenez, E. (1994). School violence among culturally diverse populations: Sociocultural and institutional considerations. *School Psychology Review, 23*(2), 216-235.

Spears, R., Doosje, B., & Ellemers, N. (1997). Self-stereotyping in the face of threats to group status and distinctiveness: The role of group identification. *Personality and Social Psychology Bulletin, 23,* 538-553.

Sue, D. W., Ivey, A. E., & Pedersen, P. B. (1996). (Eds.). *A theory of multicultural counseling and therapy.* New York: Brooks/Cole.

Sue, D. W., & Sue, D. (1990). *Counseling the culturally different: Theory and practice* (2nd ed.). New York: John Wiley.

Sue, D. W., & Sue, D. (1999). *Counseling the culturally different: Theory and practice* (3rd ed.). New York: John Wiley.

Sue, S. (1999). Science, ethnicity, and bias: Where have we gone wrong? *American Psychologist, 54,* 1070-1077.

Takaki, R. (1993). *A different mirror: A history of multicultural America.* Boston: Little, Brown.

Thompson, B. (1994). Food, bodies, and growing up female: Childhood lessons about culture, race, and class. In P. Fallon, M. A. Katzman, & S. C. Wooley (Eds.), *Feminist perspectives on eating disorders* (pp. 355-378). New York: Guilford.

Thompson, E. P. (1995). The making of class. In P. Joyce (Ed.), *Class* (pp. 131-133). New York: Oxford University Press.

Tracey, T. J. G. (1997). The structure of interests and self-efficacy expectations: An expanded examination of the spherical model of interests. *Journal of Counseling Psychology, 44,* 32-43.

Triandis, H. C. (1989). Cross-cultural studies of individualism and collectivism. In J. J. Berman (Ed.), *Nebraska symposium on motivation: Vol. 37. Cross cultural perspectives* (pp. 41-134). Lincoln: University of Nebraska Press.

Tulkin, S. R. (1973). Social class differences in attachment behaviors of ten-month-old infants. *Child Development, 44,* 171-174.

Tulkin, S. R., & Kagan, J. (1972). Mother-child interaction in the first year of life. *Child Development, 43,* 31-41.

Tyler, B. M. (1989). Black jive and White repression. *Journal of Ethnic Studies, 16*(4), 31-66.

Vobejda, B., & Chandler, C. (1997, September 30). Household incomes rise again. *The Washington Post,* pp. A1, A8.

Walker, K. (1995). "Always there for me": Friendship patterns and expectations among middle- and working-class men and women. *Sociological Forum, 10,* 273-296.

Watts, R. J. (1994). Paradigms of diversity. In E. J. Trickett, R. J. Watts, & D. Birman (Eds.), *Human diversity: Perspectives on people in context* (pp. 49-80). San Francisco: Jossey-Bass.

Weber, M. (1995). The distribution of power: Class, status, party. In P. Joyce (Ed.), *Class* (pp. 31-40). New York: Oxford University Press.

Weiss, K. R. (2000, January 9). New test taking skill; working the system. *Los Angeles Times,* pp. A1, A20, A21.

Wright, E. D. (1978). Race, class, and income inequality. *American Journal of Sociology, 83,* 1368-1397.

Ying, Y. (1988). Depressive symptomatology among Chinese-Americans as measured by the CES-D. *Journal of Clinical Psychology, 44,* 739-746.

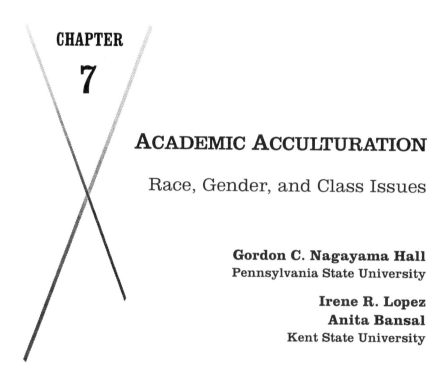

CHAPTER

7

ACADEMIC ACCULTURATION

Race, Gender, and Class Issues

Gordon C. Nagayama Hall
Pennsylvania State University

Irene R. Lopez
Anita Bansal
Kent State University

At the beginning of the 21st century, the United States is increasingly becoming a multicultural society. As of 2000, persons of color comprised 29% of the United States population, and within 50 years, nearly one half will be persons of color (U.S. Bureau of the Census, 1992). However, American psychology has been a reflection of the dominance of European American men over other groups in society (D'Andrea & Daniels, 1991; Sue, Arredondo, & McDavis, 1992). Thus, the structure of most graduate training programs in psychology reflects middle- to upper-class European American male values. The finished products of such training are also not necessarily relevant to the needs of the diverse clientele that they will serve (Hall, 1997). Thus, acculturation to the standards of traditional academic psychology may not adequately equip a trainee for the challenges of a multicultural 21st century. Making training sufficiently versatile to serve an increasingly diverse population should be a priority for training programs, whether they are internally (e.g., humanitarianism, interest in diversity) or externally (e.g., legal, professional mandates) motivated to do so (Ridley, Mendoza, & Kanitz, 1994). The provision of psychological services that are responsive to the needs of individuals of diverse backgrounds is emphasized in ethical mandates and in accreditation requirements for training programs (American Psychological Association, 1986; American Psychological Association, Office of Ethnic Minority Affairs, 1993; Sue et al., 1992). The purpose of this chapter is to examine the limitations of monocultural graduate programs in training students to serve multicultural populations. We will provide a conceptual framework to help understand monoculturalism, multiculturalism, and the necessary steps toward change. Within the context of LaFromboise, Coleman, and Gerton's (1993) models of acculturation, we will discuss how monocultural academic training may be a form of acculturation that presents challenges to students and new faculty. Several models of program change will be reviewed (Atkinson, Morten, & Sue, 1993; D'Andrea & Daniels, 1991; Ridley et al., 1994). Finally, we will articulate a mechanism for changing programs from a monocultural to a multicultural focus.

THE PROBLEM: MONOCULTURAL TRAINING IN A MULTICULTURAL SOCIETY

Academia is a culture, and those who receive academic training become acculturated to the culture of academia. Triandis (1996) defined culture as

> shared elements . . . that provide the standards for perceiving, believing, evaluating, communicating, and acting among those who share a language, a historic period, and a geographic location. The shared elements are transmitted from generation to generation with modifications. They include unexamined assumptions and standard operating procedures that reflect "what has worked" at one point in the history of a cultural group. (p. 408)

Acculturation has been defined as "the changes that groups and individuals undergo when they come into contact with another culture" (Williams & Berry, 1991, p. 632). One of the major changes involves gaining competence in the second culture (LaFromboise et al., 1993).

A shared language is one of the components of Triandis's (1996) definition of culture. The shared language in academic psychology has been developed primarily by upper-class European American men. The shared historic period

TABLE 7.1 Collectivist Versus Individualist Values

Collectivist	Individualist
Harmony and interrelatedness of nature and the universe	Dualism—mind and body are separate
Interdependence	Independence
Personal integrity is important	Personal resources such as possessions and expertise are important
Interpersonal sensitivity, compassion	Low need for affiliation
Family orientation	Individual orientation
Cooperation, equity	Competition, dominance
Respect for authority	Individual rights
Spirituality, acknowledgment of a higher, nonmaterial power that permeates all forms of life	Internal locus of control, view that life is not controlled by forces external to the self

NOTE: These values are summarized from Boykin (1983); Malgady, Rogler, and Constantino (1987); Markus and Kitayama (1991); Sue and Sue (1990); Triandis (1996); Uba (1994); and Wise and Miller (1983).

is the past century, and the shared geographic location is North America and Europe. Because of its relatively short history, most psychologists can trace their academic genealogy to European roots. The closer that trainees adhere to European American male middle- to upper-class values, the more likely they will be successful in their training and subsequent careers. Unique aspects of a trainee's background, such as cultural knowledge, have traditionally not been considered strengths (see Table 7.1).

One dimension along which European American men and others differ is individualism-collectivism (Greenfield, 1994). Whereas mainstream American culture tends to be individualistic, approximately 70% of the world's population tends to be collectivist (Triandis, 1989). Individuals of color in the United States also tend to have collectivist orientations (Greenfield, 1994). Collectivists identify themselves in terms of a group with whom they share a common fate (e.g., family, workgroup), individualists in terms of the individual (Triandis, 1996; Triandis, McCusker, & Hui, 1990). Actions that enhance the individual, such as competition, are valued by individualists, whereas actions that enhance group cohesiveness, such as cooperation, are valued by collectivists. Group norms and sanctions guide behavior across situations in collectivist groups. Personal attitudes, which may be more situation specific, are more important for individualists (Triandis, 1996).

Academic psychology is based on Western individualist assumptions and methods (Greenfield, 1994) and may create a form of culture shock for those trainees who do not share those assumptions. For example, a first-generation American college student may feel intimidated by professors and may be reluctant to share their ideas or challenge the ideas of a professor. A person of color whose goal is to provide psychological services for his or her cultural community may not perceive training in individual counseling as relevant to the community's needs. A woman may perceive a relative lack of interpersonal sensitivity in counseling methods developed by men and presented by male faculty and supervisors. A person from a lower socioeconomic background may perceive economic and political change as more relevant solutions than intrapsychic exploration.

Many of the skills offered by monocultural training programs may appear irrelevant along dimensions of gender, ethnicity, and social class. Nevertheless, the credentials that such programs offer are still necessary to function in society as a helping professional. Without such credentials (e.g., training that is necessary for licensure), it may be difficult to provide services to ethnic minority and lower socioeconomic status communities.

What has worked during the past century is becoming less relevant as a new century has arrived in which most of American society does not consist of European American men (Hall, 1997). Most training that is being provided may not be adequately responsive to the needs of a diverse clientele insofar as clients' ethnicity, social class, and gender may create certain clinical judgment biases that may affect the quality of care received (Garb, 1997; Snowden & Cheung, 1990; Sue & Zane, 1987). A generic or universal training model may be inappropriate because all cultural groups do not uniformly benefit from psychological services (Snowden & Cheung, 1990; Sue & Zane, 1987).

Perhaps these biases are associated with the training environment. Although European American men and women are well represented as faculty in graduate departments of psychology (Pion et al., 1996), only about 5% of graduate faculty members are individuals of color (Bernal & Castro, 1994). The presence of faculty of color may increase attention to multicultural issues, although this is not necessarily a causal relationship (Bernal & Castro, 1994). Because most faculty of color have not had mentors of color, unless they make a concerted effort to change, they may also be susceptible to perpetuating culturally unresponsive training environments.

Although the importance of multicultural training should be self-evident (Arredondo, 1994; Essandoh, 1996; Ridley et al., 1994; Yutrzenka, 1995), multicultural training may not be a priority for many, if not most, graduate training programs (Myers, Echemendia, & Trimble, 1991). Most graduate programs probably do not deliberately train students to hold ethnic, gender, and social class biases (Ridley, 1995). However, most faculty are European Americans who typically do not view themselves in terms of cultural identity (Helms, 1990). Thus, they may view themselves as individuals, not as European American or White. Moreover, graduate faculty may regard what they do as psychology, not a European American middle- to upper-class male psychology. They may regard the training they provide as universal or scientifically based. Indeed, individualist views of the self, which are typical of European American middle-class men, are often assumed in psychology to be universal (Markus & Kitayama, 1991). Even when cultural and feminist issues are considered, they tend to be treated as peripheral and not as part of the core training curriculum (D'Andrea & Daniels, 1991; Hall & Barongan, 1997; Leach & Carlton, 1997). Because of these biases, many programs may, in fact, train students to hold ethnic, gender, or social class biases. For training programs that do attempt to address multicultural issues, the last day of a course or a single course (that may not even be required) may become the repository or "ghetto" for the multiple issues that concern all "special" populations. Nevertheless, a lack of awareness of the sociocultural context and impact of training practices or a neglect of these issues may produce biases (Garb, 1997; Hall, 1990; Snowden & Cheung, 1990).

Not only are traditional models inadequate to address the issues of non-European Americans, but these models may even not adequately address some European American problems. For example, the United States is the most violent nation in the world (Lore & Schultz, 1993). Self-control methods have been proposed to control violent behavior (e.g., Novaco, 1976). Such methods are individualistic because they depend on individuals' ability to monitor situations and control their own behavior. An individual who views controlling violent behavior to be in his or her best interests, such as to save a marriage or job, may be motivated to do so. However, when there is little incentive to control violent behavior, a person may not be motivated to do so even if he or she has acquired the requisite self-control skills. It is possible that collectivist approaches may be more effective than individualist approaches in reducing violent behavior (Hall & Barongan, 1997). In addition, poverty is one of the strongest predictors of violent behavior (Sampson, 1993). Poverty and concomitant violence might be dramatically reduced if economic resources in the United States were more equitably shared. Moreover, inculcating young children with norms of empathy, cooperation, and interdependence could result in less of a tendency to aggressively strive for one's personal goals at the expense of others (Hall & Barongan, 1997). Thus, strengths may exist in nonindividualistic cultures that protect against certain forms of psychopathology. A Western monocultural approach to training may restrict trainees' capacity to become optimally effective in preventing and reducing psychological problems (Sue et al., 1992).

MODELS OF ACCULTURATION

Academic acculturation can be conceptualized in terms of the experiences of an individual from one culture who acquires competence in the second culture. Acculturation varies to the extent that an individual (a) retains his or her culture of origin, (b) becomes part of the second culture, and (c) becomes part of a third culture that results from a fusion of the first two cultures. LaFromboise et al. (1993) have described models of acculturation that may reflect acculturation experiences in academic training environments.

The *assimilation* model of acculturation involves absorption into the dominant or more desirable culture (LaFromboise et al., 1993). Acculturation assumes that effects of one's culture of origin persist and continue to affect a person's interactions with a second culture. The assimilation model assumes that one can leave his or her culture of origin behind and become part of a new culture. Individuals who immigrate to a second culture by choice may be more likely to desire to assimilate than involuntary immigrants who are forced to immigrate (e.g., slaves, refugees) (Ogbu, 1994). The cultural distance between one's culture of origin and the second culture may mediate one's ability to assimilate. An individual whose culture of origin is similar to the second culture may be able to assimilate easily into the second culture. Although a new identity is acquired in the second culture, dangers of assimilation are a loss of one's original cultural identity and rejection by both one's culture of origin and the second culture.

Assimilation into a second culture may not be possible for an individual who has salient differences (e.g., skin color, cultural practices) from those in the second culture (Williams & Berry, 1991). The acculturation model accounts for the individual who is unable to assimilate completely into a second culture (LaFromboise et al., 1993). Although the individual may become a competent participant in the second culture, he or she will always be identified as a member of the minority culture. He or she also may be relegated to a lower status within the second culture and not completely accepted. When a person fails to assimilate into a second culture, he or she may become marginalized and not identify with either his or her culture of origin or the new second culture (Berry, 1984). A second possibility is separatism, in which individuals or a group remain independent of the second culture (Berry, 1984). Both marginalization and separatism are associated with high levels of stress (Berry, Kim, Minde, & Mok, 1987).

In the *alternation* model of acculturation, an individual becomes competent in two cultures (LaFromboise et al., 1993). The two cultures are regarded as equal, rather than hierarchical, and the individual has positive relationships with both cultures without having to choose between them. A biculturally competent individual alters his or her behavior to fit a particular sociocultural context. For example, an individual may make a request of a Western individual in an assertive, direct manner, whereas he or she may make a request of an individual from an Asian background in a more deferential, indirect manner.

A pluralistic approach in which individuals maintain distinct cultural identities while cultures are tied together within a single multicultural social structure characterizes the *multicultural* model (LaFromboise et al., 1993). Individuals from one culture cooperate with those of other cultures to serve common needs. It is likely that groups will intermingle, leading to the evolution of a new culture.

The *fusion* model of acculturation posits that cultures sharing an economic, political, or geographic space will fuse together until they are indistinguishable and form a new culture (LaFromboise et al., 1993). This model differs from the assimilation model insofar as aspects of the culture of origin are integrated into the new culture. It also differs from the multicultural model in that cultures of origin are not distinctively maintained. What typically occurs, however, when there are cultural minority groups is that the minority groups become assimilated into the majority group at the price of their cultural identity.

In summary, these models of acculturation involve varying levels of retention of one's culture of origin as well as varying levels of incorporation of a second culture. Acceptance into the second culture is determined by one's similarities to those in the second culture, with some persons who are different not being accepted. Some models involve acceptance and integration of more than one culture.

ACADEMIC ACCULTURATION

Academic institutions serve as agents of socialization and tend to acculturate students to the status quo. When students and institutions use the same methods to cope with institutional acculturation, their expectations converge, and acculturation may occur without much difficulty (Coleman, 1995). For example, a student who expects to assimilate into academic culture and is accepted by the academic culture may not experience conflict. Conversely, a student who is interested in developing a personal cultural identity in an academic culture that does not accept other cultures may experience more conflict.

D'Andrea and Daniels (1991) and Ridley et al. (1994) have discussed differing stages of multicultural counselor training that are analogous to stages of acculturation. D'Andrea and Daniels's Level 1 (*cultural encapsulation*), Stage 1 (*cultural entrenchment*) and Ridley et al.'s (1994) *generic* framework of multicultural counseling training are analogous to the assimilation model (LaFromboise et al., 1993). Theories are taught from a monocultural perspective and assumed to be universally applicable and value neutral. The persons providing training in such programs often have negligible experience in working with persons of different cultural or socioeconomic backgrounds (D'Andrea & Daniels, 1991). Nevertheless, individuals are viewed as having similar concerns that are independent of gender, culture, and socioeconomic status and are expected to assimilate into the dominant culture. At this stage, theories of psychology and models of training are perceived as being universal and should not be adapted to accommodate "special" groups. Similarly, multiculturalism is simply viewed as an extension of the political correctness movement (Leach & Carlton, 1997).

Ethnocentric faculty may regard themselves as expert purveyors of knowledge, having little to gain from discussions with students, particularly those who differ from themselves (see D'Andrea & Daniels, 1991). Difficulties that students experience in applying Western methods to clients for whom these methods may be ineffective may be attributed by faculty to deficits in the students or clients. Rather than question the utility of the established methods, it is much easier to blame the student for a lack of skill or the student or client for being resistant or defensive.

The assimilation model describes the expectations in many psychology training programs. Students are expected to become part of the academic psychology culture. Students are voluntary immigrants (Ogbu, 1994) to the extent that they are not forced to be in school. Therefore, many students may desire to assimilate into the academic culture. It is possible that those individuals who are accepted into mainstream academic training have the least amount of identification with their culture of origin to begin with. These individuals may be more similar on many dimensions than those who are not accepted by the faculty who are training them and thus may find it relatively easy to assimilate (Williams & Berry, 1991). Assimilation may, however, come at the expense of a student's culture of origin. Gloria and Pope-Davis (1997) have pointed out that traditional faculty may prefer traditional students who are able to devote nearly all their time to academic pursuits; a graduate student who is a single parent may be viewed as neglecting his or her academic work when he or she is spending time caring for the family. The student also risks family rejection by devoting too much time to academic work. Similar rejection may occur from the student's cultural group of origin for assuming a "White identity."

A psychologist who is not accepted by the mainstream may have limited options. Distance from the values of one's culture of origin may occur during academic training, particularly if that culture of origin is not European American and male. Thus, an academically trained psychologist may not readily find acceptance in his or her culture of origin. Because psychology is currently dominated by European American men, separatism also may be a relatively unviable option. Credentialing (e.g., licensure) and much of the market for a psychologist's skills lie within the mainstream.

The term *separatism* may be laden with negative connotations. However, forms of separatism exist in psychology. For example, one who specializes in his or her training in a certain area of psychology (e.g., child clinical psychology, neuropsychology) and immerses himself or herself in this area to the relative exclusion of other areas of psychology might be considered a "separatist." If separatism is conceptualized as specialization, then a separatist could conceivably target his or her training and professional experiences to emphasize women's, ethnic minority, or class and urban issues to the relative exclusion of European American men's issues. However, one would need to be in a large, supportive, non-European male community to survive as a separatist. Nevertheless, as non-European male communities increase in size, separatism may become increasingly viable for those psychologists who are not accepted by the mainstream. Several graduate programs are already developing multicultural specialty training (Ponterotto, 1997). Thus, specializing in areas other than European American male psychology eventually may become as plausible as any other type of specialization.

The *interdisciplinary* training design—in which a student receives training in psychology as well as training in another discipline, such as ethnic studies and anthropology, to acquire multicultural skills (Ridley et al., 1994)—is analogous to the alternation model of acculturation (LaFromboise et al., 1993). Psychology programs that allow or encourage interdisciplinary training recognize that their own program may not provide all the necessary training. Interdisciplinary training allows the student to develop expertise in at least two substantive areas. However, most training may occur outside the program, and the psychology program may not view itself as responsible for multicultural training (Ridley et al., 1994). Moreover, if social and political changes are the solutions to some problems, many psychologists may question whether such change can be accomplished within psychology.

The student's professional identity in the interdisciplinary approach tends to be fragmented, and he or she may find it difficult to integrate cultural principles directly into psychological theory, research, and practice. There also is a natural tendency for individuals exposed to two cultures to identify with one more than the other (Phinney & Alipuria, 1996). A variation of the interdisciplinary approach within a psychology department is the *area of concentration* training design (Ridley et al., 1994). This allows the student to develop a specialty in multicultural issues by receiving multicultural training. However, multicultural expertise tends not to be regarded as a core component of training, and a student may elect not to be involved in such training.

D'Andrea and Daniels's (1991) Level 2 (*conscientious level*), Stage 3 (*cultural integrity stage*); Ridley et al.'s (1994) *integration* design; and Atkinson et al.'s (1993) *synergystic stage,* in which there is an infusion of multicultural training into all areas of the training program, are analogous to the multicultural model of acculturation (LaFromboise et al., 1993). A step further is D'Andrea and Daniels's Level 2 (*conscientious level*), Stage 4 (*infusion stage*), in which multicultural training becomes more synonymous with generic counseling (Leach & Carlton, 1997). This next step is analogous to the fusion model of acculturation (LaFromboise et al., 1993). In these integrative approaches, multiculturalism is not only valued but also becomes the mainstream. The creation of new cultural structures and beliefs is emphasized rather than preexisting cultural similarities or differences among groups (Coleman, 1995). Such integration of multicultural issues is difficult to implement both in society and in graduate training (LaFromboise et al., 1993; Leach & Carlton, 1997). Although such multicultural integration may be necessary for the demands of a multicultural society, changes at multiple levels in society would be necessary for such approaches to become widely influential. Nevertheless, the development of integrated multicultural training in multiple training programs may be a major step toward increasing the influence of the approach.

DOMAINS OF CULTURAL COMPETENCE

A multicultural psychology will best serve the needs of a multicultural society. Yet, there is much work to be done for psychology to become multicultural. This work means taking some personal risks as well as supporting others who are willing to do so. Otherwise, psychology will continue to be dictated by the inertia of the monocultural status quo. The purpose of this section is to identify some specific domains in which training programs can become increasingly culturally competent.

Sue et al. (1992) have identified three domains of cultural competency: (a) beliefs and attitudes, (b) knowledge, and (c) skills. To develop a training program in psychology that is appropriate for a multicultural society, a program must find ways to provide students competence in each of those domains. Beliefs and attitudes involve an awareness of personal biases and stereotypes that may hinder effectiveness in multicultural contexts. Moreover, beliefs and attitudes include the development of a positive attitude toward multiple cultural groups. Knowledge of one's worldview and the worldviews of others is the second dimension (see Landrine, 1992). The third dimension, skills, involves the intervention techniques and strategies necessary for effective work in multicultural contexts. Although these dimensions of cultural competency were proposed for individual counselors (Sue et al., 1992), they are also applicable to training programs.

Beliefs and Attitudes

A first step in changing a monocultural perspective may be an awareness of personal biases that may negatively affect others (D'Andrea & Daniels, 1991; Sue et al., 1992). Personal biases are not unique to European American men. Any person may hold ethnocentric biases. However, it is particularly incumbent on European American men in psychology to become aware of personal biases because they hold and have held positions of power in the profession. People of color, women, and persons from particular socioeconomic backgrounds also may hold negative stereotypes about their own group or other groups. These stereotypes are perpetrated in society and need to be overcome.

Knowledge

Another initial step would be to seek experiences involving persons of diverse backgrounds. This could be accomplished on personal and professional levels by joining organizations that address gender, cultural, and class issues. Within the American Psychological Association, Divisions 9 (Social Issues), 27 (Community), 35 (Women), 44 (Gay/Lesbian/Bisexual), and 45 (Ethnic Minorities) are some relevant groups. Following this initial awareness should come a realization that any individual's efforts—particularly if that person is not a woman, an ethnic minority, or from a lower socioeconomic background—will be inadequate to fully address gender, cultural, and class issues. Thus, women, ethnic minority persons, and persons from different socioeconomic backgrounds will need to be recruited to help change monocultural environments.

It is generally unappealing to enter an organization as the only minority person. Sometimes, the organization's effort to recruit a minority person is token and may preclude the possibility of recruiting additional minority persons. An even more insidious approach involves the recruitment of a minority person in an effort to demonstrate failure: "See, we gave a minority person a chance, but it didn't work." There typically does not exist much professional or social support for minority persons in monocultural organizations. Yet those monocultural organizations that are the least appealing to minority persons are the very organizations that need minority persons the most. Indeed, there is evidence that although entry-level standards tend to be set lower for ethnic minority persons than for those from the majority, standards for success tend to be set higher for ethnic minority than for majority persons (Biernat & Kobrynowicz, 1997). Thus, there may be built-in barriers in some monocultural organizations that limit the amount of success that ethnic minority persons are capable of achieving.

It is more likely that a person will successfully adapt to a second culture if there are mechanisms of social support (Williams & Berry, 1991). Such social support can be created by institutions in hiring more than one minority person at a time (Ridley, 1991). Another such mechanism could be hiring a person and his or her spouse or significant other. Perhaps the most impact on the workplace environment would be created by hiring minority persons at senior and administrative levels who can effectively change the environment.

Students and junior faculty are often advised for their survival to avoid becoming involved in organizational politics (e.g., Zanna & Darley, 1987). It is probably unwise and possibly dangerous to demand wholesale changes on entering a new organization. Nevertheless, organizational politics is the primary vehicle for change in most organizations. Students and faculty are likely to have the strongest political influence if they are able to establish themselves as valued colleagues on the basis of their productivity and contributions to the organization. However, there may be a danger that the strength of one's own values will become diluted while attempting to conform to organizational values in a monocultural organization. It may become increasingly difficult to "bite the hand that feeds you" as one becomes co-opted by an organization. Competence and acceptance in a second culture can occur to the detriment of one's culture of origin. Thus, it is important to maintain a multicultural perspective. Personal success in a monocultural organization should not preclude one's collective responsibility for multicultural change. Competence and acceptance within a monocultural organization should provide a platform for change. Rather than becoming absorbed by the system, it is important to infuse the system with the multicultural emphasis described earlier in some of the acculturation models.

Often, change at the national level can facilitate local change (Ridley et al., 1994). Professional organizations can exert pressure on local organizations to change. For example, the American Psychological Association (APA) accredits graduate programs in psychology. It is critical that the accreditation process requires attention to issues of diversity. Thus, participation within APA of persons committed to multicultural principles is critical. A lack of participation by minorities in mainstream psychology, however, may be a victory for those who prefer to ignore multicultural issues (Lu, 1996).

Another arena in which change is necessary is managed care. Managed care corporations typically do not recognize multicultural expertise as a specialty. Moreover, psychologists who are approved by managed care panels tend to be the most experienced. The most experienced psychologists often are not women, ethnic minority men, or those from lower socioeconomic backgrounds. Insofar as multicultural health care providers may effectively reduce and prevent psychological problems among multicultural persons, a multicultural health care workforce makes economic sense. Therefore, psychology must demonstrate and emphasize the benefits of multicultural expertise. For example, there is preliminary evidence that multicultural training improves treatment outcome with clients of color (Yutrzenka, 1995). Even more effective may be the participation of multicultural administrators within managed care corporations.

Individual support of national organizations that advocate multicultural issues is critical if there is to be national attention to multicultural issues. Several
of these organizations within the American Psychological Association are
mentioned above. In addition, there are the Asian American Psychological Association, the Association of Black Psychologists, the National Hispanic Psychological Association, and the Society of Indian Psychologists. These organizations can also offer professional and social support to minority persons who
work in isolated environments.

Skills

By recruiting students and faculty of diverse backgrounds, a training program can achieve diversity. However, achieving a multicultural environment in
which multiple cultural approaches are not only tolerated but also valued may
be much more difficult (Atkinson, Brown, & Casas, 1996; Sue, 1996). Simply
recruiting diverse faculty and students to a program and even providing financial incentives are not adequate substitutes for creating a supportive environment in which mentoring occurs (Atkinson et al., 1996). A deliberate integration of gender, cultural, and class issues into all aspects of a curriculum and an
evaluation of the extent to which such integration is successful are critical for
effective training. Several innovative methods for evaluating multicultural
competence have been proposed (Pope-Davis & Coleman, 1997).

Access to training experiences with diverse populations in terms of gender,
ethnicity, and social class, including appropriate supervision, should be the responsibility of all graduate training programs in counseling, clinical, and professional psychology. One method of increasing multicultural awareness issues
in graduate programs is to actively seek minority clientele. Gaining access to
ethnic minority populations may be more difficult in some geographic locations. However, with extra effort, some success may be achieved. For example,
students and a professor at a Midwestern graduate program initiated a clinical
practicum opportunity at an African American church in a nearby community.
Endeavors such as this should be encouraged and facilitated by both students
and faculty.

The process of changing a monocultural program to be multicultural may
seem to be an abstract endeavor, particularly for the majority of psychologists
who have not had access to multicultural training. Thus, concrete examples of
model multicultural programs are needed. Several model programs have been

identified (Ponterotto, 1997). Particularly helpful is an article on the evolution of the counseling psychology program at the University of California, Santa Barbara into a multicultural program (Atkinson et al., 1996).

The supply of psychologists who have been trained in programs committed to multicultural training falls far short of society's demand for multicultural psychological services. Most psychologists who provide training and services have not received multicultural training. Thus, postdoctoral and continuing education programs need to emphasize multicultural training. As with the APA accreditation process, efforts are necessary to ensure that all states require multicultural continuing education to maintain licensure. The National College of Professional Psychology has developed training in the understanding and treatment of substance abuse disorders for psychologists who did not have access to such training in their own graduate education. This training was developed in large part because of market demands for psychologists to provide services for substance abusers. The market for psychologists with expertise in multicultural issues is also expanding. Thus, large-scale continuing programs, possibly as part of the National College of Professional Psychology, should be developed for gender, cultural, and class issues.

Conclusion

The identification of traditional Western psychology as the source of gender, cultural, and class difficulties and a concomitant call for change may be viewed as provocative. However, the existing power structure has long tended to project the blame for these difficulties onto women, persons of color, and those of lower socioeconomic status. There are many reasons for the unresponsiveness of traditional Western psychology to persons who are not European American middle- to upper-class men. Some traditionalists may be oblivious to the changes that have already been occurring in American society during the past four decades. Others may recognize that society is changing but may hope to preserve their dominance and may be unwilling to relinquish power. Still others may sense a need to change but may not know how. Our goal is not simply to displace those in power but to work together to create a psychology that is responsive to all persons in society by integrating the best aspects of multiple approaches, both Western and non-Western (Hall & Barongan, 1997). We strongly believe that multicultural training should not be regarded simply as an

ideal but as a basic requirement for all training in psychology. Accommodation
in academic training should be to multiple cultures, not just to a single one.

References

American Psychological Association (APA). (1986). *Accreditation handbook* (Rev. ed.). Washington, DC: APA Committee on Accreditation and Accreditation Office.
American Psychological Association, Office of Ethnic Minority Affairs. (1993). Guidelines for
providers of psychological services to ethnic, linguistic, and culturally diverse populations.
American Psychologist, 48, 45-48.
Arredondo, P. (1994). Multicultural training: A response. *The Counseling Psychologist, 22,*
308-314.
Atkinson, D. R., Brown, M. T., & Casas, J. M. (1996). Achieving ethnic parity in counseling psy-
chology. *The Counseling Psychologist, 24,* 230-258.
Atkinson, D. R., Morten, G., & Sue, D. W. (Eds.). (1993). *Counseling American minorities: A
cross-cultural perspective* (4th ed.). Dubuque, IA: Brown & Benchmark.
Bernal, M. E., & Castro, F. G. (1994). Are clinical psychologists prepared for service and research
with ethnic minorities? Report of a decade of progress. *American Psychologist, 49,* 797-805.
Berry, J. W. (1984). Cultural relations in plural societies: Alternatives to segregation and their
socio-psychological implications. In M. Brewer & N. Miller (Eds.), *Groups in contact*
(pp. 11-27). San Diego, CA: Academic Press.
Berry, J. W., Kim, U., Minde, T., & Mok, D. (1987). Comparative studies of acculturative stress.
International Migration Review, 21, 491-511.
Biernat, M., & Kobrynowicz, D. (1997). Gender- and race-based standards of competence: Lower
minimum standards but higher ability standards for devalued groups. *Journal of Personality
and Social Psychology, 72,* 544-557.
Boykin, A. W. (1983). On academic task performance and Afro-American children. In J. R.
Spencer (Ed.), *Achievement and achievement motives* (pp. 324-371). New York: Freeman.
Coleman, H. L. K. (1995). Strategies for coping with cultural diversity. *The Counseling Psycholo-
gist, 23,* 722-740.
D'Andrea, M., & Daniels, J. (1991). Exploring the different levels of multicultural counseling
training in counselor education. *Journal of Counseling and Development, 70,* 78-85.
Essandoh, P. K. (1996). Multicultural challenges in graduate counseling psychology programs:
Timely reminders. *The Counseling Psychologist, 24,* 273-278.
Garb, H. N. (1997). Race bias, social class bias, and gender bias in clinical judgment. *Clinical Psy-
chology: Science and Practice, 4,* 99-120.
Gloria, A. M., & Pope-Davis, D. B. (1997). Cultural ambience: The importance of a culturally
aware learning environment in the training and education of counselors. In D. B. Pope-Davis &
H. L. K. Coleman (Eds.), *Multicultural counseling competencies: Assessment, education and
training, and supervision* (pp. 242-259). Thousand Oaks, CA: Sage.
Greenfield, P. M. (1994). Independence and interdependence as developmental scripts: Implications for theory, research, and practice. In P. M. Greenfield & R. R. Cocking (Eds.), *Cross-
cultural roots of minority child development* (pp. 1-37). Hillsdale, NJ: Lawrence Erlbaum.
Hall, C. C. I. (1990). Qualified minorities are encouraged to apply: The recruitment of ethnic minority and female psychologists. In G. Stricker, E. Davis-Russell, E. Bourg, E. Duran, W. R.
Hammond, J. McHolland, K. Polite, & B. E. Vaughn (Eds.), *Toward ethnic diversification in*

psychology education and training (pp. 105-111). Washington, DC: American Psychological Association.

Hall, C. C. I. (1997). Cultural malpractice: The growing obsolescence of psychology with the changing U.S. population. *American Psychologist, 52,* 642-651.

Hall, G. C. N., & Barongan, C. (1997). Prevention of sexual aggression: Sociocultural risk and protective factors. *American Psychologist, 52,* 5-14.

Helms, J. E. (Ed.). (1990). *Black and White racial identity: Theory, research, and practice.* Westport, CT: Greenwood.

LaFromboise, T., Coleman, H. L. K., & Gerton, J. (1993). Psychological impact of biculturalism: Evidence and theory. *Psychological Bulletin, 114,* 395-412.

Landrine, H. (1992). Clinical implications of cultural differences: The referential versus the indexical self. *Clinical Psychology Review, 12,* 401-415.

Leach, M. M., & Carlton, M. A. (1997). Toward defining a multicultural training philosophy. In D. B. Pope-Davis & H. L. K. Coleman (Eds.), *Multicultural counseling competencies: Assessment, education and training, and supervision* (pp. 184-208). Thousand Oaks, CA: Sage.

Lore, R. K., & Schultz, L. A. (1993). Control of human aggression: A comparative perspective. *American Psychologist, 48,* 16-25.

Lu, E. G. (1996, August). *Historical perspectives on the clinical psychology of ethnic minorities.* Symposium presented at the 104th Annual Convention of the American Psychological Association, Toronto.

Malgady, R. G., Rogler, L. H., & Constantino, G. (1987). Ethnocultural and linguistic bias in mental health evaluation of Hispanics. *American Psychologist, 42,* 228-234.

Markus, H. R., & Kitayama, S. (1991). Culture and the self: Implications for cognition, emotion, and motivation. *Psychological Review, 98,* 224-253.

Myers, H. F., Echemendia, R. J., & Trimble, J. E. (1991). The need for training ethnic minority psychologists. In H. F. Myers, P. Wohlford, L. P. Guzman, & R. J. Echemendia (Eds.), *Ethnic minority perspectives on clinical training and services in psychology* (pp. 3-11). Washington, DC: American Psychological Association.

Novaco, R. W. (1976). Treatment of chronic anger through cognitive and relaxation controls. *Journal of Consulting and Clinical Psychology, 44,* 681.

Ogbu, J. U. (1994). From cultural differences to differences in cultural frame of reference. In P. M. Greenfield & R. R. Cocking (Eds.), *Cross-cultural roots of minority child development* (pp. 365-391). Hillsdale, NJ: Lawrence Erlbaum.

Phinney, J. S., & Alipuria, L. (1996). At the interface of culture: Multiethnic/multiracial high school and college students. *Journal of Social Psychology, 136,* 139-158.

Pion, G. M., Mednick, M. T., Astin, H. S., Hall, C. C. I., Kenkel, M. B., Keita, G. P., Kohout, J. L., & Kelleher, J. C. (1996). The shifting gender composition of psychology: Trends and implications for the discipline. *American Psychologist, 51,* 509-528.

Ponterotto, J. G. (1997). Multicultural counseling training: A competency model and national survey. In D. B. Pope-Davis & H. L. K. Coleman (Eds.), *Multicultural counseling competencies: Assessment, education and training, and supervision* (pp. 111-130). Thousand Oaks, CA: Sage.

Pope-Davis, D. B., & Coleman, H. L. K. (1997). *Multicultural counseling competencies: Assessment, education and training, and supervision.* Thousand Oaks, CA: Sage.

Ridley, C. R. (1995). *Overcoming unintentional racism in counseling and therapy: A practitioner's guide to intentional intervention.* Thousand Oaks, CA: Sage.

Ridley, C. R., Mendoza, D. W., & Kanitz, B. E. (1994). Multicultural training: Reexamination, operationalization, and integration. *The Counseling Psychologist, 22,* 227-289.

Ridley, S. E. (1991). Faculty development and retraining: Some committee recommendations. In H. F. Myers, P. Wohlford, L. P. Guzman, & R. J. Echemendia (Eds.), *Ethnic minority perspectives on clinical training and services in psychology* (pp. 165-168). Washington, DC: American Psychological Association.

Sampson, R. J. (1993). The community context of violent crime. In W. J. Wilson (Ed.), *Sociology and the public agency* (pp. 259-286). Newbury Park, CA: Sage.

Snowden, L. R., & Cheung, F. K. (1990). Use of inpatient mental health services by members of ethnic minority groups. *American Psychologist, 45,* 347-355.

Sue, D. W. (1996). Multicultural counseling: Models, methods, and actions. *The Counseling Psychologist, 24,* 279-284.

Sue, D. W., Arredondo, P., & McDavis, R. J. (1992). Multicultural counseling competencies and standards: A call to the profession. *Journal of Counseling and Development, 70,* 477-486.

Sue, D. W., & Sue, D. (1990). *Counseling the culturally different: Theory and practice* (2nd ed.). New York: John Wiley.

Sue, S., & Zane, N. (1987). The role of culture and cultural techniques in psychotherapy: A critique and reformulation. *American Psychologist, 42,* 37-45.

Triandis, H. C. (1989). Cross-cultural studies of individualism and collectivism. *Nebraska Symposium on Motivation, 37,* 41-133.

Triandis, H. C. (1996). The psychological measurement of cultural syndromes. *American Psychologist, 51,* 407-415.

Triandis, H. C., McCusker, C., & Hui, C. H. (1990). Multimethod probes of individualism and collectivism. *Journal of Personality and Social Psychology, 59,* 1006-1020.

Uba, L. (1994). *Asian Americans: Personality patterns, identity, and mental health.* New York: Guilford.

U.S. Bureau of the Census. (1992). *Current population reports.* Washington, DC: Author.

Williams, C. L., & Berry, J. W. (1991). Primary prevention of acculturative stress among refugees: Application of psychological theory and practice. *American Psychologist, 46,* 632-641.

Wise, F., & Miller, N. B. (1983). The mental health of American Indian children. In G. J. Powell, J. Yamamoto, A. Romero, & A. Morales (Eds.), *The psychosocial development of minority group children* (pp. 344-361). New York: Brunner/Mazel.

Yutrzenka, B. A. (1995). Making a case for training in ethnic and cultural diversity in increasing treatment efficacy. *Journal of Consulting and Clinical Psychology, 63,* 197-206.

Zanna, M. P., & Darley, J. M. (1987). *The compleat academic: A practical guide for the beginning social scientist.* New York: Random House.

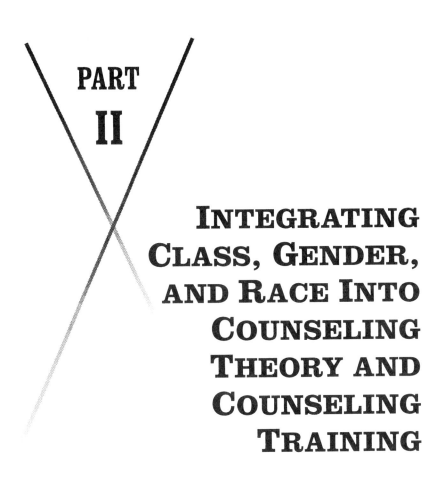

PART
II

INTEGRATING
CLASS, GENDER,
AND RACE INTO
COUNSELING
THEORY AND
COUNSELING
TRAINING

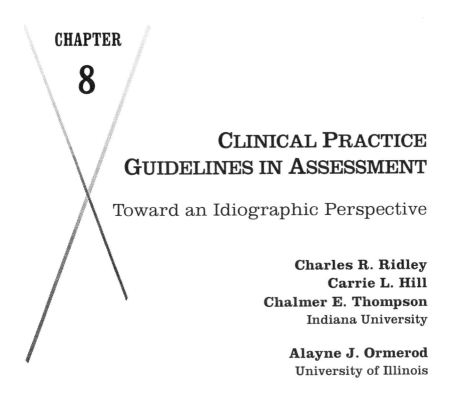

CLINICAL PRACTICE
GUIDELINES IN ASSESSMENT

Toward an Idiographic Perspective

Charles R. Ridley
Carrie L. Hill
Chalmer E. Thompson
Indiana University

Alayne J. Ormerod
University of Illinois

Clinical practice guidelines have emerged as an important feature of mental health service delivery. In many clinical settings, especially managed care facilities, the use of practice guidelines is required. According to the Institute of Medicine, guidelines for clinical practice are defined as "systemically developed statements to assist practitioner and patient decisions about appropriate health care for specific clinical circumstances" (Field & Lohr, 1990, p. 38). The fundamental purpose of practice guidelines is to improve the quality of primary care practice (Schulberg & Rush, 1994). Elaborating on this purpose, Clinton, McCormick, and Besteman (1994) stated that guidelines

> assist health care practitioners in the prevention, diagnosis, treatment, and management of clinical conditions and [provide the] performance mea-

sures, standards of quality, and review criteria by which health care practitioners and others may review health care to insure its quality. (p. 30)

The need to ensure high-quality health care arises out of a practice environment facing many significant problems and challenges, including (a) pressures for cost containment that frustrate the overall goal for quality assurance, (b) significant and unexplained variations in the management of specific health conditions, (c) the lack of consensus among practitioners about what constitutes effective practices, (d) patient misinformation about treatment options, and (e) continual disparities in treatment based on factors such as race/ethnicity, social class, and gender (Clinton et al., 1994; Gilbert & Scher, 1999; Munoz, Hollon, McGrath, Rehm, & Vanden Bos, 1994; Russell, Fujino, Sue, Cheung, & Snowden, 1996; Schulberg & Rush, 1994; Zhang, Snowden, & Sue, 1998). In light of these problems and challenges, we believe that the adoption of clinical practice guidelines could greatly improve the quality of mental health care, and we argue for this need in mental health delivery systems. Furthermore, we assert that the need is especially pressing in the area of psychological assessment. Butcher (1997), for example, reported that many clinicians fail to obtain an initial assessment or behavioral baseline. Ridley, Li, and Hill (1998) added that the failure of practitioners to conduct thorough assessments is enigmatic. A confluence of social and psychological variables is often unaccounted for by clinicians.

Therefore, the process of making sound assessment decisions requires an ability to ascertain which among a vast array of variables are significant for making judgments about treatment, prognosis, and the management of clinical conditions. In particular, knowledge about the socialization of clients on the basis of variables such as gender, race, culture, age, sexual orientation, and socioeconomic status is crucial to psychological assessment and practice. Yet, within the context of a societal zeitgeist that tends to minimize the relevance of these variables to psychological functioning, clinicians are prone to making assessment decisions that are inaccurate, incomplete, or otherwise hindered by a lack of cultural self-processing, poor motivation, or cultural insensitivity (see Ridley, Mendoza, Kanitz, Angermeier, & Zenk, 1994). The problem of making unsound assessment decisions is exacerbated when clinicians attempt to assess clients whose backgrounds are distinctly different from their own. These differences in background between therapists and clients may interfere with counselors' effectiveness in clinical decision making.

The purpose of this chapter is to propose clinical practice guidelines that could assist clinicians in making idiographic conceptualizations of clients. We assert that quality of care can be strengthened when practitioners develop a working knowledge of the cultural and sociopolitical influences on human behavior and development. In this chapter, we emphasize five undeniable features of human psychological functioning that can be obscured in psychological assessment. These features are race/ethnicity, gender, sexual orientation, age, and socioeconomic status.

The chapter is organized as follows. First, we describe the idiographic perspective of clinical assessment. Second, we describe the aforementioned cultural and sociopolitical features of human behavior and development as they pertain to psychological assessment. Third, we summarize what we perceive to be essential characteristics of clinical practice guidelines. Fourth, we propose a set of aspirational guidelines that can optimally lead to competent idiographic assessments. We conclude with some recommendations for employing the guidelines in a meaningful and systematic fashion.

WHAT IS THE IDIOGRAPHIC PERSPECTIVE?

The concept of idiographic is derived from the Greek word *idios,* meaning unique or individual. This perspective emphasizes the need to perceive each client as a unique individual rather than a person reduced to one or more sets of characteristics. In urging practitioners to strive for idiographic assessments of their clients, we are not suggesting that information about group characteristics that pertain to individual clients is not valuable. Indeed, this information is necessary to help guide practitioners' understanding of important issues that affect clients' psychological functioning. However, we do suggest that practitioners may tend to make generalizations about clients based on race, gender, age, sexual orientation, and socioeconomic status without fully exploring the nuances of these qualities in the lives of individual clients.

Although generalizations can be problematic during clinical assessment, other problems result from a lack of understanding about particular groups. For example, divisions that occur among people on the basis of race and sexual orientation can especially create misunderstandings and foster attendant feelings of fear, anger, or hatred. Consequently, practitioners who perceive themselves as different from their clients may possess biased beliefs, attitudes, or feelings toward them. These biases are based on past restrictive associations with members of the client's group, and they are fueled by stereotypes (Shih, Pittinsky, & Ambody, 1999). As a result, counselors may not consider the actual effects of socializing factors such as race, gender, age, sexual orientation, and socioeconomic status and consequently exclude such factors during an assessment. The idiographic perspective attempts to balance these clinical risks by urging practitioners to broaden their knowledge base and challenge their biases.

Ridley (1995) set forth five idiographic principles that are relevant to assessment. First, every client should be understood from his or her personal frame of reference. Second, normative information does not necessarily fit each client who is identified as a member of a particular group. Third, everyone is a dynamic blend of multiple social identities (Hewstone, 1996), and these social identities are critical to assessment and treatment (Hays, 1996; McBride, 1990; Persons, 1991; Reid & Comas-Díaz, 1990; Ridley et al., 1994; Robinson, 1993; Sinacore-Guinn, 1995). Fourth, the idiographic perspective is compatible with the biopsychosocial model of mental health. Fifth, the idiographic perspective is transtheoretical.

The idiographic perspective is illustrated by the use of a fictitious client, Lasako Woodward. Lasako is a 47-year-old woman. She is biracial. Her father is Caucasian, and her mother is Japanese. She is from a middle-class background and heterosexual in her sexual orientation. Certainly, she has other identities such as the fact that she is divorced, and she is Unitarian in her religious affiliation. Figure 8.1 depicts Lasako idiographically.

Clinicians attempting to assess Lasako holistically and as a unique person need to explore all seven of her social identities. If Lasako is considered from the perspective of having only one or a few social identities without regard to the interaction of these identities, it is likely that the assessment will be incomplete and inaccurate. Each social identity is important. However, each one examined separately offers a limited view of what it means to be Lasako as a unique person. On the other hand, Lasako's idiographic experience sets her apart from every other biracial individual who is female, heterosexual, middle aged, middle class, divorced, and Unitarian. Clinicians who have a genuine appreciation and understanding of the varied social identities that inform Lasako's personhood may still make judgmental and inferential errors, but the successful integration of all these aspects increases the chances of making a sound assessment.

To make a sound clinical judgment about Lasako, clinicians should focus their assessment on the center of the diagram. This area has been referred to as

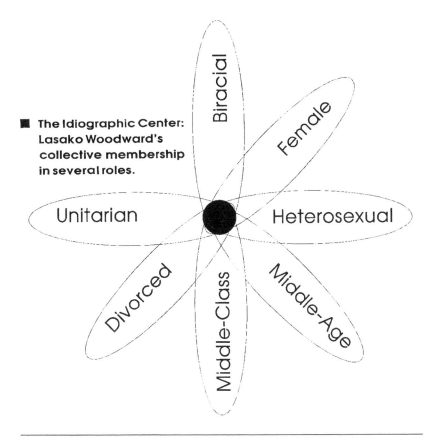

The Idiographic Center:
Lasako Woodward's
collective membership
in several roles.

Figure 8.1. An Idiographic Conceptualization of Lasako Woodward

the idiographic center (Ridley et al., 1994) or the indivisible intersection (Robinson, 1993). The area represents Lasako's personal experience based on the interaction of her seven social identities. Therefore, in making a sound assessment, clinicians "must discover the cultural groups to which a client belongs and then strive to discern the individual's personal frame of reference for his or her participation in these different groups" (Ridley et al., 1994, p. 129).

Recognizing the importance of the idiographic perspective in assessment is a desirable initial step in making comprehensive, accurate assessment decisions. This recognition, however, is not enough. Clinicians can begin to learn this process by becoming informed about the socializing influences that help shape a client's identity. In the following section, we focus on those influences that can often go unexplored or unrecognized. These socializing forces include race/ethnicity, sexual orientation, gender, socioeconomic status, and age.

SOCIALIZING FORCES THAT INFLUENCE MENTAL HEALTH FUNCTIONING

Race/Ethnicity

Individuals undergo a variety of developmental processes as they experience themselves as racial and ethnic beings. Three important processes that frequently emerge in the literature are acculturation, racial identity development, and biculturalism. *Acculturation* is the degree to which individuals integrate new cultural patterns into original cultural patterns (Dana, 1993). *Racial identity* is the degree to which individuals accept themselves and others as social beings and ostensibly the social implications of their racial group membership (Ponterotto & Pedersen, 1993). *Biculturalism* is the capacity to function in more than one culture (LaFromboise, Coleman, & Gerton, 1993). There is considerable overlap between these variables.

Clinicians should attempt to determine their clients' development in these areas. They should try to uncover any conflicts clients may have in these areas. These conflicts might arise as primary areas of concern for clients or as insidious factors associated with other symptomatology such as anxiety or depression. Drawing on these data, clinicians might also assess clients' strengths in coping and relating to others around them. Clinicians can employ inventories and instruments that have been developed to that end as well as address these issues during the clinical interview.

Another insidious factor that can affect psychological functioning is *racial victimization*. This form of trauma is particularly debilitating for people of color who are subject to overt and covert forms of racism (Ridley, 1995). Racial victimization also creates psychological problems for White people. They must deal with the psychological issues stemming from their own racism or failure to confront racism (Thompson & Neville, 1999).

Clinicians should recognize that racial victimization is an invisible wound of immense psychological proportion. When conducting an assessment, they need to maintain the delicate balance of not blaming the victim for his or her loss of status or excusing the victim from personal responsibility. They should also realize that highly prejudiced and racist individuals harbor deep-seated unresolved psychological issues.

Gender

Gender is viewed as a category holding social and political meaning about individual behavior and interrelationships. Assessment, diagnosis, and test interpretation should be undertaken with an understanding of the gender meanings and assumptions that underlie the clinician's theoretical stance and practices. Gender role analysis (Brown, 1994) should be used as a means of understanding a client's self-concept, behavior, and interrelationships within the context of the other categories that make up the individual's life and worldview.

Brown (1994) reminded us that psychological tests often have specific norm groups and purposes that may not extend to gendered experiences (e.g., understanding psychological reactions to physical or sexual violence). She suggested that clinicians ask, "What do we know about how people with this particular experience respond to this specific psychological test?" as a way of determining whether a test is appropriate for the individual and referral question.

Brown (1986) noted that for women, both participation in and deviation from the feminine gender role can lead them to being diagnosed with some form of pathology. Robertson and Fitzgerald (1990) found that men who deviate from traditional gender role behavior are more likely to receive attributions of pathology than men who engage in gender-traditional roles. Brown (1994) suggested,

> Feminist therapists must question what they mean by "male" and "female," and what beliefs and stereotypes they hold about what is "normal," "natural," and "to be expected." They must inquire how, from whom, and in what context they learned certain supposedly eternal verities [and beg the question] to what degree is this context heavily invested in maintaining a sexist, racist, classist, heterosexist status quo? (p. 99)

Psychological test data are best interpreted in the context of gender role analysis (Brown, 1994). Practitioners should seek research that includes an understanding of testing in the context of gender (e.g., see Dutton, 1992, for uses of personality testing with battered women and Fitzgerald, Buchanan-Biddle, Collinsworth, Magley, & Ramos, 1999, for uses of personality testing with women who have been sexually harassed).

Direct trauma, such as sexual or physical assault, is experienced by alarmingly high numbers of women (Koss et al., 1994). Women with a history of sexual or physical abuse are likely to experience higher rates of psychological consequences (Koss et al., 1994). When trauma (direct, indirect, or insidious) (Root, 1992) is present, it is important to understand and interpret current behavior within the context of the trauma.

Gender role analysis should include an understanding of the meaning of gender within the culture of the individual. Greene (1994) noted that a therapist should assess a culture's traditional gender role stereotypes and their relative fluidity or rigidity. Comas-Díaz (1994) concurred with this recommendation, suggesting that the experiences and definitions of womanhood vary among and within women of color.

Sexual Orientation

Lesbian, gay, and bisexual individuals are members of a cultural minority whose sexual identities are typically not visible. Consequently, clinicians may assume that clients are heterosexual unless clients volunteer otherwise. This bias toward heterosexuality can set a tone of expectant "normalcy," whereby clients who have to correct the therapist may feel as though they are admitting to a form of pathology. Assessments that contain heterosexist bias ignore other forms of sexual identity and, by implication, pathologize those who are not heterosexual. Clinicians should not assume a heterosexual orientation when assessing a client. They should also consider whether a potentially useful psychological test is based on any assumptions about roles and relationships (e.g., marriage or heterosexual relationships) that may not be appropriate for sexual minorities (Prince, 1997).

Clinicians also may hold inaccurate or negatively biased attitudes toward lesbian, gay, and bisexual individuals. Clinicians need to possess an affirming attitude and the necessary competence to work with individuals who are sexual minorities. This includes specialized knowledge about sexual identity development, an understanding of the effects of stressors related to living in a hostile sociocultural context, and knowledge about lesbians, gays, and bisexuals as distinct groups of individuals.

Age

Clinicians should gather information from clients in such a way that is sensitive to variables such as age and stage of development. For example, a client who identifies with the "baby-boomer" generation may have more liberal views about psychotherapy than an older adult who was socialized in an era when mental health treatment was considered more of a "taboo." A standard clinical interview may be sufficient to obtain a thorough biopsychosocial assessment of the baby-boomer. However, an older client may prefer to complete a paper-and-pencil exercise that contains biopsychosocial inquiries because this method seems more formal and less threatening than an immediate face-to-face interaction.

Clinicians are advised to gather assessment data from multiple sources contingent on the client's age and developmental circumstances. Possible sources include medical or mental health records, educational or occupational records, family members, caregivers, guardians, and staff members if the client is living in an institutional environment. Permission must be granted from the client or the person legally responsible for the client to seek information from any external sources.

Several age-relevant environmental stressors can affect the client's psychological functioning. Such stressors include (a) social roles and expectations, (b) career and educational issues, and (c) family and peer relationships (Blocher, 1974). The environmental stressors experienced by different age groups can vary widely. For example, a 12-year-old child entering a new school and a 40-year-old adult recently fired from a job are both experiencing many environmental stressors. Each person is confronted with new social roles and expectations, changes in educational or career plans, the loss of old peer relationships, and the challenge of forming new ones. However, the specific problems and individual experiences of these stressors are probably quite different because the 12-year-old and 40-year-old are at vastly different developmental stages and living under very different circumstances. Clinicians are urged to explore possible stressors the client is experiencing that are related to the interaction between the client's age and the environment.

Socioeconomic Status

Practitioners need to explore stressors related to socioeconomic status (SES) that are affecting their clients' functioning. These include but are not limited to access to health care, quality of family environment, quality of education, and physical and emotional safety. Socioeconomic stressors can affect clients of any socioeconomic background. For instance, a low SES client may have limited access to health care, have few opportunities for a high-quality education, and live in an unsafe neighborhood. On the other hand, a high SES client may have to negotiate between competing social and family expectations and creating extremely stressful career, social, and family environments. Therefore, clinicians should pay attention to socioeconomic variables regardless of the client's socioeconomic background.

Unfortunately, problems that are related to socioeconomic status are not always considered in assessment because they are masked by more salient variables. Some of these variables include age, race, gender, and sexual orientation. Although all of these variables are important to idiographic assessment, it has been suggested that mental health differences related to age, race, or sex are modest in comparison to socioeconomic differences (Basic Behavioral Science Task Force of the National Advisory Mental Health Council, 1996). Because many psychosocial risk factors are more prevalent at lower socioeconomic levels, it is important for clinicians to consider clients' socioeconomic status as well as their age, race, gender, and sexual orientation. Otherwise, problems may be attributed to alternative factors when SES is the actual source of difficulty. Consequently, treatment planning is misdirected, and outcomes are unfavorable at best.

Clinicians should consider the complete spectrum of socioeconomic status. In this way, overpathologizing clients from lower socioeconomic backgrounds is avoided, and underpathologizing "YAVIS" (i.e., young, attractive, verbal, intelligent, successful) clients (Schofield, 1964) is less likely. Both pitfalls can result from engaging in representativeness, or the tendency to rely on stereotypes, and fail to consider base rates when making assessment decisions (Spengler, Strohmer, Dixon, & Shivy, 1995). Clinicians may hold stereotypes about members of different socioeconomic groups that influence their assessment decisions. This is highly dangerous in the absence of base rate consideration. Therefore, clinicians must be vigilant while making assessment decisions and use base rates to counteract the potential of stereotyping.

CHARACTERISTICS OF GOOD PRACTICE GUIDELINES

Before describing our proposed guidelines for idiographic assessment, we think readers would benefit from knowing the defining characteristics of clinical practice guidelines. Admittedly, practice guidelines represent a "best judgment at the time"—a judgment, however, based on state-of-the-science information (Rush, Trivedi, Schriger, & Petty, 1992). Revision of guidelines is required as knowledge advances in the areas of assessment and treatment. With this proviso in mind, we paraphrase the eight attributes of practice guidelines (from *Clinical Practice Guidelines,* Field & Lohr, 1990). We regard these qualities as aspirational for our guidelines.

1. *Validity.* This is considered the most critical attribute and relates most directly to outcome. Practice guidelines are valid if, when followed, they improve health outcomes. Validity is determined through evaluative evidence.

2. *Reliability-reproducibility.* This characteristic establishes that, given the same evidence and methods for development, another set of experts can develop essentially the same guidelines. Moreover, given similar clinical circumstances, practitioners can fairly evenly and consistently interpret and apply the guidelines.

3. *Clinical applicability.* Practice guidelines explicitly define the patient populations for which the treatment is intended. Clinical applicability is based on data derived from subject populations that the treatment has benefited, as well as expert judgment.

4. *Clinical flexibility.* The application of good practice can yield different outcomes as a result of a myriad variables, including client, therapist, and client-therapist factors and extraneous variables. Clinical flexibility refers to the identification of known or generally expected exceptions to guideline recommendations.

5. *Clarity.* Guidelines use unambiguous language, clearly defined terms, and a logical, easy-to-follow style of presentation.

6. *Multidisciplinary process.* The development of practice guidelines includes participation by representatives of affected provider groups.

7. *Scheduled review.* Practice guidelines indicate a review period to determine the need for revisions.

8. *Documentation.* The entire process of the development and content of practice guidelines is meticulously documented and described.

CLINICAL GUIDELINES FOR ASSESSMENT

This section enfolds our discussions of socializing forces and ideal guidelines for practice. We present guidelines to which practitioners can aspire, combining knowledge about the forces that influence psychological functioning and strategies for making sound assessment decisions about a wide variety of clients.

> *Guideline 1:* Psychological functioning always involves an interaction of a person's multiple identities. Among the numerous identities people assume are those related to gender, socioeconomic status, race/ethnicity, age, and sexual orientation. These are core components of every individual's overall identity formation (Robinson, 1993). These identities are important throughout the life span and help shape a person's sense of self in the world.

Any psychological assessment that fails to consider the person's important identities is incomplete. In addition, any psychological assessment that fails to examine the interaction among these variables is inaccurate. Christian (1989), for example, noted the flaw in treating gender and race as though these are pure and exhaustive categories. In accordance with the overarching idiographic principle, clinicians must place priority on understanding a client's personal frame of reference.

> *Guideline 2:* Individuals must be evaluated within their sociocultural and sociopolitical contexts. These influences are powerful determinants of behavior. Indeed, without evaluating a person's interaction with the social environment, an accurate assessment is not possible.

Clinicians must assess the influence of sociocultural stressors on the psychological functioning of clients. On this subject, Watzlawick, Beavin, and Jackson (1967) stated that a phenomenon remains unexplainable as long as the range of observation is not wide enough to include the context in which the phenomenon occurs. Failure to realize the intricacies of the relationships between an event and the matrix in which it takes place, between an organism and its environment, either confronts the observer with something "mysterious" or induces him to attribute to his object of study certain properties the object may not possess. (pp. 20-21)

Prominent social stressors include poverty, racial or sex discrimination, xenophobia, threats of violence, recent immigrant status, inaccessibility to health care, and inadequate educational systems (Canino & Spurlock, 1994). A helpful suggestion for exploring environmental influences comes from the work of Szapocznik and Kurtines (1993). They introduced the concept of embeddedness of the individual within the context of the family within the context of culture.

> *Guideline 3:* People are holistic, consisting of a variety of assets, limitations, resources, and potentialities. Everyone exhibits potentialities and vulnerabilities in varying degrees and responds to life's challenges with a variety of coping styles.

Psychological assessment should portray a balanced case conceptualization. Clinicians should describe a client's assets and positive resources as well as liabilities. In addition, clinicians should guard themselves against the tendencies of either overpathologizing or underpathologizing clients. This applies especially to clients from marginalized groups.

> *Guideline 4:* Trauma can have a debilitating influence on psychological functioning (Root, 1992). It can lead to numerous psychological problems such as anxiety, panic, depression, multiple personalities, paranoia, anger, and sleep problems. It can also lead to suicidality, irritability, mood swings, and bizarre rituals. Finally, it can lead to relationship difficulties, general despair, aimlessness, and hopelessness. Some sources of trauma are obvious, but others are less obvious. The abstruse sources of trauma complicate the clinical picture, making it more difficult for clinicians to render sound judgments.

Idiographic assessment must ascertain the impact of trauma on the client. Root (1992) conceptualized three categories of traumatic impact that should be useful to clinicians:

1. *Direct trauma.* This is the easiest type of trauma to link to symptomatology. It includes forms of maliciously perpetrated violence, war experiences, industrial accidents, and natural disasters.
2. *Indirect trauma.* This includes the vicarious experience of trauma sustained by another person, witnessing trauma, and receiving information about devastation or violence. Females are more likely than males to experience indirect trauma.
3. *Insidious trauma.* This involves the devaluing of one's social status by those in power. Often present throughout a lifetime, prominent examples are related to gender, race, sexual orientation, and physical disability.

Guideline 5: Psychological symptoms can result from a variety of sources, including a general medical condition. Unfortunately, physical factors can be overlooked or discounted in a psychological assessment. For example, a mental disorder can be the first manifestation of a cerebral disease (American Psychiatric Association, 1994). In addition, a mental disorder can persist after the medical condition has been resolved.

Clinicians must be conscientious in their efforts to include or rule out a medical condition in their assessments. They should be especially attentive to this need in lower socioeconomic clients who often have less access to health care services or whose medical conditions have emerged as a result of impoverishment. When necessary, they should seek medical consultation.

Guideline 6: Because everyone possesses a variety of identities, some of these may be more salient than others. Salient identities supercede other qualities in the person's life because of their central influence on the phenomenological experience. Salient identities can change depending on the situation or the circumstances that arise in the person's life at a particular time.

Idiographic assessment requires an identification and examination of clients' salient identities. This exploration can lead to an understanding of how clients organize their lives. Clients often are unaware of the impact of a salient quality, even though they may have some awareness of that quality. For example, Elpin and Gawelek (1992) noted that White middle-class women tend not to recognize the impact of White privilege on their lives. Some of these women may identify more strongly with their identities as women in general. They may succumb to a climate of color blindness (see Carr, 1997; Thompson & Neville, 1999), whereby race is deemed unimportant or irrelevant to their identities and lives. Yet, their Whiteness powerfully determines their self-experiences. In contrast to some White women, Elpin and Gawelek (1992) suggested that race or class rather than gender may be a more centrally determining factor in the identity of some women of color.

People with a healthy sense of self probably are aware of all of their identities. Consequently, their identification of a salient quality or identity does not necessarily mean that other qualities are clouded or obscured. But the obscuring of identities can have mental health implications in that the people may anticipate pain in facing an identity that they would prefer not to have. For example, recognizing that one has a romantic attraction exclusively toward members of the same sex may cause some clients to experience distress and to deny any identification with gay or lesbian people. This is not difficult to understand considering the stigma that surrounds a gay, lesbian, or bisexual lifestyle. However, the developmental nature of sexual identity most likely interacts with a client's age, race/ethnicity, socioeconomic status, and unique life circumstances to define the client's process of recognition and acceptance of his or her sexual identity. In cases such as this, the clinician's ability to consider both the client's salient qualities or identities and the client's less prominent identities is integral to effective assessment.

> *Guideline 7:* The idiographic perspective is paramount when conducting a psychological assessment. However, base rate data are still an important source of clinical information and should be applied in the context of the client's idiographic blend of multiple identities. Base rate data indicate "the general prevalence of a behavior or event in the population" (Gambrill, 1990, pp. 280-281).

Clinicians must ascertain the probabilities that their clients experience particular disorders depending on how often such conditions normally occur in the population. Without considering this scientific information, clinical interpretations may be skewed. As a result, inaccurate assessment decisions will be made.

Using base rate data is not analogous to stereotyping. Base rate consideration differentiates itself from stereotyping by recognizing that clinical phenomena and circumstances unique to the individual client can always override probabilities.

> *Guideline 8:* Psychological conditions may co-occur with other psychological conditions. For example, alcoholism and depression are distinct clinical entities, but the comorbidity of these disorders is reportedly high (U.S. Department of Health and Human Services, 1993).

There are several steps clinicians can take to tease out the complicated etiology of many psychological conditions:

- Use *DSM-IV* criteria when making diagnostic decisions
- Explore gender role stressors (e.g., effects of sexual violence on depression)
- Explore racial/cultural stressors (e.g., effects of racism and discrimination on reactions of guardedness and suspiciousness)

> *Guideline 9:* Psychological testing is a valuable method of evaluating clinical hypotheses. Unfortunately, psychological testing is often employed in an exploratory manner early in the assessment process. This has been compared to an unfocused fishing expedition that usually results in a dearth of viable hypotheses (Spengler et al., 1995). To reach the soundest assessment decisions, one should form working hypotheses from clinical data gathered through a biopsychosocial assessment and subsequently test those hypotheses with appropriate psychological tests.

Prince (1997) noted that in the "Ethical Principles of Psychologists and Code of Conduct" (American Psychological Association, 1992), it is stated that psychologists

> attempt to identify situations in which particular interventions or assessment techniques or norms may not be applicable or may require adjustment in administration or interpretation because of factors such as individuals' gender, age, race, ethnicity, national origin, religion, sexual orientation, disability, language, or socioeconomic status. (p. 1603)

Prince (1997) offered additional recommendations for using psychological testing with gay, lesbian, and bisexual clients, suggesting that to avoid bias, test users should critically examine test materials for terminology, content, construct, and response bias. Terminology refers to biased language or language that does not positively recognize nonheterosexual respondents. A test user should also consider whether the content of a test is reflective solely of a heterosexual perspective, which can be limited and exclusionary at the item and scale levels (e.g., omitting questions about sexual identity development in a life history questionnaire). Measured constructs also should be meaningful to the experiences and lives of lesbian, gay, and bisexual individuals. Likewise, it is important to consider an individual's attitude toward testing and the possibility of response bias given that psychological testing has been used in the past as a means to diagnose sexual minorities as mentally ill. Lesbian, gay, and bisexual people also may experience concern about revealing sexual orientation when testing is used for selection or evaluative purposes.

> *Guideline 10:* Bias can obscure clinical judgment. Bias exists when the accuracy of a clinician's judgments varies as a function of a client's isomorphic category such as race, social class, or gender as opposed to the client's actual mental health status (Garb, 1997). Research reveals the existence of (a) race bias in the differential diagnosis of schizophrenia and psychotic affective disorders, (b) gender bias in the differential diagnosis of histrionic and antisocial personality disorders, (c) race and gender bias in the prediction of violence, (d) social class bias in the referral of clients to psychotherapy, and (e) heterosexist bias in advocating for conversion therapy (for a comprehensive review of the research on these topics, see Garb, 1997).

Clinicians should be aware of the major reasons for their inaccurate judgments. Their diagnostic criteria can be biased. They may use a biased self-report personality inventory. They may formulate hypotheses based on stereotypes and fail to consider base rate data. They may show bias in the way they integrate idiographic and normative data. To overcome bias, Garb (1997) makes the following recommendations: (a) be aware of when biases are likely to occur, (b) adhere to diagnostic criteria, (c) generate multiple hypotheses, and (d) exercise a general approach of cognitive complexity. *Cognitive complexity* is an information-processing variable defined as an individual difference in "the capacity to construe social behavior in a multidimensional way. A more cognitively complex person has available a more differentiated system of dimensions for perceiving others' behavior than does a less cognitively complex individual" (Bieri et al., 1966, p. 185).

Recommendations and Conclusions

We believe that Garb's (1997) recommendations can help practitioners employ our clinical practice guidelines in a meaningful and systematic fashion. If clinicians are mindful of when their biases are likely to occur, they can conduct more thorough biopsychosocial interviews that fully explore the range of roles and identities experienced by their clients. If they approach their assessments with cognitive complexity, they can successfully determine their clients' most salient identities and balance these decisions with the confluence of socializing forces that shape their clients' identities holistically. If clinicians generate multiple hypotheses based on their understanding of their clients' idiographic centers, they more likely will consider possibilities that include relevant base rate data and the prospect of comorbidity. And if they adhere to valid diagnostic criteria, they will test their hypotheses with a level of scientific rigor that will ensure more sound assessment decisions.

In this chapter, we have described an idiographic perspective that clinicians can use to understand the many cultural and sociopolitical features of human behavior and development that influence psychological functioning. Grounded in this perspective, we delineated a set of aspirational guidelines that can be applied to the practice of psychological assessment. It is hoped that the guidelines will lead to more competent idiographic assessment conclusions and related treatment interventions. We encourage researchers and clinicians to evaluate empirically and practically the usefulness and effectiveness of these guidelines and to participate in the modification of them to ultimately improve psychological assessment and treatment.

References

American Psychiatric Association. (1994). *Diagnostic and statistical manual of mental disorders* (4th ed.). Washington, DC: Author.
American Psychological Association. (1992). Ethical principles of psychologists and code of conduct. *American Psychologist, 47,* 1597-1611.

Basic Behavioral Science Task Force of the National Advisory Mental Health Council. (1996). Basic behavioral science research for mental health: Sociocultural and environmental processes. *American Psychologist, 51,* 722-731.

Bieri, J., Atkins, A. L., Briar, S., Leamen, R. L., Miller, H., & Tripodi, T. (1966). *Clinical and social judgment: The discrimination of behavioral information.* New York: John Wiley.

Blocher, D. H. (1974). *Developmental counseling.* New York: Ronald.

Brown, L. S. (1986). The meaning of multicultural perspective for theory building in feminist therapy. In L. S. Brown & M. P. P. Root (Eds.), *Diversity and complexity in feminist theory* (pp. 1-21). Binghamton, NY: Haworth.

Brown, L. S. (1994). *Subversive dialogues: Theory in feminist therapy.* New York: Basic Books.

Butcher, J. N. (1997). Introduction to the special section on assessment in psychological treatment: A necessary step for effective intervention. *Psychological Assessment, 9,* 331-333.

Canino, I. A., & Spurlock, J. (1994). *Culturally diverse children and adolescents: Assessments, diagnosis, and treatment.* New York: Guilford.

Carr, L. G. (1997). *"Color-blind" racism.* Thousand Oaks, CA: Sage.

Christian, B. (1989). But who do you really belong to Black studies or women's studies? *Women's Studies, 17,* 17-23.

Clinton, J. J., McCormick, K., & Besteman, J. (1994). Enhancing clinical practice: The role of practice guidelines. *American Psychologist, 49*(1), 30-33.

Comas-Díaz, L. (1994). An integrative approach. In L. Comas-Díaz & B. Greene (Eds.), *Women of color: Integrating ethnic and gender identities in psychotherapy* (pp. 287-318). New York: Guilford.

Dana, R. H. (1993). *Multicultural assessment perspectives for professional psychology.* Boston: Allyn & Bacon.

Dutton, M. A. (1992). *Empowering and healing the battered woman.* New York: Springer.

Elpin, O. M., & Gawelek, M. A. (1992). Women's diversity: Ethnicity, race, class, and gender in theories of feminist psychology. In L. S. Brown & M. Ballou (Eds.), *Personality and psychotherapy: Feminist reappraisals* (pp. 88-107). New York: Guilford.

Field, M. J., & Lohr, K. N. (Eds.). (1990). *Clinical practice guidelines: Directions for a new program.* Washington, DC: National Academy Press.

Fitzgerald, L. F., Buchanan-Biddle, N. T., Collinsworth, L. L., Magley, V. J., & Ramos, A. M. (1999). Junk logic: The abuse defense in sexual harassment litigation. *Psychology, Public Policy, and the Law, 5,* 730-759.

Gambrill, E. (1990). *Critical thinking in clinical practice.* San Francisco: Jossey-Bass.

Garb, H. N. (1997). Race bias, social class bias, and gender bias in clinical judgment. *Clinical Psychology: Science and Practice, 4*(2), 99-120.

Gilbert, L., & Scher, M. (1999). *Gender and sex in counseling and psychotherapy.* Boston: Allyn & Bacon.

Greene, B. (1994). Lesbian women of color: Triple jeopardy. In L. Comas-Díaz & B. Greene (Eds.), *Women of color: Integrating ethnic and gender identities in psychotherapy* (pp. 389-427). New York: Guilford.

Hays, P. A. (1996). Culturally responsive assessment with diverse older clients. *Professional Psychology: Research and Practice, 27*(2), 188-193.

Hewstone, M. (1996). Contact and categorization: Social psychological interventions to change intergroup relations. In C. N. Macrae, C. Strangor, & M. Hewstone (Eds.), *Stereotypes and stereotyping* (pp. 323-368). New York: Guilford.

Koss, M. P., Goodman, L. A., Browne, A., Fitzgerald, L. F., Keita, G. P., & Russo, N. F. (1994). *No safe haven: Male violence against women at home, at work, and in the community.* Washington, DC: American Psychological Association.

LaFromboise, T., Coleman, H. L. K., & Gerton, J. (1993). Psychological impact of biculturalism: Evidence and theory. *Psychological Bulletin, 114*, 395-412.

McBride, A. B. (1990). Mental health effects of women's multiple roles. *American Psychologist, 45*(3), 381-384.

Munoz, R. F., Hollon, S. D., McGrath, E., Rehm, L. P., & Vanden Bos, G. R. (1994). On the AHCPR depression in primary care guidelines: Further consideration for practitioners. *American Psychologist, 49*(1), 42-61.

Persons, J. B. (1991). Psychotherapy outcome studies do not accurately represent current models of psychotherapy: A proposed remedy. *American Psychologist, 46*(2), 99-106.

Ponterotto, J. G., & Pedersen, P. B. (1993). *Preventing prejudice: A guide for counselors and educators*. Newbury Park, CA: Sage.

Prince, J. P. (1997). Career assessment with lesbian, gay, and bisexual individuals. *Journal of Career Assessment, 5*, 225-238.

Reid, P. T., & Comaz-Díaz, L. (1990). Gender and ethnicity: Perspectives on dual status. *Sex Roles, 22*, 397-408.

Ridley, C. R. (1995). *Overcoming unintentional racism in counseling and therapy: A practitioner's guide to intentional intervention*. Thousand Oaks, CA: Sage.

Ridley, C. R., Li, L. C., & Hill, C. L. (1998). Multicultural assessment: Reexamination, reconceptualization, and practical application. *The Counseling Psychologist, 26*, 827-910.

Ridley, C. R., Mendoza, D. W., Kanitz, B. E., Angermeier, L., & Zenk, R. (1994). Cultural sensitivity in multicultural counseling: A perceptual schema model. *Journal of Counseling Psychology, 41*(2), 125-136.

Robertson, J., & Fitzgerald, L. F. (1990). The (mis)treatment of men: Effects of client gender role and life-style on diagnosis and attribution of pathology. *Journal of Counseling Psychology, 37*, 3-9.

Robinson, T. (1993). The intersection of gender, class, race, and culture: On seeing clients whole. *Journal of Multicultural Counseling and Development, 21*, 50-58.

Root, M. P. P. (1992). Reconstructing the impact of trauma on personality. In L. S. Brown & M. Ballou (Eds.), *Personality and psychopathology: Feminist reappraisals* (pp. 229-265). New York: Guilford.

Rush, A. J., Trivedi, M., Schriger, D., & Petty, F. (1992). The development of clinical practice guidelines for the diagnosis and treatment of depression. *General Hospital Psychiatry, 14*, 230-236.

Russell, G. L., Fujino, D. C., Sue, S., Cheung, M. K., & Snowden, L. R. (1996). The effects of therapist-client match in the assessment of mental health functioning. *Journal of Cross-Cultural Psychology, 27*, 598-615.

Schofield, W. (1964). *Psychotherapy: The purchase of friendship*. Englewood Cliffs, NJ: Prentice Hall.

Schulberg, H. C., & Rush, A. J. (1994). Clinical practice guidelines for managing major depression in primary care practice: Implications for psychologists. *American Psychologist, 49*(1), 34-41.

Shih, M., Pittinsky, T. L., & Ambody, N. (1999). Stereotype susceptibility: Identity salience and shifts in quantitative performance. *Psychological Science, 10*(1), 80-83.

Sinacore-Guinn, A. L. (1995). The diagnostic window: Culture- and gender-sensitive diagnosis and training. *Counselor Education and Supervision, 35*, 18-31.

Spengler, P. M., Strohmer, D. C., Dixon, D. N., & Shivy, V. A. (1995). A scientist-practitioner model of psychological assessment: Implications for training, practice, and research. *The Counseling Psychologist, 23*, 506-534.

Szapocznik, J., & Kurtines, W. M. (1993). Family psychology and cultural diversity: Opportunities for theory, research, and application. *American Psychologist, 48*(4), 400-407.

Thompson, C. E., & Neville, H. A. (1999). Racism, mental health, and mental health practice. *The Counseling Psychologist, 27,* 155-223.

U.S. Department of Health and Human Services. (1993). *Depression in primary care: Detection, diagnosis, and treatment.* Rockville, MD: Agency for Health Care Policy and Research.

Watzlawick, P., Beavin, J. H., & Jackson, D. D. (1967). *Pragmatics of human communication: A study of interactional patterns, pathologies, and paradoxes.* New York: Norton.

Zhang, A. Y., Snowden, L. R., & Sue, S. (1998). Differences between Asian and White Americans' helpseeking and utilization patterns in the Los Angeles area. *Journal of Community Psychology, 26,* 317-326.

CHAPTER 9

DETERMINING CULTURAL VALIDITY OF PERSONALITY ASSESSMENT

Some Guidelines

Gargi Roysircar-Sodowsky
Antioch New England Graduate School

Phoebe Y. Kuo
University of Nevada, Las Vegas

The primary objective of conducting an assessment is to formulate a diagnosis that will, in turn, determine the nature of treatment intervention. The assessment process, however, is a complicated task that involves weaving a comprehensive and integrated clinical picture of the client from various sources of information, whose different pieces of data may sometimes even be discrepant. Assessment entails the process of collecting information from clients. This includes qualitative data obtained from clinical interviews, such as pretreatment intake assessments and mental status exams, and quantitative data obtained from standardized measures. When one is doing assessments with racial and ethnic minorities, assessment interpretation should be modified by an understanding of research findings in relevant multicultural constructs, as these might be related to what the selected tests purport to measure.

The focus of this chapter is on qualitative assessment and objective measurement with culturally diverse clients. First, professional policy with regard to multicultural assessment is addressed. Second, a discussion of the barriers of culture that interact with the process of personality assessment is presented. These cultural barriers are differentiated as assessor barriers, environmental barriers, and assessee barriers. Assessee cultural barriers to accurate assessment and interpretation are further illustrated through a case study. Third, multicultural assessment guidelines are recommended. Fourth, multicultural psychometric constructs are presented. To illustrate the applications of these constructs, we evaluate a few widely used mainstream personality measures.

Professional Policy for
Multicultural Assessment

Counseling professionals have been called on to address the reality of the increasing diversity trend in the United States. The prediction for the year 2010 is that almost every major metropolitan area in the United States will be composed of a majority of individuals from non-White, non-European backgrounds. Furthermore, by the year 2050, racial and ethnic minorities will become the numerical majority in the United States (U.S. Bureau of the Census, 1996). Thus, working with American racial and ethnic minorities will become the norm rather than the exception. The need to develop multicultural competency has been recognized at the professional policy level, such as by the American Psychological Association's (APA's) "Ethical Principles of Psychologists and Code of Conduct" (APA, 1992).

Multicultural competency in assessment is explicitly addressed by the *enforceable* Ethical Standard 2.04(c) of the Ethics Code (APA, 1992), which requires psychologists to consider factors such as gender, age, race, ethnicity, national origin, religion, language, and socioeconomic status in deciding what tests to administer. On the basis of such factors, according to this standard, certain tests should not be used, or it may be necessary to adjust one's administration or interpretation of results. The "Guidelines for Providers of Services to Ethnic, Linguistic, and Culturally Diverse Populations" (APA, 1993) expands on this standard. For instance, psychologists are to consider the impact of adverse social, environmental, and political factors when assessing problems; provide written information, along with oral explanations, in language understandable to the client; and document culturally and sociopolitically relevant factors in the records that, for immigrants, would also include number of generations in the country, fluency in English, community resources, level of education, and level of stress related to acculturation. In the *Standards for Educational and Psychological Testing* (APA, 1985), Standard 6.10 states that educators and users of tests should not attempt to evaluate test takers whose age, linguistic, or cultural background is outside the range of their academic training or supervised experience, or the test user should seek consultations from a professional who has had relevant experience with test selection, testing modification procedures, and core interpretation.

The importance of culturally responsive assessment is further indicated in the fourth edition of the *Diagnostic and Statistical Manual of Mental Disorders (DSM-IV)* (American Psychiatric Association, 1994). There are five major improvements in the *DSM-IV*: (a) inclusion of specific cultural information with certain disorders; (b) an outline of cultural formulation to assist clinicians in evaluating the impact of cultural variables such as ethnic identity; (c) a glossary of culture-bound syndromes; (d) broader definitions of Axis IV to encompass psychosocial and environmental factors, such as problems related to acculturation and discrimination; and (e) addition of culturally sensitive "V codes." An example of (a) is the category of Dissociative Trance Disorder as a subcategory of Dissociative Disorder Not Otherwise Specified. This addition was reportedly made to include culture-specific dissociative pathologies that might otherwise be misdiagnosed as psychosis. It is noted that Dissociative Trance Disorder is specific to disorders that are "not a normal part of an accepted collective culture or religious practice and cause clinically significant distress or functional impairment" (American Psychiatric Association, 1994, p. 727). Examples of such disorders designated in the *DSM-IV* are bebainan, a disorder recognized in Indonesia, and possession, a disorder recognized in India.

The *DSM-IV* states that it includes the

> best-studied culture-bound syndromes and idioms of distress that may be encountered in clinical practice in North America and includes relevant DSM-IV categories when data suggest that they [the culture-bound syndrome] should be considered in diagnostic formulation. (American Psychiatric Association, 1994, pp. 844-845)

Culture-bound syndromes are described as recurrent patterns of divergent and troubling behavior that are specific to and influenced by the locality's cultural factors. (It is necessary to note that they are not necessarily considered to be pathological locally.) Culture-bound dissociative phenomena include the following:

amok (becoming violent or aggressive following an episode of feeling insulted or slighted), which is an experience recognized in Malaysia, Laos, the Philippines, Polynesia, Papua New Guinea, Puerto Rico, and among the Navajo;

falling out (hearing or understanding what is going on around one but feeling powerless to move), which is an experience recognized by southern U.S. and Caribbean groups;

susto (being so frightened by an event that one's soul leaves the body), which is an experience recognized by Hispanics/Latinos in the United States and Latin America;

pibloktoq (becoming very excited, followed by convulsive seizures or coma), which is an experience recognized by Eskimo groups;

qi-gong psychotic reaction, which is an experience recognized in China;

shin-byung (being possessed by ancestral or other spirits, powers, or deities), which is an experience recognized in Korea; and

zar (having a long-term relationship with a spirit that has possessed one), which is an experience recognized by African and Middle Eastern groups.

Although the expansion of the *DSM-IV* is appreciated, the *DSM-IV* glossary of culture-bound syndromes may not be helpful in the actual diagnostic process. This is because the *DSM* includes the disclaimer that some culture-bound syndromes are not considered pathological locally. In addition, the *DSM* uses a categorical assessment procedure, which means seeing symptoms as either present or absent. More helpful would be the use of a continuum for a rating scale (as used for the *DSM* Axes IV and V) with any indigenous illness or affliction, regardless of whether it is a locally recognized pathology. The indigenous affliction could be recommended for inclusion in a *DSM* diagnostic formulation if its rating on the continuum reflects a high degree of distress and psychosocial impairment in the individual's functioning in U.S. society.

It appears that the culture-bound syndromes are traditional expressions, applicable to rural, less educated, poorer classes of people in developing societies. Urban, educated, middle-class people from developing societies who have immigrated to the United States could be expected to express their adjustment difficulties differently, such as through acculturative stress, as they attempt to negotiate psychologically the presses of their original culture and those of their adopted country. However, despite the *DSM-IV*'s lack of comprehensiveness and clear directions in addressing multicultural issues, it nevertheless represents an important first step in alerting psychologists to account for cultural variables in the assessment of racial and ethnic minorities.

CULTURAL BARRIERS TO ACCURATE ASSESSMENT

Notwithstanding professional mandates, cultural barriers and disparities between the assessor (e.g., clinician or instrument) and the assessee present a difficult challenge. Inadvertent misdiagnoses may occur due to a lack of cultural knowledge, inadequate cross-cultural communication skills, and low empathy for issues of subordinate minority status. The variables of assessor barriers, environmental barriers, and assessee cultural barriers are identified below.

Assessor Barriers. Diagnostic activities are guided by the clinician's own values and theoretical orientations, both of which are likely to be biased toward the White American culture because psychology is grounded in the assumptions, values, and analytical cognitions of Western culture. When clinicians remain bound to the White American perspective, they run the risk of equating culturally different behaviors as psychopathology, which leads to overdiagnoses. For example, a clinician may misattribute a lower-class Asian immigrant's culturally derived, superstitious beliefs about omens, curses, and astrological events to a delusional disorder. Conversely, cultural misunderstanding can lead to the underdiagnoses of ethnically diverse clients. Clinicians may underdiagnose due to a lack of knowledge of culture-bound syndromes (e.g., the somatization of stress by Asians). A clinician may miss the cues of the headaches, stomachaches, and other pains presented by an Asian client.

Cultural stereotyping, which involves dismissing actual symptoms of psychopathology as being normative of a cultural group, can also contribute to underdiagnosis. For instance, by saying that a minority client has "healthy paranoia" instead of actual symptoms of paranoid schizophrenia, a psychologist may fail at accurate diagnosis. In the name of multicultural "sensitivity," which, in this case, is superficial, the psychologist sacrifices skills for cultural empathy, which connects one to the minority client's fears, suspicions, pains, and alienation. One needs to distinguish between healthy paranoia of minorities and functional paranoia. Whereas the former refers to an adaptive reaction to an oppressive and discriminatory environment, the latter stems from true psychopathology.

Furthermore, accurate diagnoses can be hampered by selective information processing in which clinicians selectively attend to conspicuous and dramatic symptoms while missing subtle manifestations of a disorder. Although selective information processing can occur in any assessment process, the likelihood of it occurring is greater in multicultural assessments in which the social or empathic distance between the clinician and the client is greater.

Environmental Barriers. Assessment needs to take into account external environmental barriers to a person's development. For instance, Helms (1996) has proposed the term *sociorace* to replace the term *race* because in the United States, race decides who is permitted to access societal resources and defines the manner in which such access can occur. To date, extant career instruments (a) fail to account for the effects of race and social class on career development and career choice; (b) do not account for immigrant sociocultural, environmental, and economic forces on individual choice; (c) assume that all individuals have an array of choices open to them; and (d) place a heavy emphasis on the role of traits. The implication of these limitations in career instruments is that psychologists need to address career assessment at both individual and system levels.

Coleman and Barker (1992) and Leong and Chou (1994) list a host of environmental barriers to the career development and choice for racial and ethnic minorities, such as occupational stereotypes, racism and discrimination, few role models, and occupational segregation. Hotchkiss and Borow (1996) contend that for all minority persons, the degree of control over one's career satisfaction and attainment is impeded by a set of longstanding social, institutional, and career barriers. Discrimination may lead many racial and ethnic minority individuals to restrict the scope of occupations they will consider. Many African Americans may exercise restrictive vocational choice patterns as a result of inadequate academic preparation and less developed interests, career planning knowledge, or opportunities (Bowman, 1993). According to an analysis of 1970 census data, Gottfredson (1978) asserted that the occupational pattern among African Americans was quite limited. That is, African Americans were overrepresented in low-paying realistic and social occupations and underrepresented in enterprising and investigative occupations (according to Holland's [1973] occupational classification system). Discrimination may lead to negative or inaccurate vocational self-concept and eventually a sense of helplessness regarding one's occupational future.

Luzzo (1993) states that career counselors must take into account the impact of ethnicity on college students' career development, specifically with regard to their perceived barriers in this process. In Luzzo's study, 25% of Asian Americans and 13% of Filipinos listed their ethnicity as a barrier to their past and future successes, and a significant number in both Asian groups listed a lack of training in study skills as a barrier to achieving their goals. In comparison, fewer than 5% of Caucasians perceived these as barriers. Helms and Piper (1994) and Parham and Austin (1994) proposed that career counseling can be enhanced by understanding how an African American's racial identity interacts with his or her career interests, career values, career choices, work satisfaction and satisfactoriness, perceptions of opportunities, and decision-making styles. These authors contended that career assessment with an African American needs to include the assessment of the client's Black racial identity.

Career assessment must take into account the social construction of gender. For example, men and women are typically found in different occupations; women earn significantly less than men; and positions of power and leadership continue to be dominated by men. In addition, women have encountered the "glass ceiling," a subtle and yet strong barrier that has prevented women and minorities from moving beyond middle management (Gilbert, 1992). There is an interaction of race with gender in the career development of African Americans, with women having higher educational and occupational aspirations and attainment than men. Just as race is sociopolitically defined, gender is socially constructed. In assessment, neither should be regarded simply as a client's given demographics, related to biological sex, phenotype, or genotype. The psychology of race and gender needs to be taken into account in multicultural assessment.

Assessee Cultural Barriers. Significant client cultural variables are the client's ethnic identification; acculturation adaptation, degree of acculturative stress, and worldview orientations; culturally sanctioned modes of symptom expression; culturally determined response sets; and socioeconomic barriers associated with minority group status. These variables underscore the heterogeneity that exists, both among and within ethnic groups. Clinicians need to account for how these factors may influence the multicultural assessment process with an individual client (Sodowsky, Kuo-Jackson, & Loya, 1997). For instance, a more acculturated client may be assessed differently from the way a less acculturated client is assessed. Clinicians also need to account for these client factors when interpreting their assessment results. A case study is presented to illustrate how cultural variables of a client may be taken into account in assessment.

A CASE STUDY

A comprehensive assessment of an Asian Indian client's psychological functioning was conducted in a county jail. The assessment process included many sources of information, including several interviews, administration and interpretation of a variety of personality and cognitive tests, reviews of employment and academic records, interviews with the client's White American wife and in-laws, and a telephone interview with a sister living in India. The client was incarcerated and convicted of his crimes, and the assessment report did not reduce the sentencing. At best, the purpose of the report was to provide a cultural understanding of the client to the judge and jury. An understanding of select acculturation variables and Asian cultural values was integrated in the assessment report. Additional explanations based on culture-specific research literature were appended to the report to enhance cultural aspects of the interpretation. Below is a summary of the report.

Background Information

T. K. is a 25-year-old Asian Indian. He has lived in the United States for 5 years. A jury convicted T. K. on charges of robbery, weapon possession, and bus hijacking. Witnesses testified at the trial that T. K. had told his co-conspirators that he did not want to take part in the crime. They further testified that the co-conspirators had threatened T. K., telling him that they had killed a man before and buried his body (this murder being also discovered at the trial) and that they would do the same to T. K. and his family. The prosecutors and the conspirators argued that T. K. was a helper in the crime because he needed money.

T. K., the eldest of two children, was born in India to middle-class parents who separated when he was 5 or 6 years old and subsequently divorced. Divorce carries a stigma in Indian society, where arranged marriages are the norm, and large, intact families and extended families form the basic structure of society. T. K., as the eldest son, grew to be protective of his mother and sister. He did not have many peer relationships. T. K.'s financial needs were taken care of by his father, an Indian Air Force fighter pilot, a prestigious occupation in India. T. K.'s father died when T. K. was in his adolescence, but this did not create financial hardships. T. K.'s grandmother, a poet and a person who is well connected to high political circles in India, was very supportive of T. K.

At age 18, after having obtained his private pilot license in India, T. K. came to the United States to receive flight training and experience. He obtained his commercial pilot license and returned to India. In India, he did some work as a flight instructor for 2 years. He returned to the United States to accelerate his accumulation of flight hours so that he would be eligible to be a pilot for a major commercial airline. When he returned to the United States, he had approximately 1,100 of the 1,500 hours necessary for that status.

In the United States, T. K. continued his additional flight training and experience while supporting himself by working as a cashier at convenience stores and gas stations. T. K.'s financial status dropped significantly. Apparently, T. K. had very little vocational preparation for jobs in the United States other than being motivated by his career interest to become a pilot. T. K. married a White American woman and developed a close relationship with his wife's family. He started a restaurant business and employed his wife's family. In this restaurant business, T. K. was under severe stress. He worked 100 to 110 hours a week, and he was unable to balance the demands of family life and business. Moreover, his in-laws may have misappropriated some of his restaurant income.

T. K. "walked away" from his business responsibilities and returned to working in gas stations and convenience stores so that he could be more available to his wife and son. After almost a year of successful work as a cashier, then as a manager, he had conflicts with his supervisor and reportedly quit because he experienced humiliation or what is known in Asian societies as "loss of face." He then pieced together other jobs as cashier and pizza delivery driver, again working up to 100 hours a week.

He was within 70 hours of completing his required 1,500 hours of flight experience when he quit training. At the time of his arrest, T. K. had decided to work at only one restaurant to spend more time with his infant son and with his wife, who was pregnant with their second child. Although he worked long hours, T. K. was very involved in the daily caretaking of his infant son. He devoted most of his time away from work to parenting tasks. This was confirmed by his wife and in-laws.

T. K. did not have a history of reckless or aggressive behavior. Except for a few speeding tickets as a pizza delivery driver, there were no records of confrontation with police or legal authorities. There was acknowledgment of only moderate consumption of alcohol except on two occasions. When T. K. was separated from his wife, he engaged in heavy drinking (e.g., six beers per night) for a period of 2 to 3 weeks. T. K.'s second episode of heavy drinking occurred 2 days prior to his crime and arrest. During this time, he was acting nervous, smoking twice as much as usual, and drinking an increased amount of beer and hard liquor, consumption of the latter being unusual for T. K.

Test Results and Interpretation

Cognitive testing (including the Wechsler Adult Intelligence Scale [WAIS]) indicated that T. K.'s current intellectual functioning was in the average range at about the 55th percentile of the normal population. His reading comprehension (included the Nelson-Denny Reading Test) was at the high school level. Tests of memory and of nonverbal problem solving were generally within the average range and indicated no obvious impairment. The fact that T. K. was tested in a language and culture different from those of his rearing and in circumstances very different from his middle-class upbringing in India would suggest that his cognitive abilities might have been underestimated.

Personality testing using a variety of instruments (including the 16 Personality Factors, Rorschach, and Thematic Apperception Test) revealed no apparent attempts to employ deceptiveness in his responses. There were no indications of significant psychopathology. However, on two of the tests, there was an indication of some increased suspiciousness or a tendency to be hypervigilant. Nevertheless, the level of suspiciousness did not rise to that associated with significant distress or mental disorder. T. K.'s suspiciousness was to be expected. He had experienced an unpredictable series of job changes and failures. His in-laws had deceived him. He had discovered that his acquaintances were criminals who coerced him into committing a crime. He was in jail when he believed he was innocent. T. K.'s suspiciousness also indicated acculturative stress. Research shows that the first 5 years of arrival in the United States are marked with adaptation difficulties (Sodowsky, Lai, & Plake, 1991). T. K.'s experiences were the antithesis of his original purpose of entering the United States for professional training. He was displaced from middle-class status in India to difficult immigrant conditions in the United States.

Testing indicated that T. K.'s interpersonal style seemed to be strongly influenced by his emotions and that he probably made decisions from an emotional and interpersonal point of view. T. K.'s responses to his wife, family demands, and employment decisions appeared to give evidence to emotional-interpersonal reactions. T. K. expected harmony in relationships and among people. There were indications that T. K. was also introspective with high expectations of himself. Perhaps as a result of such expectations and a sense of responsibility, but with limited environmental resources in an unfamiliar culture, T. K. experienced a great deal of inner tension. Although this tension did not seem to be debilitating, it was likely to be associated with introspection and self-doubt. There was also indication that T. K.'s decision-making style was more piecemeal than systematic. His problem-solving ability was characterized by a trial-and-error approach rather than a well-thought-out plan and integration of factors. T. K. did not appear to engage in independent, logical problem solving that is commonly practiced by Americans in decision making. T. K.'s personality factors associated with introspection, very high expectations of self, and inner tension were not consistent with the personality factors associated with psychopaths or manipulative deviants.

T. K. was a child of divorce, something shameful in his culture of origin, India. T. K. said, "I always missed my family being together. I just wanted to get married as soon as I could and have kids and keep them together." Despite his efforts to form and maintain a family, T. K. was not able to have the family he wanted.

Additional Variables of Cultural
Values Considered in the Interpretation

Communal Living. In India, there is a basic cultural expectation that one belongs to a family or group. Decision making, problem solving, and crisis resolution are not only within the purview of the group, but they are also expected functions of the group. A cross-cultural study indicated that Indian adolescents perceived their fathers and extended families to have more power, authority, and control than did adolescents in the United States or Australia (Poole, Sundberg, & Tyler, 1982). Thus, one's seniors and extended family are expected to help an Indian youth with decision making. It may be difficult for White Americans to understand that this attachment to elders and relatives in the family is not encumbering but sustaining; it does not restrict ambition but rather enables success. It is within the context of collective or communal living and thinking that it is believed that a person is able to develop and flourish. Verma (1987), a psychologist in India, said,

> The social self that Indians value is one that belongs to a collectivity and undermines autonomy, initiative, and individualism. It thrives on the care and concerns shown by the ingroup and is almost ineffective in handling demanding situations independently. Asking and giving are highly emotional, and one is likely to feel disappointed and hurt if ignored. The world around the social self is a network of obligations that become the source of joy and sorrow. (p. 331)

In the United States, T. K. did not have an in-group or extended family to turn to for support and decision making. When he came to the United States as an 18-year-old adolescent, he was presumably socialized in an interpersonal orientation. He probably experienced considerable acculturative stress adjusting to a Western host culture (enhanced by the stresses of adolescence) when he found himself in a society that emphasizes personal control of the environment and individualism. Acculturative stress and not having access to group decision making perhaps caused T. K. to be ineffective in handling demanding situations at work, marriage, and family life in the United States. Verma's (1987) statement that Indians are very interpersonally oriented "so much so that they are willing to forgo task and context-relevant behavior if it means maintaining a relationship" (p. 334) is a relevant explanation of T. K.'s scattered pattern of work behaviors to satisfy his need to serve his wife and son.

Although Indians may be less autonomous and independent than Americans and may see authority and decision making as communal, they do not have a lower sense of personal responsibility than Americans. Shejwal and Palsane (1986) found that under conditions of high distress, there is a coexisting belief in Indians that one has a high degree of impact and responsibility for what happens to one in life. This is related to the moral principle of actively serving "Dharma" or one's duty. Likewise, although T. K. showed ineffective problem-solving and decision-making skills, he did not surrender his responsibility but, in fact, felt an enhanced sense of responsibility to this family in the face of various environmental threats.

Law Adherence Versus Affiliation in Decision Making. At Yale University, psychologists have extensively studied the process of decision making of the individual within the cultural context. Miller and Bersoff (1992) examined how American and Indian adults and children made decisions in situations when there was conflict between law and affiliation or rules and friendship. Participants were asked to give their resolution to situations, such as whether to steal a train ticket discreetly after having been robbed and stranded while en route to deliver wedding rings for a friend's marriage ceremony. Across a variety of hypothetical vignettes involving minor, moderate, or extreme degrees of conflict, the Indian participants tended to resolve the conflict in favor of interpersonal affiliations and commitment far more frequently (84% Indians vs. 34% Americans) than did Americans, who tended to resolve the vignettes more in the direction of justice and rule adherence. This difference in perspective between the two cultural groups could not be explained by differing views on the seriousness of justice-breaching behaviors because participants in both groups tended to agree to the seriousness of such breaches. It appears that T. K. chose affiliation and protection for his family over obeying the law.

Moral Accountability Under Duress. Bersoff and Miller (1993) found that Indians more frequently absolved the agents of moral accountability under conditions of duress when compared to Americans. In response to vignettes that described persons violating rules or laws due to duress and fear, adult American participants reported that individuals in the vignettes were not accountable for their actions 45% of the time compared to the same response given by adult Indian participants 85% of the time. In response to the same vignettes, Americans considered the persons bound by moral code 36% of the time compared to about 13% of the time for Indian participants. However, the results could not be explained by saying that Americans find everyone accountable but Indians do not, because both groups showed 100% choice of nonaccountability when there was no control on the part of the actor. Bersoff and Miller (1993) stated,

> Results revealed that Indians were more prone than Americans to absolve agents of accountability for justice breaches rather than to categorize such breaches as moral violations. This difference was interpreted as reflecting

the contrasting cultural conceptions of the person emphasized in each culture, with American cultural views stressing the person's capacity to resist
contextual pressures and the Indian cultural views emphasizing vulnerability to contextual influences. (p. 665)

T. K.'s belief in his innocence and continued good spirits while awaiting sentencing could be related to his Indian cultural tendency to understand his breach
of justice within the context of a threatening situation. (*Note:* The above test interpretation was prepared for T. K.'s court trial and was made available for the
judge and jury. The trial ended in a conviction verdict with maximum penalty.)

Multicultural Guidelines for the Use of Personality Tests

The previous theoretical discussion and case study of the interactions of culture
with the assessor, assessee, and the environment leads to the next step of formu-
lating specific guidelines for the use of personality instruments in multicultural
assessment. The guidelines are presented in two sections: general procedural
guidelines and specific psychometric issues.

Fifteen Procedural Guidelines
in Multicultural Assessment

The following list highlights 15 general guidelines for multicultural assessment procedures:

1. Clinicians should establish rapport with the client to facilitate the assessment process. Good rapport will help to reduce the minority client's level of
cultural mistrust for an unfamiliar assessment process that is uniquely
Euro-American and often offered by a culturally different professional. Note
that establishing rapport requires suspending disbelief about unfamiliar
worldviews and practices of the client, abandoning racist attitudes, keeping in
check White value assumptions, listening and asking questions with respect
and sensitivity, and forming a cultural alliance with the client.

2. Helping the client to understand the assessment process and the purpose of the test(s). This will increase the client's motivation to respond more openly.

3. A pretesting assessment should be conducted to determine whether the use of mainstream tests is appropriate. At the pretesting phase, a qualitative intake should be done, collecting information on acculturation level, English proficiency, country of origin, immigration status, ethnic identification, family structure, prominent cultural values and religious beliefs, preimmigration and immigration history, and relevant socioeconomic variables such as education level and employment status. Culture-bound syndromes also should be assessed. Note that recent immigrants and clients who know limited English are likely to need alternative assessment procedures. A review of the client's mental health records, work records, and academic records may also yield important information.

4. The selection of appropriate measures should be based on the referral question, cultural information elicited from the pretesting interview, any available studies using the measure with racial and ethnic groups, and whether the measure's standardization sample included the specific cultural group of the client and approximated the group's composition, as according to the current U.S. census. If the measure's standardization sample does not have a representative sampling of the client's cultural group, results need to be interpreted with caution. Note that such measures may still be useful in that they reflect the client's culturally different behaviors under standardized White American examination conditions.

5. A question to ask is whether the instrument used adequately represents the range of the construct of interest. Multiple measures may be important to cover the range of the construct, but if the measures all use the same data-gathering method, bias may be introduced. If constructs are measured in the same way, such as through paper-and-pencil self-report instruments, similar scores between variables could result due to lack of method variance.

6. Because reliabilities are based on the scores and not on the instrument itself, it is important to keep in mind that an instrument can perform well with one type of individual and not another or under some conditions and not others.

7. Because many extant measures have not been validated on racial and ethnic minority groups, test results should be used to generate hypotheses for further testing. Multiple hypothesis testing is viewed as an essential compo-

nent in the application of a scientist-practitioner approach to psychological assessment.

8. Translated measures should demonstrate stimulus (linguistic) and conceptual equivalence. Butcher and Pancheri (1976) delineate a number of issues to consider when using translated measures, including determining whether the constructs of interest exist in the client's culture, whether the response format is meaningful to the client (e.g., forced choice, true-false format), whether validity issues have been examined with the translated version, and whether the response format of the translated version deviates from the original version. When there are significant differences in response formats, inaccurate interpretations may result due to incomparable test profiles. (However, Standard 2.04 of the APA's [1992] Ethics Code, Use of Assessment in General and With Special Populations, states that "psychologists attempt to identify situations in which particular interventions or assessment techniques or norms may not be applicable or may require adjustment in administration or interpretation.") If translated measures are used, this fact should be noted in the psychological report.

9. Observation of the client's test-taking behaviors may provide critical information regarding the client's level of understanding of and comfort level with the testing process.

10. Use of multiple methods of assessment, such as self-descriptions, behavioral ratings, review of records, and interviews with extended family members, may confirm test results.

11. There is some controversy over the use of computer-generated reports. Although they may control for clinician bias, they do not account for culture, ethnicity, and socioracial effects as these are related to the client's presentation. Thus, results from computer-generated reports should be interpreted in light of the client's cultural background and socioracial experiences.

12. Computerized reports of clinical instruments have a strong negative emphasis. They do not identify any strengths, which leads to the tendency to overinterpret or overpathologize problems of even White American clients. With racial and ethnic minority clients, the already existing problem of overdiagnosis is compounded by the built-in negativity of computerized reports. If computerized reports are used because of their time-saving convenience, psychologists must add an addendum modifying the given interpretation with insights obtained from the research literature on the client's cultural and socioracial group and through consultation with racial and ethnic minority professionals.

13. Racial and ethnic consultants must be sought for assistance in test interpretation.

14. Extra-assessment information available in the research literature on the racial or ethnic minority group of interest must be used when interpreting tests results.

15. Except in situations that preclude the explanation of results and about which the client has been informed in advance, appropriate explanations of results are given to clients in a language understandable to the client.

Five Psychometric Concerns in Multicultural Assessment

Although studies of cultural bias in psychological measures have found inconsistent results, these findings do not preclude misdiagnoses resulting from the inappropriate use and interpretation of quantitative tests with individual ethnic clients. There are several reasons why psychometrically sound measures may be used inappropriately. These are discussed below.

1. *Nonequivalent constructs.* Constructs are not equivalent across cultures in the way in which they are conceptualized or behaviorally operationalized. For example, the way in which good decision making is operationalized differs between White American and Asian cultures. In the White American culture, good decision making is based on personal, independent thinking. Conversely, Asian societies, which are collectivistic, may perceive good decision making as being based on what is best for the family. Thus, although the definition of the construct, good decision making, is equivalent between cultures, the specific behaviors that exemplify good decision making in the respective cultures are not equivalent. A related issue is that many psychological constructs are culture specific in that they do not have relevance in other cultures. For example, in developing the Vietnamese Depression Scale (VDS), Kinzie et al. (1982) found that only 4 of the 42 items retained in the VDS were from the Beck Depression Inventory.

2. *Score interpretability.* The interpretation of a score obtained from one cultural group does not hold the same meaning when the same score is obtained from a different cultural group or from a translated version of the same measurement. This issue is particularly relevant when interpretations are based on cutoff scores. Cutoff scores derived from one culture may not have the same in-

terpretive significance when the same cutoff scores are applied to individuals from a different culture.

3. *Nonrepresentative samples.* The use of nonrepresentative or inappropriate normative samples is another primary concern. Most psychological measures are norm referenced, with the normative data being based on middle-class White Americans. When such measures are used with ethnic minority clients, their performances are explicitly evaluated against the White majority yardstick. Also, when mean differences between ethnic groups are found, these do not provide meaningful answers. For example, mean differences between ethnic groups found in psychological instruments can have two possible interpretations: (a) one group may indeed be experiencing greater psychopathology, or (b) group differences are due to psychometric nonequivalence arising from an artifact of the measure.

4. *Selection criteria.* The use of separate ethnic norms may not solve the previously mentioned concerns. Ethnic normative groups are often of limited sample size, and the selection criteria for inclusion may be questionable in terms of representativeness. For example, when individuals are selected based on categorizations such as family names and U.S. census categorization, this type of selection disregards the complex interplay of acculturation, ethnic identity, and sociocultural variables (generational status, socioeconomic status, and anguage dominance) that may interact with the constructs that are being measured. Other common methods of selecting cross-validation samples are also problematic. Studies that employ the most extreme populations (i.e., inpatient clients) may not provide comparable outcomes due to differential access to mental health facilities, which is moderated by cultural modes of help seeking, as well as by socioeconomic barriers. Moreover, the criteria for admission to psychiatric facilities may be contaminated by cultural misdiagnoses. On the other hand, when criterion groups are based on self-selection or self-referral, problems may arise due to cultural variations in the patterns of mental health use, as well as help-seeking behaviors. Thus, the nature and selection criteria of the criterion group should be considered. As stated in the *Standards for Educational and Psychological Testing* (APA, 1985), "The value of a criterion-related study depends on the relevance of the criterion measure that is used" (p. 11).

5. *Response sets.* Cultural response sets can also influence the validity of the instrument. For Asian Americans, the cultural response sets of acquiescence (e.g., tendency to agree with statements) and fear of loss of face, resulting in a tendency toward a positive self-presentation may account for mean differences between Asians and other racial and ethnic groups. Psychometric mea-

sures need to provide culturally relevant controls (e.g., appropriate validity indexes) to account for differential response sets across ethnic groups (see Sodowsky, Kuo-Jackson, Richardson, & Corey, 1998).

Culture-Specific Measures

In considering the above psychometric concerns, it appears that emic (culture-specific) measures may be more appropriate in the assessment of ethnic clients for intrapersonal analyses and interpretations than established standardized measures, which are hypothesized to have universal meanings and thus restrict the user to etic or normtive comparisons. However, such instruments, although increasing in number, are mostly research measures. They are not practical for use with the U.S. mental health system, which is primarily concerned with identifying abnormality. The results obtained from emic measures are not comparable with those of other cultural groups, and they will not provide a common language across professional disciplines. Moreover, third-party payers and mental health institutions often require the use of mainstream instruments.

In conclusion, rather than abolishing the use of existing measures with ethnically diverse clients, the clinician needs to take a flexible approach by integrating information obtained from quantitative assessment, qualitative assessment, and research literature on the cultural group to which the client belongs. The case study that was presented in a previous section ("Assessee Cultural Barriers") used this method. This integrative approach necessitates a cultural decision-making process in which data from qualitative assessment and culture-specific research literature are used to determine which cultural limitations of the instrument are to be treated with more caution than others for a particular client.

As an illustration, the previously mentioned multicultural assessment concerns are being used to evaluate the cultural validity of widely used objective personality instruments. Note that classical validity and reliability indexes of each instrument will not be described. The instruments will not be described because such information is easily available in test manuals.

Minnesota Multiphasic Personality Inventory–2

The Minnesota Multiphasic Personality Inventory–2 (MMPI-2) (Hathaway, McKinley, & Butcher, 1990) represents the revision of the original instrument, the MMPI, which was published in 1943. The MMPI-2 is designed to assess a number of major patterns of personality and emotional disorders for ages 18 and older. The multicultural assessment concerns about the MMPI-2 are given below.

Nonrepresentative Samples. The restandardization samples are numerically representative of only two ethnic groups, African Americans and Native Indians. Latinos and Asian Americans continue to be underrepresented. This is a major limitation because these two groups are the most rapidly growing ethnic groups in the United States. The norms that are provided will not be applicable for use in another 20 years. Even the current normative data do not reflect the cultural and socioeconomic differences in the United States.

Native Americans in the norming sample were recruited only from Tacoma, Washington. African Americans were recruited from military bases. Also, the authors of the test noted that to conform to the U.S. census, "Hispanic" individuals in the normative group were arbitrarily classified as 56% White and 44% Other. The ethnic minority groups are not likely to be representative in terms of geographic location, acculturation, ethnic identity, and socioeconomic status. The sample exceeded the 1980 census values for education and occupational status. Roughly 50% of males and 42% of females reported an educational level of a bachelor's degree or higher, compared with 20% males and 13% females in the 1980 U.S. census data.

Score Interpretability. All tests or inventories are in some ways a test of English proficiency. The MMPI-2 requires an eighth-grade reading level compared to the MMPI, which requires a sixth-grade reading level. In this, the MMPI-2 is not an improvement on the MMPI. For minority clients, assessing adequate reading level is especially important because their English verbal fluency may not be commensurate with their ability to read English. Moreover, minority clients may be reluctant to disclose this deficiency and may complete the inventory without adequate comprehension. How are their scores to be interpreted?

Elevated scores on any given scale may not have the same pathological implications or behavioral correlates for different ethnic groups. Ethnic individuals may endorse some MMPI-2 items based on culturally patterned behaviors, beliefs, and feelings. Scale elevations for some ethnic individuals may reflect distress associated with experiences of racism and discrimination rather than actual pathology. For instance, Anderson (1995) noted that Whites with high elevations on the F scale indicate severe psychopathology, but this did not hold true for African Americans with high F scale elevations. The lowering of the cutoff scores for psychopathology ($T = 65$ for MMPI-2 from $T = 70$ for the MMPI) increases the already existing problems of minority clients being overdiagnosed and pathologized.

The F validity scale of the MMPI, viewed as elevating too fast, now goes up even faster, partly as a consequence of eliminating high F protocols from the restandardization sample. This effect is especially dramatic for females. T scores of 70, 80, and 90 on the F scale on the MMPI become 79, 92, and 109 on the MMPI-2, respectively. The L scale, considered sluggish by MMPI experts, now elevates much more briskly on the MMPI-2. In the MMPI manual, there are far more negative interpretation descriptors for women who score higher on masculine gender (GM) role or on feminine gender (GF) role than for men who have similar high scores on either of the scales.

Millon Clinical Multiaxial Inventory–II

Similar to the MMPI-2, the Millon Clinical Multiaxial Inventory–II (MCMI-II) (Millon, 1987) is designed to assess pathological personality and symptom dynamics for the purpose of aiding in diagnosis and treatment interventions. The MCMI-II is constructed to correspond with the *DSM-III-R* categories of personality disorders (Axis II) and clinical syndromes (Axis I). There are several multicultural assessment concerns with the use of MCMI-II.

Nonrepresentative Samples. Ethnic groups were either underrepresented or not even included in the normative sample (87.7% White, 6.9% African American, and 4.3% Hispanic). More important, the sampling method used to form the normative groups is questionable. Rather than using a population-proportionate sampling technique, the author sampled from a population of referred individuals who were typically administered the MCMI-II. Studies have shown that there are variations in the patterns of help-seeking behaviors both within and among ethnic groups. For example, Asian Americans who are less acculturated are more likely to underuse mental health services due to the stigma of shame attached to them in the Asian culture. Thus, ethnic groups in the standardization sample are not representative of ethnic individuals.

Selection Criteria. Another limitation of the MCMI-II concerns the validity of the 22 clinical scales for racial and ethnic minority groups. In the scaling of the

22 clinical scales of the MCMI-II, the author relied heavily on the base rate esti-
mations of Axis I and Axis II disorders in the *DSM-III-R*. The utility of these
scales is limited to the extent that the base rates accurately reflect diverse ethnic
groups.

Caution should be used when using the computerized interpretive reports.
The tendency to overinterpret or overpathologize is likely because the reports
have a strong negative emphasis without any identifying strengths. With racial
and ethnic minority clients, these reports may compound the problem of
overdiagnoses.

Multidimensional Self-Concept Scale

The Multidimensional Self-Concept Scale (MSCS) (Bracken, 1992) is designed to assess six domains of self-concept: social, competence, affect, academic, family, and physical. It is intended to be used for children and adolescents in Grades 5 through 12. The MSCS can be used for research or clinical
purposes. The MSCS requires a third-grade reading level. Response bias is controlled by positively and negatively worded items.

Representative Sampling. There are certain advantages to using the MSCS over
other similar instruments such as the Tennessee Self-Concept Scale. First, the
standardization sample is larger and more representative than that of other
self-concept instruments. The norming sample, consisting of 2,501 individuals,
was closely matched with the 1990 U.S. census data. In addition, respondents
were recruited from relatively more diverse geographical regions in the United
States (e.g., from rural and major cities). Analysis of raw scores on each
subscale and total scale by demographic variables revealed no significant differences. This suggests that the MSCS is less likely to be culturally biased.

Score Interpretability. The items are grouped by their respective scales, which
allows for the independent administration of MSCS subscales. The advantage
of this is that clinicians have the flexibility to not use certain subscales that are
judged to be culturally inappropriate. Similarly, the results obtained can be interpreted, using norm-referenced criteria or an ipsative method in which the individual's performance on a given subscale is compared with his or her overall
performance. This interpretative system allows the clinician to account for the
conceptual and metric equivalence of the instrument for a particular client.

NEO Personality Inventory

The NEO Personality Inventory (NEO-PI) (Costa & McCrae, 1992) is designed to assess five major dimensions of normal adult personality. The five domains are consistent with the five-factor model of personality: neuroticism (N), extraversion (E), openness to experience, agreeableness (A), and conscientiousness (C). It requires a sixth-grade reading level and takes approximately 30 to 40 minutes to complete.

Nonequivalent Constructs. Although minority groups are represented in the norms and there are various translated versions available, the assumption that the five-factor model of personality is equally applicable across the diverse ethnic groups is tentative at best. In different cultures and languages, other factors of personality may be more salient, resulting in different models of personality dimensions. For instance, for Asian cultures, the construct loss of face, defined as the threat or loss of one's social integrity (Sodowsky et al., 1998), has been found to be a key factor in Asian interpersonal relations. Loss of face also has been found to be independent of social desirability and predictive of certain behaviors among Asian Americans. The authors of the NEO-PI also do not explicate the method in which the instrument was translated.

Other disadvantages in using the NEO-PI include lack of adequate validity indicators and the use of English vernacular in certain statements. For instance, the idiom "bubbling with happiness" may have little meaning for English-limited Asian immigrants. The meaning of certain words varies across cultures. For example, *self-consciousness,* a facet of the neuroticism domain, may have a more positive connotation for Asian Americans, whose cultural values emphasize self-restraint and formality.

Rotter Incomplete Sentence Blank

The second edition of the Rotter Incomplete Sentence Blank (RISB) (Rotter, Lah, & Rafferty, 1992) is a soft-projective personality instrument that uses a semiobjective scoring system to assess for overall adjustment. There are potential advantages and disadvantages in using the RISB. The semiobjective scoring method involves rating client-generated sentences on a 7-point ordinal scale, with higher scores suggesting greater maladjustment.

Score Interpretability. Scores are rated on the basis of omissions, incomplete responses, conflict responses, positive responses, and neutral responses. Separate scoring examples for men and women are provided in the manual. Obviously, this method of scoring is highly open to subjective scoring and interpretation and, consequently, to cultural bias. Nevertheless, the RISB may serve as a useful and efficient way to elicit culturally relevant and personally meaningful information from ethnic clients themselves.

Strong Interest Inventory, Fourth Edition

The Strong Interest Inventory (SCII) (Strong, Campbell, & Hansen, 1985) compares a person's interests with interests of people happily employed in a wide variety of occupations. The SCII has a long, venerable history of use, in part because its authors have responded to social changes.

Representative Sampling. The major revisions of the 1985 version made the SCII more inclusive, being now relevant to noncollege individuals and those who are not from the middle class. For instance, the occupational scales were extended to reduce the previous overemphasis on professional occupations. Of the 106 occupations represented, 32% have mean educational levels of less than 16 years or do not require a college degree. The older occupational scales have been renormed, with all 207 scales reasonably current. The normative sample was expanded, testing 142,610 people to get 48,238 sample members. However, there is no information on the racial and ethnic composition of the large normative sample.

Equivalent Constructs. The extensive research that culminated in the 1985 revision was largely a result of the women's movement, which focused attention not only on inequities in the job market but also on inequities in the SCII's use of different occupational scales for men and women. In the current SCII, of the 106 occupations represented, 101 have scales for females and males. The authors conclude that substantial gender differences exist even between men and women in the same occupation. However, they caution that separate scales and separate norms must be used as a means of expanding options and not limiting them. The authors encourage men and women to consider occupations heretofore dominated by the opposite sex.

CONCLUSION

There are two primary issues in multicultural assessment: (a) how the data obtained will be interpreted and (b) how the interpretation will be used in treatment or interventions. The challenge lies with the multiculturally competent clinician to interpret test results in light of cultural variables that affect assessment outcomes, keeping in mind that the primary purpose of such outcomes is to use effective treatment intervention.

As stated by Spengler, Strohmer, Dixon, and Shivy (1995), "Assessments are accurate to the extent that they are based on what is known, do not overlook important client data, and lead to efficacious interventions" (p. 508). The ultimate test of "correctness," however, is when plausible alternative hypotheses are ruled out. This can be facilitated by having a critical awareness that every diagnosis always occurs in a broad sociocultural, political, linguistic, and economic context.

Thus, clinicians are urged to apply their scientist-practitioner training in multicultural assessment. They need to develop the skillful art of integrating qualitative data with quantitative results from mainstream psychological instruments, as well as with research findings on ethnic minority groups in areas of related constructs. In addition, several short multicultural instruments are available to assess specific psychological aspects of ethnic clients, such as acculturation, acculturative stress, and immigrant variables, including generational status, family influences, and social and ethnic identity (see Roysircar-Sodowsky & Maestas, 2000). Information from these multicultural measures will help with the interpretation of test data. Such an integrative approach will provide relevant cultural as well as comparative and normative information (Sodowsky, Gonzales, & Kuo-Jackson, 1997).

References

American Psychiatric Association. (1994). *Diagnostic and statistical manual of mental disorders* (4th ed.). Washington, DC: Author.

American Psychological Association (APA). (1985). *Standards for educational and psychological testing.* Washington, DC: Author.

American Psychological Association (APA). (1992). Ethical principles of psychologists and code of conduct. *American Psychologist, 47,* 1597-1611.

American Psychological Association (APA). (1993). Guidelines for providers of services to ethnic, linguistic, and culturally diverse populations. *American Psychologist, 48,* 45-48.

Anderson, W. P. (1995). Ethnic and cross-cultural differences on the MMPI-2. In J. C. Duckworth & W. P. Anderson (Eds.), *MMPI & MMPI-2: Interpretation manual for counselors and clinicians* (4th ed., pp. 439-460). Bristol, PA: Accelerated Development.

Bersoff, D. N., & Miller, J. G. (1993). Culture, context, and the development of moral accountability judgements. *Development Psychology, 29,* 664-676.

Bowman, S. L. (1993). Career intervention strategies for ethnic minorities. *Career Development Quarterly, 42,* 14-25.

Bracken, B. A. (1992). *Multidimensional Self Concept Scale.* Austin, TX: PRO-ED.

Butcher, J. N., & Pancheri, P. (1976). *A handbook of cross-national MMPI research.* Minneapolis: University of Minnesota Press.

Coleman, V. D., & Barker, S. A. (1992). A model of career development for a multicultural work force. *International Journal for the Advancement of Counseling, 15,* 187-195.

Costa, P. T., & McCrae, R. R. (1992). *Revised NEO Personality Inventory.* Odessa, FL: Psychological Assessment Resource.

Gilbert, L. A. (1992). Gender and counseling psychology: Current knowledge and directions for research and social action. In S. D. Brown & R. W. Lent (Eds.), *Handbook of counseling psychology* (2nd ed., pp. 383-416). New York: John Wiley.

Gottfredson, L. S. (1978). An analytical description of employment according to race, sex, prestige, and Holland type of work. *Journal of Vocational Behavior, 13,* 210-221.

Hathaway, S. R., McKinley, J. C., & Butcher, J. N. (1990). *Minnesota Multiphasic Personality Inventory-2 (MMPI-2).* Minneapolis: University of Minnesota Press, National Computer Systems.

Helms, J. E. (1996). Toward a methodology for measuring and assessing racial as distinguished from ethnic identity. In G. R. Sodowsky & J. C. Impara (Eds.), *Multicultural assessment in counseling on clinical psychology* (pp. 143-192). Lincoln, NE: Buros Institute of Mental Measurements.

Helms, J. E., & Piper, R. E. (1994). Implications of racial identity for vocational psychology. *Journal of Vocational Behavior, 44,* 124-138.

Holland, J. L. (1973). *Making vocational choices: A theory of careers.* Englewood Cliffs, NJ: Prentice Hall.

Hotchkiss, L., & Borow, H. (1996). Sociological perspectives on work and career development. In D. Brown, L. Brooks, & Associates (Eds.), *Career choice and development* (pp. 281-334). San Francisco: Jossey-Bass.

Kinzie, J. D., Manson, S. M., Vinh, D. T., Tolan, N. T., Anh, B., & Pho, T. N. (1982). Development and validation of a Vietnamese-language depression rating scale. *American Journal of Psychiatry, 139,* 1276-1281.

Leong, F. T. L., & Chou, E. L. (1994). The role of ethnic identity and acculturation in the vocational behavior of Asian Americans: An integrative review. *Journal of Vocational Behavior, 44,* 155-172.

Luzzo, D. A. (1993). Ethnic differences in college students' perceptions of barriers to career development. *Journal of Multicultural Counseling and Development, 21*(4), 227-236.

Miller, J. G., & Bersoff, D. M. (1992). Culture and moral judgement: How are conflicts between justice and interpersonal responsibilities resolved? *Journal of Personality and Social Psychology, 62,* 541-554.

Millon, T. (1987). *Millon Clinical Multiaxial Inventory-II.* Minneapolis, MN: Professional Assessment Services Division, National Computer Systems.

Parham, T. A., & Austin, N. L. (1994). Career development and African Americans: A contextual reappraisal using the nigrescence construct. *Journal of Vocational Behavior, 44,* 139-154.

Poole, M. E., Sundberg, N. D., & Tyler, L. E. (1982). Adolescent perceptions of family decision-making and autonomy in India, Australia and the United States. *Journal of Comparative Family Studies, 13,* 349-357.

Rotter, J. B., Lah, M. I., & Rafferty, J. E. (1992). *Rotter Incomplete Sentences Blank* (2nd ed.). San Antonio, TX: The Psychological Corporation.

Roysircar-Sodowsky, G., & Maestas, M. V. (2000). Acculturation, ethnic identity, and acculturative stress: Evidence and measurement. In R. H. Dana (Ed.), *Handbook of cross-cultural and multicultural personality assessment* (pp. 131-172). Mahwah, NJ: Lawrence Erlbaum.

Shejwal, B. R., & Palsane, M. N. (1986). Locus of control: A personality correlate of life events stress. *Psychological Studies, 31,* 177-180.

Sodowsky, G. R., Gonzales, J., & Kuo-Jackson, P. Y. (1997). Multicultural assessment and the Buros Institute of Mental Measurements: On the cutting edge of measurements concerns. In R. S. Samuda (Ed.), *Advancements in cross-cultural assessment* (pp. 242-273). Thousand Oaks, CA: Sage.

Sodowsky, G. R., Kuo-Jackson, P. Y., & Loya, G. J. (1997). Outcome of training in the philosophy of assessment: Multicultural counseling competencies. In D. B. Pope-Davis & H. L. K. Coleman (Eds.), *Multicultural counseling competencies: Assessment, education and training, and supervision* (pp. 3-42). Thousand Oaks, CA: Sage.

Sodowsky, G. R., Kuo-Jackson, P. Y., Richardson, M. F., & Corey, A. T. (1998). Correlates of self-reported multicultural counseling competencies: Counselor multicultural social desirability, race, social inadequacy, locus of control racial ideology, and multicultural training. *Journal of Counseling Psychology, 45,* 256-264.

Sodowsky, G. R., Lai, E. M. W., & Plake, B. S. (1991). Moderating effects on sociocultural variables on acculturation attitudes of Hispanics and Asian Americans. *Journal of Counseling and Development, 70,* 194-204.

Spengler, P. M., Strohmer, D. C., Dixon, D. N., & Shivy, V. A. (1995). A scientist-practitioner model of psychological assessment: Implications for training, practice and research. *The Counseling Psychologist, 23*(3), 506-534.

Strong, E. K., Campbell, D. P., & Hansen, J. C. (1985). *Strong Interest Inventory* (4th ed.). Palo Alto, CA: Consulting Psychologists Press.

U.S. Bureau of Census. (1996). *Statistical abstract of the United States.* Washington, DC: Government Printing Office.

Verma, J. (1987). Some observations by an Indian visitor to the United States. *International Journal of Intercultural Relations, 11,* 327-335.

CHALLENGES IN "UNPACKING" THE UNIVERSAL, GROUP, AND INDIVIDUAL DIMENSIONS OF CROSS-CULTURAL COUNSELING AND PSYCHOTHERAPY

Openness to Experience as a Critical Dimension

Frederick T. L. Leong
Aditya Bhagwat
The Ohio State University

In discussing the intersection of race, gender, and class and their implications for counseling, we would like to position those variables within a broader integrative framework for cross-cultural counseling and psychotherapy proposed by Leong (1996). To achieve this goal, we will summarize the integrative model and link it to the race, gender, and class variables that form the basis of this book. Next, the major social-cognitive barriers to using an integrative model and, by extension, the recognition and management of the race, gender, and class interactions in cross-cultural counseling and psychotherapy will be discussed. Finally, one of the major dimensions of the Big Five factor model of personality—namely, openness to experience—will be proposed as a critical dimension to understand how and when counselors will be able to deal with the complexity of race, gender, and class variables in the cross-cultural counseling encounter.

Race, GENDER, AND CLASS AS GROUP VARIABLES

Leong (1996) has recently proposed a multidimensional and integrative model of cross-cultural counseling and psychotherapy. In that model, using Kluckhohn and Murray's (1950) tripartite framework, Leong proposed that cross-cultural counselors and therapists need to attend to all three major dimensions of human personality and identity—namely, the universal, the group, and the individual dimensions. The universal dimension is based on the knowledge base generated by mainstream psychology and the "universal laws" of human behavior that have been identified (e.g., the universal "fight-or-flight" response in humans to physical threat). The group dimension has been the domain of cross-cultural psychology as well as ethnic minority psychology and the study of gender differences. The third and final dimension concerns unique individual differences and characteristics. The individual dimension is more often covered by behavioral and existential theories in which individual learning histories and personal phenomenology are proposed as critical elements in the understanding of human behavior. Leong's (1996) integrative model proposes that all three dimensions are equally important in understanding human experiences and should be attended to by the counselor in an integrative fashion.

Although one dimension should not be emphasized at the expense of the others, the focus of the present volume is on the role of the race, gender, and class variables in counseling. It is clear from Leong's (1996) integrative model that these variables of race, gender, and class fall within the domain of the group dimension. Before discussing how these group variables may be understood within the cross-cultural counseling relationship, it would be important to summarize the basic tenets of the integrative model proposed by Leong.

The INTEGRATIVE MODEL: UNIVERSAL, GROUP, AND INDIVIDUAL DIMENSIONS

As the ethnic minority population of the United States continues to grow (Triandis, Dunnette, & Hough, 1994), the number of culturally different clients seen by counseling and clinical psychologists will increase (e.g., see Pedersen, Draguns, Lonner, & Trimble, 1989; Sue & Sue, 1994). Other than a few mid-range models about acculturation (e.g., Berry, 1980; Padillla, 1980) and racial and cultural identity (e.g., Atkinson, Morten, & Sue, 1989; Cross, 1991; Helms, 1993), there are few integrative theoretical models available to the field of psychology. The purpose of Leong's (1996) integrative model is to remedy this situation by creating a model that can be used for cross-cultural counseling and psychotherapy.

The Integrative Model

Leong (1996) used a famous quote from Kluckhohn and Murray's (1950) influential article on "Personality Formation: The Determinants," published in their book *Personality in Nature, Society, and Culture,* as the beginning point for his integrative model. The quote was as follows: "Every man is in certain respects: a) like all other men, b) like some other men, and c) like no other man" (p. 35). In this quote, Kluckhohn and Murray are pointing out that some of the determinants of personality are common features found in the genetic makeup of all people. This addresses the biological aspect of the biopsychosocial model generally used in today's medical sciences. For certain features of personality, Kluckhohn and Murray state that most men are like some other men, showing the importance of social grouping, whether that grouping is based on culture, race, ethnicity, gender, or social class. Last, they say that "each individual's modes of perceiving, feeling, need, and behaving have characteristic patterns which are not precisely duplicated by those of any other individual" (p. 37). Each person's individuality, often the focus of social learning theories and models, is thus expressed in the last part of the quote. It accentuates the fact that all persons have distinct social learning experiences that can influence their values, beliefs, and cognitive schemas.

The model developed by Kluckhohn and Murray (1950) has been visible in anthropological and cross-cultural circles but has not made much of a showing in the fields of cross-cultural counseling and psychotherapy (Leong, 1996). When the model is discussed in counseling literature, it is usually used to describe the multidimensional nature of human beings rather than to show its influence on the process of cross-cultural counseling and the outcomes thereof (e.g., Speight, Myers, Cox, & Highlen, 1991).

The Universal Component of Personality

All persons are like all other persons. This statement accentuates the idea
that all human beings share some characteristics, whether they are physical or
psychological. There is much evidence to support this notion because all humans develop physically in similar fashions, learn to talk in similar fashions,
and learn to think in similar fashions (e.g., Piaget's conservation experiments).
This notion has been thoroughly accepted by the medical community because
group and individual differences are often not seen as important in medical
treatment. It also has been accepted by many in the psychological community,
however. This is seen in models such as the common factors model (Frank,
1961), which points out that the effective aspects of counseling and psychotherapy are shared by many cultures.

   The universal dimension of personality plays an important role in counseling and psychotherapy. One can see in any culture that a person who is in psychological distress looks to form a relationship with another person who is
thought to possess an expertise in healing such suffering. Traditional Western
models of counseling and psychotherapy capitalize on this notion. It is felt that
all human beings at some point are going to have periods in which they suffer
from psychological distress and that this distress will not differ qualitatively
from the distress of others. It stands to reason, then, that persons from different
cultures may be treated in similar fashions. This thought was advanced by Carl
Rogers, who felt that unconditional positive regard was a necessary and sufficient component of psychotherapy. Outcome studies of different approaches to
psychotherapy provide further support of the universal component, as it is seen
that there is no significant difference in the efficacy of various approaches to
performing counseling and psychotherapy.

   Simply focusing on the universal dimension, however, completely ignores
the group and individual components that are absolutely necessary for effective
counseling. Although the universal dimension in counseling is very important
to the integrative model, it is necessary but not sufficient (Leong, 1996). Sue
and Sue (1994) have done some research to show that ethnic minorities often
underuse counseling and psychotherapy, and if they do use it, they often end up
prematurely terminating the counseling relationship. Research such as this
helps to show that although there may be common factors in psychotherapy,
they are not enough to provide service to all consumers. Therefore, it is clear
that the integrative model must incorporate the other two components of personality, the group and the individual.

The Group Component

All persons are like some other persons. This statement serves to explain the idea that although we all share many commonalities, the human population can be subdivided into groups. These groupings may be based on culture, race, ethnicity, social class, occupation, or even gender. All persons in one group will share some type of bond with other members of the group, and at the same time, this bond will distinguish the group members from all other groups. It is further believed that belonging to a group will be a major determinant of a person's personality.

Membership in a group can affect an individual in many ways, and these ways can become the focus of counseling and psychotherapy. For example, persons who have suffered from oppression because of their religion or race will need to address these feelings. They will no longer be speaking from a universal perspective because their experiences have not been shared by all persons. A therapist who tries to relate to these types of clients on a universal level will be doing a disservice, and this will most likely lead to premature termination of the therapeutic relationship.

Another aspect of the group dimension is the existence of different types of societies, such as individualistic versus collectivistic societies. Individualistic societies are seen as those where the needs of the individual are put before the needs of the group. Western societies are traditionally seen as being individualistic. Collectivistic societies generally put the needs of the group before the needs of the individual. Eastern societies are seen as collectivistic in nature (Hofstede, 1980). The type of society one is raised in affects many aspects of a person's life, including the manner in which one communicates, what life choices one makes, and how one copes with stress. All of these are extremely pertinent in counseling situations and, if not attended to, may lead to premature termination.

The group component of personality is especially important when discussing cross-cultural counseling and psychotherapy. There have been many models of racial identity that focus on the group component. Other important constructs related to the group dimension include racial/ethnic identity, acculturation, and value preferences. A competent counselor must be able to look at all these variables from the standpoint of his or her client, especially if the client is a member of a different group. Not doing so would make it impossible to accurately conceptualize the psychological state the client is in, which in turn would make effective therapy impossible.

There has been much research looking at the experiences of different groups. Although multicultural research is growing in importance currently, there is also a substantial literature looking at the differences in experiences of men and women. Many dynamics must be taken into consideration in counseling situations involving a client and therapist of different genders. Each must have some awareness of the experiences of the other to be able to form a relationship. This is especially true for the therapist. A therapist operating only at the universal level may alienate his or her client. Although the two may not have shared experiences in their backgrounds, the counselor must be able to address issues that involve groups other than his or her own.

Although it is often better to relate at the group level than the universal level, this orientation still may not be ideal. A risk one takes when operating at the group level is to assume homogeneity in other groups. It would not be advantageous or professional to assume that because one has a lot of experience with a certain ethnic group, one can guess at the problems a client of the same ethnicity will present. For example, someone working in a university counseling center may have Asian clients who are distressed because they are pursuing degrees in their fields solely because of parental pressure. It would be a mistake, however, to always assume this to be the case. If that therapist decided to focus only on the family dynamics with his or her next Asian client, he or she may miss a very important aspect—namely, the client's own ambivalence. Although being able to relate at the universal and group levels is necessary, it should not be at the cost of being able to relate at the individual level. All three must be attended to for effective counseling.

The Individual Component

All persons are like no other person. This statement shows the beauty of humanity, the individuality of every person. Although it is true that we all share some commonalities, as seen by looking at the universal component, no two persons are identical in every way. The medical community can look at humans from a genetic perspective to show how all humans are completely alike. Psychologists, on the other hand, can look at persons from an environmental perspective to show how no two humans are completely alike. Kluckhohn and Murray (1950) said, "Each individual's modes of perceiving, feeling, need, and behaving have characteristic patterns which are not precisely duplicated by those of any other individual" (p. 37).

Kluckhohn and Murray (1950) seem to be referring to an idea akin to the concept of the "psychological environment" (Lewin, 1951). Lewin was trying to show that although two people may share the same physical space, they may not share the same psychological space. For example, take the case of identical twins. Identical twins share the exact same genetic information. If they are raised together, they also share the same physical space (same parents, same schools, etc.). However, identical twins can grow up to be very different people. Although they have shared genetic information and physical space, they have not shared the same psychological space. It is this difference that allows them to have their individuality. This is one of the basic tenets of social learning theories and models.

Because counseling psychology adopts many notions from social psychology into its theoretical frameworks, there is often a tendency to relate to persons at the individual level. Although this may be appropriate in many cases, it overlooks the effects of group influences. There may be aspects of a person's personality they are not aware of that are strongly affected by group affiliations. It is up to the therapist to find these aspects and bring them to light. If the focus remains at the individual level, however, this will not happen, and the person may not get optimum treatment. Even worse, the individual may be quite aware of the effects of being in their group (racism, discrimination, etc.), yet the therapist may not attend to them because they are concentrating on the individual component. This will also lead to less than optimum treatment, as well as possible premature termination.

The integrative model of cross-cultural counseling proposed by Leong (1996) has as one of its fundamental bases the notion that the individual client must exist at three levels: the universal, the group, and the individualistic. The problem with much of the past research done in the field of multicultural counseling is that the focus has been on only one of the three levels, ignoring the influence of the other levels in the counseling situation. Leong's integrative model includes all three dimensions of personality as well as their dynamic interactions and thus will have better incremental validity than any model that focuses on only one of the three levels. The integrative model for cross-cultural counseling and psychotherapy was conceived to show a more complex conception of a very dynamic enterprise in counseling. It is also a call to begin research using this model and the components and complex elements that are integral to the model.

Main EFFECTS AND INTERACTIONS: RACE, GENDER, AND CLASS INTERACTIONS

In cross-cultural counseling and psychotherapy, the same variables that have been found to be important in mainstream counseling and psychotherapy are also important when the client and counselor come from different cultural backgrounds. By mainstream counseling and psychotherapy, we are referring to the body of literature on psychotherapy research that has been reviewed in the *Handbook of Psychotherapy and Behavior Change* (Bergin & Garfield, 1994). These same variables happen to interact with cultural variables in cross-cultural counseling and psychotherapy. This is the interaction of the universal and group dimensions in the integrative model (Leong, 1996). At the same time, the universal dimension also interacts with the individual dimension just as the group dimension would be expected to interact with the individual dimension. In one sense, the three dimensions of universal, group, and individual factors exert their influence in cross-cultural counseling encounters as both main effects and as interaction effects. This is precisely why Leong (1996) proposed that it is important to include complexity theory in analyzing and understanding the cross-cultural counseling relationship.

Just as the three major dimensions of the integrative model can interact with each other, the variables of race, gender, and class can also exert their influence in the cross-cultural counseling relationship as both main effects and as complex interactions. Instead of delineating the complex interactions of the race, gender, and class variables in this chapter, we have chosen instead to provide a broader conceptual analysis. According to our analysis of the implications of the possible interactions of race, gender, and class variables in the cross-cultural counseling encounter, a major problem in the counselor's ability to deal with these complex interactions among these three dimensions is the host of social-cognitive barriers that works against the use of an integrative and multidimensional approach to cross-cultural counseling.

Social-COGNITIVE BARRIERS TO INTEGRATION

The integrative model of cross-cultural counseling and psychotherapy described by Leong (1996) introduced a novel way of conceptualizing the therapeutic process when dealing with clients of differing cultures. This model seems to be able to describe how to envision the entire personality of individuals and shows the sequential and dynamic interaction that occurs between the client and counselor previously ignored in the literature. It also takes into account other factors, such as complementarity, to create a better model. However, despite the gains in understanding made by this model, many social-cognitive barriers may still inhibit the acceptance of multiculturalism as a force in psychology.

One of the barriers discussed by Leong (1996) is the *out-group homogeneity effect*. This term from social psychology refers to the tendency of humans to perceive other groups as being more homogeneous while perceiving one's own group to be more heterogeneous. This can have a negative impact in counseling relationships. As discussed in the model presented above, it is important for counselors to be able to shift from one level of personality to another (universal, individual, and group). The out-group homogeneity effect would impede a counselor's ability to effectively shift out of the group level, possibly leading to premature termination by the client. This effect also can have a negative impact in social relationships. The out-group homogeneity effect stops members of one ethnic group from truly understanding individual members of other groups because judgments are made assuming that all members of the other group are alike. These judgments do not necessarily have to be negative, but if someone has had a negative experience with one member of a group, that person may expect all other group members to behave in a similar manner. This is, of course, one of the reasons that negative stereotypes get advanced and may greatly limit the movement toward an integrated multicultural society.

Another major barrier to integration is *ethnocentrism*. Ethnocentrism is a natural human tendency that advances the notion of dissimilarity between two ethnic groups. Each group evaluates the other as to how similar or different the group is from its own. The more similar they are, the greater the acceptance. The more dissimilar the other group is, the more negative stereotyping will occur. This stereotyping can then lead to misunderstandings and possibly hostility. Brislin (1993) stated,

> Ethnocentric judgments, then, are based on feelings that one's own group is the center of what is reasonable and proper in life. . . . An implication of the judgments is that one group is clearly better, even superior, than the other since its members practice proper and correct behaviors. (p. 38)

It is one's own group that is seen to be the better one, of course.

Ethnocentrism is a major obstacle in the field of counseling and psycho-therapy for two reasons. First, one of the world's leading centers of research and practice in the area of counseling and therapy is the United States. Second, the dominant theories adhered to in the United States are those of European Americans, and most of the population of the United States is of European extraction. The net result is that although there may be greater attention paid to the growth of minority populations in the United States, ethnocentrism is halting the institution of any real changes to be made in the field, as can be seen by the actions or (inactions) of the American Psychological Association (APA) (Leong & Santiago-Rivera, 1999). Because social psychology shows us that ethnocentrism is a fundamental part of human nature, it will be a difficult force to overcome.

A construct similar to ethnocentrism that also may hinder integration is the *false consensus effect*. This effect occurs when a person sees his or her behavior as being representative of others' behavior. In essence, one sees one's own behavior as the norm, and thus the expectation is that under similar circumstances, most people would behave in a similar manner. There are various reasons as to why this may occur. There is an old saying: "Birds of a feather flock together." This means that people search out and associate with those who have similar ideals and beliefs. It is then not surprising that this group of people may act in similar fashions, thus reinforcing the notion that one's behavior is typical of the majority (Fiske & Taylor, 1991).

Like ethnocentrism, it is easy to see how this effect could hurt multiculturalism. In fact, it is in some respects the antithesis of multiculturalism in that it assumes homogeneity in others rather than looking for and accepting differences. Because this is a human tendency, it is safe to assume that it exists just as much in mental health professionals as the general population. The false consensus effect may then lead to a continuing adherence to European perspectives in psychology while ignoring newer models that may try to incorporate multicultural perspectives. The difficult part to overcome here is that there is no overt negative reaction to integration; rather, it is a subtle phenomenon difficult to pinpoint and attend to.

A phenomenon that shows how the field of psychology itself could hurt the process of integration is Schneider's (1987) attraction-selection-attrition (ASA) framework. The ASA framework helps to point out that "organizations define the characteristics of people who enter them" (Leong & Santiago-Rivera, 1999). In other words, persons choose to join an organization (attraction), some are selected by the organization (selection), and some then choose to leave the organization (attrition). Those who are left in the organization will, more likely than not, be very similar in their ideas, thus creating a very homogeneous organization. This can occur in the field of psychology and indeed may have.

The field, as it stands now, is still made up of a majority of psychologists who cling to the traditional, Western perspectives. According to the ASA framework, it is then psychologists of a similar mind who will be attracted to the field and thus perpetuate that way of thinking. Because of the orientation of the field of psychology as it currently stands, along with the effects of the ASA framework, multiculturalism may have a hard time gaining importance and increased study.

Another phenomenon that could create a barrier to multiculturalism is psychological reactance. Brehm (1966) states that psychological reactance is a motivation to work to abolish threats to our freedom or to regain or restore freedoms that may have been lost. In effect, any change that one has to make can be seen as a threat to freedom. In this case, the change required of psychologists would be to open themselves to the concept of multiculturalism and to begin seeing multicultural issues as important issues in counseling. Because of psychological reactance, many psychologists may be averse to this notion.

Multiculturalism would be seen as a threat to the established ways of performing therapy. The focus would shift from solely looking at the individual or universal components to also looking at the group component. The reaction from some professionals may amount to "My way has worked for me so far, so why should I change?" They may feel that they are being forced to think and feel a certain way about culturally different clients, and they will be resistant. This resistance may be due to the fact that professionals may not want to change their methods of counseling, but it could also attack a sometimes strongly held notion that all people are alike. This is the basis of the universal component presented earlier. Although there are merits to this viewpoint, it is also damaging in that many important aspects of personality will be lost. Psychological reactance then could be a force stemming from professionals in psychology against the idea of studying multiculturalism, a change that would undoubtedly advance the field. The trick for proponents of multiculturalism is to advance the idea without arousing reactance or else to have strategies ready to deal with reactance if it occurs.

Leong and Santiago-Rivera (1999) propose another social-cognitive barrier to integration called the *values-belief fallacy.* Values are our conceptions of those things that are desirable, whereas beliefs are seen as truths. A major difference between the two is that values can evolve and change, but because beliefs are held to be truths, they are immutable. The values-belief fallacy occurs when members of a culture meld the two together and begin to think that their values are actually beliefs. In other words, their preferences become truths. This can be seen in any conflict based on religious differences. Each side thinks that their preference of religion is the truth and cannot tolerate the existence of a contrary truth. Two immutable beliefs clash, and a war results.

This type of clashing can be seen in the field of psychology as well, especially when looking at multiculturalism. Psychologists often believe that the results of experimentation and the theories they propose are uncovering truths. In other words, they are finding universal concepts, ones that relate to the universal component in all persons. Because they are speaking to the universal component, group factors then are ignored. Cultural differences are seen as nuisance variables or variables not worth considering. Leong and Santiago-Rivera (1999) provide support for this notion by showing that before the creation of the Society for the Psychological Study of Racial and Ethnic Minority Issues in Psychology (Division 45 of the APA), racial and cultural differences were not considered important. Also, even as introductory psychology classes are taught today, multiculturalism plays a small role in the curriculum.

Another example of a constraint to integration is the human tendency toward conformity. Much research has shown that human beings tend to feel a great deal of stress if their opinions deviate from the majority viewpoint. To reduce this distress, individuals tend to shift their opinions so that they are more in line with what the majority believes. This can have negative consequences as far as the furthering of multiculturalism is concerned. First, because most of the United States is Caucasian, the Caucasian viewpoint will dominate. That will serve to not only silence minority opinions but also discourage members of the majority from speaking out. Second, because having views that deviate from the majority often causes distress, fewer members of minority groups will feel comfortable pushing for their views. In either case, proponents of multiculturalism will be facing an uphill battle.

It seems clear that attention must be paid to the group component of personality, in addition to the universal and individual components. One of the major aspects of the group component is an individual's ethnicity. Multiculturalism is an important factor in psychology, but it has not yet been embraced by the psychological community. Even though some attention has been paid to the importance of group differences, many countervailing forces prevent multiculturalism from gaining prominence. It is important, however, that the minority proponents of multiculturalism continue to further the issue and learn strategies to overcome all of the social-cognitive factors working against them.

It can be seen from the above discussion that many of the factors that are hindering the acceptance of multiculturalism (ethnocentrism, false consensus effect, and psychological reactance, to name a few) seem to involve a lack of flexibility on the part of current professionals in the field. These factors remain as strong as they are because of a resistance to change and an unwillingness to investigate new ideas. A construct borrowed from the five-factor model of personality, openness to experience, can be seen as an important aspect of this resistance, as well as an integral facet in the personality of a cross-culturally competent counselor. The importance of openness to experience in using the integrative model of cross-cultural counseling and psychotherapy, as well as in overcoming social-cognitive barriers, will be discussed more thoroughly in the next section.

OPENNESS TO EXPERIENCE AS A CRITICAL DIMENSION

We would like to propose that openness to experience is a critical dimension in a counselor's ability to use an integrative approach to cross-cultural counseling. The counselor who has a high level of openness to experience will be able to attend to the race, gender, and class dimensions within their clients as well as the complex interactions between these dimensions. Because ethnic or cultural identity plays such a central role in understanding the cross-cultural counseling encounter (e.g., see Helms, 1993; Sue & Sue, 1994), the value of the construct of openness to experience to effective cross-cultural counseling will be illustrated by integrating the construct of openness to experience with the ego psychology models of Loevinger (1976).

Ego Psychology of the Effective Counselor

It may be worthwhile to examine Loevinger's (1976) model of ego development, which may help us understand why certain characteristics would make for effective and noneffective cross-cultural counselors. It should be noted that ego psychology provides one possible model, and there may be others. A central thesis of ego psychology is that the maturity of various ego functions (e.g., reasoning, perception of reality, object relations) of the individual determines the level of that individual's successful adaptation to his or her life, whether in the domain of work, relationships, or mental health.

In a sense, Loevinger's (1976) model and other models of ego psychology overlap considerably with various models of racial and ethnic identity (e.g., see Leong & Chou, 1994). Loevinger's (1976) model of ego development posits a series of stages that include presocial, self-protected, conformist, conscientious, individualistic, autonomous, and integrated. The early stages of presocial and self-protected are primarily experiences in childhood, with the latter stages of conformist, conscientious, individualistic, autonomous, and integrated being more variable within adulthood. She posits certain characteristics along four dimensions of these stages, and it may be worthwhile to examine the various stages with regards to these dimensions. The first dimension is impulse control, second is interpersonal style, third is conscious preoccupations, and fourth is cognitive style.

In the presocial stage, the impulse control of individuals is characterized by impulsiveness and fear of retaliation. The self-protected individual, on the other hand, fears being caught, tends to externalize blame, and is generally opportunistic. The impulse control of the conformist is characterized by conforming to external rules and feeling shame and guilt for breaking those rules. The conscientious individual, on the other hand, tends to have self-evaluated standards, self-criticisms, guilt for consequences, and long-term goals and ideals. The individualistic individual's impulse control, on the other hand, is similar to that of the conscientious individual, with the additional element of respect for individuality. The autonomous individual has the characteristics of the conscientious and individualistic persons' control pattern but is also able to cope with conflicting inner needs and toleration. Finally, the integrated individual is able to reconcile inner conflicts and renunciation of the unattainable.

Moving on to the interpersonal style, the presocial individual is characterized by being artistic, symbiotically receiving and being dependent and exploited. The self-protected individual, on the other hand, is wary, manipulative, and exploitative. The conformist tends to focus on belonging and superficial niceness. The conscientious individual tends to be intensive in his or her personal-interpersonal style, responsible, mutual, and concerned about communication. The individualistic person's interpersonal style is similar to that of the conscientious person but has the added element of dependence as an emotional problem. The autonomous individual's interpersonal style is characterized by an additional element of respect for autonomy and recognition of interdependency of relationships. Finally, the integrated individual's interpersonal style has the elements of the conscientious, individualistic, and autonomous, with the added developmental dimension of cherishing individuality.

Moving on to conscious preoccupation, the presocial individual is primarily concerned with self versus nonself and bodily feelings, especially sexual and aggressive ones. The self-protected individual is concerned with self-protection from trouble, wishes and things, and advantage and control. The conformist is concerned with appearance, social acceptability, and banal feelings and behavior. The conscientious individual tends to have different feelings and motives for behavior, self-respect, achievement, certain traits, and expression. The individualistic person has the components of the conscientious person with the additional element of social problems and differentiation of inner life from outer life; the autonomous individual has the added elements of vividly conveying those feelings, integration of the physiological and psychological, role conception, self-fulfillment, and a sense of self within a social context. Finally, the integrated individual has all the elements of the preceding stages as well as a well-established sense of identity.

Finally, the last relevant dimension is cognitive style. The presocial individual is characterized by the use of stereotyping and conceptual confusion. The conformist's cognitive style is characterized by conceptual simplicity, stereotypes, and cliques. The conscientious individual is characterized by conceptual complexity and the ideas of patterns. The individualistic person has the characteristic cognitive style of the conscientious individual plus the added dimension of distinction of process and outcome. The autonomous individual has all of the above plus the element of increasing conceptual complexity, complex patterns, toleration for ambiguity, broad scope, and objectivity. The cognitive style of the integrated individual is similar to that of the autonomous individual.

If one were to apply Loevinger's (1976) model of ego development to the characteristics of effective cross-cultural counselors, one can easily see that the levels of ego development at the self-protective, conformist, or conscientious stage may be quite problematical. One would hope and look for characteristics of ego development in the cross-cultural competent counselor more at the individualistic, autonomous, or integrated level. One common thread that seems to run through the descriptions in Loevinger's model of ego development as well as models of racial/ethnic identity is that of openness to experience, a dimension that recently has been identified in the five-factor model of personality.

Five-Factor Model of Personality

This five-factor model of personality has a long history, and it has been operationalized in the instrument the NEO Personality Inventory (NEO-PI) by Costa and McCrae (1985). Of the five factors of personality that include neuroticism, extroversion, openness to experience, agreeableness, and conscientiousness, one can see that the profile of the effective counselors could easily be described. It would be an individual who is low on neuroticism, in the moderate ranges of either extroversion or intraversion with no extremes on that dimension. A cross-culturally competent counselor is also one who is high on open to experience, agreeableness, and conscientiousness.

Of these five dimensions, the concept of openness to experience is worthy of further exploration in understanding the ego psychology of the cross-culturally competent counselor. In this section, we will describe the development of the concept of openness to experience, what it is, how it has been measured, what are its correlates, what are its consequences, and how that characteristic can serve as a unifying dimension for an understanding of the ego psychology of cross-culturally competent counselors.

Openness to Experience

According to Costa and McCrae (see Leong & Dollinger, 1990), openness to experience assesses proactive seeking and appreciation of experience for its own sake as well as toleration for and exploration of the unfamiliar. As with the other four factors within the NEO-PI, the openness-to-experience domain has various facets that include openness to fantasy, aesthetics, feelings, actions, ideas, and values. It may be worthwhile to describe the characteristics of the high scorer on openness to experience along the preceding facets. In terms of fantasy, the individual scoring high on this dimension is imaginative, enjoys daydreaming, and elaborates fantasies. In terms of aesthetics, the high scorer values aesthetic experience and is moved by art and beauty. In terms of feelings, the high scorer is emotionally responsive, empathic, and values his or her own feelings. In terms of action, the high scorer seeks novelty and variety and tries new activities. In terms of ideas, the high scorer is intellectually curious, theoretically oriented, and analytical. In terms of values, the high scorer is broad-minded, tolerant, nonconforming, and open-minded (see Costa & McCrae, 1985).

It also may be useful to describe the characteristics of the low scorer along the various dimensions. In general, the low scorer could be described as one who prefers realistic thinking, is practical, avoids daydreaming, is insensitive to beauty, is unappreciative of art, has a narrow range of emotions, is insensitive to surroundings, prefers the familiar, follows strict routines, is set in his or her own ways, tends to be pragmatic, is factually oriented, and does not enjoy intellectual challenges. The closed-to-experience individual is also dogmatic, conforming, narrow-minded, and conservative.

Correlates of Openness to Experience

Leong and Dollinger's (1990) review of the NEO Personality Inventory (NEO-PI) has found some significant correlates to openness that will help us understand the concept of openness better. For example, the NEO-PI openness scale was found to relate to intellectual interests factors in the Minnesota Multiphasic Personality Inventory (MMPI), with rs of .38 and .48 (Costa, Busch, Zonderman, & McCrae, 1986) and .39 with the thoughtfulness scale of the Guilford-Zimmerman Temperament Survey (GZTS) (Costa & McCrae, 1985). Openness also correlated .72 and .69 for men and women with the intuition score of the Myers Briggs Type Indicator (MBTI) (McCrae & Costa, 1989), .62 with an openness factor in the California Q Set (CQS) (McCrae, Costa, & Busch, 1986), and .45 with Zuckerman's sensation-seeking scale (McCrae, 1987).

The NEO-PI openness scale also has been shown to predict open-ended or projective-type criteria. One such criterion is ego developmental level. This is a broad construct reflecting overall level of cognitive integration ranging from the impulsive and self-protective ego levels up to the autonomous and integrated. Ego level is measured by a sentence completion technique, with responses coded individually into levels and the total protocol being categorized into one of many levels or sublevels (Loevinger, 1976). Although neuroticism and extraversion failed to predict ego level, openness did so; $r = .23$, $n = 230$, $p < .001$ (McCrae & Costa, 1980). Similarly, the facets of values, aesthetics, actions, and ideas predicted ego level.

Leong and Dollinger (1990) pointed out that if Loevinger's (1976) ego development construct is taken as one measure of maturity, another is offered by maturity of moral judgment. Using the Defining Issues Test to measure principled moral reasoning, Lonky, Kaus, and Roodin (1984) found that principled reasoners were more open than conventional reasoners ($r = .58$). Other studies have related openness to interview-based ratings of ego identity. For example, Whitbourne (1986) related NEO-PI openness to identity flexibility, defined as considering life changes in the future. In a sample of 57 adults, openness correlated .44 with identity flexibility, .45 with number of areas of flexibility, and .26 with actual life changes made by the 12-month follow-up. Relatedly, Tesch and Cameron (1987) interviewed 59 young adults to assess identity development in terms of occupation, religion, politics, and sex roles. Individuals already committed to an identity were *less* open ($r = -.40$), whereas those engaged in more current ego identity exploration were more open ($r = .27$).

Finally, McCrae (1987) postdicted divergent thinking from the NEO-PI. These tasks measure abilities such as imagining unusual and creative consequences of unusual situations. Self-reported, peer-rated, and spouse-rated openness correlated significantly with performance on total divergent thinking and most subscales, with *r*s typically in the .30s. Other factors in the NEO-PI failed to predict divergent thinking consistently. Openness was also significantly related to the California Psychological Inventory (CPI) Creative Personality Scale ($r = .44$, $N = 86\text{-}137$, $p < .001$).

Value of Openness to Experience to the
Cross-Culturally Competent Counselor

In this section, we will propose that openness to experience is a higher-order factor that underlies the various dimensions of the models of cross-culturally competent counseling (e.g., Sue & Sue, 1994)—namely, that openness to experience is a critical dimension for a counselor's ability to deal with the complexity of race, gender, and class as salient variables in the counseling relationship.

Loevinger's (1976) model of ego development describes the more mature person as autonomous or integrated, characterized as

> respecting autonomy and interdependence, cherishing individuality, coping with and reconciling conflicting inner needs, toleration . . . vividly conveying those feelings, integrating of physiological and psychological, role conception, self-fulfillment, and a sense of self within a social context . . . conceptual complexity, recognition of complex patterns, toleration for ambiguity, broad scope, and objectivity. (p. 25)

Loevinger (1976) might as well have been describing the highly open-to-experience individual. Let us reexamine the description of the person high on openness to experience:

> The individual scoring high on this dimension would be imaginative, enjoys daydreaming, and elaborates fantasies . . . values aesthetic experience, is moved by art and beauty . . . is emotionally responsive, empathic, and values own feelings . . . seeks novelty and variety and tries new activities . . . is intellectually curious, theoretically-oriented, and analytical . . . is broadminded, tolerant, non-conforming, and open-minded. (Costa & McCrae, 1985, p. 15)

The unifying characteristic of the openness-to-experience dimension of the cross-culturally competent counselor is not limited to only Loevinger's (1976) model. Keeping in mind Costa and McCrae's (1985) description of the open-to-experience individual, observe the parallels between their description and either Jahoda's conceptualization of positive mental health or Vaillant's (1977) model of psychosocial maturity. According to Jahoda's model (as reviewed in Loevinger, 1976, pp. 147-150), there are six dimensions of positive mental health. The first is concerned with "the attitudes of the person toward his or her self which includes: the accessibility of the self to consciousness, correctness of the self-concept, acceptance of the self, and a sense of identity." The second dimension "refers to growth, development, and self-actualization which includes investment in work and in social values beyond what yields immediate personal gain. . . . The inclusion of commitment to values outside oneself keeps this criterion from being interpreted as an egocentric one." Integration, as the third category, includes

> such ideas as balance of psychic forces and flexibility . . . reconciliation of two conflicting tendencies, that toward self-extension or commitment to the world and that toward self-objectification or detachment in respect to oneself. A final aspect of integration is resistance to stress.

Autonomy, as the fourth dimension, includes "regulation of behavior from within and a trend towards independence from the pressures of the immediate environment . . . the capacity for conformity when appropriate." Jahoda's fifth dimension relates to perception of reality, which is concerned with "empathy or social sensitivity and freedom of perception from distortion by the person's own needs. . . . It always concerns the reality provided by other people." The sixth dimension, environmental mastery, includes "adequacy in interpersonal relations; capacity for and adequacy in love work, and play; and capacity for adaptation, adjustment, and problem solving."

Observe the parallel between Vaillant's (1977) model of psychosocial maturity and the dimension of openness to experience. According to Vaillant, the adults in his Grant study of Harvard men exhibited a hierarchical system of defenses that characterized their adaptation to their life circumstances. Level 1 consisted of *psychotic defenses,* which included specific defenses such as denial of reality, distortions, and delusional projections. Level 2 consisted of *immature defenses* such as projection, hypochondriasis, and passive-aggressive behaviors. Level 3 consisted of *neurotic defenses,* which included intellectualization, reaction formation, and displacement. Level 4 consisted of *mature defenses,* which included sublimation, anticipation, and suppression. Vaillant found that the men who predominantly used mature defenses were the most well-adjusted and successful individuals in his study.

Taking the defense of sublimation as an illustration of the psychosocially mature individual, note the role of openness to experience in Vaillant's (1977) formulations:

The task of a successful defense is to resolve conflict. As the lives of the Grant study men illustrated, the ideal resolution is never achieved by *sweeping distress under the rug,* nor by arbitrary compromise between instinct and conscience, or by the cowardly purchase of intimacy by masochistic sacrifice. No, the sign of a successful defense is neither careful cost accounting nor shrewd compromise, but rather *synthetic and creative transmutations. . . .* But sublimation does more than make instinct acceptable; it also *makes ideas fun.* Displacement, which separates emotion from its object, and intellectualization, which separates emotion from ideas, can lead to arid lives unless they evolve into sublimation; for *sublimation permits idea, object, and attenuated emotion to remain together in overt behavior.* (pp. 91, 97)

It is not too difficult to see that the counselor who is high on openness to fantasy, aesthetics, feelings, actions, ideas, and values would be able to undertake the creative transmutations and integrate ideas, emotions, instincts, and objects in a sublimated approach to love (human relations) and work. It is precisely such an individual who is likely to manage well the intersection of race, gender, and class and who will be a cross-culturally competent counselor.

Why Openness to Experience?

Any of the five dimensions in the five-factor model of personality from Costa and McCrae (1985) could have been used as a critical concept. Given that most models of mental health and positive adjustment are multidimensional and could be readily used to predict cross-culturally competent counseling, why single out openness to experience as a central issue in the definition of the effective counselor? To answer this question, we need to turn to some key challenges facing the cross-culturally competent counselor.

First, as outlined above, there are many social-cognitive barriers to the multiculturalism movement. Many of these social-cognitive processes operate in clients, coworkers, and the counselors themselves. As Leong and Santiago-Rivera (1999) have pointed out, taking a multicultural attitude or perspective in one's work as a counselor is not an easy task. And yet the counselor who is high on openness to experience is most likely to be able to counter the social-cognitive barriers to taking the multicultural perspective outlined above. Cross-culturally competent counselors are not only able to counter these social-cognitive barriers in themselves but are also willing and able to deal with their clients' and other people's resistances to multiculturalism. For example, in counseling training programs, the counseling faculty who are high on openness to experience are most likely to study and integrate cultural material and the multicultural perspective into their courses as well as their research and service activities.

Whether it is ethnocentrism, false consensus, psychological reactance, or conformity, many of these social-cognitive factors support and maintain a resistance toward change. The resistance to change is a resistance against shifting from a monocultural to a multicultural perspective or approach in what we do and how we do it. Industrial/organizational psychology has a long history of dealing with this problem of resistance to innovation and changes within organizations. The nature of this resistance is well illustrated in a book exploring factors believed to be responsible for the underuse of research. According to Simmons (1992), part of the problem with U.S. industries is their failure to use new technologies and integrate new information into their practices. This resistance to integration is due to a pattern observed by Rothman (1980), who provides some very useful insights about the model of "two worlds" in organizations: "the notion that the world of research and the world of administrative practice have essential differences in language, values, methods, and points of view" (Havelock, 1980, pp. 11-12).

As a function of these two opposing communities, Rothman (1980) provides an excellent discussion of some of the factors responsible for practitioners' resistance to research. For example, one factor is forces of custom: "It was said that a certain inertia and unthinking conservatism exists in agency situations. As one director put it: 'Things get repeated based on custom. The system runs itself, but it doesn't criticize itself'" (p. 99). Another factor is defensiveness against criticism: "One of the major blocks to serious attention to research, it was said, is the tendency of operational people to feel threatened by information that implies a criticism of their practices" (p. 100). These and other factors discussed by Rothman (e.g., attachment to particular services) illustrate the costs associated with lack of openness to experience among our organizations' leaders. Inertia, unthinking conservatism, defensiveness, and blind attachment to the status quo are the hallmark of counselors who are closed to experience. These same patterns can be found among counseling researchers, practitioners, and educators. Openness to experience is a very important counterbalancing force to this resistance to change.

The second major challenge facing cross-culturally competent counselors is that cross-cultural counseling is extremely complex and requires a great deal of hard work (see Leong, 1996). To integrate the three dimensions in cross-cultural counseling and attend to the universal, group, and individual elements in the cross-cultural counseling encounter, the counselor has to have a high level of creativity and mindfulness (Leong, 1996). The counselor who has a high level of openness to experience is the one who will likely have this cognitive mind-set of tolerance, divergent thinking, creativity, and mindfulness. The cross-culturally competent counselor is open to the client's multidimensional cultural identity and readily explores the multifaceted nature of his or her client's personality and the full range of "possible selves" within the client.

On the other hand, the dominant Eurocentric paradigm in counseling is problematic on several fronts. As mentioned earlier in the discussion on the integrative tripartite model, the Eurocentric model suffers from being a unidimensional model that ignores group and individual differences. When unchallenged or supported by the social-cognitive factors mentioned above, it can usually create a "client uniformity myth" among counselors and clinicians that is ineffective at best and harmful at worst when applied to culturally different clients. The client uniformity myth is based on the assumption that the knowledge developed in psychology, which is heavily Eurocentric, is culture free and can be readily applied to everyone regardless of cultural background. When applied mindlessly to all persons, this approach is usually culturally inappropriate for racial and ethnic minorities. For a variety of reasons, counselors who are low on openness to experience will be less open to their clients' complex cultural identities and their multidimensional personalities. In addition, these counselors are also less able to deal with the culturally disjunctive experiences in the cross-cultural counseling encounters. They are likely to view the clients' attempts to integrate cultural (race, class, or gender) issues into the counseling relationship as unnecessary complications. When the clients persist or actually criticize the counselors for not attending to these important cultural dimensions in their problems, these counselors are likely to view their clients' responses as threats to their competence and professional self-esteem. We would like to propose that the counselor who is high on openness to experience will have the cognitively complex mind-set to use an integrative and multidimensional approach to cross-cultural counseling.

Third, it is our thesis that although openness to experience may be a personality trait, it is also a trainable cognitive orientation. If we can select and train more counselors to be more open to experience, we will go a long way toward addressing the challenge of providing culturally effective and culturally relevant counseling to the increasing number of culturally different clients.

We would hypothesize that counselors who enter training with a high level of openness to experience will have a much easier time in learning cross-cultural counseling. Because they will be more comfortable in dealing with culturally different clients, they will also acquire more experience in working with these clients and be even better at it toward the end of their training. This group will require the least effort in training them to be cross-culturally competent.

On the other hand, counselors who are low on openness to experience will be more resistant to learning cross-cultural counseling. They will also be more likely to revert to using the Eurocentric approaches to counseling, even with culturally different clients. This, in turn, is likely to lead to many of their culturally different clients having negative experiences, resisting their interventions, or prematurely terminating from the treatment. With such a cycle in place, these counselors will have a low level of self-efficacy in dealing with culturally different clients and select to work with nonminority clients. This group would be most resistant to the need to modify their approaches when counseling culturally different clients.

Counselors with a medium level of openness to experience will likely be the majority or modal group in any graduate training program. This is the group in which training to be more open to experience would be possible. They will be somewhat uncomfortable in working with culturally different clients but open to learning and could be challenged to change their orientation. This group will be more tentative and reluctant about cross-cultural counseling but not resistant like the low openness-to-experience group. With appropriate training and supervision, this group can learn to be cross-culturally competent counselors.

In conclusion, we have proposed that an integrative approach to cross-cultural counseling is the most appropriate strategy to use in understanding how counselors will deal with the intersection of race, gender, and class. We also identified a series of social-cognitive barriers to using an integrative approach in cross-cultural counseling. Finally, we proposed that the personality dimension of openness to experience is critical to identifying those who will become cross-culturally competent counselors, those who will resist cross-cultural counseling approaches, and those who can be readily trained to take on the challenge of complexity of cross-cultural counseling. Most, if not all, of the propositions in this chapter are testable hypotheses that can and should be subjected to empirical examination.

References

Atkinson, D. R., Morten, G., & Sue, D. W. (1989). *Counseling American minorities: A cross-cultural perspective* (3rd ed.). Dubuque, IA: William C. Brown.

Bergin, A. E., & Garfield, S. L. (1994). *Handbook of psychotherapy and behavior change* (4th ed.). New York: John Wiley.

Berry, J. W. (1980). Acculturation as varieties of adaptation. In A. Padilla (Ed.), *Acculturation: Theory, models and some new findings* (pp. 9-25). Boulder, CO: Westview.

Brehm, J. W. (1966). *A theory of psychological reactance.* New York: Academic Press.

Brislin, R. W. (1993). *Understanding culture's influence on behavior.* Fort Worth, TX: Harcourt Brace.

Costa, P. T., Jr., Busch, C. M., Zonderman, A. B., & McCrae, R. R. (1986). Correlations of MMPI factor scales with measures of the five-factor model of personality. *Journal of Personality Assessment, 50,* 640-650.

Costa, P. T., Jr., & McCrae, R. R. (1985). *The NEO Personality Inventory Manual.* Odessa, FL: Psychological Assessment Resources.

Cross, W. E., Jr. (1991). *Shades of Black: Diversity in African American identity.* Philadelphia: Temple University Press.

Fiske, S. T., & Taylor, S. F. (1991). *Social cognition* (2nd ed.). New York: McGraw-Hill.

Frank, J. D. (1961). *Persuasion and healing.* Baltimore: Johns Hopkins University Press.

Havelock, R. (1980). Foreword. In J. Rothman, *Using research in organizations: A guide to successful application.* Beverly Hills, CA: Sage.

Helms, J. E. (Ed.). (1993). *Black and White racial identity.* Westport, CT: Praeger.

Hofstede, G. (1980). *Culture's consequences: International differences in work-related values.* Beverly Hills, CA: Sage.

Kluckhohn, C., & Murray, H. A. (1950). Personality fromation: The determinants. In C. Kluckhohn & H. A. Murray (Eds.), *Personality in nature, society, and culture* (pp. 35-48). New York: Knopf.

Leong, F. T. L. (1996). Toward an integrative model for cross-cultural counseling and psychotherapy. *Applied and Preventive Psychology, 5,* 189-209.

Leong, F. T. L., & Chou, E. L. (1994). The role of ethnic identity and acculturation in the vocational behavior of Asian Americans: An integrative review. *Journal of Vocational Behavior, 44,* 155-172.

Leong, F. T. L., & Dollinger, S. J. (1990). NEO-Personality Inventory. In D. J. Keyser & R. C. Sweetland (Eds.), *Test critiques* (Vol. 8, pp. 527-539). Austin, TX: PRO-ED.

Leong, F. T. L., & Santiago-Rivera, A. (1999). Climbing the multiculturalism summit: Challenges and pitfalls. In P. Pedersen (Ed.), *Multiculturalism as a fourth force* (pp. 61-72). New York: Brunner/Mazel.

Lewin, K. (1951). *Field theory in social science: Selected theoretical papers.* New York: Harper & Row.

Loevinger, J. (1976). *Ego development.* San Francisco: Jossey-Bass.

Lonky, E., Kaus, C. R., & Roodin, P. A. (1984). Life experience and mode of coping: Relation to moral judgement in adulthood. *Developmental Psychology, 20,* 1159-1167.

McCrae, R. R. (1987). Creativity, divergent thinking, and openness to experience. *Journal of Personality and Social Psychology, 52,* 1258-1265.

McCrae, R. R., & Costa, P. T., Jr. (1980). Openness to experience and ego level in Loevinger's Sentence Completion Test: Dispositional contributions to developmental models of personality. *Journal of Personality and Social Psychology, 39,* 1179-1190.

McCrae, R. R., & Costa, P. T., Jr. (1989). Reinterpreting the Myers-Briggs Type Indicator from the perspective of the five-factor model of personality. *Journal of Personality, 57,* 17-40.

McCrae, R. R., Costa, P. T., Jr., & Busch, C. M. (1986). Evaluating comprehensiveness in personality systems: The California Q-Set and the five-factor model. *Journal of Personality, 54,* 430-446.

Padilla, A. (Ed.). (1980). *Acculturation: Theory, models and some new findings.* Boulder, CO: Westview.

Pedersen, P. B., Draguns, J. G., Lonner, W. J., & Trimble, J. E. (1989). *Counseling across cultures* (3rd ed.). Honolulu: University of Hawaii Press.

Rothman, J. (1980). *Using research in organizations: A guide to successful application.* Beverly Hills, CA: Sage.

Schneider, B. (1987). The people make the place. *Personnel Psychology, 40,* 437-453.

Simmons, L. (1992, June 1). New computers "fuzzy" just like the real world. *The Columbus Dispatch,* p. 4A.

Speight, S. L., Myers, L. J., Cox, C. I., & Highlen, P. S. (1991). A redefinition of multicultural counseling. *Journal of Counseling and Development, 70,* 29-36.

Sue, D. W., & Sue, D. (1994). *Counseling the culturally different* (3rd ed.). New York: John Wiley.

Tesch, S. A., & Cameron, K. A. (1987). Openness to experience and development of adult identity. *Journal of Personality, 55,* 615-630.

Triandis, H. C., Dunnette, M. D., & Hough, L. M. (1994). *Handbook of industrial/organizational psychology* (2nd ed., Vol. 4). Palo Alto, CA: Consulting Psychologists Press.

Vaillant, G. E. (1977). *Adaptation to life.* Boston: Little, Brown.

Whitbourne, S. K. (1986). Openness to experience, identity flexibility, and life change in adults. *Journal of Personality and Social Psychology, 50,* 163-168.

CHAPTER 11

DIVERSITY AT WORK

Research Issues
in Vocational Development

Ruth E. Fassinger
University of Maryland

With the rise of attention to multiculturalism as the "fourth force" in counseling (Pedersen, 1991), it has become almost axiomatic to assert that research is inadequate or flawed in terms of what we know about cultural groups that are anything other than White and European in background. Indeed, in a recent volume on the career behavior of racial and ethnic minorities (Leong, 1995), our state of knowledge in the area of career theory was described as "a mixture of knowledge and ignorance" (Osipow & Littlejohn, 1995, p. 252), and of career assessment and intervention, "what we do not know far exceeds what we know" (Betz & Fitzgerald, 1995, p. 268). These comments, reflective of a literature still largely in its infant stages, are reminiscent of statements made several decades ago in regard to women's career development, about which we have learned a great deal in the ensuing years (Betz & Fitzgerald, 1987; Fitzgerald, Fassinger, & Betz, 1995). Moreover, in the critical intersection of race/ethnicity and gender, such comments still are made routinely, suggesting the ongoing invisibility of women of color in the vocational literature on women (Betz & Fitzgerald, 1995; Fitzgerald & Betz, 1994; Fitzgerald et al., 1995).

However, it is encouraging to note that extensive attempts currently are being made to fill in these gaps, and the sheer volume of books, special journal issues, and articles on multicultural vocational issues has burgeoned during the past decade. For example, there have been special issues of the *Journal of Vocational Behavior* (1994), *Career Development Quarterly* (1991, 1993), and the *Journal of Career Assessment* (1994) devoted to multicultural career development. Several seminal books have appeared (e.g., Hsia, 1988; Leong, 1995) that focus on multicultural career issues, as well as chapters included in other vocational books (e.g., Bingham & Ward, 1994; Carter & Cook, 1992; Fitzgerald & Betz, 1994; Fouad & Bingham, 1995; Gottfredson, 1986; Leong & Brown, 1995) and individual journal articles too numerous to cite here (for reviews, see Arbona, 1990, 1995; Atkinson & Thompson, 1992; Bowman, 1995; Brown, 1995; Fouad, 1995; Johnson, Swartz, & Martin, 1995; Leong & Brown, 1995; Leong & Gim-Chung, 1995; Leong & Serafica, 1995; Martin, 1995; Smith, 1983). Some of the literature on women's career development also has begun to reflect greater attention to women of color (e.g., Fassinger & Richie, 1997; Gainor & Forrest, 1991; Gomez, Fassinger, & Prosser, 1997; Hackett & Byars, 1996; Hackett & Lonborg, 1993; McWhirter, Hackett, & Bandalos, 1998; Richie, Fassinger, Linn, Johnson, Prosser, & Robinson,1997; Ward & Bingham, 1993; Yang, 1991). Indeed, it has been argued that gender is so inextricably linked to individuals' experiences of race and ethnicity that it *must* be integrated effectively into multicultural theory, research, and intervention (Betz & Fitzgerald, 1995; Fassinger & Richie, 1997; Fitzgerald et al., 1995; Leong & Brown, 1995).

This chapter represents an attempt to describe and synthesize the state of knowledge on diversity in vocational development, particularly in the critical intersection of race, ethnicity, class, and gender. The chapter is organized into three major sections in discussing issues that arise in studying the career development and work behavior of culturally diverse populations: theoretical, methodological, and psychometric considerations. The chapter concludes with a brief discussion of the implications of these issues for vocational counseling and intervention with diverse clients. Due to space limitations, the emphasis of the chapter is on presenting a general overview of problems and issues, rather than a detailed review of individual empirical studies; for detailed reviews, the reader is referred to the many excellent works cited throughout this chapter.

Vocational Research Issues in Diverse Populations

As noted earlier, it is generally agreed that an alarming paucity of research addresses the intersection of race, ethnicity, class, and gender in career development and counseling. All of these demographic variables are critically important to vocational development because all shape the perceptions of oneself and one's social location, which, in turn, dramatically affect one's vocational attitudes and behaviors. We need only think about the possible differences between any four hypothetical diverse children to grasp this critical juncture. Imagine, for example, a Black/African American boy growing up in the Boston suburbs whose father is a Harvard economist and whose mother is a prominent attorney; a White/Euro-American girl growing up in rural West Virginia whose father is a former miner, currently unemployed, and whose mother died in childbirth; a Vietnamese/Asian American boy growing up in urban San Francisco whose parents are recent immigrants with limited English skills working in a restaurant with relatives; and a Latina/Mexican American girl being raised by aging grandparents in the Los Angeles barrio whose older sisters are unmarried with children and whose older brothers belong to gangs. We can easily see that the combined impact of social class, gender, race, and ethnicity is likely to be critical in forming the vocational ideas and plans of these four hypothetical children. Are they equally likely to think about future jobs or careers as they grow up? Are they equally likely to have access to and value education? Are they equally likely to develop complex self-understandings (including racial/ethnic awareness) that allow vocational planning to occur? Are they equally likely to learn about a wide variety of jobs and careers? Are they equally likely to experience encouragement or pressure regarding careers? Are they equally likely to have the means to explore interests and abilities? The answer to all of these questions is, of course, a resounding no. However, because we know very little, empirically, about the career development of diverse groups, making predictions about developmental trajectories and knowing how to facilitate the career planning of each of these children are difficult. Because relevant research and effective practice are assumed to be grounded in appropriate theory, we begin our discussion with theoretical considerations.

Theoretical Considerations

Useful, relevant theories are expected to be comprehensive yet parsimonious explanations of particular phenomena, with clearly defined and measurable constructs that lend themselves to empirical investigation and verification and contain discernible directions for application. Thus, career theories should concisely but thoroughly take into account the vocational issues and realities of *all* people, include constructs that pertain to the specific concerns of diverse groups, and be useful in guiding vocational counseling and intervention.

Osipow and Fitzgerald (1996) point to the importance of distinguishing between theoretical and social problems in critiques of theory vis-à-vis their applicability to diverse groups. By way of example, Osipow and Fitzgerald note that the disproportionate racial/ethnic distribution of workers across occupations (e.g., Hispanics being concentrated in low-level jobs) may reflect real differences in skills and training and therefore is not inconsistent with theoretical predictions that more advanced training and skill levels lead to higher-level jobs. This, then, suggests not a theoretical problem but a collection of social problems (e.g., racism, poverty) that lead to disproportionate occupational representation.

Theoretical questions, then, must focus on the tenets and applicability of theories. Three main issues noted by scholars (e.g., Brown, 1995; Fitzgerald & Betz, 1994; Leong & Brown, 1995) may compromise the use of existing theories with diverse groups: the questionable relevance of basic theoretical assumptions to the experiences of diverse groups (e.g., the concept of career development itself), the lack of attention to particular groups and concomitant questions about whether specific theoretical concepts (e.g., career maturity) apply to those groups, and the lack of inclusion of additional theoretical postulates that address important determinants of career behavior in diverse groups (e.g., acculturation). Leong and Brown (1995) also point out quite accurately that it is not necessarily the case that existing theories *lack* cultural validity, but rather that we do not *know* whether they are culturally valid because we have inadequate data by which to make such judgments—that is, there simply has not been enough research on vocational behavior in diverse groups to draw firm conclusions about any theory.

Nevertheless, if we examine the most widely used theories of career development, their roots in the vocational experiences of middle-class White men become quite obvious, and their adequacy in accounting for the occupational behavior of diverse populations becomes questionable (Arbona, 1995; Brown,

1995; Johnson et al., 1995; Leong & Brown, 1995; Leong & Serafica, 1995). For example, developmental theory (Super, 1957, 1980) assumes the centrality of work as a source of personal fulfillment in one's life and outlines the various developmental tasks that must be undertaken at each life stage to ensure that effective implementation of the self-concept is attained in various life roles. However, Super's theory fails to address the role of disadvantage (e.g., poverty, discrimination) in the development of the self-concept and the overdetermining aspects of external factors such as racism, opportunity structure, and family roles in directing the occupational behavior of individuals within particular racial, ethnic, cultural, socioeconomic, and gender locations (Leong & Brown, 1995). For example, the theory does not account for the experience of work as simply a necessity for ensuring basic life needs (food, shelter, safety), which is typically the case for individuals of low socioeconomic status. Additional relevant developmental variables that need to be accounted for in making Super's theory more applicable to diverse groups include socioeconomic factors, racial/ethnic self-concept, acculturation, values, and family structures (Leong & Brown, 1995).

In addition, scholars have observed that Super's (1957, 1980) stages of development are confounded by socioeconomic status and discrimination and may be applicable only to those members of diverse racial/ethnic groups who are the most acculturated or similar to the dominant (White male) culture (Arbona, 1995; Leong & Brown, 1995; Leong & Serafica, 1995), although it is also important to note the error in assuming that all oppressed individuals react to discrimination and disadvantage the same way and that it is always detrimental (Leong & Brown, 1995). Also, the concept of career maturity is thought to be profoundly affected by socioeconomic status, and it is easy to pathologize (e.g., label as "immature") developmental trajectories of individuals who simply have not had the opportunity to engage in occupational imagination or exploration. Moreover, it has been noted that attainment of vocational maturity by members of diverse racial/ethnic groups may include additional developmental tasks not accounted for in Super's theory, such as addressing racial/ethnic identity or developing strategies for coping with racism (Brown, 1995; Leong & Brown, 1995). Osipow and Fitzgerald (1996) assert that alternative or expanded notions of vocational self-concept are not only possible but important to explore.

Super's (1957, 1980) developmental theory also does not appear to consider anything other than traditionally defined occupations as appropriate vocational roles, ignoring the salience of other meaningful vocational roles in which people might participate. Richardson (1993), for example, raises unsettling questions about the basic assumption that *career development,* as it traditionally has been defined, is relevant to the vast majority of workers. Richardson presents an interesting example of motherhood as the only available role that permits implementation of the self-concept for many teenage girls in the lowest socioeconomic strata of society.

A final criticism of developmental theory is its emphasis on individual self-fulfillment and actualization, which may be at odds with family-oriented, group-oriented, collectivist values mentioned frequently in discussions of many racial, ethnic, and cultural groups, as well as of women. In fact, it has been suggested (Osipow & Fitzgerald, 1996) that collectivist value assumptions may constitute the single greatest challenge to existing career development theories, in which "the development of individual identity, goals, and desires, culminating in a career that maximizes person-environment fit, personal achievement, and satisfaction, has been considered the *sine qua non* of successful career development from the days of Parsons (1909)" (p. 276).

Person-environment fit (also termed *trait-factor* or *congruence*) theories (e.g., Dawis & Lofquist, 1984; Holland, 1985) assume that a careful process of matching one's interests, abilities, and values with occupational rewards and demands will ensure individual fit (and therefore satisfaction) with a chosen career and that careful assessment is the key to a maximally effective matching process. However, it has been noted that all people do not have the means to affect their career choices (Leong & Brown, 1995), and discrimination, poverty, lack of education, and stereotypes are the kinds of structural factors that inhibit or moderate the ability-success relationship implicit in person-environment fit theories (Fitzgerald & Betz, 1994). That is, many people are trapped by social locations that prevent the development of natural abilities and interests or the enactment of individual occupational preferences, and therefore they cannot really express anything remotely resembling "career choice."

Another problematic issue is the fit-satisfaction relationship. Brown (1995) points out that fit or congruence actually accounts for a relatively small amount of variance in occupational satisfaction and suggests that racial discrimination—particularly as it dictates the opportunity structure—may account for more variance than individual capabilities. As Brown accurately notes, there is no theoretical reason to expect congruence or fit between workers and jobs when entry into an occupation is determined more by the opportunity structure than by individual preferences. Moreover, occupational fit is likely moderated or limited by negative work climates that are characterized by sexism, racism, and other forms of discrimination; that is, an *apparent* fit based on interests, abilities, and occupational rewards and demands can be compromised by the atmosphere in a particular job setting. The assumption in person-environment fit theories that occupations require certain traits for success also raises the question of whether all cultural groups need the same set of traits to be successful (Leong & Brown, 1995). For example, occupational success may require additional skills for racial/ethnic minority workers; in addition to the basic abilities required for a specific job, the presence or likelihood of discrimination and harassment may dictate the need for additional skills, attitudes, and personality characteristics on the part of diverse individuals in managing difficult workplace realities. In addition, there is evidence that members of diverse populations often develop inaccurate self-perceptions due to the internalization of environmental oppression and stereotyping (see Leong, 1995), thus compromising theoretical assumptions regarding congruence that rest on accurate trait expression.

Finally, because person-environment fit theories rely heavily on formal assessment, it is important to examine whether traditional assessment tools are applicable or appropriate for use with diverse populations. Although this issue is discussed in more detail below, it is important to note that research is very limited, and a great deal remains unknown in the area of assessing person-environment fit variables. There is conflicting and inconclusive evidence, for example, regarding whether Holland's (1985) RIASEC (realistic, investigative, artistic, social, enterprising, and conventional) structure, which forms the basis for many of the most widely used measures of occupational interests, is applicable to all racial/ethnic groups (see Leong, 1995; Osipow & Fitzgerald, 1996). Moreover, as many scholars note (e.g., Betz & Fitzgerald, 1995; Bowman, 1995; Fouad, 1995; Leong & Gim-Chung, 1995; Martin, 1995), assessment instruments may not even exist for many of the variables that are beginning to be identified consistently as salient to the vocational behavior of diverse populations (e.g., career choice barriers, values and worldviews, home-career conflict and management, family roles and demands). However, Osipow and Fitzgerald (1996) remind us that existing congruence theories do have variables such as values and work salience embedded in them (albeit often overlooked in the focus on interests and abilities) and assert that

> the development of multiple, culturally sensitive, and even individually chosen criteria for realism of career choice does not prove an insuperable task for either researchers or counselors once it is realized that at least

some of the traditional criteria of vocational adjustment are *values*, not givens. (p. 276)

Cognitive, self-efficacy, and social learning theories (Betz & Hackett, 1983, 1996; Hackett & Betz, 1981; Krumboltz, 1979; Krumboltz & Nichols, 1990; Lent, Brown, & Hackett, 1994) assume the centrality of cognition and learning as critical factors in occupational development and posit various difficulties one might experience in thwarted learning experiences, inadequate modeling and encouragement, insufficient skills and practice in necessary cognitive tasks (e.g., decision-making and task approach skills), and societal constraints and negative messages that lead to inaccurate or inadequate self-observation generalizations. Because these theories focus on individual cognitive and learning processes as molded by the environment, these theories may seem more immediately applicable to diverse populations; indeed, it has been argued that they may offer a great deal—particularly self-efficacy theory—in conceptualizing the experiences of women and members of various racial, ethnic, and cultural groups (Brown, 1995; Fitzgerald et al., 1995; Leong & Brown, 1995). However, as with the other classes of theories, research has been sparse, fragmented, and inconclusive regarding the cultural validity of cognitive and learning theories.

Self-efficacy theory has received the most attention in terms of patterns of vocational behavior in diverse groups. Generally, research supports the notion that across racial/ethnic groups, self-efficacy beliefs predict academic performance, combine with interests to predict occupational preferences, and are gender organized, in that males and females consistently demonstrate self-efficacy beliefs that are linked to perceived gender-appropriate tasks (Fitzgerald et al., 1995; Leong & Brown, 1995). However, the exact nature of the impact of social forces such as racism on the development and maintenance of self-efficacy beliefs in culturally diverse populations remains unknown. Moreover, outcome expectations are thought to play a critical role for members of diverse groups in moderating or limiting the demonstration of self-efficacy (Arbona, 1995; Brown, 1995; Leong & Serafica, 1995); that is, an individual may have a great deal of confidence in her or his ability to engage in a particular task (e.g., conducting herself or himself competently in a job interview) but may expect a negative outcome (e.g., not getting the job) regardless of performance and therefore may not enact the behavior about which he or she feels efficacious.

Cognitive and learning theories also may too easily pathologize the experiences of those who face "structural" (limiting societal or organizational characteristics) and "cultural" (inhibiting socialized attitudes and beliefs) (Betz & Fitzgerald, 1995) barriers to career decision making and choice. These individuals lack the richness and opportunity of learning experiences, the positive and encouraging climate, and the freedom to develop and pursue interests and abilities that characterize the privileged few on whom presumed theoretical processes are based. Labeling an individual with implied deficits can result in "blaming the victim" (Arbona, 1995, p. 57) for her or his own limited environment.

Theoretical efforts that have produced "gendered" (Fitzgerald et al., 1995) individual differences frameworks to attempt to account for women's career development (e.g., Astin, 1984; Betz & Fitzgerald, 1987; Farmer, 1985; Farmer, Wardrop, Anderson, & Risinger, 1995; Fassinger, 1985, 1990; Fitzgerald, Fassinger, & Betz, 1989; Gottfredson, 1981; O'Brien & Fassinger, 1993) have had the unexpected benefit of beginning to address the experiences of groups diverse in other demographic variables besides gender. Farmer (1985; Farmer et al., 1995), for example, has attempted to address issues of career motivation in large, diverse samples of both males and females, and Fassinger's (1985, 1990; O'Brien & Fassinger, 1993) work also has attempted to test complex models of numerous career variables on large, diverse samples of women. Gottfredson's (1981) theory has been noted as having promise in use with culturally diverse groups (Leong & Brown, 1995) because it outlines a sequential process of ever-narrowing career decisions that represent compromises dictated by the realities of external constraints. However, initial testing of Gottfredson's theory has been inconclusive (Fitzgerald et al., 1995), and much more research is needed before it can be applied with confidence to populations diverse in race, ethnicity, culture, gender, and socioeconomic status.

In summary, it would appear that existing theory may be questionable in terms of its validity with culturally diverse populations. To the extent that work is not regarded as a central life role, to the extent that options and choices are not readily available, and to the extent that societal discrimination and oppression operate to distort the effects of individual characteristics, predictions implicit in existing theories do not necessarily apply (Osipow & Fitzgerald, 1996); thus, existing constructs may not be relevant. In addition,

> Theories have failed to identify relevant dimensions of cultural difference that may help psychologists gauge an individual's level of difference from the cultural majority and that may enable psychologists to understand the assortment of factors that affect the person's career-choice behavior. (Leong & Brown, 1995, p. 154)

That is, there are constructs missing in existing theories.

Although a great deal of research is needed in verifying or challenging existing constructs and assumptions and determining their relevance, there does appear to be a growing consensus regarding which constructs are missing in existing theories and need to be included in theory and research on culturally diverse populations (Betz & Fitzgerald, 1995; Leong, 1995; Leong & Brown, 1995; Osipow & Fitzgerald, 1996). One of these variables is acculturation, which also includes information related to immigration history, occupational status in the country of origin, geographical and political location of the country of origin, and language proficiency. A second variable is cultural values, which includes cultural identification (e.g., tribal identification), worldviews (e.g., collectivism), family roles and structures (as they reflect cultural values), and any other culture-specific variables that are thought to be salient for a particular group (e.g., honor, loss of face, social roles). A third variable is racial or ethnic identity, which is thought to be especially salient in exerting influence on vocational *processes* (Leong & Brown, 1995). Finally, gender is thought to be critically important in its interaction with race and ethnicity, both because there are differences in gender socialization and expectations across racial/ethnic groups and because women of color and poor women are particularly invisible in existing theory and research (Betz & Fitzgerald, 1995; Fitzgerald et al., 1995; Osipow & Fitzgerald, 1996).

In addition to engaging in systematic investigation of existing theory to determine its applicability to diverse populations, another possibility is to develop a new theory that is grounded more deliberately in the experiences of those populations—to create theory that more accurately describes what *is* rather than how we think it *should* be (Osipow & Fitzgerald, 1996). At present, no theory specifically addresses the career development of racially, ethnically, and culturally diverse populations (Leong & Brown, 1995; Osipow & Fitzgerald, 1996). However, as mentioned earlier, there is growing agreement on important variables that must be incorporated into theoretical and empirical efforts, and there are some lines of theoretical work currently under way. For example, Fassinger and colleagues (e.g., Gomez & Fassinger, 1994; Hollingsworth, Tomlinson, & Fassinger, 1997; Noonan & Fassinger, 1999; Prosser, Chopra, & Fassinger, 1998; Richie et al., 1997) are engaged in ongoing qualitative research aimed at articulating a model of women's career development that is truly inclusive of diversity and is grounded in the experiences of women of color. Whether this work also will be applicable to men of color remains to be seen.

It should seem clear from the foregoing discussion that much research is needed in determining the applicability of existing and emerging theory in terms of addressing the vocational behavior of individuals who are diverse in race, ethnicity, culture, gender, and socioeconomic status. Research is needed that explores the utility of various theories across racial/ethnic groups, and studies comparing the usefulness of several different theories within a particular racial/ethnic group also would contribute a great deal to knowledge and understanding (Betz & Fitzgerald, 1995). However, a number of issues emerge in conducting research on diverse populations, so we now turn to a discussion of methodological considerations in vocational research with diverse populations.

Methodological Considerations

One of the primary barriers preventing the accumulation of systematic empirical findings regarding the career behavior of diverse populations is the paucity of researchers engaged in this research. This raises questions about who is adequately equipped to do this research in terms of attitudes, knowledge, skills, and demographic location—that is, who possesses the requisite multicultural competency to engage in this research? Should middle-class White men and women do research on low-income Black or Hispanic populations or on Asian immigrants? If they do undertake such research, how do they ensure sensitivity and relevance? More pragmatically, how do they enlist the cooperation and participation of populations who often have experienced negative treatment at the hands of White scientists? If they do successfully complete their data gathering, how do they ensure that they interpret and report their findings in a way that is not permeated with middle-class White bias?

It would seem that the need for research on diverse populations is too great to confine such undertakings to the few psychologists of color currently engaged in research activities. It often has been said that just as men must take responsibility for helping to eradicate the negative consequences of sexism and the invisibility of women's issues in research, Whites must work to eradicate the negative consequences of racism and the invisibility of people of color in research. Team research offers a great deal of promise in terms of equipping researchers to engage in culturally sensitive studies because teams can be constructed so that individuals are involved who are likely to possess knowledge of the issues of importance to the population(s) being studied, as well as requisite skills (e.g., language fluency) (Arbona, 1995) that aid in accessing diverse groups. In addition to ensuring a sensitive and relevant research design, a team of diverse individuals can implement data collection procedures that have a high likelihood of success and also can aid in interpreting data using multiple possible explanations of phenomena so that the research moves beyond confirming biases or leaving issues unexplained. For example, knowledgeable team members can help to avoid some common problems related to stereotyping, such as inappropriately mixing levels of analysis (e.g., blaming macrolevel racism for microlevel individual failure) or assuming that culturally relevant variables (e.g., collectivism, honor) invariably function to the *advantage* of the group in question (Leong & Brown, 1995).

A second methodological problem is related to the kinds of culturally relevant studies that are undertaken. It has been noted (Leong & Brown, 1995) that many studies of racial/ethnic minority groups have been criticized for not including comparison groups. Because this usually implies a Euro-American sample, which is then implicitly seen as the norm against which the racial/ethnic minority sample is compared (often unfavorably), it is not surprising that comparison samples often are eschewed in research. Moreover, the kinds of comparisons that often are made are too global or merely nominal to be of much value, and important group distinctions are obscured (Leong & Brown, 1995). However, Leong and Brown (1995) argue for the utility of cross-cultural comparison studies: "Without the culture-comparative approach, researchers would be forever limited to *emic* studies and a series of principles of vocational behavior that has local utility but limited generalizability" (p. 167). Cross-cultural comparisons are necessary so that researchers can begin to tease out culturally specific variables that help to explain the vocational behavior of diverse groups.

Excessive focus on intergroup comparisons, however, also is problematic. In addition to the danger of superficiality (noted above), this approach can produce a literature in which differences between cultural groups are overemphasized and important commonalities are overlooked. Moreover, such approaches reinforce erroneous assumptions of homogeneity within groups and ignore important variability within cultural groups (Leong & Brown, 1995). Many scholars (e.g., Arbona, 1995; Bowman, 1995; Johnson et al., 1995; Leong & Gim-Chung, 1995; Leong & Serafica, 1995; Martin, 1995) have noted the enormous number of subgroups that comprise the cultural groups commonly referred to as "Latino" (e.g., Puerto Rican, Cuban, Mexican, Central and South

American, Caribbean), "Asian American" (e.g., Japanese, Chinese, Vietnamese, Korean, Filipino, Asian Indian), and "Native American" (318 different Indian tribes, 200 Alaska Native entities, and nearly 200 languages). Clearly, it is foolish to assume cultural similarity within these diverse groups—indeed, Leong and Serafica (1995) point out that homogeneity cannot even be assumed *within* cultural subgroups, using the Chinese as an example of a group that may claim a wide variety of geographic origins, political heritages, and cultural traditions. Moreover, when gender, social class, and other aspects of diversity are considered (e.g., sexual orientation, disability, generational status), the potential for individual differences becomes staggering. Gender, in particular, is seen as a critical variable to include and explore in detail on research on diverse populations, in light of the fact that gender differences are more frequently found than racial/ethnic differences across groups. Only by careful examination of gender can researchers begin to sort out which effects being observed are related to gender and which are related to culture (Leong & Brown, 1995). Indeed, Betz and Fitzgerald (1995) accurately note that the concept of individual differences is just as important with racial/ethnic minorities as with Euro-Americans, and they urge care in avoiding uniformity myths.

A third methodological issue is rooted in research traditions in psychology and the specific empirical approaches taken. Most psychologists are trained in a positivist model of science that emphasizes quantitative data and normative characteristics of large samples that are thought to approximate the general population. Certainly, large samples are critical in obtaining knowledge about normative patterns—indeed, Leong and Brown (1995) advise forming national research teams working on common investigations to access samples large and diverse enough to produce accurate normative data. In addition to large, relatively homogeneous samples, cross-sectional and longitudinal studies of diverse samples also are needed in producing greater understanding of important developmental issues and processes within and across groups (Leong & Brown, 1995).

Despite the widespread use of quantitative research approaches, it has been argued that they may be inadequate for understanding the behaviors and psychological processes of populations about whom little is known and for whom existing instrumentation may be inapplicable or misleading (Denzin & Lincoln, 1994; Hoshmand, 1989). In these cases—which include racially, ethnically, and culturally diverse populations—qualitative research approaches may be more useful because these approaches often focus on richly detailed narratives of the lived experiences of individuals, producing results that demonstrate high degrees of relevance (Denzin & Lincoln, 1994; Hoshmand, 1989; Lincoln & Guba, 1985; Morrow & Smith, 2000). The utility of qualitative approaches may be most apparent in the early stages of investigation of specific phenomena, when there is little existing knowledge to guide research efforts. Given the current lack of knowledge in so many areas of vocational research on diverse populations, qualitative approaches may offer great promise in fledgling efforts to identify constructs of relevance to culturally diverse groups; qualitative studies then can be followed up with instrument development and large sample quantitative studies to establish generalizability of findings.

A final methodological issue is related to identification, definition, and operationalization of relevant variables in vocational research on diverse populations. The first step is identifying culturally relevant variables, and, as noted earlier, agreement is beginning to grow regarding some of the important cultural variables that must be included in research (e.g., racial/ethnic identity, acculturation, collectivist values, family roles). Next, clear definitions of variables must be developed and used *consistently* across studies, which in practice is rarely done (Leong & Brown, 1995). In addition, it must be remembered that the labeling of variables themselves is a cultural construction, in that the extent to which a group is described in favorable (or unfavorable) terms is essentially arbitrary and therefore subject to bias (Betz & Fitzgerald, 1995).

For example, racial identity has been identified frequently as a variable of great possible importance to the career behavior of racial/ethnic minority groups, but there is little empirical evidence so far to support or refute this claim (Osipow & Fitzgerald, 1996). Racial identity is defined and operationalized in different ways across different studies, and there is little agreement about which aspects of career behavior are expected to be influenced by racial identity (Osipow & Fitzgerald, 1996). Leong and Brown (1995, citing Helms & Piper, 1994) assert that the importance of racial identity variables ("racial salience") will be most apparent not in vocational content (e.g., interests, values) but in vocational processes (e.g., job satisfaction, career maturity). Osipow and Fitzgerald (1996), on the other hand, suggest that the important issue to be examined is the stimulus value of race for the behavior of *others* rather than the behavior of racial/ethnic minorities themselves. Similar lack of consensus exists in relation to definitions of other variables generally agreed to be culturally relevant, such as culture, family, and acculturation. Clear and consistent definitions of such variables are imperative to the development of measurement tools to assess culturally relevant variables, and this leads directly to a discussion of psychometric issues and problems.

Psychometric Considerations

The central measurement issue in career development research on diverse groups is the extent to which measurement tools are appropriate for and applicable to those groups. There has been heated debate about the psychometric adequacy and relevance of commonly used ability tests (e.g., IQ tests, tests of academic achievement such as the Scholastic Aptitude Test [SAT]) for racial/ ethnic minority groups. Much attention is focused on oft-noted patterns of mean score differences across racial and ethnic groups, which then are typically viewed as evidence of cultural bias, even if the relationship of the scores to a criterion of interest (e.g., predicting academic achievement with the SAT) is the same for both groups (Osipow & Fitzgerald, 1996). Although this issue is too complex for adequate discussion here, it is worth noting that even psychometric experts cannot reach agreement on whether existing tests accurately tap abilities in racial/ethnic minority groups. Moreover, although not as politically "loaded," similar disagreements and lack of consensus exist in relation to other vocationally relevant characteristics, such as interests and career decision making (Osipow & Fitzgerald, 1996).

It should be obvious that continued research attention must be given to developing relevant norms and establishing evidence for the validity and reliability (or lack thereof) of existing vocational measures for diverse populations. Although much of the existing psychometric research has focused on the measurement of interests, it is safe to say that even in this area, the validity of interest inventories has not been established unambiguously across cultural groups (Leong, 1995). Betz and Fitzgerald (1995) note that more cross-cultural comparisons of the utility of specific measures are needed and that detailed investigations of a class of measures (e.g., measures of work values) with one particular racial/ethnic group also would contribute a great deal to understanding career behavior within groups.

In addition, modification of existing measures also may need to be undertaken to ensure that they include content reflective of culturally relevant needs and characteristics. For example, measures of work values could incorporate items that tap work values such as unity or uplifting one's people (Betz & Fitzgerald, 1995). Also, the entire process of administering tests needs to be reexamined in light of growing speculation that some racial/ethnic groups experience considerable discomfort with structured testing (Betz & Fitzgerald, 1995; Leong & Gim-Chung, 1995). In addition, psychometric work needs to focus on linking process variables to outcome variables more clearly so that important relationships are not overlooked (Osipow & Fitzgerald, 1996), and the effectiveness of existing intervention tools (e.g., system of interactive guidance and information [SIGI], card sorts) needs to be assessed for diverse populations (Betz & Fitzgerald, 1995).

Finally, new measures that assess culturally specific variables need to be developed. Instrument development work should include non-Western as well as Western constructs (Leong & Brown, 1995) and should focus on the roles of structural and cultural factors in conceptualizing and measuring salient variables (Betz & Fitzgerald, 1995). Recent promising assessment developments include interviews and checklists as a culturally sensitive way of obtaining information (Hackett & Lonborg, 1993), and Ward and Bingham (1993) present useful decision trees and checklists to be used in determining how and where to explore racial/ethnic issues in career counseling. In addition, recent models developed to explain phenomena in one racial/ethnic group, such as Gainor and Forrest's (1991) model of African American women's self-concept, can be adapted for use with other racial/ethnic groups.

IMPLICATIONS AND CONCLUSION

In the absence of dependable theory and research in the career development of diverse populations, it is perhaps premature to make detailed recommendations for intervention and counseling. In fact, one might argue that the existing state of the literature raises more questions than it resolves. However, it seems fairly safe to outline a number of broad issues to consider in career interventions with diverse populations and to speculate about what kind of theory *might* be useful in work with a particular individual.

Let us return to the four hypothetical children from the beginning of this chapter and assume they have reached adolescence. What kinds of theoretical constructs might guide our work with them? What sorts of interventions might offer promise in helping them to clarify goals and make deliberate personal choices?

The African American boy living in the Boston suburbs, by social location and economic privilege, probably most closely resembles the kind of person that existing vocational theory was designed to help. We most likely can assume that he has grown up with the concept of career as an important life role and that he has the means and freedom to effect real choices about what he might do vocationally. He is likely to have had the kinds of developmental experiences that have prepared him for the traditional tasks of thinking about and making career decisions, and he probably possesses the ability and confidence to pursue his desired goals. Holland's (1985) person-environment fit theory may be an appropriate, effective framework for helping him to accurately assess his interests, abilities, and values, and he is likely to be familiar enough with formal testing that he will benefit from it. Identifying possible clusters of careers that he can explore on his own is appropriate because he is likely to have access to the resources (e.g., a university career center) that permit this exploration to occur. Finally, he has two parents (and perhaps extended family) who are likely to be supportive of his career-planning endeavors. We might add racial/ethnic identity and African American family and cultural values to our list of areas to assess, and we might include discussions of workplace racism in our sessions with him, but, overall, the goal of assessing and promoting person-environment congruence is likely to be relevant and useful with this individual.

The White girl from a mining family in West Virginia presents a bit of a challenge in terms of vocational intervention. If she has made it this far without dropping out of school, marrying, or becoming pregnant, perhaps she has some idea of a future that includes work outside the home. She is unlikely to have received much vocational encouragement in her immediate environment (especially if she is caring for younger siblings, which she well may be), and she probably lacks confidence in her ability to pursue a life outside of her immediate family and community. However, if she has obvious intellectual ability, she may have had a teacher who encouraged her to pursue meaningful work and tried to build her confidence. She probably does not have much in the way of financial means and is likely to be extremely constrained in her choices by very real external limitations. Developmental and congruence theories may not offer much in the way of intervention guidance for this individual because she is unlikely to have had the kinds of developmental experiences and resources that would position her for accurate self-knowledge, awareness of the work world, and a rational career decision-making process that links the two. However, cognitive and learning theories, particularly self-efficacy theory, may guide interventions that focus on providing skill mastery experiences, modeling, and encouragement that will build her vocational self-efficacy, as well as realistic information about the work world that will help her to form accurate and realistic outcome expectations about obtaining specific jobs.

The Vietnamese boy living in San Francisco is likely to benefit most from a theoretical perspective that takes into account acculturation variables and his status as a recent immigrant. It is likely that his parents are oriented strongly toward his having education and a well-paying job, and he probably is facing strong pressure toward professional (vs. working-class) roles. He is likely to have developed some English-language skills, although he may still feel somewhat uncomfortable with language-based activities (e.g., writing). Due to both cultural and economic factors, he is not likely to have had much freedom in exploring a wide variety of interests and abilities, and his developmental status may evidence foreclosure in terms of firm decisions but little internal commitment to those choices. Congruence interventions may be difficult to implement because he may be unwilling to discuss his conflicts with his family or consider alternatives to his current vocational plans; moreover, the use of existing formal assessment instruments may be questionable. Social learning concepts, on the other hand, may be useful in helping him to examine occupational preconceptions he may have as well as incomplete views of his own competencies and thus lead him to a broader consideration of vocational possibilities.

The Mexican American girl in the Los Angeles barrio evidences some similarity to the girl in the mining family, in that they both are likely to experience economic and experiential deprivation, lack of encouragement for nonstereotypically female roles, and poor modeling. This girl, however, faces the additional problem of living in a population-dense area, in which the possibilities for harmful social and interpersonal experiences (e.g., coercive sex, murder) are magnified. If she is being raised strongly Catholic or identifies with Mexican culture, she also must deal with the internalization of rigidly proscribed gender behaviors and norms. Neither developmental nor trait-factor theories are likely to offer much usefulness in the way of intervention because she probably possesses little, if any, orientation to work as an important life role and probably lacks developmental experiences that would allow her to engage in even the most basic tasks of vocational planning (e.g., identifying jobs that people have or knowing something about her own skills). In addition, the use of traditional assessment devices is questionable. Again, cognitive and social learning approaches may offer some guidance regarding intervention, particularly in helping her to become aware of her assumptions about the roles open to her based on what she has learned in her family and community. If she is open to considering vocational roles in her future, then self-efficacy probably will have to be built slowly and systematically for her even to begin vocational exploration, let alone eventually choose a specific occupation.

These examples of hypothetical clients also raise unsettling questions about how interventions ought to balance workplace realities with respect for cultural traditions and values. Osipow and Fitzgerald (1996) sum it up:

Our dilemma is how to accomplish total access and integration into the workplace for everyone, and at the same time maintain the desirable features of the workplace and economy while preserving the cultural heritages of groups that may clash with those features. (p. 253)

For example, work with the Mexican American girl probably will involve questioning cultural and religious values that sharply limit her possible roles as a female. Similarly, helping the Vietnamese boy to become aware of and reconcile his own career dreams with the demands of his parents is likely to lead to questioning his cultural values of collectivism and filial duty. Both of these individuals are likely to require skill development (e.g., assertiveness) necessary to enact occupational decisions, and these skills may be counter to cultural expectations. Thus, in both of these cases, what may be considered to be an appropriate vocational intervention sets up a direct challenge to cultural values. Moreover, even if the counselor is operating with a competent knowledge of cultural values, such knowledge does not render these dilemmas any more easily resolved. As multiculturally sensitive counselors, we must continue to live and work in the spaces between theory and culture and somehow preserve the best of both.

References

Arbona, C. (1990). Career counseling research and Hispanics: A review of the literature. *The Counseling Psychologist, 18,* 300-323.

Arbona, C. (1995). Theory and research on racial and ethnic minorities: Hispanic Americans. In F. T. L. Leong (Ed.), *Career development and vocational behavior of racial and ethnic minorities* (pp. 37-68). Hillsdale, NJ: Lawrence Erlbaum.

Astin, H. S. (1984). The meaning of work in women's lives: A sociopsychological model of career choice and work behavior. *The Counseling Psychologist, 12,* 117-126.

Atkinson, D. R., & Thompson, C. E. (1992). Racial, ethnic, and cultural variables in counseling. In S. D. Brown & R. W. Lent (Eds.), *Handbook of counseling psychology* (2nd ed., pp. 349-382). New York: John Wiley.

Betz, N. E., & Fitzgerald, L. F. (1987). *The career psychology of women.* New York: Academic Press.

Betz, N. E., & Fitzgerald, L. F. (1995). Career assessment and intervention with racial and ethnic minorities. In F. T. L. Leong (Ed.), *Career development and vocational behavior of racial and ethnic minorities* (pp. 263-279). Hillsdale, NJ: Lawrence Erlbaum.

Betz, N. E., & Hackett, G. (1983). The relationship of mathematics self-efficacy expectations to the selection of science-based college majors. *Journal of Vocational Behavior, 23,* 329-345.

Betz, N. E., & Hackett, G. (1996). Applications of self-efficacy theory to understanding career choice behavior. *Journal of Social and Clinical Psychology, 4,* 279-289.

Bingham, R. P., & Ward, C. M. (1994). Career counseling with ethnic minority women. In W. B. Walsh & S. H. Osipow (Eds.), *Career counseling for women* (pp. 165-196). Hillsdale, NJ: Lawrence Erlbaum.

Bowman, S. L. (1995). Career intervention strategies and assessment issues for African Americans. In F. T. L. Leong (Ed.), *Career development and vocational behavior of racial and ethnic minorities* (pp. 137-164). Hillsdale, NJ: Lawrence Erlbaum.

Brown, M. T. (1995). The career development of African Americans: Theoretical and empirical issues. In F. T. L. Leong (Ed.), *Career development and vocational behavior of racial and ethnic minorities* (pp. 7-36). Hillsdale, NJ: Lawrence Erlbaum.

Carter, R., & Cook, D. (1992). A culturally relevant perspective for understanding the career paths of visible racial/ethnic group people. In Z. Leibowitz & D. Lea (Eds.), *Adult career development* (pp. 192-217). Alexandria, VA: American Counseling Association.

Dawis, R. V., & Lofquist, L. H. (1984). *A psychological theory of work adjustment.* Minneapolis: University of Minnesota Press.

Denzin, N. K., & Lincoln, Y. S. (1994). *Handbook of qualitative research.* Thousand Oaks, CA: Sage.

Farmer, H. S. (1985). Model of career and achievement motivation for women and men. *Journal of Counseling Psychology, 32,* 363-390.

Farmer, H. S., Wardrop, J. S., Anderson, M. Z., & Risinger, F. (1995). Women's career choices: Focus on science, math, and technology careers. *Journal of Counseling Psychology, 42,* 155-170.

Fassinger, R. E. (1985). A causal model of career choice in college women. *Journal of Vocational Behavior, 27,* 123-153.

Fassinger, R. E. (1990). Causal models of career choice in two samples of college women. *Journal of Vocational Behavior, 36,* 225-248.

Fassinger, R. E., & Richie, B. S. (1997). Sex matters: Gender and sexual orientation in training for multicultural counseling competency. In D. B. Pope-Davis & H. Coleman (Eds.), *Multicultural counseling competencies: Assessment, education and training, and supervision* (pp. 83-110). Thousand Oaks, CA: Sage.

Fitzgerald, L. F., & Betz, N. E. (1994). Career development in cultural context: The role of gender, race, class, and sexual orientation. In M. L. Savickas & R. W. Lent (Eds.), *Convergence in theories of career choice and development* (pp. 103-118). Palo Alto, CA: Consulting Psychologists Press.

Fitzgerald, L. F., Fassinger, R. E., & Betz, N. E. (1989, August). *An individual differences model of vocational choice in college women.* Paper presented at the annual meeting of the American Psychological Association, New Orleans, LA.

Fitzgerald, L. F., Fassinger, R. E., & Betz, N. E. (1995). Theoretical advances in the study of women's career development. In W. B. Walsh & S. H. Osipow (Eds.), *Handbook of vocational psychology* (2nd ed., pp. 67-109). Hillsdale, NJ: Lawrence Erlbaum.

Fouad, N. A. (1995). Career behavior of Hispanics: Assessment and career intervention. In F. T. L. Leong (Ed.), *Career development and vocational behavior of racial and ethnic minorities* (pp. 165-192). Hillsdale, NJ: Lawrence Erlbaum.

Fouad, N. A., & Bingham, R. P. (1995). Career counseling with racial and ethnic minorities. In W. B. Walsh & S. H. Osipow (Eds.), *Handbook of vocational psychology* (2nd ed., pp. 331-336). Hillsdale, NJ: Lawrence Erlbaum.

Gainor, K. A., & Forrest, L. (1991). African American women's self-concept: Implications for career decisions and career counseling. *Career Development Quarterly, 39,* 261-272.

Gomez, M. J., & Fassinger, R. E. (1994). An initial model of Latina achievement: Acculturation, biculturalism, and achieving styles. *Journal of Counseling Psychology, 41,* 205-215.

Gomez, M. J., Fassinger, R. E., & Prosser, J. (1997, August). *The career development of Latinas: An emerging model.* Paper presented at the annual meeting of the American Psychological Association, Chicago.

Gottfredson, L. S. (1981). Circumscription and compromise: A developmental theory of career aspirations. *Journal of Counseling Psychology, 28,* 545-579.

Gottfredson, L. S. (1986). Special groups and the beneficial use of vocational interest inventories. In W. B. Walsh & S. H. Osipow (Eds.), *Advances in vocational psychology: The assessment of interests* (pp. 127-198). Hillsdale, NJ: Lawrence Erlbaum.

Hackett, G., & Betz, N. B. (1981). A self-efficacy approach to the career development of women. *Journal of Vocational Behavior, 18,* 326-339.

Hackett, G., & Byars, A. M. (1996). Social cognitive theory and the career development of African-American women. *Career Development Quarterly, 44,* 322-340.

Hackett, G., & Lonborg, S. D. (1993). Career assessment for women: Trends and issues. *Journal of Career Assessment, 1,* 197-216.

Helms, J. E., & Piper, R. E. (1994). Implications of racial identity theory for vocational psychology. *Journal of Vocational Behavior, 44,* 124-138.

Holland, J. L. (1985). *Making vocational choices: A theory of vocational personalities and work environments* (2nd ed.). Englewood Cliffs, NJ: Prentice Hall.

Hollingsworth, M. A., Tomlinson, M. J., & Fassinger, R. E. (1997, August). *Working it "out": Career development among prominent lesbian women.* Paper presented at the annual meeting of the American Psychological Association, Chicago.

Hoshmand, L. T. (1989). Alternate research paradigms: A review and teaching proposal. *The Counseling Psychologist, 17,* 3-79.

Hsia, J. (1988). *Asian Americans in higher education and at work.* Hillsdale, NJ: Lawrence Erlbaum.

Johnson, M. J., Swartz, J. L., & Martin, W. E., Jr. (1995). Applications of psychological theories for career development with Native Americans. In F. T. L. Leong (Ed.), *Career development and vocational behavior of racial and ethnic minorities* (pp. 103-133). Hillsdale, NJ: Lawrence Erlbaum.

Krumboltz, J. D. (1979). A social learning theory of career decision making. In A. M. Mitchell, G. B. Jones, & J. D. Krumboltz (Eds.), *Social learning and career decision making* (pp. 19-49). Cranston, RI: Carroll.

Krumboltz, J. D., & Nichols, C. W. (1990). Integrating the social learning theory of decision-making. In W. B. Walsh & S. H. Osipow (Eds.), *Career counseling: Contemporary topics in vocational psychology* (pp. 159-192). Hillsdale, NJ: Lawrence Erlbaum.

Lent, R. W., Brown, S. D., & Hackett, G. (1994). Toward a unifying social cognitive theory of career and academic interest, choice, and performance. *Journal of Vocational Behavior, 45,* 79-122.

Leong, F. T. L. (Ed.). (1995). *Career development and vocational behavior of racial and ethnic minorities.* Hillsdale, NJ: Lawrence Erlbaum.

Leong, F. T. L., & Brown, M. T. (1995). Theoretical issues in cross-cultural career development: Cultural validity and cultural specificity. In W. B. Walsh & S. H. Osipow (Eds.), *Handbook of vocational psychology* (2nd ed., pp. 143-180). Hillsdale, NJ: Lawrence Erlbaum.

Leong, F. T. L., & Gim-Chung, R. H. (1995). Career assessment and intervention with Asian Americans. In F. T. L. Leong (Ed.), *Career development and vocational behavior of racial and ethnic minorities* (pp. 193-226). Hillsdale, NJ: Lawrence Erlbaum.

Leong, F. T. L., & Serafica, F. C. (1995). Career development of Asian Americans: A research area in need of a good theory. In F. T. L. Leong (Ed.), *Career development and vocational behavior of racial and ethnic minorities* (pp. 67-102). Hillsdale, NJ: Lawrence Erlbaum.

Lincoln, Y. S., & Guba, E. G. (1985). *Naturalistic inquiry.* Beverly Hills, CA: Sage.

Martin, W. E. (1995). Career development assessment and intervention strategies with American Indians. In F. T. L. Leong (Ed.), *Career development and vocational behavior of racial and ethnic minorities* (pp. 227-250). Hillsdale, NJ: Lawrence Erlbaum.

McWhirter, E. H., Hackett, G., & Bandalos, D. L. (1998). A causal model of the educational plans and career expectations of Mexican American high school girls. *Jounral of Counseling Psychology, 45,* 166-181.

Morrow, S. L., & Smith, M. L. (2000). Qualitative research for counseling psychology. In S. D. Brown & R. W. Lent (Eds.), *Handbook of counseling psychology* (3rd ed., pp. 199-230). New York: John Wiley.

Noonan, B., & Fassinger, R. E. (1999, August). *Career development of highly achieving women with disabilities: An analysis.* Paper presented at the annual meeting of the American Psychological Association, Boston.

O'Brien, K. M., & Fassinger, R. E. (1993). A causal model of the career orientation and career choice of adolescent women. *Journal of Counseling Psychology, 40,* 456-469.

Osipow, S. H., & Fitzgerald, L. F. (1996). *Theories of career development* (4th ed.). Boston: Allyn & Bacon.

Osipow, S. H., & Littlejohn, E. M. (1995). Toward a multicultural theory of career development: Prospects and dilemmas. In F. T. L. Leong (Ed.), *Career development and vocational behavior of racial and ethnic minorities* (pp. 251-262). Hillsdale, NJ: Lawrence Erlbaum.

Pedersen, P. B. (Ed.). (1991). Multiculturalism as a fourth force in counseling [Special issue]. *Journal of Counseling and Development, 70*(1).

Prosser, J., Chopra, S., & Fassinger, R. E. (1998, March). *A qualitative study of the careers of prominent Asian American women.* Paper presented at the annual conference of the Association for Women in Psychology, Baltimore, MD.

Richardson, M. S. (1993). Work in people's lives: A location for counseling psychologists. *Journal of Counseling Psychology, 40,* 425-433.

Richie, B. S., Fassinger, R. E., Linn, S., Johnson, J., Prosser, J., & Robinson, S. (1997). Persistence, connection, and passion: A qualitative study of the career development of highly achieving African American/Black and White women. *Journal of Counseling Psychology, 44,* 133-148.

Smith, E. J. (1983). Issues in racial minorities' career behavior. In W. B. Walsh & S. H. Osipow (Eds.), *Handbook of vocational psychology: Vol. 1. Foundations* (pp. 161-222). Hillsdale, NJ: Lawrence Erlbaum.

Super, D. E. (1957). *The psychology of careers.* New York: Harper.

Super, D. E. (1980). A life-span, life-space approach to career development. *Journal of Vocational Behavior, 16,* 282-298.

Ward, C. M., & Bingham, R. P. (1993). Career assessment of ethnic minority women. *Journal of Career Assessment, 1,* 246-257.

Yang, J. (1991). Career counseling of Chinese American women: Are they in limbo? *Career Development Quarterly, 39,* 350-359.

CHAPTER 12

THE RELEVANCE OF VOCATIONAL PSYCHOLOGY IN A MULTICULTURAL WORKPLACE

Exploring Issues of Race/Ethnicity and Social Class

Kristin M. Vespia
Gerald L. Stone
Jason E. Kanz
University of Iowa

We live in a society in which change has become a constant in our lives. Perhaps nowhere is this more evident than the workplace. We are beginning a new century with technological marvels and occupational titles that could not have been imagined at the start of the 20th century. In the past 30 years alone, we have witnessed significant transformations in labor force composition and the nature of work. The proportion of women and racial/ethnic minorities in the workplace has increased dramatically, and their numbers are expected to rise as the share of White and male workers falls (Hattiangadi & Shaffer, 1998). Individuals' work has also changed. What was once a country filled with well-paying manufacturing jobs has become a nation in which "low end business services, health care, and retail jobs" are showing the most growth (*Current State of Manufacturing*, 1997, p. 23). Automation and technological advances that have eliminated many "blue-collar" jobs have increased the need for skilled, technical workers (Archey, 1998). Jobs once thought to be secure are moving out of the inner cities and even out of the United States (*Manufacturing Job Losses*, 1993; Ullmann, 1988). Many laborers, particularly the "unskilled," have found that employment no longer protects them from poverty. At the same time, certain types of skilled workers have flourished, and chief executives now earn an average of 93 times more than their factory workers (Reich, 1991).

While these dramatic shifts were occurring in the workplace, vocational psychology was also beginning to undergo a transformation. One need only conduct a cursory search of the literature to appreciate the marked increase in writings about the career development of women and racial/ethnic minorities in recent years. Existing theories have been modified, and new theories have been advanced to address more directly differences in vocational behavior as a function of ethnicity, gender, and social class (e.g., Gottfredson, 1981; Lent, Brown, & Hackett, 1996). Empirical work in the field has also included more investigations involving issues of diversity (e.g., Brown, Minor, & Jepsen, 1991; Day & Rounds, 1998; Solorzano, 1992). Finally, intervention strategies have been developed specifically for use with special populations (e.g., D'Andrea, 1995; Okocha, 1994).

Despite these significant efforts, it would be hard to say that vocational psychology has kept pace with the changing workplace. People of color and women make up an ever-increasing portion of the labor force. Nevertheless, many of our vocational theories were developed based largely on work with middle-class White males, and calls for investigations of their applicability to ethnic minorities continue to be issued (Arbona, 1996; Leong & Brown, 1995; Leung, 1995). Culturally sensitive intervention programs have been developed, but systematic research supporting their efficacy is lacking. In fact, despite the increase in multicultural publications, empirical work in general has tended to focus narrowly on the experiences of Caucasian college students or professionals (Arbona, 1990; Fitzgerald & Betz, 1994; Hoyt, 1989). Vocational psychology also has had little to say about unskilled laborers and the plight of those who may not feel as though the labor market permits a free choice of occupation. Thus, although progress has been made, one could legitimately question whether vocational psychology has changed to reflect the composition and realities of the labor force. In fact, one could question whether it has ever truly reflected the experiences of American workers, who have never been exclusively

White, male, professional, and middle class, as vocational psychology has largely been.

The advent of the 21st century, which promises to bring more change and diversity to the workplace, may provide us with a good opportunity to assess the current state of vocational psychology and make thoughtful decisions about its future. If we choose to make the discipline more relevant to the majority of laborers, changes will be necessary. We will need to continue to incorporate issues of diversity into theory, research, and practice, and we will also have to begin to examine the ways in which different kinds of diversity (e.g., ethnicity, gender, social class) interact with one another rather than looking at these issues as if they exist in isolation.

With this chapter, we make one such attempt by addressing the issue of how vocational behavior varies as a function both of race/ethnicity and socioeconomic status (SES). We approach the chapter with a number of goals in mind. One objective is to provide a sense of the current status of the literature on this topic. Second, we hope to demonstrate that examining the interaction of social class and ethnicity does not mean focusing solely on the cumulative disadvantages that often occur for persons of color living in poverty. It also involves addressing the privilege that comes with being Caucasian or wealthy. Third, we plan to explore the implications of the interaction of ethnicity and social class for vocational theory, research, practice, and counselor training. A final goal is to pose questions to the field with which we have struggled during the writing of this chapter. Are our existing theories and constructs relevant to most individuals? If the answer to that question is no, how might we increase the external validity of our knowledge base and practices? Finally, and perhaps most difficult, in attempting to increase the generalizability of vocational psychology, are we attempting to be all things to all people—and can we be?

A BRIEF EVALUATION OF THE EXISTING LITERATURE

As we have stated, there has been a substantial increase in publications regarding the career development of racial/ethnic minorities in recent years. It is not our intent, nor would it be possible, to include a comprehensive literature review within this chapter. We do, however, feel it necessary to provide a very selected and brief evaluation of the current work concerning both race/ethnicity and SES as they pertain to career development before we discuss their interaction. We first address the multicultural literature, but we grant more attention to the social class literature because it may be less familiar to readers.

A cursory search of recent publications that include issues of race/ethnicity quickly reveals the breadth of this literature. Topics from the generalizability of existing theories to the job experiences and career development needs of racial/ethnic minorities have been covered. It is also, however, relatively easy to identify some of the weaknesses of this body of knowledge. Studies often have been plagued by methodological problems, including small sample sizes and a failure to control for possible intervening variables, such as gender and SES. The research focus has also been on between-group more so than on within-group investigations. This neglect of within-group research can act to reinforce the false notion that racial/ethnic groups are homogeneous and not worthy of study in their own right but only as compared to the Caucasian "norm" (Atkinson, Morten, & Sue, 1993). Helms and Piper (1994) have gone further in critiquing between-group studies. They have suggested that cross-cultural studies of things such as interests and aspirations have largely focused on race as a mutually exclusive categorical variable. They argue, however, that

> unless one believes that vocational behavior is biogenetically determined and racial classification is a valid indicator of persons' biogenetic endowments, then there is no valid reason for explaining or anticipating consistent between-group differences on the basis of race per se. (p. 125)

They advocate for more research using sociopolitical definitions of race, in which "socialization in a racially oppressed or oppressing racial group is assumed to have differential implications for a person's psychological status and behaviors" (p. 124). This would seem to imply a need for more within-group investigations that address variables such as SES, discrimination, educational opportunities, and racial identity or acculturation, which may be parts of the process or the outcome of such socialization.

The state of the research base regarding SES and career development is similar in some ways to that of the multicultural literature. The calls for more empirical studies of social class mirror those for additional cross-cultural research (Arbona, 1996; Fitzgerald & Betz, 1994; Richardson, 1993). Furthermore, this literature has great breadth, covering things such as the interaction of SES and vocational interests, congruence, and career decision-making skills and attitudes (e.g., Luzzo, 1992; Slaney & Brown, 1983). Some of the same design difficulties found in multicultural research also apply to work with social class variables. Most noticeable is the relative lack of within-group studies. For example, why is it that some individuals do not benefit from the protective influence afforded by economic privilege? In contrast, what factors contribute to relatively disadvantaged persons improving their SES? Despite such remaining questions, however, it should be emphasized that there are some consistent findings in the social class literature. Socioeconomic status appears to be a good predictor of vocational aspirations and expectations, and children's career goals and ultimate attainments often fall within the same social class as their parents' occupations (Gottfredson, 1981, 1996; Hotchkiss & Borow, 1996; Solorzano, 1992).

Gottfredson (1981) has been a leader in including SES in vocational psychology. She notes that although social class has been given a place in most career theories, other relatively weaker variables, such as vocational interests, are often granted more weight in the prediction of occupational goals. In her theory, Gottfredson (1996) has focused on the "public, social aspects of the self," (p. 181) such as social class, and has attempted to systematically address SES by incorporating it as an influence on self-concept and on the compromises individuals make in their career choices. More recently, social-cognitive career theory (SCCT) has discussed SES as a contextual variable that can influence career development and its outcomes (Lent et al., 1996). Sociological theories also have contributed to the investigation of SES and career development. Status attainment theory, for example, was developed to address the causes of intergenerational occupational mobility (Hotchkiss & Borow, 1996). The research that has followed from this perspective has helped to establish the variables, such as career expectations and educational attainment, that mediate the relationship between parent and child occupational status level (Hotchkiss & Borow, 1996).

VOCATIONAL BEHAVIOR AND THE COMBINATION OF RACE/ETHNICITY AND SES

Given the continued calls for additions to the vocational literature concerning both race/ethnicity and social class, it should be evident that examinations of the interaction between these two variables are relatively rare. In fact, Leung (1995) has asserted that "exactly how career behavior is influenced by the interaction between ethnic-related variables and SES is still unclear" (pp. 552-553) in large part because most empirical work with persons of color has not controlled for social class differences. Another reason that we do not know much about the combination of these two variables may be found in Gottfredson's (1996) discussion of the difficulty of determining the source of group differences in career development. She has argued that these differences "cannot be assumed to originate—or not originate—in group membership per se" (p. 203). We cannot assume that variations in the vocational behavior of members of different racial/ethnic groups are due to that classifying variable when there are, for example, established differences in income and educational levels between many of the groups. In the same way, we cannot simply conclude that career development varies based on SES when things such as educational opportunities and differential exposure to occupations and role models may explain at least a portion of group differences. Given the complexity of exploring group differences based on one classifying variable, it is hardly surprising that more work has not been done concerning a combination of variables.

What, then, do we know? We know there is an interaction between SES and race/ethnicity in regard to career-related behaviors and outcomes. Much of the support for that statement comes not from vocational psychology but from labor market statistics. In fact, the interplay of SES and race/ethnicity might be best understood when first considered within the larger context of the labor market. This can be illustrated dramatically, if incompletely, with a few statistics. African Americans, Hispanics, and Native Americans all have appreciably lower average incomes than Caucasians and Asian Americans/Pacific Islanders, who have the highest mean income (U.S. Bureau of the Census, 1990a, 1990b, 1990c, 1990d, 1990e). Furthermore, racial/ethnic minority groups have higher poverty rates than Whites (U.S. Bureau of the Census, 1999). Even when one looks at the mean annual earnings of men with graduate/professional degrees who were well advanced in their careers (ages 45-54), group differences are apparent. White men have the highest incomes, and although not much higher than those of Hispanics or Asian Americans, their earnings are over $20,000 per year more than those of African Americans and Native Americans (U.S. Bureau of the Census, 1990a, 1990b, 1990c, 1990d, 1990e). As one might predict, unemployment also differs between groups. Unemployment rates for African American men and women are more than two times that of Caucasians (U.S. Bureau of the Census, 1999).

Not all of our information on this topic comes from labor statistics. We know from psychological and sociological literatures that members of some racial/ethnic minority groups are overrepresented in low-status jobs (Arbona, 1989; Hotchkiss & Borow, 1996; Okocha, 1994). We consistently find that vocational aspirations increase with social class, and although persons of color (specifically African Americans and Hispanics) may not have lower aspirations than Whites, they may have lower expectations of achieving their goals (Arbona, 1990; Arbona & Novy, 1991; Solorzano, 1992). We are also beginning to find that, for example, African Americans cite different causes for poverty or joblessness than Caucasians living in similar economic circumstances (Fine & Weis, 1998). Furthermore, we are aware that persons of color face many internal and external career development obstacles, and although higher SES may lessen the impact of these barriers, it does not eradicate them (McClelland, 1990; Pettigrew, 1981). Finally, we know that racial/ethnic groups have different patterns of educational attainment, which influence their range of occupational choices and, thereby, potential earning power.

What is responsible for the SES and racial/ethnic differences we have outlined? The answer to that question is, of course, not a simple one. We approach it here by providing some responses from three perspectives: economic, sociological and psychological, and educational.

Economic or Labor Market Perspectives

Part of the explanation for group variations in career development can be found in economic and labor market trends. Two such trends will be discussed here. The first is the decline in the manufacturing industry and corresponding increase in service-related jobs. Manufacturing occupations that paid, on average, 26% more per week than private-sector positions are being replaced by lower-paying service and retail jobs (*Current State of Manufacturing,* 1997). This is having a particularly devastating effect on blue-collar workers, many of whom, given differential dropout and postsecondary education rates, are likely to be persons of color (National Center for Education Statistics [NCES], 1996; U.S. Bureau of the Census, 1997a, 1997b). In contrast, the workplace automization that has led to the loss of many manufacturing jobs is increasing the demand for skilled workers to create and maintain new technological systems (Archey, 1998). These new jobs are more likely to be filled with Caucasians or Asian Americans if one considers their proportionally higher achievement of college degrees (NCES, 1998a).

The decline of manufacturing has contributed to a second marketplace trend: the movement of jobs out of inner cities and into suburban areas. Many of America's inner cities have large populations of persons of color, and as employment opportunities have moved to the suburbs, so have much of the working and middle classes. Wilson (1988) has described one major metropolitan area (Chicago) in which the net African American migration from the poorest community areas was –42% between 1970 and 1980 (p. 12). During this same time period, the poverty level of these communities increased, which Wilson attributes to an exodus of African Americans with steady, gainful employment. He has asserted that a perpetuating cycle of economic hardship may be set up for African Americans in inner cities because the flight of the working and middle classes has left a concentration of urban poor without the role models, the financial support for buffer institutions such as churches and schools, and the access to informal job networks that they once had. Movement of jobs out of the inner cities also creates new barriers to employment, such as lack of transportation.

These two labor market trends are, of course, part of a much larger economic system. Nevertheless, within them, elements of a larger social problem relevant to this interaction between race/ethnicity and class can be seen: the growing gap between the "haves" and "have-nots" in American society. In a recent nightly newscast, a story about the tax burden on the working poor and its relationship to welfare participation was immediately followed by the news that sales of certain luxury automobiles had increased 300%. As a small segment of the population—most likely Caucasians and few persons of color— amasses increasing wealth, even the employed poor have a hard time making ends meet. More than 50% of poor people, including almost two thirds of the children living in poverty, have at least one worker in their household (Reich, 1991). Even employment does not necessarily provide protection from these circumstances, and from what we know of poverty rates, those in the "have-not" position are proportionately more likely to be racial/ethnic minorities.

SOCIOLOGICAL AND PSYCHOLOGICAL PERSPECTIVES

Sociology and psychology also have provided some explanations for variations in vocational behavior by social class and racial/ethnic group membership. The interaction between SES and race/ethnicity rarely has been addressed explicitly, however. Those examining vocational behavior from a sociological perspective have lamented that "research on race and gender effects has not been matched by studies on the effects of poverty as a separate independent variable" (Hotchkiss & Borow, 1996, p. 302). As previously mentioned, status attainment theory has addressed SES by attempting to explain the relationship between parent and child occupational status levels. Extrapolating from this theory, one could assert that racial/ethnic minorities, because they have higher poverty rates, may be more likely to find themselves in the position of re-creating the low-status and low-paying occupational level of their parents unless that relationship is moderated by, for example, increased educational attainment. The differences in the occupational attainment of racial/ethnic minorities also have been discussed in structuralist theory, which asserts that persons of color may have reduced access to the most desirable jobs, partly because firms continue to make personnel decisions based on variables such as education, ethnicity, and gender (Hotchkiss & Borow, 1996). Having limited access to these jobs of course would tend to depress the average social class standing of persons from racial/ethnic minority groups while protecting the SES of Caucasians.

Discrimination

Another variable that may be used to explain the interaction of race/ethnicity and SES in vocational behavior is discrimination. Kantor (1994) asserts that discrimination may, as we usually assume, involve a general resistance to hiring persons of color. Alternatively, he suggests that it may reflect associating race/ethnicity with other variables, such as inner-city schools, which may, in turn, conjure images of inferior education, poor work ethic, and substandard work skills. Such discriminatory practices certainly limit the social class mobility of many persons of color. In addition, although discrimination may be based on race/ethnicity, it would be hard, given this conceptualization, to argue that it is not tied in some ways to SES. If, for instance, employers tie being an African American to the inner city and inferior education, then an assumption is also being made that this group is associated with the poverty that contributes to poorly funded educational facilities. One has to wonder, by extension, if being White or Asian American then brings to mind images of the middle class and well-supplied and adequately funded schools. It is also important to note that social class does not insulate individuals from the effects of discrimination; it simply may come in different forms. For example, employers may hesitate to hire persons of color to supervise Caucasians (Kantor, 1994). In addition, Pettigrew (1981) has argued that the backlash against affirmative action policies in the workplace and in higher education is attacking a major source of social mobility for middle-class racial/ethnic minorities.

Vocational Aspirations

One of the psychological variables that has been a focus of attention when attempting to explain combined racial/ethnic and SES differences in vocational behavior is career aspirations, which are seen as a major mediator of occupational attainment. As we have mentioned, the aspirations of persons of color may not be significantly different from those of Caucasians, but they may have lower expectations of achieving their goals. Another perspective is provided by Solorzano (1992), who found that students' anticipated educational attainment varied little between African Americans and Whites, but when social class was controlled, far more African American students believed that they would attend college (e.g., in the lowest SES grouping, 70.9% of African American males vs. 48.9% of White males) (Solorzano, 1992, p. 33). Results regarding occupational expectations were similar when SES was controlled. Consistent with previous findings, Solorzano also found that educational and occupational aspirations rose as social class did. He further discovered that a significant gap existed in his sample between educational aspirations and actual educational attainment when considering U.S. census data. This gap was found to be larger for African Americans than for Caucasians. Although the study was conducted with very young participants, it is still easy to look at these results and wonder if many of the differences in vocational outcomes for persons from various racial/ethnic backgrounds are actually due to patterns of SES differences. The findings also point to the differential effects of poverty on African Americans and Caucasians. In this case, it appears that African Americans are better able to retain high goals in the face of poverty. In a different examination of aspirations as they relate to race, gender, and social class, McClelland (1990) discovered that in a group of high school students who had high career aspirations, less than one fifth remained on track to achieve their goals, and the individuals most likely to stay on task were already "advantaged" (White, upper middle class).

Career Development Barriers

Career development barriers, both internal and external, have also been examined to help explain the vocational behavior of, most particularly, racial/ethnic minorities and persons from low social classes. One possible internal barrier is the perception of fewer viable career options by these at-risk individuals. Another is a lack of career-related knowledge and skills. In a national survey, Brown et al. (1991) discovered that persons of color (African Americans,

Hispanics, and Asian/Pacific Islanders) were more likely than Whites to report needing help in locating information about jobs and were more likely to indicate that, if they could start over, they would want more information about career options. A lack of career information could be related to a reduced perception of occupational alternatives and play a role in racial/ethnic minorities being underrepresented in higher-status careers. Persons of color also may have fewer chances to obtain part-time work as adolescents, thereby reducing their opportunities to gain work-related skills, work environment socialization, and access to role models and mentors (Constantine, Erickson, Banks, & Timberlake, 1998). The previously described flight of working- and middle-class persons of color from the inner cities also has been tied to a lack of role models for some of the poorest segments of the population, which may help to perpetuate those economic circumstances. Such lack of opportunity may contribute to the persistent, although inaccurate, stereotype that many poor and racial/ethnic minorities do not have an appropriate work ethic (Goodwin, 1972, 1973). The restricted opportunities afforded persons of color, particularly those from lower social classes, also may lead to fewer chances to develop a sense of self-efficacy for occupations that require higher education and lead to higher pay and social status (Constantine et al., 1998).

Some final external barriers are noteworthy. Particularly in the case of inner-city youth, who are more likely to be persons of color, concerns have been raised about exposure to chronic unemployment, inadequate health care, discrimination, and inferior educational services (Constantine et al., 1998). In these ways, poverty is believed to affect racial/ethnic minorities disproportionately and negatively by placing obstacles in their way that make free-market occupational choices based on interests, values, and abilities seem, at the very least, unrealistic.

EDUCATIONAL PERSPECTIVES

Economic and Vocational Consequences
of Educational Attainment

One of the major moderating variables used to explain SES and racial/ethnic differences in vocational behavior is education. It has been argued that it is not SES or race/ethnicity per se that influences career development; rather, group differences are the result of discrepancies in educational opportunities and achievement. Children from wealthy backgrounds may be more likely to attend well-funded schools and be exposed to a wider range of learning opportunities and career options. Children of color may face discrimination in schools or find themselves subtly, or not so subtly, prepared for and encouraged to consider a narrower range of lower-prestige work opportunities. In fact, educational achievement does differ among racial/ethnic groups, and the differences correspond with variations in the average SES of these same groups. High school dropout rates are lower for Caucasians than for African Americans or Hispanics (7.3% vs. 13% vs. 29.4%) (NCES, 1997, Table 103, p. 111). Furthermore, when examining educational attainment, Caucasians and Asian Americans/Pacific Islanders are more likely to hold bachelor's degrees than Hispanics or African Americans (U.S. Bureau of the Census, 1997a, 1997b). Educational preparation also differs by SES and race/ethnicity. High school graduates from high SES backgrounds are more likely to be academically qualified for higher education (86%) than individuals from low-income homes (53%) (NCES, 1998a). Similarly, members of ethnic minority groups, except Asian/Pacific Islanders, are less likely than Whites to be academically qualified for postsecondary education (NCES, 1998a). These facts help to explain the income gains of some groups (Asian/Pacific Islanders). They also shed light on the continuing economic disadvantage of some individuals from other groups (the poor, African Americans, Hispanics, Native Americans). We know that welfare participation and unemployment rates are higher for individuals with less education (NCES, 1998d). In addition, workforce participation and salaries tend to rise as education level does (NCES, 1998b, 1998c, 1998d). Based on the social-cognitive career theory (SCCT), we could also argue that the learning experiences available in formal education contribute to the development of self-efficacy for specific careers, particularly those requiring more training. If this self-efficacy does not develop, then it would be hypothesized that individuals would express interest in and consider a smaller range of less prestigious occupational alternatives, which we know to be the case for many persons from racial/ethnic minority and low SES groups.

Societal Functions of Education

Education influences vocational development and outcomes in other ways as well, largely because educational institutions are assigned such major responsibilities, both social and economic, in this country. The social responsibility of schools is fulfilled by educating students for a democratic society (Dewey, 1916). Specifically, racial/ethnic minorities, blue-collar families, and recent immigrants are encouraged to see education as their best hope of becoming a part of America through social mobility. This promise may seem empty for many people in these at-risk groups, given that they are proportionately less likely to advance as far in the educational system as members of more "privileged" groups. From an economic perspective, schools were organized during the Industrial Revolution as human resource allocation organizations. That is, education and school guidance programs were seen as sorting processes for managing the flow of future workers along education or work trajectories to appropriately match worker talents to the evolving needs of the workplace. In serving these different functions, education has been both an obstacle and a source of opportunity in terms of career development.

Education as Obstacle. One of the primary mechanisms in schools for accomplishing its economic responsibility, *tracking,* also has been one of the major ways in which education has served as a vocational obstacle by limiting the progress of several minority groups and the poor. Tracking was first implemented by comprehensive high schools at the turn of the century in an attempt to enhance opportunities for effective learning by matching curriculum difficulty to student ability. That same "matching philosophy" has been pervasive in the history (Parsons, 1909) and contemporary practices (Holland, 1997) of vocational guidance and counseling. Four basic tracks frequently have been identified: special (slow learner; learning disability), vocational (a terminal program of vocational preparation for high school graduates), college prep (a preparatory program for college-bound students), and gifted (honors program for gifted students) (Tanner, 1965). Research on tracking has indicated a wide range of negative effects on class composition, curriculum coverage, teachers, teacher attitudes, and student learning (see Burns & Mason, 1998). In general, those assigned to the higher academic tracks interact with higher-ability students, more educational material, and better teachers, which can ultimately translate into higher achievement, increased opportunities for further education, and higher-paying employment. Unfortunately, tracking, beginning in elementary school (see Burns & Mason, 1998), has tended to segregate students along racial/ethnic or SES lines. By the time a student reaches high school, his or her educational future may be determined in many ways. If racial/ethnic minorities and those from lower social classes are tracked more frequently into noncollege preparatory tracks, even if their overall educational achievements (e.g., high school graduation rates) increase, they may not realize proportional economic gains. By creating class compositions favorable to high-ability students and unfavorable to low-ability students, the educational system exacerbates and sustains inequalities in background and history and leads many racial/ethnic minorities and poor people to perceive education as another tool of oppression and racism rather than as a means of liberation. Development of differential curriculum and educational paths may seem to be reasonable from a management and resource allocation perspective, but such efforts also have led to inadvertent and intentional side effects: unequal learning opportunities, limited social mobility for several minorities and poor people, and maintenance of the status quo (Kershaw, 1992).

Education as Opportunity. As depressing as this picture may be, education also can be a vehicle of opportunity in terms of career development. This is another element of the educational perspective that needs to be acknowledged: Education is still believed by many to be a tool of social mobility and the key to the "American Dream." In part because many traditionally disadvantaged groups have perceived the educational system as a tool of oppression, American society, through government and educational institution initiatives, has tried to encourage students from poor families by providing access to educational opportunities. For example, federally supported programs, such as Upward Bound, provide minority and majority high school students from poor backgrounds with exposure to higher education through summer campus programs and continued encouragement through ongoing contacts during the academic year. Special programs for gifted racial/ethnic minority students from poor backgrounds have been instituted at several colleges and universities. At the University of Iowa (Connie Belin and Jacqueline Blank International Center for Gifted Education and Talent Development), programs have been initiated for preparing sensitive and competent teachers of gifted minority students, as well as for encouraging gifted students in fields such as science, math, and engineering. Affirmative action, although a subject of ongoing controversy, also has attempted to create increased access to educational opportunity for persons of color. Although standardized testing in schools has been criticized, it also has identified talented students from poor majority and minority families that may have been overlooked or discouraged from pursuing college.

Examining education as a potential source of obstacles or opportunities provides another context in which to examine the overlap of race/ethnicity and SES. That is, the obstacles are often experienced by the poor racial/ethnic minorities, whereas the opportunities, notwithstanding some of the above-described initiatives, are enjoyed primarily by middle- and upper-class White students. Comparatively speaking, less has been written about minority students from upper-class backgrounds or majority students suffering from poverty. It could be assumed that class would determine student perceptions of education: Low SES students would experience obstacles, and high SES students would experience opportunities. But such assumptions neglect the historical effects of racism that may limit educational opportunities for high SES minority students (see Kershaw, 1992).

ADDITIONAL COMPLEXITIES IN THE IMPACT OF RACE/ETHNICITY AND SES

The picture that we have painted thus far from a number of different perspectives is one of White privilege and economic disadvantage for most persons of color. Although this sadly may be true, we would argue that there are exceptions to those characterizations. Furthermore, even though that original picture is often accurate, it is also frequently very complex.

Shared Experiences and Between- and Within-Group Differences

We acknowledge that we have often spoken in generalizations in this chapter because many racial/ethnic minorities, for example, share similar experiences. African Americans, Hispanics, and Native Americans all tend to make less money than Caucasians and Asian Americans, just as these groups have higher dropout and lower college completion rates. The unfortunate reality is that members of all racial/ethnic minority groups share an increased risk of oppression and discrimination that can negatively affect educational and occupational experiences. That said, it is also obvious that homogeneity does not exist either within or between these groups and that the experience of the interaction between race/ethnicity and SES on vocational behavior will be different for members of each ethnic minority and majority group. Allow us to provide two brief and incomplete examples. Native Americans probably face more poverty and lower education rates than other minority groups, which adds to the difficulty of their vocational journey. Furthermore, within this group, income level and employability are dramatically affected by choice of residence: urban America versus the reservation (Johnson, Swartz, & Martin, 1995). The vocational experiences of African Americans, on the other hand, may be influenced by the fact that they "share a sociocultural history and experience based upon negative attributions of race" (Cheatham, 1990, p. 337). African Americans may have distinct within-group experiences based on racial identity.

Asian Americans: "The Model Minority"

Asian Americans also have found themselves in a unique position, being labeled as the "model minority." Here, then, we are to find an exception to the rule of White privilege versus racial/ethnic minority economic disadvantage. As reported earlier, Asian Americans/Pacific Islanders have higher average income levels and higher college graduation rates than Caucasians in this country. There is evidence that some Asian Americans may ascribe to the "model minority" image as well. Wong, Lai, Nagasawa, and Lin (1998) found that one sample of Asian American college students perceived themselves as performing better academically, being more motivated in college, and having a greater probability of career success than both other racial/ethnic minorities and Caucasians. These perceptions were shared by the African American, Hispanic, Native American, and White participants, who also viewed members of other racial/ethnic minority groups as performing relatively worse than Caucasians on the described dimensions. Unfortunately, this picture of success for Asian Americans is not as straightforward as it may appear. In a different study of career stereotypes, Leong and Hayes (1990) discovered that Caucasian college students rated Asian Americans as less qualified for an insurance sales position than White students with an identical profile, but they saw Asian Americans as more qualified in engineering, computer science, and math (cited in Leong & Brown, 1995). Thus, success may be expected and accepted only in certain occupations. In addition, it should be noted that the group of Asian American students from the Wong et al. (1998) study may have perceived themselves as more academically prepared, but their academic preparation and performance were actually not significantly different from the White comparison group. Given their self-perceptions and the expectations of others, however, these students may feel a great deal of pressure to excel above their peers from other racial/ethnic groups, contributing to longer hours of study and restricting occupational goals to high-prestige careers. Are these the hidden costs of being the model minority?

It is also important to note in a discussion of the successes of Asian Americans that the group, like any other, is not homogeneous—and success is not the whole picture. This group also consists of recent immigrants with poor English skills and Southeast Asian/Pacific Islanders who tend to be poorer and less educated and who may not receive the assistance they need because of the halo of Asian American achievement (Wong et al., 1998). Furthermore, although Asian Americans' average income level may be higher than Caucasians', so are their poverty rates. When income is adjusted to take into account factors such as working hours, number of employed persons in a household, education, and ethnic status, the individual earnings of Asian Americans may be lower than Caucasians who are making an equal investment in the labor market (Hurh & Kim, 1989, cited in Wong et al., 1998). Asian Americans, therefore, may be reaping some economic rewards for their educational and occupational achievement, but their gains in SES, given their input into the labor market, do not appear to be equivalent to what a White person might expect. Thus, the complexity of the interaction between SES and race/ethnicity increases.

Caucasians, Social Class, and Vocational Behavior

Another topic worthy of discussion is how racial/ethnic background and social class variables interact for Caucasians. This is a group that has enjoyed a great deal of economic privilege. They have been used as the yardstick by which the progress of minorities in this country is measured, and they generally have had access to better schools and more career options, partly because of their typically higher SES. Again, however, this is not a complete picture. Some of the labor market changes discussed earlier in this chapter, such as decreases in manufacturing jobs, actually may have affected Caucasians more than members of racial/ethnic minority groups because more Whites held the relatively high-paying jobs that were lost (see Fine & Weis, 1998). In addition, not all Caucasians come from economically privileged backgrounds, and those living in poverty may face educational obstacles and perceive a very limited range of occupational choices. That said, the experience of poverty is probably different for Caucasians than it is for members of racial/ethnic minority groups. In his review of such statistics, Wilson (1988) indicated that a large majority of impoverished Whites in America's five major urban centers lived in nonpoverty areas, a circumstance that held true only for a minority of African Americans and Hispanics. Thus, poor Caucasians may have access to better schools and more role models, informal job networks, and jobs than many of their minority counterparts. Fine and Weis (1998), in their examination of a group of poor and working-class individuals, found that Caucasians were more likely to have an apartment or house to live in as a result of family financial contributions. These contributions were made possible because family members had been able to save money or own property during the days of well-paying manufacturing jobs, which was not the case for most minority workers. The authors make the point that although people of all racial/ethnic backgrounds may experience declines in SES, the "racial sedimentation of the U.S. class structure cannot be ignored" (Fine & Weis, 1998, p. 6). Social class interacts differently with vocational behavior for Caucasians than it does for racial/ethnic minorities.

IMPLICATIONS FOR PSYCHOLOGICAL THEORY, RESEARCH, PRACTICE, AND TRAINING

Theory

Vocational theories have been widely criticized for their lack of relevance to racial/ethnic minorities and persons from lower SES groups (e.g., Arbona, 1996; Leong & Brown, 1995; Warnath, 1975). The generalizability of these theories has been questioned on many grounds: the lack of supporting research using diverse participants, the scant attention paid to environmental and cultural variables in most approaches, and the assumptions such as free vocational choice, the centrality of work, and a continuous career that may not be realities for many people (Fitzgerald & Betz, 1994). External validity has thus become a major scientific challenge for vocational psychology.

Many proposals for improving the use and generalizability of vocational theories have been advanced. One obvious suggestion has been to increase the amount and quality of research investigating the applicability of existing theoretical approaches to traditionally ignored populations. Beyond this recommendation, in thinking about the complex interrelationships between race/ethnicity and SES that we have reviewed in this chapter, it is evident to us that we are unlikely to develop a theory that will be all things to all people, and attempting to do so is probably a futile task. We may do well to think more about the work of Cheatham (1990), who has discussed how career development might be viewed from an Africentric perspective and has argued for a culture-specific, rather than universal, approach to these issues.

That said, we do not feel that recognizing realistic limitations means completely ceasing attempts to make vocational theories more broadly relevant. Fitzgerald and Betz (1994), for example, have argued convincingly for increasing applicability by considering more carefully "the roles of structural and cultural factors" (p. 113) in theories. These authors have also indicated, however, that work may not be "psychologically central to the lives of all individuals" and that "many jobs are unable to provide for needs that are more complex than those for subsistence and the structuring of time" (p. 104). It might follow, then, that vocational theories will not apply well to such persons, who one might surmise would be more likely to be low SES women and racial/ethnic minorities. Making that assertion, however, may be a reflection of White, middle-class values, and improving our theories may require reexamining those assumptions.

Work is probably not a means of self-fulfillment even for some individuals in high-status and high-paying careers; it is a means of maintaining that status. In addition, although work may be most important to vast numbers of persons as a way of putting food on the table and living from day to day, that does not mean that work is not psychologically meaningful to them. Kupers (1996) has argued that when considering whether work is fulfilling or distasteful, "the status of the job is not a sufficient explanation" (p. 29). Rather, he discusses such things as degree of employee control in the work environment (deciding work pace, how tasks will be completed, etc.) as being related to "satisfaction and positive self-regard" (p. 29). Many blue-collar workers may indeed have a fair amount of autonomy concerning work rate, who will work together on what tasks, and how to approach the completion of a job.

The meaning of work, even for those who work primarily for subsistence, also can be seen when one considers the ramifications of not having a job. We know that unemployment, particularly when it is chronic in nature, may be associated with a number of psychological and physical health problems, including decreased self-esteem and social support and increased alcohol consumption (Goldsmith, Veum, & Darity, 1997; Janlert, 1997; Roberts, Pearson, Madeley, Hanford, & Magowan, 1997). Fine and Weis (1998) have suggested that under- and unemployment may relate to a loss of both identity and dominance in the workplace and subsequent attempts to "reassert power in the home/family sphere" (p. 134). Such attempts could contribute to socially deviant behavior such as domestic violence.

Even for those who are employed but in "low-level" positions, work may have meaning that current theories do not acknowledge. Kimbrough and

Salomone (1993) talk about the high social status accorded to persons in African American communities who are employed on a consistent basis even if in "menial" positions. For those individuals, work means not only food on the table but also family and community respect. For many African Americans, a "job is a means to retain self-respect, a pathway to accumulate the goods and services that others take for granted, and a route for a better life for their children" (Kimbrough & Salomone, 1993, p. 273). Thus, we would argue that even work that professionals may see as menial, unable to offer advancement, and conducted only to sustain oneself or one's family may take on psychological importance and be critical to one's self-concept and physical and psychological health, perhaps just in different ways than our current conception of career development recognizes. Merton (1968) has asserted that the majority culture has a universal definition of success: to have a career that brings prestige and economic rewards (cited in McClelland, 1990). What we may need to realize is that this definition of success, just like majority culture definitions of what is meaningful and what constitutes a career, is not universal. Thus, vocational theories could still apply to a broad range of individuals, but only with modifications.

One potential method of theory modification may be to expand our focus of study. Richardson (1993) has suggested a move to the study of work rather than careers. This is one viable option. Perhaps it is just a semantic difference, but we would assert that another option may be to redefine some of the constructs commonly used in vocational theory so that they apply to more than a small segment of the population. We might, therefore, continue to study career development, as long as we expand our definition of that term. By focusing our empirical work on the experiences of middle-class professionals, we have reinforced the notion of career as continuous professional work that allows for occupational advancement. We know that occupations that come to be dominated by female employees often lose prestige when that happens (Ferraro, 1984). Some work may be poorly paid and low prestige simply because it is usually completed by women. By extension, we wonder if what is considered to be a "career" has come to be defined by the people who hold such positions. That is, is work on an assembly line considered a career? If not, is it because that work is incapable of being psychologically meaningful or allowing for advancement, or is it because those jobs have tended to be occupied by, for example, less educated working-class individuals? Why cannot *career* also be used to describe the work of a homemaker or the series of low-paying manual labor jobs held by a poorly educated and intermittently unemployed worker? Take employees who move from "menial" job to job over time. Might this not be an attempt to find a more satisfactory occupational "fit," be it in terms of money (values/needs), what tasks they most enjoy or can most easily tolerate (interests), or what they do best (abilities/skills)? This may not be career development or choice as we usually conceptualize it, but it may be career development as it actually exists, and our theories and practices may even provide some useful guidance to the process. With our current definition of *career*, however, vocational psychology marginalizes the experiences of groups of individuals who are already at the margins of society by virtue, many times, of their SES and race/ethnicity. Similar expansions of terms such as *success* and *satisfaction* might also be useful, particularly given our earlier discussion of the different meanings that work can take on for groups and individuals. Finally, we may wish to redefine the concept of *choice*. As early as 1969, Osipow argued that "we have been concerned with vocational preference and selection when most of mankind [humankind] appears to have little choice about his [or her] work" (p. 18). Many people may not have the range of options often assumed within existing theories, but that does not mean that they have lives devoid of choice. Even the selection between two fast-food chain positions involves choice and the possibility that theory could, in some small way, inform it.

Another way of addressing some of the theoretical concerns of vocational psychology may be to use a different measure of success for the theories themselves. When researchers discuss the multicultural applications of current theories, they tend to express concern about things such as construct validity, the ability of theoretical predictions to hold across groups, and the cross-cultural validity of vocational assessment instruments. These are all extremely valuable topics that should continue to be explored. That said, it also seems as though we have largely been concerned with the cross-cultural *equivalence* of our theories. We would assert that another factor worthy of consideration is the between- and within-group *relevance* or *utility* of theories. It is unlikely that any theory will be able to explain or predict adequately the vocational experiences of all groups and all members within those groups. That does not have to mean, however, that we discard these theoretical approaches as useless. For example, we may find that for some racial/ethnic minorities and for people from low SES backgrounds, Holland (1997) type does not predict occupational choice very effectively because these individuals face limited choices as a result of internal and external barriers that mediate the relationship between personality and occupational type. That does not mean, however, that the Holland typology has no relevance or potential usefulness for such persons. Even an individual faced with a choice between two low-skill positions may benefit from a discussion of

which job might be more congruent with his or her interests, all other things being equal. Perhaps instead of focusing on establishing universally applicable
theories, we need to determine under what circumstances elements of current
theories can still be useful to a wide range of individuals.

RESEARCH

In evaluating existing research on social class and multicultural issues in vocational psychology, we already have commented on some of the strengths and
weaknesses of the knowledge base. We need more multicultural research in vocational psychology, but more is not enough. We also need larger sample sizes;
working-class, unemployed, and less educated participants; and participants
who vary in terms of age, sex, and SES. More studies that address the generalizability of vocational theories, instruments, and interventions would also be
beneficial. To provide one example, some recent researchers (e.g., Day &
Rounds, 1998; Ryan, Tracey, & Rounds, 1996) have investigated the cross-
cultural applicability of Holland's (1997) interest structure. The studies have
been an attempt to provide evidence for the construct validity of perhaps the
most widely used vocational theory in existence. They have made a significant
contribution to the literature and, in fact, include an investigation (Ryan et al.,
1996) that examined SES and the combined factors of race/ethnicity and SES.
Nevertheless, many questions, even within this small niche of vocational theory, remain unanswered. That is, knowing that interest structure is similar
across groups does not enable us to understand whether interests are a good predictor of eventual career choice for members of different groups. Finding structural equivalencies also does not tell us if giving an interest inventory or applying Holland's theory to career counseling with ethnic minorities or members of
different SES groups will prove as helpful as it has been for middle-class White
persons.

     Another improvement that could be made to the vocational psychology re-
search literature is additional use of qualitative methodology. Many questions
about SES, race/ethnicity, and vocational behavior raised in this chapter cannot
be addressed by quantitative methods alone. Following from our discussion of
theory, it may be that redefining our theoretical terminology can be partially
achieved by conducting interviews with individuals who differ on demographic
variables. What is a career to an African American living in urban poverty?
What defines success and satisfaction on the job for that same individual? Simi-

larly, how do persons from different groups explain their vocational problems, and where would they look for solutions? These are just some of the questions that might be addressed using qualitative methods.

Finally, we would assert that multicultural research in vocational psychology must examine issues beyond race/ethnicity. As is evidenced by the complex relationships between SES and ethnicity reviewed in this chapter, these variables cannot be studied in isolation. Researchers would benefit from examining, to name a few, SES, gender, education, and racial identity or acculturation in their investigations. Additional within-group research would also provide a better understanding of the factors that contribute to the vocational behavior differences between racial/ethnic groups. There is no question that following these recommendations would make research more difficult and costly. However, the price that we pay for convenience is a body of literature with unknown relevance to much of the workforce.

PRACTICE

The practice of vocational psychology faces two challenges: acknowledging the role that it has played thus far in the lives of individuals from different racial/ethnic and SES backgrounds and deciding if and how to redefine and expand that role.

Career counseling or vocational guidance is likely a very different experience for Caucasians and individuals from high SES groups than it is for the economically disadvantaged or persons of color. A youth of color who comes from a relatively wealthy background and attends a well-staffed private school in the suburbs may be encouraged to explore a much wider range of career options than an ethnic minority youngster of equal ability who comes from a poor family and attends a large public school in the inner city. Realistically, the first adolescent may very well have a wider range of possible choices given that he or she does not have to cope with some of the internal and external career development barriers faced by the inner-city youth. Our point, however, is that even as counseling has provided encouragement and assistance to individuals from all walks of life, it has also in some ways played the role of gatekeeper and guardian of the vocational status quo (Hawks & Muha, 1991). Although usually considered to be unintentional, counseling practice is not immune to the effects of stereotyping and discrimination (Kimbrough & Salomone, 1993). Counselors, may, for example, decrease their expectations for individuals perceived to be from "disadvantaged" backgrounds and communicate those lowered standards to them (Okocha, 1994). Guidance counselors are often involved in tracking procedures that tend to guide low SES racial/ethnic minorities into vocational tracks. Furthermore, career counseling has continued to apply vocational theories, practices, and instruments of unknown cross-cultural validity or utility to groups on and for which they were not developed.

Despite the fact that some vocational services may have served to perpetuate the difficulties of persons of color and individuals from low SES groups, "career counseling is a popular and preferred source of professional help for many racial-ethnic minorities" (Lattimore & Borgen, 1999, p. 185). Thus, just as we need to acknowledge the role that vocational psychology has played in maintaining the status quo, we need to consider steps we could take to modify that role. One of the ways that we might approach doing so flows from our discussion of theory. We have asserted that vocational psychology theories and constructs do not have universal meaning. Similarly, we would like to argue that explanations for career development concerns are not universal. For example, Fine and Weis (1998) have gathered some data that indicate that working-class African Americans may blame their vocational difficulties on things such as the economy, racism, and even police harassment, whereas their Caucasian counterparts frequently view African Americans and an unfair quota system as a source of vocational problems. Where individuals locate the cause of their problems may influence where (and if) they look for solutions. Part of our job as professionals may be to help clients reframe their concerns or to tailor interventions to help address the sources of trouble that they have identified. Given that individuals locate many of their problems in external sources, this may mean assisting clients in navigating bureaucracy (e.g., helping to complete forms, connecting clients with jobs programs) and taking an advocacy role that is not always typical of counseling psychologists.

There are additional ways in which career counseling may redefine itself and its role. Arbona (1996) has suggested that traditional approaches to career counseling are not sufficient. It is not enough for professionals to be armed with assessment instruments and knowledge of vocational theory. They also must be aware of labor market trends and what training and skills are necessary for entry into specific occupations so they can assist their clients in assessing the reality of their vocational situations and the obstacles that they will face. In writing this chapter, we have become painfully aware that to understand the role of racial/ethnic background and SES in career development, one must be not only a psychologist but also a political advocate, sociologist, economist, and labor market analyst. This is not true just for career counselors. The need for cross-discipline work related to other vocational topics has already been acknowledged. For example, professionals who recognized the interaction between psychology issues and occupational health generated the idea for a new specialty (occupational health psychology) that would involve academic training in psychology, public health, medicine, nursing, and business (Schneider, Camara, Tetrick, & Stenberg, 1999). Counseling psychologists may also need to expand their notion of what knowledge and training are necessary to engage in the effective practice of career counseling.

Vocational counseling could also be improved by employing more culturally sensitive and specific interventions (Hawks & Muha, 1991; Okocha, 1994). Professionals might, for example, move the site of intervention, as well as of research and professional training, from the counseling office to the community. They could then involve businesspeople or community leaders who could act as role models in service provision. Doing so could improve services and might also help counselors achieve a better understanding of the everyday economic and other barriers many of their clients face in their career development. One example of the type of intervention we are envisioning is provided by Lingg (1995), who describes the Kmart Employment for Youth Workforce 2000 program. This initiative targeted one specific group: adolescent African Americans in the inner cities. It also provided, as one way of ameliorating common vocational barriers for this group, job skills training and free transportation to work.

Career counseling might also benefit from professionals reconsidering what constitutes an appropriate intervention. Warnath (1975) has indicated that for many laborers, work will never be fulfilling but may, at best, be made tolerable. This may be true, although we would argue that the judgment that certain kinds of work can only be rendered bearable may partially reflect the global application of White, middle-class definitions of job satisfaction and meaning. Our major point, however, is that to the extent that Warnath is correct, this predicament defines a new role for career counseling. Interventions need not solely be devoted to helping individuals reach some maximum level of self-fulfillment. Vocational psychology theory and practice could also have a legitimate place in helping clients to manage more effectively the work circumstances in which they find themselves.

A final example of redefining career counseling, particularly for traditionally neglected groups, can be seen in the school-to-work movement. In response to the past neglect of work-bound youth, formal legislation has led schools and guidance programs to develop partnerships with businesses to assist in improving the transition from school to work (School-to-Work Opportunities Act of 1994 [STWOA]). The goals of such programs have been to increase youth opportunities to gain work-relevant skills and to assist businesses in the development of a more effective workforce (see Worthington & Juntunen, 1997). The hope has been that dropout rates might decrease by making education seem more relevant and that career development barriers, such as lack of job skills, might be addressed within the education system. Whether such programs can address the problem of dropouts and ameliorate the negative effects of tracking awaits empirical scrutiny.

Having suggested ways that career counselors might alter their practices, we feel that we should conclude our recommendations by addressing their practicality and congruence with the identity of counseling psychology. Our profession traditionally has been associated with vocational psychology, and it also has long been connected to work in college counseling centers and with relatively healthy and privileged populations. Our professional identity and the location of our work have likely contributed to the fact that much vocational research has been conducted with college students and has been concerned with maximizing potential. Thus, some of our practice recommendations may seem more reasonable (increasing knowledge of specific cultural groups) than others (involvement in the school-to-work movement) to an audience of traditional counseling psychologists. On the other hand, we may need to expand traditional definitions to become more relevant to the workplace. We also recognize that some of our suggestions may be more applicable to vocational rehabilitation workers, social workers, and school guidance counselors. We make the recommendations, nonetheless, because we believe that individual counseling psychologists could legitimately follow through on any of them. We also feel that an important part of the process of improving work in vocational psychology is becoming aware of the possible directions to be taken and making thoughtful choices from among those possibilities.

Training

If the theory, research, and practice of vocational psychology are to change to address more effectively issues of race/ethnicity and SES, the training of future professionals also will need to change. We would argue that goals for *multicultural training* (we use this term to encompass both race/ethnicity and SES) need to move from general recommendations to an appreciation of the individualized context of a specific training program. In terms of training for career counseling, we need to adopt the Darwinian concept of *niche*. That is, we need to understand that the "location" (or niche) of training programs exerts demands that give shape to unique opportunities for gaining cultural competence in career counseling. One size does not fit all!

What do we mean? First, we do not imply that training programs can avoid their multicultural training responsibilities by claiming that their location reduces the relevance of multiculturalism. We often hear these laments: "We can't hire minority faculty to teach multicultural courses; we don't have any students of color; we are in a rural state populated primarily by Whites." We understand these statements because we are located in a rural state where more than 90% of the population is White. We, too, have struggled to diversify our student body, faculty, and staff. Yet, from our experience, where there is a commitment, there is a way (e.g., 35% of the students in the counseling psychology program are students of color; 25% of the counseling center staff are persons of color). Our assertion of "one size does not fit all" is not an excuse to avoid the multicultural commitments expected of all training programs: diversifying the composition of students, faculty, and staff; infusing multiculturalism throughout the curriculum, including courses, research, and practice; and creating a culturally sensitive physical environment. These commitments have been covered elsewhere (e.g., Pope-Davis & Coleman, 1997; Ridley, Mendoza, & Kanitz, 1994; Stone, 1997; Swanson, 1993) and do not need to be repeated. It is hoped that these training commitments have moved from external recommendations and mandates to an internalized soul-felt mantra: "Excellence and diversity: You cannot have one without the other."

How does the concept of a niche relate to providing career counseling training that addresses issues related to race/ethnicity and class? We believe that the advocacy of one approach for all counseling psychology programs is unrealistic. For example, recommendations about linking counseling psychology to the school-to-work movement may be more relevant to some training programs than others. Programs housed in Departments of Psychology would likely have a harder time becoming involved in such interventions than programs located in Colleges of Education. Difficulties would also ensue for the many programs that, for instance, focus on health psychology and offer few opportunities for course work, research, or practice in career counseling, yet the opportunity for fusing health and career programs is available in occupational health initiatives. Several programs are located in regions that lack large businesses or racial/ethnic populations. Does this mean that counseling psychologists have little to offer at-risk, work-bound youth? This is an empirical question, but, realistically, we believe the following recommendations make sense.

All training programs, as indicated earlier, should meet their multicultural commitments in terms of diversifying human resources and curriculum. As for training career counselors, we believe that all counseling psychology programs can offer vocational theory classes that provide opportunities for students to learn about the experiences of clients from different racial/ethnic and social class backgrounds through the use of vocational case studies (see Fine & Weis, 1998). Programs could also broaden the conceptualization of practicum to provide rich career-based experiences: work in schools with adolescents in school-to-work programs, Upward Bound, or gifted programs; work in medical or rehabilitation settings with persons with disabilities and occupational concerns; and work conducting job programs in social agencies that serve persons from lower social classes.

The niche philosophy is apparent in these training recommendations. Programs cannot provide all things, and they need to create their own particular specializations. We assume that most counseling psychology programs will continue in the traditional niche where education is viewed as a means of social mobility, and vocational counseling is provided to racial/ethnic minorities to enhance their chances of higher education. We hope, however, that programs will also address the exceptions to this traditional model in some systematic way. In addition, we are hopeful that some programs may find a niche that relates to some of the issues discussed in this chapter. For example, a few programs, strategically located and identified with K-12 education, have a unique opportunity for creative collaboration in the school-to-work movement. Others may develop specializations such as minority health care, public policy and advocacy, and consultation. Ideally, we need to move our focus from multicultural courses, curriculum, and practice to the establishment of niches that actually implement programs' multicultural commitments within the vocational arena.

CONCLUDING THOUGHTS

Although simplistic, an ethnicity (2) by class (2) design may be a useful framework for presenting some of our final thoughts. Race or ethnicity can be partitioned crudely into Caucasian and racial/ethnic minority, and then it can be crossed with high and low socioeconomic statuses to result in four categories: Caucasian, high SES; Caucasian, low SES; racial/ethnic minority, high SES; and racial/ethnic minority, low SES. Using these four categories, we have found that most of the traditional vocational literature is found in one cell of privilege: Caucasian, high SES. More recent work has expanded into the cell of oppression: racial/ethnic minority, low SES. In reviewing the complex interplay of race/ethnicity and SES in this chapter, however, we have learned that a shared focus on privilege and oppression is not enough. Poor Whites and wealthy racial/ethnic minorities also face career development issues that are unique to their particular situations. What happens to young African American students raised in poverty who become suburban professionals? Will family and friends understand their new life experiences? How will they give back to the community from which they came? These are relevant empirical and practice questions that call for the development of mini-theories based on a context-driven approach that highlights structural factors such as race and economics. From such mini-theories may come ways to understand context-specific career development (theory), as well as ways to evaluate (research), intervene (practice), and evaluate professionals (train).

Counseling psychology has long been associated with vocational psychology. The profession has contributed a great deal to its theory, research, and practice. We have asserted that to improve our contributions to the field, we will need to make fundamental changes in theories, research questions and designs, interventions, and training programs. Which of these and other potential changes are to be made, as well as how they are to be implemented, are issues best left open to debate. The questions we pose to readers, then, are these: What is the place of vocational psychology in the 21st century, and what role will counseling psychology play in defining that location?

References

Arbona, C. (1989). Hispanic employment and the Holland typology of work. *Career Development Quarterly, 37,* 257-268.

Arbona, C. (1990). Career counseling research and Hispanics: A review of the literature. *The Counseling Psychologist, 18,* 300-323.

Arbona, C. (1996). Career theory and practice in a multicultural context. In M. L. Savickas & W. B. Walsh (Eds.), *Handbook of career counseling theory and practice* (pp. 45-54). Palo Alto, CA: Davies-Black.

Arbona, C., & Novy, D. M. (1991). Career aspirations and expectations of Black, Mexican American, and White students. *Career Development Quarterly, 39,* 231-239.

Archey, W. T. (1998, April 23). *Testimony.* U.S. House of Representatives Committee on Education and the Workforce: Subcommittee on Oversight and Investigations. The American Worker at a Crossroads Project. Retrieved April 1, 1999 from the World Wide Web: www.house.gov/eeo/hearings/105th/oi/awp42398/archey.htm.

Atkinson, D. R., Morten, G., & Sue, D. W. (1993). *Counseling American minorities: A cross-cultural perspective* (4th ed.). Dubuque, IA: Brown & Benchmark.

Brown, D., Minor, C. W., & Jepsen, D. A. (1991). The opinions of minorities about preparing for work: Report of the second NCDA national survey. *Career Development Quarterly, 40,* 5-19.

Burns, R. B., & Mason, D. A. (1998). Class formation and composition in elementary schools. *American Educational Research Journal, 35,* 739-772.

Cheatham, H. E. (1990). Africentricity and career development of African Americans. *Career Development Quarterly, 38,* 334-346.

Constantine, M. G., Erickson, C. D., Banks, R. W., & Timberlake, T. L. (1998). Challenges to the career development of urban racial and ethnic minority youth: Implications for vocational intervention. *Journal of Multicultural Counseling and Development, 26,* 83-95.

Current state of manufacturing in the United States: Hearing before the Subcommittee on Manufacturing and Competitiveness of the Committee on Commerce, Science, and Transportation, United States Senate, 105th Cong., 1st Sess. (1997).

D'Andrea, M. (1995). Addressing the developmental needs of urban, African-American youth: A preventive intervention. *Journal of Multicultural Counseling and Development, 23,* 57-64.

Day, S. X., & Rounds, J. (1998). Universality of vocational interest structure among racial and ethnic minorities. *American Psychologist, 53,* 728-736.

Dewey, J. (1916). *Democracy and education.* New York: Macmillan.

Ferraro, G. A. (1984). Bridging the wage gap. *American Psychologist, 39,* 1166-1170.

Fine, M., & Weis, L. (1998). *The unknown city.* Boston: Beacon.

Fitzgerald, L. F., & Betz, N. E. (1994). Career development in cultural context. In M. L. Savickas & R. W. Lent (Eds.), *Convergence in career development theories* (pp. 103-117). Palo Alto, CA: CPP Books.

Goldsmith, A. H., Veum, J. R., & Darity, W. (1997). Unemployment, joblessness, psychological well-being and self-esteem: Theory and evidence. *Journal of Socio-Economics, 26,* 133-158.

Goodwin, L. (1972). How suburban families view the work orientations of the welfare poor: Problems in social stratification and social policy. *Social Problems, 19,* 337-348.

Goodwin, L. (1973). Middle-class misperceptions of the high life aspirations and strong work ethic held by the welfare poor. *American Journal of Orthopsychiatry, 43,* 554-564.

Gottfredson, L. S. (1981). Circumscription and compromise: A developmental theory of occupational aspirations. *Journal of Counseling Psychology, 28,* 545-579.

Gottfredson, L. S. (1996). Gottfredson's theory of circumscription and compromise. In D. Brown, L. Brooks, & Associates (Eds.), *Career choice and development* (3rd ed., pp. 179-232). San Francisco: Jossey-Bass.

Hattiangadi, A. U., & Shaffer, T. R. (1998, November 12). Future workforce will reflect increased diversity [Press release]. Retrieved April 1, 1999 from the World Wide Web: www.epfnet.org/pr981112.htm.

Hawks, B. K., & Muha, D. (1991). Facilitating the career development of minorities: Doing it differently this time. *Career Development Quarterly, 39,* 251-259.

Helms, J. E., & Piper, R. E. (1994). Implications of racial identity theory for vocational psychology. *Journal of Vocational Behavior, 44,* 124-138.

Holland, J. L. (1997). *Making vocational choices: A theory of vocational personalities and work environments* (3rd ed.). Odessa, FL: Psychological Assessment Resources.

Hotchkiss, L., & Borow, H. (1996). Sociological perspective on work and career development. In D. Brown, L. Brooks, & Associates (Eds.), *Career choice and development* (3rd ed., pp. 281-334). San Francisco: Jossey-Bass.

Hoyt, K. B. (1989). The career status of women and minority persons: A 20-year retrospective. *Career Development Quarterly, 37,* 202-212.

Hurh, W. M., & Kim, K. C. (1989). The "success" image of Asian Americans: Its validity, and its practical and theoretical implications. *Ethnic and Racial Studies, 12,* 514-561.

Janlert, U. (1997). Unemployment as a disease and diseases of the unemployed. *Scandinavian Journal of Work, Environment, and Health, 23*(Suppl. 3), 79-83.

Johnson, M. J., Swartz, J. L., & Martin, W. E. (1995). Applications of psychological theories for career development with Native Americans. In F. T. L. Leong (Ed.), *Career development and vocational behavior of racial and ethnic minorities* (pp. 103-133). Hillsdale, NJ: Lawrence Erlbaum.

Kantor, H. (1994). Managing the transition from school to work: The false promise of youth apprenticeship. *Teachers College Record, 95,* 442-461.

Kershaw, T. (1992). The effects of educational tracking on the social mobility of African-Americans. *Journal of Black Studies, 23,* 152-169.

Kimbrough, V. D., & Salomone, P. R. (1993). African Americans: Diverse people, diverse career needs. *Journal of Career Development, 19,* 265-279.

Kupers, T. A. (1996). Men at work and out of work. *Psychiatric Annals, 26,* 29-32.

Lattimore, R. R., & Borgen, F. H. (1999). Validity of the 1994 Strong Interest Inventory with racial and ethnic groups in the United States. *Journal of Counseling Psychology, 46,* 185-195.

Lent, R. W., Brown, S. D., & Hackett, G. (1996). Career development from a social cognitive perspective. In D. Brown, L. Brooks, & Associates (Eds.), *Career choice and development* (3rd ed., pp. 373-421). San Francisco: Jossey-Bass.

Leong, F. T. L., & Brown, M. T. (1995). Theoretical issues in cross-cultural career development: Cultural validity and cultural specificity. In W. B. Walsh & S. H. Osipow (Eds.), *Handbook of vocational psychology: Theory, research, and practice* (2nd ed., pp. 143-180). Hillsdale, NJ: Lawrence Erlbaum.

Leong, F. T. L., & Hayes, T. (1990). Occupational stereotyping of Asian Americans. *Career Development Quarterly, 39,* 143-154.

Leung, S. A. (1995). Career development and counseling: A multicultural perspective. In J. G. Ponterotto, J. M. Casas, L. A. Suzuki, & C. M. Alexander (Eds.), *Handbook of multicultural counseling* (pp. 549-566). Thousand Oaks, CA: Sage.

Lingg, M. (1995). Preemployment training for African American youth. *Journal of Career Development, 22,* 67-82.

Luzzo, D. A. (1992). Ethnic group and social class differences in college students' career development. *Career Development Quarterly, 41,* 161-173.

Manufacturing job losses and the future of manufacturing employment in the United States: Hearing before the Joint Economic Committee, Congress of the United States, 103rd Cong., 1st Sess. (1993).

McClelland, K. E. (1990). The social management of ambition. *The Sociological Quarterly, 31,* 225-251.

Merton, R. K. (1968). *Social theory and social structure.* New York: Free Press.

National Center for Education Statistics (NCES). (1996). Minorities in higher education. *The Condition of Education 1996.* Retrieved April 1, 1999 from the World Wide Web: www.nces.ed.gov/pubs97/97372.html.

National Center for Education Statistics (NCES). (1997). NCES fast facts. *Digest of Education Statistics 1997*, p. 111. Retrieved March 25, 1999 from the World Wide Web: nces.ed.gov/fastfacts/435a.asp?type=2#dropout.

National Center for Education Statistics (NCES). (1998a). Access to higher education. *The Condition of Education 1998*. Retrieved April 1, 1999 from the World Wide Web: nces.ed.gov/pubs98/conditions98/c9808a01.html.

National Center for Education Statistics (NCES). (1998b). Annual earnings of young adults, by educational attainment. *The Condition of Education 1998*. Retrieved April 1, 1999 from the World Wide Web: nces.ed.gov/pubs98/conditions98/c9832a01.html.

National Center for Education Statistics (NCES). (1998c). Transition from high school to work. *The Condition of Education 1998*. Retrieved from the World Wide Web: nces.ed.gov/pubs98/conditions98/c9830a01.html.

National Center for Education Statistics (NCES). (1998d). Welfare participation, by educational attainment. *The Condition of Education 1998*. Retrieved from the World Wide Web: nces.ed.gov/pubs98/conditions98/c9834a01.html.

Okocha, A. (1994). Preparing racial ethnic minorities for the work force 2000. *Journal of Multicultural Counseling and Development, 22*, 106-114.

Osipow, S. H. (1969). Some revised questions for vocational psychology. *The Counseling Psychologist, 1*, 17-19.

Parsons, F. (1909). *Choosing a vocation*. Boston: Houghton Mifflin.

Pettigrew, T. F. (1981). Race and class in the 1980s: An interactive view. *Daedalus, 110*, 233-255.

Pope-Davis, D. B., & Coleman, H. L. K. (1997). *Multicultural counseling competencies: Assessment, education and training, and supervision*. Thousand Oaks, CA: Sage.

Reich, R. B. (1991). *The work of nations*. New York: Knopf.

Richardson, M. S. (1993). Work in people's lives: A location for counseling psychologists. *Journal of Counseling Psychology, 40*, 425-433.

Ridley, C. R., Mendoza, D. W., & Kanitz, B. E. (1994). Multicultural training: Reexamination, operationalization, and integration. *The Counseling Psychologist, 22*, 227-289.

Roberts, H., Pearson, J. C. G., Madeley, R. J., Hanford, S., & Magowan, R. (1997). Unemployment and health: The quality of social support among residents in the Trent region of England. *Journal of Epidemiology and Community Health, 51*, 41-45.

Ryan, J. M., Tracey, T. J. G., & Rounds, J. (1996). Generalizability of Holland's structure of vocational interests across ethnicity, gender, and socioeconomic status. *Journal of Counseling Psychology, 43*, 330-337.

Schneider, D. L., Camara, W. J., Tetrick, L. E., & Stenberg, C. R. (1999). Training in occupational health psychology: Initial efforts and alternative models. *Professional Psychology: Research and Practice, 30*, 138-142.

Slaney, R. B., & Brown, M. T. (1983). Effects of race and socioeconomic status on career choice variables among men. *Journal of Vocational Behavior, 23*, 257-269.

Solorzano, D. G. (1992). An exploratory analysis of the effects of race, class, and gender on student and parent mobility aspirations. *Journal of Negro Education, 61*, 30-44.

Stone, G. L. (1997). Multiculturalism as a context for supervision: Perspectives, limitations, and implications. In D. B. Pope-Davis & H. L. K. Coleman (Eds.), *Multicultural counseling competencies: Assessment, education and training, and supervision* (pp. 263-289). Thousand Oaks, CA: Sage.

Swanson, J. L. (1993). Integrating a multicultural perspective into training for career counseling: Programmatic and individual intervention. *Career Development Quarterly, 42*, 41-49.

Tanner, D. (1965). *Schools for youth: Change and challenge in secondary education*. New York: Macmillan.

Ullmann, J. E. (1988). *The anatomy of industrial decline.* New York: Quorum.

U.S. Bureau of the Census. (1990a). Earnings by occupation and education 1990: Race: American Indian, Eskimo, or Aleut, not of Hispanic origin. *1990 Census of Population and Housing.* Retrieved March 27, 1999 from the World Wide Web: govinfo.kerr.orst.edu/cgi-bin/ss_dio=ANH&rjob=I49&search=&slist=&table=5.

U.S. Bureau of the Census. (1990b). Earnings by occupation and education 1990: Race: Asian or Pacific Islander, not of Hispanic origin. *1990 Census of Population and Housing.* Retrieved March 27, 1999 from the World Wide Web: govinfo.kerr.orst.edu/cgi- bin/ss_dio=PNH&rjob=K15&search=&slist=&table=5.

U.S. Bureau of the Census. (1990c). Earnings by occupation and education 1990: Race: Black, not of Hispanic origin. *1990 Census of Population and Housing.* Retrieved March 27, 1999 from the World Wide Web: govinfo.kerr.orst.edu/cgi- bin/ss_ho?rloc=X001&table=5&rjob=X01&radio=BNH.

U.S. Bureau of the Census. (1990d). Earnings by occupation and education 1990: Race: White, Hispanic origin. *1990 Census of Population and Housing.* Retrieved March 27, 1999 from the World Wide Web: govinfo.kerr.orst.edu/cgi- bin/ss_cho?rloc=X001&table=5&rjob=X01&radio=WH.

U.S. Bureau of the Census. (1990e). Earnings by occupation and education 1990: Race: White, not of Hispanic origin. *1990 Census of Population and Housing.* Retrieved March 27, 1999 from the World Wide Web: govinfo.kerr.orst.edu/cgi- bin/ss_dio=WNH&rjob=F18&search=&slist=&table=5.

U.S. Bureau of the Census (1997a, March). Selected characteristics of the population by Hispanic origin. *Current Population Survey.* Retrieved April 1, 1999 from the World Wide Web: www.bls.census.gov/cps/pub/1997/int_hisp.htm.

U.S. Bureau of the Census. (1997b, March). Selected characteristics of the population by race. *Current Population Survey.* Retrieved April 1, 1999 from the World Wide Web: www.bls.census.gov/cps/pub/1997/int_race.htm.

U.S. Bureau of the Census. (1999, February 24). Selected economic characteristics of people and families, by sex and race: March 1998. Retrieved March 28, 1999 from the World Wide Web: www.census.gov/population/socdemo/race/black/tabs98/tab02.txt.

Warnath, C. F. (1975). Vocational theories: Direction to nowhere. *Personnel and Guidance Journal, 53,* 422-428.

Wilson, W. J. (1988). The ghetto underclass and the social transformation of the inner city. *The Black Scholar, 19,* 10-17.

Wong, P., Lai, C. F., Nagasawa, R., & Lin, T. (1998). Asian Americans as a model minority: Self-perceptions and perceptions by other racial groups. *Sociological Perspectives, 41,* 95-118.

Worthington, R. L., & Juntunen, C. C. (1997). The vocational development of non-college-bound youth: Counseling psychology and the school-to-work transition. *The Counseling Psychologist, 25,* 323-363.

THE IMPACT OF PHENOTYPE ON GENDER AND CLASS FOR SOUTHWESTERN HISPANIC AMERICANS

Implications for Counselor Training

Luis A. Vázquez
Enedina García-Vázquez
New Mexico State University

It is a brisk, cold day in a small southwestern town. In a kindergarten class of 26 students sits a dark-complected Mexican American girl. She smiles often and is very friendly to all her classmates. Her name is María. Over time, María develops a very strong relationship with a little White girl named Christy. As the school year progresses, they become inseparable. Both love playing games together and sharing little stories about home. At times, you can see them holding hands as they walk each other to the bus stop, where they get on separate buses to go home. When María is at home, she often talks to her parents about her friend. Christy does the same at her house. Each of them often asks her parents if someday she can go over to her friend's house to play. Smiling, each parent assures the child that someday she can bring her friend over to play and that they would like to meet her friend. Springtime arrives and the flowers begin to bloom, the air is warm, and the children are in shorts and T-shirts at school. A very exciting event is about to occur. Christy's birthday will be next weekend. Christy and her parents begin to prepare invitations for the party. When Christy arrives at school, she begins to hand out her birthday invitations and goes running to María and hands her one. Both are very excited as they jump up and down and talk about what the birthday party will be like for everyone. Christy tells María that she cannot wait for María to see her bedroom and toys. She also tells María that her mother is really cool, and maybe they can talk her into having María spend the night. Christy invites five other girls, and throughout the week, all seven girls talk about the birthday party. The big day arrives, and María's parents have bought Christy a Barbie doll as a gift from María. María's mother dresses María in a beautiful blue dress with ruffles on the sleeves and a cute blue bow in her hair. During the car ride to Christy's house, you can see María holding the birthday gift with a big smile on her face. She looks so cute with her dark hair and dark skin, almost like a little doll herself. María and her mother arrive at Christy's house, and both walk up the sidewalk. When they reach the front door, María quickly runs up and rings the doorbell. Christy answers, and both are very happy to see each other. At that point, Christy's mother comes to the door to see who is there. Her eyes open widely, and she seems very surprised as she asks, "Who are you?" When Christy says, "Mom, it's María," her mother states, "There must be some mistake. I don't remember making Christy an invitation for you." María's mother's eyes drop as she tells María, "Come on, honey. Let's go." María tells Christy's mother, "Oh that's okay. Christy and I are best friends." Christy's mother responds by saying, "I know, but I only planned a party for five girls and Christy, but maybe you can come next time." She then pulls Christy behind the front door and closes it. By this time María is crying and yells, "I want to play with Christy!" Her mother holds her in her arms to comfort her. On the other side of the door, they hear Christy crying and yelling, "I want to play with María." Then they hear in a loud harsh voice, "Christy, we never have darkies over to the house. If you don't behave, there will be no birthday party." María's mother is outraged but at the same time realizes that she has to take care of María. It's a long, quiet ride home with María sobbing and curled up underneath her mother's right arm. At the same time, there are tears running down María's mother's cheeks, and she asks herself, "When will this ever stop?" From that day on, María and Christy are no longer friends.

No matter how often we have heard stories such as this one, it still provokes a heavy feeling inside of us. At times, a tear slips out and rolls down our cheeks.

The first racial marker that children recognize is skin color, and it is possibly the most observable phenotypic attribute (Alejandro-Wright, 1985; Holmes, 1995). According to Phinney (1996), skin color and facial features are the most notable racial characteristics. However, the notion of color is not as important as the interpretation given to skin color by children's family members (Ponterotto & Pedersen, 1993). Dennis (1981) notes that children adhere to the family's social norms relating to issues such as color. Research on White children's ethnic attitudes have found that more often than not, they have a strong preference for same-group members and negative group attitudes toward children of color (Aboud, 1987). Children of color often showed mixed results toward same-group preference and more positive attitudes toward White children. These findings suggest that both White and minority children are raised with images that fairer is better. The difference is that White children typically see themselves in these images, whereas many minority children do not.

PHENOTYPE AND AMERICAN SOCIETY

Skin color and physical characteristics, often defined as phenotype, play a major role in an individual's educational and economic status in the United States. Phenotyping is the process by which physical attributes such as skin color, hair texture, eye color, and other race-defining characteristics become the basis of the allocation of economic and psychological privileges to individuals relative to the degree those privileges are awarded to valued members of the dominant culture (Codina & Montalvo, 1994). Society's perceptions of dark skin color versus light skin color in individuals have been well documented as unfavorable in the former versus a position of privilege for the latter group (Hall, 1994). Skin color in and of itself has no true meaning until defined, often through racist and prejudiced views. Minority individuals who attain success in the dominant culture and appear to abandon the native culture are sometimes described with pejorative epithets such as "oreo," "apple," "coconut," and so on. These imply that such people are racially distinctive physically (are people of color on the outside) but have become culturally like the majority (on the inside, referring to values, beliefs, etc.).

The word *dark* has several meanings when reviewed through *Webster's II* (1995) dictionary. Some of the definitions of *dark* include the following: "of a shade tending toward black or brown," "causing gloom," "being without knowledge or enlightenment," and "evil or wicked" (p. 287). Such descriptions of *dark* when combined with the word *complexion* bring forth many connotations of bias in a society drenched with a vocabulary of discrimination and disenfranchisement of minority populations.

The issue of color has been well documented in the literature on Black populations ranging from Black identity models to economic, political, and educational opportunities (Hall, 1994). The same can be said about the Latinos as a cultural population, but there are few studies written about this population in relation to skin color. Our experiences at national conferences and private conversations with people of color confirm that this subject is often avoided in the literature and considered relevant only for the Black population.

Research on African Americans and skin color has shown that darker-skinned Blacks were more likely to be found in less prestigious occupations and lower-income categories and were three times more likely to be unemployed than lighter-skinned Blacks (Ransford, 1970). Clearly, skin color mediates the opportunities available to African Americans. The issue of skin color can be a divisive or uniting force when defined by the White population and accepted as the norm. The internalization of such perceptions creates great disparity within and between people of color. According to Vargas-Willis and Cervantes (1987), skin color prejudice has yet to be acknowledged as having an impact on Mexican Americans.

Esteva-Fabregat (1995) points out that the primary basis of racial classifications are anatomical features, primarily skin color, hair texture, eye color, and other facial features. As the Native Indian admixture heavily influences the mestizo phenotype, the mestizo (and therefore Mexican-descent Hispanics in the United States) will have dark skin and typically Indian facial features. Esteva-Fabregat (1995) estimates that 84.5% of the population of contempo-

rary Mexico is mestizo, with larger concentrations of Indians in the southern regions, and he lists Mexico as one of five countries in which the process of misce-
genation is nearly consummated.

Hall (1994) identified skin color as the "master status" that distinguishes
dark-skinned Hispanic Americans from the mainstream group by its potent effect on all aspects of an individual's life, including employment, income, and,
most important, self-concept. de Anda (1984) observed that "ethnic minorities
whose physical appearance is dissimilar are more likely to experience socialization as pressure exerted upon outsiders" (p. 106). Codina and Montalvo
(1994) combined phenotype, education, mental health, and family income.
They found that phenotypically darker Mexican American men from lower-
education and lower-income families experienced depression more often than
light-complected Mexican American men. Bobo and Hutchings (1996), in a
study examining racial group competition, found that the White population perceived Hispanics and Asians to be the most threatening to their economic
well-being. Such findings further validate the fears and biases affecting minority groups and their experiences in obtaining economic opportunities. These
fears among the White population manifest themselves in attitudes such as "re-
verse discrimination," character assassination, racism, and a projected perception of second-class citizenship for minority group members. Such a disparity
of privileges creates undue distress and a questioning of one's ethnic identity
between and within one's own group of support. Physical appearances, along
with skin color, set the stage for feelings of uncertainty, low self-worth, internalized racism, and how a person adapts to a culture different from one's own.
For Mexican Americans, the history of skin color in the Southwest is important
to consider, especially how such discriminatory practices developed toward
Mexican Americans.

THE HISTORY OF COLOR IN THE SOUTHWEST

The discrimination against the mestizo in the United States has roots in the history of the Spanish conquest in Mexico as well as in the subjugation and isolation of the Native Indian people in this country. In Mexico, the Spaniards over-
threw the Aztec empire and established a society in which the "pure" European
Spanish maintained power and status, although the process of racial mixing was
quite rapid. There were only 1,385 Spaniards in New Spain in 1545, almost all
of whom were male. The first households were composed of Spanish men and

Indian women (Esteva-Fabregat, 1995). The rapidity of the racial mixing is evident in these figures: In 1810, there were three times as many Indians as mestizos, but in 1900, there were twice as many mestizos as Indians. Today, there are nine times as many mestizos as Indians.

The Mexican-descent population in the southwestern United States is composed largely of descendants of immigrants who entered this country after the Mexican revolution in 1910. Some trace their ancestry to those Mexicans who became Americans when the territory in which they were living was annexed by the United States (Buriel, 1987). The history during the time of war between Mexico and the United States in the 1830s is very important to explore in relation to the issue of phenotype in the southwestern United States. To enforce boundary lines, the United States posted buffalo (Black) soldiers at the border, creating great animosity between the Mexican population and the buffalo soldiers. It was speculated that this was done because it was considered appropriate for a Black soldier to kill another dark-skinned individual but not a White person (Acuña, 1981).

This internalization of society's view of skin color historically has created a status differential within and between Hispanic Americans. This phenomenon is well documented in the history of New Mexico at the turn of the 20th century. Many light-complected New Mexicans called themselves Hispanos or Spanish Americans to distinguish them from the Mexican, *Mestizo,* for fear of being discriminated against by White Americans. The Spanish Americans claimed that they were descendants of the Spanish conquistadors, who were fair skinned. They believed that they were giving credibility to their light-complected status by denying their Mexican heritage in hopes of maintaining economic wealth and political power (Acuña, 1981). The unification of the light-complected Spanish American with the Anglo American provided the impetus for further discrimination against the dark-complected Mexican American. Often, intermarriages between Spanish Americans and Anglo Americans were carefully orchestrated to maintain the status quo.

Dysart (1976), in her historical account of Mexican women in the Southwest, documents White American men's descriptions of light-skinned Mexican American women as having a fair complexion and with blue eyes worthy of their hand in marriage. At the same time, they described the poorer dark-complected Mexican American women as *styled greasers* with fine figures that were kept for their amusement and sexual pleasure. In addition, many of the marriages that took place from 1837 to 1860 between White American men and light-complected Mexican American women were women from high-status wealthy families. It was speculated that at least one daughter of each rich Mexican American family from San Antonio, Texas, married an Anglo. Many times, these marriages were established for economic and political necessity because the Mexican American family would receive legal protection and freedom from being disloyal to other dark-complected Mexican Americans. However, such marriages did not stop the discrimination between White Americans and the rich Mexican Americans. "Only the women and children with Anglo surnames, light skins, and wealth had a reasonable chance to escape the stigma attached to their Mexican ancestry" (Dysart, 1976, p. 375). The poor dark-complected Mexican Americans had fewer options and for the most part remained in poverty.

Acculturation

The interaction of diverse cultures resulting in acceptance or lack of acceptance by the dominant culture is known as *acculturation* (Padilla, 1980). Acculturation is a dynamic, multifaceted process of examining cultural traits and retaining, modifying, or adopting traits of cultures in contact. This process occurs on both conscious and unconscious levels. It also can be viewed as a journey from one cultural system to another, which includes the internalization of values, language, and other cultural practices such as economics and politics of the second culture (Valencia, 1991).

LaFromboise, Coleman, and Gerton (1993) use the term *second culture acquisition* to describe an individual learning the dominant culture and the term *acculturation* to describe the outcome of what has been learned by that individual. The distinction by the various authors recognizes that even though an individual may learn many of the traits of the dominant culture he or she is encountering, he or she may never be accepted as a full member. According to Gomez and Fassinger (1994), a person must develop a behavioral episode schema that would allow him or her to learn about the dominant culture and also be able to manage the stress from this learning process. Behavioral episode schemas are strategies that an individual develops to deal with cultural diversity. These strategies are used to facilitate a positive relationship between an individual's culture of origin and the dominant culture. When there is an incongruence between a person's learned traits of the dominant culture and acceptance of these traits by the dominant culture, it results in acculturative stress (Padilla, 1980).

Phenotype and Acculturation

The acculturation literature presented by several researchers (Keefe & Padilla, 1987; Padilla, 1980; Valencia, 1991) addresses how variables such as language familiarity; usage and preference; ethnic identity and generational level; reading, writing, and cultural exposure; perceptions of discrimination; and ethnic interaction mitigate the process of acculturation among Mexican Americans. However, none of these researchers addresses the impact of phenotype, especially skin color, on the process of acculturation.

W. E. B. DuBois (1969), a sociologist, was perhaps the first to acknowledge the problems of differing shades of skin color. He called it double consciousness. Light skin was considered better, and a dark-skinned person could not offend a light-skinned person without repercussions. Having dark skin meant taking a passive role with people of light skin. A societal awareness of such issues can develop a dual perspective in an individual's interpersonal and personality style. Genuineness is sacrificed in place of survival. Researchers interested in this topic have speculated that phenotype directly affects gender socialization. According to Hall (1994), women with mestizo phenotype features or darker skin experience greater levels of discrimination and more difficulty acculturating due to the pervasive media ideal of "White beauty." He further described the bleaching syndrome, in which dark-complected women used creams to lighten their skin to physically acculturate into mainstream society. Dark-complected Mexican American women would often use these creams in hopes of becoming more like White women. Obviously, such behaviors had very little impact on physical characteristics but often resulted in self-depreciating beliefs and low self-esteem.

Findings by Maldonado (1972) suggest that Mexican American female (Latina) high school students with dark skin did not rate their physical appearance as highly positive as did those girls with light or medium skin color. This was reflected in significantly lower scores on a physical self subscale on a measure of self-concept. Also, most darker-skinned participants (male and female) showed significantly higher total conflict scores than did their lighter-skinned classmates. Maldonado interprets this as "indicating greater conflict and confusion in the self-concept of the individual with darker skin color" (p. 81).

Relethford, Stern, Gaskill, and Hazuda (1983) used a spectrophotometer to measure skin color in a study for diabetes. This investigation was also one of the first to empirically document the relationship between phenotype and the life chances of Mexican Americans. Using survey data of Mexican Americans and Anglo Americans residing in San Antonio, Texas, the authors noted that individuals with darker skin were found in the barrio sample, whereas those with lightest skin appeared in the suburban sample. As the medical team moved from the barrio to the suburbs, changes in skin color were noted. These results indicated a positive relationship between lighter complexions and higher social economic status neighborhoods.

Using data from a national survey of Chicanos, Arce, Murguia, and Frisbie (1987) also found a strong positive relationship between lighter skin and more European features (as rated by interviewers) and higher levels of both occupational prestige and education. An additional relevant finding is that those respondents with darker skin and more Indian appearance reported greater perceived discrimination than did the lighter-skinned respondents. On the other hand, Vargas-Willis and Cervantes (1987) found that light-complected high-class Mexican women enjoyed high status and position in their "home." However, when moving to the United States, these same women suffered a loss of identity and self-esteem. Both White and dark-complected Mexican Americans often questioned these fair-complected women about their cultural commitment.

The information presented indicates that phenotype directly affects individuals' acculturation process and economic life chances in the United States. These studies suggest that a darker, more Indian phenotype predisposes Mexican Americans to discriminatory practices by the dominant culture in areas such as education, economics, and class status. These discriminatory practices affect a person's occupational functioning and educational opportunities (Smart & Smart, 1995).

Skin color plays a major role in the positioning of status among the majority White culture, as well as in the Mexican American culture regardless of the traits acquired to succeed in the dominant culture. Such positioning due to skin color expands the process of acculturation from learning culturally competent traits to succeed to learning a competent behavioral episode schema to cope with the discriminatory practices from the culture of origin and the dominant culture due to phenotype.

According to Carter (1995), the issue of color continues to be used to construct the social order in the United States. Historically, the White population often has defined themselves as superior to those of a "darker" coloration. Therefore, status and achievement often have resulted due to White privilege but are described as earned fruits of effort (McIntosh, 1992). At the same time, status and achievement often have been described for Hispanics as "affirmative action" efforts rather than the ability and effort put forth by each individual to succeed.

IMPLICATIONS FOR COUNSELOR TRAINING

Although the issue of skin color is well documented with respect to African Americans, today, phenotypic characteristics are becoming equally salient features among Latino populations. As we begin the 21st century, it is critical to determine the factors that affect education and economic and political success among the minority population. With the highest increases in the Latino population, it becomes highly important to develop the best counseling and assessment practices for the group. In addition, as more recruitment efforts are conducted to increase the educational level among Latinos, the possibilities of seeing non-Whites in counseling are increased. The counselor, regardless of ethnicity, must be prepared to work effectively with a diverse clientele. Acknowledging the factors that influence our clients' lives will be the first step in providing an effective treatment and developing the best client-counselor relationships.

The physical manifestations of a counseling situation, in and of itself, represent a microcosm of White society. There is an implied power differential between the counselor and client, even though many beg to differ with this conceptualization. In addition, there is a vulnerability expected from the client for the "process" to be successful. The client is expected to be open, trusting, and honest. These are the ideals historically presented by the White culture when developing relationships with minority group members. Fascinating enough, these were also the same ideals presented to minority group members by their light- and some dark-complected colleagues throughout history. Therefore, there is historical, political, and economic evidence of the perceptions of skin color related to issues of trust and credibility that at times are displayed within counseling relationships.

Even Schofield (1964) found that counselors tend to prefer clients that resemble the YAVIS (young, attractive, verbal, intelligent, and social) syndrome. However, skin color was not part of this equation. Sundberg (1981) suggested that therapy may not be successful for people who are QUOID (quiet, ugly, old, indigent, and dissimilar culturally). Again, the issue of skin color was not addressed. What these two authors addressed is that physical characteristics (phenotype), financial status, social skills, culture, and age definitely bias the counselor's view toward clients. Such examples make necessary an experiential process-oriented curriculum to develop a multiculturally competent counselor.

The journey of developing multiculturally competent counselors is a painful and enlightening experience, to say the least. From the discussion throughout this chapter, it is apparent that people's perceptions come from sociopolitical historical events, family socialization, and personal experiences. It behooves counselor training programs to examine how people have developed such biases and to help them develop self-awareness coupled with responsibility for their perceptions. Such a training program would include the three major components often cited in the literature for training: awareness, knowledge, and skills (Sue & Sue, 1990). Knowledge is often the component most focused on in multicultural courses by counseling programs across the country. The content often reflects the "dark" history of the mental health profession toward minority group members, explanations of various models of worldview, identity development, and acculturation, along with literature related to the four major minority groups in the United States. What is interesting about this simplistic view is that it is contradictory to how people have developed their emotional, psychological, and behavioral reactions to their perceptions of phenotypical and diverse issues. The adherence to these perceptions has come through experiential learning from the family of origin, personal critical incidents, and the projections from the mass media.

It would make sense that the first step in training multiculturally competent counselors reflects the same process. For example, training would reflect an experiential versus a didactic form of learning. Students would enter the course with an informed consent that the curriculum will reflect a developmental, chronological, and emotional sequence. Such sequences are often common when training students in the practice of group counseling. The training course would reflect a strong process orientation versus a content orientation. A pre- and posttest inventory would be administered to measure overall progress throughout the course. Such inventories may include the Multicultural Awareness-Knowledge-Skills Survey (MAKSS) (D'Andrea, Daniels, & Heck, 1991), the Multicultural Counseling Inventory (MCI) (Sodowsky, Taffe, Gutkin, & Wise, 1994), or the Multicultural Counseling Awareness Scale (MCAS-B) (Ponterotto, Rieger, Barrett, & Sparks, 1994). These instruments and other forms of self-assessment would become part of an ongoing multicultural assessment portfolio (Coleman, 1996). Once the assessments are accomplished, they can provide counselors' areas of strength as well as areas for growth, facilitating goal setting in the multicultural course and other clinical training courses.

The course would begin with an exploration of the counselor's worldview. *Worldview* is defined as a person's perceptions of culture, universality, and individuality (Sue & Sue, 1990). One method to accomplish this task is through the use of the multicultural genogram (Vázquez, 1999). Such an assignment includes an exploration of family history dating back three generations. The unique quality of this particular genogram is the descriptors that are used as variables of exploration for the counselor. For example, some of the variables would include the counselor's family's perceptions across generations toward diversity and positive and negative interactions. In addition, counselors can explore their ethnic group's historical perceptions of people diverse from themselves. This area may include all the ethnicities with which the counselor identifies. Another section would include an integration of these two areas, ending with a section on areas for improvement, exploration, and probable limitations for practice. The integration of this assignment with the concept of worldview would create historical, personal awareness and possibly emotional conflicts for the counselor to examine, especially in working with multicultural populations.

Such assignments would be integrated with videotaped interviews. For example, the video *Voices* (Daniel, Aden, Davidson, & Ellis, 1990) interviews several diverse individuals and how they have experienced their interactions with other people of diversity. These assignments create an excellent catalyst for discussion and process. Other examples may include diversity awareness exercises that would include having the counselors trace their experiences chronologically, from kindergarten to their current age, about issues such as race, gender, and sexual orientation. Once this is done, the counselors can share with each other in a group format what these experiences were like for them and give each other feedback. This exercise would help counselors accept responsibility and be accountable for their beliefs. In addition, it provides the opportunity to learn from those similar to and different from themselves. The process in and of itself affords the students a multicultural experience with each other. Having experienced and processed these exercises, counselors can begin to examine their identity development.

Simply defined, *identity* is how people feel about themselves in relation to their own ethnic group and those groups diverse from themselves (Sue & Sue, 1990). It is at this level of training that the issue of phenotype is addressed through the use of various identity models (Carter, 1995; Helms, 1984). An exercise that has proven successful is the analysis of the film *Malcolm X* (Worth, Lee, & Lee, 1993) in relation to Black identity development. The counselor watches the film in a small group with other counselors, applies the appropriate identity development models and the concept of skin color to the main character, and responds in journal format to each phase of identity development from his or her own identity development perspective. This exercise allows counselors to explore how skin color and group identification mitigate their own relationships with people of color. The exercise also serves as a reflection of the counselor's own development and interactions with his or her own history of developing intimate relationships with minorities of a darker skin color and different phenotype from themselves. This assignment often has created very strong emotional reactions. These emotions are often processed during experiences in the small groups during and after the film. The reactions are also processed in the classroom environment with the instructor as facilitator in a group format.

The learning of the concepts of worldview and identity development sets the stage for the integration of the concept of acculturation and phenotype. *Acculturation* refers to the contact an individual has with a different culture and the traits adopted from that culture (Redfield, Lenton, & Herskovits, 1936). The complexity of the concept of acculturation makes it difficult to choose a comprehensive model of application. However, the multidimensional model developed by Keefe and Padilla (1987) provides a very comprehensive conceptual picture of acculturation. This model is thoroughly explored and presented by the instructor in class. The counselors are taught how to operationalize the constructs of the model in relation to assessment. Once this is accomplished, the counselors are assigned the movie *Mi Familia* (Thomas & Nava, 1995) and asked to select three characters from the movie, with one being the opposite gender from themselves. The comprehensiveness of the multidimensional model engages the counselor in an integrative process of examining the various constructs of acculturation, phenotype, and how these concepts apply to the assessment of acculturation to each of the characters. This allows the counselors to assess how phenotype may have affected the character's reaction to discrimination or acceptance into the dominant culture. The exercise is assigned as a group task. Four to five counselors watch the movie together while they process the dimensions of the acculturation model and phenotype. In addition, the assignment is processed in class with the other counselors to exchange similar and different experiences that each group encountered. These are only a few examples that can be used in providing experiential exercises for counselors learning about acculturation and phenotype.

While the counselors are engaged in these various activities, they are also journaling their reactions each week and handing them in to receive feedback from the instructor. Journal entries include information such as an incident during class or reaction to an incident, immediate emotional reactions to the incident, where the emotional reaction developed (personal history, family history, etc.), and possible suggestions to resolve or explore these reactions. The journal allows the instructor to monitor progress in the counselor's critical consciousness and awareness to multicultural issues. When these assignments are completed and the counselors have an in-depth understanding of each of these multicultural concepts, it is time to experience the application of these moderator variables in counseling situations through role-plays in the classroom. It is at this time that the counselors take the posttests to assess developmental changes in relation to multicultural awareness and competency. In our experience, counselors consistently have shown a marked increase in self-awareness and confidence in the ability to apply the multicultural concepts. There is also a thorough understanding of how a person's perception of skin color and ethnicity can affect interpersonal communication. In addition, there is an awareness of how power differentials and perceptions of skin color directly affect appropriate versus inappropriate treatment processes for counseling. The inventories validate the growth process for the counselor and serve as further areas for growth to complete the requirements for multicultural competence.

Once the multicultural competencies discussed have been achieved, it is time for the counselors to apply their multicultural awareness, knowledge, and introductory skills in their first practicum experience. Bernard and Goodyear (1992) indicate that live supervision and videotaped observations provide the best feedback for counselor training. Using training methods such as the bug-in-the-ear in live supervision, along with videotaping, can give counselors the immediate feedback necessary to achieve competence in their demonstrations of incorporating multicultural concepts in counseling. A specific technique that we have used with videotaping and bug-in-the-ear is to have an ethnically diverse client wear the bug while receiving guidance from the counselor's supervisor to have the counselor react to oppressive situations related to issues of color and ethnicity. The participants consist of both White and ethnically diverse counselors. Once the experience is completed, the supervisor and the counselor review the videotape to provide feedback for the counselor. These experiences are very powerful in developing appropriate skills and awareness of multicultural counseling situations.

Throughout the various activities, all aspects of the individual are considered. These include skin color, gender, ethnicity, and race, along with other salient issues of diversity. It is important for the counselor to know how worldview, identity, and acculturation level of an individual or client will affect their counseling relationship. Equally important is the counselor's awareness of how these same concepts in himself or herself will affect the client. After accomplishing these assignments and training at a competent level, the counselors are now ready to work with clients at identity levels consistent or lower than the counselors' levels. In addition, the counselors are now able to understand and help their clients understand that the acculturation process is a very complex issue. Issues such as phenotype, socioeconomic status, education, and discriminatory perceptions by the dominant culture and the client's culture of origin directly affect how a client may negotiate the process of acculturation.

CONCLUSION

The dear friend's personal story, historical account of color, and the research related to phenotype validate the impact that the perceptions of phenotype, especially color, have had on the acculturation process of southwestern Mexican Americans. The internalization of racist beliefs toward one's ethnic group and the physical rejection of one's color through "skin bleaching" have created a tremendous power differentiation among southwestern Mexican Americans. The belief that lighter is better has led to mistreatment within and even among family members. The ascribed privilege of being lighter complected with "acceptable" physical characteristics, as defined by the dominant culture, has created a within-group superiority status. The examination and evaluation of these issues among minority group counselors in training are of utmost importance in preparing culturally competent counselors. Just as important is the examination and evaluation of such views of superiority among White cultural group counselors in training. With a current backlash against affirmative action, unearned assumed privilege of superiority (McIntosh, 1992), along with an "us-and-them" mentality, creates undue stress between clients and White counselors in training.

References

Aboud, R. E. (1987). The development of ethnic self-identification and attitudes. In J. S. Phinney & M. J. Rotheram (Eds.), *Children's ethnic socialization: Pluralism and development* (pp. 32-55). Newbury Park, CA: Sage.

Acua, R. (1981). *Occupied America: A history of Chicanos* (2nd ed.). New York: Harper & Row.

Alejandro-Wright, M. N. (1985). The child's conceptions of racial classification: A socio-cognitive developmental model. In M. B. Spencer, G. K. Brookus, & W. R. Allen (Eds.), *Beginnings: The social and affective development of Black children* (pp. 185-200). Hillsdale, NJ: Lawrence Erlbaum.

Arce, C. H., Murguia, E., & Frisbie, W. P. (1987). Phenotype and life chances among Chicanos. *Hispanic Journal of Behavioral Science, 9,* 19-32.

Bernard, J. M., & Goodyear, R. K. (1992). *Fundamentals of clinical supervision.* Boston: Allyn & Bacon.

Bobo, L., & Hutchings, V. L. (1996). Perceptions of racial group competition: Extending Blumer's theory of group position to a multiracial social context. *American Sociological Review, 61,* 951-972.

Buriel, R. (1987). Ethnic labeling and identity among Mexican Americans. In J. S. Phinney & M. J. Rotheram (Eds.), *Children's ethnic socialization: Pluralism and development* (pp. 134-152). Newbury Park, CA: Sage.

Carter, R. T. (1995). *The influence of race and racial identity in psychotherapy: Toward a racially inclusive model.* New York: John Wiley.

Codina, G. E., & Montalvo, F. F. (1994). Chicano phenotype and depression. *Hispanic Journal of Behavioral Sciences, 16,* 296-306.

Coleman, H. L. K. (1996). Portfolio assessment of multicultural counseling competency. *The Counseling Psychologist, 24*(2), 216-229.

D'Andrea, M., K., Daniels, J., & Heck, R. (1991). Evaluating the impact of counseling training. *Journal of Counseling and Development, 70*(1), 143-150.

Daniel, J., Aden, M., Davidson, C. (Coproducers), & Ellis, M. (Director). (1990). *Voices* [Film]. (Available from Colorado State University, 7B Student Health Services, Fort Collins, CO 80523)

de Anda, D. (1984). Bicultural socialization: Factors affecting the minority experience. *Social Work, 29,* 101-107.

Dennis, R. M. (1981). Socialization and racism: The White experience. In B. P. Bowser & R. G. Hunt (Eds.), *Impacts of racism on White Americans* (pp. 71-85). Beverly Hills, CA: Sage.

DuBois, W. E. B. (1969). *The souls of Black folk.* New York: New American Library.

Dysart, J. (1976). Mexican women in San Antonio, 1830-1860: The assimilation process. *Western Historical Quarterly, 366,* 365-375.

Esteva-Fabregat, C. (1995). *Mestizaje in Ibero-America* (J. Wheat, Trans.). Tucson: University of Arizona Press.

Gomez, M. J., & Fassinger, R. E. (1994). An initial model of Latina achievement: Acculturation, biculturalism, and achieving style. *Journal of Counseling Psychology, 41,* 205-215.

Hall, P. E. (1994). The "bleaching syndrome": Implications of light skin for Hispanic American assimilation. *Hispanic Journal of Behavioral Sciences, 16,* 307-314.

Helms, J. E. (1984). Toward a theoretical model of the effects of race on counseling: A Black and White model. *The Counseling Psychologist, 12,* 152-165.

Holmes, R. M. (1995). *How young children perceive race.* Thousand Oaks, CA: Sage.

Keefe, S. E., & Padilla, A. M. (1987). *Chicano ethnicity.* Albuquerque: University of New Mexico Press.

LaFromboise, T. D., Coleman, H. L. K., & Gerton, J. (1993). Psychological impact of biculturalism: Evidence and theory. *Psychological Bulletin, 114,* 395-412.

Maldonado, B. B. (1972). *The impact of skin color on self-concept of low socio-economic level Mexican-American high school students.* Unpublished doctoral dissertation, New Mexico State University.

McIntosh, P. (1992). White privilege and male privilege: A personal account of coming to see cor-respondences through work in women's studies. In M. L. Andersen & P. H. Collins (Eds.), *Race, class, and gender: An anthology* (2nd ed., pp. 70-81). Belmont, CA: Wadsworth.

Padilla, A. M. (1980). *Acculturation: Theory, models, and some new findings.* Boulder, CO: Westview.

Phinney, J. S. (1996). When we talk about American ethnic groups, what do we mean? *American Psychologist, 51,* 918-927.

Ponterotto, J. G., & Pedersen, P. B. (1993). *Preventing prejudice: A guide for counselors and educators.* Newbury Park, CA: Sage.

Ponterotto, J. G., Rieger, B. P., Barrett, A., & Sparks, R. (1994). Assessing multicultural counsel-ing competence: A review of instrumentation. *Journal of Counseling and Development, 72,* 316-322.

Ransford, E. H. (1970). Skin color, life chances, and anti-White attitudes. *Social Problems, 18,* 164-178.

Redfield, R., Lenton, R., & Herskovits, M. J. (1936). Memorandum for the study of acculturation. *American Anthropologist, 38,* 149-152.

Relethford, J. H., Stern, M. P., Gaskill, S. P., & Hazuda, H. P. (1983). Social class, admixture, and skin color variation in Mexican-Americans and Anglo-Americans living in San Antonio, Texas. *American Journal of Physical Anthropology, 61,* 97-102.

Schofield, W. (1964). *Psychotherapy: The purchase of friendship.* Englewood Cliffs, NJ: Prentice Hall.

Smart, J. F., & Smart, D. W. (1995). Acculturative stress: The experience of the Hispanic immi-grant. *The Counseling Psychologist, 23*(1), 25-42.

Sodowsky, G. R., Taffe, R. C., Gutkin, T. B., & Wise, S. L. (1994). Development of the multicul-tural counseling inventory: A self-report measure of multicultural competencies. *Journal of Counseling Psychology, 41,* 137-148.

Sue, D. W., & Sue, D. (1990). *Counseling the culturally different: Theory and practice.* New York: John Wiley.

Sundberg, N. D. (1981). Cross-cultural counseling and psychotherapy: A research overview. In A. J. Mansella & P. B. Pedersen (Eds.), *Cross-cultural counseling and psychotherapy* (pp. 28-62). New York: Macmillan.

Thomas, A. (Producer), & Nava, G. (Director). (1995). *My family* [Film]. (Available from New Line Productions, Inc., New Line Home Video, Turner Home Entertainment)

Valencia, A. A. (1991). Acculturation for the Hispanic: A multidimensional perspective. *Journal of Educational Issues of Language Minority Students, 9,* 91-115.

Vargas-Willis, G., & Cervantes, R. C. (1987). Consideration of psychosocial stress in the treat-ment of the Latina immigrant. *Hispanic Journal of Behavioral Sciences, 9,* 315-329.

Vázquez, L. A. (1999). *The multicultural genogram: An exercise in self-awareness.* Manuscript submitted for publication.

Webster's II: New Riverside college dictionary. (1995). Boston: Houghton Mifflin.

Worth, M., Lee, S. (Coproducers), & Lee, S. (Director). (1993). *Malcolm X* [Film]. (Available from Warner Home Video, 4000 Warner Blvd., Burbank, CA 91522)

ADDRESSING RACIAL, ETHNIC, GENDER, AND SOCIAL CLASS ISSUES IN COUNSELOR TRAINING AND PRACTICE

Madonna G. Constantine
Teachers College, Columbia University

The fields of counseling and counseling psychology have taken the lead among applied mental health disciplines in attempting to incorporate multicultural issues into academic curricula (Constantine, Ladany, Inman, & Ponterotto, 1996; Ponterotto, Alexander, & Grieger, 1995; Quintana & Bernal, 1995). The integration of multicultural issues into curricula has occurred in response to the need to prepare future counselors and counseling psychologists to deal with a range of culturally diverse clients. In recent years, several components of multiculturalism have received some attention in counselor training programs, including race, ethnicity, and gender. In fact, there are proposed competencies, guidelines, and even conceptual models for addressing racial, ethnic, and gender issues in counseling (e.g., Arredondo et al., 1996; Coleman, 1996; Good, Gilbert, & Scher, 1990; Sue, Arredondo, & McDavis, 1992). However, one component of multiculturalism that is frequently overlooked or ignored by many training programs is social class, a variable that is increasingly viewed as a critical dimension in the lives of many clients who are served by mental health professionals (Ross, 1995).

The insufficient amount of attention that has been devoted in the literature and in counselor training programs to understanding social class issues and how they affect clients' lives may cause counselors in training to exit their graduate programs with inadequate levels of competence to address such issues with clients. It is apparent that issues related to clients' social class may have a significant impact on a variety of counseling-related phenomena, including clients' presenting issues and clients' motivation to seek or remain in treatment. Without additional empirically and conceptually based information concerning social class, it is unclear the extent to which this phenomenon may interact with or influence other important demographic variables such as race, ethnicity, and gender in clients' lives.

In this chapter, I will discuss the intersection of race, ethnicity, gender, and social class, emphasizing the potential impacts of these variables in individuals' lives. (Because the construct of social class has received relatively less attention in the literature, as compared to other multicultural variables, I will address this variable more deliberately in the context of this discussion.) In addition, I will elucidate the importance of addressing racial, ethnic, gender, and social class issues in counselor training programs to facilitate the development of multicultural counseling competence in students. Last, using a clinical scenario, I will illustrate the confluence of these sociodemographic variables in relation to clients' presenting concerns.

THE INTERSECTION OF RACE, ETHNICITY, GENDER, AND SOCIAL CLASS

Race, ethnicity, gender, and social class are vital elements of all individuals' identity formation (e.g., Pinderhughes, 1989; Robinson, 1993, 1999; Scher & Good, 1990). However, each of these variables in isolation fails to reflect the complexities and life experiences of most people. In particular, the importance of understanding the unique and combined contributions of each of these demographic identities on individuals' development and functioning cannot be too strongly expressed. Failing to recognize the intersections of race, ethnicity, gender, and social class is paramount to regarding them as pure and complete constructs (Christian, 1989; Robinson, 1993, 1999).

Some researchers (e.g., Mantsios, 1998a; Weber, 1998) have asserted that although constructs such as race, ethnicity, gender, and class have existed throughout history, these variables are largely contextual in that they are continuously undergoing changes as social and national systems are transformed. Such changes may be reflected, for example, in ever-evolving terminology related to issues such as racial group designations (e.g., Afro American vs. African American) and social class distinctions (e.g., lower class vs. working class). Thus, it is vital that sociodemographic variables such as race, ethnicity, gender, and social class are viewed dynamically, as opposed to statically, to reduce the likelihood of oversimplification and overgeneralization of their meanings and applications (Fandetti & Goldmeier, 1988).

With regard to social class issues, the United States is frequently viewed as a country in which (a) class differences are largely insignificant or nonexistent, and (b) all individuals have an equal opportunity to succeed if they are willing and able to work hard to obtain income and resources (Hochschild, 1995; Mantsios, 1998a). In particular, many people believe that most Americans fall within the middle class and that there are few class distinctions among Americans (Mantsios, 1998a). More realistically, however, the United States is among the most stratified nations in the industrialized world in that class distinctions pervade almost all aspects of American citizens' lives (e.g., schooling, access to health care, personal safety) (Mantsios, 1998b; Weber, 1998). The U.S. class structure is based on a capitalist economic system (i.e., a system rooted in private ownership and control of enterprises and resources) (Mantsios, 1998a). To put these social class issues into perspective, it is important to note that nearly one third of Americans are situated at one end or the other of the income continuum (U.S. Department of Commerce, 1993). Moreover, the middle class is believed to be shrinking in size, and the majority of individuals leaving middle-class ranks are falling to a lower economic position (Mantsios, 1998a). This economic polarization of the United States is predicted to continue over the next few decades (Blumberg, 1980).

Counseling professionals may tend to avoid social class issues except when assessing their clients' resources or when considering the psychological effects of clients' socioeconomic status (Ross, 1995). In addition, they may not focus on socioeconomic issues, in part, because many counselors have had no training in this realm. Moreover, some counselors may avoid social class issues because they are first-generation professionals, and clients' social class issues may too closely parallel their own experiences (Ross, 1995). Many counselors may tend to see themselves and others as belonging to the middle-class ranks. They may make attempts to be "class-blind," much like some people attempt to

be "color-blind" with regard to racial and ethnic issues. Compounding the challenge that counselors may face in dealing with social class issues is that class is
a very difficult concept to define universally.

Although race, ethnicity, gender, and social class may operate independently of each other, they are interconnected, and the impact of their intersections must be acknowledged (Mantsios, 1998a). Historically, the variables of
race, ethnicity, gender, and social class have not only represented different cultural practices, beliefs, and values but also have been conceptualized to be socially constructed power hierarchies; that is, these constructions may provide
individuals with power and opportunities in some situations but may limit their
options in other arenas (Weber, 1998). More specifically, racial, ethnic, gender,
and class systems are rooted in social relationships wherein there are dominant
and subordinate groups that struggle over the control of valuable resources.
Race, ethnicity, gender, and social class function concurrently in all social circumstances, both societally (e.g., systems of social hierarchies are embedded in
all social institutions) and individually (e.g., people develop their personal
identity based on where they fall on the continuum along various
sociodemographic dimensions) (Weber, 1998). Furthermore, it is important to
emphasize that racism and sexism intensify the impact of classism (Mantsios,
1998a). Examinations of racial, ethnic, gender, and social class issues must
consider "the ways in which the privilege of dominant groups is tied to the oppression of subordinate groups" (Weber, 1998, p. 21). Any genuine understanding of the impact of oppression on subordinate groups must be preceded by an
examination of individual and social forces in relation to various manifestations of oppression.

RACE, ETHNICITY, GENDER, AND SOCIAL CLASS ISSUES IN COUNSELING CURRICULA

Although there has been much recent attention in the literature to the importance of counselors being multiculturally competent, the process by which cultural concepts are integrated into academic curricula remains in an embryonic
stage. Some counseling and counseling psychology training programs have experienced success in incorporating multicultural issues into their curricula, but
the level at which such integration occurs may vary significantly across training
programs (Constantine et al., 1996; Quintana & Bernal, 1995). For example, a
recent survey of doctoral graduates in applied psychology revealed that only a

small number of respondents perceived themselves to possess high levels of competence in providing services to racial and ethnic minorities (Allison, Crawford, Echemendia, Robinson, & Knepp, 1994). For the most part, such surveys have tended to query respondents about their ability to work with racially and ethnically diverse clients but may not ask respondents to report their perceived competence in addressing other types of sociodemographic issues (e.g., gender, social class). The facilitation of multicultural counseling competence in trainees requires the presence of an integrated set of didactic and experiential courses and applied clinical experiences that are organized to achieve this goal.

To date, many counseling theories and interventions have been conceptualized and validated, respectively, using White, heterosexual, middle-class individuals. One of the most serious consequences of this phenomenon is the underlying assumption that White, heterosexual, middle-class persons represent the normative group. Moreover, a significant portion of the content in counseling and counseling psychology curricula is rooted in how to best work with clients who represent these specific cultural group memberships. As a proposed remedy to this predicament, the common practice in many academic courses is to devote one or two class sessions to discussing how the overall course content may relate to culturally diverse individuals. However, counselors in training would likely find it difficult at best to take concepts that have been "tried and tested" on White, heterosexual, middle-class individuals and then successfully apply them to persons who do not fit this narrow set of criteria.

Regarding the relationships among racial, ethnic, gender, and social class issues in counseling and counseling psychology training, little information in the literature comprehensively discusses this intersection. Moreover, there is no simple mathematical formula that can comprehensively capture the intricacy of the relationships among these variables (Weber, 1998). Consequently, many academicians and counselors historically have tended to compartmentalize these issues without considering the enormity and salience of their potential interactions. At times, some counselors may be reticent to consider such interactions for fear of feeling overwhelmed or ineffectual in their ability to help clients whose concerns may be potentially rooted in complex societal forces (e.g., institutional oppression). This phenomenon may be especially true for counselors whose training programs may have neglected to pay sufficient attention to multicultural issues.

In terms of counselor training programs including multicultural content in their course offerings, it is important that all instructors deliberately and systematically provide students with learning environments that reflect how the subject areas they teach may apply to various populations. Moreover, academicians may wish to consistently provide opportunities for counselors in training to explore how the intersection of salient sociodemographic constructs may affect various levels of client functioning. For example, one way that racial, ethnic, gender, and social class issues might be integrated into a couples and family therapy course is by exploring the impact of various gender role socialization and social class experiences on racially and ethnically diverse couples and familial configurations. Moreover, multicultural issues also could be addressed in the context of such a course by examining a variety of theories and interventions related to working with middle- and working-class African American, Asian American, Latino American, Native American, White American, interracial, and international couples and families. The integration of multicultural material in academic curricula is critical to the development of students' professional practice competencies, and the fruits of this labor will likely be reaped by the clients with whom these students work.

ADDRESSING RACE, ETHNICITY, GENDER, AND SOCIAL CLASS ISSUES IN COUNSELING PRACTICE: A CASE EXAMPLE

The following scenario is a clinical example of how the intersection of racial, ethnic, gender, and social class issues may be manifested in the context of marital counseling.

Victor and Elena (pseudonyms) were a married, heterosexual White South African couple who presented for counseling because they were experiencing domestic- and school-related difficulties. They were advanced doctoral students in music and anthropology, respectively, and had had a child approximately 6 months ago. Victor held a 25-hour per week job as a musician, and Elena was employed as a 20-hour per week teaching assistant in her department. Elena and Victor both complained of feeling lethargic, sleep deprived, irritable, and anxious most of the time.

In discussing their reasons for seeking counseling, Elena and Victor reported being concerned about (a) their lack of agreement regarding responsibility for various household tasks, (b) having inadequate financial resources to support their family, (c) feeling pressure from faculty advisers and family members to complete their doctoral dissertations in a timely manner, and (d) feeling a perceived lack of support from each other regarding completing their dissertations. Victor, in discussing his thoughts and feelings about their current situation, stated that he was socialized to believe that "a good wife" should cook, clean, and attend to other domestic responsibilities, including most aspects of child rearing. Furthermore, Victor believed that he was primarily responsible for being "the breadwinner" in the family and felt the need to try to work additional hours to support his wife and new child. He had hoped that Elena would temporarily postpone her doctoral studies and quit her assistantship to rear their child full-time and support him emotionally in completing his dissertation. Elena, having been reared with some similar values about domestic responsibilities, stated that although she understood and appreciated Victor's commitment to providing for his family, she did not wish to quit her teaching assistantship and postpone working on her dissertation. She reported that she felt capable of holding part-time employment, working on her dissertation, and attending to some domestic tasks. Over the past 6 months, Elena stated that she had pleaded with Victor to begin assuming some of the domestic responsibilities because she was "feeling burned out" in her attempts to take care of all the household responsibilities. She reported that Victor had consistently refused to "take on women's work." After threatening him with the possibility of a marital separation, Elena insisted that they attend counseling to address some of their concerns.

During their initial counseling sessions, Elena and Victor explored the impact of their varied socialization experiences related to their ethnic group, assumed gender roles, and social classes of origin. Although they were members of the same ethnic group, Elena and Victor became increasingly aware of how their intraethnic similarities and differences interacted with their divergent gender role socialization processes and social class of origin experiences to form their contemporary manifestations of themselves. They began to see how their various cultural group memberships intersected to form their own personal values, thoughts, perceptions, and experiences. As an example, Victor was reared by a mother who took care of their home and a father who owned and managed a large, successful family business. As such, Victor believed that, "If at all possible, it is better that women stay at home to take care of domestic tasks while their husbands work." In contrast, Elena was reared by a single mother who had worked two jobs to support Elena and her three siblings. As the oldest child, Elena had also worked part-time as a teenager and young adult to help support her family of origin. Hence, she believed that it was important for "a good wife" to contribute monetarily to her household, particularly when it was necessary to do so. Moreover, Elena stated that because of her own gender role and social class socialization experiences, she felt the need to complete her dissertation in the near future to (a) feel good about accomplishing such a prestigious educational goal as a woman and (b) provide as many employment options as possible to help support her current nuclear family.

As Victor and Elena gained insight into the ways in which their ethnic, gender, and social class of origin identities shaped their personal development, they were better able to address the concerns that prompted them to seek counseling. In particular, a heightened understanding of their own and each other's cultural group memberships enabled them to (a) appreciate the complexities of their lives, both individually and as a couple, and (b) begin negotiating their presenting issues in a satisfactory manner.

In the case example above, Elena and Victor's counselor seemed to comprehend and acknowledge the importance of examining several potential intersections of salient sociodemographic identities in relation to these clients' presenting concerns. Victor and Elena's increased understanding of how these intersections may affect various aspects of their lives seemed to encourage their progression toward addressing their issues. Counselors who are knowledgeable about and able to explore the impacts of such variables and constructs in their clients' lives may experience a great deal of success in working with a wide range of individuals.

CONCLUSIONS

Counselors must challenge themselves to strive toward in-depth understanding of how the intersections of sociodemographic variables such as race, ethnicity, gender, and social class may affect the lives of the clients with whom they work. Some counselors' resistance to examining the relationships among multicultural phenomena in their clients' lives may be related to their lack of understanding about the intersections of their own cultural group memberships. True insight and understanding about cultural phenomena will not emerge solely from intellectual, academic discussions of their potential impacts. In part, counselors' reflective analyses of their own personal demographic identities, which include explorations of issues of power, privilege, and oppression, will enable them to better serve a wider range of client populations.

In training students to work with clients in a multiculturally competent manner, academicians and supervisors must be willing to face their own personal and professional discomforts regarding helping trainees to examine the intersections of race, ethnicity, gender, social class, and other such variables. Faculty members and supervisors have an ethical and social responsibility to teach their students to provide multiculturally competent services to clients. Hence, multicultural issues must be proactively and meaningfully integrated into academic curricula and applied training experiences. Without deliberate and systematic inclusion of cultural issues into various forms of counselor training, future clinicians will not be adequately equipped to work with an increasingly diverse U.S. population.

Future research and scholarship in counseling and counseling psychology should continue to examine and discuss implications of the intersections of vital sociodemographic constructs on various aspects of clients' functioning. Information gleaned from the results of qualitative and quantitative investigations in this vein may enable counselors to work more effectively with individuals who seek their services.

References

Allison, K. W., Crawford, I., Echemendia, R., Robinson, L., & Knepp, D. (1994). Human diversity and professional competence: Training in clinical and counseling psychology revisited. *American Psychologist, 49,* 792-796.

Arredondo, P., Toporek, R., Brown, S. P., Jones, J., Locke, D., Sanchez, J., & Stadler, H. (1996). Operationalization of the multicultural counseling competencies. *Journal of Multicultural Counseling and Development, 24,* 42-78.

Blumberg, P. (1980). *Inequality in an age of decline.* New York: Oxford University Press.

Christian, B. (1989). But who do you really belong to—Black studies or women's studies? *Women's Studies, 17,* 17-23.

Coleman, H. L. K. (1996). Portfolio assessment of multicultural counseling competency. *The Counseling Psychologist, 24,* 216-229.

Constantine, M. G., Ladany, N., Inman, A. G., & Ponterotto, J. G. (1996). Students' perceptions of multicultural training in counseling psychology programs. *Journal of Multicultural Counseling and Development, 24,* 241-253.

Fandetti, D. V., & Goldmeier, J. (1988). Social workers as culture mediators in health care settings. *Health and Social Work, 13,* 171-179.

Good, G. E., Gilbert, L. A., & Scher, M. (1990). Gender aware therapy: A synthesis of feminist therapy and knowledge about gender. *Journal of Counseling and Development, 68,* 376-380.

Hochschild, J. (1995). *Facing up to the American Dream: Race, class, and the soul of the nation.* Princeton, NJ: Princeton University Press.

Mantsios, G. (1998a). Class in America: Myths and realities. In P. S. Rothenberg (Ed.), *Race, class, and gender in the United States: An integrated study* (4th ed., pp. 202-214). New York: St. Martin's.

Mantsios, G. (1998b). Media magic: Making class invisible. In P. S. Rothenberg (Ed.), *Race, class, and gender in the United States: An integrated study* (4th ed., pp. 510-519). New York: St. Martin's.

Pinderhughes, E. (1989). *Understanding race, ethnicity & power: The key to efficacy in clinical practice.* New York: Free Press.

Ponterotto, J. G., Alexander, C. M., & Grieger, I. (1995). A multicultural competency checklist for counseling training programs. *Journal of Multicultural Counseling and Development, 23,* 11-20.

Quintana, S. M., & Bernal, M. E. (1995). Ethnic minority training in counseling psychology: Comparisons with clinical psychology and proposed standards. *The Counseling Psychologist, 23,* 102-121.

Robinson, T. L. (1993). The intersections of gender, class, race, and culture: On seeing clients whole. *Journal of Multicultural Counseling and Development, 21,* 50-58.

Robinson, T. L. (1999). The intersections of dominant discourses across race, gender, and other identities. *Journal of Counseling and Development, 77,* 73-79.

Ross, J. L. (1995). Social class tensions within families. *American Journal of Family Therapy, 23,* 338-350.

Scher, M., & Good, G. E. (1990). Gender and counseling in the twenty-first century: What does the future hold? *Journal of Counseling and Development, 68,* 388-391.

Sue, D. W., Arredondo, P., & McDavis, R. J. (1992). Multicultural counseling competencies and standards: A call to the profession. *Journal of Multicultural Counseling and Development, 20,* 64-68.

U.S. Department of Commerce. (1993). *Current population reports: Consumer income: 1992.* Washington, DC: Author.

Weber, L. (1998). A conceptual framework for understanding race, class, gender, and sexuality. *Psychology of Women Quarterly, 22,* 13-32.

PART

III

THEORY TO
PRACTICE

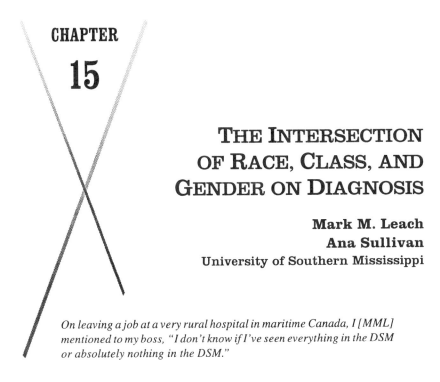

CHAPTER

15

THE INTERSECTION
OF RACE, CLASS, AND
GENDER ON DIAGNOSIS

Mark M. Leach
Ana Sullivan
University of Southern Mississippi

On leaving a job at a very rural hospital in maritime Canada, I [MML]
mentioned to my boss, "I don't know if I've seen everything in the DSM
or absolutely nothing in the DSM."

Herein lies the dilemma when using the *Diagnostic and Statistical Manual of*
Mental Disorders (*DSM*). Few clients meet all required criteria for a particular
disorder and hence diagnosis. However, diagnoses are generated by clinicians,
so we must question what diagnostic categories actually represent. The popular
diagnostic classification system in the United States, used as the basis of diagnosis, does not seem to be providing an accurate description of disorders when
applied to most individuals. Furthermore, it is less valid when applied to groups
of diverse individuals. We need not delete the *DSM* but reconsider it from a contextual framework.

It is human nature to classify in order to organize and simplify information,
and more than 200 publications have discussed different diagnostic cluster-
ings to create psychiatric classification schemes (Blashfield, 1984; Gara,
Rosenberg, & Goldberg, 1992). Although classification systems are useful, the
DSM is limited due to its dearth of emphases on sociocultural, historical, and

political factors. Until these factors are included significantly in classification systems, the *DSM* will, at best, have marginal clinical utility. At worst, it will result in inappropriate treatment and miscommunication. We understand that diagnosis is a process and a continuous entity (and the *DSM-IV* is considered to be a classification system, not a diagnostic system), but the mental health system in the United States forces clinicians into making quick diagnostic judgments based on limited information, which often results in labeling a client needlessly or inappropriately. Lipton and Simon (1985) found that although clinicians consider culture to be an important variable when diagnosing, many clinicians focus on only one behavioral indicator when making a diagnosis. For example, the *DSM* suggests that affective and organic disorders be ruled out prior to a diagnosis of schizophrenia, yet many clinicians diagnose schizophrenia based on one symptom that is consistent across affective, organic, and schizophrenia disorders. It could be argued that clinicians need to be better trained, but tools are only effective if they assist the clinician properly.

We believe that the *DSM* does have some present utility in that classification systems provide a format for communication among professionals, possible guidance for treatment and research, and reimbursement from insurance companies. However, Kutchins and Kirk (1988) reported that 35% of psychiatrists would cease using the *DSM* if allowed to do so, 90% of clinical psychologists indicated that insurance practices constituted the chief reason for employing the *DSM,* and 81% of social workers' top four reasons for using the *DSM* (insurance, agency, Medicaid, and legal requirements) were not related to clinical practice. In addition, Smith and Kraft (1983) found that more than half of all psychologists rejected the idea that a universal classification system was useful and that most preferred interpersonal and nondiagnostic analyses.

There are numerous concerns with the structure, function, and philosophical roots of the *DSM* nosology, explicated in the literature. A deficit in *DSM* criteria is the paucity of relational and contextual[1] factors in the system criteria, which would add robustness and clarity to diagnosis. Psychiatric classification systems are intertwined with cultural and social norms but do not allow for assessing the influence of these factors, instead focusing on a medico-deductive system. These psychiatric systems are revised with increased scientific knowledge, and it is now necessary to look at the knowledge that is being gained because of the influence of the cultural and social norms on diagnosis. We do not advocate that the *DSM* and other classification systems be dismissed but that future revisions include greater sociocultural emphases, beginning with a relational belief system (Kaslow, 1996a).

First, we will discuss some of the concerns with the prevailing North American diagnostic system (American Psychiatric Association, 1994) and its relationship to race, class, and gender. We fall somewhere between Szasz (1990), who is opposed to diagnosis, and the American Mental Health Fund of Jack Hinkley, whose motto is "All mental illness is a medical illness" (as cited in Albee, 1990), believing both are misguided. We believe that universally based disorders exist regardless of social and cultural differences (Draguns, 1996, 1997) and that most of the current disorders listed in the *DSM* are largely social, contextual, and relational, with little underlying biomedical cause. In essence, a large number of "mental disorders" can be conceptualized more contextually as social deviance disorders.

Second, we will present an overview of the diagnostic research with underrepresented populations, which suggests that marginalized persons are more likely to receive a mental illness diagnosis than nonmarginalized persons. Third, we will discuss symptom expression and worldviews of culturally diverse clients. Fourth, we will examine an alternative diagnostic approach that complements the *DSM,* thus maintaining the positive features of the *DSM* while increasing diagnostic validity through added contextualism. Finally, we will present an overview of factors to consider when diagnosing such as base rates, diagnostic bias, and the counselor's own cultural environment. Case studies and questions to consider will be included throughout the chapter to determine diagnostic thought processes and culturally consistent alternative diagnostic conceptualizations.

Concerns with the *DSM*

A recent shift in thinking has occurred regarding the use of the *DSM* as a taxonomy and as a tool (Gara et al., 1992). The *DSM* was not initially formulated for insurance company reimbursement purposes but has since become the diagnostic system accepted by companies, academic programs, government programs, and the public. Concerns with the *DSM* have led to alternative conceptualizations from family systems practitioners, feminists, constructivists, multiculturalists, and some practitioners within the medical community.

The *DSM* is based on a medical model determined by three culture-bound mental health/illness assumptions: (a) egocentricity of the self, (b) Cartesian dualism, and (c) culture is defined epiphenomenally. First, egocentricity of the self is the belief that normality and abnormality are contained within the self, thus excluding cultural and social variables. This neo-Darwinian perspective holds that individualism, independence, and competition are of utmost importance; most mental disorders are considered manifestations residing solely within the individual. Second, Cartesian dualism connotes that the brain and mind are exclusive, with emphasis on the importance of the brain. Finally, epiphenomenal culture implies that culture is viewed *a posteriori* to medical conditions (Lewis-Fernandez & Kleinman, 1994). For example, Swartz, Carroll, and Blazer (1989) indicated that "a social model describing the causes and nature of psychiatric illness . . . is a nonscientific position" (p. 33). From these assumptions, authors have concluded that the *DSM* may not be appropriate for culturally marginalized individuals and systems (e.g., Jacobs, 1994).

There are other reasons that the *DSM* may be inappropriate for use with culturally marginalized individuals and systems. First, some (Barney, 1994; Brown, 1990; Fabrega, 1992) propose that the *DSM* is based less in scientific outcome studies and more in political and social convention. Diagnosis is based on social norms, with the dominant cultural norms viewed as intrinsic to all disorders and classification schemes. If training programs and clinicians are to find the *DSM* to be more useful, then more research on the sociopolitical and sociocultural influences on mental disorders needs to be conducted and the results incorporated into the *DSM*. This would lead to diagnoses that would more accurately fit disorders of individuals and their natural social systems and address the factors contributing to diagnosis. Second, the borderline between mental health and mental illness continues to shift depending on the sociopolitical paradigm of the time. For example, "drapetomania" was considered a disease of African slaves whose interest it was to leave slavery, thus allowing physicians to act within social norms to maintain the oppression of African slaves (Comas-Díaz, 1996). Two hundred years ago, Benjamin Rush, the "founder of American psychiatry," identified people who were unhappy with the new political structure of the United States as experiencing "Anarchia" (Brown, 1990), a type of insanity. More than 100 years ago, masturbation was considered a behavioral symptom of "dementia," and about 30 years ago, homosexuality was considered a mental illness. Diagnoses tend to follow trends and moralities of a particular society, some of which foster oppression, especially of marginalized people (Farber, 1990).

Third, *DSM* syndromes imply a neo-Kraepelinian orderliness and contain perceived minimal overlap between diagnostic categories (Brown, 1990; Klerman, 1989). Clinicians have to determine whether they consider diagnosis to be a process or a class of illness. If it is a process, clinicians can modify their conceptualization of client issues and not be constrained by specific categories. The *DSM* often drives clinicians to focus on classifying the individual's perceived illness, leading to client labeling.

Fourth, numerous studies (e.g., Kirk & Kutchins, 1992, 1994; Wilson, 1993) using the *Kappa* coefficient showed that although interrater reliability varies depending on the criteria and the disorder under investigation, reliability coefficients using the *DSM* have been poor and have improved only slightly from the *DSM-I* to the *DSM-III-R*. Without reliability, the validity of the *DSM* is questionable.

We conducted an informal, unscientific survey of local psychologists in town who indicated that they typically do not alter their treatment plans significantly if someone bears a diagnosis of major depression versus dysthymia or other diagnoses embedded under the rubric of a general category. These clinicians maintained their general treatment plans regardless of the intensity and time frame of the depressive syndromes. Thus, diagnosis based on the *DSM* classification system does not appear to be driving the treatment plan. One could argue that once clinically based research becomes more refined, then clinical treatment differences will occur, and as the diagnostic system used is more valid, then greater treatment efficacy will occur. However, unlike medicine, the increase in the number of diagnoses is unlikely to fine-tune our treatment plans due to the ambiguity of personality constructs, social mores, and interactions between biochemical and contextual effects. Research using cluster analysis to discover the taxonomic system of the *DSM-III-R* indicated that there are several discrete symptom classes of disorders, but many psychiatric disorders transcended classes or did not fit the model at all (Gara et al., 1992). Others (Endicott & Spitzer, 1972; Spitzer, Endicott, Fleiss, & Cohen, 1970) found that factor analysis of an early *DSM* revealed 16 symptom patterns that clustered empirically but were not consistent with clinical diagnosis. These studies indicate that clinical diagnostic categories are not distinct entities and that the symptoms embedded in the taxonomic system are consistent with many diagnostic categories.

As many clinicians realize, the *DSM* emphasizes inherent factors significantly (e.g., genetics) and tends to overlook etiological and contextual issues surrounding the diagnosis. The *DSM* decontextualizes and removes meaning from the individual, including the individual's attitudes toward his or her symptomatic behaviors and the historical significance of his or her symptoms. "In an attempt to maintain the 'atheoretical' nature of the *DSM-IV*, its framers again demonstrated how tightly they cling to the outdated idea that emotional and behavioral problems occur within the vacuum of the individual" (Alexander & Pugh, 1996, p. 219). Diagnostic schemas tend to focus on the individual in isolation, although people do not live in isolation. Therefore, considering contextual factors as essential classification has become less of a process and more of a final entity. There are concerns about "category fallacy" when discussing clients who fall outside the realm of Eurocentric middle-class, male diagnostic values. The fallacy asserts that categories and symptoms are universal, even though evidence indicates that distress is conceptualized and experienced differently in different cultures (Draguns, 1996, 1997; Westermeyer, 1987).

Numerous writers (e.g., Barney, 1994) have discussed the issue that psychological research in North America is directed largely through research-granting institutions with bio-behavioral emphases. Furthermore, many funding agencies are backed by pharmaceutical companies that profit financially from perpetuating the medical view of dysfunction and diagnosis. The medical model, of course, views the use of medication as the primary approach to treatment; thus, the research being conducted is guided by the medical model. It is our view that more money is needed for contextualist research perspectives. Although this is a recognized need, there does not seem to be the same interest in funding contextualist research, possibly due to the lack of financial benefits.

Fabrega (1994) outlined five assumptions fundamental to universal, international systems of classification such as the *DSM*. First, there is an assumption that clinical categories are valid; however, this is based on the fallacy that individual psychopathological behaviors observed in one social time period apply over time. Implicit in this position is a "recovering" or "in remission" perspective instead of a "recovered" or "healthy" perspective. Second, descriptive psychopathology assumes that behaviors across cultures are scientifically and clinically equivalent. Third, there is an assumption that universal categories of behavior can be operationally defined even though the criteria are socially constructed based on a particular culture and time. Fourth, there is a belief in an optimal number of diagnostic categories, and, once identified, "science" (medicine) will eventually confirm the categories. Finally, there is an assumption that categories are fixed entities, even though recent evidence with schizophrenia and depression (among other diagnoses, see Draguns, 1997; Jacobs, 1994; Sarbin, 1990) indicates that psychosocial factors mediate the occurrence, course, and outcome of alleged biological factors.

In essence, existing categorical diagnoses have distanced the individual from social influences and place the individual within a system that decontextualizes. The demarcating line between normal and abnormal, health and ill health, becomes rigid (Kaschak, 1992). Although officially viewed as atheoretical and nonetiological, the biomedical model is strongly endorsed by many of the creators of the *DSM*. We believe that the contextual influences brandishing the *DSM* as unworkable are similar to the forces acting on applied psychology as a whole. There has been increased discussion recently between "traditional" philosophies in psychology and newer models, such as constructivism, feminism, and multiculturalism. The latter theories rely less on medico-deductive, logical positivism with its linear, cause-effect thinking and more on relational, systemic beliefs. The contextual theories do not engage in the level of reductionism typically found in medico-positivist theories and are more concerned with contextual, sociohistorical, and sociopolitical influences on the individual. Because of the concerns elaborated above, there have been alternative conceptualizations of diagnostic criteria, with calls to increase the amount of social-cultural research in diagnostic formulas.

Although politically unsavvy, the social-cultural-contextual etiology of some perceived disorders needs to be clarified in the next *DSM* iteration. The *DSM* has begun to incorporate explicitly stated contextual issues, largely due to recent research and the political influence of family and ethnic therapists (e.g., Kaslow, 1996a, 1996b). For example, the introduction includes a one-page section on ethnic and cultural considerations, the Global Assessment of Relational Functioning Scale (GARF) is included in "Criteria Sets and Axes Provided for Further Study," and "Culture-Bound Syndromes" are included in the glossary. Furthermore, "Specific Culture Features" (including age and gender) are contained briefly throughout the *DSM*. Finally, specific diagnoses incorporate contextual factors, but the medical model still focuses on the individual for the source (and therefore change agent) of most of the disorders. These cultural sections of the *DSM* indicate an increased awareness of the need to consider cultural factors, but these issues are addressed in a limited manner.

Diagnostic Research with Underrepresented Populations

Much of the research on the diagnosis of various ethnic, gender, and class groups has pitted one category against the other (e.g., class vs. race) to determine the factor that accounts for the greatest amount of variance (Kessler & Neighbors, 1986). However, these cannot be considered distinct categories. For example, minority racio-ethnic groups, women, and the lower class share a lack of social, economic, and psychological power (Kaschak, 1992). As a general rule, people who are marginalized in society (less power; women, people of color, low financial means) receive mental illness diagnoses at a significantly greater rate than people who are considered to have more power (i.e., men, Euro-Americans, middle and upper classes) (Mirowsky, 1990). This result invokes the idea that a purpose of diagnosis is to maintain societal control over "deviant" individuals and serve a gatekeeping function (Brown, 1990), given that the behavior of ethnic minorities, women, and lower socioeconomic (SES) individuals is more likely to be viewed as deviating from White, middle-class, male norms (e.g., Hare-Mustin & Marecek, 1988). Lopez (1989) asserted that clinicians hold different base rates for acceptable ranges of behavior depending on race, class, and gender. In addition, Lipton and Simon (1985) found that clinicians' diagnostic styles differed and that most clinicians focused on a single symptom (i.e., hallucinations) when generating a diagnosis.

Evidence of cultural differences in diagnosis has been summarized by Solomon (1992) and Parker, Georgaca, Harper, McLaughlin, and Stowell-Smith (1995), although it is by no means a comprehensive summary:

(a)	Blacks and Hispanics are more likely than Whites to be diagnosed with affective or personality disorders or schizophrenia (instead of affective disorders),

(b)	African American children are more likely to be diagnosed as hyperactive than White and Asian American children,

(c)	lower-class children are more likely to be diagnosed with psychoses and character disorders than middle-class children,

(d)	racio-ethnic minorities are more likely than Whites to be diagnosed with chronic disorders rather than acute disorders,

(e)	adult White males have lower admission rates to outpatient psychiatric facilities than White women and non-White men and women,

(f)	African Americans are overrepresented in secure facilities (controlling for age, gender, and class),

(g)	Puerto Ricans use mental health services at a higher rate than non–Puerto Rican populations and have higher rates of schizophrenia and alcohol abuse than other populations, and

(h)	White males are more likely to have shorter stays in psychiatric hospitals than women and people of color.

An argument could be made that there are true differences between groups when any diagnostic comparisons are made. Much has been written on the predisposition of certain groups (e.g., lower social class) to nosological disorders (e.g., affective disorders, schizophrenia) (Draguns, 1997). In essence, social forces and other extrapsychic factors predispose individuals to "intrapsychic" problems. Kessler and Neighbors (1986) maintained that the effects of racio-ethnic heritage and class are not additive as most research indicates but interactive.

The empirical data on race, class and gender, and diagnosis are difficult to discern because most of studies investigated the factors as singular constructs. For example, Leaf and Bruce (1987) found that although specific psychiatric disorders differed for men and women, overall rates of disorders did not differ by gender. Landrine (1989) found that men and women are likely to be diagnosed with disorders consistent with their societal sex role stereotypes, and Rosenfield (1982) found that clients were more likely to be committed to mental hospitals if their behaviors were inconsistent with their sex roles. In addition, women are likely to receive diagnoses of dependent, histrionic, or borderline personality disorders, whereas men are likely to receive diagnoses of narcissistic and obsessive-compulsive personality disorders (Kaschak, 1992), both consistent with accepted social sex roles. It must be questioned to what extent diagnosis reflects distinction versus more deviance from behavior currently deemed socially acceptable.

SYMPTOM EXPRESSION AND WORLDVIEWS

When examining a diagnostic system, it is important to consider how worldviews influence or guide the criteria. The *DSM* taxonomic system relies on behavioral symptom expression as a primary means of categorizing individuals. Many marginalized people in the United States (and globally) exhibit symptoms considered atypical by many clinicians, and the interpretation of these symptoms is translated into diagnoses through the worldview of the clinician. Furthermore, many marginalized people possess worldviews that differ from those of the dominant culture in the United States (Ibrahim, 1991; Katz, 1985). Clinicians unfamiliar with the symptom expression and worldviews (e.g., beliefs about time, modes of action) of various marginalized groups or clinicians whose worldview conflicts with that of marginalized groups may tend to misdiagnose. For example, many authors (Canino, 1988; Kleinman & Good,

1985; Solomon, 1992) have discussed that Mexicans, Iraquis, and Asian Indians may somaticize complaints rather than express in Western affective terms (i.e., "my stomach hurts" vs. "I'm depressed"). As another example, Egeland, Hotsetter, and Eshleman (1983) found that pressured speech among the Amish may be considered a thought disorder, another indication of culturally appropriate behavioral expression misinterpreted as pathology.

An essential cultural consideration for counselors is how the self is conceptualized. The self can be viewed as sociocentric or egocentric, the latter forming the basis of the *DSM*. Sociocentric people view the self in relation to others, thereby creating an inseparable, fluid, and interconnected context (Comas-Díaz, 1992, 1996). Sociocentric cultures value harmony with the environment, cohesion, group identity, and cooperation and attain actualization through others (Twemlow, 1995). The egocentric self characterizes the self as autonomous, individualistic, and separate from others. Egocentric, typically Western industrialized cultures create competition, master the environment, and increase self-growth and self-worth through the individualized self. Persons in these cultures engage in dualistic thinking, which is consistent with the medical model of the *DSM* (Comas-Díaz, 1996). An example of a difference between egocentric and sociocentric worldviews is illustrated below.

A colleague recently recalled his surprise while working on a National Institute of Mental Health (NIMH) grant in Miami, Florida to examine childhood anxiety disorders. As part of his assessment process, he noticed that the Hispanic families consistently reported that their 10- to 12-year-old children were sleeping in the parents' beds, whereas children of White parents slept in their own rooms. He found enough evidence that this behavior was considered typical in the Hispanic families that he saw from interviews. Consider the dominant U.S. view of the self in relation to separation from family members. Normality in U.S. psychology calls for the child to eventually individuate and separate from the parents, usually at an early age. If this process does not occur during the "right" developmental stages, then it could be argued that the child may be experiencing "separation anxiety" (a diagnosis given to children developing in "unhealthy" ways). However, in Hispanic culture, it is not unusual for children to sleep with the parents until age 11 or 12. Views of appropriate child development may differ, particularly views of individuation of the self. If a therapist is unfamiliar with Hispanic cultures, then it would be easy to consider the family as enmeshed or the child as experiencing separation anxiety. Therefore, the clients may be labeled with a diagnostic disorder and in need of treatment. The colleague began to question his views of "normal" childhood development and its relationship to anxiety disorders. The diagnostic criteria he used were subsequently modified because of cultural differences. More research on these cultural differences may lead to altering our views of "normal" childhood systems and the effects of the family system. The following example illustrates the concepts of egocentrism and sociocentrism:

> I was called to complete an evaluation of a 13-year-old White young man from a lower SES family who was diagnosed with leukemia earlier that week and was on the adolescent ward at the local hospital. The physician reported that the young man was "depressed because he has leukemia" (egocentric) and that I should speak with him regarding further treatment, "to adjust to his disease." The young man presented as an individual who engaged me in conversation, was eating and sleeping poorly, and displayed some psychomotor agitation and fatigue. After a brief discussion, it became evident that although he was depressed because of the disease, the majority of his depression stemmed from his belief that his parents would be sad and that he was responsible for their grief (sociocentric) because he held a part-time job and contributed to his family's income. The brief treatment that followed was in a family format, with both parents and the young man adjusting to the disease and subsequent responsibility issues. Although the diagnosis of depression was accurate, the etiology was based on context and not the individual child. In this example, different conceptualizations of the same category, depression, can result in different approaches to treatment, either individual or family based.

Other worldview variations can occur when different cultural conceptualizations of time are misinterpreted. For example, minority clients are often stereotyped as resistive to treatment or lazy because "they have no respect for time constraints and often are late for or miss appointments" (Solomon, 1992, p. 375). To illustrate a business example, the senior author spent a short amount of time in Turkey a few years ago and discussed with some American businessmen their frustration toward the Turks for being "lazy, avoidant, and non-business-like." The Americans were losing business opportunities to the Iranians at that time. American business practices consisted of arriving in the city, proceeding directly to the meeting place, making the deals, and leaving the same day or very early the following day. Turkish business practices consisted of greeting the businessmen, taking them back to their homes, serving them tea (or the appropriate dish) at a leisurely pace, introducing the family, and taking the Americans to their hotel for rest prior to the next day's meeting. The Turks view time in a cyclical fashion, whereas the Americans view time in a linear manner. Many racio-ethnic minorities in the United States view time in a similar fashion, and marginalized persons often receive diagnostic labels due to time value differences, not a mental health deficit. Evidence indicates that clinicians often diagnose based on limited behavioral information and one factor (Lopez & Nunez, 1987) and tend to decontextualize individuals. The use of limited information to make judgments or evaluations of others is epitomized by the old psychoanalytic joke: If you arrive early for an appointment, you're dependent; if late, you're avoidant; if on time, you're compulsive. The individual cannot be accurately understood when the relationship to others and their culture is not considered.

As illustrated above, cultural considerations are important in the diagnostic process. Lonner and Ibrahim (1996) offered contextual questions to consider when identifying the cultural identity of clients. Furthermore, clinicians can contemplate the following questions adapted from Constantine (1997) when considering worldviews and identity issues:

1. Which extrapsychic variables (e.g., gender, race/ethnicity, SES) do I consider most important, and how do these make up my cultural identities?
2. What assumptions, biases, and values do I bring to the counseling session based on my cultural identities?
3. What value systems are inherent in my diagnostic approach?
4. What knowledge do I possess about clients whose worldviews and behavioral symptom expression differ from my own?
5. What kinds of struggles and challenges must I address when working with someone from another culture?

The recognition of the need for a contextualist approach to diagnosis led to the development of relational systems of diagnosis for analyzing and conceptualizing psychological distress. Some of these systems have included feminist

(Chesler, 1990), narrative (Susko, 1994), interpersonal (Benjamin, 1993; Leary, 1957), and relational schemes (Kaslow, 1996a). Each of these systems has under development diagnostic schemes that attempt to match the theoretical orientation to those following this approach. In addition, many of these approaches attempt to consider the cultural aspects of the individual and how these influences affect diagnostic considerations. The relational model will be discussed below because of recent political advances made by a member organization coalition to increase relational diagnoses in the *DSM* (Kaslow, 1996b). Individuals are changing the future of the *DSM* also. As a former president of the American Psychiatric Association stated, "I predict that the biggest changes in *DSM-V*—in a decade or so—will be in the area of personality disorders and family or systems (relationship) diagnoses" (McIntyre, 1993, p. 3). The *DSM*, therefore, should be considered as only one of many diagnostic classification systems, and its utility with marginalized people needs to be examined.

Relational System

The relational model of diagnostic classification gained widespread approval in the past few years, in part as a reaction to the *DSM*'s minimal commitment to sociocultural influences. The relational model is a sociocentric method of conceptualizing clients, which emphasizes contextual and cultural thinking and de-emphasizes linearity, individualism, and independence. The addition of greater relational or contextual perspectives when assessing clients leads to one of two conclusions. First, context may allow for less severe diagnoses because of enhanced understanding and predictability. Culture allows for more flexibility in thinking and acceptance in beliefs. Second, even when two clinicians arrive at the same diagnosis with and without significant context, the diagnosis may be more legitimate when implementing greater context because of the increased amount of cultural information. As discussed earlier, it is difficult to determine the effects of race, class, and gender on diagnostic processes, and it is recognized that processes differ depending on the clinician's skills, biases, and awareness of internal and external cultural matters. A more likely scenario is that the therapist focuses on one or two of these extrapsychic variables.

The relational model is also a process of diagnosing clients, with some relational authors advocating additions to the *DSM* (Kaslow, 1996b) and others choosing to disregard the *DSM* (Gergen, Hoffman, & Anderson, 1996). The

DSM is stated as atheoretical and nonetiological, whereas much of the literature of relational diagnosis discusses etiology. Clients are understood with greater depth when context is accounted for, and our belief is that less severe diagnoses are frequently given to clients when greater context is implemented into the diagnostic process. Culture has been included in the *DSM* but is generally afforded second-class status (e.g., V codes) or appendices (GARF; Culture-Bound Syndromes). In essence, culture is viewed epiphenomenally in the *DSM* and does not seem to offer clinicians and researchers a means to diagnose from a culturally contextualized or relational perspective.

The movement for the incorporation of organized family and relational issues into a diagnostic system began in the 1970s. During this time, a task force was formed to prepare materials to be included in the *DSM-III-R* because of concerns that relational aspects of disorders would be relegated to Axis V or ignored completely (Kaslow, 1996a). Despite the efforts made by the task force, little attention was given to relational aspects of disorders, and they remained in Axis V. Axis IV (psychosocial and environmental problems) diagnostic information is very useful, but we believe that much of this information should be incorporated directly into Axes I and II.

Although initial efforts of the task force were unsuccessful, new efforts were mounted for the inclusion of relational diagnosis in the *DSM-IV*. The mission statement of the task force formally outlined an opposition to the view of symptomology as a result of the individual being dysfunctional (Denton & Associates, 1989). It was further stated that this view directly contradicted approaches of the family therapist. Although philosophical variability occurs among family therapists, there is an underlying link in the importance of systems theory (Haley, 1976; Selvini-Palazzoli, Boscolo, Cecchin, & Prata, 1978). Modifications to the *DSM-IV* incorporated cultural aspects intended to be useful in family and relational work, specifically in the section "Other Conditions That May Be a Focus of Clinical Attention." The *DSM* does not, however, provide guidance about how these "Other Conditions" influence diagnosis. Although there is progress, the expansion of the *DSM* to include relational issues is limited.

For clinicians attempting to include relational and cultural aspects in diagnosis, ethical dilemmas will arise when operating within the currently accepted diagnostic system. The current system may force ethical clinicians into unethical behavior because insurance companies often do not view cultural, familial, social, and political aspects as being a valid focus of treatment. Therefore, the clinician may need to choose between the "correct" diagnosis and one currently available or one currently reimbursable. For example, many clinicians are caught between administering a diagnosis compatible with insurance reimbursement policies and wanting to furnish a less severe diagnosis that may not be reimbursable. Numerous examples exist in which clients are not accepted for treatment or not provided appropriate care because they failed to meet the insurance requirements. Miscommunication among professionals is another outcome of misdiagnosis done in the interest of receiving reimbursement from insurance companies and federal agencies. A purpose of any classification system, including the *DSM*, is "to facilitate research and improve communication among clinicians and researcher" (American Psychiatric Association, 1994, p. xv); therefore, the *DSM*'s role in the mental health system assists in misclassifying individuals because of its current emphasis on the medical philosophy.

Fortunately, the *DSM* does include some diagnoses that are contextually based. For example, oppositional defiant disorder is considered contextually, but research on other childhood disorders in the United States such as attention deficit hyperactivity disorder (ADHD) exudes a biochemical emphasis (Rabian, personal communication, 1997), almost to the exclusion of social and cultural factors. Recently, Culbertson and Sivlosky (1996) examined a nonchemical preference to the ADHD diagnosis stemming from U.S. social, contextual, and cultural norms instead of neurochemical foundations. Bauermeister, Berrios, Jimenez, Acevedo, and Gordon (1990) found that some symptomatic behaviors of ADHD in the United States are considered to be signs of healthy adjustment in Puerto Rico. Other diagnostic labels (e.g., social phobia, posttraumatic stress disorder) appropriately include context when making the diagnosis, but more work throughout the *DSM* needs to occur. Because the *DSM* is not etiologically based, the *DSM* framers "have demonstrated how tightly they cling to the outdated idea that emotional and behavioral problems occur within the vacuum of the individual" (Alexander & Pugh, 1996, p. 219). It is impossible to separate etiology from diagnosis from treatment even when using a taxonomic system considered atheoretical and nonetiological. Understanding the variables assessed in the diagnostic process is critical and involves exploring client cultural factors attended to, as well as clinician self-assessment of values and bias. The following factors need to be addressed by clinicians to increase their cultural awareness and the effects this awareness, or lack of it, has on diagnosis.

Factors to Consider

Base Rates

One method of understanding how culture and group membership may affect a clinician's judgment is to examine base rates held by clinicians. Base rates are "subjective probabilities that clinicians hold about specific patient groups having certain symptoms or disorders" (Lopez, 1989, p. 195). Differential base rates occur to separate or distinguish one group from another. The idea that women suffer from depression more than men or Blacks suffer from schizophrenia more than Whites are examples of differential base rates. Some studies have examined the use of differential base rates by clinicians to differentiate the occurrence of disorders in Mexican immigrants and Anglo Americans (Lopez, 1983), among different age populations (Wolkenstein & Lopez, 1988), and some studies have examined the base rates held by physicians concerning the psychological symptoms of men and women (Bernstein & Kane, 1981).

It is critical to examine the base rates under which one operates to determine if they represent biased clinical judgment. Studies examining the overdiagnosis and underdiagnosis of mental disorders indicate that clinicians hold different base rates for Blacks, females, lower socioeconomic class clients, and the mentally retarded than White middle-class males (Lopez, 1989). One must question if these differences in diagnosis actually represent differences among the groups or if they are related to a bias in judgment or evaluations. The determination of base rates needs to be grounded in empirical research. However, with the increased inclusion of cultural issues and other contextual considerations in research studies, it is possible that base rates may shift or be reformulated. No single factor, such as gender or race, should be the primary determinant when making a diagnosis, and it is important not only to understand and evaluate the base rates under which one operates but also to evaluate the accuracy or validity of these beliefs continually. Unfortunately, impressions concerning base rates exist even when evidence contradicts those impressions. It is easy to fall prey to social stereotypes even though one may be seemingly sensitive to them. However, the following case study is an example of how stereotypes can affect the diagnosis based on base rates. Each of the following case studies in this chapter includes individuals seen for treatment by the first author.

I recall a male client whom I saw a number of years ago in therapy. I contacted a colleague after the seventh session for a consultation because of a stagnating treatment and my frustration with the client. He was a 27-year-old, lower SES, third-generation Latino who had a history of abandonment issues and identity concerns. My client was a heavy drinker, held a number of jobs over the years, and received less than satisfactory job performance appraisals. He was contemplating suicide because of a failed relationship, and later reports indicated that he had attempted suicide on two occasions in the past (unbeknown to me at that time). His mood was generally stable in sessions, although anger was not atypical, and his job performance appraisals indicated fluctuating moods. As the reader may have deduced, the client fits the criteria for borderline personality disorder (BPD), although I had missed it. Fortunately, the consultant concluded this immediately. We discussed how I could have missed such a (now) seemingly easy diagnosis and talked about how I was not "looking for that." The crux of the discussion revolved around my (then) mental block regarding men and BPD and how I had usually considered persons with BPD to be Euro-American and female. My base rate was so decontextualized that I failed to see any deviation from my norm group. This incident forced me to rethink my level of awareness and biases regarding contextual issues, stereotypes, and my diagnostic process, even though I had considered myself to be sensitive to these issues. Since then, I have continued examining my roles and identities in social context more assertively, which has caused me to consider my social and cultural history closely. This example also illustrates the question of diagnostic bias.

Diagnostic Bias

Review of the therapist bias literature concludes that there is little evidence of bias, although data indicate that people in lower SES categories appear to consistently receive more frequent and severe diagnoses than individuals in other class levels (Abramowitz & Murray, 1983; Lopez, 1989; Smith, 1980).

However, this literature incorporated an old definition of bias, which is defined as a prejudgment or prejudice, usually of women, the elderly, and ethnic minorities. Lopez (1989) analyzed data using a broader definition of bias to analyze specific types of judgment separately (i.e., overdiagnosis and underdiagnosis) within both classification (diagnosis) and continuum (severity) judgments. He concluded that when the new definition is applied, there is almost twice as much evidence of diagnostic bias as previously believed. Economic class issues yielded the most powerful effect, specifically the lower class, with race showing diagnostic bias and gender difference showing inconsistent diagnostic and severity judgments. Therefore, client characteristics such as race, class, and gender are believed to mediate diagnostic hypotheses about individuals, which lead to systematic errors for some disorders and client groups. More generally, Loring and Powell (1988) found that more severe diagnoses are applied to clients who are perceived as different from the therapist.

Iwamasa, Larrabee, and Merritt (1995) found that African Americans are likely to receive the antisocial personality disorder diagnosis, whereas Native Americans were viewed as schizotypal and Asian Americans as schizoid. Numerous investigators (e.g., Loring & Powell, 1988) have found that both the clinician's and client's race and gender influence diagnoses. For example, Hispanics are more likely to be diagnosed as schizophrenic than non-Hispanics instead of bipolar affective disorder (Mukherjee, Shukla, & Woodle, 1983). Because diagnosis relies on clinical judgment, it is likely that stereotypes and other biases intrude into the assessment process (Lopez, 1989). Therefore, a clinician can benefit from a contextual and comprehensive approach to assessment to mitigate many unconscious biases.

Cultural Factors in the Diagnostic Process

A critical component of arriving at culturally sensitive diagnoses involves an exploration and understanding of one's own and the client's culture. Evaluation of culture and its impact on the client's problems begins in the assessment phase, with the goal of increasing the validity of the conceptualization of the client's issue and thus affecting diagnosis. According to Sinacore-Guinn (1995), including cultural considerations in client conceptualization involves examining four basic categories. Examples following each of the four categories were drawn from Brown (1986), Comas-Díaz (1994, 1996), Jacobsen (1988), and Westermeyer (1993). The categories consist of (a) cultural systems and structures, (b) cultural values, (c) gender socialization, and (d) the effects of trauma. First, cultural systems and structures include factors such as racio-ethnic identities, history of (im)migration and generation from (im)migration, family of origin and multigenerational history, family scripts, and individual and family life cycle development. For example, Sinacore-Guinn indicated that clients attempting to function in two different cultures exhibit natural difficulties that may be misdiagnosed as a mental illness (e.g., adjustment disorder) instead of a "problem-in-living" (Dana, 1993).

Second, cultural values influence the perception of normality and abnormality. Kluckhohn and Strodtbeck (1961) indicated that cultures share the values of time (past, present, future), activity (doing, being, being-in-becoming), relational orientation (individual, communal, hierarchical), person-nature orientation (harmony, control, subjugation), and nature of people (good, bad, combination). For example, some lower SES Turks and Mexican Americans share a strong belief in *Mal ojo,* or the evil eye (Dana, 1993), which bestows on the person a sense of powerlessness (subjugation) and is contrary to many middle-class psychological theories that emphasize "control." Some Western therapists may view this belief as delusional if a thorough understanding of the relationship of cultures to external forces is not fully understood.

Third, gender socialization includes gender roles, sexual orientation, and gender-specific issues such as "battered wife syndrome." It is possible that clinicians unfamiliar with the similarities between homosexual and heterosexual relationships may de-emphasize partner-relational problems and emphasize a more individualistic diagnosis. Finally, the effects of trauma include issues such as the history of trauma (individual, collective), multigenerational oppression, and geopolitical history with the dominant group. For example, Paniagua (1994) discussed unique clinical issues when working with Southeast Asian (instead of Asian American and Pacific Islanders) clients regarding the possible trauma experienced in their homelands. For example, many Southeast Asian clients "come to therapy with a history of torture, killing of loved ones, missing family members, witnessed killing, and sexual abuse acts" (p. 65). An understanding of geopolitical influences on a Southeast Asian client will aid the clinician in the diagnostic process. Paniagua recommends avoiding statements or questions regarding traumatic events in the first session, but an assessment of suicide, depression, and organic brain syndrome should be completed.

In-depth awareness of the intrapersonal and interpersonal factors contributing to diagnosis will lead to more accurate and appropriate diagnosis. Clinician self-evaluation is critical, and clinicians need to examine their initial reactions to and assumptions about clients and how the behaviors or symptoms of the client may be evaluated differently based on cultural issues. Consider the following brief scenario and the questions:

> On greeting a client for the first time, a clinician notices that the client does not make direct eye contact, does not shake hands, and says hello in a mumbled voice that is barely audible. The client then walks behind the clinician to the office, looking at the ground the entire way, and sits down in the chair without once looking at the clinician.

Questions:

1. Is your working hypothesis that the client is a man or a woman? Where does this information come from?
2. Is your working hypothesis stemming from some form of pathology or health? Where did this idea originate, and is there evidence for your choice at this point?
3. Would your beliefs change if the client were a male versus a female (or vice versa)?
4. Would you view the behaviors differently if the client were African American, Hispanic, Asian, or White?
5. If you viewed the client differently depending on racio-ethnicity, did cultural context allow for more "normalizing" behaviors or offer more validity to your choice?
6. Does the person seem very different from you?
7. What are your initial reactions based on? Is there a rationale or support for these reactions or assumptions?
8. How do your own personal values, culture, and beliefs affect these judgments?
9. Is there a single factor, such as race or gender, that is over- or underinfluencing your evaluation of the client?

You have now seen the client for 20 minutes. Are you attempting to confirm your earlier hypotheses, or have they changed significantly?

Earlier, we said that incorporating more contextual information in the diagnostic process may decrease the perceived severity of the diagnosis or will add more validity to the diagnosis. Described below are examples that incorporate race, class, and gender variables. The first will focus on a less severe diagnosis given contextual variables, and the second describes a case in which the diagnosis and treatment were altered after context was taken into account.

I was called to conduct a commitment evaluation on a client who had recently attempted suicide. She had been involved with the mental health system briefly and was diagnosed by a White male physician as a schizophrenic, undifferentiated type. The only information received from the psychiatrist was her diagnosis and the fact that there was a suicide attempt. The client was a 28-year-old, low SES, Euro-American woman with a ninth-grade education and average verbal skills. She was a bit shaken, but her speech was organized, and she was coherent. She could be considered a fundamentalist in her religious beliefs, had three children, and considered herself to function in a traditional manner with regard to her family, sexuality, roles, and friends. She had had difficulty sleeping, eating, and concentrating since "the incident" with her husband 3 days earlier. The referent "incident" was that she awakened about 3:00 a.m. and found her husband masturbating to pornographic videotapes. Her identity as a Christian, woman, wife, mother, and individual was shattered because she considered pornography and masturbation as sinful and believed that she had not fulfilled her "duties" as a wife. Because of her initial crisis, she began praying and both saw and spoke to her sister who had died 2 years earlier. My client informed me that some people may perceive her as being "crazy" but that the vision actually occurred. All symptoms of schizophrenia except for the "hallucination" were negative. Furthermore, she failed to meet the criteria because schizophrenic symptoms must be manifested for 6 months, and the hallucination was ego-syntonic. Also, she did not qualify for schizophreniform disorder because of the less than 1-month duration of her symptoms, even with good prognostic features. I began to consider the religious differences between us, as well as my perception of normality between where I grew up and my geographic area now.

Prior to moving to the South, I may have considered her to be a person with schizophrenia who was maintained due to medications or some transient factor. However, having an understanding of "Southern culture" and its complex relationship with religious depth, I have now come to see certain "hallucinations" or visions as within my realm of acceptance as normal. Numerous anecdotal accounts indicate that it is acceptable for an African American woman to have experienced "visions" when spiritually close to the church, without severe (or any) diagnosis (Solomon, 1992). In fact, many religiously and spiritually devout people consider it common. Why, then, could this not occur with a Euro-American woman?

After further discussion, it was concluded that the physician had not considered her cultural background and had not followed the *DSM* criteria closely. In many cultures and religions, usually described as "non-Western," people have different ways of expressing grief, including what might be termed "hallucinations" or "hearing voices" by Westerners. Thus, her expression of grief may be culturally "normal." Furthermore, dysfunction and abnormality are not equated concepts. Any system that diagnoses without considering cultural, social, and political realities and is based on the dominant culture is inherently ethnocentric. In my view, she did not meet the criteria for major depression with psychotic features (even if she had met the required 2 weeks' duration). She also did not meet the criteria for acute stress disorder or any other "severe" disorder. Because I was confined to the *DSM,* I could choose either a depressive disorder not otherwise specified, adjustment disorder with depressed mood, or the V code, partner-relational problem. Any of these diagnoses would have had a better social and personal prognosis than schizophrenia, undifferentiated type. I was uncomfortable with the first two diagnoses because of their reliance on the individual as the inflicted party, particularly because she fit the adjustment disorder with depressed mood category well. However, my contextual approach leaned toward the partner-relational problem because of its reliance on her immediate family and her macrocultural influences. Fortunately, insurance reimbursement was not an issue.

Some therapists may disagree with my diagnosis if they closely follow the *DSM* categories. In my estimation, the partner-relational problem was the "healthiest" diagnosis and the one with the best prognosis because it curtails a pathological focus. It also took the onus of sole responsibility off of the individual client and placed it within the context of the family and church. However, although the healthiest diagnosis was partner-relational problem and the clinician may treat the client(s) as such, this diagnosis may not have been the best for the client. Many clients cannot afford counseling unless their insurance company or Medicaid reimburses the clinician. Most of the "less severe" diagnoses are not typically reimbursed; thus, the clinician providing a "less severe" diagnosis may overestimate the client's possibility of receiving services.

Mirowsky and Ross (1989) asserted that the process of diagnosis assumes four steps: (a) assessing the degree of symptoms and impaired functioning, (b) splitting the degree into two categories that either meet or do not meet the criteria, (c) tabulating the criteria, and (d) excluding cases that meet other criteria considered consummate (e.g., grief from major depression). When following the *DSM* or other existing nosological systems, culture is viewed as epiphenomenal and not central to the assessment procedure. A reason I opted for partner-relational problem instead of a more severe diagnosis was due to my emphasis on culture prior to step one. Severity of impaired functioning and symptom level are perceptually and thereby culturally based; thus, the following three steps are functionally mediated from a healthier perspective. Without cultural context, symptoms and functioning are viewed through the only lens available. Temerlin (1968) discussed the social psychology of clinical diagnosis or the effect of suggestion on whether the clinician saw psychopathology. The author concluded that the idea of a client arriving for treatment connotes to the clinician to look for pathology. It seems reasonable that if training programs emphasize cultural influences of the client and counselor to a greater extent, then the number of seemingly severe diagnoses will decrease. An example of these issues is given below.

Because of my experience with court-referred clients, I was asked to consult on a case in which the counselor, a 31-year-old White middle-class male, was seeing a low SES, 17-year-old African American man for treatment. The client was court referred for vandalizing his school after being suspended for fighting and was "highly resistive to treatment," according to the therapist. Three weeks earlier, the therapist diagnosed the young man as having conduct disorder, adolescent onset, severe. The *DSM-IV* indicates that the diagnosis of conduct disorder should be given "when the behavior in question is symptomatic of an underlying dysfunction within the individual and not simply a reaction to the immediate social context" (American Psychiatric Association, 1994, p. 88). It seems that unless one considers conduct disorder to be a manifestation of an underlying biological consideration, then it has to fall within the realm of a sociocontextual influence.

After further discussion with the therapist, it was determined that the client was one of six children, had not been in trouble with the law previously, had adequate grades, was sexually active, and smoked marijuana periodically. When queried about his family, the therapist indicated that the mother was "domineering" and recently divorced his father. The therapist was interested in how treatment might progress and mentioned that he was sensitive to cultural issues. However, when asked what some of these issues might be, he identified the obvious differences such as race, education, SES, and age but could not discuss these in detail. Further questioning of the therapist led to discussions about the client's possible history of racism and classism (although unidentified at this point), racial identity and its relationship to the therapist, and the therapist's initial views of the client. It was determined that the therapist's initial views consisted of stereotypes, which were "confirmed" by the counselor's recollection of selected criteria such as the client's "resistive" behavior, drug use, vandalism, and the mother being "domineering." He recognized positive aspects of the young man but did not give these positive traits and behaviors equal weight when considering a diagnosis. We then discussed possible culturally related process issues such as cultural mistrust, interpersonal style differences, power issues, the mother being redefined as assertive, and the perception that the therapist may be viewed as maintaining the status quo because of therapy being viewed as court-appointed punishment. We also discussed issues surrounding diagnosing someone who had similar behavioral patterns but was a Black female or a White male.

> After 3 more weeks of treatment, we reconvened to discuss the
> case, and I offhandedly asked what the counselor's diagnosis was,
> allegedly "forgetting" the previous diagnosis. The therapist
> informed me that when considering more contextual and relational
> factors, the client was viewed less diagnostically severe. We
> discussed the idea of an "adjustment disorder with disturbance of
> conduct" along with an anxiety disorder the client displayed. The
> therapist indicated that his original diagnosis would be maintained
> had the client been a White male but not a Black male or a Black
> female. This disclosure led to further discussions on class, race, and
> gender issues and on the power of diagnosing to treatment and its
> relationship to the counselor's culture. Many therapists may have
> considered an adjustment disorder to be the primary diagnosis
> initially, but this example delineates the influence that previous
> cultural myopic learning has on accurately assessing, diagnosing,
> and treating clients.

These are two examples of how issues that on the surface appear negative
may be reframed as positive or adaptive when cultural factors are taken into account (i.e., the cultural mistrust of the young man may initially be viewed as resistance but can also be perceived as understandable when cultural factors are
considered).

FUTURE DIRECTIONS AND RECOMMENDATIONS

To understand the future directions of the *DSM* and diagnosis, one must understand the current philosophy and politics that underlie the present system. It has
been well documented that science is rooted in philosophy, and the philosophy
of the *DSM* is a medico-deductive system. There is nothing wrong with that system except that it is inherently limiting because of its emphasis on individualism. At the present time, the philosophical underpinnings of a relational, multicultural, contextual approach are equally limited because they are vaguely (and
not reliably) defined. Therefore, we would not expect the *DSM* to include culture as a central focus of diagnosis presently because if the philosophy is vague,
the product becomes vague. However, we do believe that the *DSM* can be more

culturally specific than it is currently, and it is hoped that future revisions of the *DSM* will include context as a central theme. The present medical philosophy underlying the *DSM* is changing as more clinicians and physicians recognize the limiting factors inherent in any one belief system. Our concern, however, is the influence of politics and the business ethic on the future diagnosis and treatment of human beings. Numerous authors (e.g., Caplan, 1995) have indicated that the *DSM* is a political document fraught with negotiating and campaigning. Although some diagnoses are based on good clinical research, many are not. A business ethic continues to drive portions of the mental health care system in the United States. Clinicians often are caught giving inaccurate diagnoses to be paid, and pharmaceutical companies offer financial support for the medicalization of psychological issues. In many cases, this is money well spent. However, the balance between medical and nonmedical approaches has yet to be achieved.

Often, the *DSM* authors are caught in a difficult situation because of a lack of good research in numerous classification areas. The enhanced study of the differences between treatment efficacy and effectiveness could increase the specificity in clinical diagnostic criteria. Furthermore, more clinical studies are needed combining alleged diagnostic labels to determine productive treatment outcome. For example, it is likely that clients arrive with multiple diagnoses, but much of the treatment literature delineates treatment for one specific category. A recent client of the first author indicated symptoms on a well-known anxiety checklist consistent with panic disorder with agoraphobia, social phobia, and posttraumatic stress characteristics. Some researchers have combined these clinical categories in their research projects, but more research is needed that crosses these diagnostic categories to examine the relationship between them. Furthermore, more international classification research is needed to determine universal versus culture-bound diagnostic syndromes. For example, the vegetative symptoms for schizophrenia appear consistent internationally (Draguns, 1997), whereas anorexia is found in only a few Westernized societies. More research funding also is needed to examine diagnostic criteria from multiple philosophies, including family, feminist, and multicultural positions. In addition, more research using qualitative methodologies can offer valuable insight into our understanding of mental health and disorders. The future of the *DSM* must include greater input from diverse organizations. It is hoped that the American Psychological Association, the American Psychiatric Association, and other organizations (e.g., the American Association of Marriage and Family Therapists, multicultural groups) meet among themselves, along with business leaders (e.g., pharmaceutical companies, insurance companies) and political organizations to work toward a unified goal of accurate assessment and diagnosis. Philosophical and practical changes to the *DSM* are unlikely to be made from a bottom-up perspective, and federal government financial initiatives may need to be considered bringing business, educational, and political groups together before significant changes can occur.

Changing how diagnoses are made also requires changes in educational settings. Educators are in a unique position to alter traditional means of teaching diagnosis in course work. It is recommended that these instructors have a firm foundation in cultural issues prior to course instruction. First, instructors can include vignettes or videotapes depicting symptoms of a particular disorder and then ask questions that vary the race, ethnicity, gender, or class of the individual. Personal biases, multiple criteria, and cultural knowledge can be discussed prior to initiating a diagnosis. These types of exercises can help the student to understand different cultural issues and their influence on diagnosis. For example, I teach a practicum in which graduate students must read a brief vignette; answer questions that tap into their assumptions, theoretical orientation, and treatment plan; and then diagnose the client. These are altered by the factors listed above. What I have found is that diagnoses change sometimes when context is taken into account. When diagnoses do not change, the students have greater justification for the ones they make.

Second, information on base rates can be presented along with conceptual articles on which base rates are well grounded and which rates may be motivated by other means. Third, the relational model can be presented along with the *DSM* in teaching and using diagnosis, examining the similarities and differences between the two models. Although the *DSM* is used by most third-party payers, a relational scheme offers a greater contextual framework from which to diagnose. Practitioners taught with a relational model may assess using greater context, thus adding validity to the *DSM* diagnostic criteria. Finally, educators can include articles critiquing the *DSM* (and relational or other models) and its relationship to the mental health field. Balance should be strived for, with students determining the efficacy of their beliefs. Regardless of the method of teaching a diagnostic schema, new systems must come from the faculty, a top-down approach.

CONCLUSION

Procedures for diagnosing are complex and connected to social, political, and cultural factors of both the counselor and client. Although the framers of the past two iterations of the *DSM* have made strides to include more contextual factors, the existing classification system is limited in its reliability and validity and will remain so until the above recommendations are implemented. The relational model was discussed to assist in adding context to the *DSM* and illustrated through case studies. The relational model allows the clinician to consider additional factors when making a diagnosis such as sociocultural history, religion, and gender socialization to obtain an improved representation of the client. It is believed that inclusion of these factors may lead to enhanced diagnostic validity.

Note

1. Although technically not equivalent in meaning, the terms *contextual, cultural,* and *relational* will be used interchangeably.

References

Abramowitz, S. I., & Murray, J. (1983). Race effects in psychotherapy. In J. Murray & P. R. Abramson (Eds.), *Bias in psychotherapy* (pp. 215-255). New York: Academic Press.

Albee, G. W. (1990). The futility of psychotherapy. *Journal of Mind and Behavior, 11,* 369-384.

Alexander, J. F., & Pugh, C. A. (1996). Oppositional behavior and conduct disorders in children and youth. In F. W. Kaslow (Ed.), *Handbook of relational diagnosis and dysfunctional family patterns* (pp. 210-224). New York: John Wiley.

American Psychiatric Association. (1994). *Diagnostic and statistical manual of mental disorders* (4th ed.). Washington, DC: Author.

Barney, K. (1994). Limitations of the critique of the medical model. *Journal of Mind and Behavior, 15,* 19-34.

Bauermeister, J. J., Berrios, V., Jimenez, A. C., Acevedo, L., & Gordon, M. (1990). Some issues and instruments for the assessment of attention-deficit hyperactivity disorder in Puerto Rican children. *Journal of Child Clinical Psychology, 19,* 9-16.

Benjamin, L. S. (1993). *Interpersonal diagnosis and treatment of personality disorders.* New York: Guilford.

Bernstein, B., & Kane, R. (1981). Physicians' attitudes towards female patients. *Medical Care, 19,* 600-608.

Blashfield, R. K. (1984). *The classification of psychotherapy: Neo-Kraepelinian and quantitative approaches.* New York: Plenum.

Brown, L. S. (1986). Gender-role analysis: A neglected component of psychological assessment. *Psychotherapy, 23,* 243-248.

Brown, P. (1990). The name game: Toward a sociology of diagnosis. *Journal of Mind Behavior, 15,* 385-406.

Canino, I. (1988). The clinical assessment of the transcultural child. In C. Kestenbaum & D. Williams (Eds.), *Clinical assessment of children and adolescents* (pp. 1024-1042). New York: New York University Press.

Caplan, P. J. (1995). *They say you're crazy.* Reading, MA: Addison-Wesley.

Chesler, P. (1990). Twenty years since women and madness: Toward a feminist institute of mental health and healing. *Journal of Mind and Behavior, 11,* 313-322.

Comas-Díaz, L. (1992). The future of psychotherapy with ethnic minorities. *Psychotherapy, 29,* 88-94.

Comas-Díaz, L. (1994). An integrative approach. In L. Comas-Díaz & B. Greene (Eds.), *Women of color: Integrating ethnic and gender identities in psychotherapy* (pp. 347-388). New York: Basic Books.

Comas-Díaz, L. (1996). Cultural considerations in diagnosis. In F. W. Kaslow (Ed.), *Handbook of relational diagnosis and dysfunctional family pattern* (pp. 152-170). New York: John Wiley.

Constantine, M. G. (1997). Facilitating multicultural competency in counseling supervision: Operationalizing a practical framework. In D. B. Pope-Davis & H. L. K. Coleman (Eds.), *Multicultural counseling competencies* (pp. 310-324). Thousand Oaks, CA: Sage.

Culbertson, J. L., & Sivlosky, J. F. (1996). Learning disabilities and conduct disorders of children and youth. In F. W. Kaslow (Ed.), *Handbook of relational diagnosis and dysfunctional family patterns* (pp. 186-210). New York: John Wiley.

Dana, R. H. (1993). *Multicultural assessment perspectives for professional psychology.* Boston: Allyn & Bacon.

Denton, W., & Associates. (1989). *Rationale for the inclusion of relational disorders with DSM-IV.* Photocopy paper, Coalition on Family Diagnosis.

Draguns, J. G. (1996). Humanly universal and culturally distinctive: Charting the course of cultural counseling. In P. B. Pedersen, J. G. Draguns, W. J. Lonner, & J. E. Trimble (Eds.), *Counseling across cultures* (pp. 1-20). Thousand Oaks, CA: Sage.

Draguns, J. G. (1997). Abnormal behavioral patterns across cultures: Implications for counseling and psychotherapy. *International Journal of Intercultural Relations, 21*(2), 213-248.

Egeland, J. A., Hostetter, A. M., & Eshleman, S. K., III. (1983). Amish study: III. The impact of cultural factors on diagnosis of bipolar illness. *American Journal of Psychiatry, 140,* 67-71.

Endicott, J., & Spitzer, R. L. (1972). What! Another rating scale? The psychiatric evaluation form. *Journal of Nervous and Mental Disease, 154,* 88-104.

Fabrega, H. (1992). The role of culture in a theory of psychiatric illness. *Social Science in Medicine, 35,* 91-103.

Fabrega, H. (1994). International system of diagnosis in psychiatry. *Journal of Nervous and Mental Disease, 182,* 356-363.

Farber, S. (1990). Institutional mental health and social control: The ravages of epistomological hubris. *Journal of Mind and Behavior, 11*(3-4), 285-299.

Gara, M. A., Rosenberg, S., & Goldberg, L. (1992). *DSM-III-R* as a taxonomy: A cluster analysis of diagnosis and symptoms. *Journal of Nervous and Mental Disease, 180,* 11-19.

Gergen, K. J., Hoffman, L., & Anderson, H. (1996). Is diagnosis a disaster? A constructivist trialogue. In F. W. Kaslow (Ed.), *The handbook of relational diagnosis and dysfunctional family patterns* (pp. 102-118). New York: John Wiley.

Haley, J. (1976). *Problem-solving therapy.* New York: Harper & Row.

Hare-Mustin, R., & Marecek, J. (1988). The meaning of differences: Gender theory, postmodernism and psychology. *American Psychologist, 43,* 455-464.

Ibrahim, F. A. (1991). Contribution of cultural worldview to generic counseling and development. *Journal of Counseling and Development, 70,* 13-19.

Iwamasa, G. Y., Larrabee, A. L., & Merritt, R. D. (1995, August). *Are personality disorders ethnically and gender biased?* Poster presented at the annual meeting of the American Psychological Association, New York.

Jacobs, D. H. (1994). Environmental failure-oppression is the only cause of psychopathology. *Journal of Mind and Behavior, 15,* 1-18.

Jacobsen, F. M. (1988). Ethnocultural assessment. In L. Comas-Díaz & E. H. E. Griffith (Eds.), *Clinical guidelines in cross-cultural mental health* (pp. 135-147). New York: John Wiley.

Kaschak, E. (1992). *Engendered lives.* Boston: Basic Books.

Kaslow, F. W. (1996a). *Handbook of relational diagnosis and dysfunctional family patterns.* New York: John Wiley.

Kaslow, F. W. (1996b). History, rationale, and philosophic overview of issues and assumptions. In F. W. Kaslow (Ed.), *Handbook of relational diagnosis and dysfunctional family patterns* (pp. 3-18). New York: John Wiley.

Katz, J. H. (1985). The sociopolitical nature of counseling. *The Counseling Psychologist, 13,* 615-624.

Kessler, R. C., & Neighbors, H. W. (1986). A new perspective on the relationships among race, social class, and psychological distress. *Journal of Health and Social Behavior, 27,* 107-115.

Kirk, S. A., & Kutchins, H. (1992). *The selling of the DSM: The rhetoric of science in psychiatry.* New York: Guilford.

Kirk, S. A., & Kutchins, H. (1994). The myth and reliability of the *DSM. Journal of Mind and Behavior, 15,* 55-71.

Kleinman, A., & Good, B. (1985). *Culture and depression.* Berkeley: University of California Press.

Klerman, G. L. (1989). Psychiatric diagnostic categories: Issues of validity and measurement. *Journal of Health and Social Behavior, 30,* 26-32.

Kluckhohn, F. R., & Strodtbeck, F. L. (1961). *Variations in value orientation.* Evanston, IL: Row, Patterson.

Kutchins, H., & Kirk, S. (1988). The business of diagnosis: *DSM-III* and clinical social work. *Social Work, 33*(3), 215-220.

Landrine, H. (1989). The politics of personality disorder. *Psychology of Women Quarterly, 13,* 325-340.

Leaf, P. J., & Bruce, M. L. (1987). Gender differences in the use of mental health-related services: A re-examination. *Journal of Health and Social Behavior, 28,* 2-15.

Leary, T. (1957). *Interpersonal diagnosis of personality.* New York: Ronald.

Lewis-Fernandez, R., & Kleinman, A. (1994). Culture, personality, and psychopathology. *Journal of Abnormal Psychology, 103*(1), 67-71.

Lipton, A. A., & Simon, F. S. (1985). Psychiatric diagnosis in a state hospital: Manhattan State revisited. *Hospital and Community Psychiatry, 36,* 368-373.

Lonner, W. J., & Ibrahim, F. A. (1996). Appraisal and assessment in cross-cultural counseling. In P. B. Pedersen, J. G. Draguns, W. J. Lonner, & J. E. Trimble (Eds.), *Counseling across cultures* (pp. 293-322). Thousand Oaks, CA: Sage.

Lopez, S., & Nunez, J. A. (1987). Cultural factors considered on selected diagnostic criteria and interview schedules. *Journal of Abnormal Psychology, 96,* 270-272.

Lopez, S. R. (1983). *Ethnic bias in clinical judgement: An attributional analysis.* Unpublished doctoral dissertation, University of California, Los Angeles.

Lopez, S. R. (1989). Patient variable biases in clinical judgement: Conceptual overview and methodological considerations. *Psychological Bulletin, 106,* 184-203.

Loring, M., & Powell, B. (1988). Gender, race and *DSM-III*: A study of the objectivity of psychiatric diagnostic behavior. *Journal of Health and Social Behavior, 29,* 1-22.

McIntyre, J. (1993). Some highlights of APA's annual meeting. *Psychiatric News, 28,* 3.

Mirowsky, J. (1990). Subjective boundaries and combinations in psychiatric diagnosis. *Journal of Mind and Behavior, 11,* 407-424.

Mirowsky, J., & Ross, C. E. (1989). Psychiatric diagnosis as a refined measurement. *Journal of Health and Social Behavior, 30,* 11-25.

Mukherjee, S., Shukla, S., & Woodle, J. (1983). Misdiagnosis of schizophrenia in bipolar patients: A multiethnic comparison. *American Journal of Psychiatry, 140,* 1571-1574.

Paniagua, F. A. (1994). *Assessing and treating culturally diverse clients.* Thousand Oaks, CA: Sage.

Parker, I., Georgaca, E., Harper, D., McLaughlin, T., & Stowell-Smith, M. (1995). *Deconstructing psychopathology.* London: Sage.

Rosenfield, S. (1982). Sex roles and societal reactions to mental illness: Labeling a deviant deviance. *Journal of Health and Social Behavior, 23,* 18.

Sarbin, T. R. (1990). Toward the obsolescence of the schizophrenia hypothesis. *Journal of Mind and Behavior, 11,* 259-284.

Selvini-Palazzoli, M., Boscolo, L., Cecchin, G., & Prata, G. (1978). *Paradox and counterparadox.* Northvale, NJ: Jason Aronson.

Sinacore-Guinn, A. L. (1995). The diagnostic window: Culture- and gender-sensitive diagnosis and training. *Counselor Education and Supervision, 35,* 18-31.

Smith, D., & Kraft, W. A. (1983). *DSM-III:* Do psychologists really want an alternative? *American Psychologist, 38,* 777-785.

Smith, M. L. (1980). Sex bias in counseling and psychotherapy. *Psychological Bulletin, 87,* 392-407.

Solomon, A. (1992). Clinical diagnosis among diverse populations: A multicultural perspective. *Journal of Contemporary Human Services, 73,* 371-377.

Spitzer, R. L., Endicott, J., Fleiss, J. L., & Cohen, J. (1970). The psychiatric status schedule: Properties of factor-analytically derived scales. *Archives of General Psychiatry, 16,* 479-493.

Susko, M. A. (1994). Caseness and narrative: Contrasting approaches to people who are psychiatrically labeled. *Journal of Mind and Behavior, 15,* 87-112.

Swartz, M., Carroll, B., & Blazer, D. (1989). In response to "Psychiatric diagnosis as reified measurement." *Journal of Health and Social Behavior, 30,* 33-34.

Szasz, T. (1990). Law and psychiatry: The problem that will not go away. *Journal of Mind and Behavior, 11*(3-4), 557-572.

Temerlin, M. K. (1968). Suggestions effects in psychiatric diagnosis. *Journal of Nervous and Mental Disease, 147,* 349-353.

Twemlow, S. W. (1995). *DSM-IV* from a cross-cultural perspective. *Psychiatric Annuals, 25,* 46-52.

Westermeyer, J. (1987). Cultural factors in clinical assessment. *Journal of Consulting and Clinical Psychology, 55,* 471-478.

Westermeyer, J. (1993). Cross-cultural psychiatric assessment. In A. Gaw (Ed.), *Culture, ethnicity, and mental illness* (pp. 125-144). Washington, DC: American Psychiatric Press.

Wilson, M. (1993). *DSM-III* and the transformation of American psychiatry: A history. *American Journal of Psychiatry, 150,* 399-410.

Wolkenstein, B. H., & Lopez, S. (1988, August). *Underlying social cognitive processes of age bias in clinical judgement.* Paper presented at the annual meeting of the American Psychological Association, Atlanta, GA.

CHAPTER 16

ADVOCACY
IN COUNSELING

Addressing Race, Class, and Gender Oppression

Rebecca L. Toporek
University of Maryland

William M. Liu
University of Iowa

Counseling psychology has been criticized for its individualistic focus, neglect of the sociopolitical realities of clients, and reinforcement of current power structures in society (Kantrowitz & Ballou, 1992; Prilleltensky, 1997; Sarason, 1981; Sue, 1981). Detrimental effects of these conditions on people of color, women, the economically disadvantaged, and others in society with limited institutional power have been hypothesized to contribute to attrition in therapy, misaligned therapy goals, or feelings of alienation in clients (Ridley, 1995; Sue, 1977; Terrel & Terrel, 1984).

Those in feminist and multicultural counseling have challenged the limitations of the traditional client-counselor relationship and advanced the role of advocacy as an important and often necessary expansion of counseling professional roles (Atkinson, Thompson, & Grant, 1993; Enns, 1993; Esquivel & Keitel, 1990; Grevious, 1985; Sodowsky, Kuo-Jackson, & Loya, 1996).

Sodowsky et al. (1996) posited that advocacy and political activism on behalf of clients are critical components in the philosophical foundation of multicultural counseling. They further stated that multicultural competency requires that counseling professionals "be willing to integrate a component of political advocacy for minority populations into their professional identity" (p. 18). Similarly, Atkinson and Thompson (1992) suggested that counselors must develop their own political consciousness and that

> attaining a commitment to dismantling oppression as it affects all groups, reminds us of the need of psychology professionals to "leave their desks" and assume direct responsibility as change agents rather than simply functioning as purveyors of conventional services in the context of troubled environments. (p. 371)

The charge to consider new roles for counselors asserts advocacy as appropriate and necessary. The need for this new role, in part, may be a reflection of an increasing awareness of the complexity of our clients and the contextual variables that unavoidably affect their mental health and growth. Race, class, and gender represent dimensions of complex identities that clients bring to us. In addition, it is important that practice acknowledges and addresses clients' experiences of their environment and the potential oppression resulting from society's devaluation of certain race, class, gender, and other groups.

The purpose of this chapter is to begin a discussion of the changing role of counselors and psychologists, particularly the role of advocate in relation to oppression based on race, class, and gender. This chapter will examine advocacy as a continuum encompassing the related concepts of empowerment and social action. As envisioned, these roles are driven by experiences with clients and specific client issues.

We will set the foundation for our discussion by presenting a brief historical perspective of advocacy in counseling as it relates to gender, race, and class. A review of the status of advocacy in ethical guidelines and counselor training also will provide an introduction to some current challenges and dilemmas, such as the potential for conflicts with traditional counseling values, client dependency, unclear boundaries, paternalism, and politicizing counseling. Finally, case examples will help to demonstrate the holistic approach that may be taken by counselors and psychologists to address intrapsychic issues as well as external sociopolitical barriers clients may face.

Definitions: Advocacy, Empowerment, and Social Action in the Context of Race, Class, and Gender Issues

In recent years, the term *advocacy* has been increasingly used to refer to action taken in support of counseling and psychology as professions rather than advocacy of specific client issues. For our purposes, we are considering advocacy as the action a mental health professional, counselor, or psychologist takes in assisting clients and client groups to achieve therapy goals through participating in clients' environments. Advocacy may be seen as an array of roles that counseling professionals adopt in the interest of clients, including empowerment, advocacy, and social action.

Advocacy is action taken by counseling professionals to facilitate the removal of external and institutional barriers to clients' well-being. An essential component of our definition for this chapter encompasses the description of client advocacy given by Lewis, Lewis, Daniels, and D'Andrea (1998) as an indirect service aimed at strengthening socially devalued populations and working toward creating responsive helping networks. The objective of advocacy in this definition is to strengthen the impact of the individual and group by increasing their independence or interdependence and thereby their effectiveness. Lewis and Lewis (1983) distinguished between *case advocacy* as advocacy on behalf of individuals and *class advocacy* as attacks on the social, legal, economic, and governmental policies that discriminate against members of the population being served. They described three types of advocacy: (a) "here-and-now advocacy," which is a response to an immediate situation; (b) "preventive advocacy," which is an action taken to prevent injustice against a group of individuals by creating attitudes and systems that make justice the norm; and (c) "citizen advocacy," which is a movement to encourage others to take on social issues.

The term *empowerment* has been used to describe a variety of interventions used in counseling and therapy. Our definition describes empowerment as one end of an advocacy continuum and embodies the interpersonal interactions between the therapist and client working within the socioeconomic, sociocultural, and sociopolitical context (see Figure 16.1). This is in contrast to a more traditional definition of empowerment, wherein the counselor works with the client to discover or enhance the client's sense of self-efficacy during counseling, which may not include reference to the sociopolitical world of the client and does not assume counselor involvement in or recognition of that environment. Empowerment in this definition is used more generally across client groups.

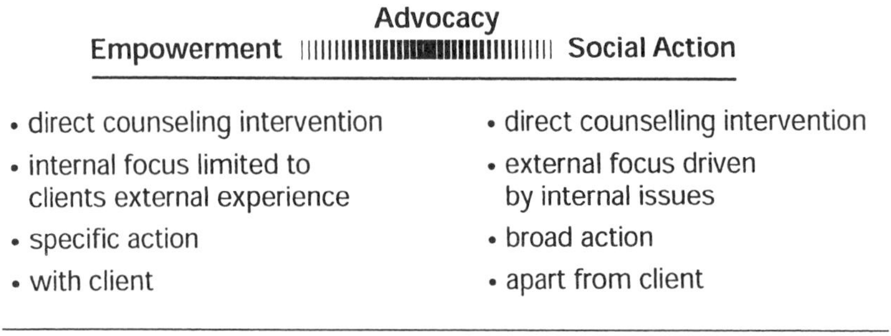

Advocacy
Empowerment ||||||||||||||||||■|||||||||||||||| Social Action

• direct counseling intervention	• direct counselling intervention
• internal focus limited to clients external experience	• external focus driven by internal issues
• specific action	• broad action
• with client	• apart from client

Figure 16.1. Advocacy Continuum in Counseling

For this chapter, the previous definition of *empowerment* is expanded with individuals who are oppressed due to their group status or their access to resources in society. Empowerment acknowledges the central role of power dynamics at societal, cultural, familial, and individual levels (Pinderhughes, 1983). However, McWhirter (1994) contended that recognizing oppression is not enough. She stated that counselors must act on oppression by expanding their traditional role and developing awareness of the social, political, and economic barriers to growth and autonomy experienced by individuals who are marginalized. Empowerment may be seen as a dimension of advocacy in which the counselor is able to help the client achieve goals by initially becoming involved in the client's environment (or one similar along salient dimensions), with the ultimate result being that the client acts independently from the counselor.

Although one end of our advocacy continuum encompasses individual and group empowerment within a sociopolitical context, social action may reflect the opposite end. In social action, the counselor may be actively engaged in facilitating the removal of barriers faced by his or her clients or client groups in the larger sociopolitical context through action external to counseling. In this definition, social action refers to advocacy at a macrosocial level (e.g., engaging in legislative or policy issues) affecting clients.

Currently, the counseling profession's perspectives range from an acceptance of advocacy as an appropriate and necessary role of the counselor or psychologist to the view that advocacy compromises the bounded relationship between the client and therapist. Although some of these differences may reflect political beliefs, many valid questions of professionalism deserve attention. It is important to note that discussions of professionalism of counselor-client relationships must be accountable within the context of race-, class-, and gender-based oppression.

A BRIEF HISTORY OF ADVOCACY IN COUNSELING PSYCHOLOGY

The concepts of advocacy, empowerment, and social action are not new to the counseling field. The profession has long debated the appropriateness of counselors and psychologists as advocates. In the wake of the social activism of the 1970s, considerable discussion took place supporting the role of advocacy for counselors and mental health professionals. Lerner (1972) felt that the difference between social action and psychotherapy was a false dichotomy and stated,

> The conflict over individual versus group methods in community mental health rests on a false dichotomy because the essential nature of constructive psychotherapy and social action is the same. So too are the goals of both: to promote effective action in one's own behalf, in the former case by removing internal psychological obstacles to such action and, in the latter, by removing external social obstacles to it. . . . The only real dichotomy is between those who work on their clients and those who work for their clients. (p. 11)

In the 1970s, the growth of community counseling brought advocacy and community organizing to the attention of the counseling profession. From this perspective, facilitation of structural changes in clients' environments was seen as a necessary and appropriate role for counselors (Lewis & Lewis, 1983). In the late 1980s and 1990s, perspectives such as these seemed to have difficulty maintaining a foothold in the profession.

In his article documenting the history of advocacy in the American Psychological Association (APA), Wright (1992) asserted that advocacy is appropriate for the profession and focused his historical review on legislative forms of advocacy. He noted that along with advocacy for the profession, counseling and mental health organizations also have been advocating for client rights and changes in public policy that directly affect clients and vulnerable groups (e.g., immigration, welfare, and education issues). However, in a review of advocacy literature, McClure and Russo (1996) noted significant movement of counseling away from activism and social change in the 1980s and early 1990s. They concluded that the focus of the profession had been redirected as a result of efforts toward achieving credibility, narrow research activities, and individualism. This shift may contribute to limited advocacy training and guidance for counselors and psychologists.

Although many authors in multicultural, feminist, and community counseling promote advocacy roles, a substantial number of authors support contrary views. These include perspectives expressing that it is an unrealistic and inappropriate role for counseling professionals to become involved in the environment directly (Weinrach & Thomas, 1998), that sociocentric views may lead the profession toward a political ideology similar to fallen communism (Ramm, 1998), and that taking on a more active role may result in authoritarianism (Sollod, 1998). In addition, there are those authors who encourage advocacy roles and raise valid cautions about the complexities of appropriate implementation. The potential for dependency building (Lee, 1998; Pinderhughes, 1983), the fostering of client powerlessness (McWhirter, 1994), and repercussions of challenging institutional policy and practice (Lee, 1998) have all been concerns voiced in the literature.

Over the past 10 years, the counseling and psychology literature has increasingly used the term *advocacy* to refer to action that professional associations, counselors, and psychologists have taken either to increase the credibility of the profession or to affect legislation. This particular kind of advocacy on behalf of the counseling profession attends to issues such as managed care, prescription privileges, and licensure (Davis & Yazak, 1996; Galassi, 1980; Wright, 1992). There has been less attention in the field to the role that counseling professionals may take as advocates for clients. Two areas of exception are feminist counseling and multicultural counseling. In each of these areas, researchers and clinicians have repeatedly suggested the need to expand counseling professionals' roles to include advocacy.

Issues of oppression and advocacy provide a unifying link between feminist and multicultural counseling literature. Mental health is affected by experiences of oppression. Research on stress indicates that factors such as gender, socioeconomic class, and racial/cultural backgrounds affect the type of contextual stressors enacted and the means by which individuals cope. Lewis et al. (1998) summarized four variables that contribute to stress among individuals identified as minority or oppressed: being one of few, effects of discrimination and prejudice, economic strain, and stressors related to group pressure. Traditionally, counselors have worked with clients on internal issues to help them cope with these stressors. However, when there is systemwide oppression, a lack of acknowledgment of the forces in that system may itself be disempowering. Counselors may need to extend beyond the intrapsychic work and begin to address the external forces that perpetuate clients' negative conditions. Race, class, and gender have been targets in discriminatory action and thus are often mitigating factors in advocacy.

In their discussion of client advocacy, Chesler, Bryant, and Crowfoot (1976) commented on the intersection of identities in oppression and noted that advocacy typically aligns the counselor with women, ethnic minorities, sexual minorities, and the poor. As indicated earlier in this chapter, most people experience more than one dimension of their identity at a time (e.g., gender, sexual orientation, race). For some individuals, this may represent a complex identity that encompasses multiple oppressions (Reynolds & Pope, 1991). For example, a woman of color who has limited economic resources may experience stress and discrimination due to her gender, racial prejudice, and class barriers. These multiple oppressions serve as mitigating factors and present the counselor-advocate with systemic as well as intrapsychic challenges. The cases and discussion at the end of this chapter provide some possibilities for appropriate counselor-advocate approaches.

The historical development of feminist and multicultural counseling reflects the growth of a sociocontextual approach and demonstrates the fluctuating tendencies in the profession. Given gender-based discrimination, feminist therapy has been one of the biggest proponents of advocacy as an appropriate and necessary role for counseling professionals. Founded in the civil rights and women's movements, feminist therapy has been, in theory, committed to social action. The recognition that many women's mental health issues were misdiagnosed or resulting from oppression led to the expectation that advocacy must be an active part of the therapy relationship.

In the initial growth of feminist therapy, consciousness-raising groups were created to encourage women to explore the impact of gender bias and systemic discrimination on their mental health, as well as to raise awareness in society in general around issues of sexism and discrimination (Atkinson & Hackett, 1995). This form of advocacy and social action subscribed to the philosophy that the "personal was political." Although these were the roots of feminist therapy, over time, the goals of social change have given way to more individualistic and conservative perspectives (Enns, 1993).

Discrimination in mental health services also has been linked to racial and cultural factors. Similar to research in feminist psychology, multicultural counseling and psychology raised questions about the equity with which mental health diagnoses were made across racial lines. Research also indicated that in counseling (social, emotional, and vocational), persons of color tended to receive differential treatment (Ridley, 1995). As a result of these and other issues, multicultural counseling has continued to assert advocacy as an important role (Atkinson, Thompson, & Grant, 1993; Grevious, 1985; Lerner, 1972; Williams & Kirkland, 1971).

A milestone in multicultural counseling was the development of competencies and standards in which Sue, Arredondo, and McDavis (1992) delineated the awareness, knowledge, and skills necessary for culturally appropriate multicultural counseling. These standards were recently adopted by Division 17 of APA, the Association of Counselor Educators and Supervision (ACES), and many divisions of the American Counseling Association (ACA), providing guidelines for competency and practice and expanding the traditional role of counseling professionals to meet the needs of diverse populations. Several of these competencies include advocacy, institutional involvement, and social action. Arredondo et al. (1996) expanded on the competency guideline that directs counselors to assess the appropriateness of intervening on behalf of clients. They stated that "[culturally competent counselors] can describe concrete examples of situations in which it is appropriate and possibly necessary for a counselor to exercise institutional intervention skills on behalf of a clients" (p. 71).

Differential diagnoses and treatment also have been discussed in relation to socioeconomic or class variables (Sutton & Kessler, 1986). However, in general, attention to class issues by the counseling profession has remained minimal over time. Although multicultural and feminist literature occasionally addresses this form of oppression, the extent of general professional activity in this area seems to encompass more legislative action (e.g., welfare reform, health care). Solomon (1976) specifically posited that advocacy in helping professions should involve assisting the oppressed and socially disenfranchised. He believed that this was necessary because the wealthy in the nation typically had agencies and institutions already advocating for them. Other segments of the helping profession, such as social work, have more adequately recognized social class and economic conditions as critical factors in mental health. Although we maintain that the counselor-advocate role is distinct from that of a social worker, future discussions about dependency building, boundaries, and other concerns could be enhanced by an examination of the social work literature and interprofessional dialogue.

Historically, oppression based on gender, race, and class has prompted feminist and multicultural counseling literature to voice the need for advocacy and social action. This support was documented in the mid-1970s and has kept some degree of presence since that time. However, widespread acceptance and implementation of these roles have not followed. Although there is currently a reemergence of literature suggesting the role of the advocate (Lee, 1998; Lewis et al., 1998; McWhirter, 1994), for the most part, the discussions of advocacy as an integral part of counselor's roles have remained on the periphery.

Issues in the Profession

The challenges posed by shifting our ideas about the role of counselors and psychologists are numerous. For instance, the lack of discussion regarding professional guidance and training for advocacy creates barriers and impedes the potential for such a shift. Changes in traditional roles also raise dilemmas affecting practice, such as conflicts with traditional counseling values, concerns about client dependency and therapist paternalism, and consequences of power and privilege in therapy. Controversy arises around whether advocacy suggests a political stance in opposition to a "objective and scientific" stance for the profession of psychology. The existence of these concerns and the assertions that advocacy is necessary warrant discussion.

The Status of Advocacy in Counseling Training and Ethical Guidelines

A review of current professional ethical standards and graduate counseling programs finds minimal guidance about advocacy in counseling and psychology. The dearth of material in introductory counseling textbooks seems to imply that the issue of advocacy is either prohibitively complex or a nonrole in the profession. In addition, counselor training programs do not typically include curricula that explore advocacy or provide guidance for students around roles of advocacy (Collison et al., 1998).

Graduate counseling programs that address issues of advocacy tend to do so through discussions of ethics or issues faced in therapy (e.g., dependency). In a note about advocacy, Thompson (1983) suggested that there are two sides

to this dilemma. On one hand, Thompson suggested that "intercession on behalf of individual clients with third parties, when it may be presumed that the
client could have accomplished much the same by herself, albeit with some
skill training and support, is also obviously dependency-building" (p. 40). This
statement is followed by a seemingly opposing view, asserting that "intercession or political activity on behalf of clients as a group or as an unfairly treated
class is advocated by many psychologists as being a social and ethical responsibility of the profession" (Thompson, 1983, p. 40). This type of statement demonstrates conflicting guidelines as to when and how advocacy is an appropriate
role.

The APA's (1992) "Ethical Principles of Psychologists and Code of Conduct" includes a section on social responsibility that directs psychologists to be
aware of "professional and scientific responsibilities to the community and the
society in which they work and live" (p. 1600). It suggests that psychologists
encourage the development of law and social policy that serve the interests of
their patients, clients, and the public, but it does not delineate how this might be
undertaken. The "Guidelines for Providers of Psychological Services to Ethnic,
Linguistic, and Culturally Diverse Populations" (APA, 1993) provide slightly
more substantive guidance. In this piece, psychologists are encouraged to address and work toward the elimination of biases, prejudices, and discriminatory
practices. Similar to the APA code of conduct, psychologists are cautioned to
be aware of their own biases and prejudices that may affect therapy, assessment,
consultation, and other areas of professional service. Problematically, however,
the guidelines do not elaborate or discuss whether this is at an individual or environmental level. Thus, this particular piece is congruent with the code of conduct yet is rhetorical because it offers no real parameters for counselor actions
outside the therapy setting. In effect, the clients' race, gender, and class differences, in respect to the counselor, are recognized but depoliticized because
these differences are disconnected from the sociopolitical and cultural environment that creates and reinforces "difference."

Brown (1988) used the National Board of Certified Counselors (NBCC,
1987) code of ethics to illustrate ethical issues presented for the counselor-
advocate. This code states that acceptance of employment implies that the
counselor agrees with the policies and principles of the institution. The code
further indicates that

> if, despite concerted efforts, the certified counselor cannot reach agreement
> with employers as to acceptable standards of conduct that allow for changes
> in institutional policy that are conducive to the positive growth and devel-

opment of clients, then terminating the affiliation would be seriously considered. (p. 1)

Because research has shown that clients report experiences of discrimination, sexism, racism, and classism within institutions, including social service
agencies, mental health agencies, and universities (Atkinson, Morten, & Sue,
1993; Bryant, 1991; Wade, 1993), counselors may be put in a position of losing
their jobs if they challenge the status quo. Brown (1988) pointed out that if the
NBCC and other ethical codes assert that counselors have as their first responsibility to promote and protect the welfare of the client in all situations, the case
for advocacy would be supported. For advocacy to be recognized as a part of
counselors' functions, existing codes of ethics must be revised to include ethical principles pertaining to advocacy.

In developing some ethical guidelines for advocacy, the multicultural
counseling competencies (Sue et al., 1992) provide essential elements, including the need for counselors to be aware, knowledgeable, and skillful in understanding clients' cultural experiences and encounters with oppression. In addition, a recent statement by the Governing Council of the ACA may provide a
general but helpful foundation.

> The practice of Professional Counseling is the application of mental health,
> psychological, or human development principles, through cognitive, affec-
> tive, behavioral or systemic intervention strategies, that address wellness,
> personal growth, or career development as well as pathology. (Lee & Walz,
> 1998, p. 307)

A set of ethical provisions for advocacy in counseling should provide guidance for addressing several issues, including the counselor-client relationship,
the counselor-helping network, and the role of the counselor within the institution or system. The following are some possible guiding statements:

1. Counselors will work to understand the societal context within which
clients and their relations live and work. Counselors will strive to comprehend
the impact that this context has, both positively and negatively, on the functioning of the individual client and his or family and community.

2. Counselors will strive to recognize oppression faced by clients and
communities, including racism, classism, sexism, and other oppressions. They
will validate the clients' experience and commit themselves to confronting oppression in their professional and personal lives. They will recognize elements

of privilege they enjoy based on their education and other factors and use that privilege only insofar as it furthers the goals of their clients.

3. Counselors will work collaboratively with clients to determine appropriate goals and activities for work within the session and in the environment for both the counselor and client. Counselors will be cognizant of their intentions in pursuing these goals and will ensure that their actions are for the benefit of the client and not for self-enhancing needs of the counselor.

4. Counselors will ensure that their actions both within and outside counseling sessions maintain the goal of increasing clients' skills and efficacy in influencing their environment and mental health as well as working to remove environmental barriers.

5. Counselors will recognize that at times, institutions and systems may be hostile toward clients and may respond more appropriately to intervention enacted in the presence of the counselor. Counselors will take appropriate action within their own or other institutions or agencies to confront individuals, practices, or policies that demean or create unreasonable barriers for clients. Counselors will work to establish policies and practices within their organizations to provide and support appropriate client advocacy and facilitate cooperation between help-giving systems.

6. Counselors will seek consultation from community groups and other helping professionals to ensure ethical advocacy. Counselors will become involved in the communities in which they provide services so they may better understand and pursue the goals of the community.

These statements are meant to provoke discussion and are not inclusive or error free. There are many difficulties in developing guidelines such as these, including the fine line between fostering dependency and taking action, and identifying one's own political agenda versus what seems to be best for the client. In addition, confrontations with organizations may result in repercussions for the counselor, and it is often difficult to affect bureaucratic systems. Some discussion about the issues in practice may promote clearer elaboration of these ideas.

Dilemmas and Challenges in Practice

Often, commitment to client advocacy, apart from legislative involvement, challenges some primary goals and traditional values of counseling psychology. Prilleltensky (1997) argued that several assumptions in psychology lead to excesses and abuses of power. Among the assumptions he listed were "knowing what is best for our clients, minimizing clients' autonomy by excluding them from decision-making processes, stigmatizing individuals with deficit-oriented labels, defining problems exclusively in intrapsychic terms, and neglecting to consider social injustices" (p. 518). This raises several issues on both sides of the advocacy controversy. On one hand, there is concern that advocacy requires the therapist to abandon principles of neutrality and minimizes client autonomy, thereby negatively affecting therapeutic effectiveness. On the other hand, the traditional focus on intrapsychic causes and remedies has been criticized as minimizing the important influence of the external environment (Atkinson et al., 1993).

Values Inherent in Traditional Counseling

The interaction of values and therapy may be considered in two different ways. First, advocacy roles may seem to conflict with values inherent in traditional counseling theory and practice. Second, advocacy requires that individual therapists examine their personal values and biases particularly in relation to race, class, or gender issues.

Typically, empowerment has been seen as a more congruent objective for counseling professionals. The intrapsychic focus of traditional therapy, client responsibility, independence, and other similar values are all easily maintained in traditional definitions of empowerment because the therapist is not called on to be actively involved in the client's environment. This view of empowerment allows for the maintenance of traditional distance between client and therapist, which in turn reinforces traditional values and infers that extrasession involvement by the therapist is neither necessary nor appropriate. The value placed on intrapsychic processes has been questioned in the multicultural counseling literature and is particularly significant when the sociopolitical involvement of advocacy is considered.

The value of autonomy, when taken to extremes in counseling, may imply that the client is responsible for his or her distress and can overcome problems through intrapsychic work. This may minimize the experience of discrimination and assumes that all individuals have equal access to power and control over their environment. In addressing this issue, counselors may need to examine how this affects their perspective of the clients, their ability to understand

the oppression faced by their clients, and their involvement in holistically addressing the clients' needs. A crucial component of this is an acknowledgment
of privilege and its impact on a counselor's feelings about clients and the systems within which clients function. For each therapist, issues of values and
privilege are unique. As a White female counselor, one author receives privilege based on socioracial characteristics as well as class privilege from education and power inherent in the therapeutic situation. As an Asian American
male counselor, one author receives privilege due to the status of his gender and
class privilege, again based on education. In advocacy, it is possible that the
type of societal change necessary may lessen the privilege that the therapist receives, thus making advocacy a very personal decision.

    Chesler et al. (1976) presented some special issues faced by counselor-
advocates, suggesting that the counselors must address their own values and intentions in counseling very clearly. They noted that because client advocacy
aligns the counselor with clients and client groups facing societal oppression,
the potential exists for value conflicts, particularly for White, middle-class, heterosexual male counselors. They emphasized that advocacy is psychologically
stressful and often results in alliances that must be able to stand the strain of
conflict.

Dependency and Paternalism Versus Collaboration

    An assumption often made is that when one advocates for clients or client
groups, it reinforces a client's view of helplessness and does not teach self-
sufficiency. Lee (1998) cautioned counselors who take social action roles, emphasizing that it is essential to remain cognizant that the potential exists for creating client dependency. This issue is complicated when considering perceived
counselor intentions in multicultural counseling.

    When oppression is salient, clients may suspect that counselors of the ma-
jority culture are providing service only insofar as it maintains the status quo.
Ivey, Ivey, and Simek-Morgan (1993) cautioned that White professionals acting on behalf of people of color may be viewed with suspicion. Vontress (1981)
also used the phrase the "Great White Father Syndrome" to describe self-enhancing needs that White counselors may be fulfilling in multicultural counseling and suggested that this leads therapists into behavior that is paternalistic and
condescending. One danger of advocacy implemented with paternalistic intentions is that it may reinforce passivity and learned helplessness in the client.

This issue is complex when one considers the literature indicating that advocacy is important, yet there is minimal guidance for providing appropriate and empowering advocacy.

These issues raise a central question: When is a counselor truly working with the client for the benefit of the client, and when is a counselor creating "dependence" (vs. interdependence)? The intent and role of the counseling professional in advocacy are important. On one hand, if I am "helping" because "there are others less fortunate than I" or because "others cannot do it without my help," the intent and outcome may be paternalistic, and actions may be seen as unintentionally racist or prejudicial (Yamato, 1995). On the other hand, if I recognize that the realities of our social system endow me with a certain power that I may use to facilitate my clients' increase of power and focus, I may be able to advocate effectively and appropriately. Awareness of privilege is crucial to make the distinction between these two different intentions.

An essential aspect of appropriate advocacy is an awareness of counselor intentions. Is the advocacy paternalistic and therapist directed or a collaborative alliance driven by the client? Is the counselor working on goals that were mutually determined or those that the counselor believes are beneficial for the client? In Keiffer's (1984) discussions of citizen empowerment, he emphasized the importance of collaboration and cautioned that "we should not seek to do for others what they must do for themselves" (p. 28). Keiffer suggested that the roles of "external enabler" and "mentor" may be useful when considering how to act in the best interest of clients. Ivey (1995) used Friere's theory of liberation and positioned the client as a colleague in the mutual dialectical process of therapy. Thus, instead of the counselor "helping" the client, the client is asked to engage, determine, and facilitate his or her own growth in therapy. As an advocate, the counselor also may help clients understand the wider sociopolitical context within which they, and all of us, exist. Another step may be to work with clients to see that they are not alone and that they may be experiencing valid feelings despite what others are telling them. Working together means moving beyond "just coping" toward a more active engagement of the milieu that may be creating the initial problem.

Politicizing the Profession

Another issue that arises when discussing client advocacy—and even more so with social action—is the concern that counseling and psychology are being used as a tool to further political causes (Lee, 1998; Weinrach & Thomas, 1998). Opinions debating this issue often may be seen in the APA's monthly news publication. The public interest directorate of the APA advocates for legislation affecting low income, immigration, education, and other social issues. However, it reports receiving regular and numerous letters from APA members expressing reactions ranging from mild discomfort to angry resignation about the social positions taken by the APA (Tomes, 1997). Thus, advocacy both on the individual and institutional levels sparks controversy that science should not be political.

Focusing on advocacy at an individual level, one may ask how to ensure that the advocacy taken is for the purpose of the client issues rather than to satisfy the political or personal needs of the therapist. This may be possible once guidelines and training explicitly address appropriate advocacy.

WHAT ARE APPROPRIATE ROLES? IMPLICATIONS FOR RACE, CLASS, AND GENDER ADVOCACY

Race, class, and gender advocacy may take various forms. On one level, advocacy may begin with knowing how to critique a situation to develop a better understanding of how to ask appropriate questions. At another level, advocacy may imply personal or professional risks and taking a visible or vocal role to change an oppressive environment. Not everyone is comfortable with the role of social activist, and it is not our intention to admonish anyone for not taking this role. Advocacy may manifest differently for various people and is highly contingent on the environment. However, competence requires that counselors are aware of the social conditions that reproduce inequities for clients and communities. The following sections provide some ideas and discuss possible roles that advocacy may play in counseling and psychology. Some of these include advocacy as a catalyst, advocacy as modeling, and advocacy in research.

Advocacy as a Catalyst for Change

Two themes emerge in the social action aspect of advocacy: legislative involvement and institutional change. Each of these represents a way in which counselors may be involved in advocating for some larger change that will affect specific client issues. Legislative action tends to be a broad and indirect way to address needs, whereas work toward institutional change is typically done at a local or organizational level and may stem directly from patterns of discrimination of particular client groups observed by the counseling professional.

Because race, class, and gender are socially constructed identities that are reified through society's laws and codes, advocacy in relation to these constructs necessitates an understanding of how historical and contemporary laws structure and reinforce these culturally bound identities. Besides the explicitly xenophobic laws on immigration and welfare, seemingly innocuous policy decisions marry easily into the dominant culture's values and norms. For example, anti-sodomy laws are used against gay, lesbian, and bisexuals; books are banned from elementary and high school classrooms because they may challenge dominant values (e.g., marriage, sexuality); and English-only legislation tacitly implies the inferiority of Latino or Asian languages.

Ponterotto and Pedersen (1993) suggested that counselors play an activist role in preventing prejudice. They described this activism as involvement on a broad social scale within professional organizations, media, and government to educate and mediate discrimination and prejudice issues. One of the most powerful motivating factors can be injustice that is observed within one's own institutions. Advocacy may be something that happens in the course of counseling professionals' work as issues stemming from client experiences in the institution clearly affect the success of therapy. This is especially notable in large institutions in which the client participates on a variety of levels (e.g., universities). Later, we will discuss case examples that will illustrate possible and appropriate action.

Arredondo et al. (1996) elaborated on the competency standard that "culturally skilled counselors are aware of institutional barriers that prevent minorities from using mental health services" (Sue et al., 1992, p. 482) and suggested that counselors take the role of change agent. They further suggested that the counselor note examples of institutional barriers that prevent people of color from using mental health services and bring these examples to the attention of colleagues and decision-making bodies within the institution. In addition, Arredondo et al. suggested that culturally competent counselors "identify and communicate possible alternatives that would reduce or eliminate existing barriers within their institutions and within local, state, and national decision-making bodies" (p. 69).

Atkinson, Morten, and Sue (1993), in reference to multicultural counseling, defined the *counselor-advocate* as someone who "speaks on behalf of the

client, often confronting the institutional sources of oppression that are contributing to the client's problem" (p. 301). They pointed out that often the institution within which the counselor works may need to be confronted because these
institutions may present barriers impeding a client's well-being. As an employee of the institution, the counselor may be in the position of addressing the
injustice or lack of support for the client by directly intervening in the system.
Possible conflicts can arise when the counselor must choose to represent the client or the institution. Thus, there exist two competing professional issues: acting for the benefit of the client and being beneficent for the institution. According to Atkinson et al. (1993), a counselor-advocate would represent the client if
the institution were being discriminatory.

Advocacy as Modeling

Although much of the discussion thus far as been fairly abstract, a more
concrete discussion may help to reinforce the therapeutic influence of advocacy. Often advocacy, empowerment, and social action can serve as effective
modeling for clients. That is, the counselor may be teaching the client how to
develop certain behavioral and attitudinal competencies that contribute to the
client's self-actualization. Thus, the client learns not only how to cope with the
distressing environment temporarily but also how to change the milieu for the
better. As Gruber and Trickett (1987) noted, the professional's knowledge
about how institutions function provides the client with the "unwritten rules" of
a particular culture that tend to marginalize those who do not understand them.

Gruber and Trickett (1987) discussed a paradox of empowerment that is
relevant to our discussion of advocacy. The paradox is that people who empower or advocate for others typically have the institutional opportunities or
cultural sanction to do so. For example, a gay, lesbian, and bisexual "allies" program seeks individuals who do not identify as gay, lesbian, or bisexual to be vis-
ibly and politically aligned with those who do. Therefore, the cultural sanction
and acceptance of heterosexuality over homosexuality is used as a tool for advocacy, empowerment, and social action for those gay, lesbian, and bisexual individuals who may be marginalized from full participation in the power structure. In this way, privilege may exist with genuine collaboration that is driven
by the issues and perspective of the oppressed group.

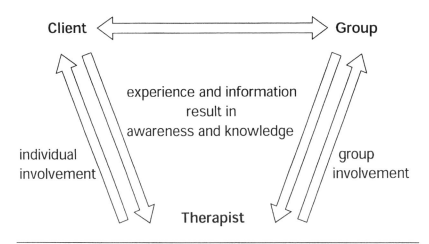

Figure 16.2. Therapist Involvement in the Client's Sociocultural, Socioeconomic, and Sociopolitical Context

To be an advocate and begin to understand the constraints and realities of clients' situations, counselors must become involved so they may hear issues from the oppressed group's perspective. The multicultural counseling competencies (Sue et al., 1992) clearly asserted that culturally competent counselors must gain knowledge and awareness of the contexts within which their clients live. We propose that the relationship formed between the client, therapist, and the client's community is interactive and collaborative (see Figure 16.2). Clients, by nature, are involved in some community that is a reflection of their race, culture, economics, gender, or other salient aspects of their identity. To understand and genuinely reflect this context, the therapist may gain insight into that experience by becoming involved in a community representative of the client's salient issue. For example, if the client is a middle-class Latino and the therapist is a middle-class African American, the therapist may want to become involved in a middle-class Latino community to the extent that they may begin to understand the issues faced from the perspective of members of that group. The therapist may also want to assess the salience of gender and whether that should also be considered in group involvement. A crucial piece of this model is that the therapist not only receives information and insight from the community but also is obliged to contribute in some way to that community through social action efforts or some other means (e.g., assisting at community functions). Although this experience will inform the therapist's ability to reflect the client's experience of the world, it is important that the issues in therapy are client driven and not driven by the experience felt by the therapist.

Throughout the discussion on advocacy, we have maintained that the counselor needs to understand the sociopolitical milieu from which the client is entering counseling and to which he or she must return. An understanding of the intrapsychic constructions of race, class, and gender are not enough if the counselor cannot make the connections to the environment. As Bronfenbrenner (1986) has pointed out, the individual exists within a complex ecology of factors (environmental) that contribute to behaviors and attitudes. In addition, the fluidity of these ecological factors means that a change or action in one part of the system will necessarily affect the individual.

Advocacy in Research

Another form of advocacy and social change may be seen in research. The rise in qualitative and phenomenological research designs was due to the perceived limitations of quantitative research methods, particularly as noted in the feminist and multicultural literature. Specifically, the quantitative, logico-positivist underpinnings of empirical designs did not fully capture the lived experiences of participants and clients. Advocating for other research methods has allowed the field of counseling psychology to add another dimension to the repertoire of research methods we currently employ. In this case, we understood the various shortcomings from our empirical methods and wanted phenomenology to add to our understanding of human behavior. Thus, if it were not for persistent and vocal advocates, empiricism would still determine our understanding of human behavior.

CASE EXAMPLES AND APPLICATIONS

In reality, our lives and our clients' lives are not affected solely along just one dimension, race, class, or gender. Rather, the intersection of these creates a complexity requiring sophisticated understanding of the impact of each on clients. These case examples, therefore, are presented in such a way that a variety of issues may be relevant. Determining appropriate roles for advocacy may require an understanding of the intersection of these and other oppressions, but the action is often motivated by the salience of just a few aspects of oppression.

Clients seen in a community mental health center may be faced with confronting large and rigid governmental structures that do not allow clients to have access to avenues of recourse. A White, middle-aged, low-income woman with children who is depressed about her situation and is facing the possibility of no federal aid may not see the relevance of career counseling or becoming a fully functioning autonomous individual if she cannot reconcile her present environmental concerns. What is the counselor-advocate to do in this situation? Much like crisis management with a suicidal client, the counselor needs to assess the immediate issues before therapy can really take place. The counselor-advocate should have some understanding of state laws and relevant sources pertaining to the population he or she is likely to see. The counselor may need to assess how well the client understands the laws that apply to her. The counselor-advocate may need to work with the client to fill out paperwork and find suitable day care and affordable housing. The counselor-advocate then may want to work with the client to call state and federal agencies and help navigate the bureaucracy. In addition, the client may want to seek the comfort of others like herself, and the counselor-advocate may want to help find an appropriate therapy group. The counselor-advocate's role does preclude counseling or therapy just as it does not end with therapy. The advocate may also find himself or herself working with others to change existing laws and regulations that jeopardize the welfare of others in a similar situation. This may mean writing letters; phoning local, state, and federal representatives; becoming a visible "ally" to this particular issue; and speaking out against these inequities. Collaboration with other helping professionals in the client's system to develop an advocacy team may also be effective. One may ask, "What is the difference between what is being proposed here and the work done by a social worker?" The question raises two different points: what needs to be done with the client for the welfare of the client and what are the professional issues that advocacy brings forth. Advocacy does entail a certain amount of involvement in the client's life outside the clinical setting, and professional issues may have to respond to these changing roles. That is, the client's welfare should be of paramount concern and not the identity of the counseling professional. Thus, advocacy challenges the role of counseling and psychology and asks how our profession may create the very issues clients come to us with.

Multicultural competency and advocacy imply an understanding of race, class, and gender issues, such that the counselor is able to ask the appropriate questions. For example, when working with a male first-generation Vietnamese American college student, the counselor may want to ask the following: What is the socioeconomic background of this person, and am I aware of the model minority myth? Is it possible that this student is suspicious of people who work for an institution due to the political history of the group? Are there particular language issues I should be aware of? What does it mean to be an Asian American male in the United States? Being a good advocate starts with understanding the client holistically. For this particular client, the counselor may find himself or herself in the position of being an active participant with the client in overcoming environmental barriers. If the client is reluctant to use various services on campus (e.g., financial aid) because of perceived prejudice (e.g., asking to see proof of citizenship), the counselor may want to assess the legitimacy of this perception and become more aware of how a specific service operates. That is, the counselor may want to understand how and why the client may have had previous negative interactions with a particular office and is now reluctant to go back or hears of negative treatment from others and is therefore reticent. The counselor may choose to speak with staff from that office and relate general concerns in hopes of changing that environment. In this manner, the counselor is able to capitalize on the particular knowledge of the institution for the benefit of the client. It is also important to note that clients may perceive that there would be repercussions if they challenged the system. Often, this perception may be accurate due to power dynamics in place. The counselor may work with clients to determine the appropriate action that will accomplish the client's goals. Sometimes, this may suggest use of the counselor's privilege recognized in the system.

Among the competencies discussed by Sue et al. (1992), several noted advocacy and social action as critical roles: "Culturally skilled counselors are able to exercise institutional intervention skills on behalf of their clients" (p. 483). Arredondo et al. (1996) provide an example of this type of intervention:

> Another hypothetical example may be that of a student of color in a large educational institution who approaches a counselor with a complaint about a faculty member, citing racial discrimination and sexual harassment. The student complains that he or she went through the grievance process but did not feel that it was satisfactorily resolved and was told that the incidents were minor and not adequate to justify taking action. The culturally competent counselor, having been approached in the past by other students with similar complaints against the same faculty member, may choose

to intervene within the institution's policies and procedures for such situations. (p. 52)

The preceding cases integrate strategies and illustrate various levels of advocacy. Additional guidance may be found in advocacy literature for college, community, and career counseling, suggesting appropriate roles for various institutional contexts.

Advocacy seems to be more concretely discussed in college counseling literature than in the general counseling psychology literature. Drum and Valdes (1988) suggested that advocacy in counseling supports student causes to increase students' power over outside influences that negatively affect their development and the quality of their lives. They described the counselor-advocate as intervening on behalf of students when discriminatory policies, unfavorable legislation, and inadequate funding create barriers. They further noted that it might be sometimes appropriate for counselors to join students in active participation in advocating for environmental change. Drum and Valdes also suggested that counselors might work toward helping students develop a sense of empowerment to overcome obstacles and institutional barriers. Hendricks (1994) and Williams and Kirkland (1971) indicated that counselors should be advocates for students of color by addressing the administration when discriminatory patterns are observed; assisting students in finding supportive networks for social action; teaching colleagues to recognize race-, class-, and gender-based bias in the institution; and challenging bureaucratic processes that inhibit the success of students.

From the community counseling literature, Lewis and Lewis (1983) gave the example of a gender and class advocacy situation in which a single, teenage parent is denied public education. They contrasted a traditional helping approach that attempts to generate possibilities such as counseling her about career options available for persons with limited education with an advocacy approach in which the counselor directly addresses the system with the goal of policy change. In this example, the counselor-advocate may work toward changing policy so that individuals such as this client are not denied education while providing career counseling. The advocacy approach is described as one that benefits not only the individual client but also others who may face similar situations.

In career counseling, one of the hallmarks of the counseling profession (Gelso & Fretz, 1992), advocacy is also needed. There is ample documentation in the multicultural counseling literature of differential treatment in vocational counseling. Vocational and occupational issues are a highly classed issue in the United States. In terms of how one determines subjective socioeconomic status, vocation is often used as a primary index (Hollingshead, 1975). Career counseling and advocacy would mean linking relevant economic and occupational issues rather than solely focusing on career-related exploration. For example, an African American male senior in college may seek career counseling to clarify interests and values. The counselor may need to also remain available to the client in the event that he or she experiences job discrimination. In this case, the counselor may capitalize on the working alliance developed between the client and counselor as a possible mechanism to challenge discrimination. Hotchkiss and Borow (1990) described a sociological perspective of career development that included, among other tasks of career counselors, the need to provide direct advocacy. One example provided was that of helping clients to complete job applications and develop strategies for dealing with discrimination. Leung (1995) described a system interventions approach in career counseling in which he asserted that counselors should be active in changing environments (i.e., reduction of barriers) with clients of color. It is hoped that these changes in the environment would facilitate better educational and career development.

Advocacy at both individual and group levels can have multiple benefits. Atkinson and Hackett (1995) suggested that advocacy on behalf of one person (e.g., gay client) can be seen as advocacy for all people of that group. From another angle, advocacy can mean drawing attention to gay, lesbian, and bisexual issues within professional events or helping to disseminate information throughout a community that in turn affects individual clients' welfare.

Do these actions cross traditional client-therapist boundaries? Yes, and we purport that they can do so appropriately. We cannot assume that we as counselors are not affected through our work with clients. The counselor-advocate may experience his or her work with clients as a kind of Freireian praxis (Freire, 1989): action and reflection. That is, as we consider the clients and understand them through our therapeutic discourse, reflection also considers the sociopolitical context from which they come. The reflection is an opportunity for the counselor to better understand how his or her sociopolitical context fits with the client's. As the counselor-advocate simultaneously considers the client and himself or herself, action should also be a tandem activity. Thus, as we work with the client to better himself or herself, we are also changed and learn from the process. If we teach clients to be reflective and action oriented, and we are also changed by the therapeutic process, why are we then not action oriented as well? Because we are all "race-ed," "class-ed," and "gender-ed" individuals, it is necessary for us to learn about and understand ourselves in terms of these so-cial constructions continuously. We would argue that detachment from these is-sues necessarily implies that many counseling professionals feel insulated from these issues and therefore are not involved. In other words, privilege offers per-ceived protection, whereas becoming involved may reflect a lessening of privi-lege. As professionals, by remaining detached from our clients and their envi-ronments, are we acting to preserve our privilege?

CONCLUSION

What we have attempted to do is provide the grounding for further discussions of advocacy within the profession of counseling. Our premise was that to work effectively with clients on issues of race, class, and gender oppression, extrasession work must be considered as important as intrasession work. Be-cause clients are race-ed, class-ed, and gender-ed individuals, focusing on a cli-ent's race, class, or gender apart from the sociopolitical context creates a disso-nance that may make it difficult to resolve the issues identified by the client.

The professional organizations that represent counselors participate in their own type of advocacy. Problematically, though, this brand of advocacy is often dominated by the development of the profession versus the betterment of the client. Although these two goals are not mutually exclusive, we have pro-posed that traditional professional roles may conflict with appropriate client advocacy and that clients' welfare should always be considered paramount. Much like the introduction of multiculturalism and feminism into the field of psychology, the formal instatement of advocacy as a crucial role for counselors will change the discipline.

Multiculturalism and feminism have exploded the various assumptions that "traditional" therapy have imposed on clients and how counseling must change to keep pace with the changing demographic realities of the United States. Advocacy may have a similar impact. Advocacy asks us to investigate the professional and therapeutic role of the counselor and whether the notion of "boundaries" is helping or hindering the development of the client. Although we do not necessarily believe that therapeutic boundaries are bad, we do ques-tion who benefits most from retaining "strict" therapy boundaries. That is, does extrasession involvement with clients necessarily mean that we are creating de-pendency between the client and counselor? One concern may be that extrasession engagement with the client is a type of unhealthy counter-

transference and that the counselor is somehow attempting to work out unresolved issues. Yet this interpretation of advocacy, as with many others, carries
with it a number of assumptions that may be incompatible with the changing
nature and role of counseling.

One task that advocacy necessitates is the development of clearer guidelines from which ethical issues may be interpreted. Another task is the incorporation of advocacy in and of itself, as a corollary element to multicultural counseling. That is, training programs are important in helping students to explore
the facets of advocacy and its form, role, and complexity when working with diverse populations.

We believe that counseling is at a turning point in its profession once again.
With the efflorescence of literature on race, class, and gender issues in counseling, coupled with the projected demographic changes in the United States,
counseling must decide how it will best adapt to these elements. On one hand, it
could attempt to assimilate diversity and multiculturalism into existing tem-
plates of therapy, or counseling can take the risk of redefining itself and therapy
to meet the new demands of our constituents.

References

American Psychological Association (APA). (1992). Ethical principles of psychologists and code
    of conduct. *American Psychologist, 47*(12), 1597-1611.
American Psychological Association (APA). (1993). Guidelines for providers of psychological
    services to ethnic, linguistic, and culturally diverse populations. *American Psychologist, 48,*
    45-48.
Arredondo, P., Toporek, R., Brown, S. P., Jones, J., Locke, D. C., Sanchez, J., & Stadler, H. (1996).
    Operationalization of the multicultural counseling competencies. *Journal of Multicultural
    Counseling & Development, 24*(1), 42-78.
Atkinson, D. R., & Hackett, G. (1995). *Counseling diverse populations.* Dubuque, IA: William C.
    Brown.
Atkinson, D. R., Morten, G., & Sue, D. W. (1993). *Counseling American minorities: A cross-cul-
    tural perspective* (4th ed.) Dubuque, IA: William C. Brown.
Atkinson, D. R., & Thompson, C. E. (1992). Racial, ethnic, and cultural variables in counseling. In
    S. D. Brown & R. W. Lent (Eds.), *Handbook of counseling psychology* (2nd ed., pp. 349-382).
    New York: John Wiley.
Atkinson, D. R., Thompson, C. E., & Grant, S. K. (1993). A three-dimensional model for counsel-
    ing racial/ethnic minorities. *The Counseling Psychologist, 21*(2), 257-277.
Bronfenbrenner, U. (1986). Ecology of the family as a context for human development: Research
    perspectives. *Developmental Psychology, 22,* 723-742.
Brown, D. (1988). Empowerment through advocacy. In D. J. Kurpius & D. Brown (Eds.), *Hand-
    book of consultation: An intervention for advocacy and outreach* (pp. 8-17). Alexandria, VA:
    Association for Counselor Education and Supervision.

Bryant, B. K. (1991). *Counseling for racial understanding.* Alexandria, VA: American Counseling Association.

Chesler, M. A., Bryant, B. I., & Crowfoot, J. E. (1976). Consultation in schools: Inevitable conflict, partisanship, and advocacy. *Professional Psychology, 7*(4), 637-645.

Collison, B. B., Osborne, J. L., Gray, L. A., House, R. M., Firth, J., & Lou, M. (1998). Preparing counselors for social action. In C. C. Lee & G. R. Walz (Eds.), *Social action: A mandate for counselors* (pp. 263-278). Alexandria, VA: American Counseling Association.

Davis, A., & Yazak, D. (1996). Goals and tasks of counselor licensing boards. *Counselor Education & Supervision, 35*(4), 308-318.

Drum, D. J., & Valdes, L. F. (1988). Advocacy and outreach: Applications to college university counseling centers. In D. J. Kurpius & D. Brown (Eds.), *Handbook of consultation: An intervention for advocacy and outreach* (pp. 38-60). Alexandria, VA: Association for Counselor Education and Supervision.

Enns, C. Z. (1993). Twenty years of feminist counseling and therapy: From naming biases to implementing multifaceted practice. *The Counseling Psychologist, 21*(1), 3-87.

Esquivel, G. B., & Keitel, M. A. (1990). Counseling immigrant children in the schools. *Elementary School Guidance and Counseling, 24,* 213-221.

Freire, P. (1989). *Pedagogy of the oppressed.* New York: Continuum.

Galassi, J. P. (1980). The concerns of counseling psychologists. *The Counseling Psychologist, 9*(1), 86-87.

Gelso, C. J., & Fretz, B. R. (1992). *Counseling psychology.* Fort Worth, TX: Harcourt Brace.

Grevious, C. (1985). The role of the family therapist with low-income Black families. *Family Therapy, 12*(2), 115-122.

Gruber, J., & Trickett, E. J. (1987). Can we empower others? The paradox of empowerment in the governing of an alternative public school. *American Journal of Community Psychology, 15*(3), 535-371.

Hendricks, F. M. (1994). Career counseling with African American college students. *Journal of Career Development, 21*(2), 117-126.

Hollingshead, A. B. (1975). *Four factor index of social status.* Unpublished manuscript, Yale University, New Haven, CT.

Hotchkiss, L., & Borow, H. (1990). Sociological perspectives on work and career development. In D. Brown, L. Brooks, & Associates (Eds.), *Career choice and development* (2nd ed., pp. 262-307). San Francisco: Jossey-Bass.

Ivey, A. E. (1995). Psychotherapy as liberation: Toward specific skills and strategies in multicultural counseling and therapy. In J. G. Ponterotto, J. M. Casas, L. A. Suzuki, & C. M. Alexander (Eds.), *Handbook of multicultural counseling* (pp. 53-72). Thousand Oaks, CA: Sage.

Ivey, A., Ivey, M., & Simek-Morgan, L. (Eds.). (1993). *Counseling psychotherapy: A multicultural perspective.* Boston: Allyn & Bacon.

Kantrowitz, R., & Ballou, M. (1992). A feminist critique of cognitive-behavioral theory. In L. S. Brown & M. Ballou (Eds.), *Personality and psychopathology: Feminist reappraisals* (pp. 70-87). New York: Guilford.

Keiffer, C. H. (1984). Citizen empowerment: A developmental perspective. In J. Rappaport, C. Swift, & R. Hess (Eds.), *Studies in empowerment: Steps toward understanding and action* (pp. 30-38). Binghamton, NY: Haworth.

Lee, C. C. (1998). Counselors as agents of social change. In C. C. Lee & G. R. Walz (Eds.), *Social action: A mandate for counselors* (pp. 3-14). Alexandria, VA: American Counseling Association.

Lee, C. C., & Walz, G. R. (1998). A summing up and call to action. In C. C. Lee & G. R. Walz (Eds.), *Social action: A mandate for counselors* (pp. 307-312). Alexandria, VA: American Counseling Association.

Lerner, B. (1972). *Therapy in the ghetto: Political impotence and personal disintegration.* Baltimore: Johns Hopkins University Press.

Leung, S. A. (1995). Career development and counseling: A multicultural perspective. In J. G. Ponterotto, J. M. Casas, L. A. Suzuki, & C. M. Alexander (Eds.), *Handbook of multicultural counseling* (pp. 549-566). Thousand Oaks, CA: Sage.

Lewis, J. A., & Lewis, M. D. (1983). *Community counseling: A human services approach.* New York: John Wiley.

Lewis, J. A., Lewis, M. D., Daniels, J. A., & D'Andrea, M. J. (1998). *Community counseling: Empowerment strategies for a diverse society* (2nd ed.). Pacific Grove, CA: Brooks/Cole.

McClure, B. A., & Russo, T. R. (1996). The politics of counseling: Looking back and forward. *Counseling & Values, 40*(3), 162-174.

McWhirter, E. H. (1994). *Counseling for empowerment.* Alexandria, VA: American Counseling Association.

National Board of Certified Counselors (NBCC). (1987). *Code of ethics.* Alexandria, VA: American Association for Counseling and Development.

Pinderhughes, E. B. (1983). Empowerment for our clients and for ourselves. *Social Casework, 64*(6), 331-338.

Ponterotto, J. G., & Pedersen, P. B. (1993). *Preventing prejudice: A guide for counselors and educators.* Newbury Park, CA: Sage.

Prilleltensky, I. (1997). Values, assumptions, and practices: Assessing the moral implications of psychological discourse and action. *American Psychologist, 52*(5), 517-535.

Ramm, D. R. (1998). Consider the scientific study of morality. *American Psychologist, 53*(3), 323-324.

Reynolds, A. L., & Pope, R. L. (1991). The complexities of diversity: Exploring multiple oppressions. *Journal of Counseling and Development, 70*(1), 174-180.

Ridley, C. R. (1995). *Overcoming unintentional racism in counseling and therapy.* Thousand Oaks, CA: Sage.

Sarason, S. B. (1981). An asocial psychology and a misdirected clinical psychology. *American Psychologist, 36,* 827-836.

Sodowsky, G. R., Kuo-Jackson, P. Y., & Loya, G. J. (1996). Outcome of training in the philosophy of assessment. In D. B. Pope-Davis & H. L. K. Coleman (Eds.), *Multicultural counseling competencies: Assessment, education and training, and supervision* (pp. 3-42). Thousand Oaks, CA: Sage.

Sollod, R. N. (1998). Unexamined religious assumptions. *American Psychologist, 53*(3), 324-325.

Solomon, B. B. (1976). *Black empowerment social work in oppressed communities.* New York: Columbia University Press.

Sue, D. W. (1981). *Counseling the culturally different: Theory and practice.* New York: John Wiley.

Sue, D. W., Arredondo, P., & McDavis, R. J. (1992). Multicultural counseling competencies and standards: A call to the profession. *Journal of Counseling and Development, 70,* 477-486.

Sue, S. (1977). Community mental health services to minority groups: Some optimism, some pessimism. *American Psychologist, 32,* 616-624.

Sutton, R. G., & Kessler, M. (1986). National study of the effects of clients' socioeconomic status on clinical psychologists' professional judgment. *Journal of Consulting and Clinical Psychology, 54*(2), 275-276.

Terrel, F., & Terrel, S. (1984). Race of counselor, client sex, cultural mistrust level, and premature termination from counseling among black clients. *Journal of Counseling Psychology, 31,* 371-375.

Thompson, A. (1983). *Ethical concerns in psychotherapy and their legal ramifications.* Lanham, MD: University Press of America.

Tomes, H. (1997). PI Directorate is home to controversy. *American Psychological Association Monitor, 28*(4), 4.

Vontress, C. E. (1981). Racial and ethnic barriers in counseling. In P. B. Pedersen, J. G. Draguns, W. J. Lonner, & J. E. Trimble (Eds.), *Counseling across cultures* (2nd ed., pp. 87-107). Honolulu: University of Hawaii Press.

Wade, J. C. (1993). Institutional racism: An analysis of the mental health system. *American Journal of Orthopsychiatry, 63*(4), 536-544.

Weinrach, S. G., & Thomas, K. R. (1998). Diversity-sensitive counseling today: A postmodern clash of values. *Journal of Counseling and Development, 76*(2), 115-122.

Williams, R. L., & Kirkland, J. (1971). The White counselor and the Black client. *The Counseling Psychologist, 2*(4), 114-117.

Wright, R. H. (1992). The American Psychological Association and the rise of advocacy. *American Psychologist, 23*(6), 443-447.

Yamato, G. (1995). Something about the subject makes it hard to name. In M. L. Andersen & P. H. Collins (Eds.), *Race, class, and gender: An anthology* (2nd ed., pp. 71-75). Belmont, CA: Wadsworth.

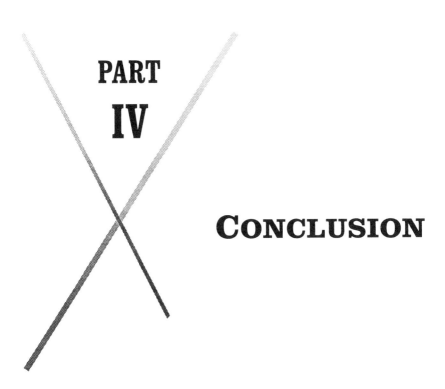

PART

IV

CONCLUSION

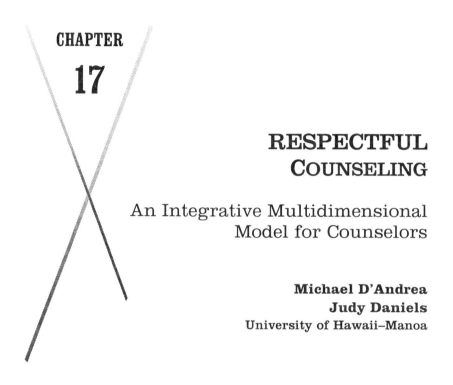

CHAPTER

17

RESPECTFUL
COUNSELING

An Integrative Multidimensional
Model for Counselors

Michael D'Andrea
Judy Daniels
University of Hawaii–Manoa

The RESPECTFUL counseling model represents a new, comprehensive, and integrative way of thinking about the persons who are directly involved in the process of counseling. This includes clients who seek professional assistance and mental health practitioners (e.g., counselors, psychologists, social workers, etc.) who are responsible for providing psychological services to persons from diverse groups and backgrounds in an effective and ethical manner. Two general assumptions represent the foundation on which this new theoretical framework is based.

The first assumption rests in the belief that the ultimate goal of counseling and psychotherapy is to promote clients' development. Counselors and psychologists commonly use different approaches in promoting clients' development. These include the following:

(a)   fostering the development of more effective decision-making
       and problem-solving competencies that can be used by clients who
       are not necessarily in crisis but are in need of acquiring more
       effective life skills,
(b)   providing crisis counseling services that are designed to help
       clients develop more effective coping strategies during times of
       heightened stress, and
(c)   using more intensive, long-term psychotherapeutic inter
       ventions that are aimed at stimulating qualitative changes in
       clients' personality development.

The second assumption involves the importance of understanding the
unique and complex multidimensionality of human development and the need
to intentionally address the multiple factors that affect clients' development in
counseling practice. The fields of counseling, psychology, and social work are
beginning to demonstrate a greater awareness of the ways in which a person's
group-referenced identities affect his or her sense of psychological health and
well-being. This increased awareness largely has been spurred by the development of new theoretical insights and a host of research findings that are helping
mental health professionals to reconstruct and expand their thinking about human development.

Increasing Our Understanding of the Impact
of Gender and Culture on Human Development

Over the past 20 years, researchers have directed increasing attention to (a)
the role a person's gender (Abbott, 1987; Gilligan, 1982; Riger, 1992) and
cultural-racial background (Locke, 1992) play in an individual's psychological
development, and (b) the ways in which these factors influence counseling and
therapeutic processes and outcomes (Fujino, Okazaki, & Young, 1994; Taussig, 1986). Recognizing that these client-counselor characteristics may have a
positive or negative impact in the process and outcome of counseling, several
experts have urged mental health practitioners to

(a)   consider the ways in which their own as well as their clients'
       personal characteristics may influence the counseling process,

(b)   acquire the types of counseling skills and competencies that are necessary to work effectively and ethically with clients from diverse populations, and

(c)   implement counseling interventions that reflect an awareness, sensitivity, and respect for their clients' unique multidimensionality (Arredondo et al., 1996; Sue, Arredondo, & McDavis, 1992).

Defining the Term *Multidimensionality*

As used in this chapter, the term *multidimensionality* refers to those multiple factors that significantly influence a person's psychological development. Although counselors and psychologists have exalted the notion of the client's individuality in the past, many mental health practitioners are beginning to become aware of the ways in which a person's group-referenced identities influence his or her sense of psychological health and personal well-being. As noted above, much of this increased understanding comes from research conducted over the past two decades that has focused on the ways in which people's gender and cultural-racial backgrounds affect the development of their attitudes, values, worldviews, and personal identity (Atkinson, Morten, & Sue, 1993; Carter, 1995; Lewis, Hayes, & Bradley, 1992).

Clearly, the feminist and multicultural movements have done much to help mental health practitioners expand their understanding of the multidimensional nature of human development. These movements also have stimulated new thinking about the need to combine traditional and nontraditional intervention strategies when working with women and persons from diverse cultural-racial backgrounds (Atkinson et al., 1993; Lee & Richardson, 1991; Sue, Ivey, & Pedersen, 1996).

However, a client's gender and cultural-racial background represent only two factors that comprise a person's total multidimensional nature. In trying to build on the advances that have been made by multicultural and feminist advocates, we have noted that mental health professionals must gain an expanded understanding of the ways in which other group-referenced factors influence a person's psychological development for them to work effectively and ethically within the context of a pluralistic 21st-century society. In essence, we suggest that mental health practitioners will continue to fall short in accurately understanding their clients' perspectives and fail to implement counseling strategies that reflect a heightened sensitivity for the multidimensional nature of human development until they become more cognizant of the ways in which other factors affect the developmental and counseling processes (D'Andrea & Daniels, 1995).

To illustrate the importance of acquiring a more expansive understanding of the multidimensional nature of human development for mental health practice, we provide the following brief case presentation and set of questions.

An African American lesbian client, whose poor socioeconomic status was directly related to her inability to secure a job because of a serious physical disability that she experienced several years earlier, sought counseling services because she was increasingly depressed with her life. During her first counseling session with a White male counselor, she indicated that her strong religious beliefs and support from her family were all "that I had left in my life." She also stated how much she hated being "poor, Black, and disabled."

Given this scenario, which aspect of this client's multidimensionality should the counselor attend to during their initial counseling session? What issues should the counselor keep in mind when addressing the client's concerns about being "poor, Black, and disabled?" How might the counselor tap into this client's religious beliefs and support from her family to foster positive counseling outcomes? In what ways might the counselor's own gender, race, or lack of any visible physical disability affect the counseling process? Does the fact that this client is a lesbian have any relevance for counseling? If so, what considerations should the counselor keep in mind about her sexual identity as they continue to work together in counseling in the future?

These questions represent some of the issues practitioners should consider when working with this particular client. They are presented to (a) underscore the importance of recognizing how the client's multidimensional nature affects the counseling process, (b) highlight some of the challenges the mental health practitioner faces in providing help to this client, and (c) encourage practitioners to consider how their own multidimensional characteristics may affect the counseling process with this and other clients with whom they may work.

The Interactional Nature of the
Multidimensionality of Human Development

The brief description of the above-mentioned client points to the interactional nature of the multiple factors that comprise a person's multidimensionality. In other words, a person's individuality is largely determined by the ways in which multiple factors (i.e., the client's sexual identity, ethnic-racial background, religious and spiritual identity, chronological age, economic class background, family history, unique physical characteristics, etc.) interface with one another. As stated above, the RESPECTFUL counseling model is based on the assumption that each client's psychological needs, attitudes, values, worldviews, and personal identity are all significantly affected by the manner in which these and other factors interface with one another.

Although the interface of these factors results in the development of uniquely different psychological perspectives, it is very important that mental health practitioners understand that these variables emerge from and reinforce a sense of group identity, which has major implications in the way a person develops. For example, from a group reference perspective, the notion of spirituality and its importance for the psychological development of Native Americans has been noted to be very different from the way that most Euro-Americans think about spirituality and the role this factor plays in their personal development (LaFromboise, 1996).

Also, many of the concerns and needs expressed by gay or lesbian teenagers are likely to differ from those manifested by gay or lesbians clients who are in middle adulthood. This is so, in part, because the psychological challenges of adolescence are markedly different from the types of challenges individuals normally experience during adulthood. Thus, to be effective when working with gay and lesbian adolescents and adults, counselors need to (a) have a working understanding of the different types of psychological characteristics and developmental challenges that are associated with adolescence and adulthood, (b) be knowledgeable of the barriers that gay and lesbian persons commonly face in realizing their own sense of psychological health and personal well-being, (c) consider how the interface of the client's sexual identity and developmental challenges results in the manifestation of different needs across the life span, and (d) reflect on the ways in which the counselor's own sexual identity (e.g., having a heterosexual vs. a bisexual or gay or lesbian identity) might influence the counseling process.

All of these examples point to the complex considerations and challenges mental health practitioners face when working with their clients. This complexity can be overwhelming for even the most experienced mental health practitioner. However, given the increasing knowledge that is available regarding the multiple factors that contribute to human development and the ways in which these factors affect the counseling process, practitioners will be increasingly challenged to (a) stretch their understanding of their clients' multidimensionality, (b) become increasingly cognizant of the ways in which these factors affect their own development, (c) develop a greater awareness of the ways in which the clients' multidimensional identity and the counselors' multidimensionality affect each other within the counseling context, and (d) implement intervention strategies that reflect a heightened level of respect and understanding of their clients' multidimensional nature.

Addressing the Need to Develop More
Complex and Integrative Counseling Models

Numerous theoretical models have emerged in the counseling literature over the past two decades that describe singular aspects of a person's multidimensionality. This includes the presentation of various racial identity development models (Carter, 1995; Helms, 1990), models related to women's development (Lewis et al., 1992), and a host of theoretical frameworks that describe the process of psychological maturity (Gilligan, 1982; Kohlberg, 1981; Loevinger, 1976). Given our increasing understanding of the complexity of human development and the counseling process, what is sorely needed at this point is a comprehensive and integrative framework that practitioners can use to understand how the client's and the counselor's multidimensionality affects the process and outcome of counseling.

The RESPECTFUL counseling model is presented to address the need for such a framework. In developing this model, we have focused on 10 different factors that affect an individual's psychological development and sense of personal well-being. This includes a person's (R) religious and spiritual identity; (E) ethnic-cultural-racial background; (S) sexual identity; (P) psychological maturity; (E) economic class standing and background; (C) chronological-developmental challenges; (T) threats to personal well-being; (F) family history, values, and dynamics; (U) unique physical characteristics; and (L) location of residence. Not only does each of these factors influence the way individuals learn to view themselves and others, but also each frequently affects the types of developmental challenges and problems clients bring to counseling. Although the factors listed above reflect many important aspects of a person's multidimensionality, they are not presented as an exhaustive list of all the possible variables that may affect a person's psychological development. However, by identifying these different dimensions, we hope to (a) identify some of the important variables that frequently influence an individual's development, (b) underscore the need to think more comprehensively and holistically when working with clients, and (c) outline strategies that effectively address our clients' multidimensional nature.

Whereas the other chapters in this book discuss the implications of the interface of race, class, and gender for counseling practice, the RESPECTFUL counseling framework is designed to extend practitioners' thinking further by exploring some of the ways in which other group-referenced identities and psychological factors affect both clients' and counselors' development. To facilitate a clearer understanding of the various components of this theoretical framework, we present the following subsections in a similar format. First, each subsection opens with a definition of key terms and concepts that are included in the RESPECTFUL counseling model. Second, we briefly discuss some of the ways in which each factor affects a person's psychological development and sense of personal well-being. Third, attention is directed to the implications that each factor has for counseling practice.

R—RELIGIOUS AND SPIRITUAL IDENTITY

Definition of Terms

As Kelly (1995) points out, defining the terms *spirituality* and *religion* is "a complex and thorny issue, full of differences and disputes" (p. 2). However, a close review of the literature related to religion and spirituality reveals a number of similarities and differences in the meanings of these concepts. In terms of their similarities, Albanese (1992) stated that both terms refer to "extraordinary" experiences—that is, experiences that go beyond the boundaries of the strictly objective, empirically perceived material world. The terms *religion* and *spirituality* are both "grounded in an affirmation of transcendence or 'otherness' that is reflected within the boundaries of everyday culture and manifested in identifiable religious forms pointing beyond the boundaries of the ordinary and tangible" (Kelly, 1995, p. 3). Thus, religion and spirituality both refer to a person's belief in a reality that transcends physical nature and provides individuals with an "extra-ordinary" meaning of life and human existence.

Although both of these terms include the affirmation of a transcendental, meta-empirical dimension of reality, they also hold different meanings. In this regard, several scholars have noted that although the term *spirituality* is often used to refer to a person's belief and affirmation of a transcendent connectedness with the universe, *religion* is commonly used to denote the specific ways in which this belief is manifested institutionally within the creeds and dogma of different religious groups and denominations (Bergin & Jensen, 1990; Kelly, 1995). As used in this chapter, the term *religious or spiritual identity* refers to the unique ways that individuals integrate their beliefs about a transcendental, extra-ordinary reality into their worldview and sense of personal identity. This may include but is not limited to a person's beliefs about the "after life" and the interconnectedness of all things in the universe as well as his or her views about the meaning of concepts such as "God," "enlightenment," and "grace." For a more detailed discussion of the distinctions between a person's "religious identity" versus "spiritual identity," the reader is encouraged to review Kelly's (1995) seminal work in this area.

The Impact of Religious and Spiritual Identity on Individuals' Psychological Development

To describe what we know about the relationship between religious and spiritual identity and a person's mental health, we should state that the research findings in this area are complex and still evolving. The complexity of the research findings is underscored by contradictory findings that have resulted from numerous investigations in this area. Although some researchers describe ways in which religion and spirituality negatively affect individuals' psychological development and sense of well-being, other social scientists have noted a host of positive effects of an individual's religious and spiritual identity.

Kelly (1995) provides a comprehensive listing of the results of numerous studies that found negative outcomes in terms of a person's religious and spiritual beliefs and affiliation. A summary of these findings reveals the following:

1. Several researchers reported a strong relationship between students' level of religiosity and feelings of personal inadequacy (Argyle & Beit-Hallahmi, 1975; Lea, 1982).
2. Dittes (1969) found that a person's religious beliefs were associated with unhealthy levels of dependence and a relatively defensive, constricted personality.
3. Lea (1982) and Sanua (1969) reported finding no compelling evidence to suggest that a person's religion correlates with his or her mental health or moral behavior or that it acts to deter deviancy or social pathology.
4. Religion was also found to be positively related to authoritarianism and negatively correlated with self-actualization, dogmatism/ tolerance, and ambiguity/rigidity. (Gartner, Larson, & Allen, 1991)

To complicate counselors' understanding of the impact that a person's religious and spiritual identity has on his or her mental health, other findings describe a broad range of positive outcomes that emerge from a person's beliefs in this area. This includes the following:

1. Investigators have reported that adults' (and especially elderly persons') religiosity and spiritual beliefs were positively correlated with measures of personal adjustment; appeared to be particularly helpful in times of crisis, and played a role in reducing and controlling compulsive behaviors (Argyle & Beit-Hallahmi, 1975; Lea, 1982).
2. Stark (1971) found that (a) psychiatric patients were far more likely than so-called normal people to be nonreligious, and (b) persons who scored high in their level of psychological inadequacies were less likely to score high on measures of religiosity and spirituality.
3. Gartner et al.'s (1991) findings that religion and spirituality had a beneficial association with suicide risk, drug use, alcohol abuse, delinquent behavior, divorce and marital satisfaction, psychological well-being, depression, and physical health and longevity.

4. Investigators reported the positive mental health effects of a person's religious and spiritual identity as measured by the absence of pathological symptoms (Batson & Ventis, 1982).

Despite the contradictory nature of the above-mentioned findings, the collective body of research related to religious and spiritual identity provides compelling evidence that this aspect of an individual's multidimensionality may indeed significantly affect that person's psychological development in many positive or negative ways.

Religion and spirituality not only affect clients' psychological development, but numerous studies also have shown that most mental health practitioners in the United States have acknowledged that religious or spiritual beliefs and values play an important part in their lives. In a recent survey that included a nationally representative sample of professional counselors, Kelly (1995) found that almost 64% of the counselors who participated in this study indicated that they believed in a personal god, whereas another 25% stated their belief in a transcendent or spiritual reality. Furthermore, approximately 70% of the counselors indicated that they had some affiliation with an organized religion, with 45% of these persons stating that they were highly active or regularly participated in religious activities.

However, differences were noted among another group of mental health practitioners in a study that was conducted by Beit-Hallahmi (1989). This investigation examined the religious and spiritual beliefs and values of clinical psychologists. The results of this study indicated that almost 30% of the clinical psychologists surveyed believed that ideas about God or the divine are illusory notions. This finding sharply contrasts with survey results that were generated from a representative sample of persons living in the United States in which 90% of the respondents stated that they believed in a god or adhered to other spiritual beliefs.

Implications for Counseling Practice

There are several important considerations that mental health practitioners should keep in mind when working with clients regarding their religious and spiritual identity. First, in light of the above-mentioned research findings, it is important that mental health practitioners understand that a person's religious and spiritual identity and beliefs may positively or negatively affect that person's psychological development. Although researchers have found that the vast majority of persons in the United States adhere to some sort of religious and spiritual beliefs (Gallup & Castelli, 1989) that influence their lives in a myriad of ways (Kelly, 1995), it is distressing to note that many professional training programs avoid addressing this important aspect of human development. Without having adequate training in this area, mental health practitioners are ill prepared to address clients' religious and spiritual identity in ways that could foster positive outcomes within counseling settings.

Second, it is important for mental health practitioners to be aware of the ways in which their own religious and spiritual identity may influence the counseling and therapeutic process. It is suggested that the counselor's own predisposition toward religion and spirituality often influences the practitioner's ability to demonstrate a high level of empathic understanding and genuine respect for clients whose religious and spiritual beliefs play an important role in their psychological development.

Commenting on the substantial number of mental health practitioners who share a nontheistic and nontranscendental view of the world, Beit-Hallahmi (1989) noted that this nonreligious and nonspiritual worldview reflects a long-lasting tension and even animosity between religion and the mental health professions. However, given the important role clients' religious and spiritual identity apparently plays in their development, it is vital that practitioners become more aware of the ways in which their own religious and spiritual beliefs and values may positively or negatively affect their ability to foster the psychological development of clients who manifest strong attachments to different types of religious and spiritual identities and beliefs.

Third, it is important for counselors to be knowledgeable of the variety of religious and spiritual traditions that exist in the United States. Acquiring this sort of knowledge will require (a) professional training programs to address this aspect of clients' multidimensionality in their curricula and (b) making a commitment to increase one's own level of understanding in this area by attending workshops and other professional development activities that address issues related to their clients' religious and spiritual beliefs and traditions.

Fourth, mental health practitioners must be able to assess clients' religious and spiritual identity development effectively. Kelly (1995) provides several frameworks that describe various stages of religious and spiritual identity development that mental health practitioners may find helpful in developing their assessment skills in this area. These frameworks include a description of several procedures and instruments that practitioners can use to assess this aspect of clients' lives.

E—ETHNIC, CULTURAL, AND RACIAL BACKGROUND

Definition of Terms

Although many persons have offered numerous definitions of the term *culture,* we have selected the following definitions because they succinctly capture a number of central ideas that have been presented by numerous anthropologists, psychologists, and multicultural counselors regarding the meaning of the term. The first definition is taken from Linton (1945), who defined culture as "the configuration of learned behavior and the results of behavior whose components and elements are shared and transmitted by members of a particular society" (p. 32). The components of culture thus include a shared language, set of values, traditions, and worldview. In his address at the 1997 American Psychological Association's annual convention, Parham further expanded our understanding of the term by stating that "culture provides a general design for living and a pattern for interpreting reality."

Although these definitions may give clarity to the meaning of this term, we have noted that individuals who come from the similar racial and ethnic groups often differ in terms of their cultural identity. For instance, although there are racial and ethnic similarities among Italians and Italian Americans, noticeable cultural differences exist among these two groups of persons. These cultural differences are often the result of the changes Italian Americans undergo as a result of being acculturated to the mainstream culture of the United States.

The term *ethnicity* is derived from the Greek word *ethnos,* meaning "nation." Thus, the term *ethnic differences* often has been used when discussing groups of persons who are distinguished by the unique social-cultural characteristics, values, and traditions that have evolved within the nation-states in which they live or from which they have descended. Similarly, Schaefer (1988) uses the term *ethnicity* to refer to individuals who are "set apart from others because of their national origin or distinctive cultural patterns" (p. 9). Atkinson et al. (1993) further expand our understanding of this term by stating that ethnic differences involve differences in nationality, customs, language, religion, and other cultural factors; physical characteristics are not necessarily germane to ethnic differences. If one accepts the view that ethnicity is the result of a shared social and cultural heritage, then Jews, for example, are an ethnic group but not a racial group. (p. 8)

As used in the multicultural literature, the term *race* is more elusive than *culture* and *ethnicity*. Historically, *race* has been used to connote both biological and social differences. From a biological perspective, people of different races have been classified into three major groups—Caucasoid, Mongoloid, and Negroid. Although these three categories have been used to distinguish individuals according to race, this approach to describing racial differences has been criticized as being a misleading and superficial way to classify persons according to phenotypic variations in skin color. As Atkinson et al. (1993) point out,

When we look beneath the superficial characteristics, we find there are more similarities between [racial] groups than differences (owing to the fact that all humans originate from a single genus species, homo sapiens), and more differences exist within racial groups than between them (Littlefield, Lieberman, & Reynolds, 1982). Race as a biological concept can be questioned on other grounds. . . . Given frequent migration, exploration, and invasions, pure gene frequencies have not existed for some time, if they ever did. (p. 6)

A more meaningful and productive way to describe terms such as *race* and *racial differences* is to focus on the social dimensions of this construct. Cox (1948) was one of earliest theorists to provide a social perspective of the term *race* by using it to describe "any group of people who are distinguished or consider themselves distinguished, in social relations with other peoples, by their physical characteristics" (p. 402). Thus, although the definition of *race* is considered to be a flawed and superficial way of describing persons from a strictly biological perspective, the notion of racial differences clearly exists from a social-political perspective. As Atkinson et al. (1993) point out, the social-political meaning of race and racial differences is clearly reflected in the way

outsiders view members of a "racial" group and how individuals within the "racial" group view themselves, members of their own group, and members of other "racial" groups. In other words, the concept of race has taken on important dimensions in terms of how individuals identify who they are. (p. 7)

How Does an Individual's Ethnic, Cultural, and Racial Background Affect His or Her Psychological Development?

The fields of counseling and psychology have been slow to address the ways in which a person's ethnic, cultural, and racial background influences his or her psychological development. The lack of attention that mental health professionals have directed to this aspect of clients' multidimensionality has had negative consequences for many persons from different cultural, ethnic, and racial groups who have sought counseling services (Fujino et al., 1994; Sue et al., 1992; Sue & Sue, 1999). The rise of the multicultural movement within the counseling profession has been largely fueled by the increasing recognition that persons from diverse cultural, ethnic, and racial backgrounds are adversely affected by psychological services that are embedded in an ethnocentric monocultural view of mental health and counseling (Daniels & D'Andrea, 1996). As Sue et al. (1996) note,

> The traditional theories of counseling and psychotherapy have arisen from a Western cultural milieu, with each emphasizing an important but narrow aspect of the human condition; given that client populations vary in their cultural identity, requiring a more integrated and holistic approach; and given that the majority of people reside outside the Euro-American hemispheres, it is little wonder that current theories of counseling may have limited applicability to culturally different populations. (p. 9)

In attempting to move the mental health professions beyond this monocultural perspective, multicultural counseling researchers and theorists have directed a great deal of time over the past 30 years to explain how a person's ethnic, cultural, and racial background influences that person's psychological development. These efforts have resulted in a clearer understanding of two important dimensions of the psychological differences that exist among persons from diverse cultural, ethnic, and racial backgrounds. First, multicultural researchers and theorists have taken time to discuss the types of between-group differences that exist among persons from diverse backgrounds.

As a result of this work, mental health practitioners now have a much greater understanding of the ways in which African Americans (Parham, 1996), Asian Americans (Leong, 1996), Euro-Americans (Carter, 1995), Latinos/Latinas (Arredondo, 1996), and Native Americans (LaFromboise, 1996) differ from one another in terms of their cultural values, attitudes, interpersonal styles, and worldviews.

Second, multicultural experts have more recently begun to describe the types of within group-differences that exist among members of each of these groups. Although a focus on between-group differences helps mental health practitioners understand some of the more general differences that are likely to exist among clients who come from diverse backgrounds, the current emphasis on within-group differences helps clarify the unique ways in which persons of the same cultural, ethnic, or racial background may psychologically differ from one another.

Two theoretical frameworks that are particularly useful in conceptualizing the types of psychological differences that differentiate persons from the same cultural-racial group include the minority identity development (Atkinson et al., 1993) and White identity development models (Carter, 1995). According to these developmental models, individuals from the same ethnic-racial group may demonstrate different psychological perspectives regarding the way they view their own cultural-racial background as well as manifesting differing attitudes about persons from other cultural, ethnic, and racial groups. These developmental differences include very negative and self-depreciating views of one's own cultural-racial background, a naive understanding of cultural differences, a highly defensive psychological disposition in which individuals become immersed in the traditions and history of their cultural-racial group, a more complex understanding of cultural differences, and an increased level of acceptance and respect for persons who come from backgrounds that are different from one's own (Carter, 1995).

Implications for Counseling Practice

The Association for Multicultural Counseling and Development (AMCD) has endorsed a set of multicultural counseling competencies that describe the types of awareness, knowledge, and skills mental health practitioners are expected to acquire before providing counseling and psychotherapeutic services to culturally and racially diverse client populations (Arredondo et al., 1996; Sue et al., 1992). Other theorists have emphasized that it is very important for mental health professionals to refer to these competencies in evaluating their own level of multicultural counseling competence prior to working with persons from ethnically diverse groups (D'Andrea & Daniels, 1997). Acquisition of these competencies is considered to be a necessary prerequisite when providing mental health services in an effective and ethical manner to persons from diverse ethnic-cultural backgrounds (Sue et al., 1992).

It is important that mental health practitioners have a working understanding of the historical background, traditions, attitudes, values, and worldview of persons who come from the five major ethnic-racial groups in the United States. This includes being knowledgeable about the differences that are noted to exist among African Americans, Asian Americans, European Americans, Latinas/ Latinos, and persons from Native American groups. Besides having an understanding of these between-group differences, it is also important for counselors to understand the within-group variation that is often manifested among persons from the same ethnic-racial groups. The minority identity development (Atkinson et al., 1993) and White identity development (Carter, 1995; Helms, 1990) models that were mentioned earlier provide mental health practitioners with a useful way of thinking about some of the within-group differences that are commonly manifested by persons who come from similar ethnic-racial backgrounds. These models also provide useful suggestions regarding the types of interventions mental health practitioners might use when working with ethnically and racially diverse persons. By using these theoretical frameworks to guide their work, practitioners are better able to implement intervention strategies that reflect greater sensitivity and respect for persons who come from culturally diverse client populations.

It has also been pointed out that counselors need to go beyond simply assessing their clients' level of racial identity development. In this regard, multicultural experts have underscored the importance of practitioners taking the time to evaluate where they themselves are operating in terms of these developmental models. This is an important step to take when working with persons from diverse ethnic-racial backgrounds because counselors, who are operating at various stages of these models, are likely to elicit antagonistic reactions from clients who are operating at stages that are marked by incompatible characteristics. For a more detailed discussion of the types of antagonisms that might result from inappropriate matching of counselors and clients who are operating at different stages of the minority identity development and White identity development models, the reader is encouraged to review our earlier published work in this area (D'Andrea & Daniels, 1997).

S—SEXUAL IDENTITY

Definition of Terms

One of the most complex though often understudied aspects of a person's psychological development involves sexual identity. As used in the RESPECTFUL counseling model, the term *sexual identity* is a broad construct that includes one's gender identity, gender roles, and sexual orientation. The term *gender identity* has been used to refer to an individual's subjective sense of being either male or female. A person's gender identity is affected by the specific roles that men and women are expected to play in a given culture. More specifically, the type of gender identity that one develops is markedly influenced by "those behaviors, attitudes, and personality traits that a society designates as masculine or feminine, that is, more 'appropriate' for or typical of the male or female role" (Savin-Williams & Cohen, 1996, p. 72).

Sexual identity can be manifested in a broad range of ways that extend beyond the narrow notion of masculinity and femininity. Transsexuals, for example, are described as individuals who are convinced that they were born the wrong biological sex. Thus, the term *transsexualism* refers to those persons who experience a discordance between their gender identity and their anatomical sex (Bailey, 1997).

The term *androgyny* refers to those individuals who manifest a combination of masculine and feminine traits and behaviors. In conducting an interesting multicultural study on this topic, Williams (1997) discussed how persons with an androgynous sexual identity were viewed in spiritual terms and referred to as "two-spirit people" by many Native American tribes. Williams further noted that

American Indian religions view androgenous persons—that is, males who are feminine or females who are masculine—as evidence that the person has been blessed with two spirits. Because both the masculine and the feminine are respected, a person who combines them is considered as higher than the average person, who only has one spirit. Therefore, persons who act like the other sex are not condemned as "deviant" but are blessed for their possession of a double dose of spirituality. They are not considered "abnormal" but "exceptional," somewhat similar to the way in which a musically or intellectually gifted person might be seen in Euro-American culture. (p. 418)

Beyond adopting various gender roles, a person's sexual identity is also influenced by sexual orientation. There are a number of ways to conceptualize this aspect of a person's sexual identity. Generally speaking, counselors should acquire a clear understanding of general concepts such as *bisexuality, heterosexuality,* and *homosexuality* and be knowledgeable of the ways in which these different sexual orientations affect clients' psychological development.

Bisexuality refers to individuals who demonstrate a sexual interest in both males and females. *Heterosexuality* refers to individuals whose sexual orientation involves persons of the opposite sex. A third way of viewing a person's sexual orientation and identity involves the concept of *homosexuality,* which is a general term that has been used to identify individuals whose sexual orientation involves persons of the same sex. Given the negative stereotypes that historically have been associated with homosexuality, the terms *gay males, gays,* and *lesbians* are considered more acceptable words to use to describe this dimension of one's sexual identity.

How Do Gender and Sexual Identity Affect a Person's Psychological Development?

Over the past 20 years, there has been a groundswell of interest among social scientists regarding the ways in which gender and sexual identity affect a person's psychological development and sense of personal well-being. Much of the research that has been done in these areas focuses on the negative impact that unfair discriminatory practices, prejudice, and stereotyping have on the way women, bisexuals, gays, and lesbians develop personally and psychologically. Researchers generally agree that the various forms of discrimination, prejudice, and stereotyping that these persons experience in their lives commonly result in differential economic rewards, varying levels of social acceptance, and heightened stress that compromise their sense of personal worth and validation in our society (Savin-Williams & Cohen, 1996).

Although it is important to acknowledge the gains that have been made in terms of removing some of the barriers that have historically limited women's ability to realize their economic and psychological potential in the past, counselors must be knowledgeable of the unique challenges women continue to experience in their lives. Despite the achievements that the women's movement has realized in terms of helping to combat many of the oppressive and unfair stereotypes to which women have been subjected, numerous types of discriminatory practices continue to be perpetuated in the United States that undermine a woman's ability to realize her personal and economic potential (National Commission on Working Women, 1990). Commenting on these gains and the challenges, Banks and McGee Banks (1997) note that

> social, economic, and political conditions for women have improved sub-stantially since the women's rights movement emerged as part of the civil rights movement of the 1960s and 1970s. However, gender discrimination and inequality still exist in schools and in society at large. In 1992, the me-dium earnings for women who were full-time workers were 71 percent of those for men, up from 70.2 percent in 1988. The status of women in the United States within the past two decades has changed substantially. More women are now working outside the home than ever before, and more women are heads of households. In 1993, 57.9 percent of women worked outside the home, making up 46 percent of the total work force. In 1990, 17 percent of households in the United States were headed by women. How-ever, a growing percentage of women and their dependents continue to con-stitute the nation's poor. In 1989, almost half of poor families in the United States were headed by women. (p. 129)

Besides the differential economic rewards that female workers receive for doing the same type of work men do, women continue to be subjected to a host of other conditions that seriously compromise their overall health and well-being. This includes the disproportionately high numbers of women who live in poverty (Children's Defense Fund, 1991; Solarz, 1992) and who are homeless in the United States (Daniels, D'Andrea, Omizo, & Pier, 1997), frequent acts of violence and sexual assaults against women that are reported annually in this country (Worell & Remer, 1992), and the lack of knowledge that many health care professionals have regarding the medical and psychological needs of women. These factors have been linked to the manifestation of high rates of de-pression, reduced levels of self-esteem, and the provision of inappropriate and ineffective health care services by professionals who lack in-depth knowledge and understanding of women's health and development (Lewis et al., 1992).

It is important to point out that women are not the only ones who are ad-versely affected by these types of oppression and discriminatory practices. Men's mental health is also undermined by maintaining negative stereotypes. Such faulty thinking reinforces distorted views of the potential contributions women can make in society and perpetuates a false sense of their own intellectual, social, and psychological superiority.

Gay, lesbian, and bisexual persons also experience a great deal of suffering as a result of the types of discriminatory and stereotypic views society places on individuals whose sexual identity deviates from a heterosexual orientation. Researchers have noted that individuals who openly lead a gay, lesbian, or bisexual lifestyle frequently confront stressors that serve as barriers in achieving a high level of mental health as a result of living in "a culture that is almost uniformly anti-homosexual" (Savin-Williams & Cohen, 1996, p. 181).

Adolescents who manifest a gay, lesbian, or bisexual orientation as part of their sexual identity are particularly prone to a host of debilitating psychological stressors that can negatively affect their psychological development and sense of personal well-being. Such stressors include being routinely exposed to various forms of verbal abuse (Martin & Hetrick, 1988), peer (D'Augelli, 1991) and adult harassment (Savin-Williams, 1990), and physical and sexual assaults (Hunter, 1990). These stressors commonly lead to a host of problems that include but are not limited to school-related difficulties (Price & Telljohann, 1991); increasing numbers of runaway and homeless gay, lesbian, and bisexual youth in the United States (National Network of Runaway and Youth Services, 1991); substance abuse (Rotheram-Borus, Hunter, & Rosario, 1992); prostitution (Coleman, 1989); and high rates of depression (Rothblum, 1990) and suicide (Rotheram-Borus et al., 1992).

Implications for Counseling Practice

Mental health practitioners need to be knowledgeable and respectful of the unique developmental needs that female clients commonly present in counseling settings. Recognizing the importance of having counselors become more knowledgeable and respectful in this area, the Division of Counseling Psychology of the American Psychological Association (APA) approved the "Principles Concerning the Counseling and Psychotherapy of Women" in 1978. Unless they have already done so, it is important that mental health practitioners familiarize themselves with these principles so that they might better understand the ethical and professional responsibilities they face when working with female clients. Among the points that are emphasized in this document include the need for counselors to

(a)   become aware of the ways in which traditional models of counseling and psychotherapy may be used to limit women from realizing their personal potential;
(b)   continue to learn about the issues that are specifically related to women, including the social problems of female subgroups (e.g., single, female parents, lesbians, etc.) throughout their careers;
(c)   become knowledgeable of the ways in which the power differential affects women in individual and counseling and psychotherapeutic settings; and
(d)   be sensitive to circumstances when it is more desirable for a female client to be seen by a female or male counselor (Fitzgerald & Nutt, 1995).

To work effectively and ethically with heterosexual, gay, lesbian, and bisexual persons, mental health practitioners need to have knowledge of the ways in which their clients' sexual identity affects their psychological development and worldview. This includes acquiring knowledge about how a client's gender roles and sexual orientation affect his or her overall mental health and sense of personal well-being. To assist mental health practitioners in becoming competent in these areas, the APA developed the Task Force on Heterosexual Bias in Psychotherapy in 1991. This task force was, in part, designed to evaluate the quality of mental health services provided to gay, lesbian, and bisexual clients in the United States. Summarizing their observations in this area, the members of the task force reported that gay, lesbian, and bisexual clients were often subjected to biased, inappropriate, and inadequate mental health treatment (Garnets, Hancock, Cochran, Goodchilds, & Peplau, 1991). Drawing on the work of this task force and of other researchers in the area (Browning, Reynolds, & Dworkin, 1991; Falco, 1991; Walsh, 1995), Browning (1996) proposed the following recommendations for mental health practitioners to consider when working with persons whose sexual identity includes a gay, lesbian, or bisexual lifestyle:

1. Practitioners should examine their own biases and values about sexual orientation.
2. Counselors need to learn about the coming-out process as well as the types of community resources that are available to support individuals who are in the process of publicly acknowledging their sexual orientation.

3. Mental health professionals need to explore how the clients' sexual orientation is related or unrelated to the presenting concern in counseling.
4. Practitioners need to understand how a client's sexual identity is affected by that person's religious and spiritual identity and cultural values.
5. Counselors should encourage gay, lesbian, and bisexual clients to participate in support groups comprising persons who are experiencing problems that are associated with their sexual identity to help break down the sense of isolation and alienation that these individuals commonly experience in their lives.
6. Practitioners should facilitate contact with other gay, lesbian, and bisexual persons in the community who may serve as role models for successful sexual identity integration.
7. Mental health professionals should assist gay, lesbian, and bisexual clients in overcoming shameful feelings about their sexual identity by increasing their understanding of internalized homophobia and the interconnections between other forms of oppression.
8. Counselors should help clients develop skills that will help them to cope with antigay discrimination in society more effectively.
9. Practitioners should work with gay, lesbian, and bisexual clients in helping them to develop more effective and satisfying dating and relationship skills.

P—PSYCHOLOGICAL MATURITY

Definition of Terms

Mental health practitioners often work with clients who share common demographic characteristics (e.g., age, gender, socioeconomic and cultural-racial backgrounds, etc.) but appear to be very different in psychological terms. In these situations, we might refer to one client as being "more psychologically mature" than another client who is the same age, identifies with the same cultural-racial reference group, and shares a similar sexual identity. Some descriptors that are commonly used by mental health professionals to describe an "immature" client include statements such as "he demonstrates limited impulse control in social interactions" or "she has a low capacity for self-awareness." In contrast, statements that are often used to describe "more mature" clients include the following: "He is able discuss his or her problems with much insight," "She is highly self-aware," and "She has developed a much broader range of interpersonal and perspective-taking skills than many of the other clients that I am working with."

Over the past three decades, there has been a tremendous increase in our understanding of the developmental stages that individuals pass through as they mature psychologically. Much of this knowledge comes from the work of a variety of structural-developmental psychologists who have presented numerous models that help explain the process of psychological maturity. This includes the work of Piaget (1977) (cognitive development), Perry (1970) (ethical development), Kohlberg (1981) and Gilligan (1982) (moral development), Selman (1980) (social and interpersonal development), and Loevinger (1976) (ego development).

Structural-developmental theories view psychological development as a process in which individuals move from simple to more complex ways of thinking about themselves and their life experiences. This movement can be traced along a set of invariant, hierarchical stages that reflect qualitatively different ways on thinking, feeling, and acting in the world (D'Andrea & Daniels, 1994). According to Young-Eisendrath (1988), each developmental stage represents a uniquely different frame of reference for meaning making. She points out that developmental stages "are not entirely dependent on chronological maturation. . . . Stages evolve with aging up to a point. However, when further development is not supported by environmental factors, a person may stop developing" (p. 71).

What Are the Characteristics of Psychological Maturity?

As stated above, the process of psychological maturity is characterized by transformational changes in the way individuals think, feel, and respond to their environment. This process involves the manifestation of a shift from simple to more complex ways of making meaning about oneself and the world in which one lives. Developmental researchers and theorists have noted that the acquisition of advanced cognitive skills is extremely important for individuals to lead productive and satisfying lives in a highly complex, rapidly changing modern society (D'Andrea, 1988; D'Andrea & Daniels, 1994). This is so, in part, because higher levels of cognitive functioning lead to a more accurate and objective assessment of experiences that individuals encounter in their daily lives (Loevinger, 1976).

The process of psychological maturity also involves moving from an ego-centric (self-centered) to a more allocentric (other-centered) view of the world. The shift from an egocentric to an allocentric perspective requires the acquisition of a set of interpersonal skills that allows individuals to understand the perspective of other persons with whom they interact more accurately. When individuals do not develop these interpersonal skills, they often manifest significant interpersonal problems with others during their adolescent and adult years (Selman, 1980).

According to Kohlberg (1981) and Gilligan (1982), advancements in a person's level of psychological maturity include the manifestation of more sophisticated moral reasoning abilities. These abilities help adolescents and adults to exhibit a greater sense of responsibility regarding school- and work-related tasks (Kuhmerker, 1991) and an increased sense of caring and responsiveness to others (Gilligan, Ward, Taylor, & Bardige, 1988).

Implications for Counseling Practice

There are several reasons why structural-developmental theories have tremendous relevance for counseling practice. First, when using developmental theories to guide their work, counselors focus on the positive dimensions of their clients' psychological disposition. In contrast to other traditional helping theories that direct much attention to clients' deficits and emphasize the need for remedial interventions, developmental theories encourage counselors to operate from a more proactive perspective by building on clients' psychological strengths as they assist them in realizing their human potential.

Second, besides providing practitioners with frameworks that can be used to assess their clients' personal strengths, structural-developmental theories encourage counselors to consider the ways in which their own level of psychological development may affect the counseling process. This is a very important consideration because, as several researchers have pointed out, clients' personal growth is optimally stimulated when they work with persons who are operating at a half stage to one full stage above their current level of development (Kohlberg, 1981; Sprinthall & Sprinthall, 1990). In building on this notion, D'Andrea (1988) discusses the important role counselors play in "pacing" their clients to higher levels of development by reframing their problems in ways that challenge them to think in more complex terms about their personal dilemmas.

However, as D'Andrea (1988) points out, this sort of "developmental pacing" requires counselors to be operating at a higher stage of psychological development than their clients. According to this researcher, little developmental change has been noted to occur in counseling situations in which the counselor is either operating at the same stage or is functioning at a stage below where the client is normally operating. Thus, in striving to promote positive counseling outcomes, it is important to be knowledgeable of both the client's and the counselor's level of psychological development. This knowledge can be particularly useful in guiding decisions that are made about counselor-client matchings in clinical settings.

Third, knowledge of structural developmental theories allows mental health practitioners to be more intentional regarding the types of counseling approaches they decide to use with clients who are operating at different stages of development. These theories provide a framework from which counselors and other mental health practitioners can implement an eclectic approach to counseling in a more disciplined and intentional manner. Swensen (1980) was one of the first theorists to discuss the ways in which knowledge of structural-developmental models could be used to guide the selection of various counseling approaches when working with clients who are operating at different stages of psychological maturity. Swensen's original model has been expanded and tested by other researchers who have reported positive client outcomes when counselors used a "developmental eclectic" approach with their clients (D'Andrea & Daniels, 1994).

Finally, the developmental theories that have been discussed in this section not only provide mental health practitioners with powerful theoretical models that can help to expand their understanding of human development, but they include assessment strategies as well. Bradley (1988) provides a comprehensive discussion of several types of developmental assessment strategies that counselors can use to assess both their clients' and their own level of psychological maturity.

E—ECONOMIC CLASS STANDING AND BACKGROUND

Definition of Terms

Social scientists have not always agreed on the definition of the term *economic class standing and background.* Part of the problem in defining this term is that definitional characteristics that were primarily conceptualized as relat-

CONCLUSION

ing to one particular socioeconomic group during a particular time are noted to occur with increasing frequency among large numbers of persons in other economic classes as a result of the significant societal changes that have taken place in the United States. Commenting on this point further, Banks and McGee Banks (1997) explain that

> during the 1950s, social scientists often attributed characteristics to the lower class that are found in the middle class today, such as single-parent and female-headed households, high divorce rates, and substance abuse. Today, these characteristics are no longer rare among the middle class though their frequency is still higher among lower-class families. (p. 19)

Although disagreement regarding the definition of this term is likely to persist in the social sciences, there are a number of characteristics that many persons agree are important criteria to use in determining an individual's economic class standing and background. These criteria include one's occupation, education, ethnicity, and lifestyle (Banks & McGee Banks, 1997; Coleman, Rainwater, & McClelland, 1978; Vontress, 1988).

Researchers historically have referred to three major economic classes in the United States—upper, middle, and lower (Berger, 1971; Farb, 1978). Given the different ways in which a person's occupation, education, ethnicity, and lifestyle may interface to determine his or her economic class standing, we believe that these broad categories need to be further differentiated to define more accurately the economic class standing and background of persons who currently live in the United States.

With this in mind, we have identified six categories that we believe more accurately describe the different positions individuals hold in terms of their economic class standing and background in the United States today. This classification system includes *poor persons* (i.e., unemployed individuals with less than a high school degree who are in need of economic assistance to meet their basic living needs), the *working poor* (i.e., individuals who have a high school or equivalency degree or some college experience, are employed as a nonskilled worker, and have annual incomes that fall below the federal poverty guidelines), *working class* (i.e., individuals who have a high school degree, some college experience, or have received a certificate or license in a particular trade; their annual incomes fall above the federal poverty guidelines), *middle-class nonprofessionals* (i.e., persons with at least a high school degree but more likely an advanced degree or specialized training in a given vocational career whose annual incomes are above the national average), *middle-class professionals* (e.g., individuals with at least a college degree but more likely having an advanced degree in some professional field such as education, law, or medicine and whose annual incomes are above the national average), and persons in the *upper class* (e.g., individuals whose annual incomes fall within the upper 10% of the national average).

A person's economic class standing can be affected by a variety of factors, including the types of policies that are enacted by corporate and government leaders. This can most clearly be seen in the negative ways in which thousands of middle-class nonprofessional and professional persons have been affected by changes that occur in the global market. Such changes include exporting many U.S. jobs to Third World countries to increase corporate profits by reducing labor costs here in the United States.

This corporate strategy has resulted in the downsizing of many U.S. businesses, which in turn has resulted in the erosion in the quality of life for hundreds of thousands of middle- and working-class people in this country over the past 30 years. In contrast to the economic boom that occurred during the post–World War II era, the 1970s, 1980s, and 1990s have been times when fewer well-paying jobs have been available, prices rose, real incomes of a large proportion of the general population fell, and an increasing number of middle-class families experienced some of the hard times that poor families have always lived with (Banks & McGee Banks, 1997; Newman, 1993; Rivlin, 1992).

How Does an Individual's Economic Class Standing and Background Affect His or Her Development?

A plethora of research examines the ways in which a person's economic class background affects the quality of one's life. These research findings consistently indicate that, to a large extent, a person's economic class standing and background determine an individual's life chances. These life chances include far-reaching factors such as life expectancy, level of education, occupational status, exposure to occupational hazards, incidence of crime victimization, and rate of incarceration. In short, class position has been found to play a critically important role in determining how long people live, whether they have a healthy life, their probability of failing in school, and the types of employment successes they will experience in adulthood.

By reporting the above findings, we do not mean to suggest that there is always a causal relationship between a person's economic class standing and his or her health. We do hope to point out, however, that research that has been conducted in this area has demonstrated that a negative correlation has been commonly noted to exist between individuals' economic class standing and their sense of personal well-being. In this regard, the incidence of suicides, violence, drug and alcohol abuse, school dropouts, and dissatisfaction with a job or career are all found to be consistently higher among persons in lower economic classes in the United States (Newman, 1993).

Mental health professionals have pointed to a host of other factors that are affected by clients' economic class standing that have direct implications for the work they do with their clients. This includes the development of different verbal and nonverbal communication styles, trust, empathy, and a willingness to self-disclose in counseling and psychotherapeutic settings among persons in different economic classes.

In elaborating on these issues further, it is generally acknowledged that the effectiveness of counseling is largely determined by the ability of the counselor to communicate effectively with her or his clients. However, as stated earlier, individuals often develop different communication styles as a result of their economic class standing and background. Vontress (1988) points out that people in different economic classes use a unique argot in their communication style. The term *argot* refers to the specialized vocabulary, idioms, secret jargon, and nonverbal gestures used by individuals of one group to distinguish themselves from members of other groups in society. Because most counselors fall into the economic class category that we have referred to as "middle-class professionals," they may experience difficulty verbally interacting with poor adolescents (especially those from non-White, non-European backgrounds) because of their lack of familiarity with these clients' vocabulary and idioms. Vontress goes on to state that "occasionally, counselors encounter two language systems used simultaneously by the same client. For example, in penal institutions, a black inmate may use the vernacular of the ghetto plus the slang of the multiracial inmate population" (p. 351).

In a study involving poor children and their families, investigators reported that these individuals consistently had difficulty demonstrating a sense of trust with other persons (Daniels et al., 1997). Vontress (1988) suggests that a heightened level of distrust is a common characteristic that many poor persons use as a defense mechanism to protect themselves against being rejected or unfairly treated by others. We would add that the combination of their impoverished living conditions and the seemingly general lack of interest that many middle- and upper-class persons exhibit toward poor persons in the United States represent additional factors that heighten the distrust that many poor persons manifest in their dealings with other people in general and in counseling in particular.

The level of trust or distrust that one manifests toward others is often affected by the degree to which one senses that he or she is being received empathically and respectfully by others. People generally have an easier time empathizing with individuals who share similar life experiences, values, attitudes, and worldviews as themselves. Because a person's life experiences, values, attitudes, and worldviews are all influenced by his or her economic class standing, it is often difficult for individuals to manifest true empathy for persons who come from an economic class background that is very different from their own. Furthermore, because the challenges individuals experience in life differ largely as a result of their economic class standing, it is difficult for members of one economic class to understand accurately how individuals in other economic classes are affected by the different stressors that characterize their lives. This empathy gap is particularly noticeable when persons from poor and working poor backgrounds seek services from mental health professional practitioners whose middle-class values and attitudes are reflected in the way they dress, talk, and even in the way they decorate their offices. These economic class differences often make it difficult for people from poor and working-class backgrounds to experience a truly empathic connection with many mental health practitioners (Vontress, 1988).

Implications for Counseling Practice

Counselors can do several things to help overcome some of the barriers that may exist between themselves and clients who come from diverse socioeconomic backgrounds. First, counselors are encouraged to become more knowledgeable about and sensitive to the ways in which economic class factors influence the process and outcome of counseling. This can be done, in part, by attending professional development workshops and conferences that specifically focus on economic class issues in counseling as well as by reading journal articles and books that focus on the ways in which a person's economic class standing influences her or his psychological development.

Besides attending professional development training workshops and reading materials that focus on the psychosocial needs of persons from diverse socioeconomic backgrounds, counseling practitioners are encouraged to participate in local community organizations that are specifically designed to meet the needs of citizens from different economic class backgrounds. Homeless shelters, labor groups, organizations that provide services for runaway youth, local church groups that provide services for economically impoverished persons, prison outreach programs, and community organizations that offer services to poor and elderly persons are particularly valuable resources that counselors may find useful in learning about the needs of economically disadvantaged persons in their own communities.

Second, it is important that mental health professionals evaluate the degree to which economic class differences that exist between themselves and their clients may interfere with the counseling process. Counselors can begin to gather information about their clients' economic class background by asking questions about their education, employment history, current employment status, family income, and general lifestyle.

Third, attention should be directed toward the client's verbal and nonverbal communication styles early in the counseling process. Counselors should respectfully ask for clarification regarding words or phrases that a client uses that they are not familiar with. It is not advisable for counselors to try to talk like their clients in attempting to create a more effective therapeutic alliance with them, especially when they are unfamiliar with the unique dialects clients bring to counseling. Such efforts may be perceived as being disrespectful and not genuine by many clients. Besides asking their clients for clarification when they use words or phrases that counselors do not understand, mental health practitioners are encouraged to consult with other members of the community who are more knowledgeable about the language styles of clients from different economic classes.

It is also important to assess the ways in which differences in the clients' and counselors' economic class backgrounds may represent barriers to successful counseling. We have noticed that mental health practitioners have a tendency to interpret problems that they have with poor and working-class clients in clinical settings to be the result of clients' resistance and lack of trust in the counseling process. Although it is indeed important for counselors to evaluate clients' receptivity to counseling, it is equally important to assess the degree to which their own economic class background may foster biases and stereotypes about persons who come from socioeconomic backgrounds that are very different from their own. This is important to do because the problems counselors encounter with clients who come from different economic backgrounds are often rooted in barriers that emerge from both the clients' sense of distrust and the counselors' own class-based biases and stereotypes (Sue & Sue, 1999).

Banks and McGee Banks (1997) list a set of actions that counselors can become engaged in to address the tremendous economic gap that exists between poor, working-class, and wealthy clients. These suggested actions include the following:

1. Working politically to increase the quality and availability of educational and mental health services to all persons in the United States, not just those who come from economic backgrounds that allow them the opportunity to afford quality services in these areas.

2. Actively promoting efforts to reduce the gross economic inequities that continue to exist in our nation. This can be done by supporting national income tax reforms that are designed to benefit poor and working-class families, opposing tax cuts for the rich, supporting job programs that assist people in securing jobs at reasonable wages, and supporting programs that provide economic aid for poor parents who are unable to secure employment.

3. Working to build economically and racially integrated communities. This can be done by choosing to live in an economically or racially integrated community oneself, supporting federal subsidies for low-income housing in mixed-income areas, and opposing efforts to restrict access to certain communities by members of particular ethnic, racial, or income groups.

C—CHRONOLOGICAL-DEVELOPMENTAL CHALLENGES

Definition of Terms

Besides the types of developmental changes that were discussed under the "Psychological Maturity" section of this chapter, individuals also undergo systematic changes that are chronologically based. These age-related changes represent what we refer to as *chronological-developmental challenges* that individuals face at different points across the life span. Mental health practitioners are familiar with many of these challenges because they represent the characteristics that we normally associate with infancy, childhood, adolescence, and adulthood.

Theorists, who explain human development from a chronological perspective, are oftentimes referred to as life span development (Craig, 1992; Havighurst, 1953; Shaffer, 1993) or maturational (Erikson, 1968) theorists. Unlike the structural-developmental theorists who tend to look at a particular aspect of a person's psychological maturity (e.g., intellectual, moral, social development), life span development theorists examine a person's growth from a more holistic perspective, which includes taking into account the types of physical, cognitive, and psychological changes that predictably occur at different times in an individual's life. One notable exception to this statement is Erik Erikson (1968). Although considered to be a maturational developmental theorist because his developmental stages are chronologically based, his work primarily focuses on a person's psychosocial development.

Another major difference distinguishes life span and maturational theorists from the structural-developmental theorists who were discussed earlier in this chapter. This important distinction is reflected in the fact that the research that the structural-developmental theorists (Kohlberg, 1981; Loevinger, 1976; Selman, 1980) have done in the past indicates that most persons do not advance to the highest stages of their models. In contrast, life span and maturational theorists operate from the premise that everyone undergoes similar developmental changes that predictably occur at specific times (e.g., infancy, childhood, adolescence, adulthood) during one's life.

Impact on Individuals' Psychological Development

The specific changes that life span researchers have noted individuals normally undergo as they develop from infancy through adulthood include physical growth (e.g., bodily changes and the sequencing of motor skills), the emergence of different cognitive competencies (e.g., the development of perceptual, language, learning, memory, and thinking skills), and the manifestation of a variety of psychological skills (e.g., including the ability to manage one's emotions and the demonstration of more effective interpersonal competencies) that occur over time (Shaffer, 1993). The ways in which individuals successfully negotiate the chronological challenges that are commonly associated with infancy, childhood, adolescence, and adulthood largely determine the degree to which they develop a positive sense of self-esteem, lead productive lives, and experience a general sense of personal satisfaction in life.

Implications for Counseling Practice

As a result of the increased knowledge that has emerged in developmental psychology over the past 30 years, mental health practitioners are able to more clearly differentiate and understand the various chronological challenges individuals normally face at predictable points during the life span. Whereas in the past, counselors have had a relatively broad understanding of the challenges that persons faced during their childhood, adolescence, and adulthood, developmental researchers and theorists have helped to refine our thinking about the challenges individuals experience at different points in their development by differentiating these challenges into subcategories. As a result of this progress, mental health professionals are increasingly able to develop intervention strategies that are intentionally designed to address the specific challenges of early, middle, and late childhood, adolescence, and adulthood.

The refinement in the way many counselors have come to think about these developmental challenges enhances their ability to implement counseling strategies that more effectively address their clients' needs. The tremendous advancements that have occurred in our understanding of the chronological tasks and challenges individuals face at different points are reflected in the widespread proliferation of numerous counseling books and articles that outline new types of interventions that are tailored to meet the developmental needs of children (Holmgren, 1996), adolescents (Carlson & Lewis, 1988), and adults (McWhirter, 1994).

Beyond gaining an increased understanding of human development as a result of acquiring new knowledge about the chronological challenges individuals face at different points across the life span, it is important that counselors also learn how to put this knowledge effectively to use in counseling practice. This includes assessing the different ways that children, adolescents, and adults relate to their changing physical health needs (Schneider & Rowe, 1990; Troll, 1985), their roles and responsibilities in society in general and within their families in particular (Aquilino, 1990), and the different economic and career-related concerns that adolescents and adults commonly express in counseling (Coe, 1988).

T—THREATS TO ONE'S PERSONAL WELL-BEING

Definition of Terms

Stress is an inevitable part of life. Although many mental health profession-als have directed much attention to the debilitating effects of stress, it is important to point out that some level of stress is necessary for growth and development to occur. However, when a person experiences stressors that exceed his or her ability to deal with them effectively, they can cause both physical and psychological harm. We have used the phrase "threats to one's personal well-being" in the RESPECTFUL counseling model to describe some of the stressful situations that put a person in imminent psychological danger or harm. This normally occurs when the stressors an individual experiences in life exceed that person's ability to deal with them in an effective and constructive manner.

The following equation provides a useful way of conceptualizing the deli-cate balance that exists between a person's personal resources and threatening life circumstances:

$$\frac{Psychological}{Health} = \frac{Organic\ Factors + Stress + Powerlessness}{Coping\ Skills + Self\ Esteem + Social\ Support + Personal\ Power}.$$

According to this equation, threats to a person's psychological well-being can be identified when the factors in the numerator are greater than the factors listed in the denominator. For a detailed description of the terms that are included in this equation, the reader is encouraged to review the work of Lewis, Lewis, Daniels, and D'Andrea (1998). For the purpose of the present discussion, it is important to note that an individual's personal resources (e.g., coping skills, self-esteem, social support, and personal power) may be overtaxed when he or she is subjected to ongoing stressors for extended periods of time. When this occurs, individuals are thought to be at risk for experiencing various types of psychological problems and a diminished sense of personal well-being.

Impact on Individuals' Psychological Development

When individuals experience stressors that persist for extended periods of time, they are collectively referred to as a vulnerable population (Lewis et al., 1998). Counselors commonly work with vulnerable populations such as poor, homeless, and unemployed people; adults and children in families undergoing divorce; pregnant teenagers; individuals with HIV or AIDS; and people victimized by ageism, racism, and sexism. Although persons who comprise these vulnerable populations differ greatly from each other, they are all likely to experience high levels of environmental stress that outweigh their personal resources and coping abilities.

Many studies confirm the widely held belief that people who are subjected to constant threats to their personal well-being are at risk for physical and mental health problems (Stokols, 1992; U.S. Department of Health and Human Services, 1990). Lewis et al. (1998) have noted that

> this is true whether the origin of the stress is linked to an immediate crisis—such as an unexpected pregnancy during adolescence—or rooted in more subtle but no less destructive forms of chronic stress—such as regular subjection to racism and sexism. (p. 87)

Implications for Counseling Practice

Mental health professionals need to adopt a multifaceted approach to address the various stressors that threaten a person's well-being. We believe that the ultimate goal of such an approach should be to promote the empowerment of those persons who seek counseling and psychotherapeutic services. Lewis et al.'s (1998) community counseling framework provides a description of one type of multifaceted approach that counselors may find useful when applying the principles associated with the RESPECTFUL counseling model to foster the empowerment of their clients.

The community counseling model emphasizes the important role mental health practitioners can play in helping to reduce the threats to their clients' personal well-being by promoting systemic and individual changes. The multifaceted approach that is reflected in this framework places a high value on preventive intervention strategies that are designed to reduce the incidence of mental health problems that commonly occur among persons whose psychological well-being is regularly threatened by various environmental factors and conditions (Lewis et al., 1998).

This multifaceted counseling model comprises four distinct service components: direct and indirect client counseling services, and direct and indirect community services.

The *direct client component* of this model includes traditional services such as individual and small group counseling as well as outreach efforts to persons in vulnerable populations.

Indirect counseling services are reflected in environmental interventions that are designed to promote the psychological health of persons who are currently experiencing various threats to their personal well-being. Mental health practitioners traditionally have used client advocacy and consultation services to help promote individual and systemic changes to reduce the types of threats many persons routinely experience as a result of being subjected to toxic environmental conditions.

Direct community services include community-wide educational programs that are aimed at fostering the development of a broad range of life skills among large numbers of persons. Preventive education programs are the most commonly used strategies in this component of the community counseling framework.

Indirect community services include efforts that are designed to make the social environment more responsive to the needs of a given population as a whole. Intervention strategies that are intentionally designed to promote systemic changes and influence public policies are included in this component of the community counseling framework.

Recognizing the broad range of factors that represent threats to clients' personal well-being, the RESPECTFUL counseling model requires practitioners to broaden their understanding of the multiple roles they can play in promoting their clients' mental health. In this regard, it is important to emphasize that although the use of individual and small group counseling services is an important aspect of the RESPECTFUL counseling model, it is insufficient to help reduce the types of threats many clients regularly experience in their lives. As a result, the RESPECTFUL counseling model embraces a more comprehensive approach to mental health that is dedicated to the empowerment of all clients (McWhirter, 1994), particularly those groups of persons who are predisposed to multiple threats to their psychological health because of their religious and spiritual identity; ethnic, cultural, and racial background; economic class background; sexual identity; location of residence; and family history.

F—FAMILY HISTORY, VALUES, AND DYNAMICS

Definition of Terms

One of the major challenges professional counselors face in the 21st century relates to their ability to develop the knowledge and skills that are necessary to meet the mental health needs of an increasingly pluralistic society. The diversification of our nation includes the increasing number of families that are different from the more traditional definition of the term. Traditionally, the concept of the *nuclear family* has been used by many mental health professionals as a standard to which all other types of families were compared. The term *nuclear family* refers to those families in which the male is the sole breadwinner; the female is the full-time homemaker, wife, and mother; and children generally defer to their parents' authority until adolescence, when they commonly manifest an expressed need for greater independence.

There is an increasing rise in the number of other types of families in which millions of persons live and grow in the United States. This includes single-parent families, divorced families (families in which one or both parents were previously divorced), blended families (families composed of children and youth who are brought together as a result their divorced parents' remarrying), extended families, and families headed by gay and lesbian parents, to name a few.

Goldenberg and Goldenberg (1994) comment on the different meanings of the term *family*, noting that

> the family, no less than other institutions, is undergoing rapid and dramatic changes in form, composition, and structure. Nontraditional families (led by single parents, for example) are becoming more commonplace and the traditional nuclear family . . . less and less the American norm. Skyrocketing divorce rates (which doubled between 1965 and 1985), the surge of women into the work force, the need to have two or more incomes in order to make ends meet, marriage postponement, the greater prevalence of step families, children living in poverty, single people living alone or with a partner of the same or opposite sex, childless families, mothers with out-of-wedlock children—these are just some of the contemporary realities in what Skolnick (1991) calls an "age of uncertainty" for the American family. (p. 3)

Impact on Individuals' Development

Regardless of the different types of families that exist in the United States, there is little doubt about the tremendous impact that family history and dynamics have on one's psychological development. This includes the ways in which an individual's family influences that person's religious and spiritual identity

(Giblin, 1996), a person's propensity for drug and alcohol use or abuse (Andrews, Hops, & Duncan, 1997), incidence of juvenile delinquency (Gorman-Smith, Tolan, Zelli, & Huesmann, 1996), relationships with other siblings during adulthood (Stocker, Lanthier, & Furman, 1997), social cognition and psychological maturity (Goodnow, 1996), and sexual identity (Katz, 1987). Given the important impact that a person's family history and dynamics play in terms of his or her psychological development, it is very important that mental health practitioners address this aspect of the RESPECTFUL counseling model when working with their clients.

Implications for Counseling Practice

We have outlined several recommendations that counselors are encouraged to keep in mind when addressing clients' family background. First, given the impact that each of our family histories has on the types of attitudes, values, and worldview we develop, it is important for mental health practitioners to take time to consider the ways in which their own family backgrounds affect the way they view clients who come from families that are very different from their own. This is an important consideration because individuals may develop and maintain positive or negative stereotypes about family structures that are different from their own. When left unexamined, these stereotypes and biases may lead counselors to make misinterpretations and inaccurate assessments of clients' development, their current level of mental health, and the availability of persons who may play a supportive role in promoting clients' sense of personal well-being.

Second, it is important that counselors develop the knowledge and skills they will need to conduct an effective appraisal of a client's family functioning. Building on the work of other family theorists (Reiss, 1980), Goldenberg and Goldenberg (1994) discuss a number of routes that practitioners can take in conducting family appraisals. This includes deciding whether to (a) adopt a cross-sectional or developmental view of families, (b) conduct a family-based or an environmental-based inquiry, (c) adopt a crisis or character orientation in the appraisal process, (d) focus on family pathology or family competence, or (e) emphasize underlying family themes or observable behavioral events. To this list, we would add the importance of being knowledgeable about the different roles individuals are expected to play in families composed of persons from diverse ethnic-racial backgrounds.

Third, counselors must acquire the skills that are necessary to evaluate a broad range of families, including but not limited to single-parent families, remarried families, cohabitating heterosexual families, and gay and lesbian couples (Goldenberg & Goldenberg, 1994). This is important so that practitioners might be able to design counseling strategies that (a) take into account a client's relationship with his or her family and (b) include specific family members in the overall intervention when such action is thought to be of potential benefit to the persons with whom counselors work.

Fourth, when counselors identify shortcomings in their own ability to accurately appraise the structure, composition, and impact that different types of families have on their clients' development, they have an ethical responsibility to seek professional training that fosters the development of these sorts of appraisal skills.

U—UNIQUE PHYSICAL CHARACTERISTICS

Definition of Terms

McWhirter (1994) notes that "one of the most disheartening and frightening phenomena in our society is the relentless and all-consuming desire for physical beauty" (p. 203). Typically, this obsession is rooted in an idealistic image of persons who are thin and muscular. In reality, few persons match up to this idealistic image. Consequently, many individuals experience a sense of reduced self-esteem and increased feelings of personal inadequacy as a result of being unable to live up to this socially constructed view of a "beautiful person" (McWhirter, 1994).

Persons who possess physical characteristics that traditionally have been referred to as "physical disabilities" are often subjected to various forms of discrimination and stigmatization whose genesis is rooted in misperceptions and stereotypes about physical beauty and health. The RESPECTFUL counseling model emphasizes the importance of being sensitive to the various ways in which society's idealized image of physical beauty negatively affects the psychological development of those persons whose physical appearance does not fit the narrow and distorted views that are promoted by our modern culture.

As used in the RESPECTFUL counseling model, the term *unique physical characteristics* is a broad construct that refers to a variety of physical traits that may include but are not limited to obvious characteristics such as being overweight or underweight or having a visual physical disability. It also includes other physical characteristics that may negatively affect a person's sense of self-esteem such as premature balding, aging, and having a physical disfigurement or even a birthmark that is visually noticeable to others.

Impact on Individuals' Psychological Development

The current societal image of physical beauty is highlighted by the slogan that "thin is in." This image is accompanied by the prevalent myth that weight loss is a simple matter of willpower and discipline. This inaccurate view exists despite an abundance of medical evidence indicating that safe and permanent weight loss is not possible for most obese people (Rothblum, Brand, Miller, & Oetjen, 1990). McWhirter (1994) adds that "for lower socioeconomic status (SES) women of color, who have higher proportions of obesity than other segments of the population, this myth adds to their experience of oppression" (p. 206). Often, this myth leads to a diminishment in these women's self-esteem and sense of personal empowerment. The increasing number of young women who are diagnosed with eating disorders and undergo cosmetic surgery further attests to the ways in which individuals are psychologically affected by the myth of the perfect body in our modern society.

It is important to note that the psychological impact of one's physical characteristics affects men as well as women. McWhirter (1994) describes society's view of the ideal body type for men as being characterized by "a mesomorphic body or the muscle man physique" (p. 208). This idealized view greatly contributes to the frequency with which men express dissatisfaction with their chest, weight, and waist. It also has been reported that short men commonly express more negative feelings about their bodies and frequently manifest greater levels of psychological distress in comparison to their average-height or tall counterparts (Martel, 1985).

Implications for Counseling Practice

When working with clients whose unique physical characteristics may be a source of stress and dissatisfaction, it is important for counselors to first reflect on the ways in which the idealized myth of physical beauty may have led them to internalize negative views and stereotypes about persons who do not fit this myth. This is important because when these types of internalized views go unchecked, they may lead to inaccurate assessments and misinterpretations of our clients' personal strengths and concerns.

Second, when working with women and men whose psychological development has been negatively affected by some unique physical characteristic, counselors need to be able to assist them in understanding the ways in which gender role socialization contributes to irrational thinking about their own sense of self-worth. Good, Gilbert, and Scher (1990) outline an intervention model that they refer to as gender-aware therapy (GAT), which provides practitioners with strategies that are useful in helping women and men become more aware of the ways in which they may be negatively affected by the effects of gender role socialization and expectations.

Third, mental health practitioners would do well to work with teachers and administrators in the public schools and universities to develop and implement preventive strategies that address many of the negative stereotypes, misconceptions, and insensitivities children, adolescents, and adults develop about persons who have unique physical characteristics. This sort of preventive intervention has much potential in terms of reducing the various forms of discrimination and disrespect that many persons who have unique physical characteristics commonly experience in their lives.

Fourth, counselors are ethically responsible for familiarizing themselves with the Americans with Disabilities Act of 1990. This important legislation is designed to (a) safeguard the rights of persons who have various types of physical disabilities and (b) ameliorate the different forms of discrimination that they have been subjected to in the past.

L—LOCATION OF RESIDENCE

Definition of Terms

The term *location of residence* refers to the geographical region and the type of setting where one resides. We have identified five general geographical areas that persons commonly refer to when talking about the major regions in the United States. These geographical areas include the northeastern, southeastern, midwestern, southwestern, and northwestern regions of the United States. These geographical locations are distinguished by the different climate patterns, geological terrain, and, to some degree, the types of occupations and industry that are available to workers who reside in these areas. We would also add that these different geographical locations are often characterized by their own unique "subcultures," which result in different types of values, attitudes, and language accents that are commonly manifested by many of the individuals who reside in these areas.

The location of one's residence also includes the type of setting in which a person lives. Mental health practitioners are generally familiar with three major types of residential settings. These include *rural, suburban,* and *urban* settings. As defined by the U.S. Bureau of the Census (1978), rural populations consist of people who live in places or towns of less than 2,500 inhabitants and in open country areas outside the closely settled suburbs of metropolitan cities. By contrast, urban areas consist of cities with 50,000 or more inhabitants.

Population experts also make the distinction between metropolitan and nonmetropolitan areas. Since 1993, the definition of these terms has been based on the designation of what is referred to as *metropolitan statistical areas* (MSAs). MSAs are defined as those areas that have a total population of at least 100,000 inhabitants, comprise one or more central cities with at least 50,000 inhabitants, and include adjoining areas that are socially and economically related to a central city (U.S. Bureau of the Census, 1988). It is important to point out that these definitions are arbitrary and that many important variables are not taken into account when distinguishing the meaning of the terms *rural, suburban,* and *urban* settings.

Impact on Individuals' Psychological Development

A person's location of residence represents an important part of an individual's total ecological system, which has a tremendous impact on one's psychological development. Bronfenbrenner (1979, 1988) has dedicated most of his career to describing how ecological factors affect human development. According to Bronfenbrenner's theory, a person's psychological development is significantly affected by four major systems that comprise his or her total ecology. This includes a client's microsystems (e.g., those immediate settings, such as family, school, and workplace, of which the individual is directly a part), mesosystems (the dynamic interactions or linkages that occur among microsystems, such as when family members and school interact on behalf of the individual), exosystems (which include those major societal institutions and settings that directly and indirectly affect persons in their microsystems), and macrosystems (those overarching societal and cultural institutions that directly and indirectly affect the way individuals develop and behave) (Bronfenbrenner, 1988).

According to these definitions, a person's residential setting is a part of his or her exosystem. Because an individual's exosystem directly and indirectly affects that person's psychological development, it is important that mental health practitioners understand the positive and negative ways that clients may be affected by their residential location. It has been noted, for example, that the combination of overcrowded living conditions, economic disadvantage, and limited opportunities for career and educational advancement causes many urban youth to develop a host of antisocial behaviors that result in violence, crime, high rates of teenage pregnancies, and drug and alcohol abuse problems (Lewis et al., 1998).

Persons living in rural settings experience a variety of different stressors that, although unique to their particular location of residence, have a significant impact on their overall psychological health and sense of personal well-being. This includes stressors that result from a heightened sense of social isolation (Murray & Keller, 1991) as well as the recent social and industrial changes that have affected thousands of persons in many rural communities across the United States.

Several social scientists have described how the restructuring of numerous rural communities in our nation has affected many persons who have been used to a different way of life. The structural changes that have occurred in many rural parts of the United States have been stimulated by technological advancements that have been made in the farming industry, industrial development projects, and an increased reliance on automobiles among persons living in sparsely populated parts of the country (Ford, 1978; Murray & Keller, 1991; Wilkinson, 1982). These changes have resulted in the erosion of rural persons' dependence on traditional social and community structures that historically provided a sense of meaning and support during times of personal stress and crisis. As Murray and Keller (1991) pointed out,

Needs that were formerly met by the small, local community are now met by distant and more formal agencies, employers, and commercial enterprises. In addition, the subtle urban transformation of many rural areas and the decline of local community service structures has also created a decline in the natural support systems that have traditionally been present in rural communities. For example, fewer rural Americans participate in cooperative problem solving granges, churches, and other civic groups. Changes in communication patterns and the geographic dispersal of extended families away from the family farm have also strained traditional sources of natural support. (p. 225)

Implications for Counseling Practice

When mental health practitioners work with persons who come from geographic regions or residential settings that are different from the ones in which they were raised, it is important that they reflect on the types of prejudices and biases they may have developed about individuals who come from these different residential settings. As is the case with the other aspects of the RESPECTFUL counseling model, this sort of self-reflection and assessment is a very important starting point because such biases and stereotypes may lead to inaccurate and negative clinical interpretations in counseling and psychotherapeutic situations.

Second, counselors need to develop the knowledge and skills that are necessary to evaluate the impact that a client's total ecology has on her or his development. Lewis et al. (1998) provide specific examples of the ways in which counselors can conduct an ecological assessment and offer suggestions regarding the types of counseling strategies that might be employed to address specific needs at each level of a client's ecological system.

Third, practitioners should be particularly sensitive to the ecological barriers that prevent individuals from using traditional mental health services and develop alternative ways of helping to meet their personal needs. Landis, Trevor, Futch, and Plaut (1995) describe an innovative and comprehensive approach to providing a broad range of health services to elderly persons and adolescents who reportedly experienced numerous barriers that impeded them from securing quality health care services in rural areas. This particular intervention was implemented in a rural part of North Carolina. It included (a) assessing the needs of the persons in the community who were considered to be at risk for a variety of physical and mental health problems, (b) prioritizing the health care needs of the community members, (c) designing and implementing health promotion interventions that were based on the input that was generated from the residents in the area, and (d) evaluating the effectiveness of the health promotion programs to enable their ongoing improvement.

Conclusion

In presenting the RESPECTFUL counseling model, we have tried to outline a comprehensive framework that will assist practitioners to conceptualize their clients' multidimensionality more effectively. In doing so, we hope to promote a greater understanding of the implications of clients' and counselors' multiple group-referenced identities when providing services that are designed to foster mental health and human development among persons from diverse client populations. One of the major challenges that practitioners face in the future involves the need to develop a clearer understanding of the ways in which the factors that are presented in the RESPECTFUL counseling model interface, resulting in even more complex and unique client perspectives and experiences. This book represents a bold step in increasing our understanding of the complex nature of the interface of race, class, and gender. However, if counselors and other mental health professionals are to provide services that more effectively, ethically, and respectfully help foster clients' mental health and personal well-being, counseling researchers and theorists will need to continue to add many more steps in our understanding of the multidimensional nature of human development in the coming decades.

References

Abbott, F. (Ed.). (1987). *New men, new minds: Breaking male tradition.* Freedom, CA: Crossing Press.

Albanese, C. L. (1992). *America: Religions and religion* (2nd ed.). Belmont, CA: Wadsworth.

Andrews, J. A., Hops, H., & Duncan, S. C. (1997). Adolescent modeling of parent substance use: The moderating effect of the relationship with the parent. *Journal of Family Psychology, 11*(3), 259-270.

Aquilino, W. S. (1990). The likelihood of parent-adult child co-residence: Effects of family structure and parental characteristics. *Journal of Marriage and the Family, 52,* 405-419.

Argyle, M., & Beit-Hallahmi, B. (1975). *The social psychology of religion.* London: Routledge & Kegan Paul.

Arredondo, P. (1996). MCT theory and Latina(o)-American populations. In D. W. Sue, A. E. Ivey, & P. B. Pedersen (Eds.), *A theory of multicultural counseling and therapy* (pp. 217-235). Pacific Grove, CA: Brooks/Cole.

Arredondo, P., Toporek, R., Brown, S., Jones, J., Locke, D. C., Sanchez, J., & Stadler, H. (1996). Operationalization of the multicultural counseling competencies. *Journal of Multicultural Counseling and Development, 24,* 42-78.

Atkinson, D. R., Morten, G., & Sue, D. W. (1993). *Counseling American minorities: A cross-cultural perspective* (4th ed.). Madison, WI: Brown & Benchmark.

CONCLUSION

Bailey, J. M. (1997). Gender identity. In R. C. Savin-Williams & K. M. Cohen (Eds.), *The lives of lesbians, gays, and bisexuals: Children to adults* (pp. 71-93). Fort Worth, TX: Harcourt Brace.

Banks, J. A., & McGee Banks, C. A. (1997). *Multicultural education: Issues and perspectives* (3rd ed.). Boston: Allyn & Bacon.

Batson, C. D., & Ventis, W. L. (1982). *The religious experience.* New York: Oxford University Press.

Beit-Hallahmi, B. (1989). *Prolegomena to the psychology of religion.* Lewisburg, PA: Bucknell University Press.

Berger, B. (1971). *Societies in change: An introduction to comparative sociology.* New York: Basic Books.

Bergin, A. E., & Jensen, J. P. (1990). Religiosity of psychotherapists: A national survey. *Psychotherapy, 27,* 3-7.

Bradley, L. J. (1988). Developmental assessment: A life-span approach. In R. Hayes & R. Aubrey (Eds.), *New directions for counseling and human development* (pp. 136-157). Denver, CO: Love.

Bronfenbrenner, U. (1979). *The ecology of human development.* Cambridge, MA: Harvard University Press.

Bronfenbrenner, U. (1988). Interacting systems in human development. In N. Bolger, A. Caspi, G. Downey, & M. Moorehouse (Eds.), *Persons in context: Developmental processes* (pp. 25-49). New York: Cambridge University Press.

Browning, C. (1996). Lesbian, gay, and bisexual identity issues. In P. B. Pedersen & D. C. Locke (Eds.), *Cultural and diversity issues in counseling* (pp. 99-102). Greensboro, NC: ERIC Counseling & Student Services Clearinghouse.

Browning, C., Reynolds, A., & Dworkin, S. (1991). Affirmative psychotherapy for lesbian women. *The Counseling Psychologist, 19*(2), 177-196.

Carlson, J., & Lewis, J. A. (Eds.). (1988). *Counseling the adolescent: Individual, family, and school interventions.* Denver, CO: Love.

Carter, R. T. (1995). *The influence of race and racial identity in psychotherapy: Toward a racially inclusive model.* New York: John Wiley.

Children's Defense Fund. (1991). *Homeless families: Failed policies and young victims.* Washington, DC: Author.

Coe, R. (1988). A longitudinal examination of poverty in the elderly years. *The Gerontologist, 28,* 540-544.

Coleman, E. (1989). The development of male prostitution activity among gay and bisexual adolescents. *Journal of Homosexuality, 17,* 131-149.

Coleman, R., Rainwater, L., & McClelland, K. (1978). *Social standing in America: New dimensions of class.* New York: Basic Books.

Cox, O. C. (1948). *Caste, class, and race.* Garden City, NY: Doubleday.

Craig, G. J. (1992). *Human development* (6th ed.). Englewood Cliffs, NJ: Prentice Hall.

D'Andrea, M. (1988). Counselor as pacer: A model for the revitalization of the counseling profession. In R. Hayes & R. Aubrey (Eds.), *New directions for counseling and human development* (pp. 22-44). Denver, CO: Love.

D'Andrea, M., & Daniels, J. (1994). Group pacing: A developmental eclectic approach to group work. *Journal of Counseling and Development, 72*(6), 585-590.

D'Andrea, M., & Daniels, J. (1995, April). *RESPECTFUL counseling: A practical framework for diversity counseling.* Paper presented at the annual meeting of the American Counseling Association, Denver, CO.

D'Andrea, M., & Daniels, J. (1997). Multicultural counseling supervision: Central issues, theoretical considerations, and practical strategies. In D. B. Pope-Davis & H. L. K. Coleman (Eds.),

Multicultural counseling competencies: Assessment, education and training, and supervision (pp. 290-309). Thousand Oaks, CA: Sage.

Daniels, J., & D'Andrea, M. (1996). MCT theory and ethnocentrism in counseling. In D. W. Sue, A. E. Ivey, & P. B. Pedersen (Eds.), *A theory of multicultural counseling and therapy* (pp. 155-173). Pacific Grove, CA: Brooks/Cole.

Daniels, J., D'Andrea, M., Omizo, M., & Pier, P. (1997). *Applying contextual considerations in group work with homeless youngsters and their mothers.* Honolulu: University of Hawaii Press.

D'Augelli, A. R. (1991). Gay men in college: Identity processes and adaptations. *Journal of College Student Development, 32,* 140-146.

Dittes, J. E. (1969). The psychology of religion. In G. Lindzey & E. Aronson (Eds.), *The handbook of social psychology* (Vol. 5, pp. 602-659). Reading, MA: Addison-Wesley.

Erikson, E. (1968). *Identity: Youth and crisis.* New York: Norton.

Falco, K. (1991). *Psychotherapy with lesbian clients: Theory into practice.* New York: Brunner/Mazel.

Farb, P. (1978). *Humankind.* Boston: Houghton Mifflin.

Fitzgerald, L. F., & Nutt, R. (1995). The Division 17 principles concerning the counseling/psychotherapy of women: Rationale and implementation. In D. R. Atkinson & G. Hackett (Eds.), *Counseling diverse populations* (pp. 229-261). Madison, WI: Brown & Benchmark.

Ford, T. R. (Ed.). (1978). *Rural USA: Persistence and change.* Ames: Iowa State University Press.

Fujino, D. C., Okazaki, S., & Young, K. (1994). Asian-American women in the mental health system: An examination of ethnic and gender match between therapist and client. *Journal of Community Psychology, 22,* 164-176.

Gallup, G., Jr., & Castelli, J. (1989). *The people's religion: American faith in the 90s.* New York: Macmillan.

Garnets, L., Hancock, K. A., Cochran, S., Goodchilds, J., & Peplau, L. A. (1991). Issues in psychotherapy with lesbians and gay men. *American Psychologist, 46,* 964-972.

Gartner, J., Larson, D. B., & Allen, G. D. (1991). Religious commitment and mental health: A review of empirical literature. *Journal of Psychology and Theology, 19,* 6-25.

Giblin, P. (1996). Spirituality, marriage, and family. *The Family Journal, 4*(1), 46-52.

Gilligan, C. (1982). *In a different voice: Psychological theory and women's development.* Cambridge, MA: Harvard University Press.

Gilligan, C., Ward, J. V., Taylor, J. M., & Bardige, B. (Eds.). (1988). *Mapping the moral domain.* Cambridge, MA: Harvard University Press.

Goldenberg, H., & Goldenberg, I. (1994). *Counseling today's families* (2nd ed.). Pacific Grove, CA: Brooks/Cole.

Good, G. E., Gilbert, L. A., & Scher, M. (1990). Gender aware therapy: A synthesis of feminist therapy and knowledge about gender. *Journal of Counseling and Development, 68*(4), 376-380.

Goodnow, J. J. (1996). Social cognition and family relationships: Comment. *Journal of Family Psychology, 10*(4), 422-430.

Gorman-Smith, D., Tolan, P. H., Zelli, A., & Huesmann, L. R. (1996). The relation of family functioning to violence among inner-city minority youths. *Journal of Family Psychology, 10*(2), 115-129.

Havighurst, R. J. (1953). *Human development and education.* New York: Longman.

Helms, J. E. (Ed.). (1990). *Black and White racial identity: Theory, research, and practice.* Westport, CT: Greenwood.

Holmgrem, V. S. (1996). *Elementary school counseling: An expanding role.* Boston: Allyn & Bacon.

Hunter, J. (1990). Violence against lesbian and gay youths. *Journal of Interpersonal Violence, 5,* 295-300.

Katz, P. A. (1987). Variations in family constellation: Effects on gender schemata. In L. S. Liben & M. L. Signorella (Eds.), *Children's gender schemata* (pp. 212-238). San Francisco: Jossey-Bass.

Kelly, E. W. (1995). *Spirituality and religion in counseling and psychotherapy: Diversity in theory and practice.* Alexandria, VA: American Counseling Association.

Kohlberg, L. (1981). *The philosophy of moral development.* San Francisco, CA: Harper & Row.

Kuhmerker, L. (Ed.). (1991). *The Kohlberg legacy: For the helping professions.* Birmingham, AL: REP.

LaFromboise, T. (1996). MCT theory and Native-American populations. In D. W. Sue, A. E. Ivey, & P. B. Pedersen (Eds.), *A theory of multicultural counseling and therapy* (pp. 192- 203). Pacific Grove, CA: Brooks/Cole.

Landis, S., Trevor, J., Futch, J., & Plaut, T. (1995). *Building a healthier tomorrow: A manual for coalition building.* Asheville, NC: Mountain Area Health Education Center.

Lea, G. (1982). Religion, mental health, and clinical issues. *Journal of Religion and Health, 21,* 336-351.

Lee, C. C., & Richardson, B. L. (Eds.). (1991). *Multicultural issues in counseling: New approaches to diversity.* Alexandria, VA: American Counseling Association.

Leong, F. T. L. (1996). MCT theory and Asian-American populations. In D. W. Sue, A. E. Ivey, & P. B. Pedersen (Eds.), *A theory of multicultural counseling and therapy* (pp. 204-216). Pacific Grove, CA: Brooks/Cole.

Lewis, J. A., Hayes, B. A., & Bradley, L. J. (Eds.). (1992). *Counseling women over the life span.* Denver, CO: Love.

Lewis, J. A., Lewis, M. D., Daniels, J., & D'Andrea, M. (1998). *Community counseling: Empowerment strategies for a diverse society.* Pacific Grove, CA: Brooks/Cole.

Linton, R. (1945). *The science of man in the world crisis.* New York: Columbia University Press.

Littlefield, A., Lieberman, L., & Reynolds, L. T. (1982). Redefining race: The potential demise of a concept in anthropology. *Current Anthropology, 23,* 641-647.

Locke, D. C. (1992). *Increasing multicultural understanding: A comprehensive model.* Newbury Park, CA: Sage.

Loevinger, J. (1976). *Ego development.* San Francisco: Jossey-Bass.

Martel, L. F. (1985). *Short stature in Caucasian males: Personality correlates and social attribution.* Unpublished doctoral dissertation, University of Rhode Island.

Martin, A. D., & Hetrick, E. S. (1988). The stigmatization of the gay and lesbian adolescent. *Journal of Homosexuality, 15,* 163-183.

McWhirter, E. H. (1994). *Counseling for empowerment.* Alexandria, VA: American Counseling Association.

Mishkind, M. E., Rodin, J., Silberstein, L. R., & Striegel-Moore, R. H. (1986). The embodiment of masculinity: Cultural, psychological, and behavioral dimensions. *American Behavioral Scientist, 29*(5), 545-562.

Murray, J. D., & Keller, P. A. (1991). Psychology and rural America: Current status and future directions. *American Psychologist, 46*(3), 220-231.

National Commission on Working Women. (1990). *Wider opportunities for women.* Washington, DC: Women and Work.

National Network of Runaway and Youth Services. (1991). *To whom do they belong? Runaway, homeless and other youth in high-risk situations in the 1990s.* Washington, DC: Author.

Newman, K. S. (1993). *Declining fortunes: The withering of the American dream.* New York: Basic Books.

Parham, T. (1996). MCT theory and African-American populations. In D. W. Sue, A. E. Ivey, & P. B. Pedersen (Eds.), *A theory of multicultural counseling and therapy* (pp. 177-191). Pacific Grove, CA: Brooks/Cole.

Parham, T. (1997, August). *Transformation of the racist mentality: From isfet to maat.* Paper presented at the annual meeting of the American Psychological Association, Chicago.

Perry, W. G. (1970). *Forms of intellectual and ethical development in the college years: A scheme.* New York: Holt, Rinehart, & Winston.

Piaget, J. (1977). *The development of thought: Equilibrium of cognitive structure.* New York: Viking.

Price, J. H., & Telljohann, S. K. (1991). School counselors' perceptions of adolescent homosexuals. *Journal of School Health, 61,* 433-438.

Reiss, D. (1980). Pathways to assessing the family: Some choice points and a sample route. In C. K. Hofling & J. M. Lewis (Eds.), *The family: Evaluation and treatment* (pp. 192-233). New York: Brunner/Mazel.

Riger, S. (1992). Epistemological debates, feminist voices: Science, social values, and the study of women. *American Psychologist, 47*(6), 730-740.

Rivlin, A. M. (1992). *Reviving the American Dream: The economy, the states, and the federal government.* Washington, DC: Brookings Institution.

Rothblum, E. D. (1990). Depression among lesbians: An invisible and unresearched phenomenon. *Journal of Gay & Lesbian Psychotherapy, 1,* 67-87.

Rothblum, E. D., Brand, P. A., Miller, C. T., & Oetjen, H. A. (1990). The relationship between obesity, employment discrimination, and employment-related victimization. *Journal of Vocational Behavior, 37,* 251-266.

Rotheram-Borus, M. J., Hunter, J., & Rosario, M. (1992). *Suicidal behavior and gay-related stress among gay men and bisexual adolescents.* Unpublished manuscript, Columbia University, New York.

Sanua, V. D. (1969). Religion, mental health, and personality: A review of empirical studies. *American Journal of Psychiatry, 125,* 1203-1213.

Savin-Williams, R. C. (1990). *Gay and lesbian youths: Expressions of identity.* New York: Hemisphere.

Savin-Williams, R. C., & Cohen, K. M. (Eds.). (1996). *The lives of lesbians, gays, and bisexuals: Children to adults.* Fort Worth, TX: Harcourt Brace.

Schaefer, R. T. (1988). *Racial and ethnic groups* (3rd ed.). Glenview, IL: Scott, Foresman.

Schneider, E., & Rowe, J. (Eds.). (1990). *Handbook of the biology of aging.* San Diego, CA: Academic Press.

Selman, R. (1980). *The growth of interpersonal understanding: Developmental and clinical analysis.* New York: Academic Press.

Shaffer, D. R. (1993). *Developmental psychology: Childhood and adolescence* (3rd ed.). Pacific Grove, CA: Brooks/Cole.

Skolnick, A. (1991). *Embattled paradise: The American family in an age of uncertainty.* New York: Basic Books.

Solarz, A. L. (1992). To be young and homeless: Implications of homelessness for children. In M. J. Robertson & M. Greenblatt (Eds.), *Homelessness: A national perspective* (pp. 275-286). New York: Plenum.

Sprinthall, N. A., & Sprinthall, R. C. (1990). *Educational psychology: A developmental approach* (5th ed.). New York: McGraw-Hill.

Stark, R. (1971). Psychopathology and religious commitment. *Review of Religious Research, 12,* 165-176.

Stocker, C. M., Lanthier, R. P., & Furman, W. (1997). Sibling relationships in early adulthood. *Journal of Family Psychology, 11*(2), 210-221.

Stokols, D. (1992). Establishing and maintaining healthy environments: Toward a social ecology of health promotion. *American Psychologist, 47*(1), 6-22.

Sue, D. W., Arredondo, P., & McDavis, R. J. (1992). Multicultural counseling competencies and standards: A call to the profession. *Journal of Counseling and Development, 70*, 477-486.

Sue, D. W., Ivey, A. E., & Pedersen, P. B. (Eds.). (1996). *A theory of multicultural counseling and therapy.* Pacific Grove, CA: Brooks/Cole.

Sue, D. W., & Sue, D. (1999). *Counseling the culturally different: Theory and practice* (3rd ed.). New York: John Wiley.

Swensen, C. H. (1980). Ego development and a general model for counseling and psychotherapy. *Personnel & Guidance Journal, 58*(5), 373-381.

Taussig, I. M. (1986). Comparative responses of Mexican Americans and Anglo-Americans to early goal setting in a public mental health clinic. *Journal of Counseling Psychology 34*(2), 214-217.

Troll, L. E. (1985). *Early and middle adulthood* (2nd ed.). Monterey, CA: Brooks/Cole.

U.S. Bureau of the Census. (1978). *Geographic tools* (Fact finder for the nation). Washington, DC: Government Printing Office.

U.S. Bureau of the Census. (1988). *Statistical abstract of the United States: 1989* (104th ed.). Washington, DC: Printing Office.

U.S. Department of Health and Human Services. (1990). *Healthy people 2000: National health promotion and disease prevention objectives* (PHS Publication No. 91-50212). Washington, DC: Author.

Vontress, C. E. (1988). Social class influences on counseling. In R. Hayes & R. Aubrey (Eds.), *New directions for counseling and development* (pp. 346-364). Denver, CO: Love.

Walsh, P. (1995). *Biased and affirmative practice with lesbian and gay clients.* Unpublished master's thesis, California State University, Long Beach.

Wilkinson, K. P. (1982). Changing rural communities. In K. P. Keller & J. D. Murray (Eds.), *Handbook of rural community mental health* (pp. 20-28). New York: Human Sciences Press.

Williams, W. L. (1997). Two-spirit persons: Gender nonconformity among Native American and native Hawaiian youths. In R. C. Savin-Williams & K. M. Cohen (Eds.), *The lives of lesbians, gays, and bisexuals: Children to adults* (pp. 416-435). Fort Worth, TX: Harcourt Brace.

Worell, J., & Remer, P. (1992). *Feminist perspectives in therapy: An empowerment model for women.* Chichester, UK: Wiley.

Young-Eisendrath, P. (1988). Making use of human development theories in counseling. In R. Hayes & R. Aubrey (Eds.), *New directions for counseling and human development* (pp. 66-84). Denver, CO: Love.

Index

Abrahams, N., 11
ACA. *See* American Counseling Association
Academic acculturation, 172, 177-180
Acculturation:
  academic, 172, 177-180
  alternation, 177, 180
  application to minority group members, 107
  assimilation, 91, 92, 176
  career development and, 276
  definitions, 172, 196, 329
  forced, 108
  fusion, 177, 180
  integration, 90-91, 92, 107
  marginalization, 91-92, 176-177
  models, 90-92, 176, 335
  multiculturalism, 177, 180
  of Mexican Americans, 330
  phenotype and, 330-332, 335
  segregation, 91, 92

separation, 91, 177, 179
stress related to, 91-92, 96, 371
ACES. *See* Association of Counselor Educators and Supervision
Addictions counseling, xi
ADHD. *See* Attention deficit hyperactivity disorder
Adolescents:
  African American, 44, 313
  African American female, 29-30, 45-46
  career development programs, 313
  gay and lesbian, 421-422, 436
  identity development, 26
  Latinas, 28, 330
  phenotype and self-concept, 330
  relationships with parents, 34, 44-45
Advocacy for counseling profession, 387, 390
Advocacy in counseling:
  as catalyst for change, 400-402

ABOUT THE EDITORS

Donald B. Pope-Davis is Professor in the Counseling Psychology Program, Department of Psychology, University of Notre Dame. He received his doctorate in Counseling Psychology from Stanford University. He is currently the editor of the *Journal of Multicultural Counseling and Development* and coordinator of the Center for Multicultural Research, Department of Psychology, University of Notre Dame. He is the author of numerous texts and articles in the areas of multicultural counseling competencies, training and education, and identity development.

Hardin L. K. Coleman is Associate Professor of Counseling Psychology in the School of Education at the University of Wisconsin–Madison. He received his doctorate in Counseling Psychology from Stanford University. He is on the editorial board of several journals. He is the author of numerous texts and articles in the areas of multicultural counseling, training and education, counselor competence, and cultural identity development.

ABOUT THE CONTRIBUTORS

Va Lecia L. Adams, Executive Director of the Stanford University Medical Youth Science Program, received her doctorate in counseling psychology from Stanford University. She conducts workshops on mother-daughter relationships and racial identity development. Her research focuses on the psychological and academic development of ethnic minority youth within community contexts.

Anita Bansal is a graduate student at Kent State University, Kent, Ohio. Her interests lie in ethnic minority issues as they relate to psychosocial adaptation. More specifically, she is interested in examining how individuals' cultural values and familial relationships influence subsequent generations. Additional interests include women's health risk behaviors such as high-risk sexual activity, eating disorders, and coping strategies.

Aditya Bhagwat is a doctoral student in counseling psychology at The Ohio State University. He received his M.A. in counseling psychology from The

Ohio State University. His research interests include identity formation in Asian Americans, as well as making the delivery of mental health services more effective with minority populations. He is also interested in the process of acculturation and how it differentially affects members of a minority population. He plans to pursue a career in academia coupled with providing mental health services to minority populations.

Madonna G. Constantine is Associate Professor of Psychology and Education in the Department of Counseling and Clinical Psychology at Teachers College, Columbia University. She received her Ph.D. in counseling psychology from the University of Memphis. Her professional interests include multicultural issues in counseling, training, and supervision; professional development issues of people of color and counselors in training; and the vocational and psychological issues of underserved populations.

Michael D'Andrea is Professor in the Department of Counselor Education at the University of Hawaii. He has authored or coauthored more than 100 journal articles, book chapters, books, and other scholarly works on a broad range of issues related to multicultural counseling. Besides his extensive research in the area of multicultural counseling, he is best known for his political and social activism in the counseling profession.

Judy Daniels is Professor in the Department of Counselor Education at the University of Hawaii. Her research and publications primarily focus on issues related to multicultural counseling, the needs of homeless children, and the psychology of White racism. She is well known for her efforts to promote changes in the counseling profession that reflect an increased level of understanding, sensitivity, and respect for cultural differences.

Ruth E. Fassinger is Associate Professor in the Counseling Psychology Program at the University of Maryland, affiliate faculty in Women's Studies, and Director of the College of Education Honors Program. She received her Ph.D. from The Ohio State University in 1987. Her primary scholarly work is in the psychology of women and gender, particularly women's career development, and in the development of sexuality and sexual orientation. She is a Fellow of Division 17 and Division 44 of the American Psychological Association and serves on the editorial board of *Psychology of Women Quarterly*.

She also maintains a psychotherapy and consultation practice specializing in issues related to gender, work, and sexuality.

Enedina García-Vázquez is Associate Professor in the Counseling and Educational Psychology Department at New Mexico State University. Her research interests focus on acculturation, ethnicity, skin color, academic success, and various psychological variables such as self-esteem, stress, and expressiveness. She has written several chapters and is author of a number of refereed manuscripts. She received her doctorate in school psychology from the University of Iowa. She also has served as a consultant in the area of assessment and evaluation for the state of New Mexico.

Alberta M. Gloria is Associate Professor in the Department of Counseling Psychology at the University of Wisconsin–Madison. She has published and presented in areas related to educational issues for racial and ethnic minority students in higher education, particularly for Latino undergraduates, and professional practice issues for counselors in training. She is an active member of the American Psychological Association and secretary for APA's Division 17 (Counseling Psychology) Section on Ethnic and Racial Diversity and the National Association for Chicana and Chicano Studies. She is an editorial board member for the *Journal of Multicultural Counseling and Development* and the *Journal of Counseling and Development.* Some of her recent journal articles are published in *The Counseling Psychologist, Education and Urban Society, Professional Psychology,* and the *Hispanic Journal of Behavioral Sciences.*

Gordon C. Nagayama Hall is Professor of Psychology at Pennsylvania State University. His interests are in ethnicity and psychopathology, including the influence of culture on sexually aggressive behavior and other forms of violent behavior.

Carrie L. Hill is a doctoral candidate in the Counseling Psychology Program of the Department of Counseling and Educational Psychology, Indiana University, Bloomington. She has published in the areas of multicultural assessment and counseling, clinical judgment, and geropsychology.

Farah A. Ibrahim is Professor in the Counseling Psychology Program, Department of Human Development and Psychoeducational Studies at Howard

University, Washington, D.C. She received her doctorate from the Department of Counseling and Educational Psychology at Pennsylvania State University. She is on the editorial boards of *Journal for Multicultural Counseling and Development* and *International Journal for the Advancement of Counseling (IJAC)* and is book editor for the *IJAC*. She is the author of *Scale to Assess Worldview* and has published articles and book chapters on cultural issues in counseling and psychotherapy, psychology of women, Asian American identity issues, and curriculum development in counseling psychology.

Lisa R. Jackson is Assistant Professor in the Department of Counseling, Developmental and Educational Psychology in the School of Education at Boston College. She does research examining the role of racial and gender identity in the development of self-concept in people of color. Her most recent work seeks to understand and improve school engagement and academic performance for adolescents of color. She received her doctorate degree from Stanford University.

Jason E. Kanz is a doctoral student in the Counseling Psychology Program, College of Education, University of Iowa. He received a master's degree in Community Counseling from Mankato State University prior to attending the University of Iowa. He has research interests in the areas of multiculturalism, religious issues in counseling, and psychological assessment.

Phoebe Y. Kuo is a counseling psychologist at the Counseling Center of the University of Nevada, Las Vegas. She has a Ph.D. in counseling psychology from the University of Nebraska–Lincoln. Her dissertation topic was "Minority Experiences Across Asian American Ethnic Groups and Generational Levels: Ethnic Identity, Bicultural Stress, Perceived Prejudice, and Racial Consciousness." Her research and professional interests include multicultural assessment, counseling, and supervision; personality assessment; dynamic psychotherapy; women's issues; and identity development.

Teresa D. LaFromboise is Associate Professor in the Counseling Psychology Program, School of Education, Stanford University. She received her doctorate in counseling psychology from the University of Oklahoma. She is currently Associate Editor of *Cultural Diversity and Ethnic Minority Psychology* and faculty adviser of the Stanford Counseling Institute. She teaches courses in the Counseling Psychology Program and the Center for Comparative Studies of Race and Ethnicity. She is the author of numerous social skills curricula and articles on interventions for American Indian well-being, biculturalism, and multicultural competence.

Mark M. Leach is Associate Professor in the Department of Psychology at the University of Southern Mississippi and consults with a local mental health center. His professional interests include racial identity, suicide, religion and counseling, group counseling, and international issues. He received his Ph.D. from the University of Oklahoma.

Frederick T. L. Leong is Professor of Psychology at The Ohio State University and serves as a faculty member in both the Counseling and Industrial/Organizational Psychology Programs. He obtained his Ph.D. from the University of Maryland with a double specialty in counseling and industrial/organizational psychology. He has authored or coauthored more than 80 publications in various counseling and psychology journals and 40 book chapters. He was the editor of *Career Development and Vocational Behavior of Racial and Ethnic Minorities* (1995). His latest book is *The Psychology Research Handbook: A Guide for Graduate Students and Research Assistants* (coedited with James Austin). He is also Associate Editor of the *Encyclopedia of Psychology.* He is the editor of the Sage book series, *Racial and Ethnic Minority Psychology.* He is a Fellow of the American Psychological Association (Divisions 2, 17, 45, and 52). His major research interests are in vocational psychology (career development of ethnic minorities), cross-cultural psychology (particularly culture and mental health and cross-cultural psychotherapy), Asian American psychology, and organizational behavior.

William M. Liu is Assistant Professor of Counseling Psychology at the University of Iowa. He received a master's degree in College Student Personnel from the University of Maryland, where he also served as Assistant Director of Asian American Studies, and earned a doctorate in counseling psychology from the University of Maryland at College Park. He has taught courses in Asian American history, gender issues, counseling, and education. His research interests are in the areas of Asian American masculinity, multicultural training and competency, and social class. His dissertation focuses on racial identity, masculinity, and prejudicial attitudes.

Irene R. Lopez is a graduate student at Kent State University, Kent, Ohio. Her interests are generally in minority mental health and specifically in Puerto Rican mental health. She is also interested in women's issues and in the application of anthropology and sociology into psychology.

Hifumi Ohnishi is a counseling psychologist at the Michigan State University, Multi-Ethnic Counseling Center Alliance of the Counseling Center. She received her doctorate from the University of Connecticut from the Counseling Psychology Program in the Department of Educational Psychology. She has researched and published articles on counseling Japanese nationals, Asian American identity, career development in a diverse society, women and depression, and the Factor Structure of the Objective Measure of Ego-Identity Status (OMEIS) Scale.

Alayne J. Ormerod is Assistant Professor in the Division of Counseling Psychology at the University of Illinois at Urbana-Champaign. She previously served on the faculty at Indiana University and received her Ph.D. from the University of Illinois. Her research interests include the career psychology of women, particularly the influence of gender, race, and ethnicity, and sexual orientation on career choice and adjustment; the study of racial discrimination and harassment in the workplace; and sexual harassment.

Charles R. Ridley is Professor in the Counseling Psychology Program and Associate Dean of Research and the University Graduate School at Indiana University. He received his doctorate in counseling psychology from the University of Minnesota. He has published extensively in the areas of multicultural counseling, organizational consultation, and the integration of psychology and theology. As a licensed psychologist, he consults with a variety of organizations.

Gargi Roysircar-Sodowsky is Professor in the Department of Clinical Psychology, Antioch New England Graduate School, and Director of the Antioch New England Multicultural Center for Research and Practice. A first-generation immigrant from India, she does research on acculturation, acculturative stress, and ethnic identity of immigrant and later-generation Asian Americans; worldview differences; multicultural counseling competencies and multicultural training in professional psychology; and multicultural assessment and instrument development. She is the coeditor of the book

Multicultural Assessment in Counseling and Clinical Psychology (1996). She is President-Elect of the Association for Multicultural Counseling and Development and senior associate editor of the *Journal of Multicultural Counseling and Development.*

Gerald L. Stone is Professor in the Counseling Psychology Program, College of Education, and Director of the University Counseling Service at the University of Iowa. He is the former editor of *The Counseling Psychologist* and a past president of Division 17 (Counseling Psychology) of the American Psychological Association. His current research interests are in the areas of mental health policy in higher education and multicultural education and training.

Ana Sullivan is a doctoral candidate in the Counseling Psychology Program at the University of Southern Mississippi and is working at Behavioral Health Systems in Birmingham, Alabama. She received her M.S. in psychology in 1995 from Auburn University at Montgomery. Her interests include multicultural counseling, eating disorders, relational diagnosis, holistic counseling, and the effects of stress on health.

Chalmer E. Thompson is Associate Professor in the Department of Counseling and Educational Psychology and Director of Training of the Counseling Psychology Program at Indiana University. Her areas of research interest include the elaboration and application of racial identity theory, the psychology of oppression, and liberatory change processes within individuals in psychotherapy and within the educational arena and communities. She is a licensed psychologist in the state of Indiana.

Rebecca L. Toporek is a doctoral student in counseling psychology at the University of Maryland, College Park (UMCP) and a predoctoral intern at the University of California, Berkeley, Counseling and Psychological Services. She received a master's degree in counseling psychology from the University of Oregon in 1987. Prior to entering the doctoral program at UMCP, she was a community college counselor in Cupertino, California. She served for two years as Assistant Editor for the *Journal of Multicultural Counseling and Development* and Assistant Coordinator for UMCP's overseas counseling psychology master's program. Her research interests include multicultural counseling, career development, and advocacy and social action in counseling.

Luis A. Vázquez is Associate Professor in the Counseling and Educational Psychology Department at New Mexico State University. His research and publications focus on the impact of phenotype on issues such as acculturation and identity development. He also has written in the area of multicultural attitudes in curriculum development. In addition, he has developed multicultural training videos used across the country in counseling programs. He received his doctorate in counseling psychology from the University of Iowa. He has also served as a consultant to higher education, school districts, and agencies in their multicultural development and policies.

Kristin M. Vespia is a doctoral candidate in counseling psychology at the University of Iowa. She is currently completing her predoctoral internship in professional psychology at Illinois State University's Student Counseling Services. Her doctoral dissertation is a longitudinal study focusing on the relationship between vocational interests and career aspirations across individual difference dimensions. In addition to work in vocational psychology, she has coauthored articles and presented at national conferences in the areas of clinical supervision and college student mental health.

Vivian Ota Wang is Assistant Professor in the Counseling/Counseling Psychology Programs and Director of the Asian Cultural Studies Program in the Division of Psychology in Education at Arizona State University. Prior to receiving her Ph.D. in counseling psychology at Columbia University, she was a board-certified genetic counselor. Her research and clinical interests focus on social justice issues related to multicultural education program development and evaluation in genetics and psychology, racial-cultural identity, and health psychology in the United States and China.